THE
BOOK ®

Honda Civic
Service and Repair Manual

Martynn Randall

(4050 - 272)

Models covered

Hatchback, Saloon, Aerodeck (Estate) & Coupe, including special/limited editions
1.4 litre (1396cc), 1.5 litre (1493cc), 1.6 litre (1590 & 1595cc) & 1.8 litre (1797cc) petrol

Also covers Civic models of this range first registered during 2001

Does NOT cover revised Civic range introduced January 2001

© Haynes Publishing 2003

ABCDE
FGHIJ
KLMN

A book in the **Haynes Service and Repair Manual Series**

ISBN 1 84425 050 4

British Library Cataloguing in Publication Data
A catalogue record for this book is available from the British Library.

Printed in the USA

Haynes Publishing
Sparkford, Yeovil, Somerset BA22 7JJ, England

Haynes North America, Inc
861 Lawrence Drive, Newbury Park, California 91320, USA

Editions Haynes
4, Rue de l'Abreuvoir
92415 COURBEVOIE CEDEX, France

Haynes Publishing Nordiska AB
Box 1504, 751 45 UPPSALA, Sverige

Contents

Contents

REPAIRS & OVERHAUL

REFERENCE

Advanced driving

Many people see the words 'advanced driving' and believe that it won't interest them or that it is a style of driving beyond their own abilities. Nothing could be further from the truth. Advanced driving is straightforward safe, sensible driving - the sort of driving we should all do every time we get behind the wheel.

An average of 10 people are killed every day on UK roads and 870 more are injured, some seriously. Lives are ruined daily, usually because somebody did something stupid. Something like 95% of all accidents are due to human error, mostly driver failure. Sometimes we make genuine mistakes - everyone does. Sometimes we have lapses of concentration. Sometimes we deliberately take risks.

For many people, the process of 'learning to drive' doesn't go much further than learning how to pass the driving test because of a common belief that good drivers are made by 'experience'.

Learning to drive by 'experience' teaches three driving skills:

- ☐ Quick reactions. (Whoops, that was close!)
- ☐ Good handling skills. (Horn, swerve, brake, horn).
- ☐ Reliance on vehicle technology. (Great stuff this ABS, stop in no distance even in the wet...)

Drivers whose skills are 'experience based' generally have a lot of near misses and the odd accident. The results can be seen every day in our courts and our hospital casualty departments.

Advanced drivers have learnt to control the risks by controlling the position and speed of their vehicle. They avoid accidents and near misses, even if the drivers around them make mistakes.

The key skills of advanced driving are **concentration**, effective all-round **observation, anticipation** and **planning.** When **good vehicle handling** is added to these skills, all driving situations can be approached and negotiated in a safe, methodical way, leaving nothing to chance.

Concentration means applying your mind to safe driving, completely excluding anything that's not relevant. Driving is usually the most dangerous activity that most of us undertake in our daily routines. It deserves our full attention.

Observation means not just looking, but seeing and seeking out the information found in the driving environment.

Anticipation means asking yourself what is happening, what you can reasonably expect to happen and what could happen unexpectedly. (One of the commonest words used in compiling accident reports is 'suddenly'.)

Planning is the link between seeing something and taking the appropriate action. For many drivers, planning is the missing link.

If you want to become a safer and more skilful driver and you want to enjoy your driving more, contact the Institute of Advanced Motorists at www.iam.org.uk, phone 0208 996 9600, or write to IAM House, 510 Chiswick High Road, London W4 5RG for an information pack.

Working on your car can be dangerous. This page shows just some of the potential risks and hazards, with the aim of creating a safety-conscious attitude.

General hazards

Scalding

• Don't remove the radiator or expansion tank cap while the engine is hot.
• Engine oil, automatic transmission fluid or power steering fluid may also be dangerously hot if the engine has recently been running.

Burning

• Beware of burns from the exhaust system and from any part of the engine. Brake discs and drums can also be extremely hot immediately after use.

Crushing

• When working under or near a raised vehicle, always supplement the jack with axle stands, or use drive-on ramps. *Never venture under a car which is only supported by a jack.*
• Take care if loosening or tightening high-torque nuts when the vehicle is on stands. Initial loosening and final tightening should be done with the wheels on the ground.

Fire

• Fuel is highly flammable; fuel vapour is explosive.
• Don't let fuel spill onto a hot engine.
• Do not smoke or allow naked lights (including pilot lights) anywhere near a vehicle being worked on. Also beware of creating sparks (electrically or by use of tools).
• Fuel vapour is heavier than air, so don't work on the fuel system with the vehicle over an inspection pit.
• Another cause of fire is an electrical overload or short-circuit. Take care when repairing or modifying the vehicle wiring.
• Keep a fire extinguisher handy, of a type suitable for use on fuel and electrical fires.

Electric shock

• Ignition HT voltage can be dangerous, especially to people with heart problems or a pacemaker. Don't work on or near the ignition system with the engine running or the ignition switched on.

• Mains voltage is also dangerous. Make sure that any mains-operated equipment is correctly earthed. Mains power points should be protected by a residual current device (RCD) circuit breaker.

Fume or gas intoxication

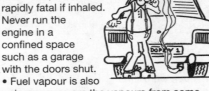

• Exhaust fumes are poisonous; they often contain carbon monoxide, which is rapidly fatal if inhaled. Never run the engine in a confined space such as a garage with the doors shut.
• Fuel vapour is also poisonous, as are the vapours from some cleaning solvents and paint thinners.

Poisonous or irritant substances

• Avoid skin contact with battery acid and with any fuel, fluid or lubricant, especially antifreeze, brake hydraulic fluid and Diesel fuel. Don't syphon them by mouth. If such a substance is swallowed or gets into the eyes, seek medical advice.
• Prolonged contact with used engine oil can cause skin cancer. Wear gloves or use a barrier cream if necessary. Change out of oil-soaked clothes and do not keep oily rags in your pocket.
• Air conditioning refrigerant forms a poisonous gas if exposed to a naked flame (including a cigarette). It can also cause skin burns on contact.

Asbestos

• Asbestos dust can cause cancer if inhaled or swallowed. Asbestos may be found in gaskets and in brake and clutch linings. When dealing with such components it is safest to assume that they contain asbestos.

Special hazards

Hydrofluoric acid

• This extremely corrosive acid is formed when certain types of synthetic rubber, found in some O-rings, oil seals, fuel hoses etc, are exposed to temperatures above 400°C. The rubber changes into a charred or sticky substance containing the acid. *Once formed, the acid remains dangerous for years. If it gets onto the skin, it may be necessary to amputate the limb concerned.*
• When dealing with a vehicle which has suffered a fire, or with components salvaged from such a vehicle, wear protective gloves and discard them after use.

The battery

• Batteries contain sulphuric acid, which attacks clothing, eyes and skin. Take care when topping-up or carrying the battery.
• The hydrogen gas given off by the battery is highly explosive. Never cause a spark or allow a naked light nearby. Be careful when connecting and disconnecting battery chargers or jump leads.

Air bags

• Air bags can cause injury if they go off accidentally. Take care when removing the steering wheel and/or facia. Special storage instructions may apply.

Diesel injection equipment

• Diesel injection pumps supply fuel at very high pressure. Take care when working on the fuel injectors and fuel pipes.

⚠ *Warning: Never expose the hands, face or any other part of the body to injector spray; the fuel can penetrate the skin with potentially fatal results.*

Remember...

DO

• Do use eye protection when using power tools, and when working under the vehicle.

• Do wear gloves or use barrier cream to protect your hands when necessary.

• Do get someone to check periodically that all is well when working alone on the vehicle.

• Do keep loose clothing and long hair well out of the way of moving mechanical parts.

• Do remove rings, wristwatch etc, before working on the vehicle – especially the electrical system.

• Do ensure that any lifting or jacking equipment has a safe working load rating adequate for the job.

DON'T

• Don't attempt to lift a heavy component which may be beyond your capability – get assistance.

• Don't rush to finish a job, or take unverified short cuts.

• Don't use ill-fitting tools which may slip and cause injury.

• Don't leave tools or parts lying around where someone can trip over them. Mop up oil and fuel spills at once.

• Don't allow children or pets to play in or near a vehicle being worked on.

The Honda Civic models covered by this manual were first introduced to the UK in March 1995. The Civic was available as a 2-door Coupe, 3-door Hatchback, 4-door Saloon, 5-door Hatchback and 5-door Estate, and equipped with a variety of engine sizes. This manual covers the 4-cylinder petrol engine models. Five petrol engines were available: a 1396cc, 1493cc or 1590cc SOHC 16-valve unit, or a 1595cc or 1797cc DOHC 16-valve unit. The 1.5 litre, 1.6 litre and 1.8 litre units could be specified with Hondas V-TEC or VTEC-E systems, whereby the valve timing and duration were altered automatically as the engine speed changed, to obtain greater drivability (torque) at lower engine speeds, and greater power output at higher engine speeds. All of the engines are fuel injected, with an integrated engine management system.

Fully-independent front suspension is fitted, with upper and lower control arms, shock absorber/coil spring assemblies, and an anti-roll bar. The rear suspension uses trailing arms, upper and lower control arms, compensator arms, shock absorber/coil spring assemblies and, on some models, an anti-roll bar.

A five-speed manual gearbox is fitted as standard to all models, with a four-speed automatic unit available on all SOHC models. A Constantly Variable Transmission (CVT) was available on 1.6 litre SOHC models.

A wide range of standard and optional equipment is available within the model range to suit most tastes, including an anti-lock braking system and air conditioning.

For the home mechanic, the Civic is quite straightforward to maintain, and most of the items requiring frequent attention are easily accessible.

Your Honda Civic Manual

The aim of this manual is to help you get the best value from your vehicle. It can do so in several ways. It can help you decide what work must be done (even should you choose to get it done by a garage). It will also provide information on routine maintenance and servicing, and give a logical course of action and diagnosis when random faults occur. However, it is hoped that you will use the manual by tackling the work yourself. On simpler jobs it may even be quicker than booking the car into a garage and going there twice, to leave and collect it. Perhaps most important, a lot of money can be saved by avoiding the costs a garage must charge to cover its labour and overheads.

The manual has drawings and descriptions to show the function of the various components so that their layout can be understood. Tasks are described and photographed in a clear step-by-step sequence. The illustrations are numbered by the Section number and paragraph number to which they relate – if there is more than one illustration per paragraph, the sequence is denoted alphabetically.

References to the 'left' or 'right' of the vehicle are in the sense of a person in the driver's seat, facing forwards.

Acknowledgements

Thanks are due to Draper Tools Limited, who provided some of the workshop tools, and to all those people at Sparkford who helped in the production of this manual.

We take great pride in the accuracy of information given in this manual, but vehicle manufacturers make alterations and design changes during the production run of a particular vehicle of which they do not inform us. No liability can be accepted by the authors or publishers for loss, damage or injury caused by any errors in, or omissions from, the information given.

Project vehicles

The main vehicle used in the preparation of this manual, and which appears in many of the photographic sequences, was a 1996 1.6 litre 3-door Hatchback. Also included was a 1999 1.4 litre 5-door Hatchback, 4-door Saloon and a 5-door Estate model.

The following pages are intended to help in dealing with common roadside emergencies and breakdowns. You will find more detailed fault finding information at the back of the manual, and repair information in the main chapters.

If your car won't start and the starter motor doesn't turn

- [ ] If it's a model with automatic transmission, make sure the selector is in P or N.
- [ ] Open the bonnet and make sure that the battery terminals are clean and tight.
- [ ] Switch on the headlights and try to start the engine. If the headlights go very dim when you're trying to start, the battery is probably flat. Get out of trouble by jump starting (see next page) using a friend's car.

If your car won't start even though the starter motor turns as normal

- [ ] Is there fuel in the tank?
- [ ] Is there moisture on electrical components under the bonnet? Switch off the ignition, then wipe off any obvious dampness with a dry cloth. Spray a water-repellent aerosol product (WD-40 or equivalent) on ignition and fuel system electrical connectors like those shown in the photos. Pay special attention to the ignition coil wiring connector and HT leads.

A Check the condition and security of the battery connections

B Check the fuel injection system wiring is secure

C Check the ignition system distributor wiring is secure

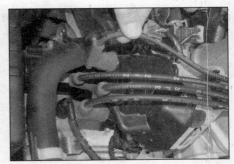

D Check that the HT leads are securely connected to the spark plugs and the distributor cap

Check that electrical connections are secure (with the ignition switched off) and spray them with a water dispersant spray like WD-40 if you suspect a problem due to damp

Jump starting

When jump-starting a car using a booster battery, observe the following precautions:

✔ Before connecting the booster battery, make sure that the ignition is switched off.

✔ Ensure that all electrical equipment (lights, heater, wipers, etc) is switched off.

✔ Take note of any special precautions printed on the battery case.

✔ Make sure that the booster battery is the same voltage as the discharged one in the vehicle.

✔ If the battery is being jump-started from the battery in another vehicle, the two vehicles MUST NOT TOUCH each other.

✔ Make sure that the transmission is in neutral (or PARK, in the case of automatic transmission).

HAYNES HiNT *Jump starting will get you out of trouble, but you must correct whatever made the battery go flat in the first place. There are three possibilities:*

1 *The battery has been drained by repeated attempts to start, or by leaving the lights on.*

2 *The charging system is not working properly (alternator drivebelt slack or broken, alternator wiring fault or alternator itself faulty).*

3 *The battery itself is at fault (electrolyte low, or battery worn out).*

1 Connect one end of the red jump lead to the positive (+) terminal of the flat battery

2 Connect the other end of the red lead to the positive (+) terminal of the booster battery.

3 Connect one end of the black jump lead to the negative (-) terminal of the booster battery

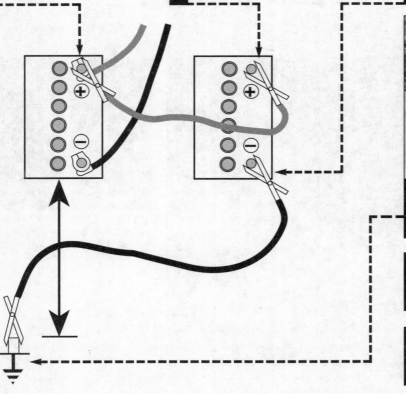

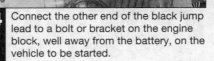

4 Connect the other end of the black jump lead to a bolt or bracket on the engine block, well away from the battery, on the vehicle to be started.

5 Make sure that the jump leads will not come into contact with the fan, drivebelts or other moving parts of the engine.

6 Start the engine using the booster battery and run it at idle speed. Switch on the lights, rear window demister and heater blower motor, then disconnect the jump leads in the reverse order of connection. Turn off the lights etc.

Wheel changing

 Warning: Do not change a wheel in a situation where you risk being hit by another vehicle. On busy roads, try to stop in a lay-by or a gateway. Be wary of passing traffic while changing the wheel – it is easy to become distracted by the job in hand.

Preparation

- ☐ When a puncture occurs, stop as soon as it is safe to do so.
- ☐ Park on firm level ground, if possible, and well out of the way of other traffic.
- ☐ Use hazard warning lights if necessary.

- ☐ If you have one, use a warning triangle to alert other drivers of your presence.
- ☐ Apply the handbrake and engage first or reverse gear (or Park on models with automatic transmission).

- ☐ Chock the wheel diagonally opposite the one being removed – a couple of large stones will do for this.
- ☐ If the ground is soft, use a flat piece of wood to spread the load under the jack.

Changing the wheel

1 The vehicle jack and tools are stored under the floor in the luggage compartment/boot. Open boot/tailgate, lift the luggage compartment/boot floor lid. The spare wheel is retained by a wing bolt, and the vehicle jack is stored alongside or on top of the spare wheel.

2 Undo the wing bolt and lift out the spare wheel and toolkit/vehicle jack. On some models the jack needs to be 'wound down' to release it from the storage compartment.

3 Loosen each wheel bolt by half a turn. Use the special adapter where a locking wheel bolt is fitted.

4 Locate the jack head below the reinforced jacking point nearest the wheel to be changed. On most models, the jacking points are indicated by small arrow shaped indentations pressed into the sill. On a vehicle fitted with sill trims, remove the jacking point covers from the sill by pulling them up, and out. Turn the handle to raise the wheel clear of the ground.

5 Remove the bolts and lift the wheel from the vehicle. Place the wheel beneath the sill as a precaution against the jack failing.

6 Fit the spare wheel, insert the bolts and then tighten them moderately with the wheel brace. Lower the vehicle to the ground, then finally tighten the wheel bolts in a diagonal sequence.

Finally...

- ☐ Remove the wheel chocks.

- ☐ Stow the jack and tools in the correct locations in the car.

- ☐ Check the tyre pressure on the wheel just fitted. If it is low, or if you don't have a pressure gauge with you, drive slowly to the nearest garage and inflate the tyre to the right pressure.

- ☐ The wheel bolts should be tightened to the specified torque at the earliest opportunity.

- ☐ Have the damaged tyre or wheel repaired as soon as possible.

Identifying leaks

Puddles on the garage floor or drive, or obvious wetness under the bonnet or underneath the car, suggest a leak that needs investigating. It can sometimes be difficult to decide where the leak is coming from, especially if the engine bay is very dirty already. Leaking oil or fluid can also be blown rearwards by the passage of air under the car, giving a false impression of where the problem lies.

 Warning: Most automotive oils and fluids are poisonous. Wash them off skin, and change out of contaminated clothing, without delay.

HAYNES HiNT *The smell of a fluid leaking from the car may provide a clue to what's leaking. Some fluids are distictively coloured. It may help to clean the car carefully and to park it over some clean paper overnight as an aid to locating the source of the leak.*
Remember that some leaks may only occur while the engine is running.

Sump oil

Engine oil may leak from the drain plug...

Oil from filter

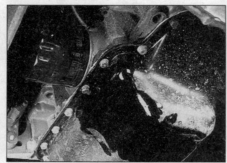

...or from the base of the oil filter.

Gearbox oil

Gearbox oil can leak from the seals at the inboard ends of the driveshafts.

Antifreeze

Leaking antifreeze often leaves a crystalline deposit like this.

Brake fluid

A leak occurring at a wheel is almost certainly brake fluid.

Power steering fluid

Power steering fluid may leak from the pipe connectors on the steering rack.

Towing

When all else fails, you may find yourself having to get a tow home – or of course you may be helping somebody else. Long-distance recovery should only be done by a garage or breakdown service. For shorter distances, DIY towing using another car is easy enough, but observe the following points:

☐ Use a proper tow-rope – they are not expensive. The vehicle being towed must display an ON TOW sign in its rear window.
☐ Always turn the ignition key to the ON position when the vehicle is being towed, so that the steering lock is released, and that the direction indicator and brake lights will work.

☐ Before being towed, release the handbrake and select neutral on the transmission (manual transmission or CVT).
☐ On models with automatic transmission, special precautions apply. Check the transmission fluid level (see Chapter 1). If the level is below the HOT line on the dipstick, add fluid or use a towing 'dolly' (front wheels off the ground). Start the engine, move the selector lever to D4, then to neutral, turn off the engine. Road speed must not exceed 30 mph (50 kmh), and towed distance must not exceed 30 miles (50 km). Never tow the vehicle from the rear with the front wheels on the ground.

☐ Note that greater than usual pedal pressure will be required to operate the brakes, since the vacuum servo unit is only operational with the engine running.
☐ On models with power steering, greater than usual steering effort will also be required.
☐ The driver of the car being towed must keep the tow-rope taut at all times to avoid snatching.
☐ Make sure that both drivers know the route before setting off.
☐ Only drive at moderate speeds and keep the distance towed to a minimum. Drive smoothly and allow plenty of time for slowing down at junctions.

Introduction

There are some very simple checks which need only take a few minutes to carry out, but which could save you a lot of inconvenience and expense.

These *Weekly checks* require no great skill or special tools, and the small amount of time they take to perform could prove to be very well spent, for example:

☐ Keeping an eye on tyre condition and pressures, will not only help to stop them wearing out prematurely, but could also save your life.

☐ Many breakdowns are caused by electrical problems. Battery-related faults are particularly common, and a quick check on a regular basis will often prevent the majority of these.

☐ If your car develops a brake fluid leak, the first time you might know about it is when your brakes don't work properly. Checking the level regularly will give advance warning of this kind of problem.

☐ If the oil or coolant levels run low, the cost of repairing any engine damage will be far greater than fixing the leak.

Underbonnet check points

◀ **SOHC engines**

A *Engine oil level dipstick*

B *Engine oil filler cap*

C *Coolant expansion tank*

D *Brake fluid reservoir*

E *Clutch fluid reservoir*

F *Screen washer fluid reservoir*

G *Battery*

H *Power steering fluid reservoir*

◀ **DOHC engines**

A *Engine oil level dipstick*

B *Engine oil filler cap*

C *Coolant expansion tank*

D *Brake fluid reservoir*

E *Clutch fluid reservoir*

F *Screen washer fluid reservoir*

G *Battery*

H *Power steering fluid reservoir*

Engine oil level

Before you start

✔ Make sure that your car is on level ground.
✔ Check the oil level before the car is driven, or at least 5 minutes after the engine has been switched off.

 If the oil is checked immediately after driving the vehicle, some of the oil will remain in the upper engine components, resulting in an inaccurate reading on the dipstick.

The correct oil

Modern engines place great demands on their oil. It is very important that the correct oil for your car is used (see 'Lubricants and fluids').

Car Care

● If you have to add oil frequently, you should check whether you have any oil leaks. Place some clean paper under the car overnight, and check for stains in the morning. If there are no leaks, the engine may be burning oil.
● Always maintain the level between the upper and lower dipstick marks (see photo 2). If the level is too low severe engine damage may occur. Oil seal and/or catalytic converter failure may result if the engine is overfilled by adding too much oil.

1 The dipstick is located on the front of the engine (DOHC engines) or at the front left-hand corner of the engine (SOHC engines) and has an orange handle (see *Underbonnet check points* for exact location). Withdraw the dipstick, and using a clean rag or paper towel, wipe all oil from the dipstick. Insert the clean dipstick into the tube as far as it will go, then withdraw it again.

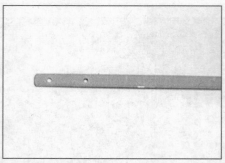

2 Note the oil level on the end of the dipstick, which should be between the upper and lower mark. Approximately 0.5 litre of oil will raise the level from the lower mark to the upper mark.

3 Oil is added through the filler cap on top of the engine. Turn the cap anticlockwise and withdraw it. Top-up the level. A funnel may help to reduce spillage. Add the oil slowly, checking the level on the dipstick often. Do not overfill.

Coolant level

⚠ *Warning: DO NOT attempt to remove the expansion tank pressure cap when the engine is hot, as there is a very great risk of scalding. Do not leave open containers of coolant about, as it is poisonous.*

Car Care

● With a sealed-type cooling system, adding coolant should not be necessary on a regular basis. If frequent topping-up is required, it is likely there is a leak. Check the radiator, all hoses and joint faces for signs of staining or wetness, and rectify as necessary.
● It is important that antifreeze is used in the cooling system all year round, not just during the winter months. Don't top-up with water alone, as the antifreeze will become too diluted.

1 The coolant level varies with the temperature of the engine. When the engine is cold, the coolant level should be between the MIN and MAX marks.

2 If topping-up is necessary, wait until the engine is cold. Slowly unscrew the cap to release any pressure present in the cooling system, and remove the cap.

3 Add a mixture of water and antifreeze to the expansion tank until the coolant level is on the MAX mark.

Brake and clutch fluid level

Warning:
● *Brake/clutch fluid can harm your eyes and damage painted surfaces, so use extreme caution when handling and pouring it.*

● *Do not use fluid that has been standing open for some time, as it absorbs moisture from the air, which can cause a dangerous loss of braking effectiveness.*

• *Make sure that your car is on level ground.*
• *The fluid level in the reservoir will drop slightly as the brake pads wear down, but the fluid level must never be allowed to drop below the MIN mark.*

Safety First!

● If the reservoirs require repeated topping-up this is an indication of a fluid leak somewhere in the system, which should be investigated immediately.

● If a leak is suspected, the car should not be driven until the braking/clutch system has been checked. Never take any risks where brakes are concerned.

1 The MIN and MAX marks are indicated on the reservoirs. The fluid level must be kept between the marks at all times. This is the brake fluid reservoir . . .

2 . . . and the clutch fluid reservoir.

3 If topping-up is necessary, first wipe clean the area around the filler cap to prevent dirt entering the hydraulic system. Unscrew the reservoir cap.

4 Carefully add fluid, taking care not to spill it onto the surrounding components. Use only the specified fluid; mixing different types can cause damage to the system. On completion, securely refit the cap and wipe away any spilt fluid.

Wiper blades

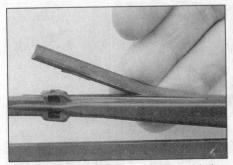

1 Check the condition of the wiper blades. If they are cracked or show any signs of deterioration, or if the glass swept area is smeared, renew them. For maximum clarity of vision, wiper blades should be renewed annually, as a matter of course.

2 To remove a windscreen wiper blade, pull the arm fully away from the screen until it locks. Swivel the blade through 90º, then depress the locking tab with a screwdriver or your fingers.

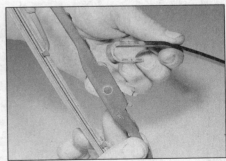

3 Slide the wiper blade out of the hooked end of the arm, then feed the arm through the hole in the blade. When fitting the new blade, make sure that the blade locks securely into the arm, and that the blade is orientated correctly.

Power steering fluid level

Before you start

✔ Park the vehicle on level ground.
✔ With the engine idling, turn the steering wheel slowly from lock-to-lock 2 or 3 times and set the front wheels at the straight-ahead position, then stop the engine. The steering must not be turned once the engine has been stopped.

Safety first!

● The need for frequent topping-up indicates a leak, which should be investigated immediately.

1 The power steering fluid reservoir is located on the left-hand side of the engine compartment. Only check the fluid level when the engine/fluid is **cold**.

2 The fluid level must be between the upper and lower level as indicated on the reservoir.

3 Where topping-up is required, add the specified type of fluid until the level reaches the maximum mark. On completion refit and tighten the cap.

Washer fluid level

Screenwash additives not only keep the windscreen clean during foul weather, they also prevent the washer system freezing in cold weather – which is when you are likely to need it most. Don't top-up using plain water, as the screenwash will become too diluted, and will freeze during cold weather.

On no account use coolant antifreeze in the washer system – this could discolour or damage paintwork.

1 The reservoir for the windscreen and headlight washer systems is on the front left-hand side of the engine compartment.

2 A screenwash additive should be added in the quantities recommended on the bottle.

Tyre condition and pressure

It is very important that tyres are in good condition, and at the correct pressure - having a tyre failure at any speed is highly dangerous. Tyre wear is influenced by driving style - harsh braking and acceleration, or fast cornering, will all produce more rapid tyre wear. As a general rule, the front tyres wear out faster than the rears. Interchanging the tyres from front to rear ("rotating" the tyres) may result in more even wear. However, if this is completely effective, you may have the expense of replacing all four tyres at once! Remove any nails or stones embedded in the tread before they penetrate the tyre to cause deflation. If removal of a nail does reveal that the tyre has been punctured, refit the nail so that its point of penetration is marked. Then immediately change the wheel, and have the tyre repaired by a tyre dealer.

Regularly check the tyres for damage in the form of cuts or bulges, especially in the sidewalls. Periodically remove the wheels, and clean any dirt or mud from the inside and outside surfaces. Examine the wheel rims for signs of rusting, corrosion or other damage. Light alloy wheels are easily damaged by "kerbing" whilst parking; steel wheels may also become dented or buckled. A new wheel is very often the only way to overcome severe damage.

New tyres should be balanced when they are fitted, but it may become necessary to re-balance them as they wear, or if the balance weights fitted to the wheel rim should fall off. Unbalanced tyres will wear more quickly, as will the steering and suspension components. Wheel imbalance is normally signified by vibration, particularly at a certain speed (typically around 50 mph). If this vibration is felt only through the steering, then it is likely that just the front wheels need balancing. If, however, the vibration is felt through the whole car, the rear wheels could be out of balance. Wheel balancing should be carried out by a tyre dealer or garage.

1 Tread Depth - visual check
The original tyres have tread wear safety bands (B), which will appear when the tread depth reaches approximately 1.6 mm. The band positions are indicated by a triangular mark on the tyre sidewall (A).

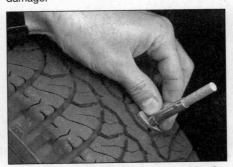

2 Tread Depth - manual check
Alternatively, tread wear can be monitored with a simple, inexpensive device known as a tread depth indicator gauge.

3 Tyre Pressure Check
Check the tyre pressures regularly with the tyres cold. Do not adjust the tyre pressures immediately after the vehicle has been used, or an inaccurate setting will result.

Tyre tread wear patterns

Shoulder Wear

Underinflation (wear on both sides)
Under-inflation will cause overheating of the tyre, because the tyre will flex too much, and the tread will not sit correctly on the road surface. This will cause a loss of grip and excessive wear, not to mention the danger of sudden tyre failure due to heat build-up.
Check and adjust pressures
Incorrect wheel camber (wear on one side)
Repair or renew suspension parts
Hard cornering
Reduce speed!

Centre Wear

Overinflation
Over-inflation will cause rapid wear of the centre part of the tyre tread, coupled with reduced grip, harsher ride, and the danger of shock damage occurring in the tyre casing.
Check and adjust pressures

If you sometimes have to inflate your car's tyres to the higher pressures specified for maximum load or sustained high speed, don't forget to reduce the pressures to normal afterwards.

Uneven Wear

Front tyres may wear unevenly as a result of wheel misalignment. Most tyre dealers and garages can check and adjust the wheel alignment (or "tracking") for a modest charge.
Incorrect camber or castor
Repair or renew suspension parts
Malfunctioning suspension
Repair or renew suspension parts
Unbalanced wheel
Balance tyres
Incorrect toe setting
Adjust front wheel alignment
Note: *The feathered edge of the tread which typifies toe wear is best checked by feel.*

Battery

Caution: Before carrying out any work on the vehicle battery, read the precautions given in 'Safety first!' at the start of this manual.

✔ Make sure that the battery tray is in good condition, and that the clamp is tight. Corrosion on the tray, retaining clamp and the battery itself can be removed with a solution of water and baking soda. Thoroughly rinse all cleaned areas with water. Any metal parts damaged by corrosion should be covered with a zinc-based primer, then painted.

✔ Periodically (approximately every three months), check the charge condition of the battery as described in Chapter 5A.

✔ If the battery is flat, and you need to jump start your vehicle, see *Roadside repairs*.

1   The battery is located on the left-hand side of the engine compartment.

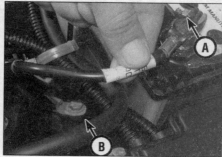

2   Check the tightness of battery clamps (A) to ensure good electrical connections. You should not be able to move them. Also check each cable (B) for cracks and frayed conductors.

HAYNES HINT

Battery corrosion can be kept to a minimum by applying a layer of petroleum jelly to the clamps and terminals after they are reconnected.

3   If corrosion (white, fluffy deposits) is evident, remove the cables from the battery terminals, clean them with a small wire brush, then refit them. Automotive stores sell a tool for cleaning the battery post . . .

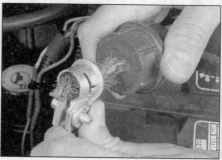

4   . . . as well as the battery cable clamps

Electrical systems

✔ Check all external lights and the horn. Refer to the appropriate Sections of Chapter 12 for details if any of the circuits are found to be inoperative.

✔ Visually check all accessible wiring connectors, harnesses and retaining clips for security, and for signs of chafing or damage.

HAYNES HINT

If you need to check your brake lights and indicators unaided, back up to a wall or garage door and operate the lights. The reflected light should show if they are working properly.

1   If a single indicator light, brake light or headlight has failed, it is likely that a bulb has blown and will need to be renewed. Refer to Chapter 12 for details. If both brake lights have failed, it is possible that the brake light switch operated by the brake pedal has failed. Refer to Chapter 9 for details.

2   If more than one indicator light or headlight has failed, it is likely that either a fuse has blown or that there is a fault in the circuit (see Chapter 12). The main fusebox is located behind the storage compartment on the driver's side of the facia panel; further fuses are located in the left-hand corner of the engine compartment.

3   To renew a blown fuse, pull it from its location in the fusebox. Fit a new fuse of the same rating, available from car accessory shops.

Lubricants and fluids

Engine	Engine oil to specification ACEA B2:96, CCMC PD2, API Service SG, SH or SJ, viscosity SAE 10W-40
Cooling system	Honda anti-freeze
Manual transmission	Honda MTF. SAE 10W-40 engine oil may be used, but higher gearchange effort may be required
Automatic transmission	Honda ATF, or Dexron II or III
Constantly Variable Transmission (CVT)	Honda CVT fluid
Braking system	Hydraulic fluid to DOT 3 or DOT 4
Clutch system	Hydraulic fluid to DOT 3 or DOT 4
Power steering system	Honda power steering fluid

Choosing your engine oil

Engines need oil, not only to lubricate moving parts and minimise wear, but also to maximise power output and to improve fuel economy.

HOW ENGINE OIL WORKS

• Beating friction

Without oil, the moving surfaces inside your engine will rub together, heat up and melt, quickly causing the engine to seize. Engine oil creates a film which separates these moving parts, preventing wear and heat build-up.

• Cooling hot-spots

Temperatures inside the engine can exceed 1000° C. The engine oil circulates and acts as a coolant, transferring heat from the hot-spots to the sump.

• Cleaning the engine internally

Good quality engine oils clean the inside of your engine, collecting and dispersing combustion deposits and controlling them until they are trapped by the oil filter or flushed out at oil change.

OIL CARE - FOLLOW THE CODE

To handle and dispose of used engine oil safely, always:

0800 66 33 66
www.oilbankline.org.uk

- *Avoid skin contact with used engine oil. Repeated or prolonged contact can be harmful.*
- *Dispose of used oil and empty packs in a responsible manner in an authorised disposal site. Call 0800 663366 to find the one nearest to you. Never tip oil down drains or onto the ground.*

Tyre pressures

The tyre pressures are given on a label affixed to the driver's door aperture.

Chapter 1
Routine maintenance and servicing

Contents

Degrees of difficulty

 Easy, suitable for novice with little experience

 Fairly easy, suitable for beginner with some experience

Fairly difficult, suitable for competent DIY mechanic

Difficult, suitable for experienced DIY mechanic

Very difficult, suitable for expert DIY or professional

Lubricants and fluids

Refer to *Weekly checks*

Capacities*

Engine oil

Including oil filter:
SOHC engines	3.5 litres
DOHC engines	4.0 litres

Cooling system
SOHC engines	4.2 litres
DOHC engines	5.0 litres

Transmission

Manual transmission:
SOHC engines	1.8 litres
DOHC engines	2.2 litres

Automatic transmission:
At fluid change	2.5 litres
Constantly Variable Transmission (CVT)	3.9 litres

Washer fluid reservoir
Without headlight washers	4.5 litres
With headlight washers	6.5 litres

Fuel tank
3-door & 4-door models	45 litres
5-door & Estate models	55 litres

All capacities are approximate. Add as necessary to bring to appropriate level

Engine

Engine codes	See Chapter 2A or 2B

Valve clearances (engine cold):

SOHC engines:
Intake	0.18 to 0.22 mm (0.007 to 0.009 in)
Exhaust	0.23 to 0.27 mm (0.009 to 0.011 in)

DOHC engines:
Intake	0.15 to 0.19 mm (0.006 to 0.007 in)
Exhaust	0.17 to 0.21 mm (0.007 to 0.008 in)

Cooling system

Antifreeze mixture:
50% antifreeze	Protection down to –35°C
55% antifreeze	Protection down to –45°C

Note: *Refer to antifreeze manufacturer for latest recommendations.*

Ignition system

	Type	Electrode gap
Spark plugs:		
SOHC engines	Bosch FR 78 X	Not adjustable
	NGK ZFR5J-11	1.0 to 1.1 mm
	NGK BKR5E-11	1.0 to 1.1 mm
DOHC engines	Bosch FR 78 X	Not adjustable
	NGK BKR6E-N-11	1.0 to 1.1 mm
HT lead resistance	Less than 25 000 ohms	

Brakes

Friction material minimum thickness:
Front brake pads	1.6 mm
Rear brake pads	1.6 mm
Rear brake shoes	2.0 mm

Disc minimum thickness:
Front disc	19.0 mm
Rear disc	8.0 mm
Handbrake adjustment	6 to 10 clicks

Idle speed

SOHC engines	750 ± 50 rpm
DOHC engines	800 ± 50 rpm

Auxiliary drivebelt tension

	Deflection	Tension
Power steering pump belt:		
Used belt	8.0 to 12.0 mm	340 to 490 N
New belt	5.5 to 8.5 mm	590 to 785 N
Alternator belt:		
Used belt	7.0 to 10.5 mm	340 to 490 N
New belt	5.0 to 7.0 mm	640 to 785 N
Air conditioning compressor belt:		
Used belt	7.5 to 9.5 mm	340 to 490 N
New belt	5.0 to 7.0 mm	740 to 880N

Note: *A used belt is one which has been run for 5 minutes or more.*

Torque wrench settings

	Nm	lbf ft
Automatic/Constantly Variable transmission drain plug	50	37
Fuel filter:		
Banjo bolt	15	11
Banjo nut	22	16
Manual transmission oil drain plug	39	29
Manual transmission oil filler plug	44	32
Oil filter cartridge	22	16
Roadwheel nuts	110	81
Spark plugs	18	13
Sump drain plug:		
Aluminium sump	39	29
Steel sump	44	32

Underbonnet view (SOHC model)

1 Engine oil filler cap
2 Air cleaner
3 Brake fluid reservoir
4 Spark plugs
5 Battery
6 Coolant expansion tank
7 Engine oil level dipstick
8 Alternator
9 Washer fluid reservoir
10 Power steering fluid
   reservoir
11 Clutch fluid reservoir

Front underbody view

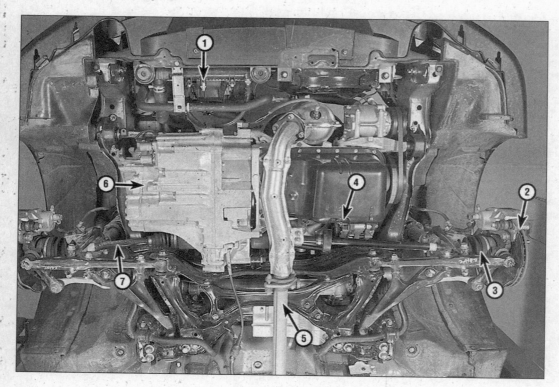

1 Radiator drain plug
2 Front brake caliper
3 Outer driveshaft gaiter
4 Engine oil drain plug
5 Exhaust pipe
6 Transmission drain plug
7 Driveshaft

Rear underbody view

1 Exhaust pipe
2 Fuel tank
3 Handbrake cable
4 Rear disc brake caliper
5 Silencer
6 Brake hose
7 Shock absorber and
   spring assembly

The maintenance intervals in this manual are provided with the assumption that you, not the dealer, will be carrying out the work. These are the minimum maintenance intervals recommended by us for vehicles driven daily. If you wish to keep your vehicle in peak condition at all times, you may wish to perform some of these procedures more often. We encourage frequent maintenance, because it enhances the efficiency, performance and resale value of your vehicle.

If the vehicle is driven in dusty areas, used to tow a trailer, or driven frequently at slow speeds (idling in traffic) or on short journeys, more frequent maintenance intervals are recommended.

When the vehicle is new, it should be serviced by a factory-authorised dealer service department, in order to preserve the factory warranty.

Every 6000 miles (10 000 km) or 6 months, whichever comes first

☐ Renew the engine oil and filter (Section 4)

Note: *Honda recommend that the engine oil and filter are changed every 12 000 miles or 12 months. However, oil and filter changes are good for the engine and we recommend that the oil and filter are renewed more frequently, especially if the vehicle is used on a lot of short journeys.*

Every 12 000 miles (20 000 km) or 12 months, whichever comes first

☐ Auxiliary drivebelt check, adjustment and renewal (Section 5)
☐ Exhaust emission test (Section 6)
☐ Check the operation of all electrical systems (Section 7)*
☐ Check and if necessary adjust the engine idle speed (Section 8)
☐ Check the braking system (Section 9)*
☐ Check the exhaust system (Section 10)*
☐ Check all components, pipes and hoses for fluid leaks (Section 11)
☐ Check the steering and suspension components for condition and security (Section 12)
☐ Check the condition of the driveshaft gaiters (Section 12)
☐ Renew the pollen filter (Section 13)*
☐ Check the automatic transmission/CVT fluid level (Section 14)
☐ Check the manual transmission oil level (Section 15)
☐ Carry out a road test (Section 16)*

* *On vehicles covering a high mileage (more than 20 000 miles/ 30 000 km annually) carry out the items marked with an asterisk every 10 000 miles/15 000 km, regardless of time, and carry out the items not marked with an asterisk at the 12 month interval.*

Every 24 000 miles (40 000 km) or 2 years, whichever comes first

☐ Check and if necessary adjust the engine valve clearances (Section 17)
☐ Renew the air cleaner element (Section 18)
☐ Renew the fuel filter (Section 19)
☐ Lubricate all door locks and hinges, door stops, bonnet lock and release, and tailgate lock and hinges (Section 20)
☐ Renew the spark plugs (Section 21)
☐ Check the ignition system (Section 22)

Every 36 000 miles (60 000 km) or 3 years, whichever comes first

☐ Renew the transmission oil (Section 23 or 24 as applicable)

Every 48 000 miles (80 000 km) or 4 years, whichever comes first

☐ Renew the coolant (Section 25)

Every 60 000 miles (100 000 km) or 5 years, whichever comes first

☐ Renew the timing belt (Section 26)

Note: *Honda recommend that the interval for timing belt renewal is 60 000 (100 000 km) or 5 years. However, if the vehicle is used mainly for short journeys or a lot of stop-start driving it is recommended that the renewal interval is shortened. The actual belt renewal interval is very much up to the individual owner but, bearing in mind that severe engine damage will result if the belt breaks in use, we recommend you err on the side of caution.*

Every 2 years, regardless of mileage

☐ Renew the brake fluid (Section 27)
☐ Renew the remote control handset batteries (Section 28)

1 General information

1 This Chapter is designed to help the home mechanic maintain his/her vehicle for safety, economy, long life and peak performance.

2 The Chapter contains a master maintenance schedule, followed by Sections dealing specifically with each task in the schedule. Visual checks, adjustments, component renewal and other helpful items are included. Refer to the accompanying illustrations of the engine compartment and the underside of the vehicle for the locations of the various components.

3 Servicing your vehicle in accordance with the mileage/time maintenance schedule and the following Sections will provide a planned maintenance programme, which should result in a long and reliable service life. This is a comprehensive plan, so maintaining some items but not others at the specified service intervals, will not produce the same results.

4 As you service your vehicle, you will discover that many of the procedures can – and should – be grouped together, because of the particular procedure being performed, or because of the proximity of two otherwise-unrelated components to one another. For example, if the vehicle is raised for any reason, the exhaust can be inspected at the same time as the suspension and steering components.

5 The first step in this maintenance programme is to prepare yourself before the actual work begins. Read through all the Sections relevant to the work to be carried out, then make a list and gather all the parts and tools required. If a problem is encountered, seek advice from a parts specialist, or a dealer service department.

2 Regular maintenance

1 If, from the time the vehicle is new, the routine maintenance schedule is followed closely, and frequent checks are made of fluid levels and high-wear items, as suggested throughout this manual, the engine will be kept in relatively good running condition, and the need for additional work will be minimised.

2 It is possible that there will be times when the engine is running poorly due to the lack of regular maintenance. This is even more likely if a used vehicle, which has not received regular and frequent maintenance checks, is purchased. In such cases, additional work may need to be carried out, outside of the regular maintenance intervals.

3 If engine wear is suspected, a compression test (refer to Chapter 2A or 2B) will provide valuable information regarding the overall performance of the main internal components. Such a test can be used as a basis to decide on the extent of the work to be carried out. If, for example, a compression test indicates serious internal engine wear, conventional maintenance as described in this Chapter will not greatly improve the performance of the engine, and may prove a waste of time and money, unless extensive overhaul work is carried out first.

4 The following series of operations are those most often required to improve the performance of a generally poor-running engine:

Primary operations

a) Clean, inspect and test the battery (refer to 'Weekly checks').
b) Check all the engine-related fluids (refer to 'Weekly checks').
c) Check the condition and tension of the auxiliary drivebelt (Section 5).
d) Renew the spark plugs (Section 21).
e) Check the condition of the air filter, and renew if necessary (Section 18).
f) Renew the fuel filter (Section 19).
g) Check the condition of all hoses, and check for fluid leaks (Section 11).

5 If the above operations do not prove fully effective, carry out the following secondary operations:

Secondary operations

All items listed under *Primary operations*, plus the following:

a) Check the charging system (refer to Chapter 5A).
b) Check the ignition system (refer to Chapter 5B).
c) Check the fuel system (refer to Chapter 4A).

3 Maintenance Required Indicator reset

1 Some Civic models are quipped with a Maintenance Required Indicator (MRI), mounted in the lower half of the speedometer in the instrument panel. The display will indicate that the next service will soon be due. After having carried out the required service, the MRI can be reset by inserting the ignition key in the slot in the dash.

Every 6000 miles (10 000 km) or 6 months, whichever comes first

4 Engine oil and filter renewal

1 Frequent oil and filter changes are the most important preventative maintenance procedures which can be undertaken by the DIY owner. As engine oil ages, it becomes diluted and contaminated, which leads to premature engine wear.

2 Before starting this procedure, gather together all the necessary tools and materials. Also make sure that you have plenty of clean rags and newspapers handy, to mop-up any spills. Ideally, the engine oil should be warm, as it will drain more easily, and more built-up sludge will be removed with it. Take care not to touch the exhaust or any other hot parts of the engine when working under the vehicle.

To avoid any possibility of scalding, and to protect yourself from possible skin irritants and other harmful contaminants in used engine oils, it is advisable to wear gloves when carrying out this work.

3 Firmly apply the handbrake then jack up the front of the vehicle and support it on axle stands (see *Jacking and vehicle support*).

4 Remove the oil filler cap **(see illustration)**.

5 Using a spanner, or preferably a suitable socket and bar, slacken the drain plug about half a turn **(see illustration)**. Position the

4.4 Unscrew the oil filler cap

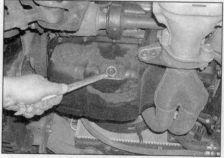
4.5 Slacken the drain plug

As the drain plug releases from the threads, move it away quickly so that the stream of oil running out of the sump goes into the drain pan and not up your sleeve

4.9 Use an oil filter removal tool to slacken the filter

4.11 Apply a light coat of clean engine oil to the filter seal

draining container under the drain plug, then remove the plug completely **(see Haynes Hint)**.

6 Allow some time for the oil to drain, noting that it may be necessary to reposition the container as the oil flow slows to a trickle.

7 After all the oil has drained, wipe the drain plug and the sealing washer with a clean rag. Examine the condition of the sealing washer, and renew it if it shows signs of scoring or other damage which may prevent an oil-tight seal. Clean the area around the drain plug opening, and refit the plug complete with the washer and tighten it to the specified torque.

8 Move the container into position under the oil filter. On all engines, the filter is located on the rear face of the cylinder block, above the left-hand side driveshaft.

9 Use an oil filter removal tool to slacken the filter initially, then unscrew it by hand the rest of the way **(see illustration)**. Empty the oil

from the old filter into the container. In order to ensure that all the old oil is removed, puncture the 'dome' of the filter in two places, and allow the oil to drain from the filter completely.

10 Use a clean rag to remove all oil, dirt and sludge from the filter sealing area on the engine.

11 Apply a light coating of clean engine oil to the sealing ring on the new filter, then screw the filter into position on the engine. Tighten the filter firmly by hand only – **do not** use any tools. If a genuine filter is being fitted and the special oil filter tool (a socket which fits over the end of the filter) is available, tighten the filter to the specified torque **(see illustration)**.

12 Remove the old oil and all tools from under the vehicle then lower the vehicle to the ground.

13 Fill the engine through the filler hole, using the correct grade and type of oil (refer to *Weekly Checks* for details of topping-up). Pour in half the specified quantity of oil first,

then wait a few minutes for the oil to drain into the sump. Continue to add oil, a small quantity at a time, until the level is up to the lower mark on the dipstick.

14 Start the engine and run it for a few minutes, while checking for leaks around the oil filter seal and the sump drain plug. Note that there may be a delay of a few seconds before the low oil pressure warning light goes out when the engine is first started, as the oil circulates through the new oil filter and the engine oil galleries before the pressure builds-up.

15 Stop the engine, and wait a few minutes for the oil to settle in the sump once more. With the new oil circulated and the filter now completely full, recheck the level on the dipstick, and add more oil as necessary.

16 Dispose of the used engine oil safely with reference to *General repair procedures*. It should be noted that used oil filters should not be included with domestic waste. Most local authority used oil 'banks' also have used filter disposal points alongside.

Every 12 000 miles (20 000 km) or 12 months, whichever comes first

5 Auxiliary drivebelt check, adjustment and renewal

Checking

1 Due to their function and material makeup, drivebelts are prone to failure after a long period of time and should therefore be inspected regularly.

2 With the engine stopped, inspect the full length of the drivebelts for cracks and separation of the belt plies. It will be necessary to turn the engine (using a spanner or socket and bar on the crankshaft pulley bolt) in order to move the belts from the pulleys so that the belts can be inspected thoroughly. Twist the belts between the pulleys so that both sides can be viewed. Also

check for fraying, and glazing which gives the belts a shiny appearance. Check the pulleys for nicks, cracks, distortion and corrosion.

3 The tension of each belt is checked by pushing the belt at a distance halfway between the pulleys. Push firmly with your thumb and see how much the belt moves (deflects) **(see illustration)**. Alternatively, if a tension gauge is available, measure the tension of the belts halfway between the pulleys. Compare the deflection obtained with the figures given in the Specifications at the beginning of this Chapter.

4 Renew the belt if it shows any sign of wear or damage.

Adjustment

5 If it is necessary to adjust the belt tension, either to make the belt tighter or looser, it is done by moving the belt-driven accessory on the bracket (PAS pump belt and alternator

belt), or by repositioning the idler pulley (air conditioning compressor belt).

6 The alternator drivebelt is adjusted by

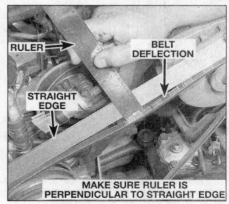

5.3 Measuring the belt deflection

5.6a Slacken the bolts or nuts (arrowed), then move the alternator in or out to adjust the drivebelt tension

5.6b The air conditioning compressor uses an adjustable idler pulley on some models to adjust the belt tension – slacken the idler pulley (A), then turn the adjusting bolt (B) to slacken or tighten the belt

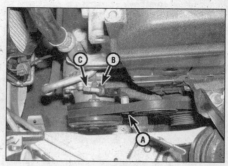

5.6c On other models the air conditioning compressor belt is adjusted by slackening the pivot bolt (A) and locknut (B), then turning the adjusting bolt (C)

loosening the pivot and adjusting bolts and moving the alternator to tension the drivebelt **(see illustration)**. After adjustment, tighten the pivot and adjusting bolts. The air conditioning compressor on some models is rigidly mounted and uses an adjustable idler pulley which is mounted between the components to tension the belt. On other models the compressor must be moved in its bracket to tension the belt **(see illustrations)**. The power steering pump is adjusted by loosening the adjusting bolt(s) and moving the pump in its bracket to tension the belt **(see illustrations)**.

7 After the bolts have been loosened, move the component away from the engine to tighten the belt or toward the engine to loosen the belt. Measure the belt tension in accordance with the above methods. Repeat this step until the drivebelt is adjusted.

Renewal

8 To renew a belt, follow the above procedures for drivebelt adjustment but slip the belt off the crankshaft pulley and remove it. Since belts tend to wear out more or less at the same time, its a good idea to renew them

all at the same time. Mark each belt and the corresponding pulley groove so the belts can be installed properly.

9 Take the old belts with you when purchasing new ones in order to make a direct comparison for length, width and design.

10 Adjust the belts as described earlier in this Section.

6 Exhaust emission check

1 Honda specify that this check should be carried out annually on vehicles which are subject to intensive use (eg, taxis/hire cars) and every 3 years on other vehicles. The check involves checking the engine management system operation by plugging an electronic tester into the system diagnostic socket to check the electronic control module (ECM) memory for faults (see Chapter 4A).

2 In reality, if the vehicle is running correctly and the engine management warning light in the instrument panel is functioning normally, then this check need not be carried out.

7 Electrical systems check

1 Check the operation of all electrical equipment, ie, lights, direction indicators, horn, wash/wipe system, etc. Refer to the appropriate Sections of Chapter 12 for details if any of the circuits are found to be inoperative.

2 Visually check all accessible wiring connectors, harnesses and retaining clips for security, and for signs of chafing or damage. Rectify any faults found.

8 Idle speed check and adjustment

1 Engine idle speed is the speed at which the engine operates when no accelerator pedal pressure is applied, as when stopped at a traffic light. The speed is critical to the performance of the engine itself, as well as

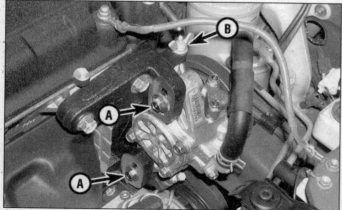

5.6d The power steering pump belt requires loosening the adjusting bolts (A) and turning the wingnut (B) on some models . . .

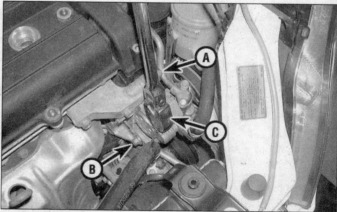

5.6e . . . while on other models the power steering pump belt is adjusted by loosening the pivot bolt (A) and adjusting bolt (B), then inserting a 3/8-inch drive ratchet (C) into the square hole and pivoting the pump in its bracket

many subsystems. Before checking or adjusting the idle speed make sure the Malfunction Indicator Light is not on, the air cleaner and spark plugs are in good condition, the PCV system is operating properly and the ignition timing is correct.

2 Connect a hand-held tachometer in accordance with the tool manufacturer's instructions.

3 Set the handbrake firmly and block the wheels to prevent the vehicle from rolling. Place the transmission in Neutral (manual transmission) or Park (automatic transmission).

4 Start the engine and run it at 3000 rpm until it warms-up to normal operating temperature (the cooling fan comes on), then allow the engine to idle.

5 On SOHC engine codes D14A2, D15Z3, D15Z6, D15Z8, D16Y2, D16Y3, D16Y5, D16Y6, D16Y8, and all DOHC models proceed as follows:

a) *Stop the engine and disconnect the electrical connector from the Idle Air Control (IAC) valve (see Chapter 4A).*

b) *Start the engine with the accelerator slightly depressed and stabilize the idle at 1000 rpm. Slowly release the accelerator and allow the engine to idle. Make sure all accessories are turned off and the radiator fan and air conditioning are not operating.*

c) *The idle speed should be:*
D14A2, D15Z3, D16Y2, D16Y3
– 550 ± 50 rpm.
D15Z6, D15Z8, D16Y5, D16Y6, D16Y8
and all DOHC models – 480 ± 50 rpm.

d) *If the idle speed is too low or too high, remove the cap and turn the idle adjust screw to obtain the specified idle speed* **(see illustration)**. *Make changes slowly in 1/4-turn increments only.*

e) *Turn off the engine and connect the electrical wiring plug to the IAC valve.*

f) *Remove the 7.5 amp BACK UP fuse from the underbonnet fuse block for ten seconds. This will clear any trouble codes from the ECM memory.* **Note:** *Unplugging the BACK UP fuse also cancels the radio preset stations and the clock setting. Be sure to make a note of the various radio*

stations that are programmed into the memory before removing the fuse.

g) *Start the engine and allow the idle to stabilize for one minute. Note the idle speed on the tachometer and compare it to that listed in this Chapter's Specifications.*

6 On the following engine codes: D14A3, D14A4, D14A7, D14A8, D15Z4, D15Z5, D16B2, D16Y4, D16Y9, DO NOT disconnect the IAC valve and proceed as follows:

a) *Start the engine and allow the idle to stabilize for one minute. Note the idle speed on the tachometer and compare it to that listed in this Chapter's Specifications.*

b) *If the idle speed is too low or too high, remove the cap and turn the idle adjust screw to obtain the specified idle speed. Make changes slowly in 1/4-turn increments only.*

7 On all models, turn the air conditioning on and place the heater blower fan to the High position. The idle should increase 50 to 100 rpm. If it doesn't there could be a problem with the IAC valve (see Chapter 4A).

9 Braking system inspection

![warning] *Warning: The dust created by the brake system is harmful to your health. Never blow it out with compressed air and don't inhale any of it. An approved filtering mask should be worn when working on the brakes. Do not, under any circumstances, use petroleum-based solvents to clean brake parts. Use brake system cleaner only. Try to use non-asbestos parts whenever possible.*

1 In addition to the specified intervals, the brakes should be inspected every time the wheels are removed or whenever a defect is suspected.

2 Any of the following symptoms could indicate a potential brake system defect:

a) *The vehicle pulls to one side when the brake pedal is depressed.*

b) *The brakes make squealing or dragging noises when applied.*

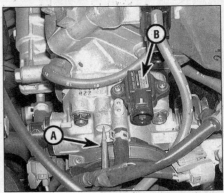

8.5 Prise off the cap and turn the adjusting screw (A) until the idle speed is correct with the IAC valve connector (B) disconnected on most models – see text

c) *Brake pedal travel is excessive.*
d) *The brake pedal pulsates when applied.*
e) *Brake fluid leaks, usually onto the inside of the tyre or wheel.*

3 Loosen the wheel nuts.

4 Raise the vehicle and place it securely on axle stands (see *Jacking and vehicle support*).

5 Remove the wheels.

Disc brakes

6 There are two pads (an outer and an inner) in each caliper. The pads are visible through inspection holes in each caliper **(see illustration)**.

7 Check the pad thickness by looking at each end of the caliper and through the inspection hole in the caliper body **(see illustration)**. If the lining material is less than the thickness listed in this Chapter's Specifications, renew the pads. **Note:** *Keep in mind that the lining material is bonded to a metal backing plate and the metal plate is not included in this measurement.*

8 If it is difficult to determine the exact thickness of the remaining pad material by the above method, or if you are at all concerned about the condition of the pads, remove the caliper(s), then remove the pads from the calipers for further inspection (refer to Chapter 9).

9 Once the pads are removed from the calipers, clean them with brake cleaner and remeasure them with a ruler or a vernier caliper.

10 Measure the disc thickness with a micrometer to make sure that it still has service life remaining. If any disc is thinner than the specified minimum thickness, renew it (refer to Chapter 9). Even if the disc has service life remaining, check its condition. Look for scoring, gouging and burned spots. If these conditions exist, remove the disc and have it resurfaced (see Chapter 9).

11 Before installing the wheels, check all brake pipes and hoses for damage, wear, deformation, cracks, corrosion, leakage, bends and twists, particularly in the vicinity of the rubber hoses at the calipers **(see**

9.6 Place a ruler across the inspection hole and determine the thickness of the remaining pad material

9.7 The amount of brake pad material remaining on the outer pad can be checked by looking at the end of the pad

9.11 Check all brake pipes and hoses for damage, wear and deformation, especially in the vicinity of the rubber hose at the caliper (arrowed)

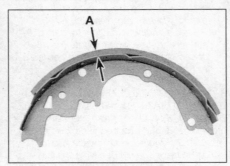

9.15 Measure the brake shoe lining thickness (A)

illustration). Check the clamps for tightness and the connections for leakage. Make sure that all hoses and pipes are clear of sharp edges, moving parts and the exhaust system. If any of the above conditions are noted, repair, reroute or renew the pipes and/or fittings as necessary (see Chapter 9).

Drum brakes

12 On rear drum brakes, make sure the handbrake is off then proceed to tap on the outside of the drum with a rubber mallet to loosen it.
13 Remove the brake drums (see Chapter 9).
14 With the drums removed, carefully clean the brake assembly with brake system cleaner.

⚠️ *Warning: Don't blow the dust out with compressed air and don't inhale any of it (it may contain asbestos, which is harmful to your health).*

15 Note the thickness of the lining material on both front and rear brake shoes. If the material has worn away to within 2.0 mm of the metal backing the shoes should be renewed (see illustration). The shoes should also be renewed if they're cracked, glazed (shiny areas), or covered with brake fluid.

16 Make sure all the brake assembly springs are connected and in good condition (see illustration).
17 Check the brake components for signs of fluid leakage. With your finger or a small screwdriver, carefully pry back the rubber cups on the wheel cylinder located at the top of the brake shoes (see illustration). Any leakage here is an indication that the wheel cylinders should be renewed immediately (see Chapter 9). Also, check all hoses and connections for signs of leakage.
18 Wipe the inside of the drum with a clean rag and brake system cleaner. Again, be careful not to breathe the dangerous asbestos dust.
19 Check the inside of the drum for cracks, score marks, deep scratches and 'hard spots' which will appear as small discoloured areas. If imperfections cannot be removed with fine emery cloth, the drum must be taken to an automotive machine shop for resurfacing.
20 Repeat the procedure for the remaining wheel. If the inspection reveals that all parts are in good condition, reinstall the brake drums, install the wheels and lower the vehicle to the ground.

Brake servo check

21 Sit in the driver's seat and perform the following sequence of tests.

22 With the brake fully depressed, start the engine – the pedal should move down a little when the engine starts.
23 With the engine running, depress the brake pedal several times – the travel distance should not change.
24 Depress the brake, stop the engine and hold the pedal in for about 30 seconds – the pedal should neither sink nor rise.
25 Restart the engine, run it for about a minute and turn it off. Then firmly depress the brake several times – the pedal travel should decrease with each application.
26 If your brakes do not operate as described, the brake servo may have failed. Refer to Chapter 9 for the renewal procedure.

Handbrake

27 Slowly pull up on the handbrake and count the number of clicks you hear until the handle is up as far as it will go. The adjustment is correct if you hear the specified number of clicks (see this Chapter's Specifications). If you hear more or fewer clicks, it's time to adjust the handbrake (see Chapter 9).

10 Exhaust system inspection

1 With the engine cold (at least three hours after the vehicle has been driven), check the complete exhaust system from the engine to the end of the tailpipe. Ideally, the inspection should be done with the vehicle on a hoist to permit unrestricted access. If a hoist isn't available, raise the vehicle and support it securely on axle stands (see *Jacking and vehicle support*).
2 Check the exhaust pipes and connections for evidence of leaks, severe corrosion and damage. Make sure that all brackets and

9.16 Typical assembled view of a rear drum brake (right-hand side)

9.17 Check the wheel cylinders for leaking fluid

10.2a Check the exhaust pipe flange at the exhaust manifold (arrowed) for leakage

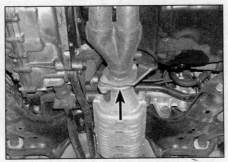

10.2b Inspect the exhaust pipe connection at the catalytic converter (arrowed) for leaks – also check that the retaining nuts and bolts are securely tightened

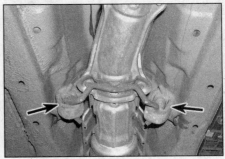

10.2c Check the exhaust system mountings (arrowed) for damage or deterioration

hangers are in good condition and tight **(see illustrations)**.

3 At the same time, inspect the underside of the body for holes, corrosion, open seams, etc, which may allow exhaust gases to enter the passenger compartment. Seal all body openings with silicone or body filler.

4 Rattles and other noises can often be traced to the exhaust system, especially the mounts and hangers. Try to move the pipes, silencer and catalytic converter. If the components can come in contact with the body or suspension parts, secure the exhaust system with new mounts.

11 Hose and fluid leak check

1 Visually inspect the engine joint faces, gaskets and seals for any signs of water or oil leaks. Pay particular attention to the areas around the cylinder head cover, cylinder head, oil filter and sump joint faces. Bear in mind that, over a period of time, some very slight seepage from these areas is to be expected – what you are really looking for is any indication of a serious leak. Should a leak be found, renew the offending gasket or oil seal by referring to the appropriate Chapters in this manual.

2 Also check the security and condition of all the engine-related pipes and hoses, and all braking system pipes and hoses and fuel lines. Ensure that all cable ties or securing clips are in place, and in good condition. Clips which are broken or missing can lead to chafing of the hoses, pipes or wiring, which could cause more serious problems in the future.

3 Carefully check the radiator hoses and heater hoses along their entire length. Renew any hose which is cracked, swollen or deteriorated. Cracks will show up better if the hose is squeezed. Pay close attention to the hose clips that secure the hoses to the cooling system components. Hose clips can pinch and puncture hoses, resulting in cooling system leaks. If the crimped-type hose clips are used, it may be a good idea to substitute standard worm-drive clips.

4 Inspect all the cooling system components (hoses, joint faces, etc) for leaks.

5 Where any problems are found on system components, renew the component or gasket with reference to Chapter 3.

6 With the vehicle raised, inspect the fuel tank and filler neck for punctures, cracks and other damage. The connection between the filler neck and tank is especially critical. Sometimes a rubber filler neck or connecting hose will leak due to loose retaining clamps or deteriorated rubber.

7 Carefully check all rubber hoses and metal fuel lines leading away from the fuel tank. Check for loose connections, deteriorated hoses, crimped lines, and other damage. Pay particular attention to the vent pipes and hoses, which often loop up around the filler neck and can become blocked or crimped. Follow the lines to the front of the vehicle, carefully inspecting them all the way. Renew damaged sections as necessary. Similarly, whilst the vehicle is raised, take the opportunity to inspect all underbody brake fluid pipes and hoses.

8 From within the engine compartment, check the security of all fuel, vacuum and brake hose attachments and pipe unions, and inspect all hoses for kinks, chafing and deterioration.

9 Check the condition of the power steering and, where applicable, the automatic transmission fluid pipes and hoses.

12 Suspension, steering and driveshaft gaiter inspection

Front suspension & steering

1 Raise the front of the vehicle, and securely support it on axle stands (see *Jacking and vehicle support*).

2 Visually inspect the balljoint dust covers and the steering rack-and-pinion gaiters for splits, chafing or deterioration. Any wear of these components will cause loss of lubricant, together with dirt and water entry, resulting in

rapid deterioration of the balljoints or steering gear.

3 Check the power steering fluid hoses for chafing or deterioration, and the pipe and hose unions for fluid leaks. Also check for signs of fluid leakage under pressure from the steering gear rubber gaiters, which would indicate failed fluid seals within the steering gear.

4 Grasp the roadwheel at the 12 o'clock and 6 o'clock positions, and try to rock it **(see illustration)**. Very slight free play may be felt, but if the movement is appreciable, further investigation is necessary to determine the source. Continue rocking the wheel while an assistant depresses the footbrake. If the movement is now eliminated or significantly reduced, it is likely that the hub bearings are at fault. If the free play is still evident with the footbrake depressed, then there is wear in the suspension joints or mountings.

5 Now grasp the wheel at the 9 o'clock and 3 o'clock positions, and try to rock it as before. Any movement felt now may again be caused by wear in the hub bearings or the steering track rod balljoints. If the outer balljoint is worn, the visual movement will be obvious. If the inner joint is suspect, it can be felt by placing a hand over the rack-and-pinion rubber gaiter and gripping the track rod. If the wheel is now rocked, movement will be felt at the inner joint if wear has taken place.

6 Using a large screwdriver or flat bar, check for wear in the suspension mounting bushes

12.4 Check for signs of wear in the wheel bearings by grasping the roadwheel at the 12 o'clock and 6 o'clock positions, and trying to rock it

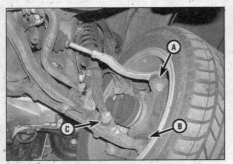

12.6a Inspect the track rod ends (A) and the lower balljoints (B) for torn grease seals – inspect the lower shock fork bushes (C) for deterioration

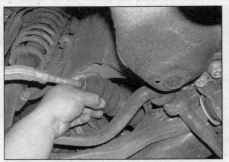

12.6b Check the steering rack gaiters for cracks and leaking steering fluid

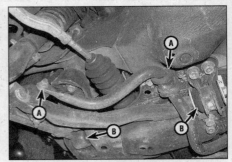

12.6c Check the anti-roll bar bushes and connectors (A) and the lower control arm bushes (B) for damage or distortion

by levering between the relevant suspension component and its attachment point. Some movement is to be expected, as the mountings are made of rubber, but excessive wear should be obvious. Also check the condition of any visible rubber bushes, looking for splits, cracks or contamination of the rubber **(see illustrations)**.

7 With the car standing on its wheels, have an assistant turn the steering wheel back-and-forth, about an eighth of a turn each way. There should be very little, if any, lost movement between the steering wheel and roadwheels. If this is not the case, closely observe the joints and mountings previously described. In addition, check the steering column universal joints for wear, and also check the rack-and-pinion steering gear itself.

Rear suspension

8 Chock the front wheels, then jack up the rear of the vehicle and support securely on axle stands (see *Jacking and vehicle support*).
9 Working as described previously for the front suspension, check the rear hub bearings, the suspension bushes and the strut or shock absorber mountings (as applicable) for wear.

Shock absorber

10 Check for any signs of fluid leakage around the shock absorber body, or from the rubber gaiter around the piston rod **(see illustration)**. Should any fluid be noticed, the shock absorber is defective internally, and should be renewed. **Note:** *Shock absorbers should always be renewed in pairs on the same axle.*
11 The efficiency of the shock absorber may be checked by bouncing the vehicle at each corner. Generally speaking, the body will return to its normal position and stop after being depressed. If it rises and returns on a rebound, the shock absorber is probably suspect. Also examine the shock absorber upper and lower mountings for any signs of wear.

Driveshaft gaiter

12 With the vehicle raised and securely supported on stands, turn the steering onto full lock then slowly rotate the roadwheel. Inspect

12.10 Check the shock absorbers for leakage where the rod enters the tube (arrowed)

the condition of the outer constant velocity (CV) joint rubber gaiters while squeezing the gaiters to open out the folds **(see illustration)**. Check for signs of cracking, splits or deterioration of the rubber which may allow the grease to escape and lead to water and grit entry into the joint. Also check the security and condition of the retaining clips. Repeat these checks on the inner CV joints. If any damage or deterioration is found, the gaiters should be renewed as described in Chapter 8.
13 At the same time, check the general condition of the CV joints themselves by first holding the driveshaft and attempting to rotate the wheel. Repeat this check by holding the inner joint and attempting to rotate the driveshaft. Any appreciable movement indicates wear in the joints, wear in the driveshaft splines or loose driveshaft retaining nut.

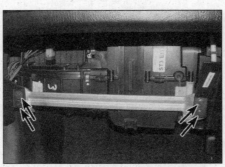

13.3 Undo the retaining bolts (arrowed) and remove the glovebox aperture brace

12.12 Flex the driveshaft gaiters to check for tears, cracks and leaking grease

13 Pollen filter renewal

1 Some models are equipped with a filter under the dash that cleans the air entering the vehicle through the ventilation system, as well as recirculated air.
2 Remove the glovebox (see Chapter 11, Section 23).
3 Undo the retaining bolts and remove the glovebox aperture brace **(see illustration)**.
4 Pull off the filter lid and slide the filter out of the housing. Note how the filter is fitted **(see illustrations)**.
5 Wipe the inside of the housing clean, then install the new filter by reversing the removal procedure.

13.4a Pull of the filter lid . . .

13.4b ... and remove the pollen filter

14.5a The automatic transmission fluid dipstick (arrowed) is located on the right-hand side of the engine compartment

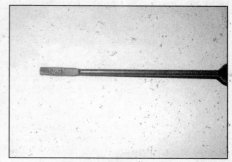

14.5b The automatic transmission fluid level should be in the cross-hatched area on the dipstick

14 Automatic transmission and Constantly Variable Transmission fluid level check

1 The level of the automatic or Constantly Variable transmission fluid should be carefully maintained. Low fluid level can lead to slipping or loss of drive, while overfilling can cause foaming, loss of fluid and transmission damage.
2 The transmission fluid level should only be checked on level ground within one minute of the engine being shut off.
3 Remove the dipstick – it's located down low on the front of the transmission (in the right-hand side of the engine compartment).
4 Wipe the fluid from the dipstick with a clean rag and reinsert it.
5 Pull the dipstick out again and note the fluid level (see illustration). The level should be between the upper and lower marks on the dipstick (see illustration). If the level is low, add the specified automatic transmission fluid through the dipstick opening with a funnel.
6 Add just enough of the specified fluid to fill the transmission to the proper level. It takes about 0.8 litre to raise the level from the lower mark to the upper mark, so add the fluid a little at a time and keep checking the level until it is correct.

7 The condition of the fluid should also be checked along with the level. If the fluid at the end of the dipstick is black or a dark reddish brown colour, or if it emits a burned smell, the fluid should be changed (see Section 23). If you are in doubt about the condition of the fluid, purchase some new fluid and compare the two for colour and smell.

15 Manual transmission fluid level check

1 The manual transmission does not have a dipstick. To check the fluid level, raise the vehicle and support it securely on axle stands (see *Jacking and Vehicle support*). The filler/level plug is on the right-hand side of the transmission housing (see illustration). Remove the plug, if the lubricant level is correct, it should be up to the lower edge of the hole.
2 If the transmission needs more lubricant (if the level is not up to the hole), use a funnel to add more (see illustrations). Stop filling the transmission when the lubricant begins to run out the hole.
3 Refit the plug and tighten it securely. Drive the vehicle a short distance, then check for leaks.

16 Road test

Instruments & electrical equipment

1 Check the operation of all instruments and electrical equipment.
2 Make sure that all instruments read correctly, and switch on all electrical equipment in turn, to check that it functions properly.

Steering & suspension

3 Check for any abnormalities in the steering, suspension, handling or road 'feel'.
4 Drive the vehicle, and check that there are no unusual vibrations or noises.
5 Check that the steering feels positive, with no excessive 'sloppiness', or roughness, and check for any suspension noises when cornering and driving over bumps.

Drivetrain

6 Check the performance of the engine, clutch, transmission and driveshafts.
7 Listen for any unusual noises from the engine, clutch and transmission.
8 Make sure that the engine runs smoothly when idling, and that there is no hesitation when accelerating.

15.1 The manual transmission filler/level plug is located on the right-hand side of the transmission

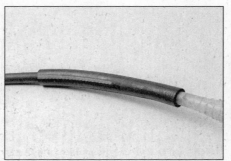

15.2a Use two different size pieces of hose to make an adapter on the funnel ...

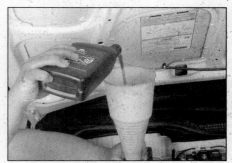

15.2b ... so you can easily add lubricant to the transmission from above

9 Check that, where applicable, the clutch action is smooth and progressive, that the drive is taken up smoothly, and that the pedal travel is not excessive. Also listen for any noises when the clutch pedal is depressed.

10 Check that all gears can be engaged smoothly without noise, and that the gear lever action is smooth and not abnormally vague or 'notchy'.

11 On automatic transmission models, make sure that all gearchanges occur smoothly, without snatching, and without an increase in engine speed between changes. Check that all of the gear positions can be selected with the vehicle at rest. If any problems are found, they should be referred to a Honda dealer or specialist.

12 On CVT models, check that all of the gear positions can be selected with the vehicle at rest. If any problems are found, they should be referred to a Honda dealer or specialist.

13 Listen for a metallic clicking sound from the front of the vehicle, as the vehicle is driven slowly in a circle with the steering on full-lock. Carry out this check in both directions. If a clicking noise is heard, this indicates wear in a driveshaft joint (see Chapter 8).

Braking system

14 Make sure that the vehicle does not pull to one side when braking, and that the wheels do not lock when braking hard.

15 Check that there is no vibration through the steering when braking.

16 Check that the handbrake operates correctly, without excessive movement of the lever, and that it holds the vehicle stationary on a slope.

Every 24 000 miles (40 000 km) or 2 years, whichever comes first

17 Valve clearance check and adjustment

Check

1 Valve clearances generally do not need adjustment unless valvetrain components have been renewed, or the assembly has been removed.

2 The simplest check for proper valve adjustment is to listen carefully to the engine running with the bonnet open. If the valvetrain is noisy, adjustment is necessary.

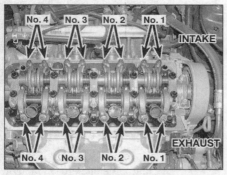

17.6 Valve layout (SOHC; DOHC similar)

Adjustment

3 The valve clearance must be checked and adjusted with the engine cold.

4 Remove the camshaft cover (see Chapter 2A or 2B).

5 Place the number one piston (closest to the drivebelt end of the engine) at Top Dead Centre (TDC) on the compression stroke. This is accomplished by rotating the crankshaft in the normal direction of rotation (which is anti-clockwise on these models) until the white TDC mark on the crankshaft pulley aligns with the timing pointer on the lower timing belt cover and the UP mark on the camshaft sprocket(s) are at the twelve o'clock position.

6 With the engine in this position, the number one cylinder valve adjustment can be checked and adjusted (**see illustration**).

7 Start with the intake valve clearance. Insert a feeler gauge of the correct thickness (see this Chapter's Specifications) between the valve stem and the rocker arm on single overhead camshaft (SOHC) engines or an intake camshaft lobe and the rocker arm on double overhead camshaft (DOHC) engines (**see illustrations**). Withdraw it; you should feel a slight drag. If there's no drag or a heavy drag, loosen the adjuster nut and undo the adjuster screw. Carefully tighten the adjuster screw until you can feel a slight drag on the feeler gauge as you withdraw it.

8 Hold the adjuster screw with a screwdriver (to keep it from turning) and tighten the locknut (**see illustration**). Recheck the clearance to make sure it hasn't changed. Repeat the procedure in this Step and the previous Step on the other intake valve, then on the two exhaust valves.

9 Rotate the crankshaft pulley 180-degrees anti-clockwise (the camshaft pulley will turn 90-degrees) until the number three cylinder is at TDC. With the number three cylinder at TDC, the UP mark on the camshaft sprocket(s) will be at the nine o'clock position. Check and adjust the number three cylinder valves.

10 Rotate the crankshaft pulley 180-degrees anti-clockwise until the number four cylinder is at TDC. With the number four cylinder at TDC, the UP mark on the camshaft sprocket(s) will be pointed straight down. Check and adjust the number four cylinder valves.

11 Rotate the crankshaft pulley 180-degrees anti-clockwise to bring the number two cylinder to TDC. The UP mark on the camshaft sprocket(s) should be at the three o'clock position. Check and adjust the number two cylinder valves.

12 Install the camshaft cover.

17.7a To make sure the adjusting screw doesn't move when the locknut is tightened, use a box end spanner and have a good grip on the screwdriver

17.7b On DOHC engines, insert the feeler gauge between the camshaft lobe and the rocker arm

17.8 On DOHC engines, a special tool is available to making tightening of the locknuts easier

18.2a On some models the air cleaner housing cover is secured by four clips (arrowed) . . .

18.2b . . . or two clips (arrowed) . . .

18.2c . . . or four screws (arrowed)

18.4a Lift the cover (D16Y7 engine) . . .

18.4b . . . and remove the filter (D14A2 engine)

4 Place rags around and under the filter. Remove the banjo bolt, unscrew the threaded fitting, remove the clamp bolt and lift the filter from the engine compartment **(see illustrations)**.

5 Installation is the reverse of removal. Use new sealing washers on either side of the banjo fitting and tighten the banjo bolt to the torque listed in this Chapter's Specifications. Tighten the threaded pipe fitting securely. Start the engine and check for leaks.

18 Air cleaner element renewal

1 At the specified intervals, the air filter should be renewed.
2 Detach the clips or loosen the air cleaner cover screws **(see illustrations)**.
3 Lift the cover up.
4 Lift the air filter element out of the housing and wipe out the inside of the air cleaner housing with a clean rag **(see illustrations)**.
5 While the air cleaner cover is off, be careful not to drop anything down into the air cleaner assembly.
6 Place the new filter in the air cleaner

housing. Make sure it seats properly in the housing.
7 Install the air cleaner cover and tighten the screws or refit the clips securely.

19 Fuel filter renewal

1 This job should be done with the engine cold (after sitting at least three hours).
2 The fuel filter is located on the bulkhead in the engine compartment.
3 Relieve the fuel system pressure as described in Chapter 4A, then disconnect the cable from the negative terminal of the battery – see Chapter 5A.

20 Hinge and lock lubrication

1 Work around the vehicle and lubricate the hinges of the bonnet, doors and tailgate with a light machine oil.
2 Lightly lubricate the bonnet release mechanism and exposed section of inner cable with a smear of grease.
3 Check the security and operation of all hinges, latches and locks, adjusting them where required. Check the operation of the central locking system.
4 Check the condition and operation of the tailgate struts, renewing them both if either is leaking or no longer able to support the tailgate securely when raised.

19. 4a Unscrew the banjo bolt (it isn't necessary to remove the small service port in the centre of the banjo bolt on models so equipped) . . .

19.4b . . . use a brake pipe spanner, if available, to disconnect the fuel pipe . . .

19.4c . . . then undo the filter clamp bolt

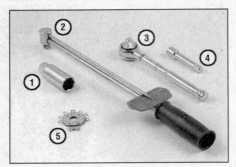

21.2 Tools required for changing spark plugs

1 *Spark plug socket* 4 *Extension*
2 *Torque wrench* 5 *Spark plug gap*
3 *Ratchet* *gauge*

21 Spark plug renewal

Note: *If the original spark plugs are to be removed and reinstalled in the engine, the spark plugs must be marked and reinstalled in the original cylinder from which they were removed.*

1 All vehicles covered by this manual are equipped with transversely mounted engines which locate the spark plugs on the top.

2 In most cases, the tools necessary for spark plug renewal include a spark plug socket, which fits onto a ratchet (spark plug sockets are padded inside to prevent damage to the

21.6 On DOHC engines, remove the spark plug cover

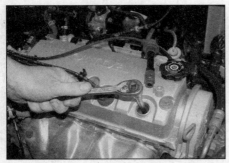

21.8 Because they are deeply recessed, an extension will be required when removing or fitting the spark plugs

21.5a Spark plug manufacturers recommend using a wire-type gauge when checking the gap – if the wire does not slide between the electrodes with a slight drag, adjustment is required

porcelain insulators on the new plugs), various extensions and a gap gauge to check and adjust the gaps on the new plugs **(see illustration)**. A special HT lead removal tool is available for separating the lead gaiters from the spark plugs, and is a good idea on these models because the gaiters fit very tightly. A torque wrench should be used to tighten the new plugs. It is a good idea to allow the engine to cool before removing or installing the spark plugs.

3 The best approach when renewing the spark plugs is to purchase the new ones in advance, adjust them to the proper gap and fit the plugs one at a time. When buying the new spark plugs, be sure to obtain the correct plug type for your particular engine. The plug type can be found in the Specifications at the front of this Chapter.

4 Allow the engine to cool completely before attempting to remove any of the plugs. While you are waiting for the engine to cool, check the new plugs for defects and adjust the gaps.

5 On plugs which can be adjusted, check the gap by inserting the proper thickness gauge between the electrodes at the tip of the plug **(see illustration)**. The gap between the electrodes should be the same as the one specified in this Chapter's Specifications. The wire should slide between the electrodes with a slight amount of drag. If the gap is incorrect, use the adjuster on the gauge body to bend

21.9 A light coat of anti-seize compound applied to the threads of the spark plugs will keep the threads in the cylinder head from being damaged the next time the plugs are removed

21.5b To change a gap, bend the side electrode only, as indicated by the arrows, and be very careful not to crack or chip the porcelain insulator surrounding the centre electrode

the curved side electrode slightly until the proper gap is obtained **(see illustration)**. If the side electrode is not exactly over the centre electrode, bend it with the adjuster until it is. Check for cracks in the porcelain insulator (if any are found, the plug should not be used).

6 On DOHC models, remove the spark plug cover **(see illustration)**. With the engine cool, remove the HT lead from one spark plug. Pull only on the gaiter at the end of the HT lead – do not pull on the lead. A plug lead removal tool should be used if available.

7 If compressed air is available, use it to blow any dirt or foreign material away from the spark plug hole. A common bicycle pump will also work. The idea here is to eliminate the possibility of debris falling into the cylinder as the spark plug is removed.

8 The spark plugs on these models are recessed so a spark plug socket incorporating a long extension will be necessary. Place the spark plug socket over the plug and remove it from the engine by turning it in an anti-clockwise direction **(see illustration)**.

9 Before installing the new plugs, it is a good idea to apply a thin coat of anti-seize compound to the threads **(see illustration)**.

10 Thread one of the new plugs into the hole until you can no longer turn it with your fingers, then tighten it with a torque wrench (if available) or the ratchet. It's a good idea to slip a short length of rubber hose over the end of the plug to use as a tool to thread it into place **(see illustration)**. The hose will grip the

21.10 A piece of rubber hose will help get the spark plug started in the hole

22.11a Undo the retaining screws and remove the distributor cap

22.11b Inspect the outside of the distributor cap for carbon tracks, broken or cracked towers and damage (if in doubt about its condition, fit a new one)

22.11c Check the inside of the distributor cap for carbon tracks, charred or eroded terminals and a worn or eroded button (if in doubt about its condition, fit a new one)

plug well enough to turn it, but will start to slip if the plug begins to cross-thread in the hole – this will prevent damaged threads and the accompanying repair costs.

11 Before pushing the HT lead connector onto the end of the plug, inspect it following the procedures outlined in the next Section.

12 Attach the HT lead connector to the new spark plug, using a twisting motion on the gaiter until it's seated on the spark plug.

13 Repeat the procedure for the remaining spark plugs, renewing them one at a time to prevent mixing up the HT leads.

22 Ignition system inspection

1 The spark HT leads should be checked whenever new spark plugs are installed.

2 Begin this procedure by making a visual check of the spark plug wires while the engine is running. In a darkened garage (make sure there is ventilation) start the engine and observe each HT lead. Be careful not to come into contact with any moving engine parts. If there is a break in the lead, you will see arcing or a small spark at the damaged area. If arcing is noticed, make a note to obtain new leads, then allow the engine to cool and check the distributor cap and rotor.

3 The spark plug HT leads should be inspected one at a time to prevent mixing up

the order, which is essential for proper engine operation. Each original HT lead should be numbered to help identify its location. If the number is illegible, a piece of tape can be marked with the correct number and wrapped around the plug wire.

4 Disconnect the plug HT lead from the spark plug. A removal tool can be used for this purpose or you can grasp the rubber gaiter, twist the gaiter half a turn and pull the it free. Do not pull on the lead itself.

5 Check inside the gaiter for corrosion, which will look like a white crusty powder.

6 Push the HT lead and gaiter back onto the end of the spark plug. It should fit tightly onto the end of the plug. If it doesn't, remove the lead and use pliers to carefully crimp the metal connector inside the lead gaiter until the fit is snug.

7 Using a clean rag, wipe the entire length of the lead to remove built-up dirt and grease. Once the wire is clean, check for burns, cracks and other damage. Do not bend the lead sharply, because the conductor might break.

8 Disconnect the HT lead from the distributor. Again, pull only on the rubber gaiter. Check for corrosion and a tight fit. Refit the HT lead in the distributor.

9 Inspect the remaining spark plug HT leads, making sure that each one is securely fastened at the distributor and spark plug when the check is complete.

10 If new spark plug HT leads are required, purchase a set for your specific engine model. Precut leads sets with the gaiters already installed are available. Remove and refit the HT leads one at a time to avoid mix-ups in the firing order.

11 Detach the distributor cap by removing the cap retaining screws **(see illustration)**. Check the outside for cracks and damage **(see illustration)**, then look inside it for cracks, carbon tracks and worn, burned or loose contacts **(see illustration)**.

12 Loosen the retaining screw and pull the rotor off the distributor shaft **(see illustration)**. It may be necessary to use a small screwdriver to gently pry off the rotor and examine it for cracks and carbon tracks **(see illustration)**. Renew the cap and rotor if any damage or defects are noted.

13 It is common practice to install a new cap and rotor whenever new spark plug HT leads are installed, but if you wish to continue using the old cap, check the resistance between the spark plug wires and the cap first. If the indicated resistance is more than the specified maximum value (see this Chapter's Specifications), refit the cap and/or HT leads.

14 When installing a new cap, remove the HT leads from the old cap one at a time and attach them to the new cap in the exact same location.

22.12a Slacken the retaining screw and remove the distributor rotor

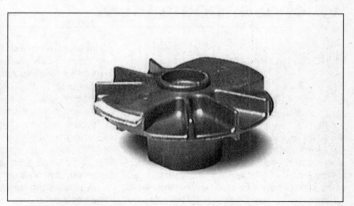

22.12b Check the distributor rotor for cracks and an eroded or worn tip (if in doubt about its condition, fit a new one)

Every 36 000 miles (60 000 km) or 3 years, whichever comes first

23 Automatic and Constantly Variable Transmission (CVT) fluid renewal

1 At the specified time intervals, the automatic/CVT transmission fluid should be drained and renewed.

2 Before beginning work, purchase the specified transmission fluid (see *Lubricants and fluids*).

3 Other tools necessary for this job include axle stands to support the vehicle in a raised position, a 3/8-inch drive ratchet and extension, a drain pan capable of holding at least five litres, newspapers and clean rags.

4 The fluid should be drained immediately after the vehicle has been driven. Hot fluid is more effective than cold fluid at removing built-up sediment.

⚠ *Warning: Fluid temperature can exceed 120°C in a hot transmission. Wear protective gloves.*

5 After the vehicle has been driven to warm-up the fluid, raise it and place it on axle stands for access to the transmission drain plug (see *Jacking and vehicle support*).

6 Move the necessary equipment under the vehicle, being careful not to touch any of the hot exhaust components.

7 Place the drain pan under the transmission and remove the drain plug – it's located on the right-hand side of the transmission, near the bottom **(see illustration)**. Be sure the drain pan is in position, as fluid will come out with some force. Once the fluid is drained, clean the drain plug and reinstall it securely.

8 Lower the vehicle.

9 With the engine off, pull out the dipstick, then add new fluid to the transmission through the dipstick tube. Use a funnel to prevent spills. It is best to add a little fluid at a time, continually checking the level with the dipstick (see Section 14).

10 Start the engine and slowly shift the selector into all positions, then shift into P and apply the handbrake.

11 Turn off the engine and check the fluid level. Add fluid to bring the level into the cross-hatched area on the dipstick.

24 Manual transmission fluid renewal

1 At the specified time intervals, the manual transmission lubricant should be drained and renewed.

2 Before beginning work, purchase the specified transmission lubricant (see *Lubricants and fluids*).

3 Other tools necessary for this job include axle stands to support the vehicle in a raised position, 3/8-inch drive ratchet, a drain pan capable of holding at least five litres, newspapers and clean rags.

4 After the vehicle has been driven to warm-up the fluid, raise it and place it on axle stands for access to the transmission drain plug (see *Jacking and vehicle support*). Remove the

23.7 The automatic/CVT drain plug is located on the right-hand end of the transmission

24.4 Manual transmission drain plug (arrowed)

drain plug and allow the old lubricant to drain into a drain pan **(see illustration)**.

5 Reinstall the drain plug securely.

6 Add new lubricant until it begins to run out of the filler hole (see Section 15).

7 Lower the vehicle.

Every 48 000 miles (80 000 km) or 4 years, whichever comes first

25 Coolant renewal

⚠ *Warning: Do not allow antifreeze to come in contact with your skin or painted surfaces of the vehicle. Rinse off spills immediately with plenty of water. Antifreeze is highly toxic if ingested. Never leave antifreeze lying around in an open container or in puddles on the floor; children and pets are attracted by it's sweet smell and may drink it. Check with local authorities about disposing of used antifreeze. Non-toxic antifreeze solutions are now widely available, but even these should be disposed of properly.*

1 Periodically, the cooling system should be drained, flushed and refilled to replenish the antifreeze mixture and prevent formation of rust and corrosion, which can impair the performance of the cooling system and cause engine damage.

2 At the same time the cooling system is serviced, all hoses and the radiator cap should be inspected and renewed if defective (see Section 11).

3 Since antifreeze is a corrosive and poisonous solution, be careful not to spill any of the coolant mixture on the vehicle's paint or your skin. If this happens, rinse it off immediately with plenty of clean water. Consult local authorities about where to recycle or dispose of antifreeze before draining the cooling system.

Draining

4 Apply the handbrake and chock the wheels.

⚠ *Warning: If the vehicle has just been driven, wait several hours to allow the engine to cool down before beginning this procedure.*

5 Once the engine is completely cool, remove

25.5 Remove the radiator cap with the engine cool to the touch

25.6 On most models you will have to remove a cover to access the radiator drain plug located at the base of the radiator (arrowed)

the radiator cap and the reservoir cap **(see illustration)**.

6 Drain the radiator by opening the drain plug at the bottom of the radiator **(see illustration)**. If the drain plug is corroded and can't be turned easily, or if the radiator isn't equipped with a plug, disconnect the lower radiator hose (see Chapter 3) to allow the coolant to drain. Be careful not to get antifreeze on your skin or in your eyes.

7 After the coolant stops flowing out of the radiator, remove the lower radiator hose and allow the remaining fluid in the upper half of the engine block to drain.

8 While the coolant is draining from the engine block, disconnect the hose from the coolant reservoir and remove the reservoir (see Chapter 3 if necessary). Flush the reservoir out with water until it's clean, and if necessary, wash the inside with soapy water and a brush to make reading the fluid level easier.

9 While the coolant is draining, check the condition of the radiator hoses, heater hoses and clamps (refer to Section 11 if necessary).

10 Renew any damaged clips or hoses (refer to Chapter 3 for detailed renewal procedures).

Flushing

11 Once the system is completely drained, remove the thermostat from the engine (see Chapter 3). Then reinstall the thermostat housing without the thermostat. This will allow the system to be flushed.

12 Reinstall the lower radiator hose and tighten the radiator drain plug. Turn your heating system controls to Hot, so that the heater core will be flushed at the same time as the rest of the cooling system.

13 Disconnect the upper radiator hose, then place a garden hose in the upper radiator inlet

and flush the system until the water runs clear at the upper radiator hose **(see illustration)**.

14 In severe cases of contamination or clogging of the radiator, remove the radiator (see Chapter 3) and have a radiator repair workshop clean and repair it if necessary.

15 Many deposits can be removed by the chemical action of a cleaner available at automotive accessory stores. Follow the procedure outlined in the manufacturer's instructions. **Note:** *When the coolant is regularly drained and the system refilled with the correct antifreeze/water mixture, there should be no need to use chemical cleaners or descalers.*

Refilling

16 To refill the system, install the thermostat, reconnect any radiator hoses and install the reservoir and the overflow hose.

17 Place the heater temperature control in the maximum heat position.

18 Be sure to use the proper coolant listed in *Lubricants and fluids*. Slowly fill the radiator with the recommended mixture of antifreeze and water to the base of the filler neck. Where fitted, loosen the air bleed screw, located on the side of the thermostat housing and make sure a steady, bubble-free stream flows out, then tighten the bolt securely **(see illustration)**. Add coolant to the reservoir until it reaches the FULL COLD mark. Wait five minutes and recheck the coolant level in the radiator, adding if necessary.

19 Leave the radiator cap off and run the engine in a well-ventilated area until the thermostat opens (coolant will begin flowing through the radiator and the upper radiator hose will become hot).

20 Turn the engine off and let it cool. Add more coolant mixture to bring the level back up to the base of the filler neck.

21 Squeeze the upper radiator hose to expel air, then add more coolant mixture if necessary. Refit the radiator cap.

22 Place the heater temperature control and the blower motor speed control to their maximum setting.

23 Start the engine, allow it to reach normal operating temperature and check for leaks.

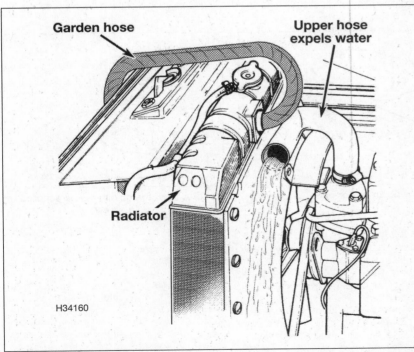

25.13 With the thermostat removed, disconnect the upper radiator hose and flush the radiator and engine block with a garden hose

25.18 The air bleed screw is located on the thermostat housing – use a spanner to open it during the filling process to bleed air from the system (pre '97 5-door models only)

Every 60 000 miles (100 000 km) or 5 years, whichever comes first

26 Timing belt renewal

Refer to the information given in Chapter 2A (SOHC engine) or 2B (DOHC engine).

Every 2 years, regardless of mileage

27 Brake fluid renewal

⚠️ **Warning: Brake hydraulic fluid can harm your eyes and damage painted surfaces, so use extreme caution when handling and pouring it. Do not use fluid that has been standing open for some time, as it absorbs moisture from the air. Excess moisture can cause a dangerous loss of braking effectiveness.**

1 The procedure is similar to that for the bleeding of the hydraulic system as described in Chapter 9.

2 Working as described in Chapter 9, open the first bleed screw in the sequence, and pump the brake pedal gently until nearly all the old fluid has been emptied from the master cylinder reservoir. Top-up to the MAX level with new fluid, and continue pumping until only the new fluid remains in the reservoir, and new fluid can be seen emerging from the bleed screw. Tighten the screw, and top the reservoir level up to the MAX level line.

 HAYNES HiNT *Old hydraulic fluid is invariably much darker in colour than the new, making it easy to distinguish the two.*

3 Work through all the remaining bleed screws in the sequence until new fluid can be seen at all of them. Be careful to keep the master cylinder reservoir topped-up to above the MIN level at all times, or air may enter the system and greatly increase the length of the task.

4 When the operation is complete, check that all bleed screws are securely tightened, and that their dust caps are refitted. Wash off all traces of spilt fluid, and recheck the master cylinder reservoir fluid level.

5 Check the operation of the brakes before taking the car on the road.

28 Remote control handset battery renewal

1 Undo the screw (where applicable) and prise the cover from the transmitter.

2 Depending on the transmitter type, one or two batteries may be fitted. Note the polarity of the battery(s), and remove it **(see illustrations)**.

3 Fit the new battery(s), and refit the cover. Where applicable, tighten the cover screw.

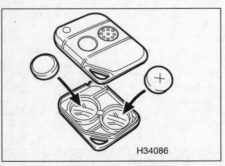

28.2a Two batteries may be fitted . . .

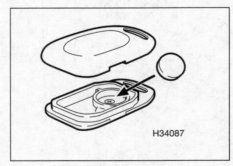

28.2b . . . or one . . .

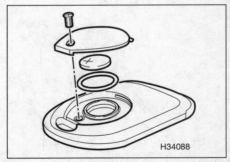

28.2c . . . and the cover may be secured by a screw

Chapter 2 Part A:
SOHC engine in-car repair procedures

Contents

Degrees of difficulty

Easy, suitable for novice with little experience	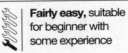	Fairly easy, suitable for beginner with some experience		Fairly difficult, suitable for competent DIY mechanic	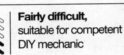	Difficult, suitable for experienced DIY mechanic		Very difficult, suitable for expert DIY or professional	

Specifications

General specifications

Engine type	Four-cylinder, in-line, water-cooled. Single overhead camshaft, 4 valves per cylinder
Manufacturer's engine codes*:	
1.4 litre	D14A2, D14A3, D14A4, D14A8
1.5 litre	D15Z3, D15Z6, D15Z8
1.6 litre	D16Y2, D16Y3, D16Y5, D16Y6, D16Y7, D16Y8, D16B2
Capacity:	
1.4 litre	1396cc
1.5 litre	1493cc
1.6 litre	1590cc
Firing order	1-3-4-2 (No 1 cylinder at timing belt end)
Direction of crankshaft rotation	Anti-clockwise (viewed from timing belt end of engine)
Compression ratio:	
D14A2	9.2:1
D14A3, D14A4	9.1:1
D14A7, D14A8	9.0:1
D15Z3	9.3:1
D15Z6	9.6:1
D15Z8	9.6:1
D16B2	9.6:1
D16Y2	9.5:1
D16Y3	9.1:1
D16Y5, D16Y7	9.4:1
D16Y6, D16Y8	9.2:1

* See 'Vehicle identification' in the Reference section

Compression pressures

Nominal	13.0 bar
Minimum	9.5 bar
Maximum difference between any two cylinders	2.0 bar

Camshaft
Endfloat .... 0.05 to 0.15 mm

Lubrication system
Oil pump type .... Rotor type, driven directly from crankshaft
Minimum permissible oil pressure with engine at operating temperature (oil temperature of at least 80°C):
  At idle speed .... 0.7 bar
  At 3000 rpm .... 3.5 bar
Oil pump clearances:
  Inner-to-outer rotor radial clearance .... 0.20 mm maximum
  Outer rotor-to-body radial clearance .... 0.20 mm maximum
  Rotor endfloat .... 0.15 mm maximum

Torque wrench settings

	Nm	lbf ft
Auxiliary drivebelt idler pulley bolt	24	18
Baffle plate	11	8
Camshaft cover bolts	10	7
Camshaft sprocket bolt	37	27
Camshaft bearing caps	12	8
Connecting rod big-end bearing cap*	31	23
Crankshaft pulley bolt:		
D14A8, D15Z8, D16B2:		
Stage 1	20	15
Stage 2	Angle-tighten a further 90°	
All other engines	181	134
Crankshaft sensor mounting bracket bolt	12	9
Crankshaft transmission end oil seal housing	11	8
Cylinder head bolts:		
D15Z3, D16Y2:		
Stage 1	29	21
Stage 2	72	53
D14A2, D16Y3:		
Stage 1	29	21
Stage 2	64	47
All other engines:		
Stage 1	20	15
Stage 2	49	36
Stage 3	67	49
Stage 4	67	49
Driveplate bolts	74	55
Exhaust front pipe-to-manifold nuts*	54	40
Exhaust manifold nuts*	31	23
Flywheel bolts	118	87
Intake manifold bolts/nuts	23	17
Lost motion assembly holder	20	15
Main bearing cap bolts:		
1.4 and 1.5 litre engines	44	32
1.6 litre engines	51	38
Oil pump:		
Retaining bolts	11	8
Pump cover screws	6	4
Oil pressure relief valve bolt	39	29
Oil pump pick-up/strainer bolts	11	8
Oil pressure switch	18	13
Roadwheel nuts	108	80
Rocker arm assembly	12	9
Sump bolts:		
Sump-to-cylinder block/oil pump bolts	12	9
Drain plug:		
Steel sump	44	32
Aluminium sump	39	29
Timing belt cover bolts	10	7
Timing belt tensioner bolt	44	32

Use new bolts

1 General information

How to use this Chapter

This Part of Chapter 2 is devoted to in-car repair procedures for the SOHC (Single Overhead Camshaft) engine. All procedures concerning engine removal and refitting, and engine block/cylinder head overhaul can be found in Chapter 2C.

Most of the operations included in this Part are based on the assumption that the engine is still fitted in the car. Therefore, if this information is being used during a complete engine overhaul, with the engine already removed, many of the steps included here will not apply.

The Specifications included in this Part of Chapter 2 apply only to the procedures contained in this chapter. Chapter 2C contains the Specifications necessary for cylinder head and engine block rebuilding.

Engine description

Three different versions of this engine have been produced by Honda for the Civic product line, all of which are covered in this Part of Chapter 2. All versions of this engine utilize a Single Overhead Camshaft (SOHC), with 4 valves per cylinder (16V). Two versions of this engine incorporate the VTEC (Variable Valve Timing and lift Electronic Control) system, which electronically alters valve timing to enhance engine performance. For more information on the VTEC system, see Section 7 of this Chapter.

The SOHC engines are lightweight in design with an aluminium alloy block (with steel cylinder liners) and an aluminium alloy cylinder head. The crankshaft rides in a single carriage unit that houses the renewable insert-type main bearings, with separate thrust bearings at the number four position assigned the task of controlling crankshaft endplay.

The pistons have two compression rings and one oil control ring. The semi-floating piston pins are press fitted into the small end of the connecting rod. The connecting rod big-ends are also equipped with renewable insert-type plain bearings.

The engine is liquid-cooled, utilizing a centrifugal impeller-type pump, driven by the timing belt, to circulate coolant around the cylinders and combustion chambers and through the intake manifold.

Lubrication is handled by a rotor-type oil pump mounted on the front of the engine under the timing belt cover. It is driven directly by the crankshaft. The oil is filtered continuously by a cartridge-type filter mounted on the rear of the engine.

Repair operations possible with the engine in the car

The following operations can be carried out without having to remove the engine from the vehicle:

a) Removal and refitting of the cylinder head.

b) Removal and refitting of the timing belt and sprockets.

c) Renewal of the camshaft oil seal.

d) Removal and refitting of the camshaft housing and camshaft.

e) Removal and refitting of the sump.

f) Removal and refitting of the connecting rods and pistons*.

g) Removal and refitting of the oil pump.

h) Renewal of the crankshaft oil seals.

i) Renewal of the engine mountings.

j) Removal and refitting of the flywheel/driveplate.

* Although the operation marked with an asterisk can be carried out with the engine in the car after removal of the sump, it is better for the engine to be removed, in the interests of cleanliness and improved access. For this reason, the procedure is described in Chapter 2C.

Caution: If the radio in your vehicle is equipped with an anti-theft system, make sure you have the correct activation code before disconnecting the battery.

2 Compression test – description and interpretation

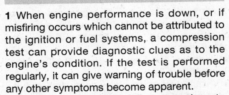

1 When engine performance is down, or if misfiring occurs which cannot be attributed to the ignition or fuel systems, a compression test can provide diagnostic clues as to the engine's condition. If the test is performed regularly, it can give warning of trouble before any other symptoms become apparent.

2 The engine must be fully warmed-up to normal operating temperature, the battery must be fully charged, and the spark plugs must be removed (see Chapter 1). The aid of an assistant will also be required.

3 Disable the ignition system by disconnecting the wiring connector from the ignition distributor, and the fuel system by removing the main fuel injection relay fuse from the engine compartment fuse box (2, 3 and 4-door models) or the fuel pump fuse from the passenger compartment fusebox (5-door models).

4 Fit a compression tester to the number 1 cylinder spark plug hole. The type of tester which screws into the plug thread is to be preferred.

5 Have the assistant hold the throttle wide open and crank the engine on the starter motor; after one or two revolutions, the compression pressure should build-up to a maximum figure, and then stabilise. Record the highest reading obtained.

6 Repeat the test on the remaining cylinders, recording the pressure in each.

7 All cylinders should produce very similar pressures; any difference greater than that specified indicates the existence of a fault. Note that the compression should build-up quickly in a healthy engine. Low compression on the first stroke, followed by gradually-increasing pressure on successive strokes, indicates worn piston rings. A low compression reading on the first stroke, which does not build-up during successive strokes, indicates leaking valves or a blown head gasket (a cracked head could also be the cause). Deposits on the undersides of the valve heads can also cause low compression.

8 If the pressure in any cylinder is reduced to the specified minimum or less, carry out the following test to isolate the cause. Introduce a teaspoonful of clean oil into that cylinder through its spark plug hole, and repeat the test.

9 If the addition of oil temporarily improves the compression pressure, this indicates that bore or piston wear is responsible for the pressure loss. No improvement suggests that leaking or burnt valves, or a blown head gasket, may be to blame.

10 A low reading from two adjacent cylinders is almost certainly due to the head gasket having blown between them; the presence of coolant in the engine oil will confirm this.

11 If one cylinder is about 20 per cent lower than the others, and the engine has a slightly rough idle, a worn camshaft lobe could be the cause.

12 If the compression reading is unusually high, the combustion chambers are probably coated with carbon deposits. If this is the case, the cylinder head should be removed and decarbonised.

13 On completion of the test, refit the spark plugs (see Chapter 1), refit the main fuel injection relay fuse and reconnect the wiring connector to the distributor.

3 Top Dead Centre (TDC) for number 1 piston – locating

Note: The following procedure is based on the assumption that the distributor is correctly fitted. If you are trying to locate TDC to refit the distributor correctly, piston position must be determined by feeling for compression at the number one spark plug hole, then aligning the TDC mark on the crankshaft pulley with the pointer on the lower timing cover as described in paragraph 8.

1 Top Dead Centre (TDC) is the highest point in the cylinder that each piston reaches as it travels up-and-down when the crankshaft turns. Each piston reaches TDC on the compression stroke and again on the exhaust stroke, but TDC generally refers to piston position on the compression stroke.

2 Positioning the number one piston at TDC is an essential part of many procedures, such as camshaft, timing belt or distributor removal.

3 Before beginning this procedure, be sure to place the transmission in Neutral and apply

3.6 Make a mark on the distributor housing directly beneath the number 1 spark plug HT terminal on the distributor cap

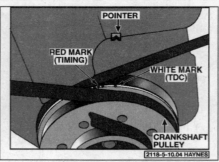

3.8 Align the white (TDC) mark on the crankshaft pulley with the pointer on the timing belt cover – note that the TDC mark is the mark farthest to the right

3.9 With the engine at TDC for the number 1 piston, the rotor should be pointing at the mark (arrowed) made on the distributor housing

the handbrake or block the rear wheels. Also, remove the spark plugs (see Chapter 1).

4 In order to bring any piston to TDC, the crankshaft must be turned using the method outlined below. When looking at the auxiliary drivebelt end of the engine, normal crankshaft rotation is anti-clockwise. Always rotate the engine anti-clockwise; clockwise rotation may cause incorrect adjustment of the timing belt. The preferred method is to turn the crankshaft with a socket and ratchet attached to the bolt threaded into the front of the crankshaft.

5 Note the position of the terminal for the number one spark plug HT lead on the distributor cap. If the terminal isn't marked, follow the HT lead from the number one cylinder spark plug to the cap.

6 Use a felt-tip pen or chalk to make a mark on the distributor body directly under the number one terminal (see illustration).

7 Undo the screws and detach the cap from the distributor and set it aside.

8 Turn the crankshaft (see Paragraph 4) until the white (TDC) notch in the crankshaft pulley is aligned with the pointer on the timing belt cover (see illustration).

9 Look at the distributor rotor – it should be pointing directly at the mark you made on the distributor body (see illustration).

10 If the rotor is 180° out, the number one piston is at TDC on the exhaust stroke. In which case, to get the piston to TDC on the compression stroke, turn the crankshaft one complete revolution (360°) anti-clockwise. The rotor should now be pointing at the mark on the distributor. When the rotor is pointing at the number 1 spark plug HT lead terminal in the distributor cap and the TDC marks are aligned, the number 1 piston is at TDC on the compression stroke.

11 After the number one piston has been positioned at TDC on the compression stroke, TDC for any of the remaining cylinders can be located by turning the crankshaft in 180° increments and following the firing order (refer to the Specifications). Rotating the engine 180° past TDC for cylinder number 1 will put the engine at TDC compression for cylinder number 3.

4 Camshaft cover – removal and refitting

Removal

1 Disconnect the cable from the negative terminal of the battery (see Chapter 5A).

2 Remove the HT leads from the spark plugs and the retaining clips on the valve cover (see Chapter 1), then position the HT leads aside. Be sure to mark each lead for correct refitting.

3 Mark and detach any hoses or wires from the throttle body or valve cover that will interfere with the removal of the valve cover.

4 Wipe off the valve cover thoroughly to prevent debris from falling onto the exposed cylinder head or camshaft/valvetrain assembly.

5 Remove the valve cover bolts (see illustration 4.9).

6 Carefully lift off the valve cover and gasket. If the gasket is stuck to the cylinder head, tap it with a rubber mallet to break the seal. Do not pry between the cover and cylinder head or you'll damage the gasket mating surfaces.

Refitting

7 Remove the old gasket and clean the mating surfaces of the cylinder head and the valve cover. Clean the surfaces with a rag soaked in cellulose thinners or use gasket remover.

8 Fit a new moulded rubber gasket into the groove around the valve cover perimeter. Apply beads of liquid sealant (available from Honda dealers) to the corners where the cylinder head mates with the rocker arm assembly (see illustration). Note: The cover must be fitted within five minutes of applying the sealant. If more time has elapsed, remove the old residue and re-apply the sealant.

9 Refit the valve cover sealing grommets, lubricate them with soapy water and tighten the bolts in the recommended sequence to the torque listed in this Chapter's Specifications (see illustration). Note: After assembly, wait at least 20 minutes to allow the sealant to set.

10 The remainder of refitting is the reverse of removal. Make sure the rubber spark plug seals are in position before connecting the spark plug leads.

5 Intake manifold – removal and refitting

Removal

1 Disconnect the cable from the negative terminal of the battery (see Chapter 5A).

2 Drain the cooling system (see Chapter 1).

3 Remove the intake air duct and air cleaner housing (see Chapter 4A, Section 9).

4 Clearly label and detach any vacuum lines

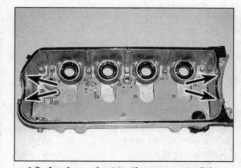

4.8 Apply sealant to the corners of the camshaft cover gasket (arrowed)

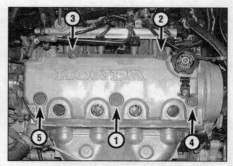

4.9 Camshaft cover bolts tightening sequence

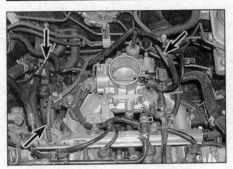

5.4 Disconnect the vacuum hoses (arrowed)

5.8 Remove the bolts (arrowed) and remove the brace from the intake manifold

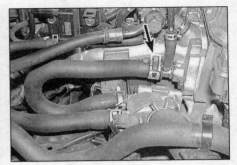

5.9 Disconnect the coolant bypass hose (arrowed)

and electrical connectors, which will interfere with removal of the manifold **(see illustration)**.

5 Detach the accelerator cable from the throttle lever (see Chapter 4A).

6 Remove the coolant hoses from the throttle body.

7 Relieve the fuel system pressure and disconnect the fuel feed and return lines at the fuel rail (see Chapter 4A).

8 Working from underneath the engine compartment, remove the brace that supports the intake manifold **(see illustration)**.

9 Disconnect the coolant bypass hose from the intake manifold **(see illustration)**.

10 Remove the intake manifold nuts and remove the manifold from the engine **(see illustration)**.

Refitting

11 Check the mating surfaces of the manifold for flatness with a ruler and feeler gauges.

12 Inspect the manifold for cracks and distortion. If the manifold is cracked or warped, renew it or see if it can be resurfaced at an automotive engineering workshop.

13 Check carefully for any damaged manifold studs/nuts/bolts. Renew any defective fasteners with new parts.

14 Using a scraper, remove all traces of old gasket material from the cylinder head and manifold mating surfaces.

15 Refit the intake manifold with a new gasket and tighten all the nuts finger-tight. Following the recommended sequence,

5.10 Intake manifold mounting nuts (arrowed) (non-VTEC; others similar)

tighten the nuts to the torque listed in this Chapter's Specifications **(see illustration)**.

16 The remainder of refitting is the reverse of removal. Refer to Chapter 1 and refill the cooling system.

6 Exhaust manifold – removal and refitting

Removal

1 Disconnect the cable from the negative terminal of the battery (see Chapter 5A).

2 Raise the front of the vehicle and support it securely on axle stands (see *Jacking and vehicle support*). Disconnect the oxygen sensor electrical connectors (two connectors

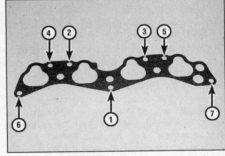

5.15 Intake manifold fastener tightening sequence

on some models). Detach the exhaust pipe from the exhaust manifold **(see illustration)**. Apply penetrating oil to the fastener threads if they are difficult to remove.

3 Remove the heat shield from the exhaust manifold **(see illustration)**. Be sure to soak the bolts and nuts with penetrating oil before attempting to remove them from the manifold.

4 Remove the exhaust manifold nuts **(see illustration)** and detach the exhaust manifold from the cylinder head. **Note:** *Be sure to remove the bolts from the lower brace located near the flange of the exhaust manifold.*

Refitting

5 Discard the old gasket and use a scraper to clean the gasket mating surfaces on the exhaust manifold and cylinder head.

6 Position the new gasket on the cylinder head.

6.2 Remove the exhaust pipe flange nuts (arrowed)

6.3 Remove the heat shield retaining bolts (arrowed)

6.4 Exhaust manifold mounting nuts (arrowed)

7 Place the exhaust manifold in position on the cylinder head and fit the nuts. Starting at the centre and working out to the ends, tighten the nuts to the torque listed in this Chapter's Specifications.

8 The remainder of refitting is the reverse of removal.

9 Start the engine and check for exhaust leaks between the manifold and the cylinder head and between the manifold and the exhaust pipe.

7 VTEC systems – description and component checks

Description

1 The VTEC system (Variable Valve Timing and lift Electronic Control) is used on several models throughout the Honda vehicle line. Single Overhead cam (SOHC) engines may be equipped with one of two different VTEC systems, the VTEC or the VTEC-E. The VTEC-E is Honda's designation for Enhanced Performance.

2 The differences between the non-VTEC engines and the VTEC counterparts are strictly in the components and operation of the valvetrain. The engine block, oiling and cooling systems are identical, as are all attached components. Models equipped with VTEC systems can be distinguished by the letters VTEC moulded into the top of the valve cover.

3 The engine management computer has the ability to alter valve lift and timing through the use of different camshaft intake valve lobes. The computer turns the system on or off, depending on sensor input.

4 The following are used on both systems to determine VTEC operation:
Engine speed (rpm).
Vehicle speed (mph).
Throttle position sensor output.
Engine load measured by the manifold absolute pressure sensor.
Coolant temperature.

5 The components and method of operation are slightly different between the VTEC and VTEC-E systems. The following describes the differences in the way the two systems operate.

VTEC

6 The camshaft used in the VTEC system has identical primary and secondary intake lobes and has an additional third lobe and rocker arm placed between the primary and secondary. This third, or Mid, lobe has larger lift and longer duration than the primary and secondary camshaft lobes.

7 During low speed operation both intake valves operate on their own camshaft lobes. Both camshaft lobes have the same specifications for lift and duration (unlike the VTEC-E). As performance is required, the primary and secondary rocker arms are locked to the Mid rocker arm through the use of an electrically-controlled, hydraulic system. Both intake valves now operate on the Mid intake camshaft lobe. **Note:** *The primary and secondary rocker arms no longer contact their respective camshaft lobes until the Mid rocker arm is disengaged.* This provides good torque at both low and high speeds by using the camshaft lobe profile that most matches driving needs at any given speed and load.

VTEC-E

8 The camshaft used in the VTEC-E system has different primary and secondary intake valve lobe profiles (lift and duration specifications).

9 At low speeds, the secondary valve operates on its own camshaft lobe, which has very low lift and duration (compared to the primary valve). The opening is intended to be just enough to keep atomised fuel from puddling at the valve head. This limited valve operation provides good low-end torque and responsiveness.

10 When performance is needed, the secondary rocker arm is locked together (through the use of an electrically-controlled, hydraulic system) with the primary rocker arm. **Note:** *The secondary rocker arm no longer contacts its own camshaft lobe, until the system is disengaged.* When activated, both valves open to the full lift and duration of the primary camshaft lobe, increasing performance at higher engine speeds.

Component checks

Lock-up control solenoid valve

11 A problem in the VTEC solenoid valve circuit will turn on the Malfunction Indicator Light (MIL) and store a diagnostic trouble code. Testing of the lock-up control solenoid and the VTEC oil pressure switch are basically the same (except for the location of the solenoid) as the Double Overhead Cam (DOHC) VTEC models. For tests of the solenoid and oil pressure switch, refer to Part B of this Chapter. **Note:** *On SOHC engines, the VTEC solenoid valve is located at the rear of the cylinder head on the driver's side of the vehicle. Also when checking oil pressure of the VTEC system, it will be necessary to remove the VTEC oil pressure switch from the lock-up solenoid and connect an adapter between the switch and the solenoid, since SOHC engines are not equipped with an oil pressure test port on the cylinder head.*

Rocker arms, synchronizing assemblies and oil control orifice

12 Remove the camshaft cover (see Section 4) and place the number 1 cylinder at TDC (see Section 3).

13 On VTEC engines, press on the mid intake rocker arm with a finger. It should move separately from the primary and secondary rocker arms.

14 On VTEC-E engines, press on the secondary rocker arm with a finger. It should move separately from the primary rocker arm.

15 Following the firing order, check the movement of the VTEC (intake) rocker arms for the remaining cylinders with the piston at TDC for the cylinder you're checking (see Section 3).

16 If the rocker arms do not move freely as described, remove and dismantle the rocker arms for inspection (see Section 8).

17 Once the rocker arm assemblies have been removed and dismantled (see Section 8), separate the rocker arms and the synchronizing pistons **(see illustrations)**.

18 Inspect all other parts (rocker arms and synchronizing pistons) for wear, scoring or signs of overheating (bluish in colour). Renew any parts necessary.

19 On VTEC engines, remove the individual lost motion assemblies from the holder.

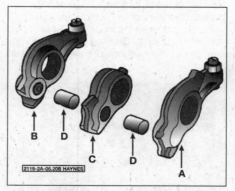

7.17a Rocker arms and synchronising assembly (VTEC)

A Primary rocker arm
B Secondary rocker arm
C Mid rocker arm
D Synchronising piston

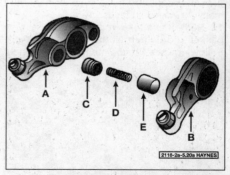

7.17b Rocker arms and synchronising assembly (VTEC-E)

A Primary rocker arm
B Secondary rocker arm
C Timing piston
D Timing spring
E Synchronising piston

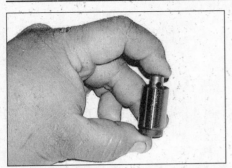

7.19 Check the lost motion assemblies for free movement (VTEC)

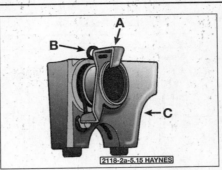

7.20 Timing plate synchronising assembly (VTEC-E)

A Timing plate
B Return spring
C Cam holder

8.4 Remove the camshaft bearing caps, bolts and rocker arm assembly

Check for free movement of the lost motion assemblies (4 required). Press down on the plunger with your finger **(see illustration)**. If the plunger does not move smoothly up-and-down in its bore, renew the lost motion assembly.

20 On VTEC-E engines, check the condition of the timing plate, collar and return spring. The timing plate and return spring **(see illustration)** are assembled to the camshaft holder on the intake rocker shaft (4 required). Check that the timing plate moves freely in the collar and that the spring returns the timing plate to the stop on the camshaft holder.

21 Remove the oil control orifice in the cylinder head (see Section 8). Clean and refit it back into the cylinder head.

22 Reassemble the rocker arms as described in Section 8. **Note:** *Secure each cylinder's components with a rubber band before trying to reassemble them on the rocker shaft.*

---

8 Rocker arm assembly – removal, inspection and refitting

Note: *The camshaft bearing caps are removed together with the rocker arm assembly. To prevent the transmission end of*

the camshaft from popping up from timing belt tension after the assembly is removed, have an assistant hold the camshaft down, then refit the bearing cap on that end to hold it in place until reassembly (assuming the timing belt remains fitted).

Removal

1 Remove the camshaft cover (see Section 4).

2 Position the number 1 piston at Top Dead Centre (see Section 3) and remove the distributor (see Chapter 5B).

3 Have an assistant hold down the transmission end of the camshaft, then loosen the camshaft bearing cap bolts 1/4-turn at a time, in the correct order, until the spring pressure is relieved **(see illustration 8.12)**.

4 Lift the rocker arm and shaft assembly from the cylinder head **(see illustration)**.

Oil control orifice

5 Pull the orifice from the cylinder head **(see illustration)**.

Inspection

6 If you wish to dismantle and inspect the rocker arm assembly (a good idea as long as

you have them removed), remove the retaining bolts and slip the rocker arms, springs, collars and bearing caps off the shafts. Mark the relationship of the shafts to the bearing caps and keep the components in order. They must be reassembled in the same positions they were removed from.

Caution: On VTEC engines, it is a good idea to bundle the intake rocker arms together with rubber bands.

7 Thoroughly clean the components and inspect them for wear and damage. Check the rocker arm faces that contact the camshaft and the rocker arm tips **(see illustration)**. Check the surfaces of the shafts that the rocker arms ride on, as well as the bearing surfaces inside the rocker arms, for scoring and excessive wear. Renew any parts that are damaged or excessively worn. Also, make sure the oil holes in the shafts are not blocked.

8 Clean the orifice so there are no obstructions and oil flows freely through the orifice.

Refitting

9 Lubricate all components with clean engine oil and reassemble rocker arms on to the shafts. When refitting the rocker arms, shafts and springs, note the markings and the

8.5 To remove the oil orifice for cleaning, thread a screw into the top and pull up on the orifice (arrowed)

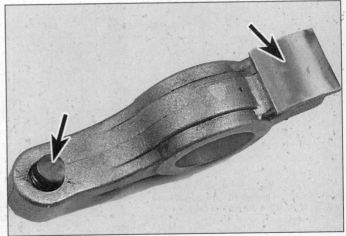

8.7 Check the contact face and adjuster tip for damage or wear (arrowed)

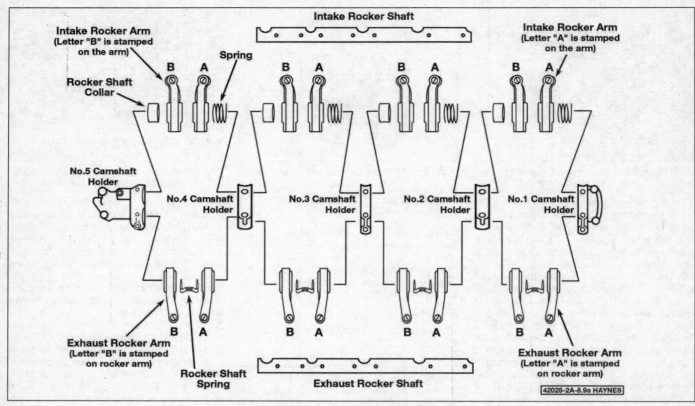

8.9a Exploded view of the rocker arms and shafts (non-VTEC)

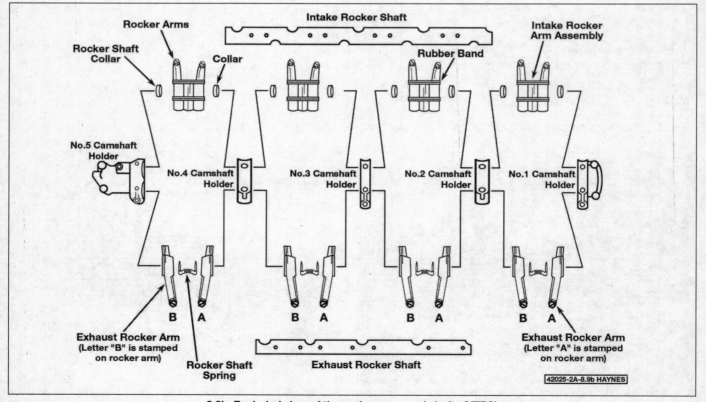

8.9b Exploded view of the rocker arms and shafts (VTEC)

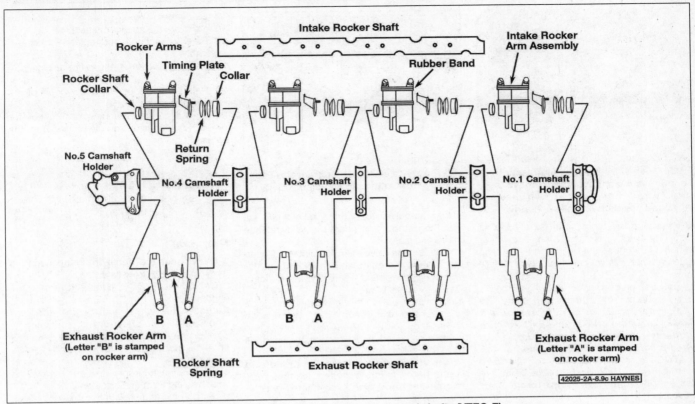

8.9c Exploded view of the rocker arms and shafts (VTEC-E)

difference between the left and right side components **(see illustrations)**.

10 Renew the O-ring on the oil control orifice, then refit the orifice in the cylinder head.

11 Coat the camshaft lobes and journals with camshaft clean engine oil. Apply suitable liquid sealant (available from Honda dealers) to the cylinder head contact surfaces of bearing caps 1 and 5 and refit the rocker arm assembly.

12 Tighten the camshaft bearing cap bolts a little at a time, in the proper sequence **(see illustration)** to the torque listed in this Chapter's Specifications.

13 The remainder of refitting is the reverse of removal. Adjust the valve clearance, if necessary (see Chapter 1).

14 Run the engine and check for oil leaks and proper operation.

9 Valve springs, retainers and seals – renewal

Note: *Broken valve springs and defective valve stem seals can be renewed without removing the cylinder heads. Two special tools and a compressed air source are normally required to perform this operation, so read through this Section carefully and rent or buy the tools before beginning the job.*

1 Refer to Section 4 and remove the camshaft cover.

2 Remove the spark plug from the cylinder that has the defective component. If all of the valve stem seals are being renewed, all of the spark plugs should be removed (see Chapter 1).

3 Turn the crankshaft until the piston in the affected cylinder is at TDC on the compression stroke (refer to Section 3 for instructions). If you're renewing all of the valve stem seals, begin with cylinder number 1 and work on the valves for one cylinder at a time. Move from cylinder-to-cylinder following the firing order sequence (see this Chapter's Specifications).

4 Remove the rocker arms and shafts (see Section 8).

5 Thread an adapter into the spark plug hole and connect an air hose from a compressed air source to it **(see illustration)**. Most

8.12 Rocker arm assembly bolt tightening sequence

9.5 Spark plug hole-to-air hose adapter

9.8 Use a valve spring compressor to compress the springs, then remove the collets from the valve stem with needle-nosed pliers or a small screwdriver

automotive parts stores can supply the air hose adapter. **Note:** *Many cylinder compression gauges utilise a screw-in fitting that may work with your air hose quick-release fitting.*

6 Apply compressed air to the cylinder.

⚠️ **Warning: The piston may be forced down by compressed air, causing the crankshaft to turn suddenly. If the spanner/socket used when positioning the number one piston at TDC is still attached to the bolt in the crankshaft end, it could cause damage or injury when the crankshaft moves.**

7 The valves should be held in place by the air pressure.

8 Push rags into the cylinder head holes around the valves to prevent parts and tools from falling into the engine, then use a valve spring compressor to compress the spring **(see illustration).**

9 Remove the collets with small needle-nose pliers or a small screwdriver.

10 Remove the spring retainer, and valve spring, then remove the valve guide seal using pliers or similar. **Note:** *If air pressure fails to hold the valve in the closed position during this operation, the valve face or seat is probably damaged. If so, the cylinder head will have to be removed for additional repair operations.*

11 Wrap a rubber band or tape around the

9.17 Apply a small dab of grease to each collet to hold it in place

top of the valve stem so the valve won't fall into the combustion chamber, then release the air pressure.

12 Inspect the valve stem for damage. Rotate the valve in the guide and check the end for eccentric movement, which would indicate that the valve is bent.

13 Move the valve up-and-down in the guide and make sure it doesn't bind. If the valve stem binds, either the valve is bent or the guide is damaged. In either case, the head will have to be removed for repair.

14 Reapply air pressure to the cylinder to retain the valve in the closed position, then remove the tape or rubber band from the valve stem.

15 Lubricate the valve stem with clean engine oil and fit a new guide seal, using a suitably-sized socket which bears only on the hard outer edge of the seal. **Note:** *The springs on the valve stem seals are colour-coded; white for the intake valves and black for the exhaust valves.*

16 Refit the spring in position over the valve. Place the end of the spring with the closely-wound coils toward the cylinder head.

17 Refit the valve spring retainer. Compress the valve spring and carefully position the collets in the groove. Apply a small dab of grease to the inside of each collet to hold it in place **(see illustration).**

18 Remove the pressure from the spring tool and make sure the keepers are seated.

19 Disconnect the air hose and remove the adapter from the spark plug hole.

20 Refer to Section 8 and refit the rocker arm assembly.

21 Refer to Section 4 and refit the camshaft cover.

22 Refit the spark plug(s) and reconnect the HT lead(s).

23 Start and run the engine, then check for oil leaks and unusual sounds coming from the camshaft cover area.

10 Timing belt and sprockets – removal, inspection and refitting

Removal

1 Disconnect the cable from the negative terminal of the battery (see Chapter 5A).

2 Chock the rear wheels and apply the handbrake.

3 Loosen the wheel nuts on the left front wheel and raise the front of the vehicle. Support the front of the vehicle securely on axle stands (see *Jacking and vehicle support*).

4 Remove the left front wheel and remove the splash shield from under the engine.

5 Support the engine with a trolley jack. Place a wood block between the jack pad and the sump to avoid damaging the sump.

6 Remove the upper left-hand engine mounting bracket (see Section 18).

7 Remove the spark plugs and the auxiliary drivebelts (see Chapter 1).

8 Unbolt the power steering pump without disconnecting the hoses and set it aside (see Chapter 10).

9 Remove the engine oil dipstick.

10 Position the number one piston at Top Dead Centre (see Section 3).

Caution: Always rotate the crankshaft anti-clockwise (viewed from the pulley end of the engine). Clockwise rotation may cause incorrect adjustment of the timing belt.

11 Undo the two bolts and remove the upper timing belt cover **(see illustration).** Recover the rubber seal.

12 Remove the auxiliary drivebelt idler pulley and bracket from the front of the engine.

13 Using a strap spanner or chain spanner to hold the crankshaft pulley stationary, loosen the crankshaft pulley bolt with a socket and breaker bar **(see illustration).**

14 Slip the pulley off the crankshaft.

15 Remove the dipstick tube from the front of the engine.

16 Undo the bolts and remove the lower timing belt cover. Recover the rubber seals.

17 If you intend to re-use the timing belt, use white paint or chalk to make match marks to align the sprockets with the belt and an arrow

10.11 Timing cover upper cover bolts (arrowed)

10.13 Hold the crankshaft pulley while you slacken the pulley bolt – a chain wrench can be used if you first wrap a length of old drivebelt around the pulley

10.17 If you intend to re-use the belt, make an arrow mark to indicate the direction of rotation, and marks to align the sprocket with the belt (arrowed)

10.18 Location of the timing belt tensioner bolt (upper arrow) and crankshaft speed fluctuation sensor (lower arrow)

10.20 Check the belt tensioner pulley for rough operation, bearing play and freedom of movement

to indicate the direction of rotation **(see illustration)**.

18 Loosen the timing belt tensioner bolt **(see illustration)**. Push on the tensioner to release the tension on the belt, then retighten the bolt. Where fitted, undo the retaining bolt and remove the crankshaft speed fluctuation sensor. Slip the timing belt from the pulleys. If you're renewing the crankshaft oil seal, slip the sprocket and inner belt guide off the crankshaft (see Section 11).

19 If you're renewing the camshaft or camshaft oil seal, slip a large screwdriver through the camshaft sprocket to keep it from rotating and remove the bolt, then pull off the sprocket. Do not allow the camshaft sprocket to rotate. Remove the Woodruff key.

Inspection

20 Rotate the belt tensioner pulley by hand and move it from side-to-side, checking for play and rough rotation **(see illustration)**. Renew it if roughness or play is detected.

21 Check the timing belt for wear (especially on the thrust side of the teeth), cracks, splits, fraying and oil contamination **(see illustration)**. Renew the belt if any of these conditions are noted. **Note:** *Unless the engine has very low mileage, it's common practice to renew the timing belt every time it's removed. Don't refit the original belt unless it's in like-new condition. Never refit a belt in questionable condition.*

Refitting

22 If you removed the sprockets, refit them. Don't forget the Woodruff key for the camshaft sprocket and the inner belt guide for the crankshaft sprocket. Tighten the camshaft sprocket bolt to the torque listed in this Chapter's specifications.

23 Before refitting the timing belt, make sure the dot or UP mark on the camshaft sprocket is at the top. The two timing marks on the sprocket must align with the upper surface of the cylinder head, or the two pointers on the rear cover depending on engine code. On engine codes D16Y2 and D16Y3, the single timing mark must align with the pointer on the rear cover **(see illustrations)**.

24 Temporarily refit the crankshaft pulley and bolt and turn the crankshaft (if it was disturbed) until the timing mark on the crankshaft sprocket and the pointer on the oil pump are aligned **(see illustration)**.

25 Fit the timing belt tightly around the

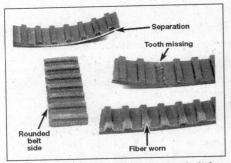

10.21 Carefully inspect the timing belt for cracked or missing teeth – wear on one side of the belt indicated sprocket misalignment problems

10.23a Ensure the UP mark is at the twelve o'clock position, and the marks arrowed align with the cylinder head surface . . .

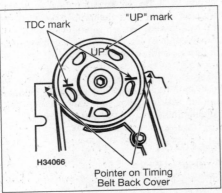

10.23b . . . or the two pointers on the rear cover

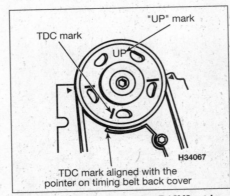

10.23c On engine codes D16Y2 and D16Y3, the single timing mark must align with the pointer on the rear cover

10.24 Align the mark on the crankshaft sprocket with the pointer on the oil pump (arrowed)

10.25 Routing of the timing belt around the belt tensioner and water pump

11.2a Remove the crankshaft sprocket . . .

11.2b . . . and the inner belt guide – note that the curved edge faces away from the timing belt

crankshaft sprocket, then around the tensioner pulley, water pump pulley and camshaft sprocket in sequence (see illustration).

26 Loosen the belt tensioner bolt, allowing the tensioner to tension the belt, then temporarily tighten the bolt.

27 Carefully turn the crankshaft anti-clockwise six revolutions and recheck the timing marks and camshaft sprocket index marks for proper alignment. If the crankshaft binds or seems to hit something, do not force it, as the valves may be hitting the pistons. If this happens, valve timing is incorrect. Remove the belt and repeat the refitting procedure and verify that the refitting is correct.

28 To properly tension the timing belt, loosen the tensioner bolt 1/2 turn (180°), rotate the

crankshaft anti-clockwise until the camshaft pulley is three teeth past TDC and tighten the tensioner bolt to the torque listed in this Chapter's Specifications.

29 Refit the remaining parts in the reverse order of removal.

30 Refer to Chapter 1 and adjust the auxiliary drivebelts.

31 Start the engine and check for proper operation.

11 Crankshaft timing belt end oil seal – renewal

1 Remove the timing belt (see Section 10).

2 Remove the outer belt guide (where fitted), followed by the crankshaft sprocket and the inner belt guide. Recover the Woodruff key (see illustrations).

3 Carefully prise the seal out of the oil pump housing with a seal removal tool or a screwdriver (see illustration). Don't scratch the seal bore or damage the crankshaft in the process (if the crankshaft is damaged, the new seal will end up leaking).

4 Clean the bore in the oil pump housing and coat the outer edge of the new seal with engine oil or multi-purpose grease. Using a socket with an outside diameter slightly smaller than the outside diameter of the seal, carefully drive the seal into place with a hammer, with the seal spring towards the engine (see illustration). If a socket is not

available, a short section of a large diameter pipe will work.

5 Refit the inner belt guide, crankshaft sprocket and, where fitted, the outer belt guide. Ensure that the curved edges of the belt guides face away from the belt, and that the timing mark on the sprocket faces away from the engine.

6 Refit the timing belt (see Section 10).

7 Start the engine and check for leaks.

12 Camshaft – removal, inspection and refitting

Removal

1 Remove the camshaft cover (see Section 4).

2 Set the engine at TDC for cylinder number one (see Section 3) and remove the timing belt (see Section 10).

3 Remove the distributor (see Chapter 5B).

4 If it necessary to separate the sprocket from the camshaft, remove the camshaft sprocket bolt, pull the sprocket from the camshaft and recover the Woodruff key. Note: Prevent the camshaft from turning by inserting a screwdriver through one of the holes in the sprocket.

5 Remove the rocker arm assembly (see Section 8). If the camshaft bearing caps are removed from the assembly and they don't have numbers on them, number them before removal. Be sure to put the marks on the same ends of all the caps to prevent incorrect orientation of the caps during refitting.

6 Lift out the camshaft (see illustration), wipe it off with a clean rag, remove the camshaft seal and set the camshaft aside.

Inspection

Endfloat check

7 To check camshaft endfloat:
  a) Refit the camshaft and secure it with the caps.
  b) Mount a dial indicator on the cylinder

11.3 Carefully prise the oil seal out with a removal tool or screwdriver

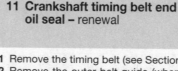

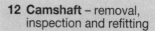

11.4 Drive in a new seal with a socket the same diameter as the seal

12.6 Lift the camshaft from the cylinder head

12.7 Check the camshaft endfloat using a DTI gauge

head with the pointer resting on the camshaft nose **(see illustration)**.

c) *Using a large screwdriver as a lever at the opposite end, move the camshaft forward-and-backward and note the dial indicator reading.*

d) *Compare the reading with the endfloat listed in this Chapter's Specifications.*

e) *If the indicated reading is excessive, either the camshaft or the cylinder head is worn. Renew parts as necessary.*

8 Check the camshaft bearing journals and caps for scoring and signs of wear. If they are worn, exchange the cylinder head with a new or rebuilt assembly.

9 Check the cam lobes for wear:

a) *Check the toe and ramp areas of each cam lobe for score marks and uneven wear. Also check for flaking and pitting.*

b) *If there's wear on the toe or the ramp, renew the camshaft, but first try to find the cause of the wear. Look for abrasive substances in the oil and inspect the oil pump and oil passages for blockage. Lobe wear is usually caused by inadequate lubrication or dirty oil.*

10 Inspect the rocker arms for wear, scoring and pitting of the contact surfaces (see Section 8).

11 If any of the conditions described above are noted, the cylinder head is probably getting insufficient lubrication or dirty oil. Make sure you track down the cause of this problem (low oil level, low oil pump capacity, clogged oil passage, etc) before refitting a new cylinder head, camshaft or rocker arm assembly.

Refitting

12 Thoroughly clean the camshaft, the bearing surfaces in the head and caps and the rocker arms. Remove all sludge and dirt. Wipe off all components with a clean, lint-free cloth.

13 Lubricate the camshaft bearing surfaces in the head and the bearing journals and lobes on the camshaft with clean engine oil.

Caution: Failure to adequately lubricate the camshaft and related components can cause serious damage to bearing and friction surfaces during the first few seconds after engine start-up, when the oil pressure is low or nonexistent.

14 Carefully lower the camshaft into position,

with the keyway in the 12 o'clock position. Using an appropriate-sized driver, deep socket or section of pipe, fit a new camshaft seal with the open (spring) side facing in.

15 Refit the rocker arm assembly (see Section 8).

16 Rotate the camshaft as necessary and refit the camshaft sprocket with the UP mark stamped on the camshaft sprocket at the twelve o'clock position **(see illustrations 10.23a, 10.23b and 10.23c)**.

17 Refit the timing belt and related components as described in Section 10.

Caution: If the crankshaft position was disturbed, be sure to realign the crankshaft sprocket before refitting the timing belt (see illustration 10.24).

18 Rotate the crankshaft anti-clockwise slowly by hand through two complete revolutions and recheck the alignment marks on the sprockets. The timing marks should still be aligned. If they're not, remove the timing belt and set all the timing marks again.

Caution: If you feel resistance while rotating the crankshaft, stop immediately.

19 The remainder of refitting is the reverse of removal.

13 Cylinder head – removal and refitting

Caution: Allow the engine to cool completely before beginning this procedure.

Removal

1 Position the number one piston at Top Dead Centre (see Section 3).

2 Disconnect the cable from the negative terminal of the battery (see Chapter 5A).

3 Drain the cooling system and remove the spark plugs (see Chapter 1).

4 Remove the air cleaner duct and housing (see Chapter 4A).

5 Remove the auxiliary drivebelts (see Chapter 1). Unbolt the power steering pump and set it aside without disconnecting any hoses, then remove the power steering pump bracket (see Chapter 10).

6 Disconnect the throttle cable from the throttle body and relieve the fuel system pressure (see Chapter 4A).

7 Disconnect the following hoses and pipes:

a) *Fuel feed hose.*

b) *Evaporative emission control hose.*

c) *Breather hose.*

d) *PCV hose.*

8 Disconnect the coolant bypass hose, heater hose and upper radiator hose (see Chapter 3).

9 Disconnect the following electrical connectors:

a) *Fuel injectors.*

b) *Engine coolant temperature sensor.*

c) *Engine coolant temperature switch.*

d) *Temperature gauge sender.*

e) *Throttle position sensor.*

f) *Manifold absolute pressure sensor.*

g) *Oxygen sensor(s).*

h) *EGR valve lift sensor (where fitted).*

i) *VTEC solenoid (where fitted).*

j) *VTEC pressure switch (where fitted).*

k) *Idle air control valve.*

l) *Intake air temperature sensor.*

10 Support the engine with a trolley jack. Place a wood block between the jack pad and the oil sump to avoid damaging the sump. Remove the left-hand engine mounting bracket (see Section 18).

11 Remove the intake manifold brace and exhaust manifold flange bolts. **Note:** *You may wish to detach the intake manifold (see Section 5) and/or exhaust manifold (see Section 6), rather than removing it with the cylinder head, to make the cylinder head easier to handle.*

12 Remove the camshaft cover (see Section 4).

13 Remove the distributor (see Chapter 5B), including the cap and HT leads.

14 Remove the timing belt (see Section 10), rocker arm assembly (see Section 8) and the camshaft (see Section 12).

15 Loosen the cylinder head bolts in 1/4-turn increments until they can be removed by hand. Work in a pattern that's the reverse of the tightening sequence to avoid warping the cylinder head **(see illustration 13.23)**. Note where each bolt goes so it can be returned to the same location on refitting.

16 Lift the cylinder head off the engine. If resistance is felt, don't prise between the head and block gasket mating surfaces – damage to the mating surfaces will result. Instead, prise between the power steering pump bracket and the engine block. Set the head on blocks of wood to prevent damage to the gasket sealing surfaces.

17 Cylinder head dismantling and inspection procedures are covered in detail in Chapter 2C. Check the cylinder head for warpage.

Refitting

18 The mating surfaces of the cylinder head and block must be perfectly clean when the head is refitted.

19 Use a gasket scraper to remove all traces of carbon and old gasket material, then clean the mating surfaces with gasket remover or cellulose thinners. If there's oil on the mating surfaces when the cylinder head is fitted, the gasket may not seal correctly and leaks may develop. When working on the engine block, fill the cylinders with clean rags to keep out debris. Use a vacuum cleaner to remove material that falls into the cylinders. Since the cylinder head and engine block are made of aluminium, aggressive scraping can cause damage. Be extra careful not to scratch or gouge the mating surfaces with the scraper.

20 Check the block and cylinder head mating surfaces for nicks, deep scratches and other damage. If damage is slight, it can be removed with a fine file; if it's excessive, machining may be the only alternative.

21 Use a tap of the correct size to clean the threads in the cylinder head bolt holes. Use a wire brush to remove corrosion and clean the

13.23 Cylinder head bolt tightening sequence

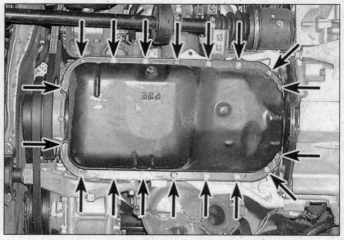

14.3 Remove the sump retaining bolts (arrowed)

bolt threads. Dirt, corrosion, sealant and damaged threads will affect torque readings.

22 Place a new gasket on the engine block. Check to see if there are any markings (such as TOP) on the gasket to indicate how it is to be fitted. Those identification marks must face up. Also, apply sealant to the edges of the timing chain cover where it mates with the engine block. Set the cylinder head in position.

23 Lubricate the threads and the seats of the cylinder head bolts with clean engine oil, then refit them. Tighten the bolts in the recommended sequence, in stages, to the torque listed in this Chapter's Specifications **(see illustration)**. Because of the critical function of cylinder head bolts, the manufacturer specifies the following conditions for tightening them:

 a) *A beam-type or dial-type torque wrench is preferable to a preset (click-stop) torque wrench. If you use a preset torque wrench, tighten slowly and be careful not to overtighten the bolts.*

 b) *If a bolt makes any sound while you're tightening it (squeaking, clicking, etc), loosen it completely and tighten it again in the specified stages.*

24 Attach the camshaft sprocket to the camshaft and refit the timing belt (see Section 10).

25 Rotate the crankshaft anti-clockwise slowly by hand through two complete revolutions and recheck the alignment marks on the sprockets.

Caution: If you feel any resistance while turning the engine over, stop and recheck the camshaft timing. The valves may be hitting the pistons.

26 Refit the remaining parts in the reverse order of removal.

27 Be sure to refill the cooling system and check all fluid levels.

28 Run the engine until normal operating temperature is reached. Check for leaks and proper operation.

14 Sump –
removed and refitting

Removal

1 Warm-up the engine, then drain the oil and renew the oil filter (see Chapter 1).

2 Raise the vehicle and support it securely on axle stands (see *Jacking and vehicle support*). Remove the splash shield from under the engine.

3 Remove the bolts securing the sump to the engine block **(see illustration)**.

4 Tap on the sump with a soft-face hammer to break the gasket seal, then detach the sump from the engine. Don't prise between the block and sump mating surfaces.

Refitting

5 Using a gasket scraper, remove all traces of old gasket and/or sealant from the engine

block and the sump. Also make sure the threaded bolt holes in the block are clean.

6 Thoroughly clean the sump. On engines with a steel sump, check the gasket flanges for distortion, particularly around the bolt holes. If necessary, place the pan on a wood block and use a hammer to flatten and restore the gasket surface.

7 Clean the mating surfaces on the engine block and remove any oil residue which will prevent the new gasket from sealing properly.

8 Apply a 2 mm wide bead of liquid sealant (available from Honda dealers) to the corners of the sump where they meet the rear oil seal retainer and the oil pump, then fit the gasket onto the sump.

9 On non-VTEC engines, apply additional 2 mm wide beads of liquid sealant (4 places) to the engine block where the rear oil seal retainer and the oil pump meet the cylinder block **(see illustration)**. On VTEC engines, apply additional 2 mm beads of liquid sealant (two places) to the top of the sump gasket

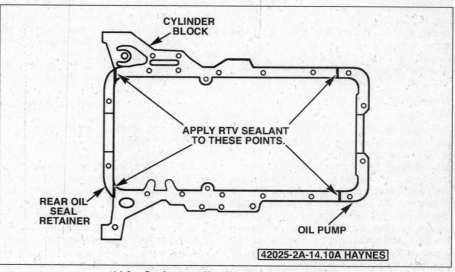

14.9a Sealant application details (non-VTEC)

where the oil pump and the rear oil seal retainer mate (see illustration). Once the sealant is applied, the sump must be fitted within five minutes, or the residue removed and fresh sealant applied.

10 Carefully place the sump in position and refit the bolts finger tight.

11 Starting with the bolts closest to the centre of the sump and working outward in a criss-cross pattern, tighten the bolts in three equal steps to the torque listed in this Chapter's Specifications. Don't overtighten them or leakage may occur.

12 Wait at least 20 minutes before adding oil (see Chapter 1), then start the engine and check for oil leaks.

15 Oil pump – removal, inspection and refitting

Removal

1 Remove the timing belt. Recover the guide plate(s) and slide the sprocket from the crankshaft (see Section 10).

2 Remove the sump (see Section 14).

3 Remove the oil pick-up tube and filter from the pump housing and the main bearing cap bridge (see illustration).

4 Remove the bolts from the oil pump housing and separate the assembly from the engine (see illustration).

5 Undo the screws and dismantle the oil

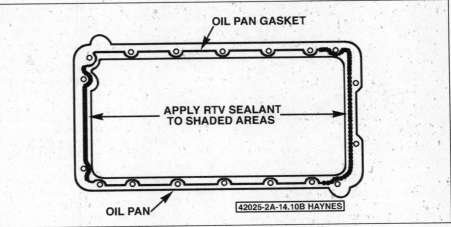

14.9b Sealant application details (VTEC and VTEC-E)

pump (see illustration). You may need to use an impact screwdriver to loosen the pump cover screws without stripping the heads.

Inspection

6 Check the oil pump rotor-to-cover-clearance, tooth tip clearance and rotor-to-body clearance (see illustrations). Compare your measurements to the figures listed in this Chapter's Specifications. Renew the pump if any of the measurements exceed the specified limits.

7 Remove the pressure relief valve bolt and extract the spring and pressure relief valve plunger from the pump housing. Check the

spring for distortion and the relief valve plunger for scoring. Renew parts as necessary.

8 Refit the pump rotors. Pack the spaces between the rotors with petroleum jelly (this will prime the pump).

9 Apply thread-locking compound to the pump cover screws, refit the cover and tighten the screws to the torque listed in this Chapter's Specifications. Refit the oil pressure relief valve and spring assembly. Use a new sealing washer on the plug and tighten the bolt to the specified torque.

Refitting

10 Apply a thin coat of liquid sealant

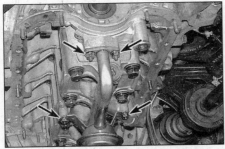

15.3 Remove the oil pick-up tube bolts (arrowed) from the oil pump and main bearing cap bridge

15.4 Remove the retaining bolts (circled) and remove the oil pump

15.5 Remove the oil pump cover screws (arrowed)

15.6a Use a feeler gauge and straight-edge to check the clearance between the rotors and the cover

15.6b Use a feeler gauge to check the tooth tip clearance between the inner and outer rotors

15.6c Use a feeler gauge to check the outer rotor-to-pump body clearance

16.3 Remove the flywheel/driveplate bolts (arrowed)

(available from Honda dealers) to the pump housing-to-block sealing surface and a new O-ring in the pump housing. Refit the pump housing to the engine block and tighten the bolts to the torque listed in this Chapter's Specifications.

11 Refit the oil pick-up tube and filter, using a new gasket. Tighten the bolts to the torque listed in this Chapter's Specifications.

12 Refit the sump (see Section 14).

13 The remainder of refitting is the reverse of removal. Add the specified type and quantity of oil and coolant (see Chapter 1), start the engine and check for leaks.

16 Flywheel/driveplate – removal and refitting

Removal

1 Raise the vehicle and support it securely on axle stands (see *Jacking and vehicle support*), then refer to the appropriate Part of Chapter 7 and remove the transmission.

2 If the vehicle is equipped with a manual transmission, remove the pressure plate and clutch disc (see Chapter 6) Now is a good time to check/renew the clutch components and pilot bearing.

3 Remove the bolts that secure the flywheel/driveplate to the crankshaft **(see illustration)**. If the crankshaft turns, wedge a screwdriver in the ring gear teeth (manual transmission models), or insert a long punch through one of the holes in the driveplate and allow it to rest against a projection on the engine block (automatic transmission models).

4 Remove the flywheel/driveplate from the crankshaft. Since the flywheel is heavy, be sure to support it while removing the last bolt.

5 Clean the flywheel to remove grease and oil. Inspect the surface for cracks, rivet grooves, burned areas and score marks. Light scoring can be removed with emery cloth. Check for cracked and broken ring gear teeth. Lay the flywheel on a flat surface and use a straight-edge to check for warpage.

6 Clean and inspect the mating surfaces of the flywheel/driveplate and the crankshaft. If the oil seal is leaking, renew it before refitting the flywheel/driveplate (see Section 17).

Refitting

7 Position the flywheel/driveplate against the crankshaft. Note that some engines have an alignment dowel or staggered bolt holes to ensure correct refitting. Before refitting the bolts, apply thread-locking compound to the threads.

8 Prevent the flywheel/driveplate from turning by using one of the methods described in Paragraph 3. Using a crossing pattern, tighten the bolts to the torque listed in this Chapter's Specifications.

9 The remainder of refitting is the reverse of the removal procedure.

17 Crankshaft transmission end oil seal – renewal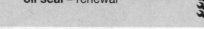

Note: *Renewal of the oil seal and retainer as a unit are covered in Chapter 2C.*

1 Remove the flywheel/driveplate (see Section 16).

2 Before removing the seal, it is very important that the clearance between the seal and the outside edge of the retainer is checked. Use a small ruler or caliper and record the distance. The new seal must not be driven in past this measurement.

3 The seal can be renewed without removing the sump or seal retainer. Use a screwdriver and a rag to carefully pry the seal out of the housing **(see illustration)**. Use the rag to be sure no nicks are made in the crankshaft seal surface.

4 Apply a film of clean oil to the crankshaft seal journal and the lip of the new seal and carefully tap the seal into place. The lip is stiff so carefully work it onto the seal journal of the crankshaft with a smooth object like the end of a socket extension **(see illustration)**. Tap the seal into the retainer with a seal driver. If a seal driver isn't available, a large socket or piece of pipe, with an outside diameter slightly smaller than that of the seal, can be used. Don't rush it or you may damage the seal.

5 The remaining steps are the reverse of removal.

6 Start the engine and check for oil leaks.

18 Engine mountings – inspection and renewal

1 Engine mounts seldom require attention, but broken or deteriorated mounts should be renewed immediately or the added strain placed on the drivetrain components may cause damage or wear.

Inspection

2 During the inspection, the engine must be raised slightly to remove the weight from the mountings.

3 Raise the vehicle and support it securely on axle stands (see *Jacking and vehicle support*),

17.3 Carefully prise out the oil seal with a removal tool or screwdriver

17.4 Lubricate the journal and the seal lip with clean engine oil, and carefully work the seal over the journal with a smooth, blunt object

18.9a Left-hand side engine mounting (arrowed)

18.9b Right-hand side transmission mounting (arrowed)

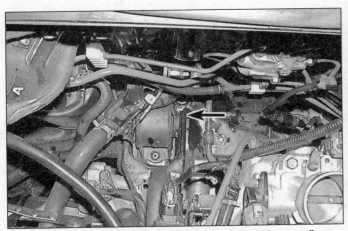

18.9c Rear engine mounting at the bulkhead (arrowed)

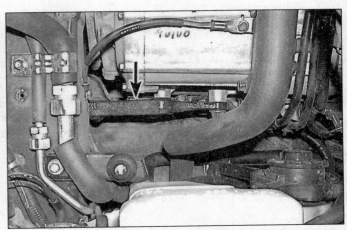

18.9d Right-hand front mounting and bracket at the transmission (arrowed)

then position a trolley jack under the engine sump. Place a large wood block between the jack head and the sump, then carefully raise the engine just enough to take the weight off the mountings.

Warning: DO NOT place any part of your body under the engine when it's supported only by a jack.

4 Check the mountings insulators to see if the rubber is cracked, hardened or separated from the metal in the centre of the mount.

5 Check for relative movement between the mounting plates and the engine or frame (use a large screwdriver or pry bar to attempt to move the mounts). If movement is noted, lower the engine and tighten the mount fasteners.

6 Rubber preservative should be applied to the insulators to slow deterioration.

Renewal

7 Disconnect the cable from the negative terminal of the battery (see Chapter 5A). Raise the vehicle and support it securely on axle stands (see *Jacking and vehicle support*). Support the engine as described in Paragraph 3.

8 Remove the fasteners, raise the engine with the jack and detach the mounting from the bracket and engine.

9 Fit the new mounting, making sure it is correctly positioned in its bracket **(see illustrations)**. Refit the fasteners and tighten them securely.

Chapter 2 Part B:
DOHC engine in-car repair procedures

Contents

Degrees of difficulty

Easy, suitable for novice with little experience		Fairly easy, suitable for beginner with some experience		Fairly difficult, suitable for competent DIY mechanic		Difficult, suitable for experienced DIY mechanic		Very difficult, suitable for expert DIY or professional	

Specifications

General

Engine type	Four-cylinder, in-line, water-cooled. Double overhead camshaft, 4 valves per cylinder
Manufacturer's engine codes*:	
1.6 litre	B16A2
1.8 litre	B18C4
Capacity:	
1.6 litre	1595cc
1.8 litre	1797cc
Firing order	1-3-4-2 (No 1 cylinder at timing belt end)
Direction of crankshaft rotation	Anti-clockwise (viewed from timing belt end of engine)
Compression ratio:	
1.6 litre	10.4:1
1.8 litre	10.0:1

See 'Vehicle identification' in the Reference section

Compression pressures

Nominal	15.5 bar
Minimum	9.5 bar
Maximum difference between any two cylinders	2.0 bar

Camshaft

Endfloat	0.5 mm maximum

Lubrication system

Oil pump type	Rotor type, driven directly from crankshaft
Minimum permissible oil pressure with engine at operating temperature (oil temperature of at least 80°C):	
At idle speed	0.7 bar
At 3000 rpm	3.5 bar
Oil pump clearances:	
Inner-to-outer rotor radial clearance	0.20 mm maximum
Outer rotor-to-body radial clearance	0.20 mm maximum
Rotor endfloat	0.15 mm maximum

Torque wrench settings

	Nm	lbf ft
Baffle plate	11	8
Camshaft cover nuts	10	7
Camshaft holder bolts:		
6 mm bolts	10	7
8 mm bolts	27	20
Camshaft sprocket bolts	56	41
Connecting rod big-end bearing cap*	40	30
Crankshaft pulley bolt	177	131
Crankshaft transmission end oil seal housing bolts	11	8
Cylinder head bolts:		
Stage 1	29	21
Stage 2:		
1.6 litre engine	83	61
1.8 litre engine	85	63
Driveplate-to-crankshaft bolts	74	55
Exhaust manifold-to-cylinder head nuts*	31	23
Exhaust pipe-to-manifold nuts*	54	40
Flywheel-to-crankshaft bolts	103	76
Intake manifold bolts/nuts	23	17
Main bearing bridge (B18C4)	63	46
Main bearing caps	74	55
Oil drain plug	44	32
Oil jet bolts	16	12
Oil pressure switch	18	13
Oil pump cover to housing	7	5
Oil pump housing-to-block bolts:		
6 mm bolts	11	8
8 mm bolts	24	18
Oil pump pick-up tube to pump housing nuts	11	8
Oil pump relief valve plug	39	29
Spark plug cover	10	7
Sump bolts	12	9
Timing belt cover bolts	10	7
Timing belt tensioner bolt	54	40
VTEC lock-up solenoid bolts	12	9

*Do not re-use

1 General information

This Part of Chapter 2 is devoted to in-vehicle repair procedures for the 1.6 litre and 1.8 litre Double Overhead Camshaft (DOHC), 16-valve, fuel injected, four cylinder engines. Both of the engines covered in this Chapter incorporate the VTEC (Variable Valve Timing and lift Electronic Control) system, which electronically alters valve timing to enhance engine performance. For more information on the VTEC system, see Section 9 of this Chapter.

The following repair procedures are based on the assumption that the engine is fitted in the vehicle. If the engine has been removed from the vehicle and mounted on a stand, many of the steps outlined in this Part of Chapter 2 will not apply.

The Specifications included in this Part of Chapter 2 apply only to the procedures contained in this chapter. Chapter 2C contains the Specifications necessary for cylinder head and engine block rebuilding.

The DOHC engines are lightweight in design with an aluminium alloy block (with steel cylinder liners) and an aluminium alloy cylinder head. The crankshaft rides in a single carriage unit that houses the renewable insert-type main bearings, with separate thrust bearings at the number four bearing position assigned the task of controlling crankshaft endfloat.

The pistons have two compression rings and one oil control ring. The semi-floating piston gudgeon pins are press fitted into the small end of the connecting rod. The connecting rod big-ends are also equipped with renewable insert-type plain bearings.

The engine is liquid-cooled, utilising a centrifugal impeller-type water pump, driven by the timing belt, to circulate coolant around the cylinders and combustion chambers and through the intake manifold.

Lubrication is handled by a rotor-type oil pump mounted on the front of the engine under the timing belt cover. It is driven directly by the crankshaft. The oil is filtered continuously by a cartridge-type filter mounted on the rear of the engine.

Repair operations possible with the engine in the car

The following operations can be carried out without having to remove the engine from the vehicle:

a) Removal and refitting of the cylinder head.
b) Removal and refitting of the timing belt and sprockets.
c) Renewal of the camshaft oil seal.
d) Removal and refitting of the camshaft housing and camshaft.
e) Removal and refitting of the sump.
f) Removal and refitting of the connecting rods and pistons*.
g) Removal and refitting of the oil pump.
h) Renewal of the crankshaft oil seals.
i) Renewal of the engine mountings.
j) Removal and refitting of the flywheel/driveplate.

* Although the operation marked with an asterisk can be carried out with the engine in the car after removal of the sump, it is better for the engine to be removed, in the interests of cleanliness and improved access. For this reason, the procedure is described in Chapter 2C.

Caution: If the radio in your vehicle is equipped with an anti-theft system, make sure you have the correct activation code before disconnecting the battery.

2 Compression test – description and interpretation

1 When engine performance is down, or if misfiring occurs which cannot be attributed to the ignition or fuel systems, a compression test can provide diagnostic clues as to the engine's condition. If the test is performed regularly, it can give warning of trouble before any other symptoms become apparent.

2 The engine must be fully warmed-up to normal operating temperature, the battery must be fully charged, and the spark plugs must be removed (see Chapter 1). The aid of an assistant will also be required.

3 Disable the ignition system by disconnecting the wiring connector from the ignition distributor, and the fuel system by removing the main fuel injection relay fuse from the engine compartment fuse box (see Chapter 12).

4 Fit a compression tester to the number 1 cylinder spark plug hole. The type of tester which screws into the plug thread is to be preferred.

5 Have the assistant hold the throttle wide open and crank the engine on the starter motor; after one or two revolutions, the compression pressure should build-up to a maximum figure, and then stabilise. Record the highest reading obtained.

6 Repeat the test on the remaining cylinders, recording the pressure in each.

7 All cylinders should produce very similar pressures; any difference greater than that specified indicates the existence of a fault. Note that the compression should build-up quickly in a healthy engine. Low compression on the first stroke, followed by gradually-increasing pressure on successive strokes, indicates worn piston rings. A low compression reading on the first stroke, which does not build-up during successive strokes, indicates leaking valves or a blown head gasket (a cracked head could also be the cause). Deposits on the undersides of the valve heads can also cause low compression.

8 If the pressure in any cylinder is reduced to the specified minimum or less, carry out the following test to isolate the cause. Introduce a teaspoonful of clean oil into that cylinder through its spark plug hole, and repeat the test.

9 If the addition of oil temporarily improves the compression pressure, this indicates that bore or piston wear is responsible for the pressure loss. No improvement suggests that leaking or burnt valves, or a blown head gasket, may be to blame.

10 A low reading from two adjacent cylinders is almost certainly due to the head gasket having blown between them; the presence of coolant in the engine oil will confirm this.

11 If one cylinder is about 20 per cent lower than the others, and the engine has a slightly rough idle, a worn camshaft lobe could be the cause.

12 If the compression reading is unusually high, the combustion chambers are probably coated with carbon deposits. If this is the case, the cylinder head should be removed and decarbonised.

13 On completion of the test, refit the spark plugs (see Chapter 1), refit the main fuel injection relay fuse and reconnect the wiring connector to the distributor.

3 Top Dead Centre (TDC) for number 1 piston – locating

Note: *The following procedure is based on the assumption that the distributor is correctly fitted. If you are trying to locate TDC to refit the distributor correctly, piston position must be determined by feeling for compression at the number 1 spark plug hole, then aligning the TDC mark on the crankshaft pulley with the pointer on the lower timing cover as described in Paragraph 8.*

1 Top Dead Centre (TDC) is the highest point in the cylinder that each piston reaches as it travels up-and-down when the crankshaft turns. Each piston reaches TDC on the compression stroke and again on the exhaust stroke, but TDC generally refers to piston position on the compression stroke.

2 Positioning the number 1 piston at TDC is an essential part of many procedures, such as camshaft, timing belt or distributor removal.

3 Before beginning this procedure, be sure to place the transmission in Neutral and apply the handbrake or chock the rear wheels. Remove the spark plugs (see Chapter 1).

4 In order to bring any piston to TDC, the crankshaft must be turned using the method outlined below. When looking at the auxiliary drivebelt end of the engine, normal crankshaft rotation is anti-clockwise. Always rotate the engine anti-clockwise; clockwise rotation may cause incorrect adjustment of the timing belt. The preferred method is to turn the crankshaft with a socket and ratchet attached to the bolt threaded into the front of the crankshaft.

5 Note the position of the terminal for the number 1 spark plug HT lead on the distributor cap. If the terminal isn't marked, follow the HT lead from the number 1 cylinder spark plug to the cap.

6 Use a felt-tip pen or chalk to make a mark on the distributor body directly under the number 1 terminal of the distributor cap **(see illustration)**.

7 Detach the cap from the distributor and set it aside.

8 Turn the crankshaft (see Paragraph 4) until the white (TDC) notch in the crankshaft pulley is aligned with the pointer on the timing belt cover **(see illustration)**.

9 Look at the distributor rotor – it should be pointing directly at the mark you made on the distributor body **(see illustration)**.

10 If the rotor is 180° out, the number 1 piston is at TDC on the exhaust stroke. In which case, to get the piston to TDC on the compression stroke, turn the crankshaft one complete revolution (360°) anti-clockwise. The rotor should now be pointing at the mark on the distributor. When the rotor is pointing at the number 1 spark plug HT lead terminal in the distributor cap and the TDC marks are aligned, the number 1 piston is at TDC on the compression stroke.

11 After the number 1 piston has been positioned at TDC on the compression stroke, TDC for any of the remaining cylinders can be located by turning the crankshaft in 180° increments and following the firing order (refer

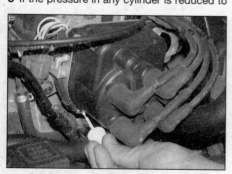

3.6 Make a mark (arrowed) on the distributor housing directly below the number 1 HT lead terminal on the distributor cap

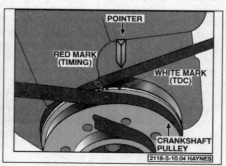

3.8 Align the white (TDC) mark on the crankshaft pulley with the pointer on the timing belt cover – note that the TDC mark is the mark farthest to the right

3.9 When the engine is at TDC for the number 1 piston, the rotor should be pointing at the mark (arrowed) made on the distributor housing

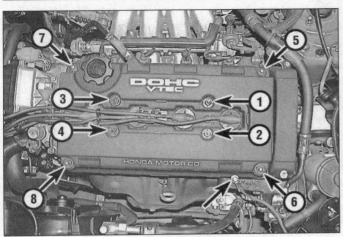

4.10 Camshaft cover bolts tightening sequence

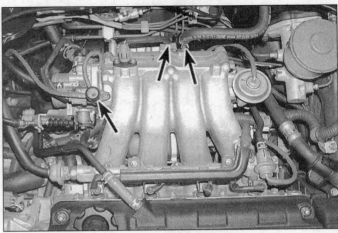

5.4 Disconnect the vacuum hoses (arrowed)

to the Specifications). Rotating the engine 180° past TDC for cylinder number 1 will put the engine at TDC compression for cylinder number 3.

4 Camshaft cover –
removal and refitting

Removal

1 Disconnect the cable from the negative terminal of the battery (see Chapter 5A).
2 Remove the distributor cap and HT leads from their cylinder head and camshaft cover connections (see Chapter 1). Be sure to mark each lead for correct refitting.
3 Mark and detach any hoses or wires from the throttle body or camshaft cover that will interfere with the removal of the cover.
4 Wipe off the camshaft cover thoroughly to prevent debris from falling onto the exposed cylinder head or camshaft/valvetrain assembly.
5 Remove the camshaft cover nuts and washers (see illustration 4.10).
6 Carefully lift off the camshaft cover and gasket. If the gasket is stuck to the cylinder head, tap it with a rubber mallet to break the seal. Do not prise between the cover and cylinder head or you'll damage the gasket mating surfaces.

Refitting

7 Remove the old gasket and clean the mating surfaces of the cylinder head and the camshaft cover. Clean the surfaces with a rag soaked in cellulose thinners or gasket remover.
8 Inspect the sealing grommets and the rubber seals that fit at the bottoms of the spark plug wells. Renew them if they're cracked or flattened, or if the rubber has hardened. Make sure the rubber spark plug seals are in position before refitting the camshaft cover.

9 Apply a bead of liquid sealant (available from Honda dealers) to the corners where the cylinder head mates with the rocker arm assembly. **Note:** *The cover must be fitted within five minutes of applying the sealant. If more time has elapsed, remove the old residue and re-apply the sealant.*
10 Fit a new moulded rubber gasket into the groove around the perimeter of the camshaft cover and refit the cover. Refit the camshaft cover sealing grommets and nuts. Following the recommended sequence, tighten the nuts to the torque listed in this Chapter's Specifications (see illustration). **Note:** *After assembly, wait at least 20 minutes to allow the sealant to set.*
11 The remainder of refitting is the reverse of removal.

5 Intake manifold –
removal and refitting

> *Warning: Wait until the engine is completely cool before beginning this procedure.*

Removal

1 Disconnect the cable from the negative

terminal of the battery (see Chapter 5A).
2 Drain the cooling system (see Chapter 1).
3 Remove the intake air duct and air cleaner housing (see Chapter 4A, Section 9).
4 Clearly label and detach any vacuum lines and electrical connectors which will interfere with removal of the manifold and the throttle body (see illustration).
5 Detach the accelerator cable and, if equipped, the cruise control cable from the throttle lever (see Chapter 4A).
6 Remove the coolant hoses from the throttle body. Also disconnect the coolant hoses from the Idle Air Control (IAC) valve.
7 Relieve the fuel system pressure and disconnect the fuel feed and return lines at the fuel rail (see Chapter 4A).
8 Working from underneath the engine compartment, remove the brace that supports the intake manifold (see illustration).
9 Disconnect the coolant bypass hose from the timing belt end of the intake manifold (see illustration).
10 Remove the intake manifold nuts and remove the manifold from the engine (see illustration 5.9).
11 On 1.8 litre models, the intake manifold chamber can be separated from the manifold by undoing the bolts/nuts (see

5.8 Remove the bolts (arrowed) and remove the brace from the intake manifold

5.9 Disconnect the coolant bypass hose and remove the intake manifold mounting nuts (arrowed)

5.11 On 1.8 litre models, the intake manifold chamber can be separated from the manifold by undoing the bolts/nuts

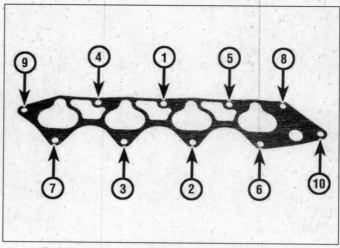

5.16 Intake manifold fastener tightening sequence

illustration). As the chamber is removed, recover the gaskets and separate the intake air bypass valve body.

Refitting

12 Check the mating surfaces of the manifold for flatness with a precision straight-edge and feeler gauge.

13 Inspect the manifold for cracks and distortion. If the manifold is cracked or warped, renew it.

14 Check carefully for any stripped or broken intake manifold bolts/studs. Renew any defective fasteners with new parts.

15 Using a scraper, remove all traces of old gasket material from the cylinder head and manifold mating surfaces. Clean the surfaces with cellulose thinners or gasket remover.

16 Refit the intake manifold with a new gasket and tighten the nuts finger-tight. Following the recommended sequence, tighten the nuts to the torque listed in this Chapter's Specifications **(see illustration)**.

17 The remainder of the refitting procedure is the reverse of removal. Refer to Chapter 1 and refill the cooling system.

6 Exhaust manifold – removal and refitting

Removal

1 Disconnect the battery cable from the negative battery terminal (see Chapter 5A).

2 Raise the front of the vehicle and support it securely on axle stands (see *Jacking and vehicle support*). Unbolt the bracket and detach the exhaust pipe from the exhaust manifold **(see illustration)**. Apply penetrating oil to the fastener threads if they are difficult to remove.

3 Remove the heat shield from the exhaust manifold **(see illustration)**. Be sure to soak the bolts and nuts with penetrating oil before attempting to remove them from the manifold.

4 Remove the exhaust manifold nuts **(see illustration)** and detach the exhaust manifold from the cylinder head.

Refitting

5 Discard the old gasket and use a scraper to clean the gasket mating surfaces on the manifold and cylinder head.

6 Place a new gasket on the cylinder head, fit the exhaust manifold in position, and fit the new nuts. Starting at the centre, tighten the nuts in a criss-cross pattern to the torque listed in this Chapter's Specifications.

7 The remainder of refitting is the reverse of removal.

8 Start the engine and check for exhaust leaks between the manifold and the cylinder head, and between the manifold and the exhaust pipe.

7 Timing belt and sprockets – removal, inspection and refitting

Removal

1 Loosen the wheel nuts on the left-hand front wheel and raise the front of the vehicle. Support the front of the vehicle securely on axle stands (see *Jacking and vehicle support*).

2 Remove the left front wheel and remove the splash shield from under the engine.

3 Support the engine with a trolley jack. Place a wood block between the jack pad and the sump to avoid damaging the sump.

6.2 Remove the exhaust pipe flange and bracket bolts (arrowed), then lower the exhaust pipe

6.3 Remove the bolts (arrowed) and remove the heat shield

6.4 Exhaust manifold retaining nuts (arrowed)

7.10 Hold the crankshaft pulley with a strap wrench and remove the bolt – a chain wrench can be used if you first wrap a length of old drivebelt around the pulley

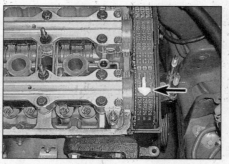

7.13 If you intend to re-use the belt, make an arrow mark to indicate direction of rotation and match marks to align the sprockets with the belt

7.14a Centre timing belt cover bolts (arrowed)

4 Remove the spark plugs and drivebelts (see Chapter 1).

5 On 1.8 litre models, remove the upper left-hand engine mounting (see Section 17).

6 Unbolt the power steering pump without disconnecting the hoses and set it aside (see Chapter 10).

7 On 1.6 litre models, remove the upper left-hand engine mounting bracket, and the power steering pump lower bracket.

8 On all models, remove the camshaft cover (see Section 4).

9 Position the number 1 piston at Top Dead Centre (see Section 3).

Caution: Always rotate the crankshaft anti-clockwise (viewed from the pulley end of the engine). Clockwise rotation may cause incorrect adjustment of the timing belt.

10 Using a strap spanner or chain spanner to hold the crankshaft pulley stationary, loosen the crankshaft pulley bolt with a socket and breaker bar **(see illustration)**.

11 Slip the pulley off the crankshaft. If it is loose, recover the locating key from the crankshaft.

12 Remove the drivebelt idler pulley and bracket from the front of the engine.

13 If you intend to re-use the timing belt, use white paint or chalk to make match marks to align the sprockets with the belt and an arrow

to indicate the direction of rotation **(see illustration)**.

14 Undo the bolts, and remove the centre and lower timing belt covers **(see illustrations)**.

15 Loosen the belt tensioner bolt 1/2 turn **(see illustration)**. Push the tensioner away from the belt to loosen it, then tighten the bolt to hold the tensioner. Slip the belt off the sprockets and remove it from the engine. If you're renewing the crankshaft oil seal, slip the outer belt guide, sprocket and inner belt guide off the crankshaft (see Section 8).

16 If you're renewing the camshafts or camshaft oil seals, slip a large screwdriver through the camshaft sprocket to keep it from rotating and remove the bolt, then pull off the sprocket. Also remove the Woodruff key.

Inspection

Caution: Do not rotate the camshaft or crankshaft sprockets with the timing belt off or valve damage may result from valves hitting the tops of pistons.

17 Rotate the belt tensioner pulley by hand and move it from side-to-side, checking for play and rough rotation **(see illustration 7.15)**. Renew it if roughness or play is detected.

18 Check the timing belt for wear (especially on the thrust side of the teeth), cracks, splits,

fraying and oil contamination **(see illustration 10.21 in Chapter 2A)**. Renew the belt if any of these conditions are noted. **Note:** *Unless the engine has very low mileage, it's common practice to renew the timing belt with a new one every time it's removed. Don't refit the original belt unless it's in like-new condition. Never refit a belt in questionable condition.*

19 Whilst the belt is removed, check the condition of the coolant pump. Rotate the pump sprocket checking for play, roughness or partial seizure. If necessary, renew the pump as described in Chapter 3.

Refitting

20 If you removed the sprockets, refit them. Don't forget the Woodruff keys for the camshaft sprockets and the inner belt guide for the crankshaft sprocket. Ensure that the guide is fitted with the curved edge facing away from the belt. Tighten the camshaft sprocket bolts to the torque listed in this Chapter's specifications.

21 Before fitting the timing belt, make sure the UP marks on the camshaft sprockets are at the top and the two timing marks are aligned with the pointer on the rear cover **(see illustration)**.

22 Temporarily refit the crankshaft pulley and bolt and turn the crankshaft (if it was

7.14b Lower timing belt cover bolts (arrowed)

7.15 Timing belt tensioner (arrowed)

7.21 Ensure the word UP is at the twelve o'clock position and the two timing marks (arrowed) are aligned with the pointer on the rear cover

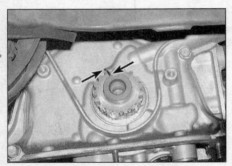

7.22 Align the mark on the crankshaft sprocket with the pointer on the oil pump housing (arrowed)

disturbed) until the timing mark on the crankshaft sprocket and the pointer on the oil pump housing are aligned **(see illustration)**. *Caution: If you feel resistance, stop turning the crankshaft. The pistons may be contacting open valves, and continued turning may bend the valves. Carefully reposition the camshaft sprockets and try rotating the crankshaft again.*

23 Refit the timing belt, making sure there is no slack, first on the crankshaft sprocket, then around the tensioner pulley, water pump pulley, exhaust camshaft sprocket and intake camshaft sprocket in sequence. Loosen the belt tensioner bolt, allowing the tensioner to tension the belt and temporarily tighten the bolt.

24 Carefully turn the crankshaft through six

revolutions and recheck the timing marks and camshaft sprocket index marks for proper alignment **(see illustrations 7.21 and 7.22)**. If the crankshaft binds or seems to hit something, do not force it, as the valves may be hitting the pistons. If this happens, valve timing is incorrect. Remove the belt and repeat the refitting procedure and verify that the fitting is correct.

25 To properly tension the timing belt, loosen the tensioner bolt 1/2 turn (180°), rotate the crankshaft anti-clockwise until the camshaft pulley is three teeth past TDC and tighten the tensioner bolt to the torque listed in this Chapter's Specifications.

26 Refit the remaining parts in the reverse order of removal.

27 Refer to Chapter 1 and adjust the auxiliary drivebelts.

28 Start the engine and check for correct operation.

8 Crankshaft timing belt end oil seal – renewal

1 Remove the timing belt (see Section 7).

2 Remove the outer belt guide and crankshaft sprocket from the crankshaft. Also remove the inner belt guide **(see illustrations)**.

3 Carefully pry the seal out of the oil pump housing with a seal removal tool or a screwdriver **(see illustration)**. Don't scratch

the seal bore or damage the crankshaft in the process (if the crankshaft is damaged, the new seal will end up leaking).

4 Clean the bore in the oil pump housing and coat the inner edge of the new seal with engine oil or multi-purpose grease. Using a socket with an outside diameter slightly smaller than the outside diameter of the seal, carefully drive the seal into place with a hammer, ensuring that the spring side of the seal faces inwards **(see illustration 11.4 in Chapter 2A)**. If a socket is not available, a short section of a large diameter pipe will work.

5 Refit the inner belt guide, crankshaft sprocket and outer belt guide. Make sure the curved edges of the guides face away from the belt.

6 Refit the timing belt (see Section 7).

7 Lubricate the sleeve of the crankshaft pulley with engine oil or multi-purpose grease, then refit the crankshaft pulley. The remainder of refitting is the reverse of removal.

8 Start the engine and check for leaks.

9 VTEC system – general information and components checks

General information

1 The VTEC system (Variable Valve Timing and lift Electronic Control) is used on various models throughout the Honda vehicle range.

2 The differences between the base engines and their VTEC counterparts is strictly in the components and operation of the valve train. The engine block, oiling and cooling systems are identical, as are all attached components. Models equipped with VTEC systems can be distinguished by the letters VTEC moulded into the top of the camshaft cover.

3 The Powertrain Control Module (PCM) has the ability to alter valve lift and timing during different engine operating conditions. The PCM turns the system on or off, depending on sensor input.

4 The following are used to determine VTEC operation:

   a) Engine speed (rpm).
   b) Vehicle speed (mph).
   c) Throttle position sensor output.
   d) Engine load measured by manifold absolute pressure sensor.
   e) Coolant temperature.

5 The VTEC system on Double Overhead Camshaft (DOHC) engines operates both the intake and exhaust valves unlike SOHC engines, where the VTEC system operates the intake valves only. Double Overhead camshaft (DOHC) engines have three camshaft lobes for each pair of intake and exhaust valves in a given cylinder. This equates to six camshaft lobes (three intake and three exhaust) for every four valves (two intake and two exhaust) in a cylinder.

6 The camshafts used on DOHC VTEC

8.2a Remove the outer belt guide – note that the curved outer edge faces away from the belt

8.2b Slide the sprocket off the crankshaft

8.2c After removing the sprocket, slide off the inner belt guide (where fitted); the curved edge faces away from the timing belt

8.3 Carefully prise the oil seal out with a removal tool or a screwdriver

9.11 VTEC oil pressure switch connector (upper arrow) and solenoid connector (lower arrow)

9.16 Connect an oil pressure gauge to the VTEC solenoid port (arrowed)

systems also have different primary and secondary valve lobe profiles (lift and duration specifications) and an additional third lobe and rocker arm placed between the primary and secondary. This third, or Mid, lobe has larger lift and longer duration than the primary and secondary camshaft lobes.

7 During low speed operation, the primary and secondary rocker arms (on the intake and exhaust camshafts) operate on their own camshaft lobes allowing the valves to be opened at a smaller lift. This limited valve operation is designed to provide good low-end torque and responsiveness.

8 As performance is required, the primary and secondary rocker arms are locked to the Mid rocker arm through the use of an electrically-controlled, hydraulic system. Both the intake and exhaust valves now operate on the Mid camshaft lobe of their respective camshaft. **Note:** *The primary and secondary rocker arms no longer contact their respective camshaft lobes until the Mid rocker arm is disengaged.* This provides good torque at both low and high speeds by using the camshaft lobe profile that most matches driving needs at any given speed and load.

Component checks

Lock-up solenoid valve/ pressure switch

9 The lock-up VTEC solenoid valve and the

oil pressure switch on DOHC engines is mounted on the end of the cylinder head next to the distributor.

10 A problem in either the VTEC solenoid valve circuit or VTEC pressure switch circuit will turn on the Malfunction Indicator Light (MIL) and set a diagnostic trouble code. Refer to Chapter 4A for more information on accessing trouble codes.

11 Disconnect the round electrical connector from the pressure switch **(see illustration)**.

12 Connect an ohmmeter between the terminals of the switch. There should be continuity. If there is no continuity, renew the switch.

13 Connect a voltmeter between body earth and the blue-black wire terminal in the harness side of the connector. With the ignition key ON (engine not running), there should be approximately 12 volts. If not, look for a break or bad connection in the blue-black wire between the connector and its terminal at the PCM.

14 Once you've got the correct voltage at the blue-black wire terminal in the connector, connect the voltmeter between both of the terminals in the harness side of the connector (blue-black and black wires). With the key ON, there should still be approximately 12 volts. If not, check the black wire (which supplies the earth for this circuit) for a break or bad connection between the connector and body earth.

15 With the ignition key OFF, disconnect the single-pin connector from the VTEC solenoid **(see illustration 9.11)**. Connect an ohmmeter between the terminal pin in the solenoid (not in the harness) and body earth. If the ohmmeter doesn't indicate 14 to 30 ohms, renew the solenoid as described below.

16 Remove the 10 mm bolt from the oil pressure test port on the solenoid. Attach a mechanical oil pressure gauge, using an appropriate adapter **(see illustration)**.

17 Warm the engine to normal operating temperature (until the electric cooling fan comes on).

18 Briefly run the engine at 1000 rpm, 3000 rpm and 5000 rpm, noting the oil pressure reading at each engine speed.

Caution: Don't run the engine for more than one minute at no-load.

19 The oil pressure should be less than 7 psi. If it isn't, inspect the VTEC solenoid.

20 Connect a length of wire between the battery positive terminal and the VTEC solenoid terminal **(see illustration 9.11)**. Briefly run the engine at 5000 rpm (no more than one minute) and check the oil pressure reading. It should now be 57 psi or more. If not, remove the solenoid valve assembly **(see illustration)** from the cylinder head and inspect the VTEC solenoid valve filter.

21 Check the filter/O-ring for clogging. Clean and refit the filter with a new O-ring. If the filter was clogged, change the engine oil and filter to keep it from clogging again **(see illustration)**.

22 Unbolt the solenoid from the solenoid valve assembly and push on the solenoid plunger to check for free movement **(see illustration)**. Use a new O-ring when refitting the solenoid.

Rocker arms and oil control orifices

23 Refer to Section 4 and remove the camshaft cover. Starting with the number 1 cylinder, place the number 1 piston at TDC (see Section 3).

9.20 VTEC solenoid mounting bolts (arrowed)

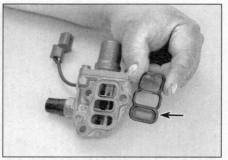

9.21 Whenever problems in the VTEC system are suspected, check the filter and the O-ring (arrowed) located between the solenoid valve and the cylinder head

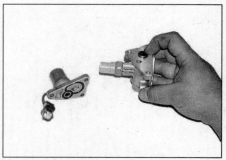

9.22 Push on the solenoid plunger and check for free movement

9.24 Press the mid rocker arm with a finger; it should move independently of the others

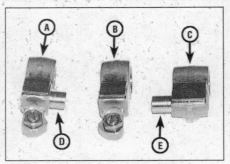

9.25 Rocker arms and synchronising assembly (VTEC)

A Primary rocker arm	*D Short piston*
B Mid rocker arm	*E Long piston*
C Secondary rocker arm	

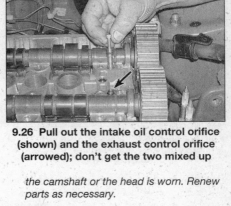

9.26 Pull out the intake oil control orifice (shown) and the exhaust control orifice (arrowed); don't get the two mixed up

24 Press on the (intake and exhaust) mid rocker arms for the number 1 cylinder and check for free movement **(see illustration)**. They should move separately from the primary and secondary rocker arms. Check the remaining mid rocker arms by following the firing order and placing each piston at TDC before checking the rocker arms. If any of the mid rocker arms do not move freely, remove and dismantle the rocker arms for inspection (see Section 10).

25 Once the rocker arm assemblies have been removed and dismantled (see Section 10), separate the rocker arms and synchronising pistons **(see illustration)**.

26 Inspect all other parts (rocker arms and synchronising pistons) for wear, scoring or signs of overheating (bluish in colour). Renew any parts necessary. Remove the oil control orifice from the intake and exhaust sides of the cylinder head **(see illustration)**, clean and refit them.

27 Reassembly is the reverse of removal. **Note:** *Reassemble and secure with a rubber band each cylinder's components before trying to assemble on the rocker shaft (see Section 10).*

Lost motion assemblies

28 The lost motion assemblies sit in pockets in the cylinder head.

29 Remove the individual lost motion assemblies from the cylinder head (see Section 10).

30 Test each lost motion assembly by pushing the plunger with your finger **(see illustration)**. A light pressure should move the plunger slightly, and firmer pressure will move it further. If the assembly doesn't move smoothly, renew it.

---

10 Camshafts and rocker arms – removal, inspection and refitting

Endfloat check

1 To check camshaft endfloat:

a) *Refit the camshaft and secure it with the caps.*

b) *Mount a dial indicator (DTI) on the cylinder head with the gauge plunger touching the nose of the camshaft (see illustration).*

c) *Using a large screwdriver as a lever at the opposite end, move the camshaft forward-and-backward and note the dial indicator reading.*

d) *Compare the reading with the endfloat listed in this Chapter's Specifications.*

e) *If the indicated reading is higher, either*

the camshaft or the head is worn. Renew parts as necessary.

Removal

2 Remove the timing belt and sprockets (see Section 7).

3 Remove the air cleaner housing and the air intake duct (see Chapter 4A). Also remove the distributor (see Chapter 5B).

4 Loosen the valve adjustment locknuts and back off the screws all the way.

5 Check the camshaft bearing caps for arrow marks pointing to the timing belt end of the engine. If you can't see them, make your own marks with a sharp scribe. Also number the bearing caps (1 through 5, starting at the timing belt end of the engine) and label them with an I for intake or E for exhaust.

Caution: Refitting the camshaft holders in the wrong positions (or turned around backwards) may cause the camshaft to seize.

6 Loosen the camshaft holder plate and bearing cap bolts 1/4-turn at a time, starting from the centre and working outward, until the spring pressure is relieved **(see illustration 10.22)**. Lift off the holder plates and bearing caps. There's a dowel with an O-ring in the underside of the No 3 (centre) bearing cap. Locate these so they won't be lost.

7 Lift the camshafts from the cylinder head.

8 Wrap each set of rocker arms with a rubber band before you remove them so the sets can be kept together **(see illustration)**.

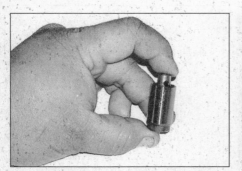

9.30 Check the lost motion assemblies for free movement

10.1 Check the endfloat using a DTI gauge on the end of the camshaft

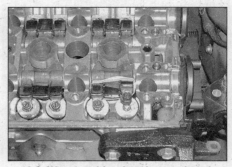

10.8 Wrap a rubber band around each rocker arm set to hold the components together

10.10a One of the rocker shafts (arrowed) is secured by a threaded plug

10.10b Thread a bolt into each rocker shaft and use it to pull the shaft out

10.11 Remove the lost motion assemblies (arrowed) from their bores in the cylinder head

9 Remove the oil control orifice from each rocker shaft **(see illustration 9.26)**.

10 Thread a 12 mm bolt into the end of each rocker shaft and use it to pull the rocker shafts from the head **(see illustrations)**.

11 Remove the lost motion assemblies from the head **(see illustration)**. Inspect them as described in Section 9.

Inspection

12 Thoroughly clean the parts and inspect them for wear and damage. Check the rocker arm faces that contact the camshaft and the rocker arm tips. Check the surfaces of the shafts that the rocker arms ride on, as well as the bearing surfaces inside the rocker arms, for scoring and excessive wear. Renew any parts that are damaged or excessively worn.

Also, make sure the oil holes in the shafts are not blocked.

13 Check the camshaft lobes for wear:
a) *Check the toe and ramp areas of each cam lobe for score marks or uneven wear. Also check for flaking and pitting.*
b) *If there's wear on the toe or the ramp, renew the camshaft, but first try to find the cause of the wear. Look for abrasive substances in the oil and inspect the oil pump and oil passages for blockage. Lobe wear is usually caused by inadequate lubrication or dirty oil.*

14 Check the camshaft bearing journals and caps for signs of scoring and wear. If they are worn, renew the cylinder head with a new or rebuilt unit.

15 Dismantle each set of rocker arms and check the rocker arms and synchronising pistons as described in Section 9. Be sure to keep the components from each set together. Reassemble the sets after inspection if you're going to refit them, then secure each set together with a rubber band.

Refitting

16 Refit the lost motion assemblies **(see illustration 10.11)**.

17 Lubricate all components with engine assembly lubricant or clean engine oil. Loosen the valve adjusting screws all the way. Lay the assembled rocker arms in their original locations, then refit the shafts. There's a bore in each rocker shaft that accepts the oil control orifice. If the bores aren't aligned after

the rocker shafts are fitted, insert a 12 mm bolt into the end of the rocker shaft and use it as a handle to move the rocker shaft around until they align.

18 Renew the O-ring on each oil control orifice, then refit all the orifices in the cylinder head **(see Section 9)**. Be sure to refit the intake and exhaust orifices in the correct locations. Also make sure the orifices fit into their bores in the rocker shafts. They should prevent the rocker shafts from turning when correctly refitted.

19 Coat the cam lobes and journals with clean engine oil. Lay the camshafts in their bearings, making sure the intake and exhaust camshafts are fitted in the correct side of the head.

20 Make sure the oil seal contact surfaces of the cylinder head are clean and dry and fit new oil seals **(see illustration)**. The oil seal springs face toward the cylinder head.

21 Apply liquid sealant (available from Honda dealers) to the cylinder head contact surfaces of bearing caps 1 and 5 and Refit the bearing caps **(see illustration)**.

22 Refit the holders on the bearing caps. Tighten the caps evenly in stages, in the correct sequence, to the torque listed in this Chapter's Specifications **(see illustration)**.

23 Refit the sealing plug in the number 5 journal of the exhaust camshaft **(see illustration)**. The remainder of refitting is the reverse of removal. Adjust the valve clearance (see Chapter 1). Check and adjust the ignition timing (see Chapter 5B).

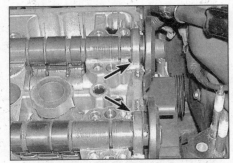

10.20 Fit new oil seals (arrowed) on the camshafts at the timing belt end of the engine

10.21 Apply sealant to the cylinder head contact surfaces of the outer bearing caps

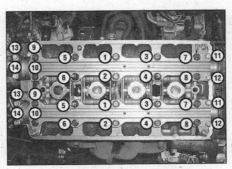

10.22 Camshaft holder tightening sequence

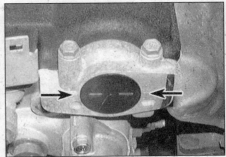

10.23 Fit the exhaust camshaft sealing plug with the alignment marks (arrowed) running parallel to the cap mating surface

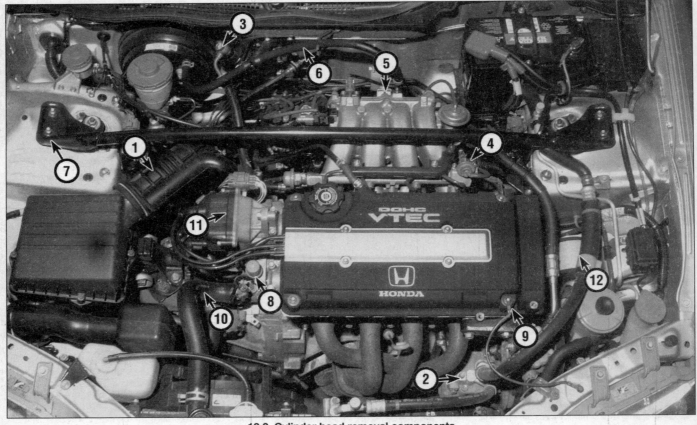

12.2 Cylinder head removal components

1 Air intake duct	4 Fuel return pipe	7 Strut brace fasteners	10 Coolant hose
2 Power steering pump	5 PCV hose	8 VTEC solenoid/pressure switch	11 Distributor
3 Fuel feed pipe	6 Brake servo vacuum hose	9 Engine earth cable	12 Upper engine mounting

24 Start the engine and check for oil leaks and proper operation.

11 Valve springs, retainers and seals – removal and refitting

Renewing broken valve springs and defective valve stem seals requires removing the head from the engine. Remove the camshafts and cylinder head, then refer to Chapter 2C, to remove the valves, valve springs and stem seals.

12 Cylinder head – removal and refitting

 Warning: Allow the engine to cool completely before beginning this procedure.

Removal

1 Position the number 1 piston at Top Dead Centre (see Section 3).
2 Disconnect the cable from the negative terminal of the battery (see Chapter 5A). Also disconnect the earth cable from the engine **(see illustration)**.
3 Drain the cooling system and remove the spark plugs (see Chapter 1).
4 Remove the air cleaner duct and housing (see Chapter 4A).
5 Remove the auxiliary drivebelts (see Chapter 1). Unbolt the power steering pump and set it aside without disconnecting any hoses, then remove the power steering pump bracket (see Chapter 10).
6 Disconnect the throttle cable and relieve the fuel system pressure (see Chapter 4A).
7 Disconnect the following hoses and pipes (see Chapters 4 and 9):
a) Fuel feed and return hoses.
b) Evaporative emission control hose.
c) Breather hose.
d) PCV hose.
e) Brake servo vacuum hose.
8 Disconnect the coolant bypass hose, heater hose and upper radiator hose (see Chapter 3).
9 Remove the strut brace that passes across the engine compartment **(see illustration 12.2)**.

10 Disconnect the following electrical connectors:
a) Fuel injectors.
b) Engine coolant temperature sensor.
c) Temperature gauge sender.
d) TDC/crankshaft/camshaft position sensor.
e) Oxygen sensor(s).
f) Ignition coil.
g) Throttle position sensor.
h) Manifold absolute pressure sensor.
i) EVAP purge control solenoid.
j) VTEC solenoid.
k) VTEC pressure switch.
l) Idle air control valve.
m) Intake air bypass control solenoid (1.8 litre engines).
11 Remove the splash shield from under the engine compartment.
12 Support the engine with a trolley jack. Place a wood block between the jack pad and the sump to avoid damaging the sump. On 1.6 litre models remove the upper left-hand engine mounting bracket. On 1.8 litre models, remove the upper left-hand engine mounting (see Section 17).
13 Remove the intake manifold brace and exhaust manifold flange bolts. **Note:** *You may wish to detach the intake manifold (see*

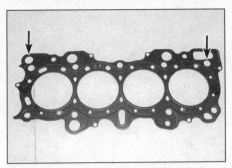

12.25 Cylinder head dowel locations (arrowed)

Section 5) and/or exhaust manifold (see Section 6), rather than removing it with the cylinder head, to make the cylinder head easier to handle.

14 Remove the camshaft cover (see Section 4).

15 Remove the distributor (see Chapter 5B), including the cap and HT leads.

16 Remove the timing belt (see Section 7) and the camshafts (see Section 10).

17 Loosen the head bolts in 1/4-turn increments until they can be removed by hand. Work in a pattern that's the reverse of the tightening sequence **(see illustration 12.26)** to avoid warping the head. Note where each bolt goes so it can be returned to the same location on refitting.

18 Lift the head off the engine. If resistance is felt, don't lever between the head and block gasket mating surfaces – damage to the mating surfaces will result. Instead, prise between the power steering pump bracket and the engine block. Set the head on blocks of wood to prevent damage to the gasket sealing surfaces. If necessary, remove the rocker arms and shafts from the cylinder head after the cylinder head has been removed from the engine.

19 Cylinder head dismantling and inspection procedures are covered in detail in Chapter 2C. Check the cylinder head for warpage.

Refitting

20 The mating surfaces of the cylinder head and block must be perfectly clean when the head is refitted.

21 Use a gasket scraper to remove all traces of carbon and old gasket material, then clean the mating surfaces with cellulose thinners or gasket remover. If there's oil on the mating surfaces when the head is refitted, the gasket may not seal correctly and leaks may develop. When working on the engine block, pack the cylinders with clean rags to keep out debris. Use a vacuum cleaner to remove material that falls into the cylinders. Since the cylinder head and block are made of aluminium, aggressive scraping can cause damage. Be extra careful not to nick or gouge the mating surfaces with the scraper.

22 Check the engine block and cylinder head mating surfaces for nicks, deep scratches and other damage. If damage is slight, it can be removed with a fine file; if it's excessive, machining may be the only alternative. Also remove the cylinder head oil control orifice from the engine block and clean it thoroughly with compressed air, then refit the oil control orifice back into the block with a new O-ring.

23 Use a tap of the correct size to clean the threads in the head bolt holes. Use a wire brush to remove corrosion and clean the threads of each head bolt. Dirt, corrosion, sealant and damaged threads will affect torque readings.

24 Refit the rocker arm assemblies in the cylinder head with the head on the bench (see Section 10).

25 Place a new gasket on the engine block. Check to see if there are any markings (such as TOP) on the gasket that indicate how it is to be fitted. Those identification marks must face up. Make sure the dowels are in the correct locations **(see illustration)** and set the cylinder head in position.

26 Lubricate the threads and the seats of the cylinder head bolts with clean engine oil, then fit them. Following the recommended sequence, tighten the cylinder head bolts to the torque listed in this Chapter's Specifications **(see illustration)**.

27 Refit the camshafts (see Section 10) and the timing belt (see Section 7).

28 Rotate the crankshaft anti-clockwise slowly by hand through two complete revolutions.

Caution: If you feel any resistance while turning the engine over, stop and recheck the camshaft timing. The valves may be hitting the pistons.

29 Refit the remaining parts in the reverse order of removal.

30 Be sure to refill the cooling system and check all fluid levels (see Chapter 1). Start the engine and check the ignition timing (see Chapter 5B).

31 Start the engine until normal operating temperature is reached. Check for leaks and proper operation.

13 Sump – removal and refitting

Removal

1 Warm-up the engine, then drain the oil and renew the oil filter (see Chapter 1).

2 Raise the vehicle and support it securely on axle stands (see *Jacking and vehicle support*). Remove the splash shield from under the engine.

3 Remove the front exhaust pipe (see Chapter 4A).

4 Remove the bolts securing the sump to the engine block **(see illustration)**.

5 Tap on the sump with a soft-face hammer to break the gasket seal, then detach the sump from the engine. Don't lever between the block and sump mating surfaces.

6 Using a gasket scraper, remove all traces of old gasket and/or sealant from the engine block and sump. Remove the seals from each end of the engine block or sump. Clean the

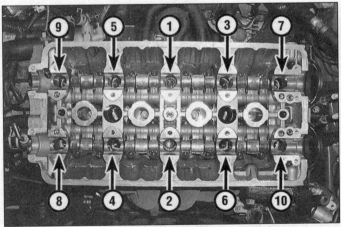

12.26 Cylinder head bolt tightening sequence

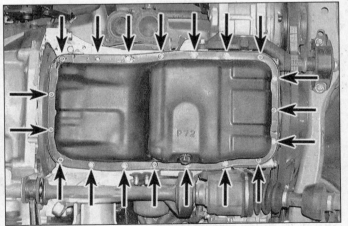

13.4 Oil sump bolt locations (arrowed)

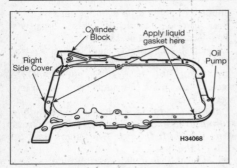

13.8 Apply a 2 mm wide dead of sealant

14.4 Oil pump bolt locations (arrowed)

14.5 Remove the oil pump cover screws (arrowed)

mating surfaces. Make sure the threaded bolt holes in the block are clean.

Refitting

7 Clean the sump and dry it thoroughly. Check the gasket flanges for distortion, particularly around the bolt holes. If necessary, place the sump on a wood block and use a hammer to flatten and restore the gasket surfaces.

8 Apply a 2 mm wide bead of liquid sealant (available from Honda dealers) to the engine block/oil pump gasket surfaces **(see illustration)**.

9 Position a new gasket on the sump.

10 Carefully place the sump in position.

11 Refit the bolts and tighten them in small increments to the torque listed in this Chapter's Specifications. Start with the bolts closest to the centre of the pan and work out in a spiral pattern. Don't overtighten them or leakage may occur.

12 Add oil (see Chapter 1), start the engine and check for oil leaks.

14 Oil pump – removal, inspection and refitting

Removal

1 Remove the timing belt (see Section 7).

2 Remove the sump (see Section 13).

3 Undo the bolts/nuts, then remove the oil pick-up tube and filter from the pump housing

and the main bearing cap bridge/cylinder block.

4 Remove the bolts from the oil pump housing and separate the assembly from the engine **(see illustration)**.

5 Remove the screws and dismantle the oil pump **(see illustration)**. You may need to use an impact screwdriver to loosen the pump cover screws without stripping the heads.

Inspection

6 Check the oil pump rotor-to-cover-clearance, tooth tip clearance and rotor-to-body clearance **(see illustrations)**. Compare your measurements to the figures listed in this Chapter's Specifications. Renew the pump if any of the measurements are outside of the specified limits.

7 Remove the pressure relief valve bolt and extract the spring and pressure relief valve plunger from the pump housing. Check the spring for distortion and the relief valve plunger for scoring. Renew parts as necessary.

8 Refit the pump rotors. Pack the spaces between the rotors with petroleum jelly (this will prime the pump).

9 Apply thread-locking compound to the pump cover screws, refit the cover and tighten the screws to the torque listed in this Chapter's Specifications. Refit the oil pressure relief valve and spring assembly. Use a new sealing washer on the plug and tighten the plug securely.

Refitting

10 Apply a thin coat of liquid sealant

(available from Honda dealers) to the pump housing-to-block sealing surface and a new O-ring in the pump housing. Refit the pump housing to the engine block. Apply liquid gasket to the threads, and tighten the bolts to the torque listed in this Chapter's Specifications. The pump must be fitted within five minutes of applying the sealant, otherwise the residue must be removed and fresh sealant applied.

11 Refit the oil pick-up tube and filter, using a new gasket. Tighten the bolts to the torque listed in this Chapter's Specifications.

12 Refit the sump (see Section 13). Wait at least 20 minutes for the sealant to set before adding the engine oil.

13 The remainder of refitting is the reverse of removal. Add the specified type and quantity of oil and coolant (see Chapter 1), start the engine and check for leaks.

15 Flywheel/driveplate – removal, inspection and refitting

Refer to Chapter 2A, for this procedure.

16 Crankshaft transmission end oil seal – renewal

Refer to Chapter 2A, for this procedure.

14.6a Use a feeler gauge and straight-edge to check the clearance between the rotors and the cover

14.6b Use a feeler gauge to check the tooth tip clearance between the inner and outer rotors

14.6c Use a feeler gauge to check the outer rotor-to-pump body clearance

17.9a Upper left-hand engine mounting (arrowed) – 5-door models

17.9b Upper left-hand engine mounting (A) and bracket (B) – 2, 3 and 4-door models

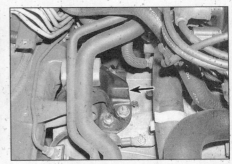

17.9c Right-hand side transmission mounting (arrowed)

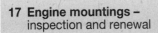

17 Engine mountings – inspection and renewal

1 Engine mountings seldom require attention, but broken or deteriorated mountings should be renewed immediately or the added strain placed on the driveline components may cause damage or wear.

Inspection

2 During the inspection, the engine must be raised slightly to remove the weight from the mountings.

3 Raise the vehicle and support it securely on axle stands (see *Jacking and vehicle support*), then position a jack under the engine sump. Place a large wood block between the jack head and the sump, then carefully raise the engine just enough to take the weight off the mountings.

 Warning: DO NOT place any part of your body under the engine when it's supported only by a jack.

4 Check the mounting insulators to see if the rubber is cracked, hardened or separated from the metal in the centre of the mounting.

5 Check for relative movement between the mounting and the engine or body (use a large screwdriver or lever bar to attempt to move the mountings). If movement is noted, lower the engine and tighten the mounting fasteners.

6 Rubber preservative should be applied to the insulators to slow deterioration.

Renewal

7 Raise the vehicle and support it securely on axle stands (see *Jacking and vehicle support*). Support the engine as described in Paragraph 3.

8 Remove the fasteners, raise the engine with

17.9d Right-hand front transmission mounting (arrowed)

17.9f Rear engine mounting at the bulkhead (arrowed)

the jack and detach the mounting from the bracket and engine.

9 Refit the new mounting, making sure it is correctly positioned in its bracket **(see illustrations)**. Refit the fasteners and tighten them securely.

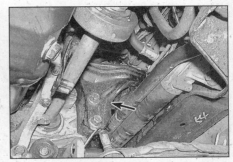

17.9e Rear engine mounting bracket at the engine (arrowed)

17.9g Lower left-hand engine mounting (arrowed)

Chapter 2 Part C:
Engine removal and overhaul procedures

Contents

Degrees of difficulty

| Easy, suitable for novice with little experience | | Fairly easy, suitable for beginner with some experience | | Fairly difficult, suitable for competent DIY mechanic | 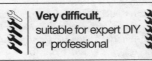 | Difficult, suitable for experienced DIY mechanic | | Very difficult, suitable for expert DIY or professional | |

Specifications

General

Manufacturer's engine codes*:

1.4 litre:	
D14A2, D14A3, D14A4, D14A8	66 kW SOHC 16V non-VTEC
1.5 litre:	
D15Z3, D15Z6, D15Z8	85 kW SOHC 16V VTEC-E
1.6 litre:	
D16Y2	93 kW SOHC 16V VTEC
D16Y3, D16B2	83 kW SOHC 16V non-VTEC
D16Y5	86 kW SOHC 16V VTEC-E
D16Y6, D16Y8	92 kW SOHC 16V VTEC
D16Y7	78 kW SOHC 16V non-VTEC
B16A2	118 kW DOHC 16V VTEC
1.8 litre:	
B18C4	125 kW DOHC 16V VTEC

* See 'Vehicle identification' in the Reference section

Engine block

Bore:	
SOHC engines	75.0 mm (nominal)
DOHC engines	81.0 mm (nominal)
Stroke:	
1.4 litre engines	79.0 mm
1.5 litre engines	84.5 mm
1.6 litre:	
SOHC engines	90.0 mm
DOHC engines	77.4 mm
1.8 litre DOHC engines	87.2 mm
Block surface warp limit	0.10 mm maximum

Pistons and rings

Piston diameter:
SOHC engines .... 74.98 to 74.99 mm
DOHC engines .... 80.98 to 80.99 mm
Diameter measurement point (from bottom):
SOHC engines .... 5 mm
DOHC engines .... 15 mm
Piston ring end gap:
SOHC engines:
Top ring .... 0.15 to 0.30 mm
Service limit .... 0.61 mm
Second ring .... 0.30 to 0.45 mm
Service limit .... 0.71 mm
Oil control ring .... N/A*
DOHC engines:
Top ring .... 0.20 to 0.35 mm
Service limit .... 0.61 mm
Second ring .... 0.40 to 0.55 mm
Service limit .... 0.71 mm
Oil control ring .... 0.20 to 0.50 mm
Service limit .... 0.71 mm
Information not available at the time of writing – refer to dealer or specialist

Connecting rods

Big-end shell-to-journal clearance:
SOHC engines .... 0.05 mm maximum
DOHC engines .... 0.06 mm maximum
Big-end bearing endfloat .... 0.40 mm maximum

Crankshaft

Endfloat .... 0.45 mm maximum
Main bearing shell-to journal clearance:
SOHC engines .... 0.05 mm maximum
DOHC engines .... 0.06 mm maximum

Cylinder head

Head warpage limit:
Maximum without resurfacing .... 0.05 mm
Service limit .... 0.08 mm
Cylinder head height:
SOHC engines .... 92.95 to 93.05 mm
DOHC engines .... 141.95 to 142.05 mm
Resurfacing limit .... 0.20 mm

Valves

	Inlet	Exhaust
Valve spring free length:		
D14A2, D16Y3 engine codes	48.58 mm	49.19 mm
D15Z3 engine code	54.78 mm	58.24 mm
D15Z8 engine code	56.50 mm	58.70 mm
D15Z6, D16Y5, D16Y6 engine codes	56.50 mm	57.90 mm
D14A3, D14A4, D14A8, D16B2 engine codes	58.70 mm	58.70 mm
D16Y2 engine code	57.97 mm	58.41 mm
D16Y7 engine code	57.90 mm	57.90 mm
D16Y8 engine code	58.00 mm	58.70 mm
B16A2 engine code:		
Inner spring	36.71 mm	41.95 mm
Outer spring	40.91 mm	
B18C4 engine code:		
Inner spring	36.16 mm	41.95 mm
Outer spring	41.05 mm	
Maximum valve head deflection (valve extended 10 mm out from seat):		
SOHC engines:		
Inlet valve	0.16 mm	
Exhaust valve	0.22 mm	
DOHC engines:		
Inlet valve	0.15 mm	
Exhaust valve	0.24 mm	

Torque wrench settings

Refer to Chapter 2A and 2B Specifications

1 General information

Included in this portion of Chapter 2 are the general overhaul procedures for the cylinder head and internal engine components.

The information ranges from advice concerning preparation for an overhaul and the purchase of new parts to detailed, step-by-step procedures covering removal and refitting of internal engine components and the inspection of parts.

After Section 5, the information has been written based on the assumption that the engine has been removed from the vehicle. For information concerning in-vehicle engine repair, as well as removal and refitting of the external components necessary for the overhaul, see Chapter 2A or 2B.

The Specifications included in this Part are only those necessary for the inspection and overhaul procedures which follow. Refer to Chapter 2A or 2B, for additional Specifications, and all torque wrench settings.

It's not always easy to determine when, or if, an engine should be completely overhauled, as a number of factors must be considered.

High mileage is not necessarily an indication that an overhaul is needed, while low mileage doesn't preclude the need for an overhaul. Frequency of servicing is probably the most important consideration. An engine that's had regular and frequent oil and filter changes, as well as other required maintenance, will most likely give many thousands of miles of reliable service. Conversely, a neglected engine may require an overhaul very early in its life.

Excessive oil consumption is an indication that piston rings, valve seals and/or valve guides are in need of attention. Make sure that oil leaks aren't responsible before deciding that the rings and/or guides are defective. Perform a cylinder compression check to determine the extent of the work required (see Chapter 2A or 2B as applicable).

Loss of power, rough running, knocking or metallic engine noises, excessive valve train noise and high fuel consumption rates may also point to the need for an overhaul, especially if they're all present at the same time. If a complete service doesn't remedy the situation, major mechanical work is the only solution.

An engine overhaul involves restoring the internal parts to the specifications of a new engine. During an overhaul, the piston rings are renewed and the cylinder walls are reconditioned (rebored and/or honed). If a rebore is done by an automotive engineering workshop, new oversize pistons (where available) will also be fitted. The main bearings and connecting rod bearings are generally renewed and, if necessary, the crankshaft may be reground to restore the journals.

Generally, the valves are serviced as well, since they're usually in less-than-perfect condition at this point. While the engine is being overhauled, other components, such as the distributor, starter and alternator, can be rebuilt as well. The end result should be a like new engine that will give many trouble free miles. **Note:** *Critical cooling system components such as the hoses, auxiliary drivebelts, thermostat and water pump should be renewed when an engine is overhauled. The radiator should be checked carefully to ensure that it isn't blocked or leaking (see Chapter 3). If you purchase a rebuilt engine or short block, some reconditioners will not warranty their engines unless the radiator has been professionally flushed. Also, be sure to check the oil pump carefully, as described in Chapter 2A or 2B.*

Before beginning the engine overhaul, read through the entire procedure to familiarise yourself with the scope and requirements of the job. Overhauling an engine isn't difficult, but it is time-consuming. Plan on the vehicle being tied up for a minimum of two weeks, especially if parts must be taken to an automotive engineering workshop for repair or reconditioning. Check on availability of parts and make sure that any necessary special tools and equipment are obtained in advance. Most work can be done with typical hand tools, although a number of precision measuring tools are required for inspecting parts to determine if they must be renewed. Often an automotive engineering workshop will carry out the inspection of parts and offer advice concerning reconditioning and renewal. **Note:** *Always wait until the engine has been completely dismantled and all components, especially the engine block, have been inspected before deciding what service and repair operations must be performed by an automotive engineering workshop.* Since the block's condition will be the major factor to consider when determining whether to overhaul the original engine or buy a rebuilt one, never purchase parts or have machine work done on other components until the block has been thoroughly inspected. As a general rule, time is the primary cost of an overhaul, so it doesn't pay to refit worn or substandard parts.

As a final note, to ensure maximum life and minimum trouble from a rebuilt engine, everything must be assembled with care in a spotlessly-clean environment.

2 Engine removal – methods and precautions

If you've decided the engine must be removed for overhaul or major repair work, several preliminary steps should be taken.

Locating a suitable place to work is extremely important. Adequate work space, along with storage space for the vehicle, will be needed. If a workshop or garage isn't available, at the very least a flat, level, clean work surface made of concrete or tarmac is required.

Cleaning the engine compartment and engine before beginning the removal procedure will help keep tools clean and organised.

An engine hoist or A-frame will also be necessary. Make sure the equipment is rated in excess of the combined weight of the engine/transmission and its accessories. Safety is of primary importance, considering the potential hazards involved in lifting the engine out of the vehicle.

If the engine is being removed by a novice, a helper should be available. Advice and aid from someone more experienced would also be helpful. There are many instances when one person cannot simultaneously perform all of the operations required when lifting the engine out of the vehicle.

Plan the operation ahead of time. Arrange for or obtain all of the tools and equipment you'll need prior to beginning the job. Some of the equipment necessary to perform engine removal and refitting safely and with relative ease are (in addition to an engine hoist) a heavy duty trolley jack, complete sets of spanners and sockets as described in the rear of this manual, wooden blocks and plenty of rags and cleaning material for mopping-up spilled oil, coolant and petrol. If the hoist must be hired, be sure to arrange for it in advance and perform all of the operations possible without it beforehand. This will save you money and time.

Plan for the vehicle to be out of use for quite a while. A engineering workshop will be required to perform some of the work the DIY-er can't accomplish without special equipment. These workshops often have a busy schedule, so it would be a good idea to consult them before removing the engine in order to accurately estimate the amount of time required to rebuild or repair components that may need work.

Always be extremely careful when removing and refitting the engine. Serious injury can result from careless actions. Plan ahead, take your time and a job of this nature, although major, can be accomplished successfully.

3 Engine – removal and refitting

Note: *The engine and transmission must be removed together, as a single unit. Read through the following steps carefully and familiarise yourself with the procedure before beginning work. Also at this point it may be helpful to use a penetrating fluid or spray on nuts and bolts that may be difficult to remove, such as exhaust manifolds, engine mountings, etc.*

3.4 Remove the nuts at each end of the strut brace (arrowed) and remove the brace

Removal

1 Refer to Chapter 4A and relieve the fuel system pressure.
2 Remove the battery, as described in Chapter 5A.
3 Cover the wings and cowl and remove the bonnet (see Chapter 11). Special pads are available to protect the wings, but an old bedspread or blanket will also work.
4 Where fitted, remove the engine compartment strut brace **(see illustration)**.
5 Remove the air cleaner assembly (see Chapter 4A), and the air intake duct.
6 Label the vacuum lines, emissions system hoses, electrical connectors, earth straps and fuel pipes to ensure correct refitting. Pieces of masking tape with numbers or letters written on them work well. If there's any possibility of confusion, make a sketch of the engine compartment and clearly label the pipes, hoses and wires.
7 Disconnect the electrical connectors from the following components:

  a) *Fuel injectors.*
  b) *Engine coolant temperature sensor.*
  c) *Engine coolant temperature switch.*
  d) *Throttle position sensor.*
  e) *Manifold absolute pressure sensor.*
  f) *Idle air control valve.*
  g *Intake air temperature sensor.*
  h) *Distributor.*
  i) *EGR valve lift sensor (where fitted).*
  j) *VTEC solenoid and pressure switch (VTEC engines).*

  k) *Evaporative emission solenoid valve.*
  l) *Crankshaft speed fluctuation sensor.*
  m) *Power steering pressure switch.*
  n) *Oxygen sensor(s).*
  o) *Knock sensor (where fitted).*
  p) *Vehicle speed sensor.*
  q) *Oil pressure switch.*
  r) *Alternator.*

After the components have been disconnected, detach the main wiring harness from the rear of the engine and the connectors at the bulkhead **(see illustrations)**. Position the main wiring harness aside so it won't interfere with engine removal.
8 Disconnect the fuel pipes running from the engine to the chassis (see Chapter 4A). Plug or cap all open fittings and lines. Also disconnect the vacuum lines and the earth strap from the engine.
9 Drain the cooling system (see Chapter 1). Label and detach all coolant hoses from the engine. Remove the coolant reservoir, cooling fan, shroud and radiator (see Chapter 3).
10 Remove the auxiliary drivebelt(s) and idler, if equipped (see Chapter 1).
11 Disconnect the accelerator cable from the engine (see Chapter 4A).
12 Unbolt the power steering pump and set it aside (see Chapter 10). Leave the pipes/hoses attached and make sure the pump is kept in an upright position in the engine compartment.
13 Unbolt the air conditioning compressor (see Chapter 3) and set it aside. Do not disconnect the hoses.
14 Unbolt the alternator and mounting bracket and set it aside (see Chapter 5A).
15 Raise the vehicle and support it securely on axle stands (see *Jacking and vehicle support*).
16 Remove the splash shield from the underside of the engine compartment.
17 Drain the engine oil and remove the filter (see Chapter 1).
18 Remove the starter (see Chapter 5A).
19 On automatic transmission models, disconnect the throttle control cable from the transmission. Also, disconnect the electrical

connectors and selector cable from the transmission (see Chapter 7B).
20 On automatic transmission models, disconnect the cooler pipes from the transmission. Be prepared for fluid spillage.
21 Remove the crankshaft pulley and refit the bolt.
22 Disconnect the exhaust system from the manifold (see Chapter 4A)
23 Support the transmission with a trolley jack. Position a wood block on the jack head to prevent damage to the transmission.
24 Attach lifting straps or a length of chain to the lifting brackets on the engine **(see illustration)**.
25 Roll the engine hoist into position and connect the straps/chain to it. Take up the slack in the strap/chain, but don't lift the engine.

> ⚠️ **Warning: DO NOT place any part of your body under the engine when it's supported only by a hoist or other lifting device.**

26 Remove the driveshafts (see Chapter 8).
27 If you're working on a model equipped with a manual transmission, unbolt the clutch release cylinder (don't disconnect the hydraulic pipe) and pipe support bracket, then position it out of the way (see Chapter 6). Disconnect the transmission gearchange linkage (see Chapter 7A).
28 Remove the engine mounting-to-body nuts/bolts (see Chapter 2A or 2B).
29 Recheck to be sure nothing is still connecting the engine to the vehicle. Disconnect anything still remaining.
30 Raise the engine slightly to disengage the mountings. Also, slightly raise the jack supporting the transmission. Slowly raise the engine/transmission assembly out of the engine compartment, turning it sideways, as necessary, for clearance. Check carefully to make sure nothing is trapped or damaged as the hoist is raised.
31 Lower the engine/transmission assembly to the ground and support it with wood blocks. Remove the clutch and flywheel or driveplate.
32 Separate the transmission from the engine at this time.

3.7a The main wiring harness connector on 2, 3 and 4-door models is located on the right-hand side of the engine compartment (arrowed) . . .

3.7b . . . while the main harness connectors on 5-door models are on the left-hand side (arrowed)

3.24 Attach lifting straps or chains to the lifting brackets on the engine (arrowed)

Refitting

33 Check the engine and transmission mountings. If they're worn or damaged, renew them.

34 If you're working on a manual transmission vehicle, refit the clutch and pressure plate (see Chapter 6). Now is a good time to fit a new clutch. Apply a dab of clutch shaft grease to the input shaft.

35 Attach the transmission to the engine. **Caution: DO NOT use the bolts to force the transmission and engine together. If you're working on an automatic transmission vehicle, take great care when refitting the torque converter, following the procedure outlined in Chapter 7B.**

36 Attach the hoist to the engine/transmission and lower the assembly into the engine compartment. Align the holes in the engine mountings with the body and refit the bolts, tightening them securely.

37 The remainder of refitting is the reverse of the removal steps.

38 Add coolant, oil, power steering and transmission fluid as needed.

39 Start the engine and check for leaks and proper operation of all accessories, then refit the bonnet (if removed) and test drive the vehicle.

40 If the air conditioning system was discharged, have it evacuated, recharged and leak tested by the specialist that discharged it.

4 Engine rebuilding alternatives

Note: *The costs of alternatives described in this Section can vary, depending upon quality of parts, machine work required and the necessary tools and equipment to correctly do the work. Some automotive parts stores carry complete assemblies (long and short block) in addition to individual repair parts. Consult the local parts store on price and availability to make the final repair/renew decision.*

The home mechanic is faced with a number of options when performing an engine overhaul. The decision to renew the engine block, piston/connecting rod assemblies and crankshaft depends on a number of factors, with the number one consideration being the condition of the block. Other considerations are cost, access to engineering workshop facilities, parts availability, time required to complete the project and the extent of prior mechanical experience.

Give careful thought to which alternative is best for you and discuss the situation with local automotive engineering workshops, automotive parts dealers and experienced reconditioners before ordering or purchasing renewal parts.

Some of the rebuilding alternatives include:

Individual parts

If the inspection procedures reveal the engine block and most engine components are in re-usable condition, purchasing individual parts may be the most economical alternative. The block, crankshaft and piston/connecting rod assemblies should all be inspected carefully. Even if the block shows little wear, the cylinder bores should be surface honed.

Short block

A short block consists of an engine block with a crankshaft and piston/connecting rod assemblies already refitted. All new bearings are incorporated and all clearances will be correct. The existing camshaft, valvetrain components, cylinder head(s) and external parts can be bolted to the short block with little or no engineering work necessary.

Long block

A long block consists of a short block plus an oil pump, sump, cylinder head, camshaft cover, camshaft and valve train components, timing sprockets and belt. All components are installed with new bearings, seals and gaskets incorporated throughout. The refitting of manifolds and external parts is all that's necessary.

5 Engine overhaul – dismantling sequence

1 It's much easier to dismantle and work on the engine if it's mounted on a portable engine stand. A stand can often be hired quite cheaply from an equipment hire workshop. Before it's mounted on a stand, the flywheel/driveplate should be removed from the engine.

2 If a stand isn't available, it's possible to dismantle the engine with it blocked up on the floor. Be extra careful not to tip or drop the engine when working without a stand.

3 If you're going to obtain a rebuilt engine, all external components must first be removed, to be transferred to the new engine, just as they will if you're doing a complete engine overhaul yourself. These include:

Alternator and brackets.
Power steering pump and brackets.
Emissions control components.
Distributor, HT leads and spark plugs.
Thermostat and housing cover.
Water pump bypass hose.
Fuel injection components.
Intake/exhaust manifolds.
Oil filter.
Engine mountings.
Clutch and flywheel, or driveplate.

Note: *When removing the external components from the engine, pay close attention to details that may be helpful or important during refitting. Note the fitted position of gaskets, seals, spacers, pins, brackets, washers, bolts, wiring and other small items.*

4 If you're obtaining a short block, which consists of the engine block, crankshaft, pistons and connecting rods all assembled, then the cylinder head, sump and oil pump will have to be removed as well. See *Engine rebuilding*

alternatives for additional information regarding the different possibilities to be considered.

5 If you're planning a complete overhaul, the engine must be dismantled and the internal components removed in the following general order:

Intake and exhaust manifolds.
Camshaft cover.
Timing belt covers and bolts.
Timing belt and sprockets.
Rocker arm assembly and camshaft(s).
Cylinder head.
Water pump.
Sump.
Oil jets (DOHC engines).
Oil pump and pick-up tube.
Rear main oil seal retainer.
*Main bearing caps (or bearing cap bridge)
    and lower main bearings.*
Piston/connecting rod assemblies.
Crankshaft and upper main bearings.

6 Cylinder head – dismantling

Note: *New and rebuilt cylinder heads are commonly available for most engines at dealer parts departments and some automotive reconditioning specialists. Due to the fact that some specialised tools are necessary for the dismantling and inspection procedures, and new parts aren't always readily available, it may be more practical and economical for the home mechanic to purchase an exchange head rather than taking the time to dismantle, inspect and recondition the original.*

1 Cylinder head dismantling involves removal of the intake and exhaust valves and related components. The rocker arm assemblies and camshaft(s) must be removed before beginning the cylinder head dismantling procedure (see Part A or B of this Chapter). Label the parts or store them separately so they can be refitted in their original locations.

2 Before the valves are removed, arrange to label and store them, along with their related components, so they can be kept separate and refitted in their original locations **(see illustration)**.

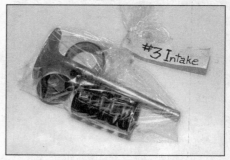

6.2 A plastic bag, with an appropriate label, can be used to store the valvetrain components so they can be kept together and refitted in their original positions

6.3 Use a valve spring compressor to compress the springs then remove the collets from the valve stem with a magnet or small needle-nose pliers

3 Compress the springs on the first valve with a spring compressor and remove the collets **(see illustration)**. Carefully release the valve spring compressor and remove the retainer, the spring and the spring seat (if used). **Note:** *On DOHC engines, use an adapter with the compressor to reach the recessed valve spring.*

4 Pull the valve out of the head, then remove the oil seal from the guide. If the valve binds in the guide (won't pull through), push it back into the head and deburr the area around the stem and the collet groove with a fine file or fine emery cloth **(see illustration)**.

5 Repeat the procedure for the remaining valves. Remember to keep all the parts for each valve together so they can be refitted in the same locations. **Note:** *On VTEC models only, remember to remove the oil control orifice and O-ring from the cylinder head (see Chapter 2A or 2B).*

6 Once the valves and related components have been removed and stored in an organised manner, the head should be thoroughly cleaned and inspected. If a complete engine overhaul is being done, finish the engine dismantling procedures before beginning the cylinder head cleaning and inspection process.

7 Cylinder head – cleaning and inspection

1 Thorough cleaning of the cylinder head and related valvetrain components, followed by a detailed inspection, will enable you to decide how much valve service work must be done during the engine overhaul. **Note:** *If the engine was severely overheated, the cylinder head is probably warped.*

Cleaning

2 Scrape all traces of old gasket material and sealant off the head gasket, intake manifold and exhaust manifold mating surfaces. Be very careful not to gouge the cylinder head. Special gasket removal solvents that soften

6.4 If the valve stem won't pull through the guide, deburr the edge of the stem end and the area around the top of the collet groove with a file or fine emery cloth

gaskets and make removal much easier are available at automotive parts stores.

3 Remove all built-up scale from the coolant passages.

4 Push a stiff wire brush through the various holes to remove deposits that may have formed in them.

5 Run an appropriate size tap into each of the threaded holes to remove corrosion and thread sealant that may be present. If compressed air is available, use it to clear the holes of debris produced by this operation.

 Warning: Wear eye protection when using compressed air.

6 Clean the camshaft bearing cap bolt threads with a wire brush.

7 Clean the cylinder head with degreaser and dry it thoroughly. Compressed air will speed the drying process and ensure that all holes and recessed areas are clean. **Note:** *Decarbonising chemicals are available and may prove very useful when cleaning cylinder heads and valvetrain components. They're very caustic and should be used with caution. Be sure to follow the instructions on the container.*

8 Clean the rocker arms and bearing caps with degrease and dry them thoroughly (don't mix them up during the cleaning process). Compressed air will speed the drying process and can be used to clean out the oil passages.

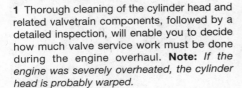

7.12 Check the cylinder head gasket for warpage by trying to slip a feeler gauge under the straight-edge

9 Clean all the valve springs, spring seats, collets and retainers with degreaser and dry them thoroughly. Do the components from one valve at a time to avoid mixing up the parts.

10 Scrape off any heavy deposits that may have formed on the valves, then use a motorised wire brush to remove deposits from the valve heads and stems. Again, make sure the valves don't get mixed up.

Inspection

Cylinder head

11 Inspect the head very carefully for cracks, evidence of coolant leakage and other damage. If cracks are found, check with an automotive engineering workshop concerning repair. If repair isn't possible, a new/reconditioned cylinder head should be obtained.

12 Using a straight-edge and feeler gauge, check the head gasket mating surface for warpage **(see illustration)**. If the warpage exceeds the limit in this Chapter's Specifications, it may be resurfaced at an automotive engineering workshop.

13 Examine the valve seats in each of the combustion chambers. If they're pitted, cracked or burned, the head will require engineering work that's beyond the scope of the home mechanic.

14 Check the valve stem-to-guide clearance by measuring the lateral movement of the valve head with a dial indicator gauge (DTI) attached securely to the head **(see illustration)**. The valve must be in the guide and approximately 10 mm off the seat. After this is done, if there's still some doubt regarding the condition of the valve guides, they should be checked by an automotive engineering workshop (the cost should be minimal).

Valves

15 Carefully inspect each valve face for uneven wear, deformation, cracks, pits and burned areas. Check the valve stem for scuffing and the neck for cracks. Rotate the

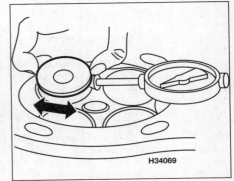

7.14 Check the valve stem-to-guide clearance by measuring the lateral movement of the valve head with a dial indicator gauge

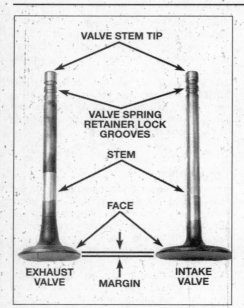

7.15 Check for valve wear at the points shown here

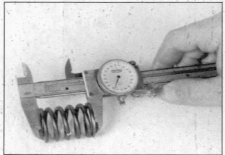

7.16 Measure the free length of each valve spring

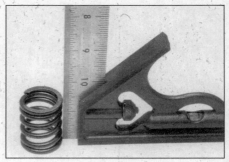

7.17 Check each valve spring for squareness

valve and check for any obvious indication that it's bent. Look for pits and excessive wear on the end of the stem (see illustration). The presence of any of these conditions indicates the need for valve reconditioning by an automotive engineering workshop.

Valve components

16 Check each valve spring for wear (on the ends) and pits. Measure the free length and compare it to this Chapter's Specifications (see illustration). Any springs that are shorter than specified have sagged and shouldn't be re-used.

17 Stand each spring on a flat surface and check it for squareness with a carpenter's square (see illustration). If any of the springs are distorted or sagged, renew all of them with new parts.

18 Check the spring retainers and collets for obvious wear and cracks. Any questionable parts should be renewed, as extensive damage will occur if they fail during engine operation.

8 Valves and seats – reconditioning

1 If the valves are in satisfactory condition, they should be ground (lapped) into their respective seats, to ensure a smooth gas-tight seal. If the seat is only lightly pitted, or if it has been recut, fine grinding compound only should be used to produce the required finish. Coarse valve-grinding compound should not be used unless a seat is badly burned or deeply pitted; if this is the case, the cylinder head and valves should be inspected by an expert to decide whether seat recutting, or even the renewal of the valve or seat insert, is required.

2 Valve grinding is carried out as follows. Place the cylinder head upside-down on a bench.

3 Smear a trace of the appropriate grade of valve-grinding compound on the seat face, and press a suction grinding tool onto the valve head. With a semi-rotary action, grind the valve head to its seat, lifting the valve occasionally to redistribute the grinding compound (see illustration). A light spring placed under the valve head will greatly ease this operation.

4 If coarse grinding compound is being used, work only until a dull, matt even surface is produced on both the valve seat

and the valve, then wipe off the used compound and repeat the process with fine compound. When a smooth unbroken ring of light grey matt finish is produced on both the valve and seat, the grinding operation is complete. Do not grind in the valves any further than absolutely necessary, or the seat will be prematurely sunk into the cylinder head.

5 When all the valves have been ground-in, carefully wash off all traces of grinding compound using paraffin or a suitable degreaser before reassembly of the cylinder head.

9 Cylinder head – reassembly

1 Ensure that the cylinder head is completely clean before attempting reassembly.

2 Refit the spring seats before the valve seals (see illustration).

3 Fit new seals on each of the valve guides. Using a hammer and a deep socket or seal refitting tool, gently tap each seal into place until it's completely seated on the guide (see illustration). Don't twist the seals during refitting or they won't seal properly on the valve stems. Note: The valve stem seals are colour-coded; white for the intake valves

8.3 Grind-in the valve with a reciprocating rotary motion

9.2 Refit the spring seats over the valve guides

9.3a Gently tap the valve seals into place with a seal installation tool or a deep socket and hammer

9.3b The intake valve stem seals are colour-coded white and the exhaust seals are colour-coded black (arrowed)

9.5a Fit the spring (closely-wound coils toward the head) and retainer over the valve stem

9.5b Apply a dab of grease to each collet before fitted them – it'll hold them in place on the valve stem as the spring is released

and black for the exhaust valves **(see illustration)**.

4 Beginning at one end of the head, lubricate and refit the first valve. Apply clean engine oil to the valve stem.

5 Position the valve springs and retainers over the valves **(see illustration)**. Place the end of the valve spring with the closely wound coils toward the cylinder head. On DOHC engines, inner and outer springs are fitted to the inlet valves. Compress the springs with a valve spring compressor and carefully refit the collets in the groove, then slowly release the compressor and make sure the collets seat properly. Apply a small dab of grease to each collet to hold it in place if necessary **(see illustration)**.

6 Repeat the procedure for the remaining valves. Be sure to return the components to their original locations – don't mix them up!

7 Apply clean engine oil to the rocker arm faces, the camshaft lobes and journals and the rocker shafts, then refit the camshaft, rocker arms and shafts (refer to Chapter 2A or 2B).

10 Pistons and connecting rods – removal

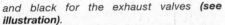

Note: Prior to removing the piston/connecting rod assemblies, remove the cylinder head, sump, oil pump pick-up tube, oil pump and baffle plate (see Chapter 2A or 2B).

1 Use your fingernail to feel if a ridge has formed at the upper limit of ring travel (about 6 mm down from the top of each cylinder). If carbon deposits or cylinder wear have produced ridges, they must be completely removed with a scraper or ridge reamer **(see illustration)**. Follow the manufacturer's instructions provided with the reamer. Failure to remove the ridges before attempting to remove the piston/connecting rod assemblies may result in piston breakage.

2 After the cylinder ridges (if any) have been removed, turn the engine upside-down so the crankshaft is facing up.

3 The bearing cap bridge (where fitted) must be removed first to access the connecting rods (see Section 11).

4 Before the connecting rods are removed, check the side clearance (endfloat) with feeler gauges. Slide them between the first connecting rod and the crankshaft web until the play is removed **(see illustration)**. The endfloat is equal to the thickness of the feeler gauge(s). If the endfloat exceeds the service limit, new connecting rods will be required. If new rods (or a new crankshaft) are installed, the endfloat may be inadequate (if it is, the rods will have to be machined to restore it – consult an automotive engineering workshop for advice if

necessary). Repeat the procedure for the remaining connecting rods.

5 The existing numbers on the connecting rods indicate the rod bore size, not the position in the engine **(see illustration)**. Use a small centre punch to make the appropriate number of indentations on each rod and cap (1, 2, 3, etc, depending on the cylinder they're associated with) **(see illustration)**.

6 Loosen each of the connecting rod cap nuts 1/2-turn at a time until they can be removed by hand. Remove the number 1 connecting rod cap and bearing insert. Don't drop the bearing insert out of the cap.

7 Slip a short length of plastic or rubber hose over each connecting rod cap bolt to protect

10.1 A ridge reamer is required to remove the ridge from the top of each cylinder

10.4 Check the connecting rod endfloat with a feeler gauge

10.5a Do not confuse the stamped numbers on the parting surface, such as this 3 (arrowed) with the cylinder numbers – the numbers indicates the big-end bore size

10.5b Mark the cylinder number on each connecting rod and cap with a centre punch before removing them

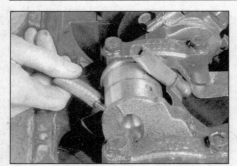

10.7 To prevent damage to the crankshaft journals and cylinder bores, slip sections of rubber or plastic hose over the rod bolts before removing the pistons

11.1 Place a DTI gauge against the end of the crankshaft and lever the crankshaft back-and-forth to check endfloat

11.3 The endfloat can also be checked with a feeler gauge at the thrustwasher journal

the crankshaft journal and cylinder wall as the piston is removed **(see illustration)**.

8 Remove the bearing insert and push the connecting rod/piston assembly out through the top of the engine. Use a wooden hammer handle to push on the upper bearing surface in the connecting rod. If resistance is felt, double-check to make sure that all of the ridge was removed from the cylinder.

9 Repeat the procedure for the remaining cylinders.

10 After removal, reassemble the connecting rod caps and bearing inserts in their respective connecting rods and fit the cap nuts finger tight. Leaving the old bearing inserts in place until reassembly will help prevent the connecting rod bearing surfaces from being accidentally scratched or gouged.

11 Don't separate the pistons from the connecting rods.

11 Crankshaft – removal

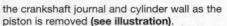

Note: *The crankshaft can be removed only after the engine has been removed from the vehicle. It's assumed that the flywheel or driveplate, timing belt, sump, oil pick-up tube and oil pump, and baffle plate have already been removed. The oil seal retainer must be*

11.4 The main bearing caps should have arrows pointing to the timing belt end and numbers indicating position – make your own marks if they aren't visible

unbolted and separated from the block before proceeding with crankshaft removal.

1 Before the crankshaft is removed, check the endfloat. Mount a dial indicator gauge (DTI) with the stem in line with the crankshaft and touching the end **(see illustration)**. **Note:** *The main caps and main-cap bridge should be in place and torqued to Specifications.*

2 Push the crankshaft all the way to the rear and zero the dial indicator gauge. Next, lever the crankshaft to the front as far as possible and check the reading on the dial indicator gauge. The distance that it moves is the endfloat. If it's greater than specified, check the crankshaft thrust surfaces for wear. If no wear is evident, new thrust washers should correct the endfloat.

3 If a dial indicator gauge isn't available, feeler gauges can be used. Gently lever or push the crankshaft all the way to the left of the engine. Slip feeler gauges between the crankshaft and the back face of the front thrustwasher to determine the clearance **(see illustration)**. The thrustwasher is fitted to journal number 4.

4 If you're working on a DOHC engine, check the main bearing caps to see if they're marked to indicate their locations. They should be numbered consecutively from the left of the engine to the right **(see illustration)**. If they aren't, mark them with number-stamping dies or a centre punch. Main bearing caps generally have a cast-in arrow, which points

12.2 DOHC engines are equipped with oil jets (arrowed)

to the left of the engine. Loosen the main bearing cap and/or bridge assembly bolts 1/4-turn at a time each, working around the engine until they can be removed by hand **(see illustration 19.14a or 19.14b)**. Make sure all bolts are removed before trying to remove the caps and/or bridge assembly.

5 Remove the main bearing caps and or bridge assembly. If you're working on a DOHC engine, gently tap the remaining caps with a soft-face hammer and separate them from the engine block. If necessary, use the bolts as levers to remove the caps. Try not to drop the bearing inserts if they come out with the caps.

6 Carefully lift the crankshaft out of the engine. It may be a good idea to have an assistant available, since the crankshaft is quite heavy. With the bearing inserts in place in the engine block, return the caps to their respective locations on the engine block, refit the main bearing cap bridge and tighten the bolts finger tight.

12 Engine block – cleaning

1 On SOHC engines, remove the main bearing cap bridge. On DOHC engines, remove the caps and bridge (where fitted). Separate the bearing inserts from the caps and the engine block. Label the bearings, indicating which cylinder they were removed from and whether they were in the cap or the block, then set them aside.

2 If you're working on a DOHC engine, unbolt the oil jets from the block and remove them **(see illustration)**. The spout holes in the oil jets are 1.2 mm in diameter and you should be able to fit a 1.1 mm drill into them. Insert the shank end of the drill bit into the oil inlet and push against the non-return ball. It should move freely and return with spring pressure. If the spring seems weak, test it with by blowing compressed air into the oil inlet. It should take at least 2 bar to push the non-return ball off its seat against the spring pressure. If the oil jet fails any of these tests, renew it.

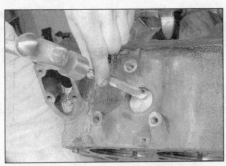

12.5a A hammer and a large punch can be used to knock the core plugs sideways in their bores

12.5b Pull the core plugs from the block pliers

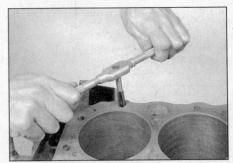

12.9 All bolt holes in the block (particularly the main bearing cap cylinder head bolt holes) should be cleaned and restored with a tap

3 Using a gasket scraper, remove all traces of gasket material from the engine block. Be very careful not to scratch or gouge the gasket sealing surfaces.

4 Remove all of the covers and threaded oil gallery plugs from the block. The plugs are usually very tight – they may have to be drilled out and the holes retapped. Use new plugs when the engine is reassembled.

5 Remove the core plugs from the engine block. To do this, knock one side of the plug into the block with a hammer and a punch, then grasp them with large pliers and pull them out (see illustrations).

6 If any of the castings are extremely dirty, all should be steam-cleaned.

7 After the block is steam-cleaned, clean all oil holes and oil galleries one more time. Brushes specifically designed for this purpose are available at most automotive parts stores. Flush the passages with warm water until the water runs clear, dry the block thoroughly and wipe all machined surfaces with a light, rust preventive oil. If you have access to compressed air, use it to speed the drying process and blow out all the oil holes and galleries.

 Warning: Wear eye protection when using compressed air.

8 If the block isn't extremely dirty or sludged up, you can do an adequate cleaning job with hot soapy water and a stiff brush. Take plenty

of time and do a thorough job. Regardless of the cleaning method used, be sure to clean all oil holes and galleries very thoroughly, dry the block completely and coat all machined surfaces with light oil.

9 The threaded holes in the block must be clean to ensure accurate torque readings during reassembly. Run the proper size tap into each of the holes to remove rust, corrosion, thread sealant or sludge and restore damaged threads (see illustration). If possible, use compressed air to clear the holes of debris produced by this operation. Now is a good time to clean the threads on the head bolts and the main bearing cap bolts as well.

10 Refit the main bearing caps and tighten the bolts finger tight.

11 After coating the sealing surfaces of the new core plugs with sealant, fit them in the engine block (see illustration). Make sure they're driven in straight and seated properly or leakage could result. Special tools are available for this purpose, but a large socket, with an outside diameter that will just slip into the core plug, a 1/2-inch drive extension and a hammer will work just as well.

12 Apply sealant to the new oil gallery plugs and thread them into the holes in the block. Make sure they're tightened securely.

13 If the engine isn't going to be reassembled right away, cover it to keep it clean.

13 Engine block – inspection

1 Before the block is inspected, it should be cleaned as described in Section 12.

2 Visually check the block for cracks, rust and corrosion. Look for stripped threads in the threaded holes. It's also a good idea to have the block checked for hidden cracks by an automotive engineering workshop that has the special equipment to do this type of work. If defects are found, have the block repaired, if possible, or renewed.

3 Check the cylinder bores for scuffing and scoring.

4 Measuring the cylinder bores for ovality, tapering and wear should be entrusted to an automotive engineering workshop or specialist. Not only are specialist tools required, but also the experience to operate them.

5 If the cylinder walls are badly scuffed or scored, or if they're oval or tapered beyond the limits (refer to a dealer or specialist), have the engine block rebored and honed at an automotive engineering workshop. If a rebore is done, oversize pistons and rings will be required.

6 Using a precision straight-edge and feeler gauge, check the block gasket surface (the surface that mates with the cylinder head) for distortions (see illustrations).

12.11 A large socket on an extension can be used to drive the new core plugs into the bores

13.6a Check the block gasket surface with a precision straight-edge and feeler gauges

13.6b Lay the straight-edge across the block, diagonally and from end-to-end when making the check

7 If the cylinders are in reasonably good condition and not worn to the outside of the limits, and if the piston-to-cylinder clearances can be maintained properly, then they don't have to be rebored. Honing is all that's necessary – ask at an automotive engineering workshop or specialist.

14 Pistons and connecting rods – inspection

1 Before the inspection process can be carried out, the piston/connecting rod assemblies must be cleaned and the original piston rings removed from the pistons. **Note:** *Always use new piston rings when the engine is reassembled.*

2 Using a piston ring expander tool, carefully remove the rings from the pistons. Be careful not to scratch or gouge the pistons in the process.

3 Scrape all traces of carbon from the top of the piston. A hand held wire brush or a piece of fine emery cloth can be used once the majority of the deposits have been scraped away. Do not, under any circumstances, use a wire brush mounted in a drill motor to remove deposits from the pistons. The piston material is soft and may be eroded away by the wire brush.

4 Use a piston ring groove cleaning tool to remove carbon deposits from the ring grooves. If a tool isn't available, a piece broken off the old ring will do the job. Be very careful to remove only the carbon deposits – don't remove any metal and do not scratch the sides of the ring grooves **(see illustrations)**.

5 Once the deposits have been removed, clean the piston/rod assemblies with degreaser and dry them with compressed air (if available). Make sure the oil return holes in the back sides of the ring grooves are clear.

 Warning: Wear eye protection when using compressed air.

6 If the pistons and cylinder walls aren't damaged or worn excessively, and if the engine block isn't rebored, new pistons won't be necessary. Normal piston wear appears as

even vertical wear on the piston thrust surfaces and slight looseness of the top ring in its groove. New piston rings, however, should always be used when an engine is rebuilt.

7 Carefully inspect each piston for cracks around the skirt, at the pin bosses and at the ring lands.

8 Look for scoring and scuffing on the thrust faces of the skirt, holes in the piston crown and burned areas at the edge of the crown. If the skirt is scored or scuffed, the engine may have been suffering from overheating and/or abnormal combustion, which caused excessively high operating temperatures. The cooling and lubrication systems should be checked thoroughly. A hole in the piston crown is an indication that abnormal combustion (pre-ignition) was occurring. Burned areas at the edge of the piston crown are usually evidence of spark knock (detonation). If any of the above problems exist, the causes must be corrected or the damage will occur again. The causes may include intake air leaks, incorrect fuel/air mixture, low octane fuel, ignition timing and EGR system malfunctions.

9 Corrosion of the piston, in the form of small pits, indicates coolant is leaking into the combustion chamber and/or the crankcase. Again, the cause must be corrected or the problem may persist in the rebuilt engine.

10 Measure the piston across the skirt, at a 90° angle to the gudgeon pin, at the height from the bottom of the skirt listed in this Chapter's Specifications **(see illustration)**.

11 Check the piston-to-rod clearance by twisting the piston and rod in opposite directions. Any noticeable play indicates excessive wear, which must be corrected. The piston/connecting rod assemblies should be taken to an automotive engineering workshop or specialist to have the pistons and rods resized and new gudgeon pins installed. Renewing the gudgeon pins requires several special tools including a hydraulic press.

12 If the pistons must be removed from the connecting rods for any reason, they should be taken to an automotive engineering workshop or specialist. While they are there have the connecting rods checked for bend and twist, since they have special equipment

for this purpose. **Note:** *Unless new pistons and/or connecting rods must be installed, do not dismantle the pistons and connecting rods.*

13 Check the connecting rods for cracks and other damage. Temporarily remove the rod caps, lift out the old bearing inserts, wipe the rod and cap bearing surfaces clean and inspect them for gouges and scratches. After checking the rods, renew the old bearings, slip the caps into place and tighten the nuts finger tight. **Note:** *If the engine is being rebuilt because of a connecting rod knock, be sure to fit new rods.*

15 Crankshaft – inspection

1 Clean the crankshaft using paraffin or a suitable degreaser, and dry it, preferably with compressed air if available. Be sure to clean the oil holes with a pipe cleaner or similar probe, to ensure that they are not obstructed.

 Warning: Wear eye protection when using compressed air.

2 Check the main and big-end bearing journals for uneven wear, scoring, pitting and cracking.

3 Big-end bearing wear is accompanied by distinct metallic knocking when the engine is running (particularly noticeable when the engine is pulling from low speed) and some loss of oil pressure.

4 Main bearing wear is accompanied by severe engine vibration and rumble – getting progressively worse as engine speed increases – and again by loss of oil pressure.

5 Check the bearing journal for roughness by running a finger lightly over the bearing surface. Any roughness (which will be accompanied by obvious bearing wear) indicates that the crankshaft requires regrinding (where possible) or renewal.

6 Check for burrs around the crankshaft oil holes (the holes are usually chamfered, so burrs should not be a problem unless regrinding has been carried out carelessly). Remove any burrs with a fine file or scraper, and thoroughly clean the oil holes as described previously.

14.4a The piston ring grooves can be cleaned with a special tool, as shown here . . .

14.4b . . . or a section of a broken ring

14.10 Measure the piston diameter at a 90° angle to the gudgeon pin, at the specified distance from the bottom of the skirt

7 Accurate measuring of the crankshaft bearing journals requires special tools and the experience to use them. Consequently, it is recommended that the task be entrusted to an automotive engineering workshop or specialist. If the crankshaft requires machining, they will be able to carry out the work and supply suitable oversize bearing inserts.

8 Check the oil seal contact surfaces at each end of the crankshaft for wear and damage. If the seal has worn a deep groove in the surface of the crankshaft, consult an engine overhaul specialist; repair may be possible, but otherwise a new crankshaft will be required.

16 Main and big-end bearings – inspection

1 Even though the main and big-end bearings should be renewed during the engine overhaul, the old bearings should be retained for close examination, as they may reveal valuable information about the condition of the engine (see illustration).

2 Bearing failure can occur due to lack of lubrication, the presence of dirt or other foreign particles, overloading the engine, or corrosion. Regardless of the cause of bearing failure, the cause must be corrected (where applicable) before the engine is reassembled, to prevent it from happening again.

3 When examining the bearing shells, remove them from the cylinder block, the main bearing caps, the connecting rods and the connecting rod big-end bearing caps. Lay them out on a clean surface in the same general position as their location in the engine. This will enable you to match any bearing problems with the corresponding crankshaft journal.

4 Dirt and other foreign matter gets into the engine in a variety of ways. It may be left in the engine during assembly, or it may pass through filters or the crankcase ventilation system. It may get into the oil, and from there into the bearings. Metal chips from machining operations and normal engine wear are often present. Abrasives are sometimes left in engine components after reconditioning, especially when parts are not thoroughly cleaned using the proper cleaning methods. Whatever the source, these foreign objects often end up embedded in the soft bearing material, and are easily recognised. Large particles will not embed in the bearing, and will score or gouge the bearing and journal. The best prevention for this cause of bearing failure is to clean all parts thoroughly, and keep everything spotlessly-clean during engine assembly. Frequent and regular engine oil and filter changes are also recommended.

5 Lack of lubrication (or lubrication breakdown) has a number of interrelated causes. Excessive heat (which thins the oil), overloading (which squeezes the oil from the bearing face) and oil leakage (from excessive bearing clearances, worn oil pump or high engine speeds) all contribute to lubrication breakdown. Blocked oil passages, which usually are the result of misaligned oil holes in a bearing shell, will also oil-starve a bearing, and destroy it. When lack of lubrication is the cause of bearing failure, the bearing material is wiped or extruded from the steel backing of the bearing. Temperatures may increase to the point where the steel backing turns blue from overheating.

6 Driving habits can have a definite effect on bearing life. Full-throttle, low-speed operation (labouring the engine) puts very high loads on bearings, tending to squeeze out the oil film. These loads cause the bearings to flex, which produces fine cracks in the bearing face (fatigue failure). Eventually, the bearing material will loosen in pieces, and tear away from the steel backing.

7 Short-distance driving leads to corrosion of bearings, because insufficient engine heat is produced to drive off the condensed water and corrosive gases. These products collect in the engine oil, forming acid and sludge. As the oil is carried to the engine bearings, the acid attacks and corrodes the bearing material.

8 Incorrect bearing refitting during engine assembly will lead to bearing failure as well.

Tight-fitting bearings leave insufficient bearing running clearance, and will result in oil starvation. Dirt or foreign particles trapped behind a bearing shell result in high spots on the bearing, which lead to failure.

9 As mentioned at the beginning of this Section, the bearing shells should be renewed as a matter of course during engine overhaul; to do otherwise is false economy.

17 Engine overhaul – reassembly sequence

1 Before reassembly begins, ensure that all new parts have been obtained, and that all necessary tools are available. Read through the entire procedure to familiarise yourself with the work involved, and to ensure that all items necessary for reassembly of the engine are at hand. In addition to all normal tools and materials, thread-locking compound will be needed. A good quality tube of liquid sealant will also be required for the joint faces that are fitted without gaskets.

2 To save time and avoid problems, engine reassembly must be done in the following general order:

Piston/connecting rod assemblies.
Crankshaft and main bearings.
Crankshaft transmission end oil seal and retainer.
Oil baffle.
Oil pump and oil pump pick-up.
Oil sump.
Cylinder head.
Camshaft(s) and rocker arm assembly.
Coolant pump.
Timing belt and sprockets.
Intake and exhaust manifolds.
Timing belt covers.
Camshaft cover.
Flywheel/driveplate.

3 At this stage, all engine components should be absolutely clean and dry, with all faults repaired. The components should be laid out (or in individual containers) on a completely clean work surface.

18 Piston rings – refitting

1 Before fitting the new piston rings, the ring end gaps must be checked.

2 Lay out the piston/connecting rod assemblies and the new ring sets so the ring sets will be matched with the same piston and cylinder during the end gap measurement and engine assembly.

3 Insert the top (number 1) ring into the first cylinder and square it up with the cylinder walls by pushing it in with the top of the piston (see illustration). The ring should be near the bottom of the cylinder, at the lower limit of ring travel.

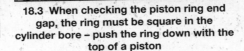

18.3 When checking the piston ring end gap, the ring must be square in the cylinder bore – push the ring down with the top of a piston

16.1 Typical bearing failures

CRATERS OR POCKETS
FATIGUE FAILURE

BRIGHT (POLISHED) SECTIONS
IMPROPER SEATING

SCRATCHES
DIRT IMBEDDED INTO BEARING MATERIAL
SCRATCHED BY DIRT

OVERLAY WIPED OUT
LACK OF OIL

OVERLAY GONE FROM ENTIRE SURFACE
EXCESSIVE WEAR

RADIUS RIDE
TAPERED JOURNAL

4 To measure the end gap, slip feeler gauges between the ends of the ring until a gauge equal to the gap width is found **(see illustration)**. The feeler gauge should slide between the ring ends with a slight amount of drag. Compare the measurement to this Chapter's Specifications. If the gap is larger or smaller than specified, double-check to make sure you have the correct rings before proceeding.

5 If the gap is too small, it must be enlarged or the ring ends may come in contact with each other during engine operation, which can cause serious engine damage. The end gap can be increased by filing the ring ends very carefully with a fine file. Mount the file in a vice equipped with soft jaws, slip the ring over the file with the ends contacting the file teeth and slowly move the ring to remove material from the ends. When performing this operation, file only from the outside in.

6 Excess end gap isn't critical unless it's greater than the service limit listed in this Chapter's Specifications. Again, double-check to make sure you have the correct rings for the engine.

7 Repeat the procedure for each ring that will be fitted in the first cylinder and for each ring in the remaining cylinders. Remember to keep rings, pistons and cylinders matched up.

8 Once the ring end gaps have been checked/corrected, the rings can be fitted on the pistons.

9 The oil control ring (lowest one on the

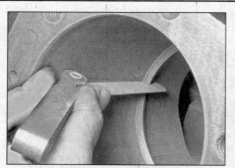

18.4 With the ring square in the cylinder, measure the end gap with a feeler gauge

piston) is usually installed first. It's composed of three separate components. Slip the spacer/expander into the groove **(see illustration)**. If an anti-rotation tang is used, make sure it's inserted into the drilled hole in the ring groove. Next, fit the lower side rail. Don't use a piston ring refitting tool on the oil ring side rails, as they may be damaged. Instead, place one end of the side rail into the groove between the spacer/expander and the ring land, hold it firmly in place and slide a finger around the piston while pushing the rail into the groove **(see illustration)**. Next, fit the upper side rail in the same manner.

10 After the three oil ring components have been fitted, check to make sure both the upper and lower side rails can be turned smoothly in the ring groove.

11 The number 2 (middle) compression ring is installed next. It's usually stamped with a mark, which must face up, toward the top of the piston. **Note:** *Always follow the instructions printed on the ring package or box – different manufacturers may require different approaches. Don't mix up the top and middle rings, as they have different cross-sections.*

12 Use a piston ring refitting tool and make sure the identification mark is facing the top of the piston, then slip the ring into the middle groove on the piston **(see illustration)**. Don't expand the ring any more than necessary to slide it over the piston.

13 Fit the number 1 (top) compression ring in the same manner. Make sure the mark is facing up. Be careful not to confuse the number 1 and number 2 rings.

14 Repeat the procedure for the remaining pistons and rings.

19 Crankshaft – refitting

Note: *It is recommended that new main bearing shells are fitted regardless of the condition of the original ones.*

Note: *If you're working on an engine with a main bearing cap bridge, fit the piston/connecting rod assemblies first (see Section 21), placing all of the pistons at Top Dead Centre so the connecting rods don't interfere with crankshaft refitting.*

1 It's assumed at this point that the engine block and crankshaft have been cleaned, inspected and repaired or reconditioned.

2 Position the engine with the bottom facing up.

3 Remove the main bearing caps and/or bridge assembly.

4 Remove the original bearing inserts from the block and the main bearing caps. Wipe the bearing surfaces of the block and caps with a clean, lint-free cloth. They must be kept spotlessly clean. **Note:** *Don't touch the faces of the new bearing inserts with your fingers. Oil and acids from your skin can etch the bearings.*

5 Clean the back sides of the new main bearing inserts and lay one in each main bearing saddle in the block. If one of the bearing inserts from each set has a large groove in it, make sure the grooved insert is fitted in the block. Lay the other bearing from each set in the corresponding main bearing cap. Make sure the tab on the bearing insert fits into the recess in the block or cap.

6 The flanged thrustwashers must be fitted in the number 4 cap and saddle (counting from the left of the engine) **(see illustration)**.

7 Clean the faces of the bearings in the block and the crankshaft main bearing journals with a clean, lint-free cloth.

8 Check or clean the oil holes in the

18.9a Fit the spacer/expander into the oil control ring groove

18.9b Do not use a piston ring fitting tool when fitting the oil control ring side rails

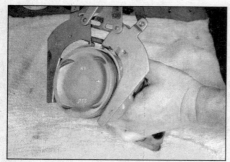

18.12 Fitting the compression rings with a ring expander – the mark on the ring must face up

19.6 The thrustwashers (arrowed) must be fitted to the number four main bearing journal – the grooved sides face out

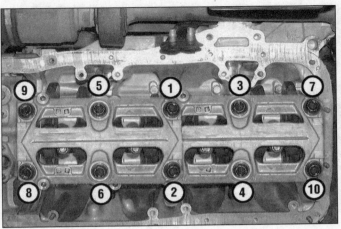

19.14a Main bearing cap bridge assembly tightening sequence (SOHC)

19.14b Main bearing cap and bridge assembly tightening sequence (DOHC)

crankshaft, as any dirt here can go only one way – straight through the new bearings.

9 Clean the bearing faces in the block, then apply a thin, uniform layer of clean engine oil to each of the bearing surfaces. Be sure to coat the thrust faces as well as the journal face of the thrust bearing.

10 Make sure the crankshaft journals are clean, then lay the crankshaft back in place in the block.

11 Clean the faces of the bearings in the caps, then apply lubricant to them.

12 Refit the main bearing caps and/or bridge assembly.

13 Refit the bolts.

14 Following the recommended sequence, tighten all main bearing cap bolts to the torque listed in Chapter 2A or 2B Specifications **(see illustrations)**.

15 Rotate the crankshaft a number of times by hand to check for any obvious binding.

16 Check the crankshaft endfloat with feeler gauges or a dial indicator gauge (DTI) as described in Section 11. The endfloat should be correct if the crankshaft thrust faces aren't worn or damaged and new bearings have been fitted.

17 Refer to Section 20 and fit the new oil seal.

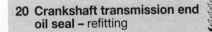

20 Crankshaft transmission end oil seal – refitting

Note: *The crankshaft must be fitted and the main bearing caps bolted in place before the new seal and retainer assembly can be bolted to the block.*

1 Remove the old seal from the retainer with a hammer and punch by driving it out from the rear side **(see illustration)**. Be sure to note how far it's recessed into the retainer bore before removing it; the new seal will have to be recessed an equal amount. Be very careful not to scratch or otherwise damage the bore in the retainer or oil leaks could develop.

2 Make sure the retainer is clean. The seal must be pressed squarely into the retainer bore, so hammering it into place isn't recommended. If you don't have access to a press, sandwich the retainer and seal between two smooth pieces of wood and press the seal into place with the jaws of a large vice. If you don't have a vice big enough, lay the retainer on a workbench and drive the seal into place with a wood block and hammer **(see illustration)**. The piece of wood must be thick enough to distribute the force evenly around

the entire circumference of the seal. Work slowly and make sure the seal enters the bore squarely. **Note:** *Using a feeler gauge, confirm that the clearance between the seal and the retainer is equal all the way around* **(see illustration)**. *It should be 0.5 to 0.8 mm.*

3 Place a thin coat of liquid sealant (available from Honda dealers) to the entire edge of the retainer.

4 Lubricate the seal lips with multi-purpose grease or engine oil before you slip the seal/retainer over the crankshaft and bolt it to the block. Be sure to use a new gasket. **Note:** *Apply a film of liquid sealant to both sides of the gasket before refitting.*

5 Tighten the retainer bolts, a little at a time, to the torque listed in the Chapter 2A or 2B Specifications. Trim the gasket flush with the sump gasket surface, being careful not to scratch it.

21 Pistons and connecting rods – refitting

1 Before fitting the piston/connecting rod assemblies, the cylinder walls must be perfectly clean, the top edge of each cylinder

20.1 Support the retainer on wood blocks and drive out the oil seal with a punch and a hammer

20.2a Drive the new seal into the retainer with a wood block or a section of pipe, if you have one large enough – ensure the seal is driven in squarely

20.2b Check the clearance between the seal and retainer using a feeler gauge

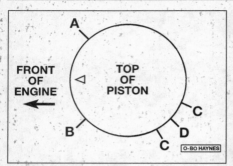

21.5 Ring end gap positions – align the oil control sing spacer gap at D, the oil control ring side rails at C, the second compression ring at A, and the top compression ring at B

21.9 Using a piston ring compressor, fit the pistons with the mark (arrowed) toward the timing belt end of the engine

21.11 Drive the piston gently into the cylinder bore with the end of a wooden or plastic hammer handle

must be chamfered, and the crankshaft must be in place.

2 Remove the cap from the end of the number 1 connecting rod (check the marks made during removal). Remove the original bearing inserts and wipe the bearing surfaces of the connecting rod and cap with a clean, lint-free cloth. They must be kept spotlessly clean. **Note:** *Don't touch the faces of the new bearing inserts with your fingers. Oil and acids from your skin can etch the bearings.*

3 Clean the back side of the new upper bearing insert, then lay it in place in the connecting rod. Make sure the tab on the bearing fits into the recess in the rod. Don't hammer the bearing insert into place and be very careful not to scratch or gouge the bearing face. Lubricate the bearing face with clean engine oil.

4 Clean the back side of the other bearing insert and fit it in the rod cap. Again, make sure the tab on the bearing fits into the recess in the cap, and lubricate the bearing face with clean engine oil.

5 Position the piston ring gaps at intervals around the piston **(see illustration)**. *Caution: DON'T position any ring gap in-line with the gudgeon pin hole or at piston thrust surfaces (90° to gudgeon pin).*

6 Slip a section of plastic or rubber hose over each connecting rod cap bolt.

7 Lubricate the piston and rings with clean engine oil and attach a piston ring compressor to the piston. Leave the skirt protruding about 6 mm to guide the piston into the cylinder. The rings must be compressed until they're flush with the piston.

8 Rotate the crankshaft until the number 1 connecting rod journal is at BDC (bottom dead centre) and apply a coat of engine oil to the cylinder bores.

9 With the mark or notch on top of the piston facing the timing belt end of the engine **(see illustration)**, gently insert the piston/connecting rod assembly into the number 1 cylinder bore and rest the bottom edge of the ring compressor on the engine block.

10 Tap the top edge of the ring compressor

to make sure it's contacting the block around its entire circumference.

11 Gently tap on the top of the piston with the end of a wooden or plastic hammer handle **(see illustration)** while guiding the end of the connecting rod into place on the crankshaft journal. The piston rings may try to pop out of the ring compressor just before entering the cylinder bore, so keep some pressure on the ring compressor. Work slowly, and if any resistance is felt as the piston enters the cylinder, stop immediately. Find out what's catching and fix it before proceeding. Do not, for any reason, force the piston into the cylinder – you might break a ring and/or the piston.

12 Slide the connecting rod into place on the journal, remove the protective hoses from the rod cap bolts, fit the rod cap and tighten the nuts to the torque listed in Chapter 2A or 2B Specifications. Work up to the torque in two steps and make sure the mating mark on the cap is on the same side as the mark on the connecting rod.

13 Repeat the entire procedure for the remaining pistons/connecting rods.

14 The important points to remember are:
a) Keep the back sides of the bearing inserts and the insides of the connecting rods and caps perfectly clean when assembling them.
b) Make sure you have the correct piston/rod assembly for each cylinder.
c) The arrow or mark on the piston must face the timing belt end of the engine.
d) Lubricate the cylinder bores with clean oil.
e) Lubricate the bearing faces when fitting the rod caps.
f) Where fitted, refit the main bearing cap bridge assembly before proceeding to the next Step.

15 After all the piston/connecting rod assemblies and the main bearing cap bridge (if fitted) have been properly fitted, rotate the crankshaft a number of times by hand to check for any obvious binding.

16 As a final step, the connecting rod endfloat must be checked. Refer to Section 10 for this procedure.

17 Compare the measured endfloat to this Chapter's Specifications to make sure it's correct. If it was correct before dismantling and the original crankshaft and rods were refitted, it should still be right. If new rods or a new crankshaft were fitted, the endfloat may be inadequate. If so, the rods will have to be removed and taken to an automotive engineering workshop or specialist for resizing.

22 Initial start-up and running-in after overhaul

1 With the engine refitted in the vehicle, double-check the engine oil and coolant levels. Make a final check that everything has been reconnected, and that there are no tools or rags left in the engine compartment.

2 With the spark plugs out of the engine and the ignition system and fuel system disabled (see *Compression check* in Chapter 2A or 2B), crank the engine until oil pressure registers on the gauge or the light goes out.

3 Refit the spark plugs, and HT leads, then restore the ignition and fuel system functions.

4 Start the engine as normal noting that this may take a little longer than usual, due to the fuel system components having been disturbed.

5 While the engine is idling, check for fuel, water and oil leaks. Don't be alarmed if there are some odd smells and smoke from parts getting hot and burning off oil deposits.

6 Assuming all is well, keep the engine idling until hot water is felt circulating through the top hose, then switch off the engine.

7 Allow the engine to cool then recheck the oil and coolant levels as described in *Weekly Checks*, and top-up as necessary.

8 If new pistons, rings or crankshaft bearings have been fitted, the engine must be treated as new, and run-in for the first 500 miles (800 km). *Do not* operate the engine at full-throttle, or allow it to labour at low engine speeds in any gear. It is recommended that the oil and filter be changed at the end of this period.

Chapter 3
Cooling, heating and air conditioning systems

Contents

Degrees of difficulty

Easy, suitable for novice with little experience	Fairly easy, suitable for beginner with some experience	Fairly difficult, suitable for competent DIY mechanic	Difficult, suitable for experienced DIY mechanic	Very difficult, suitable for expert DIY or professional

Specifications

General

Coolant capacity	See Chapter 1
Cooling fan:	
On at	91 to 95°C
Off at	3 to 8° below 'On' temperature
Drivebelt tension	See Chapter 1
Radiator pressure cap rating	0.95 to 1.25 bar
Thermostat:	
Opens at	76 to 80°C
Fully open at	90°C
Valve lift at fully open	8.0 mm (minimum)
Refrigerant type	R-134a
Refrigerant oil added for component renewal:	
Compressor	120 to 140 ml
Condenser	15 ml
Evaporator	25 ml
Receiver-drier	10 ml
Pipe or hose	10 ml

Torque specifications

	Nm	lbf ft
Alternator adjustment bracket-to-water pump bolt	44	32
Coolant pump-to-block bolts	12	9
Coolant temperature gauge sender	10	7
Coolant temperature switch	24	18
Thermostat housing cover bolts	12	9
Thermostat housing-to-block bolts	12	9
Upper radiator hose fitting-to-block bolts	10	7

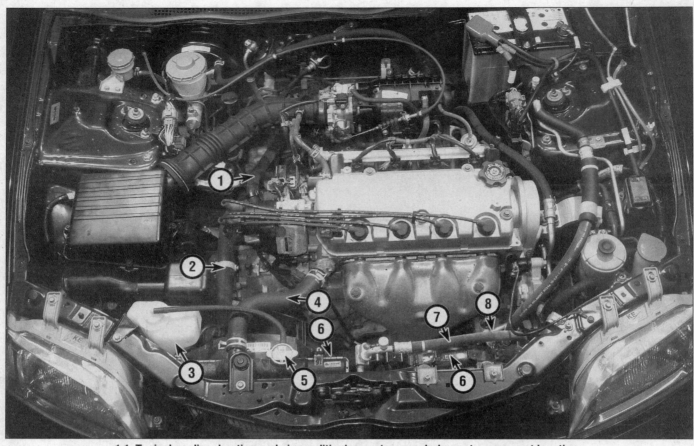

1.1 Typical cooling, heating and air conditioning systems underbonnet component locations

1 Heater hoses	3 Coolant reservoir	5 Radiator cap	7 Air conditioning refrigerant hose
2 Lower radiator hose	4 Upper radiator hose	6 Cooling fans	8 Air conditioning compressor

1 General information and precautions

Engine cooling system

All vehicles covered by this manual employ a pressurised engine cooling system with thermostatically-controlled coolant circulation **(see illustration)**. An impeller-type water pump mounted on the engine block pumps coolant through the engine. The coolant flows around each cylinder and toward the rear of the engine. Cast-in coolant passages direct coolant around the intake and exhaust ports, near the spark plug areas and in close proximity to the exhaust valve guides.

A wax pellet type thermostat controls engine coolant temperature. During warm-up, the closed thermostat prevents coolant from circulating through the radiator. As the engine nears normal operating temperature, the thermostat opens and allows hot coolant to travel through the radiator, where it's cooled before returning to the engine.

The cooling system is sealed by a pressure-type radiator cap, which raises the boiling point of the coolant and increases the cooling efficiency of the radiator. If the system pressure exceeds the cap pressure relief value, the excess pressure in the system forces the spring-loaded valve inside the cap off its seat and allows the coolant to escape through the overflow tube into a coolant reservoir. When the system cools the excess coolant is automatically drawn from the reservoir back into the radiator.

The coolant reservoir serves as both the point at which fresh coolant is added to the cooling system to maintain the proper fluid level and as a holding tank for overheated coolant.

This type of cooling system is known as a closed design because coolant that escapes past the pressure cap is saved and re-used.

Heating system

The heating system consists of a blower fan and heater matrix located in the heater housing, the hoses connecting the heater matrix to the engine cooling system and the heater/air conditioning control panel on the dashboard. Hot engine coolant is circulated through the heater matrix. When the heater mode is activated, a flap door opens to expose the heater box to the passenger compartment. A fan switch on the control panel activates the blower motor, which forces air through the matrix, heating the air.

Air conditioning system

The air conditioning system consists of a condenser mounted in front of the radiator, an evaporator mounted adjacent to the heater matrix, a compressor mounted on the engine, a receiver-drier which contains a high pressure relief valve and the plumbing connecting all of the above components.

A blower fan forces the warmer air of the passenger compartment through the evaporator matrix (sort of a radiator-in-reverse), transferring the heat from the air to the refrigerant. The liquid refrigerant boils off into low pressure vapour, taking the heat with it when it leaves the evaporator.

Precautions

 Warning: Do not attempt to remove the expansion tank filler cap or disturb any part of the

cooling system while the engine is hot, as there is a high risk of scalding. If the expansion tank filler cap must be removed before the engine and radiator have fully cooled (even though this is not recommended) the pressure in the cooling system must first be relieved. Cover the cap with a thick layer of cloth, to avoid scalding, and slowly unscrew the filler cap until a hissing sound can be heard. When the hissing has stopped, indicating that the pressure has reduced, slowly unscrew the filler cap until it can be removed; if more hissing sounds are heard, wait until they have stopped before unscrewing the cap completely. At all times keep well away from the filler cap opening.

Do not allow antifreeze to come into contact with skin or painted surfaces of the vehicle. Rinse off spills immediately with plenty of water. Never leave antifreeze lying around in an open container or in a puddle in the driveway or on the garage floor. Children and pets are attracted by its sweet smell. Antifreeze can be fatal if ingested.

If the engine is hot, the electric cooling fan may start rotating even if the engine is not running, so be careful to keep hands, hair and loose clothing well clear when working in the engine compartment.

If the radio in your vehicle is equipped with an anti-theft system, make sure you have the correct activation code before disconnecting the battery.

2 Antifreeze – general information

The cooling system should be filled with a non-silicate water/ethylene glycol based antifreeze solution that is compatible with aluminium engines, which will prevent freezing down to at least −35°C. It also provides protection against corrosion and increases the coolant boiling point.

The cooling system should be drained, flushed and refilled at the specified intervals (see Chapter 1). Old or contaminated antifreeze solutions are likely to cause damage and encourage the formation of rust and scale in the system.

Before adding antifreeze, check all hose connections, because antifreeze tends to leak through very minute openings. Engines don't normally consume coolant, so if the level goes down, find the cause and correct it.

The exact mixture of antifreeze-to-water which you should use depends on the relative weather conditions. The mixture should contain at least 50% antifreeze, but should never contain more than 70% antifreeze. Consult the mixture ratio chart on the antifreeze container before adding coolant. Hydrometers are available at most automotive parts stores to test the coolant. Use antifreeze which meets the vehicle manufacturer's specifications.

3 Thermostat – removal, testing and refitting

⚠ **Warning: Do not remove the radiator cap, drain the coolant or renew the thermostat until the engine has cooled completely. Read the Warnings given in Section 1.**

Removal

1 Drain the cooling system (see Chapter 1). If the coolant is relatively new or in good condition (see Chapter 1), save and re-use it.
2 Follow the lower radiator hose to the engine to locate the thermostat housing cover.
3 Disconnect the electrical connector from the engine coolant temperature (ECT) sensor. Loosen the hose clamp, then detach the hose from the fitting **(see illustration)**. If it's stuck, grasp it near the end with a pair of adjustable pliers and twist it to break the seal, then pull it off. If the hose is old or deteriorated, cut it off and fit a new one.

4 If the outer surface of the large fitting that mates with the hose is deteriorated (corroded, pitted, etc) it may be damaged further by hose removal. If it is, the thermostat housing cover will have to be renewed.
5 Remove the thermostat cover bolts and detach the housing cover **(see illustration)**. If the cover is stuck, tap it with a soft-face hammer to jar it loose. Be prepared for some coolant to spill as the gasket seal is broken.
6 Note how it's fitted – with the bypass pin at the top – then remove the thermostat.

Testing

7 Before assuming the thermostat is to blame for a cooling system problem, check the coolant level, auxiliary drivebelt tension (see Chapter 1) and temperature gauge operation.
8 If the engine seems to be taking a long time to warm-up (based on heater output or temperature gauge operation), the thermostat is probably stuck open. Renew the thermostat.
9 If the engine runs hot, use your hand to check the temperature of the upper radiator hose. If the hose isn't hot, but the engine is, the thermostat is probably stuck closed, preventing the coolant inside the engine from escaping to the radiator. Renew the thermostat.
Caution: Don't drive the vehicle without a thermostat. The PCM may stay in open loop and emissions and fuel economy will suffer.
10 If the upper radiator hose is hot, it means that the coolant is flowing and the thermostat is open. Consult the *Fault finding* section at the rear of this manual for cooling system diagnosis.

Refitting

11 Remove all traces of old gasket material and/or sealant from the housing and cover.
12 Fit a new rubber gasket over the thermostat **(see illustration)**.
13 Fit the new thermostat in the housing without using sealant. Make sure the bypass pin, if equipped, is at the top and the spring

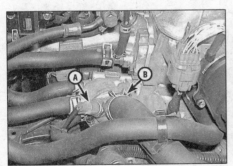

3.3 Disconnect the electrical connector from the ECT switch (A) and detach the lower radiator hose (B) from the thermostat cover (SOHC; DOHC similar)

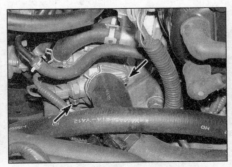

3.5 Thermostat housing cover bolts (arrowed)

3.12 Fit a new rubber gasket over the thermostat

3.13 Fit the new thermostat in the housing with the spring towards the engine and the bypass pin (arrowed) at the top

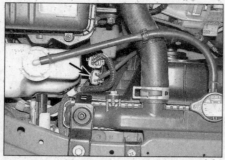

4.1a The electrical connector for the radiator cooling fan motor (arrowed) is located on the right-hand side of the vehicle

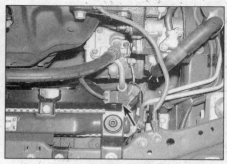

4.1b The electrical connector for the condenser fan motor (arrowed) is located on the left-hand side of the vehicle

end is directed into the engine (see illustration).

14 Refit the housing cover and bolts. Tighten the bolts to the torque listed in this Chapter's Specifications.

15 Reattach the hose and tighten the hose clamp securely. Refit all components that were removed for access.

16 Refill the cooling system (see Chapter 1).

17 Start the engine and allow it to reach normal operating temperature, then check for leaks and proper thermostat operation (as described in Paragraphs 7 to 10).

4.8a The radiator fan shroud has two lower retaining bolts (right-hand bolt) . . .

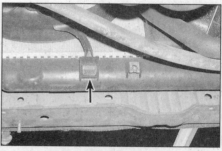

4.8b . . . but the condenser fan shroud has no bolts at the bottom; 5-door models have post that fits into a pocket on the radiator (arrowed), and on other models there are two rubber mounts that fit into holes in two brackets

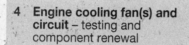

4 Engine cooling fan(s) and circuit – testing and component renewal

⚠️ **Warning: To avoid possible injury or damage, DO NOT operate the engine with a damaged fan. Do not attempt to repair fan blades – renew a damaged fan.**

Testing

Note: *Models equipped with air conditioning have two complete fan circuits – one for the condenser and one for the radiator. The following procedures apply to both.*

1 To test a fan motor, disconnect the electrical connector at the motor (see illustrations) and use bridging wires to connect the fan directly to the battery. If the fan still doesn't work, renew the motor.

2 If the motor tests OK, check the fuse and relay (see Chapter 12), the fan switch, the condenser fan relay (also mounted in the engine compartment fusebox) if equipped, or the wiring which connects the components. **Note:** *On some models, the condenser fan relay is mounted directly in front of the condenser on the driver's side of the engine compartment.*

3 To test the radiator fan switch, remove the switch electrical connector (see illustration 3.3) and, using an ohmmeter, check for continuity across the terminals of the switch with the engine cold. The switch should not have continuity while the coolant is below 91 to 95°C. Start the engine and allow the engine to reach normal operating temperature. Stop the engine and check for continuity again. The radiator fan

switch should show continuity when the coolant temperature reaches 91 to 95°C, and above. If the switch fails to show continuity above this temperature, renew it.

4 The air conditioning condenser fan is controlled by the ECM. If the condenser fan fails to operate with the air conditioning ON after all other checks have been completed, check for a low refrigerant charge or have the ECM diagnosed by a dealership service department or specialist.

Renewal

Note: *This procedure applies to either fan.*

5 Disconnect the battery cable from the negative battery terminal (see Chapter 5A).

6 Apply the handbrake and chock the rear wheels to prevent the vehicle from rolling. Raise the front of the vehicle and support it securely with axle stands (see *Jacking and*

vehicle support). Remove the lower splash pan, if equipped, from under the radiator.

7 Insert a small screwdriver into the connector to lift the locking tab and disconnect the fan wiring.

8 Remove the fan lower mounting bolt(s) (see illustrations). **Note:** *If you're removing the condenser fan on models equipped with air conditioning, unbolt the air conditioning pipe support bracket.*

9 Unbolt the fan upper mounting bolts (see illustration).

10 Carefully lift the fan out of the engine compartment (see illustration).

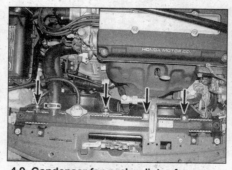

4.9 Condenser fan and radiator fan upper mounting bolts (arrowed)

4.10 To remove the condenser fan, remove the air conditioning pipe bracket bolts, push the bracket aside, then carefully lift the fan out of the engine compartment; to remove the radiator fan assembly, simply unbolt it and pull it out

4.11 To remove the fan, unscrew the nut in the centre (upper arrow), then pull the fan blade from the motor shaft (the lower arrow points to one of the motor mounting screws)

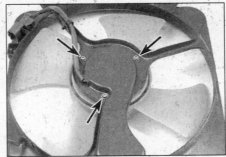

4.12 To detach the condenser fan motor from the shroud, remove these screws (arrowed)

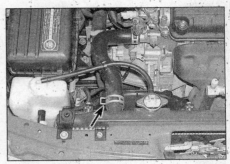

5.6a Slacken the hose clamp and detach the upper radiator hose (arrowed) . . .

11 To detach the fan from the motor, remove the motor shaft nut **(see illustration)**.

12 To detach the fan motor from the shroud, remove the mounting screws **(see illustration)**.

13 Refitting is the reverse of removal.

5 Radiator and coolant reservoir – removal and refitting

Warning: Wait until the engine is completely cool before beginning these procedures. Read the Warning at the beginning of Section 2.

Radiator

1 Disconnect the cable from the negative terminal of the battery (see Chapter 5A).

2 Apply the handbrake and chock the rear wheels. Raise the front of the vehicle and support it securely on axle stands (see *Jacking and vehicle support*). Remove the splash pan beneath the radiator.

3 Drain the cooling system (see Chapter 1). If the coolant is relatively new or in good condition, save and re-use it.

4 If the vehicle is equipped with an automatic transmission, disconnect the cooler pipes from the radiator. Use a drain pan to catch spilled fluid and plug the pipes and fittings.

5 Disconnect the electrical connector(s) for the cooling fan motor(s).

6 Loosen the hose clamps, then detach the radiator hoses from the fittings **(see illustrations)**. If they're stuck, grasp each hose near the end with a pair of slip-joint pliers and twist it to break the seal, then pull it off – be careful not to damage the radiator fittings! If the hoses are old or deteriorated, cut them off and fit new ones.

7 Remove the cooling fan(s) (see Section 4).

8 Unbolt and remove the small brackets that attach the upper end of the radiator to the radiator support **(see illustration)**.

9 Carefully lift out the radiator. Don't spill coolant on the vehicle or scratch the paint.

10 Inspect the radiator for leaks and damage. If it needs repair, have a radiator repair specialist perform the work as special techniques are required.

11 Debris and dirt can be removed from the radiator by spraying with a garden hose from the reverse.

12 Inspect the radiator mounts for deterioration and renew if necessary.

13 Refitting is the reverse of the removal procedure. Guide the radiator into the mountings until they seat properly.

14 After fitting, fill the cooling system with the proper mixture of antifreeze and water (see Chapter 1).

15 Start the engine and check for leaks. Allow the engine to reach normal operating temperature, indicated by the upper radiator hose becoming hot. Recheck the coolant level and add more if required.

16 If you're working on an automatic transmission equipped vehicle, check and add fluid as needed (see Chapter 1).

Coolant reservoir

17 The coolant reservoir is mounted adjacent to the radiator in the right-hand front corner of the engine compartment.

18 Trace the overflow hose from the radiator neck to the top of coolant reservoir. Remove the cap with the hose still attached. Lift the reservoir straight up out of the bracket.

19 Pour the coolant into a container.

20 Wash out and inspect the reservoir for cracks and chafing. Examine the reservoir closely. If it's damaged, renew it.

21 Refitting is the reverse of removal.

6 Oil cooler – removal and refitting

Warning: Allow the engine to cool completely before beginning this procedure.

Removal

1 The oil cooler used on some DOHC engines is mounted between the oil filter and engine block **(see illustration)**.

2 Remove the oil filter and drain the coolant (see Chapter 1).

3 Detach the two coolant pipes from the oil cooler. Be prepared for coolant to escape

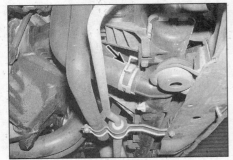

5.6b . . . then slacken the hose clamp and detach the lower radiator hose (arrowed)

5.8 Remove the upper mounting bracket (A) that secures the radiator to the radiator support – note that the air conditioning pipe support bracket (B) must also be removed

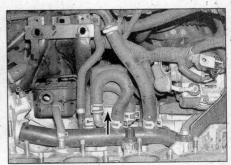

6.1 Oil cooler location (arrowed)

7.3 The 'weep' holes (arrowed) are located on the side of the coolant pump facing the bulkhead

from the open fittings. Cap or plug the open fittings.

4 Remove the large nut (actually part of the hollow retaining bolt) in the centre of the oil cooler and separate the oil cooler from the engine.

Refitting

5 Refitting is the reverse of removal. Be sure to use a new O-ring between the block and oil cooler (lubricate the O-ring with clean engine oil before refitting). Tighten the coolant hoses securely at the fittings.

6 Fit a new oil filter and change the engine oil (see Chapter 1).

7 Add coolant and oil as needed.

8 Start the engine and check for oil and coolant leaks.

9 Recheck the coolant and oil levels.

7 Coolant pump – inspection

1 A failure in the coolant pump can cause serious engine damage due to overheating.

2 There are two ways to check the operation of the coolant pump while it's fitted on the engine. If the pump is defective, it should be renewed.

3 Coolant pumps are equipped with weep (or vent) holes **(see illustration)**. If a failure occurs in the pump seal, coolant will leak from the hole. With the timing belt cover removed

(see Chapter 2A or 2B), you'll need a torch and small mirror to find the hole on the coolant pump from underneath to check for leaks. **Note:** *A small amount of 'weeping' from the hole is normal.*

4 If the coolant pump shaft bearings fail there may be a howling sound at the pump while it's running. Shaft wear can be felt with the timing belt removed if the coolant pump pulley is rocked up-and-down (with the engine not running).

8 Coolant pump – renewal

⚠ *Warning: Wait until the engine is completely cool before beginning this procedure. Read the warning at the beginning of Section 1.*

1 Drain the cooling system (see Chapter 1). If the coolant is relatively new or in good condition, save and re-use it.

2 Remove the timing belt (see Chapter 2A or 2B). On DOHC engines, also remove the camshaft pulleys from the camshafts and the rear timing cover from the cylinder head.

3 Remove any accessory brackets from the coolant pump.

4 Remove the bolts **(see illustration)** and detach the coolant pump from the engine. Note the location of any long bolts.

5 Clean the bolt threads and the threaded holes in the engine to remove corrosion and sealant.

6 Compare the new pump to the old one to make sure they're identical.

7 Remove all traces of old gasket sealant and O-ring from the engine.

8 Clean the engine and new water pump mating surfaces.

9 Carefully set a new O-ring in the groove of the pump **(see illustration)**.

10 Carefully attach the pump to the engine and thread the bolts into the holes finger-tight.

11 Refit the remaining bolts (if they also hold an accessory bracket in place, be sure to reposition the bracket at this time). Tighten them to the torque listed in this Chapter's Specifications in 1/4-turn increments. Don't

over tighten them or the pump may be distorted.

12 Refit all parts removed for access to the pump.

13 Refill and bleed the cooling system and check the auxiliary drivebelt tension (see Chapter 1). Start the engine and check for leaks.

9 Coolant temperature gauge sender unit – testing and renewal

⚠ *Warning: Wait until the engine is completely cool before beginning this procedure.*

1 The coolant temperature indicator system consists of a temperature gauge mounted in the instrument panel and a coolant temperature sender unit mounted on the engine directly below the distributor **(see illustration)**.

2 If an overheating indication occurs even when the engine is cold, check the wiring between the dash and the sender unit for a short-circuit to earth.

3 If the gauge is inoperative, test the circuit by briefly earthing the wire to the sender unit while the ignition is ON (engine not running for safety). If the gauge deflects full scale, renew the sender unit.

⚠ *Warning: This vehicle is equipped with electric cooling fans. Stay clear of the fan blades, which can come on even when the engine is not running. If the gauge doesn't respond, check for an open-circuit in the gauge wiring.*

4 If the sender unit is suspect, check the resistance of the sender with the engine cold and hot. The resistance should decrease as the temperature increases (when the engine is cool [53°C or cooler] the resistance should be approximately 140 ohms; when the engine is at normal operating temperature [85°C or warmer] the resistance should be approximately 30 to 46 ohms).

5 If the sender unit must be renewed, simply unscrew it from the engine and quickly fit the new one. Use sealant on the threads. There

8.4 Remove the coolant pump bolts (arrowed) and remove the pump

8.9 Fit a new O-ring (arrowed) into the groove

9.1 The coolant temperature sender unit (arrowed) is located near the distributor (single wire connection)

will be some coolant loss as the unit is removed, so be prepared to catch it. Check the coolant level after the renewal part has been fitted (see Chapter 1).

 Warning: Make sure the engine is completely cool before removing the sending unit.

10 Heater blower motor and circuit – testing and component renewal

Testing

1 Check the fuse (see Chapter 12) and all connections in the circuit for looseness and corrosion. Make sure the battery is fully charged.
2 Turn the ignition switch ON (engine not running).
3 Without disconnecting the blower motor, insert a bridging wire into the reverse of the blower motor connector blue/black wire **(see illustration)** and connect the other end of the bridging wire to earth. If the blower motor runs the fault lies with the blower fan switch, the blower resistor or related wiring.
4 If the motor didn't run with the bridging wire connected to earth, remove the bridging wire, disconnect the electrical connector at the blower motor and with a voltmeter measure the voltage between the connector blue/white wire and earth **(see illustration 10.3)**. If there is battery voltage present at the connector and the motor didn't run at any speed, renew

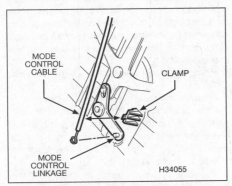

12.3a Disconnect the mode control cable . . .

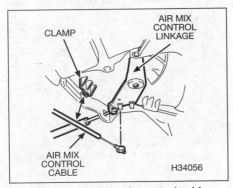

12.3b . . . and air mix control cable

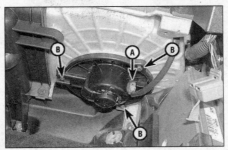

10.3 Insert a bridging wire into the rear of the blue/black wire of the blower motor connector (A) and connect it to earth – the blower motor is retained by three bolts (B)

the blower motor (see Section 11). If no battery voltage is present, check the blower motor relay or related wiring (see Chapter 12).
5 If the blower motor runs, but one or more speeds are inoperative, check the blower resistor for proper operation.
6 First remove the resistor from the heater housing (see Paragraph 7). Visually check the resistor for damage to the elements. Using an ohmmeter, check the resistor block for continuity between terminals 2 and 4 **(see illustration)**. If the resistance is not as specified or there are any open circuits, renew the blower resistor assembly.

Renewal

7 Lever out the glovebox door stops and lower the glovebox (see Chapter 11, Section 23, if necessary).
8 Remove the two screws and detach the blower motor resistor from the heater housing.
9 Refitting is the reverse of removal.

11 Heater blower motor – removal and refitting

Removal

1 Remove the passenger side glovebox, as described in Chapter 11, Section 23.

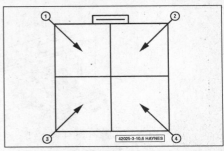

10.6 Blower motor resistor terminals – the resistance between terminals 2 and 4 should be 2 to 3 ohms

2 The blower motor unit is located under the dash, behind the glovebox.
3 Disconnect the electrical connector from the blower motor.
4 Remove the three retaining screws and remove the blower motor **(see illustration 10.3)**.
5 If you're renewing the blower motor itself, separate the blower motor from the fan wheel and place the fan on the new blower motor.

Refitting

6 Refitting is the reverse of removal. Check for proper operation.

12 Heating and air conditioning control panel – removal, refitting and cable adjustment

Removal

1 Disconnect the cable from the negative terminal of the battery (see Chapter 5A).

Heater control panel

2 Remove the driver's side lower facia panel, the glovebox and the front centre console (see Chapter 11).
3 Reach under the facia and disconnect the air mix control and mode control cable from the heater unit **(see illustrations)**.
4 Undo the four screws and pull the heater control panel out from the facia **(see illustration)**.

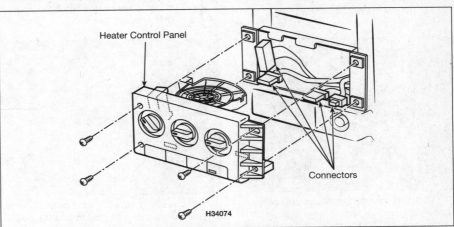

12.4 Undo the four screws and pull the heater control panel from the facia

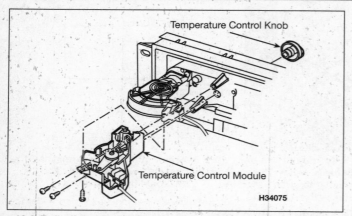

12.6 Pull off the control knob, undo the screws, and detach the control assembly from the panel

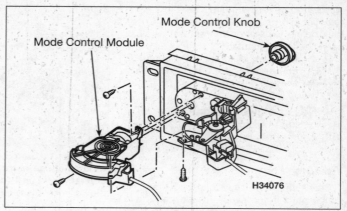

12.11 The mode control assembly is secured by three Torx screws

Disconnect the wiring plugs as the panel is withdrawn.

Air mix control cable

5 Remove the heater control panel as described earlier in this Section.

6 To remove the air mix control cable pull out the temperature control knob from the panel, undo the Torx screws, and separate the temperature control assembly from the panel **(see illustration)**.

7 Remove the two Torx screws and lift the temperature control shaft and bracket from the assembly.

8 Undo the single Torx screw, lift the temperature control lever, and remove the cable from the assembly.

Mode control cable

9 Remove the heater control panel as described earlier in this Section.

10 Pull the mode control knob from the control panel.

11 Undo the three Torx screws and separate the mode control assembly from the panel **(see illustration)**.

12 Remove the single Torx screw and clamp and lift the cable from the assembly.

Refitting

13 Refitting is the reverse of removal.

14 Run the engine and check for proper functioning of the heater and air conditioning system.

Adjustment

Temperature control cable(s)

15 To adjust the cable, disconnect the cable from the heater valve arm in the engine compartment and the air mix control arm under the dash.

16 Working in the passenger compartment, set the temperature control lever to MAX COOL.

17 Reattach the cable to the air mix control arm, then press the cable housing against the cable stop and snap the cable into the cable clamp.

18 Working in the engine compartment, turn the heater valve arm in the opposite direction of the cable clamp to the fully closed position and connect the cable to the arm. Hold the valve arm closed and remove any slack by pulling on the outer cable housing and connect the cable clamp.

13 Heater matrix – renewal

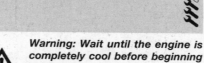

⚠ **Warning: Wait until the engine is completely cool before beginning this procedure.**

1 If the vehicle is equipped with air conditioning, have the system discharged by a dealer service department or automotive air conditioning repair facility (see Section 14). Disconnect the cable from the negative terminal of the battery (see Chapter 5A).

2 Drain the cooling system (see Chapter 1).

3 Disconnect the heater valve cable **(see illustration)**.

4 Working in the engine compartment, disconnect the heater hoses **(see illustration)** where they enter the bulkhead. Place a drain pan underneath the hoses to catch any coolant that runs out when the hoses are disconnected. Remove the heater unit mounting nut located above the heater hose inlet and outlet tubes **(see illustration)**.

Caution: Be careful not to damage or bend the fuel pipes or brake pipes when removing the nut.

5 Remove the complete facia as described in Chapter 11.

6 Remove the steering column bracket.

7 On models equipped with air conditioning, with the air conditioning system discharged, undo the two bolts and disconnect the air evaporator supply and return pipes from the bulkhead in the engine compartment.

8 Remove the wire harness clip from the heater housing, the two nuts retaining the

13.3 Detach the heater control cable (arrowed) from the heater valve using a small screwdriver to lift the cable end off the pin

13.4a Loosen the two heater hose clamps and disconnect the heater hoses (arrowed) from the heater matrix inlet and outlet pipes at the bulkhead

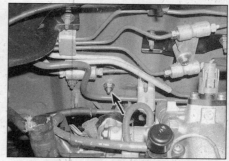

13.4b Remove the nut (arrowed) retaining the heater unit to the bulkhead

13.8 Heater unit retaining nuts (arrowed)

14.1 Evaporator housing condensation drain tube (arrowed)

14.8 Insert a thermometer into the centre air vent while operating the air conditioning system

heater housing to the bulkhead and remove the heater unit from the vehicle (see illustration).

9 Remove the screws from the heater matrix cover and the heater pipe clamp. Lift the heater matrix from the housing.

10 Refitting is the reverse of removal. Be sure to check the operation of the air control flaps. If any parts bind, correct the problem before refitting.

11 Refill and bleed the cooling system (see Chapter 1), reconnect the battery and start the engine. Check for coolant leaks and proper heater system operation. If equipped with air conditioning, have the system charged by a dealer service department or automotive air conditioning specialist.

14 Air conditioning and heating system – inspection and maintenance

⚠️ **Warning: The refrigeration circuit contains a refrigerant and it is therefore dangerous to disconnect any part of the system without specialised knowledge and equipment. The refrigerant is potentially dangerous and should only be handled by qualified persons. If it is splashed onto the skin it can cause frostbite. It is not itself poisonous, but in the presence of a naked flame (including a cigarette) it forms a poisonous gas. Uncontrolled discharging of the refrigerant is dangerous and potentially damaging to the environment.**

⚠️ **Warning: Do not operate the air conditioning system if it is known to be short of refrigerant, as this may damage the compressor.**

⚠️ **Warning: The air conditioning system is under high pressure. Do not loosen any hose fittings or remove any components until after the system has been discharged. Air conditioning refrigerant should be properly discharged at a dealer service department or by a qualified air conditioning specialist/repair facility. Always wear eye protection when disconnecting air conditioning system fittings.**

Air conditioning system

Caution: When renewing entire components, additional refrigerant oil should be added equal to the amount that is removed with the component being renewed – see the Specifications at the start of this Chapter. Be sure to read the container before adding any oil to the system, to make sure it is compatible with the R-134a system.

1 The following maintenance checks should be performed on a regular basis to ensure that the air conditioning continues to operate at peak efficiency.

 a) Inspect the condition of the compressor drivebelt. If it is worn or deteriorated, renew it (see Chapter 1).

 b) Check the drivebelt tension and, if necessary, adjust it (see Chapter 1).

 c) Inspect the system hoses. Look for cracks, bubbles, hardening and deterioration. Inspect the hoses and all fittings for oil bubbles or leakage. If there is any evidence of wear, damage or leakage, renew the hose(s).

 d) Inspect the condenser cooling fins for leaves, insects and any other foreign material that may have embedded itself in the fins. Use a 'fin comb' or compressed air to remove debris from the condenser.

 e) Make sure the system has the correct refrigerant charge.

 f) If you hear water sloshing around in the dash area or have water dripping on the carpet, slip off the evaporator housing condensation drain tube (located in the lower left-hand forward corner of the housing) and insert a piece of wire into both openings to check for blockage (see illustration).

2 It's a good idea to operate the system for about ten minutes at least once a month. This is particularly important during the winter months because long term non-use can cause hardening, and subsequent failure, of the seals. Note that using the Defrost function operates the compressor.

3 If the air conditioning system is not working properly, first make sure the compressor clutch is operating (see Section 15).

4 Because of the complexity of the air conditioning system and the special equipment necessary to service it, in-depth troubleshooting and repairs are not included in

this manual. However, simple checks and component renewal procedures are provided in this Chapter. For more complete information on the air conditioning system, refer to the *Haynes Air Conditioning Techbook*. However, simple component renewal procedures are provided in this Chapter.

5 The most common cause of poor cooling is simply a low system refrigerant charge. If a noticeable drop in system cooling ability occurs, one of the following quick checks will help you determine whether the refrigerant level is low. Should the system lose its cooling ability, the following procedure will help you pinpoint the cause.

Inspection

6 Warm the engine up to normal operating temperature.

7 Place the air conditioning temperature selector at the coldest setting and put the blower at the highest setting. Open the doors (to make sure the air conditioning system doesn't turn off as soon as it cools the passenger compartment).

8 Insert a thermometer in the centre air distribution duct (see illustration) while operating the air conditioning system – the temperature of the output air should be 19 to 25°C below the ambient air temperature (down to approximately 5°C). If the ambient (outside) air temperature is very high, say 44°C, the duct air temperature may be as high as 16°C, but generally the air conditioning is 19 to 25°C cooler than the ambient air.

9 If the air isn't as cold as it used to be, the system probably needs a charge. Further inspection or testing of the system is beyond the scope of the home mechanic and should be left to a professional.

Adding refrigerant

10 Adding refrigerant should only be carried out be a dealer service department or air conditioning specialist.

Heating systems

11 If the carpet under the heater matrix is damp, or if antifreeze vapour or steam is coming through the vents, the heater matrix is leaking. Remove it (see Section 13) and fit a new unit (most radiator repair workshops will not repair a leaking heater matrix).

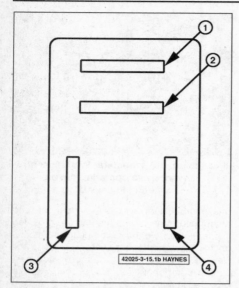

15.1a Compressor clutch relay terminals (except pre '97 5-door models) – there should be continuity between the terminals 1 and 2 with power and earth connected to terminals 3 and 4, and no continuity with the power disconnected

12 If the air coming out of the heater vents isn't hot, the problem could stem from any of the following causes:

a) *The thermostat is stuck open, preventing the engine coolant from warming-up enough to carry heat to the heater matrix. Renew the thermostat (see Section 3).*

b) *There is a blockage in the system, preventing the flow of coolant through the heater matrix. Feel both heater hoses at the bulkhead. They should be hot. If one of them is cold, there is an obstruction in one of the hoses or in the heater matrix, or the heater control valve is shut. Detach the hoses and back flush the heater matrix with a water hose. If the heater matrix is clear but circulation is impeded, remove the two hoses and flush them out with a water hose.*

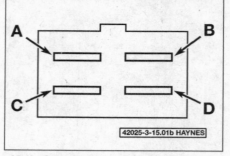

15.1b Compressor clutch relay terminals (pre '97 5-door models) – there should be continuity between terminals A and C with power and earth connected to terminals B and D, and no continuity with the power disconnected

c) *If flushing fails to remove the blockage from the heater matrix, the matrix must be renewed (see Section 13).*

15 Air conditioning compressor clutch circuit – testing

1 If the compressor clutch does not engage, the relay may be faulty. Remove the relay from the engine compartment fusebox (see Chapter 12) and check it (see illustrations).
2 If the relay is ok, check the voltage between the terminals of the relay socket and a good earth to make sure the relay is receiving power. If it isn't receiving power, there is an open-circuit that must be repaired.
3 After determining that the relay is receiving power, connect a bridging wire between terminals 1 and 2 in the relay socket and listen for a clicking sound from the compressor clutch.
4 If the compressor clutch doesn't click, remove the bridging wire, unplug the compressor clutch connector and check for continuity of the red wire that runs between the relay socket and the compressor clutch connector (see illustration). If there is an

open-circuit, repair it. If there is continuity, check the compressor clutch for damage.
5 Unplug the air conditioning low pressure switch (see illustration). Check for voltage between the pressure switch connector and a good earth with the ignition switch ON. There should be battery voltage on the blue/red wire. If there is no voltage, there is an open-circuit. If there is voltage, turn off the ignition and check for continuity between the terminals of the pressure switch itself. If there is none, there is a problem with the switch or the system pressure.

16 Air conditioning receiver-drier – removal and refitting

 Warning: The air conditioning system is under high pressure. Do not loosen any hose fittings or remove any components until after the system has been discharged. Air conditioning refrigerant should be properly discharged at a dealer service department or an automotive air conditioning specialist. Always wear eye protection when disconnecting air conditioning system fittings.
Caution: When renewing entire components, additional refrigerant oil should be added equal to the amount that is removed with the component being renewed – see the Specifications at the start of this Chapter. Be sure to read the can before adding any oil to the system, to make sure it is compatible with the R-134a system.

Removal

1 Have the refrigerant discharged (see above).
2 Disconnect the battery – see Chapter 5A.
3 Disconnect the refrigerant pipes from the receiver and plug the open fittings to prevent dirt and moisture entry (see illustration).
4 Remove the wheelarch liner, loosen the receiver-drier bracket pinch-bolt and lift the

15.4 Unplug the connector (arrowed) and check for continuity of the red wire that runs between the relay socket and the compressor clutch connector

15.5 The air conditioning pressure switch (arrowed) is located on the left-hand side of the engine compartment adjacent to the radiator on 5-door models, or on the top of the receiver-drier on other models

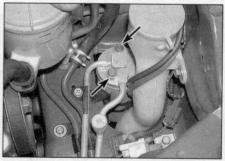

16.3 Working in the engine compartment, remove the bolts (arrowed) and disconnect both refrigerant pipe fittings from the receiver-drier

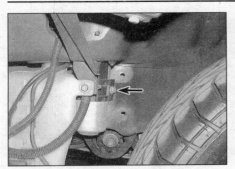

16.4 Working in the wheelarch, remove the receiver-drier bracket pinch-bolt (arrowed)

17.5 Remove the bolts (arrowed) and disconnect the pipes from the compressor

17.7 Remove the compressor mounting bolts (arrowed) and lower the compressor out from under the vehicle

receiver-drier out of the vehicle **(see illustration)**.

Refitting

5 Refitting is the reverse of removal, using new O-rings where the pipes connect to the receiver-drier.
6 Have the system evacuated, charged and leak-tested by an air conditioning specialist. If the receiver-drier was renewed, add the amount of refrigerant oil listed in the Specifications at the start of this Chapter.

17 Air conditioning compressor – removal and refitting

> ⚠ *Warning: The air conditioning system is under high pressure. Do not loosen any hose fittings or remove any components until after the system has been discharged. Air conditioning refrigerant should be properly discharged at a dealer service department or an automotive air conditioning specialist. Always wear eye protection when disconnecting air conditioning system fittings.*

Note: *The air conditioning compressor is a non-serviceable unit. It must be renewed complete. The receiver-drier should be renewed whenever the compressor is renewed.*

Removal

1 Have the air conditioning system refrigerant discharged by dealer service department or air conditioning specialist.
2 Apply the handbrake, block the rear wheels and jack up the front of the vehicle, supporting it securely on axle stands (see *Jacking and vehicle support*).
3 Remove the compressor drivebelt (see Chapter 1).
4 Remove the power steering pump (see Chapter 10).
5 Disconnect the refrigerant pipes from the compressor **(see illustration)**. Plug the open fittings to prevent entry of dirt and moisture.
6 Disconnect the compressor clutch wiring harness.

7 Unbolt the compressor **(see illustration)** from the mounting bracket and remove it from the vehicle.
8 The clutch may have to be transferred from the old compressor to the new unit.

Refitting

9 Here's how to calculate the amount of refrigerant oil for the new compressor:
a) Drain the refrigerant oil from the old compressor through the suction fitting and measure it in ml.
b) Subtract this volume from 120 ml.
c) The difference between these two figures is equal to the amount you should drain from the new compressor.
10 Refitting is otherwise the reverse of removal.
11 Have the system evacuated, recharged and leak-tested by a dealership service department or automotive air conditioning specialist.

18 Air conditioning condenser – removal and refitting

> ⚠ *Warning: The air conditioning system is under high pressure. Do not loosen any hose fittings or remove any components until after the system has been discharged. Air conditioning refrigerant should be properly discharged at a dealer service department or an automotive air conditioning specialist. Always wear eye protection when disconnecting air conditioning system fittings.*

Removal

1 Have the refrigerant discharged by a dealership service department or air conditioning specialist.
2 Disconnect the condenser fan electrical connector from the fan, then detach the fan wiring harness and the refrigerant pipe support bracket from the condenser fan shroud.
3 Disconnect the condenser hose and discharge pipe from the condenser **(see illustration)**.

4 Remove the bolt securing the condenser/compressor relay bracket.
5 Remove the condenser upper mounting bolts and or brackets. **Note:** *There is a bracket with two rubber mounts that secures the condenser to the radiator support.*
6 Lift the condenser from the vehicle. The condenser is removed with the condenser fan. Be careful not to damage the condenser fins or the radiator when removing or refitting the condenser.

Refitting

7 Refitting is the reverse of removal. **Note:** *Always renew all O-rings and lightly lubricate them with refrigerant oil before assembly.*
8 Have the system evacuated, charged and leak-tested by a dealer service department or air conditioning specialist. If a new condenser was fitted, add the correct amount of refrigerant oil (see Specifications at the start of this Chapter).

19 Air conditioning evaporator and expansion valve – removal and refitting

> ⚠ *Warning: The air conditioning system is under high pressure. Do not loosen any hose fittings or remove any components until after the system has been discharged. Air conditioning refrigerant should be properly*

18.3 Disconnect the condenser pipe and discharge pipe attaching bolts (arrowed) from the condenser

discharged into an EPA-approved recovery/recycling unit at a dealer service department or an automotive air conditioning repair facility. Always wear eye protection when disconnecting air conditioning system fittings.

Removal

1 Have the air conditioning system discharged by a dealer service department or automotive air conditioning specialist.

2 Disconnect the two pipes from the evaporator **(see illustration)**. Plug both pipes to prevent the entry of contaminants and moisture into the air conditioning system.

3 Remove the glovebox and the glovebox frame (see Chapter 11, Section 23).

4 Disconnect the electrical connector from the air conditioning thermostat and remove the wiring harness clips from the evaporator housing.

5 Remove the evaporator unit retaining screws and nuts, pull the evaporator unit out far enough to disconnect the drain hose and remove the unit from the vehicle **(see illustration)**.

6 Remove the screws and clips retaining the evaporator case halves together, remove the air conditioning thermostat and separate the housing **(see illustrations)**.

7 Remove the evaporator matrix from the housing and remove the expansion valve, if necessary.

Refitting

8 Refitting is the reverse of removal.

19.2 Disconnect the refrigerant pipes (arrowed) from the evaporator

19.5 Evaporator assembly retaining nuts and bolt locations (arrowed)

19.6a Remove the screws and detach the clips (arrowed) from the front . . .

19.6b . . . and rear of the evaporator housing

9 Have the system evacuated, charged and leak-tested by a dealer service department or automotive air conditioning specialist. If a new evaporator was fitted, add the correct amount of refrigerant oil (see the Specifications at the start of this Chapter).

Chapter 4 Part A:
Fuel and exhaust systems

Contents

Degrees of difficulty

Easy, suitable for novice with little experience	Fairly easy, suitable for beginner with some experience	Fairly difficult, suitable for competent DIY mechanic	Difficult, suitable for experienced DIY mechanic	Very difficult, suitable for expert DIY or professional

Specifications

General
Manufacturer's engine codes*:

1.4 litre:
    D14A2, D14A3, D14A4, D14A8 ....   66 kW SOHC 16V non-VTEC
1.5 litre:
    D15Z3, D15Z6, D15Z8 ....   85 kW SOHC 16V VTEC-E
1.6 litre:
    D16Y2 ....   93 kW SOHC 16V VTEC
    D16Y3, D16B2 ....   83 kW SOHC 16V non-VTEC
    D16Y5 ....   86 kW SOHC 16V VTEC-E
    D16Y6, D16Y8 ....   92 kW SOHC 16V VTEC
    D16Y7 ....   78 kW SOHC 16V non-VTEC
    B16A2 ....   118 kW DOHC 16V VTEC
1.8 litre:
    B18C4 ....   125 kW DOHC 16V VTEC

See 'Vehicle identification' in the Reference section

System type
All models ....   Honda PGM-FI (Programmable Fuel Injection) sequential injection system

Fuel system data

Fuel pump type	Electric, immersed in tank

Fuel pressure (with regulator vacuum hose disconnected):

D14A3, D14A4, D15Z6 engine codes	2.3 to 2.8 bar
D16Y5, D16Y7, D16Y8 engine codes	2.7 to 3.2 bar
D14A8, D14A2, D15Z3, D15Z8, D16Y2, D16Y3, D16Y6,	
D16B2, B16A2 engine codes	2.8 to 3.3 bar
B18C4 engine code	3.3 to 2.8 bar

Specified idle speed:

D15Z6, D16Y5 engine codes	700 ± 50 rpm
D14A2, D14A3, D14A4, D14A8, D15Z3, D15Z8, D16Y2, D16Y2,	
D16Y3, D16Y6, D16Y7, D16Y8, B16A2 engine codes	750 ± 50 rpm
B18C4 engine code	800 ± 50 rpm
Idle mixture CO content	0.1 % maximum
Injector resistance	10 to 13 ohms

Fuel level sender resistance:

Full position	3 to 5 ohms
Half position	25.5 to 39.5 ohms
Empty position	105 to 110 ohms
CKP, TDC and CYP sensor resistance (see text)	350 to 700 ohms

Recommended fuel

Minimum octane rating	95 RON unleaded (UK unleaded premium). Leaded fuel must **not** be used

Torque wrench settings

	Nm	lbf ft
Fast Idle Thermo valve	10	7
Fuel filter service bolt:		
6 mm bolt	12	9
12 mm banjo bolt (all models)	33	24
Fuel rail mounting nuts	12	9
Idle Air Control valve	16	12
Intake Air Temperature sensor	6	4
Knock sensor	31	23
Oxygen sensor	44	32
Throttle body mounting nuts/bolts	20	15

1 General information

The fuel system consists of a fuel tank, an electric fuel pump (located in the fuel tank), a fuel pump relay, the fuel rail and fuel injectors, an air cleaner assembly and a throttle body unit. All models are equipped with a Sequential Electronic Fuel Injection (SEFI) system.

Fuel injection system

Sequential Electronic Fuel Injection uses timed impulses to inject the fuel directly into the intake port of each cylinder according to its firing order. The injectors are controlled by the Powertrain Control Module (PCM). The PCM monitors various engine parameters and delivers the exact amount of fuel required into the intake ports. The throttle body serves only to control the amount of air passing into the system. Because each cylinder is equipped with its own injector, much better control of the fuel/air mixture ratio is possible **(see illustrations)**.

Fuel pump and pipes

Fuel is circulated from the fuel tank to the fuel injection system, and back to the fuel tank, through a pair of metal pipes running along the underside of the vehicle. An electric fuel pump and fuel level sender unit is located inside the fuel tank. A vapour return system routes all vapours back to the fuel tank through a separate return pipe.

The PGM-FI main relay (fuel pump relay) is equipped with a primary and secondary voltage circuit. With the ignition switch ON, the primary circuit supplies current to the PCM, the fuel injectors and the secondary circuit. The secondary circuit supplies current to the fuel pump. The secondary circuit is energised for two seconds with the ignition switch ON and the engine not running, and constantly with the engine running.

Exhaust system

The exhaust system includes an exhaust manifold, an oxygen sensor, a three-way (reduction) catalytic converter, a silencer and a tail pipe.

The catalytic converter is an emission control device added to the exhaust system to reduce pollutants. Refer to Chapter 4B for more information regarding the catalytic converter.

Caution: If the stereo in your vehicle is equipped with an anti-theft system, make sure you have the correct activation code before disconnecting the battery.

2 Fuel system depressurisation

1 Locate the fuel pump electrical connector (see Section 5). Disconnect it, then start the engine and let it run until it stalls. Detach the cable from the negative battery terminal (see Chapter 5A).
2 Unscrew the fuel filler cap to relieve pressure built-up in the fuel tank.
3 Relieve residual pressure by opening the fuel outlet pipe at the fuel filter. On some models, this is done by loosening the service bolt that's threaded into the banjo bolt on the outlet side of the fuel filter. On other models, loosen the banjo bolt (there is no separate service bolt).

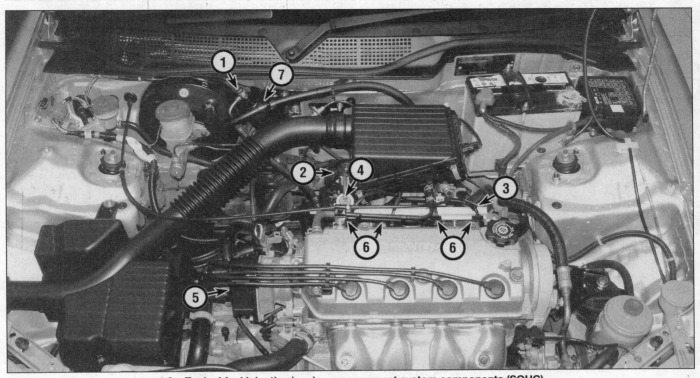

1.2a Typical fuel injection/engine management system components (SOHC)

| 1 Fuel filter banjo bolt | 3 Fuel rail | 5 Distributor | 7 Fuel filter |
| 2 Throttle body | 4 Fuel pressure regulator | 6 Fuel injectors | |

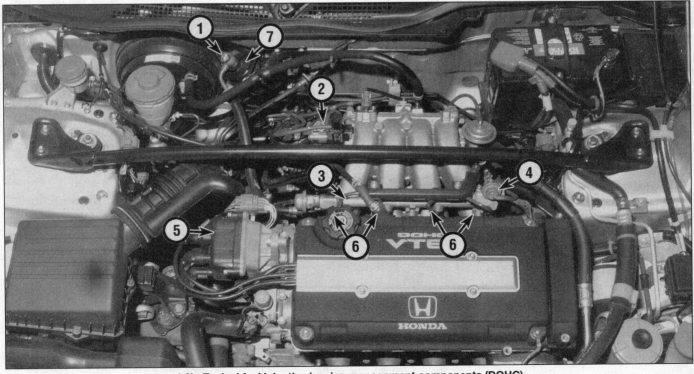

1.2b Typical fuel injection/engine management components (DOHC)

| 1 Fuel filter banjo bolt | 3 Fuel rail | 5 Distributor | 7 Fuel filter |
| 2 Throttle body | 4 Fuel pressure regulator | 6 Fuel injectors | |

2.4 When slackening the banjo bolt, use a second spanner to counterhold the fuel filter

4 You'll need two spanners for this procedure. On models with a separate service bolt, one to loosen the service bolt and one to hold the banjo bolt; on models with only a banjo bolt, one to loosen the banjo bolt and another to hold the fuel pipe fitting (see illustration).

5 Place a clean rag around the fuel pipe fitting on top of the fuel filter.

6 While holding the banjo bolt or fuel pipe fitting, slowly loosen the service bolt or banjo bolt one complete turn – fuel will begin to flow from the fitting. Allow the pressure to be relieved completely, then remove the bolt. If you're working on a vehicle with a separate service bolt, fit a new service bolt sealing washer. If you're working on a vehicle with only a banjo bolt, fit a new sealing washer on each side of the fuel pipe fitting.

7 After all work to the fuel system has been performed, refit the service bolt or banjo bolt and tighten it to the torque listed in this Chapter's Specifications.

3 Fuel pump/fuel pressure – testing

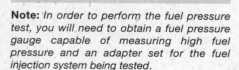

Note: In order to perform the fuel pressure test, you will need to obtain a fuel pressure gauge capable of measuring high fuel pressure and an adapter set for the fuel injection system being tested.

General checks

1 Check that there is adequate fuel in the fuel tank.

2 Verify the fuel pump actually runs. Have an assistant turn the ignition switch to ON – you should hear a brief whirring noise (approximately two seconds) as the pump comes on and pressurises the system. **Note:** The fuel pump is easily heard through the fuel tank filler neck. If there is no response from the fuel pump (makes no sound) proceed to Paragraph 9 and check the fuel pump electrical circuit.

Pump output and pressure test

3 Connect a fuel pressure gauge to the test

3.3a This aftermarket fuel pressure testing kit contains all the necessary fitting and adapters, along with a fuel pressure gauge, to test most automotive fuel systems

port on the fuel filter (see illustrations). The gauge is connected in place of the service bolt or banjo bolt (see Section 2).

4 Turn the ignition switch ON (engine not running) with the air conditioning OFF. The fuel pump should run for about two seconds – pressure should register on the gauge and should hold steady.

5 Start the engine and let it idle at normal operating temperature. The gauge reading should be approximately 0.6 bar below the value listed in this Chapter's Specifications. Now, disconnect the vacuum hose from the fuel pressure regulator – the pressure should increase immediately to the value listed in this Chapter's Specifications. If the pressures are correct, the system is operating properly.

6 If the pressure was too high with the vacuum hose connected, apply 22.4 to 26 mm of vacuum to the pressure regulator, using a hand-held vacuum pump (see illustration). If the pressure drops, repair the vacuum source to the regulator. If the pressure does not drop, renew the regulator.

7 If the fuel pressure is not within specifications, check the following:

a) If the pressure is higher than specified, check for vacuum to the fuel pressure regulator (see illustration). Vacuum must fluctuate with the increase or decrease in the engine rpm. If vacuum is present,

3.6 Connect a hand-held vacuum pump to the fuel pressure regulator and read the fuel pressure with vacuum applied. The pressure should decrease as the vacuum is increased

3.3b Connect a fuel pressure gauge to the service port or in place of the banjo bolt

check for a pinched or blocked fuel return hose or pipe. If the return pipe/hose is OK, renew the regulator.

b) If the pressure is lower than specified, change the fuel filter to rule out the possibility of a blocked filter. If the pressure is still low, fit a fuel pipe shut-off adapter between the pressure regulator and the return pipe (this can be fabricated from fuel pipe, a shut-off valve and the necessary fittings to mate with the pressure regulator and the return pipe, or, instead of a shut-off valve, use fuel hose that can be pinched with a pair of pliers). With the valve open (or the hose not pinched), start the engine (if possible) and slowly close the valve or pinch the hose (only pinch the hose on the adapter you fabricated). If the pressure rises above the maximum specified pressure, renew the regulator (see Section 14).

⚠️ **Warning: Don't allow the fuel pressure to exceed 4.0 bar. Also, don't attempt to restrict the vehicle's return line by pinching it, as the pipe will be damaged.**

c) If the pressure is still low with the fuel return pipe restricted, an injector (or injectors) may be leaking (see Section 15) or the in-tank fuel pump may be faulty.

8 After the testing is done, relieve the fuel pressure (see Section 2) and remove the fuel pressure gauge.

Pump electrical circuit check

9 If the pump does not turn on (makes no

3.7 Check for vacuum at the fuel pressure regulator hose (arrowed)

3.11a The fuel injection main relay is located under the facia on the right-hand side on 5-door models (arrowed) . . .

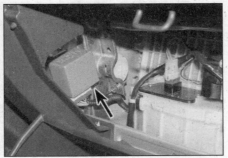

3.11b . . . and on the left-hand side (arrowed) behind the glovebox on other models

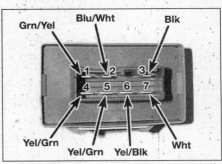

3.11c Fuel injection PGM-FI (main) relay terminals

sound) with the ignition switch in the ON position, check the fuel injection (PGM-FI) main relay fuse (see Chapter 12). If the fuse is blown, renew the fuse and see if the pump works. If the pump now works, check for a short in the circuit between the PGM-FI relay and the fuel pump.

10 If the fuel pump does not activate, check for power to the fuel pump at the fuel tank. Remove the rear seat and the fuel pump access cover (see Section 5). Disconnect the fuel pump electrical connector and check for battery voltage at the yellow/green wire terminal of the harness connector as the ignition key is turned ON and OFF. Also check for continuity to a good chassis earth point at the black or black/white wire terminal. If voltage and earth are present at the fuel pump connector and the fuel pump does not operate when connected, renew the fuel pump.

11 If no voltage is present at the pump, check the PGM-FI relay circuit. With the help of an assistant, turn the ignition key ON and OFF (engine not running) while checking for battery voltage at the relay connector (terminals 5 and 7 should have voltage with the ignition key ON) **(see illustrations)**. If battery voltage does not exist, trace the circuit for an open or shorted condition. **Note 1:** *On some vehicles, if oil pressure drops below the specified pressure level, the oil pressure switch will act as a fuel pressure cut-off device. Be sure to check the oil pressure switch and circuit in the event of a difficult problem diagnosing the fuel pump circuit (refer to the wiring diagrams at the end of Chapter 12).* **Note 2:** *The anti-theft system (where fitted) is equipped with a fuel enable circuit. If this system is malfunctioning it will not allow the PCM to signal the fuel pump relay or the engine to crank over. Be sure to check the anti-theft system and circuit in the event of a difficult problem diagnosing the fuel pump circuit.*

12 If battery voltage exists, remove and check the relay. Using jumper wires, connect battery positive voltage to terminal 2 and earth terminal 1, then, using an ohmmeter, check for continuity between terminals 4 and 5. If there is no continuity, renew the relay.

13 If there is continuity, connect the positive jumper wire to terminal 5 and earth terminal 3,

then check for continuity between terminals 6 and 7. If there is no continuity, renew the relay.

14 If there is continuity, connect the positive jumper wire to terminal 6 and earth terminal 1, then check for continuity between terminals 4 and 5. If there is no continuity, renew the relay.

4 Fuel pipes and fittings – repair and renewal

1 Because fuel pipes used on fuel-injected vehicles are under high pressure, they require special consideration. Always relieve the fuel pressure before servicing fuel pipes or fittings (see Section 2).

2 Metal fuel supply and vapour pipes extend from the fuel tank to the engine compartment. The pipes are secured to the underbody or chassis with retaining clips. Flexible hose connects the metal pipes to the fuel tank, fuel filter and fuel rail. Fuel pipes must be occasionally inspected for leaks or damage.

3 In the event of any fuel line damage, metal pipes may be repaired with steel tubing of the same diameter, provided the correct fittings are used. Never repair a damaged section of steel line with rubber hose and hose clamps. Rubber fuel hose must be renewed with fuel hose specifically designed for a high pressure fuel injection system; others may fail from the high pressures of this system. Flexible pipes with quick-connect fittings must be renewed with factory parts.

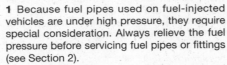

4.5 Be sure the fuel hoses (arrowed) can't rub against anything

4 If evidence of contamination is found in the system or fuel filter during dismantling, the line should be disconnected and blown through. Check the fuel filter on the fuel pump module for damage and deterioration.

5 Don't route fuel line or hose within four inches of any part of the exhaust system or within ten inches of the catalytic converter. Fuel line must never be allowed to chafe against the engine, body or frame **(see illustration)**. A minimum of 6 mm clearance must be maintained around a fuel line.

6 When renewing a fuel line, remove all fasteners attaching the fuel line to the vehicle body.

Steel tubing

7 If renewal of a steel fuel line or emission line is called for, use steel tubing meeting the manufacturer's specification.

8 Don't use aluminium tubing to renew steel tubing. This material cannot withstand normal vehicle vibration.

9 Some fuel pipes have threaded fittings with O-rings **(see illustration)**. Any time the fittings are loosened to service or renew components:

a) *Use a flare-nut spanner on the fitting nut and a counterhold spanner on the stationary portion of the fitting while loosening and tightening the fittings.*

b) *Check all O-rings for cuts, cracks and deterioration. Renew any that appear hardened, worn or damaged.*

c) *If the pipes are renewed, always use original equipment parts, or parts that meet the original equipment standards.*

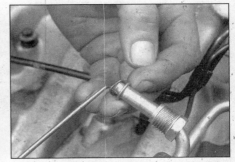

4.9 Always renew the fuel pipe O-rings (where fitted)

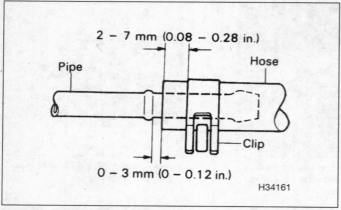

4.10 When attaching a section of rubber hose to a metal pipe, be sure to overlap the hose as shown – secure the hose to the pipe with a new hose clamp of the proper type

4.11 To disconnect a quick-connect fitting, press the tabs in and pull the fitting off the tube (arrowed)

Rubber hose

10 Note the routing of the hose and the orientation of the clamps to assure that renewal sections are installed in exactly the same manner. Do not kink or twist the hose. When attaching hoses to metal pipes overlap them **(see illustration)**. Tighten the clamp sufficiently to ensure a leak-free fit, but do not overtighten the clamp or damage to the rubber hose will result.

Quick-connect flexible hose

11 Some models may be equipped with flexible hose and quick-connect fittings **(see illustration)**. There are various methods of disconnecting the fittings, depending upon the type of quick-connect fitting installed on the fuel pipe. To disconnect a typical quick-connect fitting, push the fitting into the fuel pipe, squeeze the tabs together and pull the fitting off the fuel pipe; do not use any tools to disconnect the fitting. Clean any debris from around the fitting. Disconnect the fitting at each end of the flexible hose and carefully remove the hose from the vehicle.

Caution: Do not attempt to repair these types of fuel pipes in the event the pipe becomes damaged. Renew the entire fuel pipe as an assembly.

12 Refitting is the reverse of removal with the following additions:
 a) *Clean the quick-connect fittings with a lint-free cloth.*
 b) *Inspect the plastic retainer for damage and renew it if necessary.*
 c) *Align the tabs with the openings in the retainer and push the pipes together until the tabs click into place.*
 d) *After connecting a quick-connect fitting, check the integrity of the connection by attempting to pull the pipes apart.*
 e) *Turn the ignition key ON and OFF several times and check for leaks at the fitting, before starting the engine.*

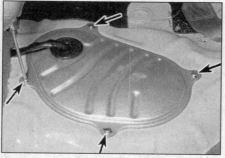

5.4a Remove the screws (arrowed) from the fuel pump/fuel level sender unit access cover; this is the 3-door cover . . .

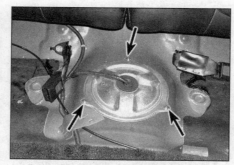

5.4b . . . and this is the 4-door cover

5.4c Unplug the electric connector and detach the fuel pipe

5.5 Remove the nuts that retain the fuel pump to the fuel tank

5 Fuel pump –
removal and refitting

Removal

1 Detach the cable from the negative battery terminal (see Chapter 5A).
2 Relieve the fuel system pressure (see Section 2).
3 On all except 3-door Hatchback and 4-door Saloon models, remove the fuel tank as described in Section 7. On 3-door Hatchback and 4-door Saloon models, remove the rear seat cushion (see Chapter 11 if necessary).
4 On 3-door Hatchback and 4-door Saloon models, remove the bolts that retain the fuel pump access cover **(see illustrations)**. Unplug the electrical connector from the fuel pump and detach the fuel pies **(see illustration)**.
5 On all models, remove the fuel pump assembly retaining nuts **(see illustration)**.

6 Remove the fuel pump from the tank (**see illustration**).

7 Remove the electrical connector protective cover (**see illustration**).

8 Remove the electrical connector from the fuel pump (**see illustration**).

9 Squeeze the hose clamps with a pair of pliers – remove the upper clamp from the hose and slide the lower clamp half-way up the hose, off the fuel pump inlet.

10 Separate the pump from the fuel pump bracket.

11 Remove the sock filter from the end of the pump (**see illustration**).

Refitting

12 Refitting is the reverse of removal with the following additions:

a) *If the fuel pipe is equipped with a banjo bolt fitting, renew the sealing washers.*

b) *If refitting a new fuel pump on a model with a quick-connect fitting, obtain a new plastic retainer and insert it into the connector on the flexible hose.*

c) *Fit a new gasket on the cover plate flange.*

---

6 Fuel level sender unit –
testing and renewal

1 Remove the rear seat (see Chapter 11).

2 Remove the fuel level sender unit protective cover (if equipped) and the access cover from the floor of the vehicle (**see illustrations**).

3 Disconnect the electrical connector from the sender unit (**see illustration**).

4 The sender unit is held in place by a locking ring, use a brass punch and tap on the locking ring (**see illustration**) until the tabs line up with the recess in the housing.

⚠️ *Warning: A steel punch shouldn't be used, since a spark could cause an explosion.*

5 Lift the fuel level sender unit from the tank (**see illustration**). Be careful not to damage the float arm.

6 Position the probes of an ohmmeter on the

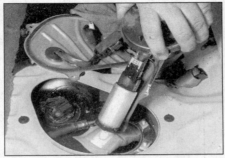

5.6 Lift the pump from the access hole. Be sure to angle it slightly to avoid damaging the pump filter attached to the base

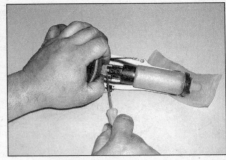

5.7 Remove the protective cover from the main electrical connector

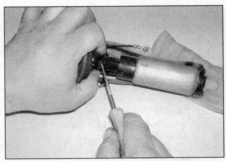

5.8 Lift the tab on the main electrical connector and disconnect it from the fuel pump

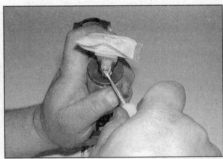

5.11 Prise off the retaining clip with a small screwdriver and detach the filter from the pump

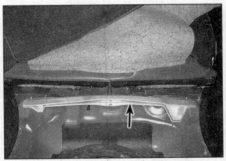

6.2a On 5-door models, remove the protective bar . . .

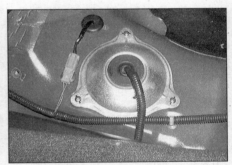

6.2b . . . and the sender unit access cover

6.3 Disconnect the electrical connector

6.4 If there's a locking ring, use a brass punch to remove it; a steel punch may cause sparks

6.5 Lift the fuel level sender unit through the access hole

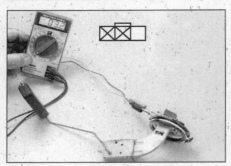

6.6 Measure the resistance of the fuel level sender unit at the indicated terminals with the float raised (full tank), halfway down and near the bottom (empty)

electrical connector terminals and check for resistance **(see illustration)**.

7 First, check the resistance of the sending unit with the float in the bottom (fuel tank empty) position. The resistance of the sending unit should be within the range listed in this Chapter's Specifications.

8 Now check the resistance of the unit with the float in the half-tank position and compare the reading to the value listed in this Chapter's Specifications.

9 Finally, lift the float to the full-tank position and measure the resistance.

10 If the readings are incorrect or there is very little change in resistance as the float travels from full to empty, renew the sending unit.

11 Refitting is the reverse of removal. Be sure to use a new gasket under the sealing flange.

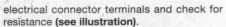

7 Fuel tank – removal and refitting

Note: *The following procedure is much easier to perform if the fuel tank is empty.*

Removal

1 Relieve the fuel system pressure (see Section 2).

2 Detach the cable from the negative terminal of the battery (see Chapter 5A).

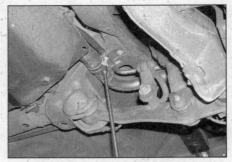

7.6 Remove the clamps that retain the rubber fuel hoses to the inlet and vent pipes

3 Remove the rear seat (see Chapter 11) and disconnect the fuel level sender unit. On 3-door Hatchback and 4-door Saloon models, disconnect the fuel pump electrical connectors and fuel hoses (see Sections 5 and 6).

4 Raise the vehicle and place it securely on axle stands (see *Jacking and vehicle support*).

5 Undo the bolts and remove the splash panel that protects the fuel filler pipe.

6 Label and disconnect the fuel hoses and any brackets that may secure them **(see illustration)**.

7 Support the fuel tank with a trolley jack. Position a wood block between the jack head and the fuel tank to protect the tank.

8 Disconnect both fuel tank retaining straps and pivot them down until they are hanging out of the way **(see illustration)**.

9 Remove the tank from the vehicle.

Refitting

10 Refitting is the reverse of removal.

8 Fuel tank cleaning and repair – general information

1 All repairs to the fuel tank or filler neck should be carried out by a specialist who has experience in this critical and potentially dangerous work. Even after cleaning and flushing of the fuel system, explosive fumes

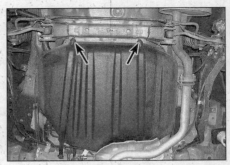

7.8 Support the fuel tank and remove the nuts from the strap bolts (arrowed)

can remain and ignite during repair of the tank.

2 If the fuel tank is removed from the vehicle, it should not be placed in an area where sparks or open flames could ignite the fumes coming out of the tank. Be especially careful inside garages where a gas-type appliance is located, because the pilot light or burner could cause an explosion.

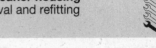

9 Air cleaner housing – removal and refitting

Removal

1 Disconnect the intake air temperature (IAT) sensor wiring where necessary.

2 Remove the air intake duct and resonator, then undo the bolts and remove the air cleaner housing **(see illustrations)**.

Refitting

3 Refitting is the reverse of removal.

10 Accelerator cable – removal, refitting and adjustment

Removal

1 Loosen the locknut and remove the

9.2a Remove the duct and resonator . . .

9.2b . . . and slacken the clamp (arrowed) to remove the air cleaner

9.2c The air cleaner housing is secured by bolts (arrowed)

accelerator cable from its bracket (see illustration).

2 Rotate the throttle shaft quadrant until the cable is out of its guide groove, and detach the cable from the quadrant (see illustration).

3 Working underneath the facia, detach the cable from the accelerator pedal (see illustration).

4 Pull the grommet from the bulkhead and pull the cable through the bulkhead from the engine compartment side.

Refitting

5 Refitting is the reverse of removal. Use the locknut and adjusting nut to get the throttle cable deflection as close as possible to the correct final setting, then adjust the cable as described below.

Adjustment

6 Start the engine and warm it up until the cooling fan comes on, then let it idle.

7 Check cable deflection (side-to-side slack) in the cable between the quadrant and the cable bracket (see illustration). Deflection should be 10 to 12 mm. If deflection is not within specifications, loosen the locknut and turn the adjusting nut until the deflection is as specified. Then tighten the locknut and turn the engine off.

8 After you have adjusted the throttle cable, have an assistant help you verify that the throttle valve opens all the way when you depress the accelerator pedal to the floor and that it returns to the idle position when you release the accelerator. Verify the cable operates smoothly. It must not bind or stick.

9 If the vehicle is equipped with an automatic transmission, adjust the transmission throttle control cable (see Chapter 7B).

11 Fuel injection system – general information

The Programmed Fuel Injection (PGM-FI) system (see illustrations 1.2a and 1.2b) consists of three sub-systems: air intake, electronic control and fuel delivery. The system uses a Powertrain Control Module (PCM) along with the sensors (coolant temperature sensor, throttle position sensor, manifold absolute pressure sensor etc) to determine the proper air/fuel ratio under all operating conditions.

The fuel injection system and the emissions control system are closely linked in function and design. For additional information, refer to Chapter 4B.

Air intake system

The air intake system consists of the air cleaner, the air intake ducts, the throttle body, the idle control system and the intake manifold. A resonator in the air intake tube provides silencing as air is drawn into the system.

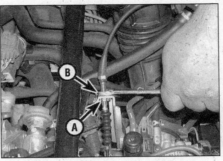

10.1 Slacken the locknut and detach the cable from its bracket

A Adjusting nut   *B Locknut*

10.3 Pull the accelerator cable end out and then lift the cable out of the recess in the pedal

The throttle body is a single barrel design; either downdraught or sidedraught depending on engine code. The lower/side portion of the throttle body is heated by engine coolant to prevent icing in cold weather. The idle adjusting screw is located on top of the throttle body. A throttle position sensor is attached to the throttle shaft to monitor changes in the throttle opening.

Electronic control system

The electronic control system consists of the Powertrain Control Module (PCM) and the following components:

a) *Heated Oxygen sensors (HO$_2$S) – The HO$_2$S generates a voltage signal that varies with the difference between the oxygen content of the exhaust and the oxygen in the surrounding air.*

b) *Crankshaft Position/Top Dead Centre/Cylinder Position (CKP/TDC/CYP) sensors – The CKP/TDC/CYP sensors are an integral part of the distributor, consisting of separate signal rotors and pick-up units for each sensor. The CKP signal is used by the PCM to determine fuel injection timing, ignition timing and engine speed (rpm). The TDC sensor signal is used by the PCM to determine ignition timing during engine starting. The CYP sensor signal is used by the PCM to determine timing for sequential fuel injection.*

c) *Crankshaft speed Fluctuation (CKF) sensor – The CKF sensor provides*

10.2 Remove the cable end from the throttle shaft quadrant (arrowed)

10.7 Measure the side-to-side cable deflection (arrowed)

information on changes in the rotational speed of the crankshaft. If the rotational speed changes beyond a set limit, the PCM concludes that a misfire has occurred.

d) *Engine Coolant Temperature (ECT) sensor – The ECT monitors engine coolant temperature and sends the PCM a voltage signal that affects PCM control of the fuel mixture, ignition timing, and EGR operation.*

e) *Intake Air Temperature (IAT) sensor – The IAT provides the PCM with intake air temperature information. The PCM uses this information to control fuel flow, ignition timing, and EGR system operation (if equipped).*

f) *Throttle Position Sensor (TPS) – The throttle position sensor (TPS) is located on the end of the throttle shaft on the throttle body. By monitoring the output voltage from the TPS, the PCM can determine fuel delivery based on throttle valve angle (driver demand). A broken or loose TPS can cause intermittent bursts of fuel from the injector and an unstable idle because the PCM thinks the throttle is moving.*

g) *Manifold Absolute Pressure (MAP) sensor – The Manifold Absolute Pressure (MAP) sensor monitors the intake manifold pressure changes resulting from changes in engine load and speed and converts the information into a voltage output. The PCM uses the MAP sensor to* control fuel delivery and ignition timing. The PCM will receive information as a voltage signal that will vary from 1.0 to 1.5 volts at closed throttle (high vacuum) and 4.0 to 4.5 volts at wide open throttle (low vacuum). The MAP sensor is located on the throttle body.

h) **Barometric pressure (BARO) sensor –** This sensor signals the atmospheric pressure to the PCM. It's built into the PCM.

i) **Vehicle Speed Sensor (VSS) –** The vehicle speed sensor provides information to the PCM to indicate vehicle speed.

j) **Power Steering Pressure (PSP) switch** – The PSP switch is used to inform the PCM when the power steering load is high. The PCM can then compensate for the added load by raising the idle speed, via the IAC valve, as necessary.

k) **Knock sensor –** The knock sensor detects the vibrations of spark knock and signals the PCM to retard the ignition timing.

l) **Transmission sensors –** In addition to the vehicle speed sensor, the PCM receives input signals from the following sensors inside the automatic transmission or connected to it: the turbine shaft speed sensor, the transmission fluid temperature sensor, and the transmission range sensor.

m) **Air conditioning clutch control switch –** When battery voltage is applied to the air conditioning compressor solenoid, a signal is sent to the PCM, which interprets the signal as an added load created by the compressor and increases engine idle speed accordingly to compensate.

n) **PGM-FI main (fuel pump) relay –** The fuel pump relay is activated by the PCM with the ignition switch in the Start or Run position. When the ignition switch is turned ON, the relay is activated to supply initial line pressure to the system. The PGM-FI main relay is in the power distribution box in the engine compartment. For more information on fuel pump check and renewal, refer to Section 3 and 5.

Fuel delivery system

The fuel delivery system consists of these components: The fuel pump, the pressure regulator, the fuel injectors, the fuel pulsation damper (some models) and the main relay.

The fuel pump is an in-tank type. Fuel is drawn through a filter into the pump, flows through the fuel delivery line, passes through another filter and is delivered to the injectors.

The pressure regulator maintains a constant fuel pressure to the injectors. Excess fuel is routed back to the fuel tank through the return line.

The injectors are solenoid-actuated, constant stroke, pintle types consisting of a solenoid, plunger, needle valve and housing. When current is applied to the solenoid coil, the needle valve raises and pressurised fuel fills the injector housing and squirts out the nozzle. The injection quantity is determined by the length of time the valve is open (the length of time during which current is supplied to the solenoid coils).

Injector open time is determined by the Powertrain Control Module (PCM). It contains a basic open time for various combinations of engine speed and air flow. This information is combined with inputs from the engine sensors to arrive at a final open time for a given set of conditions.

The main relay is installed in the left or right side of the scuttle depending on model. It contains one relay for the Powertrain Control Module (PCM), fuel injectors and the other relay. The other relay supplies power to the fuel pump.

12 Fuel injection system – inspection

1 Check all electrical connectors – especially earth connections. Loose connectors and poor earth connections can cause at least half of all engine control system problems.

2 Verify that the battery is fully-charged, because the Powertrain Control Module (PCM) and sensors cannot operate properly without adequate supply voltage.

3 Refer to Chapter 1 and check the air filter element. A dirty or partially-blocked filter will reduce performance and economy.

4 Check fuel pump operation (Section 3). If the fuel pump fuse is blown, renew it and see if it blows again. If it does, refer to Chapter 12 and the wiring diagrams and look for a wiring fault in the harness to the fuel pump.

5 Inspect the vacuum hoses connected to the intake manifold for damage, deterioration and leakage.

6 Remove the air intake duct from the throttle body and check for dirt, carbon, varnish, or other residue in the throttle body, particularly around the throttle plate. An extremely dirty throttle body requires renewal.

Caution: The throttle bodies on these engines have a protective coating on their bores, throttle plates, and shafts. Do not try to clean the throttle body, since you might damage the coating and do more harm than good.

7 With the engine running, place an automotive stethoscope against each injector, one at a time, and listen for a clicking sound that indicates operation **(see illustration)**. **Note:** *If you don't have a stethoscope, you can place the tip of a long screwdriver against the injector and listen through the handle.*

8 With the engine off and the fuel injector electrical connectors disconnected, measure the resistance of each injector with an ohmmeter **(see illustration)**. Check the specifications at the beginning of this Chapter for the correct resistance.

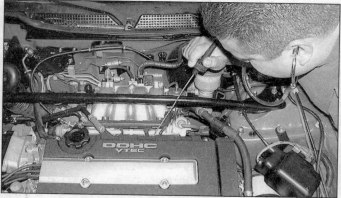

12.7 Use a stethoscope or screwdriver to determine if the injector are working properly – they should make a steady clicking sound that rises and falls with engine speed changes

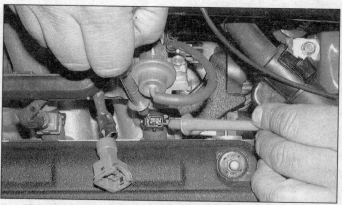

12.8 Disconnect the fuel injector electrical connector and measure the resistance of each injector

14.2a Remove the fuel pressure regulator bolts (arrowed); this is the SOHC engine . . .

14.2b . . . and this is the DOHC engine

15.3 Use a small screwdriver or scribe to lever out the retaining clip from the fuel injector electrical connector

13 Throttle body – removal and refitting

⚠️ *Warning: Wait until the engine is completely cool before beginning this procedure.*

Removal

1 Remove the air duct that connects the air cleaner assembly to the throttle body.
2 Unplug the electrical connectors from the throttle body. Also label and detach all vacuum hoses from the throttle body.
3 Detach the accelerator cable (see Section 10) and, on automatic transmission models, the transmission throttle control cable (see Chapter 7B).
4 Detach the coolant hoses from the throttle body. Plug the lines to prevent coolant loss.
5 Unscrew the mounting nuts/bolts. Remove the throttle body and gasket. Remove all traces of old gasket material from the throttle body and air intake plenum.

Refitting

6 Refitting is the reverse of removal. Be sure to use a new gasket. Tighten the mounting bolts or nuts to the torque listed in this Chapter's Specifications. Adjust the accelerator cable (see Section 10) and, if equipped, the throttle control cable (see Chapter 7B). Check the coolant level and add some, if necessary (see Chapter 1).

14 Fuel pressure regulator – renewal

1 Relieve the system fuel pressure (see Section 2).
2 Detach the vacuum hose and fuel hose from the pressure regulator, then unscrew the mounting bolts **(see illustrations)**.
3 Remove the pressure regulator.
4 Refitting is the reverse of removal. Be sure to use a new O-ring. Lubricate the O-ring with a light coat of clean engine oil before refitting.
5 Check for fuel leaks after refitting the pressure regulator.

15 Fuel injectors – removal and refitting

Removal

1 Detach the cable from the negative battery terminal (see Chapter 5A).
2 Relieve the fuel pressure (see Section 2).
3 Unplug the injector connectors **(see illustration)**.
4 Detach the vacuum hose and fuel return hose from the fuel pressure regulator (see Section 14).
5 Detach any earth cables from the fuel rail.
6 Detach the fuel feed pipe from the fuel rail.
7 Remove the mounting nuts **(see illustrations)** and detach the fuel rail from the injectors.

15.7a Remove the fuel rail mounting nuts (arrowed); this is the SOHC engine . . .

15.8a Carefully remove the injector O-rings

8 Remove the injector(s) from the bores in the intake manifold and remove and discard the O-ring, cushion ring and seal ring **(see illustrations)**. **Note:** *Whether you're renewing an injector or a leaking O-ring, it's a good idea to remove all the injectors from the intake manifold and renew all the O-rings, seal rings and cushion rings.*

Refitting

Caution: To protect the injector seals, fit all of the injectors in the fuel rail, then fit the injector and fuel rail assembly in the intake manifold.

9 Coat the new cushion rings with clean engine oil and slide them onto the injectors.
10 Coat the new O-rings with clean engine oil and fit them on the injector(s), then insert each

15.7b . . . and this is the DOHC engine

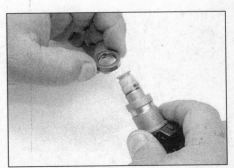

15.8b Remove the seal ring and cushion ring from the injector

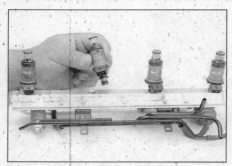

15.10 Refit the injectors in the fuel rail then refit the assembly in the intake manifold

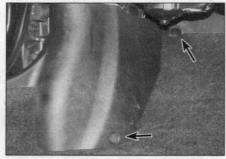

16.4a Prise out the clips (arrowed) and remove the passenger side kick panel . . .

16.4b . . . to expose the PCM

injector into its corresponding bore in the fuel rail (see illustration).

11 Coat the new seal rings with clean engine oil and press them into the injector bore(s) in the intake manifold.

12 Fit the injector and fuel rail assembly on the intake manifold. Tighten the fuel rail mounting nuts to the torque listed in this Chapter's Specifications.

13 The remainder of refitting is the reverse of removal.

14 After the injector/fuel rail assembly refitting is complete, turn the ignition switch to ON, but don't operate the starter; this activates the fuel pump for about two seconds, which builds-up fuel pressure in the fuel lines and the fuel rail. Repeat this about two or three times, then check the fuel lines, rail and injectors for fuel leakage.

---

16 Fuel injection system electronic components – removal, refitting and testing

---

Powertrain Control Module

1 The Powertrain Control Module (PCM) is located inside the passenger compartment under the dashboard behind the kick panel (left-hand side).
Caution: Avoid any static electricity damage to the computer by earthing yourself to the vehicle body before touching the PCM and using a special anti-static pad to store the PCM on once it is removed.

2 Disconnect the battery negative lead (see Chapter 5A).

3 Carefully prise up/unscrew the passenger's door sill trim panel.

4 Remove the kick panel to expose the PCM (see illustrations).

5 Remove the retaining nuts from the PCM bracket.

6 Unplug the electrical connectors from the PCM.

7 Carefully remove the PCM.

8 Refitting is the reverse of removal.

9 Testing of the PCM is not possible without specialist test equipment. If suspect, have the PCM checked by a Honda dealer or specialist.

Throttle Position Sensor

Testing

10 Follow the wiring harness from the TPS to the back of the intake manifold and remove it from the bulkhead. This will give you more room to probe the electrical terminals. Check the electrical connector at the sensor for a snug fit. Check the terminals in the connector and the wires leading to it for looseness and breaks. Repair as required.

11 Using a voltmeter, check the reference voltage from the PCM. Connect the positive probe to the yellow/blue wire and the negative probe to the green/black wire (see illustrations). It should read approximately 5.0 volts.

12 Next, check the TPS signal voltage. With the engine OFF, throttle fully closed and TPS electrical connector connected, connect the

probes of the voltmeter to the red/black wire (positive probe) and earth (negative probe) (see illustrations 16.11a and 16.11b). Note: *Use a straight pin to backprobe the connector terminal.* Gradually open the throttle valve and observe the TPS voltage. With the throttle valve fully closed, the voltage should read approximately 0.5 volts. Slowly move the throttle valve and see if the voltage changes as the sensor travels from idle to full throttle. The voltage should increase smoothly to approximately 4.5 volts. If the readings are incorrect, renew the TPS sensor.

13 A problem in any of the TPS circuits will set a DTC (Diagnostic Trouble Code) (see Section 19). Once a DTC is set, the PCM will use an artificial default value for TPS and some vehicle performance will return.

Renewal

14 The TPS is an integral part of the throttle body and must be renewed with the throttle body as a unit (see Section 13).

Manifold Absolute Pressure sensor

Testing

15 Check the electrical connector at the sensor for a snug fit. Check the terminals in the connector and the wires leading to it for looseness and breaks. Repair as required.

16 Identify the MAP sensor wires (see illustration). There are three wires.

a) Yellow/red, power to MAP sensor
b) Green/white, earth
c) Red/green, signal to PCM

16.11a SOHC Throttle Position Sensor

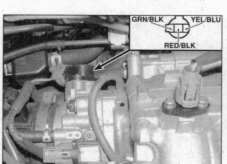

16.11b DOHC Throttle Position Sensor

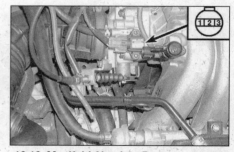

16.16 Manifold Absolute Pressure sensor (typical)

1 Power   2 Signal   3 Earth

17 Disconnect the MAP sensor connector, turn the ignition key ON (engine not running) and check for voltage between the power and earth wires in the harness side of the connector. There should be approximately 5.0 volts. If not, check the wires for breaks and poor connections and repair as necessary.

18 Remove the mounting screws and detach the sensor from the throttle body **(see illustration 16.16)**. Leave the electrical connector attached to the sensor.

19 Connect a voltmeter between the signal wire and body earth (backprobe the connector terminal with a straight pin). With the key ON and engine not running, apply vacuum to the sensor base (you'll need to remove the sensor from the throttle body to do this). Voltage should decrease as vacuum increases **(see illustration)**. If the readings are incorrect, renew the MAP sensor.

Renewal

20 Disconnect the electrical connector from the MAP sensor **(see illustration 16.16)**.

21 Undo the retaining screws and remove the sensor from the throttle body.

22 Refitting is the reverse of removal.

Intake Air Temperature sensor

Testing

23 With the ignition switch ON, disconnect the electrical connector from the IAT sensor, which is located on the intake manifold **(see illustration)**. Using an ohmmeter, measure the resistance between the two terminals of the IAT sensor with the engine cool. Reconnect the electrical connector to the sensor, start the engine and warm it up to normal operating temperature. Disconnect the connector and check the resistance again. Compare your measurements to the resistance chart **(see illustration)**.

24 With the ignition key ON (engine not running), check the supply voltage at the electrical connector (red/yellow wire) to the sensor **(see illustration 16.23a)**. It should be approximately 5.0 volts. If not, follow the red/yellow wire back to the PCM and check it for breaks or poor connections.

25 If the wiring is good and the test results are incorrect, renew the IAT sensor.

26 If the sensor seems okay but there is still a problem, have the vehicle inspected at a dealer service department or specialist, as the PCM may be malfunctioning.

Renewal

27 Unplug the electrical connector from the IAT sensor **(see illustration 16.23a)**.

28 Undo the retaining screws and remove the IAT sensor from the manifold.

29 Refitting is the reverse of removal.

Engine Coolant Temperature sensor

Testing

30 The Engine Coolant Temperature (ECT) is a thermistor (a resistor which varies its resistance in accordance with temperature changes). The change in the resistance values will directly affect the voltage signal from the ECT to the PCM. As the sensor temperature decreases, the resistance values will increase. As the sensor temperature increases, the resistance values will decrease. A DTC (Diagnostic Trouble Code) for this sensor indicates a failure in the sensor circuit, so in most cases the appropriate solution to the problem will be either repair of a wire or renewal of the sensor.

31 To check the sensor, disconnect the electrical connector from the sensor **(see illustration)**. Using an ohmmeter, measure the resistance between the two terminals of the ECT sensor with the engine cool. Reconnect the electrical connector to the sensor, start the engine and warm it up to normal operating temperature. Disconnect the connector and check the resistance again. Compare your measurements to the resistance chart **(see illustration 16.23b)**. If the sensor test results are incorrect, renew the sensor.

32 Check the supply voltage (red/white wire) with the ignition key ON (engine not running). It should be approximately 5.0 volts. If not, check for an open-circuit in the red/white wire from the sensor to the PCM.

Renewal

> ⚠ **Warning: Wait until the engine has cooled completely before beginning this procedure.**

Voltage	Vacuum (mm HG)
3.0	0
2.5	125
2.0	250
1.5	375
1.0	500
0.5	625

H34070

16.19 MAP sensor voltage should decrease as vacuum is applied

Resistance (K-ohms)	Temperature (°C)
12	-20
5.0	0
2.0	20
1.2	40
0.7	60
0.4	80

H34071

16.23b Intake Air Temperature sensor and Engine Coolant Temperature sensor resistance values should decrease as the temperature increases

33 Before fitting the new sensor, wrap the threads with PTFE sealing tape to prevent leakage and thread corrosion.

34 To remove the sensor, depress the locking tab, unplug the electrical connector, then carefully unscrew the sensor. Coolant will leak out when the sensor is removed, so fit the new sensor as quickly as possible.

Caution: Handle the coolant sensor with care. Damage to this sensor will affect the operation of the entire fuel injection system.

35 Refitting is the reverse of removal. Check the coolant level, adding as necessary (see Chapter 1).

Crankshaft Position/ Top Dead Centre/ Cylinder Position sensors

36 The Crankshaft Position/Top Dead Centre/Cylinder Position sensors are three separate sensors built into the distributor. Each sensor consists of a sensor rotor pressed onto the distributor shaft and a corresponding pick-up unit. The CKP signal is used by the PCM to determine fuel injection timing, ignition timing and engine speed (rpm). The TDC sensor signal is used by the PCM to determine ignition timing during engine starting. The CYP sensor signal is used by the PCM to determine timing for sequential fuel injection. Diagnosis of the sensors is performed by checking for DTCs (Diagnostic Trouble Codes) (see Section 19) and then

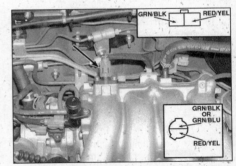

16.23a Intake Air Temperature sensor

16.31 Engine Coolant Temperature sensor (typical)

16.37a The Crankshaft Position/TDC/Cylinder Position sensor is mounted in the distributor; its connector (arrowed) is accessible from outside

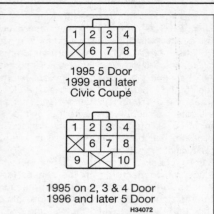

1995 5 Door
1999 and later
Civic Coupé

1995 on 2, 3 & 4 Door
1996 and later 5 Door

H34072

16.37b CKP/TDC/CYP sensor terminal identification

16.42 Location of the Crankshaft speed Fluctuation sensor (left-hand arrow) – follow the wiring harness (right-hand arrow) to find the electrical connector

checking for the proper resistance of each sensor at the electrical connector.

37 To check the sensors, disconnect the electrical connector at the distributor and measure the resistance across the following terminals with an ohmmeter (see illustrations). Compare your measurement with the resistance value listed in this Chapter's Specifications.

All except D14A3, D14A4, D14A8, and D16B2 engine codes:

a) CKP – terminals 2 and 6
b) TDC – terminals 3 and 7
c) CYP – terminals 4 and 8

38 Check for continuity to a good engine earth point on each of the test terminals. Continuity should NOT exist.

39 If the measured resistance of any sensor is not within specifications or if any sensor terminal is shorted to earth, renew the distributor (see Chapter 5B).

40 On D14A3, D14A4, D14A8 and D16B2 engine codes, diagnosis is by interpretation of any DTCs and substitution of a known good unit.

Crankshaft speed Fluctuation sensor

Note: *A CKF is only fitted to engine codes D15Z6, D15Z8, D16Y5, D16Y6 and D16Y8*

41 The crankshaft fluctuation sensor consists of a pulse rotor on the front end of the crankshaft and a pick-up sensor mounted on the engine next to the rotor. The PCM uses the signal to measure changes (fluctuations) in the rotational speed of the crankshaft. If the

changes exceed a set limit, the PCM concludes that a misfire has occurred.

Testing

42 Locate the electrical connector for the sensor at the timing belt end of the engine (see illustration). Make sure the key is in the OFF position, then disconnect the electrical connector.

43 Connect an ohmmeter between the two outer terminals in the connector (not the centre terminal). There should be 1.6 to 3.2 k-ohms. If not, renew the sensor.

44 Connect the ohmmeter between body earth and each of the sensor's outer terminals in turn (again, not to the centre terminal). If the ohmmeter shows continuity, renew the sensor.

Renewal

45 Remove the camshaft cover, crankshaft pulley and timing belt cover (see Chapter 2A).

46 Disconnect the sensor's electrical connector and remove its mounting bolt.

47 Refitting is the reverse of removal.

Electrical Load Detector

48 The ELD system detects excess amperage draw (load) on the electrical circuits that govern the headlights, fuel injection, charging system, etc. The prime symptom of an electrical overload is a driveability problem, usually occurring when the engine is idling. The ELD is mounted on the underside of the engine compartment fusebox.

Testing

49 Disconnect the electrical connector from the ELD system (see illustration).

50 Measure voltage between the power (black/white) and earth (black) wires with the ignition key ON (engine not running). There should be battery voltage. If no voltage is present, check the wiring harness back to the fusebox (under the facia) and the main fusebox (engine compartment).

51 Measure voltage with the ignition key ON (engine not running) between the green/red (+) terminal and the black terminal. There should be approximately 4.5 to 5.0 volts. If no voltage is present, check the ELD circuit between the fusebox and the PCM.

52 Switch the engine off and reconnect the three-pin connector to the ELD system. Start the engine and let it idle, then measure the voltage at the green/red terminal.

53 Now, turn on the dip beam headlights and check the amount of voltage. It should be less than in Paragraph 52. If not, renew the ELD unit.

Renewal

54 If the test results are not correct, renew the ELD unit. This requires changing the entire main fusebox. The ELD unit is not available separately.

Power Steering Pressure switch

55 The Power Steering Pressure (PSP) switch (fitted to some models), is a normally-closed switch. It is mounted in the pressure pipe near the steering rack. When steering system pressure reaches a high-pressure set point, the PSP switch sends a signal to the PCM that the PCM uses to maintain engine idle speed during parking manoeuvres. The OBD (On-Board Diagnostic) system can detect switch problems and set DTCs to indicate specific faults.

Testing

56 Check the operation of the PSP switch if the engine stalls during parking or if the engine runs continuously at high rpm.

57 Disconnect the PSP switch electrical connector.

58 Connect an ohmmeter to the terminals of the switch (see illustration).

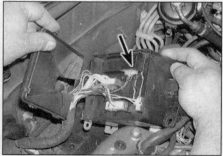

16.49 The Electrical Load Detector (ELD) is mounted under the engine compartment fusebox (arrowed)

16.58 The Power Steering Pressure (PSP) switch is mounted in the power steering pressure pipe (arrowed)

59 Start the engine and let it idle.

60 With the front wheels pointing straight-ahead, read the ohmmeter. It should indicate a continuity of close to zero ohms.

61 Turn the steering wheel to either side and watch the ohmmeter. The PSP should open as the wheel nears the steering stop on either side, and the meter should indicate an open circuit (infinite, or very high resistance).

62 If the switch fails either test, renew it. If the switch is OK, investigate the engine idle control operation if high idle speed or stalling problems continue.

Renewal

63 If necessary for access, raise the vehicle and support it securely on axle stands (see *Jacking and vehicle support*).

64 Disconnect the electrical connector from the switch and unscrew the switch from its fitting.

65 Fit and connect the new switch. Lower the vehicle to the earth if it was raised.

66 Refer to Chapter 10 and bleed air from the power steering system. Add fluid as required (see *Weekly checks*).

Oxygen sensor

67 The oxygen sensor, which is located in the exhaust manifold, monitors the oxygen content of the exhaust gas. The oxygen content in the exhaust reacts with the oxygen sensor to produce a voltage output which varies from 0.1 volts (high oxygen, lean mixture) to 0.9 volts (low oxygen, rich mixture). The PCM constantly monitors this variable voltage output to determine the ratio of oxygen-to-fuel in the mixture. The PCM alters the air/fuel mixture ratio by controlling the pulse width (open time) of the fuel injectors. A mixture ratio of 14.7 parts air to 1 part fuel is the ideal mixture ratio for minimising exhaust emissions, thus allowing the catalytic converter to operate at maximum efficiency. It is this ratio of 14.7 to 1 which the PCM and the oxygen sensor attempt to maintain at all times.

68 The oxygen sensor produces no voltage when it is below its normal operating temperature of about 300°C. During this initial period before warm-up, the PCM operates in open loop mode.

69 If the engine reaches normal operating temperature and/or has been running for two or more minutes, and if the oxygen sensor is producing a steady signal voltage below 0.45 volts at 1500 rpm or greater, the PCM will set a DTC. The PCM will also set a code if it detects any problem with the oxygen sensor heater circuit.

70 When there is a problem with the oxygen sensor or its circuit, the PCM operates in the open loop mode – that is, it controls fuel delivery in accordance with a programmed default value instead of feedback information from the oxygen sensor.

71 The proper operation of the oxygen sensor depends on four conditions:

a) **Electrical** – *The low voltages generated by the sensor depend upon good, clean connections which should be checked whenever a malfunction of the sensor is suspected or indicated.*

b) **Outside air supply** – *The sensor is designed to allow air circulation to the internal portion of the sensor. Whenever the sensor is removed and refitted or renewed, make sure the air passages are not restricted.*

c) **Proper operating temperature** – *The PCM will not react to the sensor signal until the sensor reaches approximately 300°C. This factor must be taken into consideration when evaluating the performance of the sensor.*

d) **Unleaded fuel** – *The use of unleaded fuel is essential for proper operation of the sensor. Make sure the fuel you are using is of this type.*

72 In addition to observing the above conditions, special care must be taken whenever the sensor is serviced.

a) *The oxygen sensor has permanently attached wiring and an electrical connector, which should not be removed from the sensor. Damage or removal of the wiring or electrical connector can adversely affect operation of the sensor.*

b) *Grease, dirt and other contaminants should be kept away from the electrical connector and the louvered end of the sensor.*

c) *Do not use cleaning solvents of any kind on the oxygen sensor.*

d) *Do not drop or roughly handle the sensor.*

e) *The silicone boot must be installed in the correct position to prevent the boot from being melted and to allow the sensor to operate properly.*

Testing

73 Locate the oxygen sensor electrical connector and insert a long pin into the oxygen sensor connector containing the signal voltage wire, which is the white or white/red wire (**see illustration**). **Note:** *Refer to the wiring diagrams at the end of Chapter 12 for the terminal designations, if necessary.* Connect the positive probe of a voltmeter to the pin and the negative probe to earth.

74 Monitor the voltage signal as the engine goes from cold to warm.

75 The oxygen sensor will produce a steady voltage signal at first (open loop) of approximately 0.1 to 0.2 volts with the engine cold. After a period of approximately two minutes, the engine will reach operating temperature and the oxygen sensor will start to fluctuate between 0.1 and 0.9 volts (closed loop). If the oxygen sensor fails to reach the closed loop mode or there is a very long period of time until it does switch into closed loop mode (lazy oxygen sensor), renew the oxygen sensor.

76 Also inspect the oxygen sensor heater. Disconnect the oxygen sensor electrical connector and connect an ohmmeter between the heater terminals (refer to the appropriate wiring diagrams for the proper terminals to check). It should measure 10 to 40 ohms.

77 Check for proper supply voltage to the heater. Measure the voltage on the harness side of the oxygen sensor electrical connector, with the connector unplugged (again, refer to the wiring diagrams at the end of Chapter 12). There should be battery voltage with the ignition key ON (engine not running). If there is no voltage, check the circuit between the main relay, the PCM and the sensor.

78 If the oxygen sensor fails any of the tests described, it may be defective.

Renewal

Note: *Because it is installed in the exhaust manifold which contracts when cool, the oxygen sensor may be very difficult to loosen when the engine is cold. Rather than risk damage to the sensor (assuming you are planning to re-use it in another manifold), start and run the engine for a minute or two, then turn it off. Be careful not to burn yourself during the following procedure.*

79 Raise the vehicle and place it securely on axle stands (see *Jacking and vehicle support*).

80 Disconnect the sensor's electrical connector.

81 Carefully unscrew the sensor from the exhaust manifold (**see illustration**).

82 Anti-seize compound must be used on the threads of the sensor to facilitate future removal. The threads of new sensors will

16.73 The oxygen sensor (arrowed) is mounted in the catalytic converter – follow the harness to find the electrical connector

16.81 A special socket that allows clearance for the wiring harness is recommended for oxygen sensor removal

16.88 The knock sensor is threaded into a coolant passage (arrowed) (intake manifold removed for clarity)

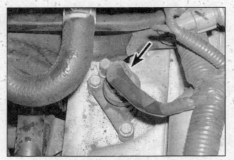

16.92 The Vehicle Speed Sensor is mounted on the transmission (arrowed)

95 Remove the retaining bolt and lift the VSS from the transmission.

96 Refitting is the reverse of removal.

Fuel shut-off inertia switch

97 The fuel shut-off switch is a safety device which automatically cuts off the fuel supply in the event of a sudden impact or collision. To reset the switch after an impact, depress the button on the top of the switch. The switch is located behind the passenger side glovebox on 3-door Hatchback, 4-door Saloon and Coupe models (accessible through the open glovebox), and behind the cigarette lighter on 5-door models (pull back the carpet and reach behind the console).

---

already be coated with this compound, but if an old sensor is removed and refitted, recoat the threads.

83 Fit the sensor and tighten it securely.

84 Reconnect the electrical connector to the main engine wiring harness.

85 Lower the vehicle, take it on a test drive and check to see that no DTCs (Diagnostic Trouble Codes) have been set.

Knock sensor

 Warning: Wait until the engine is completely cool before removing the knock sensor.

86 Knock sensors are used on engine codes D16Y5, D16Y8 and B16A2.

87 Knock sensors detect abnormal vibration in the engine. The knock control system is designed to reduce spark knock during periods of heavy detonation. This allows the engine to use maximum spark advance to improve driveability. Knock sensors produce AC output voltage which increases with the severity of the knock. The signal is fed into the PCM and the timing is retarded to compensate for the detonation.

Testing

88 To check a knock sensor, disconnect the electrical connector and unscrew it from the engine **(see illustration)**. Reconnect the wiring harness to the sensor. This type of sensor must be checked by observing voltage fluctuations with a voltmeter. Simply switch the voltmeter to the lowest AC voltage scale and connect the negative probe (–) to the sensor body and the positive (+) probe to the sensor terminal. With the voltmeter connected to the sensor, gently tap on the bottom of the knock sensor with a hammer or similar device (this simulates the knock from the engine) and observe voltage fluctuations on the meter. If no voltage fluctuations can be detected, the sensor may be defective and should be renewed with a new part. **Note:** *You may be able to perform this test without removing the sensor.*

Renewal

89 The knock sensor is threaded into the engine block coolant passage **(see illustration 16.88)**. When it is removed, coolant will drain from the block. Drain the cooling system (see Chapter 1). Place a drain

tin under the sensor, disconnect the electrical connector and unscrew the sensor.

90 New sensors are precoated with thread sealant. Don't use any additional sealant or the operation of the sensor may be affected. Fit the sensor and tighten it to the torque listed in this Chapter's Specifications. Don't over tighten the sensor or damage may occur. Plug in the electrical connector, refill the cooling system (see Chapter 1) and check for leaks.

Vehicle Speed Sensor

91 The Vehicle Speed Sensor (VSS) is located on the transmission. This sensor is a permanent magnetic variable reluctance sensor that produces a pulsing voltage whenever vehicle speed is over 3 mph. These pulses are used by the PCM to control fuel injector duration and, on automatic transmissions, shift control.

Testing

92 To check the Vehicle Speed Sensor, disconnect the electrical connector in the wiring harness at the sensor. Using a voltmeter, check for voltage at the electrical connector to the sensor **(see illustration)**. You'll need to refer to the appropriate wiring diagrams to identify the power wire. The circuit should have battery voltage available. If there is no voltage available, check for an open circuit between the VSS and the fusebox. Using an ohmmeter, check the black wire of the connector for continuity to body earth. If there's no continuity, check the black wire for breaks or poor connections.

93 Raise the front of the vehicle and place it securely on axle stands (see *Jacking and vehicle support*). Block the rear wheels and place the transmission in Neutral. Connect the electrical connector to the VSS, turn the ignition to ON and backprobe the VSS connector signal wire with a voltmeter positive lead. Connect the negative lead of the meter to body earth. While holding one wheel steady, rotate the other wheel by hand. The voltmeter should pulse between zero and 5.0 volts. If it doesn't, renew the sensor.

Renewal

94 To renew the sensor, disconnect the electrical connector from the VSS.

17 Idle Air Control system – testing and component renewal

When the engine is idling, the air/fuel ratio is controlled by the Idle Air Control system. The system consists of the Powertrain Control Module (PCM), Idle Air Control (IAC) valve and, on D14A2, D16Y2, and D16Y3 engine codes, the Fast Idle Thermo valve (FIT).

Idle air control valve

1 The IAC valve is controlled by the PCM depending upon the running conditions of the engine (air conditioning system, power steering, cold and warm running etc). This valve regulates the amount of airflow past the throttle plate and into the intake manifold. The PCM receives information from the sensors (vehicle speed, coolant temperature, air conditioning, power steering pressure, etc) and adjusts the idle speed according to the demands of the engine. Finally, to prevent rough running after the engine starts, the IAC valve is opened during cranking and immediately after starting to provide additional air into the intake manifold. Two types of IAC valves are used:

a) *All models with automatic transmission, and models with the D14A3, D14A4, D14A8, D16B2, D16Y7 engine are equipped with a rotary IAC valve mounted on the throttle body.*

b) *All other models are equipped with a linear IAC valve mounted on the intake manifold plenum (see illustration).*

17.1 Idle Air Control valve (arrowed) – D14A2 engine

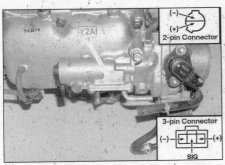

17.3a Typical linear Idle Air Control valve and 2-pin connector – the 3-pin connector is used on the rotary IAC valve

17.3b Typical DOHC engine IAC valve

17.12 The Fast Idle Thermo valve is mounted on the underside of the throttle body and is retained by three bolts (arrowed)

Testing

2 Apply the handbrake, block the wheels and place the transmission in Neutral (manual) or Park (automatic). Connect a tachometer, according to the manufacturer's instructions, to the engine. Start the engine and hold the accelerator steady at 3000 rpm until the coolant fan comes on. Return the engine to idle and disconnect the electrical connector to the IAC valve.

⚠ *Warning: Keep hands, loose clothing, etc, away from any moving engine parts while working on a running engine or personal injury may result.*

The idle speed should respond as described:

a) *On models equipped with a rotary IAC valve mounted on the throttle body, the engine speed should increase.*
b) *On models equipped with a linear IAC valve mounted on the intake manifold plenum, the engine idle speed should drop or the engine should stall.*

If the idle speed did not respond as described, the IAC valve is probably defective. If an intermittent idle problem still persists, check the wiring harness from the IAC valve to the PCM for poor connections or damaged wires.

3 Disconnect the electrical connector from the IAC valve, turn the ignition key ON (engine not running) and measure the voltage between the positive terminal of the wiring harness connector (yellow/black wire) and body earth **(see illustrations)**. There should be battery voltage present. If no voltage is present, check for an open-circuit in the yellow/black wire from the IAC valve to the PGM-FI main relay. In any case, leave the IAC valve connector disconnected for the next steps.

4 If the IAC valve has two wires in its harness (linear valve), connect the IAC valve directly to battery voltage with a pair of jumper wires (positive to black/yellow; negative to black/blue). The valve should click each time voltage is applied. If not, renew it.

Caution 1: Be very careful when applying battery voltage to an electrical component. Disconnect the component from the main wiring harness and apply voltage directly to the component or to the harness connector leading to the component. Do not apply voltage to the connector on the vehicle harness-side or damage to the Powertrain Control Module may result. Caution 2: Don't connect power any longer than is necessary to make the valve click.

5 If the IAC valve has three wires in its harness (rotary valve), connect the negative probe of an ohmmeter to the centre terminal of the connector, then connect the ohmmeter positive probe to each of the other terminals in turn. There should be 16 to 28 ohms in each case.

6 If the IAC valve tests correctly in Paragraph 4 or 5, have the PCM and the electrical circuit for the IAC valve diagnosed by a dealer service department or specialist.

Renewal

7 Disconnect the electrical connector from the IAC valve. On models with a rotary IAC valve mounted on the throttle body, disconnect and plug the coolant hoses.

8 Remove the mounting screws and remove the valve from the throttle body or air intake plenum.

9 Refitting is the reverse of removal. Be sure to fit a new O-ring. Check the coolant and refill as required.

Fast Idle Thermo valve

10 The Fast Idle Thermo (FIT) valve is used on D14A2, D16Y2 and D16Y3 engine codes equipped with an automatic transmission. The FIT valve allows additional air into the intake manifold during cold engine operation, increasing the idle speed. When the engine reaches operating temperature, the valve closes and the idle speed returns to normal. The FIT valve is mounted on the throttle body.

Testing

11 Start this procedure with the engine cold. Disconnect the air intake duct from the throttle body.

12 Start the engine and let it idle. Reach inside the throttle body and place a finger over the port that connects to the FIT valve **(see illustration)**. You should feel suction.

13 Warm the engine to normal operating temperature and check for suction at the FIT valve port again. There should not be any. If there is, the valve hasn't closed. This might be caused by a low coolant level or air bubbles in the coolant passages. Make sure the engine coolant is full and free of air bubbles.

14 If the test results weren't correct, renew the FIT valve.

Renewal

⚠ *Warning: Wait until the engine is completely cool before beginning this procedure.*

15 Disconnect the hose from the valve and unscrew the mounting bolts **(see illustration 17.12)**. Take off the valve and its O-rings. Plug the hose to prevent coolant loss.

16 Refit the valve, using new O-rings, and tighten the mounting bolts to the torque listed in this Chapter's Specifications. Renew the hose clamp with a new one if it has lost its tension.

17 Check the coolant level and add some, if necessary (see Chapter 1).

18 Intake Air Bypass system – testing and renewal

1 Models with the B18C4 engine are equipped with the Intake Air Bypass (IAB) system. The IAB system allows the intake manifold to divert the path of intake air into the combustion chamber. Two air intake paths are provided in the intake manifold to allow the option of the intake volume most favourable for the particular engine speed. Optimum performance is achieved by switching the valves from either the closed position (for high torque at low rpm) or the open position (for maximum horsepower at high rpm).

Testing

2 With the engine off, disconnect the vacuum

18.2 Apply vacuum to the IAB valve diaphragm; the rod should move

18.5 Intake Air Bypass solenoid electrical connector (arrowed)

18.7 Unscrew the mounting screws (arrowed) to remove the IAB diaphragm

hose from the IAB diaphragm and connect a vacuum pump to it **(see illustration)**. If the diaphragm rod doesn't move when vacuum is applied, renew the diaphragm.

3 With the engine idling, check for vacuum at the disconnected end of the hose. There should be vacuum at idle, and no vacuum when engine speed is raised to 6000 rpm.

4 If there isn't any vacuum at idle, follow the vacuum hose from the diaphragm to the control valve under the intake manifold, and then to the vacuum tank. Disconnect the hose that leads from the tank to the intake manifold and check for vacuum. If there isn't any, look for a blocked or cracked vacuum hose.

5 Disconnect the electrical connector from the IAB solenoid **(see illustration)**. Connect a voltmeter positive probe to the red/blue wire and the negative probe to the black wire (in the harness side of the connector). With the ignition key ON, there should be battery voltage. If not, check the wiring harness for breaks or poor connections.

6 If there's battery voltage at the wiring harness terminals and the vacuum pipes are good, but test results weren't correct in Paragraph 3, renew the solenoid.

Renewal

7 To renew the diaphragm, remove its mounting screws **(see illustration)**.

8 To renew the solenoid and vacuum tank assembly, detach it from its mounting clamp and remove it from the intake manifold **(see illustration)**.

9 Refitting is the reverse of removal.

19 On-Board Diagnostic system – general information and fault codes

General information

1 All models are equipped with an On-Board Diagnostic system (OBD). This facility is built into the PCM, and is designed to alert the driver to a system component fault which may result in higher than normal emissions of harmful exhaust/fuel vapour gases and speed-up the engine management troubleshooting procedure. Should an engine management component fail, the incorrect or (implausible) signal is recognised by the PCM, which stores a Diagnostic Trouble Code (DTC), and where appropriate, illuminates the Malfunction Indicator Light (MIL) in the instrument cluster.

Retrieving DTCs

2 In order to retrieve any stored DTCs, either a fault code reader must be connected to the vehicle's datalink connecter (located above the Service Check Connector), or read from the MIL in the instrument cluster. The Service Check Connector (2-pin) is located under the dashboard, above the passenger side kick panel **(see illustration)**. The codes can be read by bridging the two pins in the service check connector and reading the MIL on the instrument panel (all models). Vehicles from 2000 model year on are fitted with a 16-pin diagnostic connector behind the centre console on the passenger's side **(see illustration)**. A fault code reader is required to retrieve or clear codes via this connector.

3 To view any DTCs stored in the PCM memory (without a code reader), fit a bridging wire into the service check connector **(see illustration 19.2)** located in the far left-hand corner under the dash (above the PCM), then turn the ignition switch to the ON position. If any codes are present, they will blink a sequence on the MIL in the instrument panel to indicate a number or code that represents a system or component failure.

4 The MIL will blink a longer blink to represent the first digit of a two digit number and then will blink short for the second digit (for example, 1 long blink then 6 short blinks for the code 16). **Note:** *If the system has more than one problem, the codes will be displayed in sequence, then a there will be pause, then the codes will repeat.*

18.8 The IAB solenoid and vacuum tank assembly (arrowed) is mounted in a clamp on the underside of the intake manifold

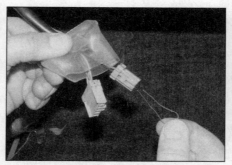

19.2a The 2-pin Service Check Connector is located under the facia above the passenger's side kick panel, bridge the terminal pins to extract the fault codes

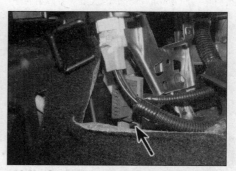

19.2b On 2000-on model year vehicles, a 16-pin diagnostic socket (arrowed) is fitted behind the centre console

Diagnostic Trouble Codes (DTCs)

Trouble code	Circuit or system	Corrective action
Code 0	Faulty PCM	Check the PCM electrical connector. If no loose connectors are found, have the PCM diagnosed by a dealer service department.
Code 1	Oxygen content	Check the oxygen sensor, heater and the oxygen sensor circuit (see Section 16).
Code 3	Manifold Absolute Pressure	Check the MAP sensor and circuit (see Section 16).
Code 4	Crankshaft Position sensor	Check the CKP sensor and circuit (see Section 16).
Code 5	Manifold Absolute Pressure	Check the MAP sensor and circuit
Code 6	Coolant temperature	Check the coolant temperature sensor and circuit (see Section 16).
Code 7	Throttle angle	Check the Throttle Position Sensor (TPS) and the circuit (see Section 16).
Code 8	TDC position	Check the TDC sensor and the circuit (see Section 16).
Code 9	No 1 cylinder position	Check the CYP sensor and the circuit (see Section 16).
Code 10	Intake Air Temperature	Check the IAT sensor and the circuit (see Section 16).
Code 12	Exhaust Gas Recirculation system	Check the hoses, the EGR valve lift sensor and the EGR valve (see Chapter 4B).
Code 14	Idle Air Control valve	Check the IAC valve and system (see Section 17).
Code 15	Ignition output signal	Check the ignition system (see Chapter 5B).
Code 17	Vehicle Speed Sensor	Check the vehicle speed sensor and circuit (see Section 16).
Code 19	Lock-up Control Solenoid	On automatic transmissions, check the solenoid (see Chapter 7B).
Code 20	Electronic Load Detector	Check the ELD system (see Section 16).
Code 21	Variable Valve Timing and Valve Lift Solenoid	See Chapter 2 VTEC Solenoid checks.
Code 23	Knock sensor	Check the knock sensor and circuit (see Section 16).
Code 41	Oxygen sensor heater	Check the heater for the proper voltage signal (see Section 16).
Code 48	Oxygen content	Check the oxygen sensor, heater, and the oxygen sensor circuit (see Section 16).
Code 54	Crankshaft speed Fluctuation sensor	Check the CKP sensor (see Section 16).

Clearing codes

5 When the PCM sets DTC, the MIL will come on and a trouble code will be stored in the memory. The trouble code will stay in the PCM memory until the voltage to the PCM is interrupted. To clear the memory, remove the BACK-UP fuse from the fuse/relay box located in the engine compartment for at least ten seconds (see Chapter 12 for fusebox location). **Note:** *Unplugging the BACK-UP fuse also cancels the radio preset stations and the clock setting. Be sure to make a note of the various radio stations that are programmed into the memory before removing the fuse.*

20 Exhaust system servicing – general information

⚠ **Warning: Inspection and repair of exhaust system components should be done only after enough time has elapsed after driving the vehicle to allow the system components to cool completely. Also, when working under the vehicle, make sure it is securely supported on axle stands (see 'Jacking and vehicle support'). Caution: All models covered by this manual**

are equipped with an exhaust system flex tube which is extremely sensitive to sharp bends. Do not allow the flex tube to hang downward during servicing or damage will occur.

1 The exhaust system consists of the exhaust manifold, the catalytic converter, the silencer, the tailpipe and all connecting pipes, brackets, mountings and clamps. The exhaust system is attached to the body with mounting brackets and rubber straps. If any of the parts are improperly installed, excessive noise and vibration will be transmitted to the body.

2 Conduct regular inspections of the exhaust system to keep it safe and quiet. Look for any damaged or bent parts, open seams, holes, loose connections, excessive corrosion or other defects which could allow exhaust fumes to enter the vehicle. Deteriorated exhaust system components should not be repaired; they should be renewed.

3 If the exhaust system components are extremely corroded or rusted together, welding equipment will probably be required to remove them. The convenient way to accomplish this is to have a exhaust specialist remove the corroded sections with a cutting torch. If, however, you want to save money by doing it yourself (and you don't have a welding

outfit with a cutting torch), simply cut off the old components with a hacksaw. If you have compressed air, special pneumatic cutting chisels can also be used. If you do decide to tackle the job at home, be sure to wear safety goggles to protect your eyes from metal chips and work gloves to protect your hands.

4 Here are some simple guidelines to follow when repairing the exhaust system **(see illustrations):**
   a) *Work from the back to the front when removing exhaust system components.*
   b) *Apply penetrating oil to the exhaust*

20.4a Be sure to apply penetrating fluid to the exhaust system fasteners before attempting to remove them

system component fasteners to make
them easier to remove.

c) Use new gaskets, rubber mountings and
clamps when refitting exhaust systems
components.

d) Apply anti-seize compound to the threads
of all exhaust system fasteners during
reassembly.

e) Be sure to allow sufficient clearance
between newly installed parts and all
points on the underbody to avoid
overheating the floorpan and possibly
damaging the interior carpet and
insulation. Pay particularly close attention
to the catalytic converter and heat shield.

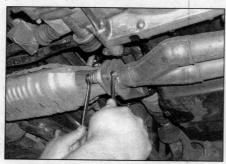

**20.4b Unscrew the exhaust system
fasteners with a pair of spanners**

**20.4c Check for any broken or missing
rubber mountings**

Chapter 4 Part B:
Emission control systems

Contents

Degrees of difficulty

Easy, suitable for novice with little experience		**Fairly easy,** suitable for beginner with some experience	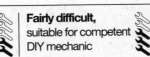	**Fairly difficult,** suitable for competent DIY mechanic		**Difficult,** suitable for experienced DIY mechanic		**Very difficult,** suitable for expert DIY or professional	

Specifications

General

Manufacturer's engine codes*:
1.4 litre:	
D14A2, D14A3, D14A4, D14A8	66 kW SOHC 16V non-VTEC
1.5 litre:	
D15Z3, D15Z6, D15Z8	85 kW SOHC 16V VTEC-E
1.6 litre:	
D16Y2	93 kW SOHC 16V VTEC
D16Y3, D16B2	83 kW SOHC 16V non-VTEC
D16Y5	86 kW SOHC 16V VTEC-E
D16Y6, D16Y8	92 kW SOHC 16V VTEC
D16Y7	78 kW SOHC 16V non-VTEC
B16A2	118 kW DOHC 16V VTEC
1.8 litre:	
B18C4	125 kW DOHC 16V VTEC

* See 'Vehicle identification' in the Reference section

Torque wrench setting

	Nm	lbf ft
Oxygen sensor	44	32

1 General information

To prevent pollution of the atmosphere from incompletely burned and evaporating gases, and to maintain good driveability and fuel economy, a number of emission control systems are incorporated. They include the:

Exhaust Gas Recirculation (EGR) system.
Evaporative Emissions Control (EVAP) system.
Positive Crankcase Ventilation (PCV) system.
Catalytic converter.

The Sections in this Chapter include general descriptions, checking procedures within the scope of the home mechanic and component renewal procedures (when possible) for each of the systems listed above.

Before assuming that an emissions control system is malfunctioning, check the fuel and ignition systems carefully. The diagnosis of some emission control devices requires specialised tools, equipment and training. If checking and servicing become too difficult or if a procedure is beyond your ability, consult a dealer service department or specialist. Remember, the most frequent cause of emissions problems is simply a loose or broken wire or vacuum hose, so always check the hose and wiring connections first.

This doesn't mean, however, that emissions control systems are particularly difficult to maintain and repair. You can quickly and easily perform many checks and do most of the regular maintenance at home with common servicing and hand tools.

Pay close attention to any special precautions outlined in this Chapter. It should be noted that the illustrations of the various systems may not exactly match the system installed on your vehicle because of changes made by the manufacturer during production or from year-to-year.

2 Positive Crankcase Ventilation system – general information and inspection

General information

1 The Positive Crankcase Ventilation (PCV) system reduces hydrocarbon emissions by scavenging crankcase vapours. It does this by circulating fresh air from the air cleaner through the crankcase, where it mixes with blow-by gases and is then rerouted through a PCV valve to the intake manifold.

2 The main components of the PCV system are the PCV valve, a blow-by filter and the vacuum hoses connecting these two components with the engine.

3 To maintain idle quality, the PCV valve restricts the flow when the intake manifold vacuum is high. If abnormal operating

2.4a The PCV valve is located on top of the engine in the intake manifold below the fuel rail (arrowed) on some models, or . . .

conditions (such as piston ring problems) arise, the system is designed to allow excessive amounts of blow-by gases to flow back through the crankcase vent tube into the air cleaner to be consumed by normal combustion.

Inspection

4 The PCV valve and hose is located in the intake manifold below the fuel injector rail at the rear of the engine, or in the valve cover, depending on model (see illustrations).

5 With the engine idling at normal operating temperature, pull the PCV valve (with hose attached) from the manifold or hose.

6 Place your finger over the valve opening or hose (see illustration). If there is no vacuum, check for a blocked hose, manifold port, or the valve itself. Renew any blocked or deteriorated hoses.

7 Turn off the engine and shake the PCV valve, listening for a rattle. If the valve doesn't rattle, renew it.

8 To renew the valve, pull it out of the end of the hose, noting its installed position and direction.

9 When purchasing a renewal PCV valve, make sure it's for your particular vehicle, model vehicle and engine size. Compare the old valve with the new one to make sure they are the same.

10 Push the valve into the end of the hose until it's seated.

11 Inspect all the rubber hoses and

2.6 Pull the PCV valve out of the rubber grommet and check for vacuum at the opening

2.4b . . . is accessible from below at the rear of the engine (arrowed) on others

grommets for damage and hardening. Renew them, if necessary.

12 Press the PCV valve and hose securely into position.

3 Exhaust Gas Recirculation system – inspection and component renewal

General description

1 To reduce oxides of nitrogen emissions, some of the exhaust gases are recirculated through the EGR valve to the intake manifold to lower combustion temperatures. Only models with the D15Z3, D15Z6, D15Z8 and D16Y5 engine codes are equipped with an EGR system.

2 The EGR system consists of the EGR valve, the EGR control solenoid valve, an EGR valve lift sensor and the Powertrain Control Module (PCM). The PCM is programmed to produce the ideal EGR valve lift for each operating condition. The EGR valve lift sensor monitors the amount of EGR valve lift and sends this information to the PCM. The PCM then compares it with the ideal EGR valve lift, which is determined by data received from the other sensors. If necessary, the PCM adjusts the amount of vacuum available to the EGR valve via the EGR control solenoid valve.

Inspection

3 Start the engine and warm it to its normal operating temperature (wait for the electric cooling fan to come on).

4 Detach the vacuum hose from the EGR valve and attach a vacuum gauge to the hose.

5 There should be no vacuum. If there is no vacuum, proceed to Paragraph 7 (D15Z3 engine code) or Paragraph 10 (D15Z6, D15Y5 and D15Z8 engine codes).

6 If vacuum exists, disconnect the electrical connector from the EGR control solenoid valve and recheck for vacuum at the vacuum hose to the EGR valve. **Note:** To find the EGR vacuum control solenoid valve, follow the vacuum hose from the EGR valve. If vacuum does not exist, have the PCM diagnosed by a technician with a fault code reader/scanner tool. If vacuum is present, check all the vacuum lines to make sure they are routed

properly. If the hoses are OK, renew the control solenoid valve.

D15Z3 engine code

7 If there originally was no vacuum, fit a hand-held vacuum pump to the EGR valve and apply 200 mmHg of vacuum to the valve and confirm that the engine stalls or runs erratically. Also, does the EGR valve hold vacuum? If not, renew the EGR valve.

8 Check for battery voltage to the EGR control solenoid valve. Disconnect the two-pin connector from the solenoid and check for battery voltage at the red wire (+) terminal on the main harness. There should be battery voltage.

9 Reconnect the vacuum gauge to the EGR vacuum hose, start the engine and allow it to idle. Connect battery positive voltage with a bridging wire to the red wire's terminal on the two-pin connector (the solenoid side, not the harness side). While observing the vacuum gauge, earth the other terminal with another bridging wire. Vacuum should increase within one second (and you should be able to hear the solenoid activate). If there is no vacuum, renew the EGR control solenoid valve.

Caution: Be very careful when applying battery voltage to an electrical component. Disconnect the component from the main wiring harness and apply voltage directly to the component or to the harness connector leading to the component. Do not apply voltage to the connector on the vehicle harness-side or damage to the Powertrain Control Module may result.

D15Z6, D15Z8 and D15Y5 engine codes

10 Disconnect the 3-pin connector from the EGR valve lift sensor, and turn the ignition on. Measure the voltage between terminals 2 and 3 of the harness plug. A voltage of 5.0 volts should be present. If not check for open-circuits in the from the PCM to the connector. If the wires are in good condition, the PCM may be faulty.

11 If the correct voltage is present during the test in Paragraph 10, connect a vacuum pump to the EGR valve, start the engine, and apply 200 mmHg of vacuum, and confirm that the engine stalls or runs erratically. If not, the EGR valve may be defective.

All engine codes

12 Further checking of the EGR control system requires a fault code reader/scanner tool. Take the vehicle to a dealer service department or specialist.

Component renewal

EGR valve

13 Unplug the electrical connector for the EGR valve lift sensor. Detach the vacuum hose.

14 Remove the two nuts that secure the EGR valve to the intake manifold and detach the EGR valve.

15 Clean the mating surfaces of the EGR valve and adapter.

16 Fit the EGR valve, using a new gasket. Tighten the nuts securely.

17 Connect the electrical connector.

EGR control solenoid

18 Locate the EGR control solenoid by following the vacuum hose from the EGR valve to the solenoid. Note their fitted locations, then detach the vacuum hoses, unplug the electrical connector, remove the mounting screws and lift the solenoid off.

19 Refitting is the reverse of removal.

---

4 Evaporative emissions control system – general information and inspection

General information

1 The fuel evaporative emissions control system absorbs fuel vapours and, during engine operation, releases them into the engine intake where they mix with the incoming air/fuel mixture.

2 Every evaporative system employs a canister filled with activated charcoal to absorb fuel vapours. The means by which these vapours are controlled, however, varies considerably from one system to another. The following descriptions of a typical system for the models covered by this manual should provide you enough information to understand the system on your vehicle. **Note:** *The following descriptions are not intended as a specific description of the evaporative*

system on your particular vehicle. Rather, they are intended as a general description of a typical system used on fuel injected vehicles. Although the following components are most likely all used on your particular system, there may also be other devices, not included here, which are unique to your system.

3 The fuel filler cap is fitted with a two-way valve as a safety device. The valve vents fuel vapours to the atmosphere if the evaporative control system fails.

4 Another fuel cut-off valve (two-way valve), mounted on the fuel tank, regulates fuel vapour flow from the fuel tank to the charcoal canister, based on the pressure or vacuum caused by temperature changes.

5 After passing through the two-way valve, fuel vapour is carried by vent hoses to the charcoal canister in the engine compartment. The activated charcoal in the canister absorbs and stores these vapours.

6 When the engine is running and warmed to a preset temperature, a purge cut-off solenoid valve near the canister closes, allowing a purge control diaphragm valve in the charcoal canister to be opened by intake manifold vacuum. Fuel vapours from the canister are then drawn through the purge control diaphragm valve by intake manifold vacuum.

Inspection

7 Always check the hoses first. A disconnected, damaged or missing hose is the most likely cause of a malfunctioning EVAP system **(see illustration)**. Repair any damaged hoses or renew any missing hoses as necessary.

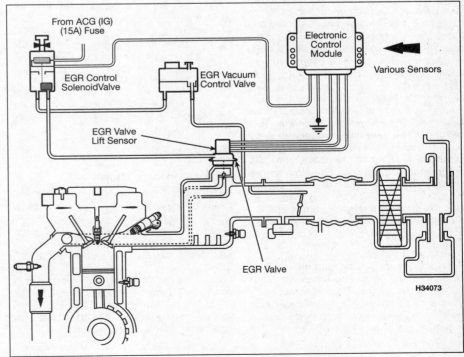

4.7 Typical EVAP system

Purge control solenoid

8 The purge control solenoid allows intake manifold vacuum to purge vapours from the canister when the engine is warm, and cuts off vacuum to the canister when the engine is cold.

9 Make sure the engine temperature is below the specified opening point of the solenoid:

D14A2, D14A3, D14A4,
   D14A8, D15Z3, D16B2,
      D16Y2, D16Y3 engine codes – 75°C.
D15Z6, D16Y5, D16Y6, D16Y7,
      D16Y8, B16A2 engine codes – 68°C.
D15Z8, B18C4 engines codes – 65°C.

10 Locate the purge hose on top of the canister **(see illustration)**. Follow the vacuum hose from the purge control valve to the canister to make sure you've got the right hose.

11 Once you've found the hose, disconnect it from the canister and connect a vacuum gauge to the disconnected end of the hose. Start the engine and allow it to idle. There should be no vacuum present.

12 Let the engine idle until it warms-up. There should now be vacuum at the end of the hose.

13 If the vacuum test results weren't correct, locate the purge control solenoid on the intake manifold and disconnect its electrical connector. Disconnect its vacuum hoses and connect a piece of rubber hose to one of the fittings on the solenoid.

14 Connect the battery directly to the solenoid with bridging wires. Try to blow into the piece of hose (through the solenoid). The solenoid should open (allowing air to flow) and close (blocking the flow of air) as the bridging wires are connected and disconnected. Some models will open when voltage is applied and close when it's removed; others will do the opposite. The important thing is that the solenoid opens and closes consistently as battery power is connected and disconnected.

Caution: Be very careful when applying battery voltage to an electrical component. Disconnect the component from the main wiring harness and apply voltage directly to the component or to the harness connector leading to the component. Do not apply voltage to the connector on the vehicle harness-side or damage to the Powertrain Control Module may result.

15 If the solenoid test results aren't correct, renew the solenoid.

Two-way valve

16 Remove the fuel filler cap.

17 Detach the vapour line from the fuel tank and connect a T-fitting into a vacuum pump and vacuum gauge **(see illustration)**.

18 Apply vacuum slowly and steadily and observe the gauge. Vacuum should stabilize momentarily at 5 to 15 mmHg. If the valve

4.10 The EVAP canister is located on the right-hand side of the engine compartment

opens (stabilises) before the correct vacuum, renew it with a new part.

19 Move the hand-held vacuum pump over to the pressure fitting (same vacuum line arrangement). Pressurise the pipe and observe the gauge. Pressure should stabilise at 12 to 37 mmHg (valve opens).

20 If the valve opens (stabilises) before or after the correct vacuum, renew it with a new part.

Canister vent shut-off valve

21 To determine whether your vehicle has a canister vent shut-off valve, look at the top of the canister. If there's a two-wire electrical connector directly on top of the canister, it has a shut-off valve.

22 Follow the hose from the shut-off valve down to the three-way valve, which is alongside the canister. Disconnect the hose from the three-way valve and attach a vacuum pump to the end of the hose.

23 Remove the shut-off valve from the canister, leaving the electrical connector and vacuum pump connected to it.

24 Switch the ignition key to ON (but don't start the engine) and apply vacuum to the hose. If the valve holds vacuum, disconnect the electrical connector. If it still holds vacuum, renew the valve with a new one.

---

5 Catalytic converter – general information and inspection

General information

1 The catalytic converter is an emission control device added to the exhaust system to reduce pollutants from the exhaust gas stream. The catalyst lowers the levels of oxides of nitrogen (NOx) as well as hydrocarbons (HC) and carbon monoxide (CO).

2 The catalytic converter is a reliable and simple device which needs no maintenance in itself, but there are some facts which an owner should be aware of if the converter is to function properly for its full service life.

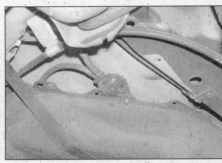

4.17 The two-way valve (where fitted) is located near the fuel tank

a) *DO NOT use leaded petrol – the lead will coat the internal precious metals, reducing their converting efficiency and will eventually destroy the converter.*

b) *Always keep the ignition and fuel systems well-maintained in accordance with the manufacturer's schedule.*

c) *If the engine develops a misfire, do not drive the car at all (or at least as little as possible) until the fault is cured.*

d) *DO NOT push- or tow-start the car – this will soak the catalytic converter in unburned fuel, causing it to overheat when the engine does start.*

e) *DO NOT switch off the ignition at high engine speeds.*

f) *The catalytic converter, used on a well-maintained and well-driven car, should last between 50 000 and 100 000 miles – if the converter is no longer effective it must be renewed.*

g) *DO NOT use fuel or engine oil additives – these may contain substances harmful to the catalytic converter.*

h) *Remember that the catalytic converter operates at very high temperatures. DO NOT, therefore, park the car in dry undergrowth, over long grass or piles of dead leaves after a long run.*

i) *Remember that the catalytic converter is FRAGILE – do not strike it with tools during servicing work.*

Inspection

3 The test equipment for a catalytic converter is expensive and highly sophisticated. If you suspect that the converter on your vehicle is malfunctioning, take it to a dealer service department or specialist for examination.

4 Whenever the vehicle is raised for servicing of underbody components, check the converter for leaks, corrosion, dents and other damage. Check the welds/flange bolts that attach the front and rear ends of the converter to the exhaust system. If damage is discovered, the converter should be renewed.

Component renewal

5 Refer to the exhaust system servicing section in Chapter 4A.

Chapter 5 Part A:
Starting and charging systems

Contents

Degrees of difficulty

Easy, suitable for novice with little experience	**Fairly easy,** suitable for beginner with some experience	**Fairly difficult,** suitable for competent DIY mechanic 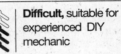	**Difficult,** suitable for experienced DIY mechanic	**Very difficult,** suitable for expert DIY or professional

Specifications

General
System type . . . . 12 volt, negative earth

Starter motor
Type:
  Hitachi (direct drive) . . . . 0.8 kW
  Mitsuba (gear reduction) . . . . 1.0 kW
  Nippondenso (direct drive) . . . . 0.8 kW
  Valeo (gear reduction) . . . . 1.0 kW

Battery
Ratings . . . . 36, 38, 47 or 92 Ah (depending on model)

Alternator
Type:
  Mitsubishi . . . . 70 or 75 amp
  Bosch . . . . 75 amp
  Denso . . . . 70, 75, 80 or 90 amp
Minimum brush length:
  Mitsubishi . . . . 14.0 mm
  Bosch . . . . 2.5 mm
  Denso . . . . 1.5 mm

Torque wrench settings	Nm	lbf ft
Alternator adjusting nut	24	18
Alternator pivot nut	44	32
Starter motor	44	32

1 General information and precautions

General information

The engine electrical system consists mainly of the charging and starting systems. Because of their engine-related functions, these are covered separately from the body electrical devices such as the lights, instruments, etc, which are covered in Chapter 12. Refer to Part B of this Chapter for information on the ignition system.

The electrical system is of the 12 volt negative earth type.

The battery may be of the low maintenance or maintenance-free (sealed for life) type and is charged by the alternator, which is belt-driven from the crankshaft pulley.

Charging system

The charging system includes the alternator, an internal voltage regulator, a charge indicator light, the battery, a fusible link and the wiring between all the components. The charging system supplies electrical power for the ignition system, the lights, the radio, etc. The alternator is driven by a drivebelt at the timing belt end of the engine.

The alternator control system within the PCM controls the voltage generated at the alternator in accordance with driving conditions. Depending upon electric load, vehicle speed, engine coolant temperature, accessories (air conditioning system, radio, cruise control, etc) and the intake air temperature, the system will adjust the amount of voltage generated, creating less load on the engine.

The purpose of the voltage regulator is to limit the alternator's voltage to a preset value. This prevents power surges, circuit overloads, etc, during peak voltage output.

The charging system doesn't ordinarily require periodic maintenance. However, the auxiliary drivebelt, battery and wires and connections should be inspected at the intervals outlined in Chapter 1.

The dashboard warning light should come on when the ignition key is turned to ON, but it should go off immediately after the engine is started. If it remains on, there is a malfunction in the charging system (see Section 4). Some vehicles are also equipped with a voltmeter. If the voltmeter indicates abnormally high or low voltage, check the charging system (see Section 4).

Starting system

The starting system consists of the battery, the starter motor, the starter solenoid and the wires connecting them. The solenoid is mounted directly on the starter motor.

The solenoid/starter motor assembly is installed at the rear of the engine, next to the transmission bellhousing.

When the ignition key is turned to the Start position, the starter solenoid is actuated through the starter control circuit. The starter solenoid then connects the battery to the starter. The battery supplies the electrical energy to the starter motor, which does the actual work of cranking the engine.

The starter motor on models equipped with manual transmissions can only be operated when the clutch pedal is depressed; the starter on models equipped with automatic transmissions can only be operated when the selector lever is in Park or Neutral.

Always observe the following precautions when working on the starting system:

Further details of the various systems are given in the relevant Sections of this Chapter. While some repair procedures are given, the usual course of action is to renew the component concerned. The owner whose interest extends beyond mere component renewal should obtain a copy of the *Automotive Electrical & Electronic Systems Manual*, available from the publishers of this manual.

Precautions

Warning: It is necessary to take extra care when working on the electrical system to avoid damage to semi-conductor devices (diodes and transistors), and to avoid the risk of personal injury. In addition to the precautions given in 'Safety first!', observe the following when working on the system:

Always remove rings, watches, etc before working on the electrical system. Even with the battery disconnected, capacitive discharge could occur if a component's live terminal is earthed through a metal object. This could cause a shock or nasty burn.

Do not reverse the battery connections. Components such as the alternator, electronic control units, or any other components having semi-conductor circuitry could be irreparably damaged.

Never disconnect the battery terminals, the alternator, any electrical wiring or any test instruments when the engine is running.

Never operate the starter motor for more than 15 seconds at a time without pausing to allow it to cool for at least two minutes. Excessive cranking of the starter motor can overheat it and cause serious damage.

Do not allow the engine to turn the alternator when the alternator is not connected.

Never test for alternator output by 'flashing' the output lead to earth.

Always ensure that the battery negative lead is disconnected when working on the electrical system.

If the engine is being started using jump leads and a slave battery, connect the batteries *positive-to-positive* and *negative-to-negative* (see *Jump starting* at the beginning of the manual). This also applies when connecting a battery charger.

Before using electric-arc welding equipment on the car, *disconnect the battery, alternator and components such as electronic control units* to protect them from the risk of damage.

Caution: The radio/cassette fitted as standard equipment has a built-in security code to deter thieves. If the power source to the unit is cut, the anti-theft system will activate. Even if the power source is immediately reconnected, the radio/cassette unit will not function until the correct security code has been entered. Therefore, if you do not know the correct security code for the radio/cassette unit, do not disconnect the battery negative terminal or remove the radio/cassette unit from the vehicle.

2 Battery – testing and charging

Testing

Standard and low-maintenance battery

1 If the vehicle covers a small annual mileage, it is worthwhile checking the specific gravity of the electrolyte every three months to determine the state of charge of the battery. Use a hydrometer to make the check, and compare the results with the following table. Note that the specific gravity readings assume an electrolyte temperature of 15°C (60°F); for every 10°C (18°F) below 15°C (60°F) subtract 0.007. For every 10°C (18°F) above 15°C (60°F) add 0.007.

	Above 25°C	Below 25°C
Fully charged	1.210 to 1.230	1.270 to 1.290
70% charged	1.170 to 1.190	1.230 to 1.250
Discharged	1.050 to 1.070	1.110 to 1.130

2 If the battery condition is suspect, first check the specific gravity of electrolyte in each cell. A variation of 0.040 or more between any cells indicates loss of electrolyte or deterioration of the internal plates.

3 If the specific gravity variation is 0.040 or more, the battery should be renewed. If the cell variation is satisfactory but the battery is discharged, it should be charged as described later in this Section.

Maintenance-free battery

4 In cases where a sealed for life maintenance-free battery is fitted, topping-up and testing of the electrolyte in each cell is not possible. The condition of the battery can therefore only be tested using a battery condition indicator or a voltmeter.

5 Certain models may be fitted with a maintenance-free battery with a built-in charge condition indicator. The indicator is located in the top of the battery casing, and indicates the condition of the battery from its colour. If the indicator shows green, then the battery is in a good state of charge. If the

indicator turns darker, eventually to black, then the battery requires charging, as described later in this Section. If the indicator shows clear/yellow, then the electrolyte level in the battery is too low to allow further use, and the battery should be renewed. **Do not** attempt to charge, load or jump start a battery when the indicator shows clear/yellow.

6 If testing the battery using a voltmeter, connect the voltmeter across the battery and note the voltage. The test is only accurate if the battery has not been subjected to any kind of charge for the previous six hours. If this is not the case, switch on the headlights for 30 seconds, then wait four to five minutes before testing the battery after switching off the headlights. All other electrical circuits must be switched off, so check that the doors and tailgate are fully shut when making the test.

7 If the voltage reading is less than 12.2 volts, then the battery is discharged, whilst a reading of 12.2 to 12.4 volts indicates a partially discharged condition.

8 If the battery is to be charged, remove it from the vehicle and charge it as described later in this Section.

Charging

Standard and low maintenance battery

Note: *The following is intended as a guide only. Always refer to the manufacturer's recommendations (often printed on a label attached to the battery) before charging a battery.*

9 Charge the battery at a rate equivalent to 10% of the battery capacity (eg, for a 45 Ah battery charge at 4.5 amps) and continue to charge the battery at this rate until no further rise in specific gravity is noted over a four-hour period.

10 Alternatively, a trickle charger charging at the rate of 1.5 amps can safely be used overnight.

11 Specially rapid boost charges which are claimed to restore the power of the battery in 1 to 2 hours are not recommended, as they can cause serious damage to the battery plates through overheating.

12 While charging the battery, note that the temperature of the electrolyte should never exceed 37.8°C (100°F).

Maintenance-free battery

Note: *The following is intended as a guide only. Always refer to the manufacturer's recommendations (often printed on a label attached to the battery) before charging a battery.*

13 This battery type takes considerably longer to fully recharge than the standard type, the time taken being dependent on the extent of discharge, but it can take anything up to three days.

14 A constant voltage type charger is required, to be set, when connected, to 13.9 to 14.9 volts with a charger current below 25 amps. Using this method, the battery should be useable within three hours, giving a voltage reading of 12.5 volts, but this is for a partially-discharged battery and, as mentioned, full charging can take far longer.

15 If the battery is to be charged from a fully-discharged state (condition reading less than 12.2 volts), have it recharged by your local automotive electrician, as the charge rate is higher and constant supervision during charging is necessary.

| 3 | Battery – disconnection, removal and refitting | |

Disconnection and removal

1 The battery is located at the left-hand side of the engine compartment **(see illustration)**.

2 Loosen the clamp nut and disconnect the battery negative (–) lead from the terminal **(see illustrations)**.

3 Lift the plastic flap where fitted, then loosen the clamp nut and disconnect the battery positive (+) lead from the terminal **(see illustration)**.

4 Unscrew the retaining nuts and remove the clamp **(see illustration)**.

5 Where fitted, disconnect the vent pipe from the battery. Note on some models the vent incorporates a flashback arrester.

6 Lift out the battery and withdraw it from the engine compartment **(see illustration)**.

Refitting

7 Clean the battery mounting.

8 Place the battery in position and refit the clamp. Tighten the nuts securely.

9 Where fitted, refit the vent pipe.

3.1 The battery is located in the left-hand corner of the engine compartment

3.2a Loosen the clamp nut . . .

3.2b . . . and disconnect the battery negative terminal

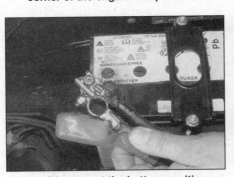

3.3 Disconnect the battery positive terminal

3.4 Undo the nuts and remove the retaining clamp

3.6 Lift the battery from the engine compartment

5.3a Loosen the adjustment bolt (arrowed) at the top of the alternator . . .

5.3b . . . and pivot bolt (arrowed) located at the bottom of the alternator

5.4 Lower the alternator from the engine

10 Reconnect the battery positive (+) lead to the terminal and tighten the clamp nut.

11 Reconnect the battery negative (–) lead to the terminal and tighten the clamp nut.

12 Re-activate the radio by inserting the security code where applicable.

4 Alternator/charging system – testing in vehicle

Note: *Refer to Section 1 of this Chapter before starting work.*

1 If the charge warning light fails to illuminate when the ignition is switched on, first check the alternator wiring connections for security. If satisfactory, check that the warning light bulb has not blown, and that the bulbholder is secure in its location in the instrument panel. If the light still fails to illuminate, check the continuity of the warning light feed wire from the alternator to the bulbholder. Check the condition of the auxiliary drivebelt. Check the condition of the regulator within the alternator as described in Section 6 of this Chapter. If all is satisfactory, the alternator is at fault and should be renewed or taken to an auto-electrician for testing and repair.

2 Similarly, if the charge warning light comes on with the ignition, but is then slow to go out when the engine is started, this may indicate an impending alternator problem. Check all the items listed in the preceding paragraph, and refer to an auto-electrical specialist if no obvious faults are found.

3 If the charge warning light illuminates when the engine is running, stop the engine and check that the drivebelt is correctly tensioned (see Chapter 1) and that the alternator connections are secure. If all is so far satisfactory, check the alternator brushes and slip-rings as described in Section 6. If the fault persists, the alternator should be renewed, or taken to an auto-electrician for testing and repair.

4 If the alternator output is suspect even though the warning light functions correctly, the regulated voltage may be checked as follows.

5 Connect a voltmeter across the battery terminals, and start the engine.

6 Increase the engine speed until the voltmeter reading remains steady; the reading should be approximately 12 to 13 volts, and no more than 14 volts.

7 Switch on as many electrical accessories (eg, the headlights, heated rear window and heater blower) as possible, and check that the alternator maintains the regulated voltage at around 13 to 14 volts.

8 If the regulated voltage is not as stated, this may be due to worn brushes, weak brush springs, a faulty voltage regulator, a faulty diode, a severed phase winding or worn or damaged slip-rings. The brushes and slip-rings may be checked (see Section 6), but if the fault persists, the alternator should be renewed or taken to an auto-electrician.

5 Alternator – removal and refitting

Removal

1 Detach the cable from the negative terminal of the battery (see Section 3).

2 Mark and detach the electrical connector and any earth straps from the alternator.

3 Loosen the alternator adjusting bolt and pivot bolt, then detach the auxiliary drivebelt **(see illustrations)**.

4 Remove the adjusting and pivot bolts and lower the alternator from the engine **(see illustration)**. If necessary, undo the bolts and remove the alternator mounting brackets from the engine block.

5 If you are renewing the alternator, take the old one with you when purchasing a renewal unit. Make sure the new/rebuilt unit looks identical to the old alternator. Look at the terminals – they should be the same in number, size and location as the terminals on the old alternator. Finally, look at the identification numbers – they will be stamped into the housing or printed on a tag attached to the housing. Make sure the numbers are the same on both alternators.

6 Many new/rebuilt alternators do not have a pulley installed, so you may have to switch the pulley from the old unit to the new/rebuilt one.

Refitting

7 Refitting is the reverse of removal.

8 After the alternator is installed, adjust the auxiliary drivebelt tension (see Chapter 1).

9 Check the charging voltage to verify proper operation of the alternator (see Section 4).

6 Alternator – brush holder/regulator module renewal

Note 1: *Some models use Mitsubishi alternators. Renewing the brushes and regulator on these alternators requires major dismantling and should be done by a suitable auto-electrical repair specialist.*

Note 2: *It's practical to renew the brushes and regulator on a Denso or Bosch alternator, but don't attempt to completely overhaul the alternator. If renewing the brushes and regulator does not solve the alternator problem, take the alternator to a dealer service department or specialist and have it rebuilt or exchange it for a rebuilt unit.*

1 Remove the alternator (see Section 5) and place it on a clean workbench.

2 Remove the rear cover nuts/bolts, the nut and terminal insulator and the rear cover **(see illustration)**.

6.2 Remove the three nuts (arrowed) and detach the rear cover from the alternator

6.3 Remove the two screws (arrowed) that retain the brush holder

6.5 Measure the exposed length of the brushes and compare your measurements to the specified minimum length to determine if they should be renewed

3 Remove the brush holder retaining screws **(see illustration)**. **Note:** *On Bosch alternators, the brush holder is integral with the voltage regulator module.*

4 Remove the brush holder from the rear end frame.

5 Measure the exposed length of the brush **(see illustration)** and compare it to the minimum length in this Chapter's Specifications. If the length of the brush is less than specified, renew the brush.

6 Make sure that each brush moves smoothly in the brush holder.

7 On Denso alternators, to remove the voltage regulator, remove the brushes as described above, then remove the mounting screws and take the regulator off **(see illustration)**.

8 Refitting is the reverse of removal. Fit the brush holder by depressing the brush with a small screwdriver to clear the shaft.

7 Starting system – testing

Note: *Refer to Section 1 of this Chapter before starting work.*

6.7 Remove the voltage regulator screws (arrowed) and remove the regulator from the alternator assembly

1 If the starter motor fails to operate when the ignition key is turned to the appropriate position, the following possible causes may be to blame:
a) *The battery is faulty.*
b) *The electrical connections between the switch, solenoid, battery and starter motor are somewhere failing to pass the necessary current from the battery through the starter to earth.*
c) *The solenoid is faulty.*
d) *The starter motor is mechanically or electrically defective.*

2 To check the battery, switch on the headlights. If they dim after a few seconds, this indicates that the battery is discharged – recharge (see Section 2) or renew the battery. If the headlights glow brightly, operate the ignition switch and observe the lights. If they dim, then this indicates that current is reaching the starter motor, therefore the fault must lie in the starter motor. If the lights continue to glow brightly (and no clicking sound can be heard from the starter motor solenoid), this indicates that there is a fault in the circuit or solenoid – see following paragraphs. If the starter motor turns slowly when operated, but the battery is in good condition, then this indicates that either the starter motor is faulty, or there is considerable resistance somewhere in the circuit.

3 If a fault in the circuit is suspected, disconnect the battery leads (including the earth connection to the body), the starter/solenoid wiring and the engine/transmission earth strap. Thoroughly clean the connections, and reconnect the leads and wiring, then use a voltmeter or test light to check that full battery voltage is available at the battery positive lead connection to the solenoid, and that the earth is sound. Smear petroleum jelly around the battery terminals to prevent corrosion – corroded connections are amongst the most frequent causes of electrical system faults.

4 If the battery and all connections are in good condition, check the circuit by disconnecting the wire from the solenoid blade terminal. Connect a voltmeter or test light between the wire end and a good earth (such as the battery negative terminal), and check that the wire is live when the ignition switch is turned to the Start position. If it is, then the circuit is sound – if not the circuit wiring can be checked as described in Chapter 12.

5 The solenoid contacts can be checked by connecting a voltmeter or test light between the battery positive feed connection on the starter side of the solenoid, and earth. When the ignition switch is turned to the start position, there should be a reading or lighted bulb, as applicable. If there is no reading or lighted bulb, the solenoid is faulty and should be renewed.

6 If the circuit and solenoid are proved sound, the fault must lie in the starter motor. Begin checking the starter motor by removing it (see Section 9), and having the brushes checked. If the fault does not lie in the brushes, the motor windings must be faulty. In this event, it may be possible to have the starter motor overhauled by a specialist, but check on the availability and cost of spares before proceeding, as it may prove more economical to obtain a new or exchange motor.

8 Starter motor – removal and refitting

Removal

1 Disconnect the cable from the negative terminal of the battery (see Section 3).

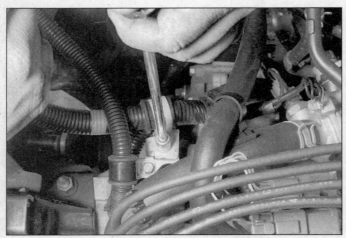

8.3a Remove the bracket assembly that retains the harness wiring loom to the transmission

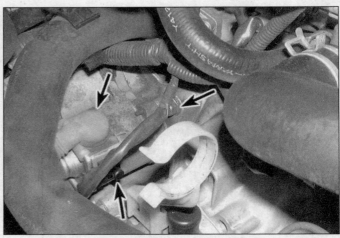

8.3b Disconnect the starter wires and remove the upper mounting bolt (arrowed) . . .

2 Remove the air duct from the air cleaner to the throttle body (see Chapter 4).

3 Clearly label, then disconnect the wires from the terminals on the starter motor solenoid. Disconnect any clips securing the wiring to the starter **(see illustrations)**.

4 Remove the mounting bolts **(see illustration)** and manoeuvre the starter from the engine compartment.

Refitting

5 Refit the starter motor by following the removal procedure in reverse. Tighten the mounting bolts to the specified torque.

9 Starter motor – testing and overhaul

If the starter motor is thought to be defective, it should be removed from the vehicle and taken to an auto-electrician for assessment. In the majority of cases, new starter motor brushes can be fitted at a reasonable cost. However, check the cost of repairs first as it may prove more economical to purchase a new or exchange motor.

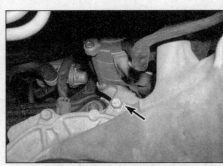

8.4 . . . and remove the lower bolt (arrowed) to separate the starter from the transmission.

Chapter 5 Part B:
Ignition system

Contents

Degrees of difficulty

Easy, suitable for novice with little experience	**Fairly easy,** suitable for beginner with some experience	**Fairly difficult,** suitable for competent DIY mechanic	**Difficult,** suitable for experienced DIY mechanic	**Very difficult,** suitable for expert DIY or professional

Specifications

System type
All models . . . . Fully-electronic under PCM control, camshaft driven distributor with integral ignition coil and control module

Firing order . . . . 1-3-4-2 (No 1 cylinder at timing belt end)

Ignition coil
Voltage . . . . 12 V
D15Z8 engine code (Lucas or Hitachi coil):
   Primary resistance . . . . 0.45 to 0.55 ohms
   Secondary resistance . . . . 22.4 to 33.6 k-ohms
D14A8, D16B2 engine codes (Lucas or Hitachi coil):
   Primary resistance . . . . 0.54 to 0.66 ohms
   Secondary resistance . . . . 13.6 to 20.4 k-ohms
All other engine codes (TEC coil):
   Primary resistance . . . . 0.63 to 0.77 ohms
   Secondary resistance . . . . 12.8 to 19.2 k-ohms

Ignition timing
D14A3, D14A4, D15Z6, D16Y5, D16Y6,
   D16Y7 and D16Y8 engine codes . . . . 12 ± 2° BTDC at idle
D14A2, D14A8, D15Z3, D15Z8, D16B2, D16Y2,
   D16Y3, B16A2 and B18C4 engine codes . . . . 16 ± 2° BTDC at idle

1 Ignition system – general information

The Programmed Ignition (PGM-IG) system provides complete control of the ignition timing by determining the optimum timing using a micro-computer in response to engine speed, coolant temperature, throttle position and vacuum pressure in the intake manifold. These parameters are relayed to the Powertrain Control Module (PCM) by the CKP/TDC/ CYP Sensor, Throttle Position Sensor (TPS), Coolant Temperature Sensor and MAP Sensor. Ignition timing is altered during warm-up, idling and warm running conditions by the PGM-IG system. This electronic ignition system also consists of the ignition switch, battery, coil, distributor, spark plug leads and spark plugs.

All distributors are driven by the camshaft (the intake camshaft on DOHC engine models). Distributors are advanced and retarded by the PCM. All models employ an ignition control module and TDC sensor which is located inside the distributor. Testing the CKP/TDC/CYP sensors is covered in Chapter 4A.

Warning: Voltages produced by an electronic ignition system are considerably higher than those produced by conventional ignition systems. Extreme care must be taken when working on the system with the ignition switched on. Persons with surgically-implanted cardiac pacemaker devices should keep well clear of the ignition circuits, components and test equipment.

Caution: If the radio in your vehicle is equipped with an anti-theft system, make sure you have the correct activation code before disconnecting the battery.

2 Ignition system – testing

1 If a fault appears in the engine management (fuel injection/ignition) system first ensure that the fault is not due to a poor electrical connection or poor maintenance; ie, check that the air cleaner filter element is clean, the spark plugs are in good condition and correctly gapped, that the engine breather hoses are clear and undamaged, referring to Chapter 1 for further information. Also check that the accelerator cable is correctly adjusted as described in Chapter 4A. If the engine is running very roughly, check the compression pressures as described in Chapter 2A or 2B.

2 If these checks fail to reveal the cause of the problem the vehicle should be taken to a suitably-equipped Honda dealer or specialist for testing. A wiring block connector is incorporated in the engine management circuit into which a special electronic diagnostic tester can be plugged. The

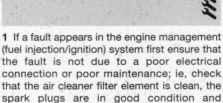

connector is located above the PCM (see Chapter 4A) in the passenger side footwell/behind the glovebox. See *On-Board Diagnostic system* in Chapter 4A.

3 The ignition system checks are detailed in Chapter 1 relating to the spark plugs, HT leads, distributor cap and rotor arm, whilst checking the ignition coil, module and ignition timing is detailed in this Chapter.

3 Ignition HT coil – testing and renewal

Testing

1 Make sure the ignition switch is turned OFF for the following checks.

2 Undo the retaining bolts and remove the distributor cap, the undo the screw and remove the rotor arm from the distributor shaft. Where fitted, remove the dust cover.

3 Disconnect the primary electrical connectors from the ignition coil.

4 Using an ohmmeter, touch the probes to the primary terminals (A and B) of the coil, measure the primary resistance and compare your reading to the value listed in this Chapter's Specifications **(see illustrations)**.

5 Touch the probes to the secondary winding terminal and the positive primary terminal (A) **(see illustrations)**, measure the secondary resistance and compare your reading to the resistance value listed in this Chapter's Specifications.

6 The readings will vary somewhat with the temperature of the coil. The specified resistance values are for a coil temperature of about 20°C.

7 If the coil fails either check, renew it.

Renewal

8 Undo the retaining bolts and remove the distributor cap, the undo the screw and remove the rotor arm from the distributor shaft. Where fitted, remove the dust cover.

9 Disconnect the wires from the coil primary terminals.

10 Remove the two screws and slide the coil out **(see illustration)**.

11 Refitting is the reverse of removal.

3.4a Disconnect the coil connectors and check resistance between the primary terminals; this is a Hitachi/Lucas distributor . . .

3.4b . . . and this is a TEC distributor

3.5a Check resistance between the coil primary and secondary terminals; this is a Hitachi/Lucas distributor . . .

3.5b . . . and this is a TEC distributor

3.10 The coil is retained by two screws (arrowed)

4.1 Check for battery voltage between the black/yellow wire and the body earth

4.3 Check for battery voltage between the white/blue wire and the body earth

4.8 Remove the screw(s) (arrowed) and pull the ICM unit straight out of the distributor body

4 Ignition Control Module – testing and renewal

Testing

1 Check for battery voltage to the Ignition Control Module (ICM). Remove the distributor cap and the rotor and disconnect the black/yellow wire from the ICM **(see illustration)**. Check for battery voltage at the harness connector with the ignition key ON (engine not running).

2 Check the ignition circuit and related components. If there is no voltage to the ICM, check the circuit from the ICM to the battery (see appropriate wiring diagram). First check the ignition system fuses in the underbonnet fuse/relay box. Follow the circuit carefully and make sure the ignition switch delivers battery voltage to the ICM with the key ON. Also check the yellow/green wire between the ICM and Powertrain Control Module (PCM), and the blue wire that connects to the tachometer or tachometer service connector. If there isn't continuity between the ends of each wire, there is a break in the wire. If there is continuity between either end of the wire and body earth, there is a short-circuit in the wire.

3 Check for battery voltage from the ignition coil to the ignition module. With the ignition key turned ON (engine not running), check for voltage between the blue wire (Lucas distributor) or white/blue wire (TEC distributor) and body earth **(see illustration)**. There should be battery voltage.

4 Check the circuit from the ignition coil to the ignition module. If there is no voltage, check the circuit between the corresponding wire and the ignition coil. Also check for an open-circuit inside the ignition coil by checking for continuity between the primary terminals of the ignition coil (see Section 3).

5 If the ignition coil and circuits are good and there is still no spark, the ICM may be defective.

Renewal

Note: *On some models, the ICM is only* available as a complete unit with the distributor.

6 Undo the retaining bolts and remove the distributor cap, the undo the screw and remove the rotor arm from the distributor shaft. Where fitted, remove the dust cover.

7 Remove all the electrical connectors from the ICM unit.

8 Remove the set screw(s) from the ICM body and pull the ICM unit straight out **(see illustration)**.

9 Refitting is the reverse of removal.

5 Distributor – removal and refitting

Removal

1 Detach the cable from the negative battery terminal (see Chapter 5A).

2 Detach any clamps and electrical connectors on the distributor. Mark the wires and hoses so they can be returned to their original locations.

3 Look for a raised number or letter on the distributor cap. This marks the location for the number 1 cylinder spark plug lead terminal. If the cap does not have a mark for the number 1 terminal, locate the number 1 spark plug and trace the wire back to the terminal on the cap.

4 Undo the bolts and remove the distributor

cap. Turn the engine over until the rotor is pointing toward the number 1 spark plug terminal (see the locating TDC procedure in Chapter 2A or 2B).

5 Make a mark on the edge of the distributor base directly below the rotor tip and in line with it (if the rotor on your engine has more than one tip, use the centre one for reference). Also, mark the distributor base and the cylinder head to ensure the distributor is refitted correctly **(see illustrations)**.

6 Remove the distributor retaining bolt(s) and pull out the distributor.

Caution: Do not turn the crankshaft while the distributor is out of the engine, or the alignment marks will be useless.

Refitting

Note: *If the crankshaft has been moved while the distributor is out, the number 1 piston must be repositioned at TDC. This can be done by feeling for compression pressure at the number 1 plug hole as the crankshaft is turned. Once compression is felt, align the ignition timing zero mark with the pointer.*

7 Fit a new O-ring on the distributor housing.

8 Insert the distributor into the cylinder head in exactly the same relationship to the head that it was when removed. **Note:** *The lugs on the end of the distributor and the corresponding grooves in the camshaft end are offset to eliminate the possibility of refitting the distributor 180° out of phase.*

9 Recheck the alignment marks between the

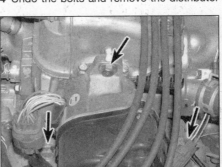

5.5a Mark the distributor position and remove the mounting bolts (arrowed); this is a SOHC engine distributor . . .

5.5b . . . and this is a DOHC engine distributor

distributor base and the cylinder head to verify the distributor is in the same position it was in before removal. Also check the rotor to see if it's aligned with the mark you made on the distributor.

10 Loosely fit the retaining bolt(s).

11 The remainder of refitting is the reverse of removal. Check the ignition timing (Section 5) and tighten the distributor retaining bolt(s) securely.

6 Ignition timing –
inspection and adjustment

1 Start the engine and allow it to reach normal operating temperature.

2 Check the engine idle speed as described in Chapter 1.

3 With the ignition OFF, connect an inductive pick-up timing light in accordance with the manufacturer's instructions. Connect the inductive pick-up lead of the timing light to the number 1 spark plug lead. On all models, number 1 is the one closest to the drivebelt end of the engine.

4 Locate the timing marks on the crankshaft pulley **(see illustration)**.

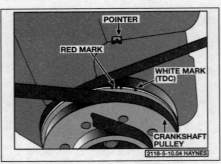

6.4 Be sure when viewing the timing mark on the pulley that you are directly above the pointer, aiming the timing light down so as not to create an extreme angle

6.5 The 2-pin Service Check Connector (arrowed) is located above the passenger's side kick panel

5 Locate the 2-pin service check connector. The service check connector is located above the passenger side kick panel behind the facia. Unclip the kick panel, reach up and locate the connector **(see illustration)**. Remove the service check connector from its holder. With the ignition OFF, connect the two terminals together with a bridging wire.

6 With the engine at normal operating temperature, start the engine and point the timing light at the timing pointer.

7 The red mark on the flywheel will appear stationary and be aligned with the pointer if the timing is correct.

8 If an adjustment is required, loosen the mounting bolts and rotate the distributor slightly until the timing is correct.

9 Tighten the mounting bolts and recheck the timing. Also recheck idle speed to make sure it hasn't changed.

10 Turn off the engine and remove the timing light.

11 Remove the bridging wire from the service check connector.

Chapter 6
Clutch

Contents

Degrees of difficulty

Easy, suitable for novice with little experience		Fairly easy, suitable for beginner with some experience		Fairly difficult, suitable for competent DIY mechanic		Difficult, suitable for experienced DIY mechanic		Very difficult, suitable for expert DIY or professional	

Specifications

General

Type	Single dry plate, diaphragm spring with spring-loaded hub
Operation	Hydraulic with release and master cylinders
Clutch pedal standard height	161 mm
Clutch pedal free play	12 to 21 mm
Friction disc minimum thickness	6.0 mm

Torque wrench settings

	Nm	lbf ft
Clutch slave cylinder mounting bolt	22	16
Pressure plate-to-flywheel bolt	25	18

1 General information

1 All vehicles with a manual transmission use a single dry-plate, diaphragm-spring type clutch. The clutch disc has a splined hub which allows it to slide along the splines of the transmission input shaft. The clutch disc and pressure plate are held in contact by spring pressure exerted by the diaphragm in the pressure plate.

2 The clutch release system is operated by hydraulic pressure. The hydraulic release system consists of the clutch pedal, a master cylinder and fluid reservoir, the hydraulic pipe, a release (or slave) cylinder which actuates the clutch release lever and the clutch release bearing.

3 When pressure is applied to the clutch pedal to release the clutch, hydraulic pressure is exerted against the outer end of the clutch release lever. As the lever pivots the shaft, fingers push against the release bearing. The bearing pushes against the fingers of the diaphragm spring of the pressure plate assembly, which in turn releases the clutch friction disc.

4 Terminology can be a problem when discussing the clutch components because common names are in some cases different from those used by the manufacturer. For example, the driven plate is also called the clutch friction plate or disc, and the release cylinder is sometimes called the operating or slave cylinder.

5 The hydraulic system requires no adjustment since the quantity of hydraulic fluid in the circuit automatically compensates for wear every time the clutch pedal is operated.

6 Other than to renew components with obvious damage, some preliminary checks should be performed to diagnose clutch problems. These checks assume that the transmission is in good working condition.

a) The first check should be of the fluid level in the clutch master cylinder (see 'Weekly Checks'). If the fluid level is low, add fluid as necessary and inspect the hydraulic system for leaks. If the master cylinder reservoir has run dry, bleed the system as described in Section 4 and retest the clutch operation.

b) To check 'clutch spin-down time,' run the engine at normal idle speed with the transmission in Neutral (clutch pedal up – engaged). Disengage the clutch (pedal down), wait several seconds and shift the transmission into Reverse. No grinding noise should be heard. A grinding noise would most likely indicate a problem in

2.2a The remote reservoir for the clutch master cylinder is located in the right-hand rear corner of the engine compartment. Remove these two bolts (arrowed) and lift the reservoir out of the way

2.2b Pinch off the fluid feed hose between the reservoir and the clutch master cylinder with a pair of locking pliers to prevent the fluid from running out of the end of the hose when you disconnect it from the clutch master cylinder

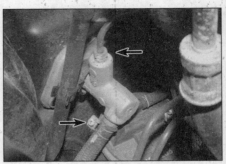

2.3 Slacken the clamp (left arrow) on the feed hose and use a brake pipe spanner to undo the pressure pipe fitting (right arrow)

the pressure plate or the clutch friction disc.

c) Visually inspect the pivot bushing at the top of the clutch pedal to make sure there is no binding or excessive play.

d) Crawl under the vehicle and make sure the clutch release lever is solidly mounted on the ball-stud.

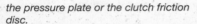

2 Master cylinder – removal, overhaul and refitting

Removal

1 Working under the facia, remove the split pin from the master cylinder pushrod clevis pin. Pull out the clevis pin to disconnect the pushrod from the pedal.

2 Detach the clutch master cylinder reservoir **(see illustration)**. Position a hose clamp or pair of locking pliers onto the clutch fluid feed hose, 50 mm downstream of the reservoir **(see illustration)**. The pliers should be just tight enough to prevent fluid flow when the hose is disconnected.

3 Disconnect the hydraulic pipes at the master cylinder **(see illustration)**. Loosen the fluid feed hose clamp and detach the hose from the cylinder. Have rags handy as some fluid will be lost as the line is removed. Cap or

plug the ends of the pipes (and/or hose) to prevent fluid leakage and the entry of contaminants.

Caution: Don't allow brake fluid to come into contact with the paint as it will damage the finish.

4 Working under the dash, unscrew the two clutch master cylinder retaining nuts **(see illustration)** and remove the cylinder.

Overhaul

5 Remove the dust cap from the end of the cylinder, hold the pushrod into the cylinder body, and prise out the circlip **(see illustration)**.

6 Ease out the pushrod, and pull out the piston assembly. If necessary use

compressed air to force the piston from the cylinder body. **Note:** *Check availability of cylinder overhaul kits prior to dismantling the old one.*

7 Carefully examine the bore of the cylinder for rust, scratches, gouges and general wear. If the bore is damaged, the complete cylinder must be renewed. If the bore is in good condition, thoroughly clean the assembly, and renew the seals as described below.

8 Take note of the seal orientation on the piston, and using a small screwdriver, lever the seals from the grooves on the piston.

9 Fit the new seals to the piston, ensuring the seal lips point towards the spring end of the piston. Smear the seals with the assembly grease supplied in the overhaul kit.

2.4 Undo the two mounting bolts (arrowed) and detach the master cylinder from the bulkhead

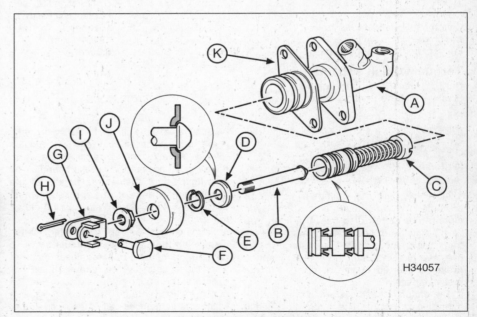

2.5 Clutch master cylinder

A Master cylinder body	E Circlip	I Lock nut
B Pushrod	F Clevis pin	J Dust seal
C Piston assembly	G Yoke	K Gasket
D Stopper washer	H Split pin	

10 Insert the piston assembly into the cylinder, spring end first. Ensure the seals lips enter the cylinder bore without catching or folding back.

11 Compress the piston with the pushrod, and fit the circlip. Squeeze some assembly grease into the dust cover, then refit cover.

Refitting

12 Place the master cylinder in position and fit the mounting nuts finger tight.

13 Connect the hydraulic pipes to the master cylinder. Move the cylinder slightly as necessary to thread the fitting into the cylinder (don't tighten the fitting yet). Attach the fluid feed hose to the cylinder and tighten the hose clamp.

14 Tighten the cylinder mounting nuts securely, then tighten the hydraulic pipe fitting securely.

15 Connect the pushrod to the clutch pedal. Use a new split pin to secure the clevis pin.

16 Remove the clamp/locking pliers from the feed hose. Fill the clutch master cylinder reservoir with brake fluid conforming to DOT 3 or DOT4 specifications and bleed the clutch system as outlined in Section 4.

3 Release cylinder – removal, overhaul and refitting

Removal

1 Raise the vehicle and support it securely on axle stands (see *Jacking and vehicle support*).

2 Disconnect the fluid hose at the release cylinder. Use a brake pipe nut spanner so you don't strip the corners off the fitting **(see illustration)**. Have a drain can and rags handy – some fluid will be spilled as the line is removed. Plug the line to prevent excessive fluid loss.

3 Remove the two release cylinder mounting bolts **(see illustration)**.

4 Remove the release cylinder.

Overhaul

5 Prise the dust cover from the cylinder body, and pull the pushrod out. Extract the piston and spring. If necessary, use compressed air to force the piston from the bore. Recover the piston spring **(see illustration)**. **Note:** *Check availability of cylinder overhaul kits prior to dismantling the old one.*

6 Carefully examine the bore of the cylinder for rust, scratches, gouges and general wear. If the bore is damaged, the complete cylinder must be renewed. If the bore is in good condition, thoroughly clean the assembly, and renew the seals as described below.

7 Note their fitted locations, then using a small screwdriver, prise the seals from the piston.

8 Fit the new seals to the piston, ensuring they are fitted as shown **(see illustration 3.5)**.

Coat the seals with assembly grease (supplied in the overhaul kit).

9 Insert the spring, large diameter end towards the cylinder bleed nipple, followed by the piston. Ensure the seals lips enter the cylinder bore without catching or folding back.

10 Squeeze some assembly grease into the dust cover, then refit the cover and pushrod.

Refitting

11 Refit the release cylinder on the clutch housing, but don't completely tighten the bolts yet. Make sure the pushrod is seated in the release fork pocket.

12 Connect the hydraulic pipe to the release cylinder, then tighten the release cylinder mounting bolts securely. Using a brake pipe nut spanner, tighten the hydraulic fitting securely.

13 Fill the clutch master cylinder with brake fluid conforming to DOT 3 or DOT 4 specifications.

14 Bleed the system as described in Section 4.

15 Lower the vehicle to the earth.

3.2 Using a brake pipe spanner, slacken the clutch fluid pipe fitting (arrowed) at the release cylinder

4 Hydraulic system – bleeding

⚠️ **Warning:** *Hydraulic fluid is poisonous; thoroughly wash off spills from bare skin without delay. Seek immediate medical advice if any fluid is swallowed or gets into the eyes. Certain types of hydraulic fluid are inflammable and may ignite when brought into contact with hot components. Hydraulic fluid is also an effective paint stripper. If spillage occurs onto painted bodywork or fittings, it should be washed off immediately, using copious quantities of cold water. It is also hygroscopic (ie, it can absorb moisture from the air) which lowers the boiling point of the fluid, rendering it dangerous to use in the hydraulic system. Old fluid will have suffered contamination, and should never be re-used.*

1 The correct operation of any hydraulic system is only possible after removing all air

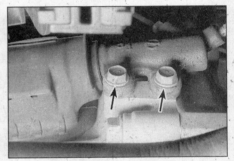

3.3 Remove the two mounting bolts (arrowed) from the clutch release cylinder

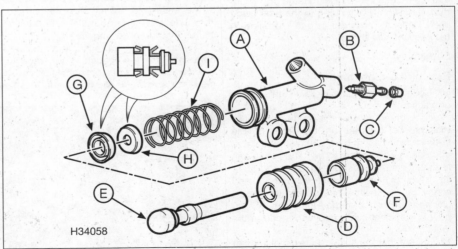

H34058

3.5 Clutch release cylinder

A	Release cylinder body	D	Gaiter	G	Piston seal
B	Bleed screw	E	Pushrod	H	Piston seal
C	Dust cap	F	Piston	I	Spring

from the components and circuit; this is achieved by bleeding the system.

2 During the bleeding procedure, add only clean, unused hydraulic fluid of the recommended type; never re-use fluid that has already been bled from the system. Ensure that sufficient fluid is available before starting work.

3 If there is any possibility of incorrect fluid being already in the system, the hydraulic circuit must be flushed completely with uncontaminated, correct fluid.

4 If hydraulic fluid has been lost from the system, or air has entered because of a leak, ensure that the fault is cured before continuing further.

5 Raise the vehicle and place it securely on axle stands (see *Jacking and vehicle support*).

6 Check that all pipes and hoses are secure, unions tight and the bleed screw is closed. The bleed screw is located on the end of the release cylinder, on the front of the transmission casing. Clean any dirt from around the bleed screw.

7 Unscrew the master cylinder fluid reservoir cap, and top the reservoir up to the upper (MAX) level line. Refit the cap loosely, and remember to maintain the fluid level at least above the lower (MIN) level line throughout the procedure, or there is a risk of further air entering the system.

8 There are a number of one-man, do-it-yourself bleeding kits currently available from motor accessory workshops. It is recommended that one of these kits is used whenever possible, as they greatly simplify the bleeding operation, and reduce the risk of expelled air and fluid being drawn back into the system. If such a kit is not available, the basic (two-man) method must be used, which is described in detail below.

9 If a kit is to be used, prepare the vehicle as described previously, and follow the kit manufacturer's instructions, as the procedure may vary slightly according to the type being used; generally, they are as outlined below in the relevant sub-section.

Bleeding

Basic (two-man) method

10 Collect a clean glass jar, a suitable length of plastic or rubber tubing which is a tight fit over the bleed screw located on the end of the release cylinder on the front of the transmission casing **(see illustration)**, and a ring spanner to fit the screw. The help of an assistant will also be required.

11 Remove the dust cap from the bleed screw. Fit the spanner and tube to the screw, place the other end of the tube in the jar, and pour in sufficient fluid to cover the end of the tube.

12 Ensure that the fluid level is maintained at least above the lower level line in the reservoir throughout the procedure.

13 Have the assistant fully depress the clutch pedal several times to build-up pressure, then maintain it on the final downstroke.

14 While pedal pressure is maintained, unscrew the bleed screw (approximately half of one turn) and allow the compressed fluid and air to flow into the jar. The assistant should maintain pedal pressure and should not release it until instructed to do so. When the flow stops, tighten the bleed screw again, have the assistant release the pedal slowly, and recheck the reservoir fluid level.

15 Repeat the steps given in paragraphs 13 and 14 until the fluid emerging from the bleed screw is free from air bubbles. If the master cylinder has been drained and refilled allow approximately five seconds between cycles for the master cylinder passages to refill.

16 When no more air bubbles appear, tighten the bleed screw securely, remove the tube and spanner, and refit the dust cap. Do not overtighten the bleed screw.

Using a one-way valve kit

17 As their name implies, these kits consist of a length of tubing with a one-way valve fitted, to prevent expelled air and fluid being drawn back into the system; some kits include a translucent container, which can be positioned so that the air bubbles can be more easily seen flowing from the end of the tube.

18 The kit is connected to the bleed screw, which is then opened. The user returns to the driver's seat, depresses the clutch pedal with a smooth, steady stroke, and slowly releases it; this is repeated until the expelled fluid is clear of air bubbles.

19 Note that these kits simplify work so much that it is easy to forget the clutch fluid reservoir level; ensure that this is maintained at least above the lower level line at all times.

Using a pressure-bleeding kit

20 These kits are usually operated by the reservoir of pressurised air contained in the spare tyre. However, note that it will probably be necessary to reduce the pressure to a lower level than normal; refer to the instructions supplied with the kit.

21 By connecting a pressurised, fluid-filled container to the clutch fluid reservoir, bleeding can be carried out simply by opening the bleed screw and allowing the fluid to flow

4.10 Push the length of plastic or rubber tubing over the end of the bleed screw, and the other end into the small container with 40 to 50 mm of clean brake fluid in it

out until no more air bubbles can be seen in the expelled fluid.

22 This method has the advantage that the large reservoir of fluid provides an additional safeguard against air being drawn into the system during bleeding.

All methods

23 When bleeding is complete, and correct pedal feel is restored, tighten the bleed screw securely and wash off any spilt fluid. Refit the dust cap to the bleed screw, and lower the vehicle to the earth.

24 Check the hydraulic fluid level in the master cylinder reservoir, and top-up if necessary (see *Weekly Checks*).

25 Discard any hydraulic fluid that has been bled from the system; it will not be fit for re-use.

26 Check the operation of the clutch pedal. If the clutch is still not operating correctly, air may still be present in the system, and further bleeding is required. Failure to bleed satisfactorily after a reasonable repetition of the bleeding procedure may be due to worn master cylinder/release cylinder seals.

| 5 | Clutch components – removal, inspection and refitting | |

 Warning: Dust produced by clutch wear and deposited on clutch components is hazardous to your health. DO NOT blow it out with compressed air and DO NOT inhale it. DO NOT use petrol or petroleum-based solvents to remove the dust. Brake system cleaner should be used to flush the dust into a drain pan.

Removal

1 Access to the clutch components is normally accomplished by removing the transmission, leaving the engine in the vehicle. If the engine is being removed for major overhaul, check the clutch for wear and renew worn components as necessary. However, the relatively low cost of the clutch components compared to the time and trouble spent gaining access to them warrants their renewal anytime the engine or transmission is removed, unless they are new or in near-perfect condition. The following procedures are based on the assumption the engine will stay in place.

2 Remove the transmission from the vehicle (see Chapter 7A). Support the engine while the transmission is out. Preferably, an engine hoist should be used to support it from above. However, if a jack is used underneath the engine, make sure a piece of wood is positioned between the jack and engine sump to spread the load.

Caution: The pick-up for the oil pump is very close to the bottom of the sump. If the sump is bent or distorted in any way, engine oil starvation could occur.

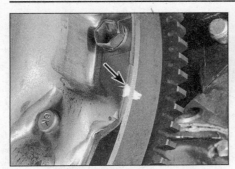

5.5 Mark the relationship of the pressure plate to the flywheel

5.6 Remove the pressure plate bolts (arrowed) gradually and evenly in a diagonal pattern

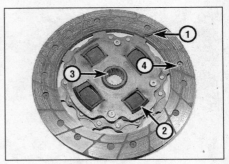

5.9 The clutch disc

1 *Lining – this will wear down in use*
2 *Springs or dampers – check for cracking and deformation*
3 *Splined hub – the splines must not be worn and should slide smoothly on the input shaft splines*
4 *Rivets – these secure the lining and will damage the flywheel or pressure plate if allowed to contact the surfaces*

3 The clutch fork and release bearing can remain attached to the transmission housing for the time being.

4 To support the clutch friction disc during removal, fit a clutch alignment tool through the friction disc hub.

5 Carefully inspect the flywheel and pressure plate for indexing marks. The marks are usually an X, an O or a white letter. If they cannot be found, scribe or paint marks yourself so the pressure plate and the flywheel will be in the same alignment during refitting **(see illustration)**.

6 Turning each bolt a little at a time, loosen the pressure plate-to-flywheel bolts **(see illustration)**. Work in a diagonal pattern until all spring pressure is relieved. Then hold the pressure plate securely and completely remove the bolts, followed by the pressure plate and friction disc.

Inspection

7 Ordinarily, when a problem occurs in the clutch, it can be attributed to wear of the clutch friction disc. However, all components should be inspected at this time.

8 Inspect the flywheel for cracks, heat distortion, grooves and other obvious defects. If the imperfections are slight, a engineering workshop can machine the surface flat and smooth, which is highly recommended regardless of the surface appearance. Refer to Chapter 2A for the flywheel removal and refitting procedure.

9 Inspect the lining on the clutch disc. There should be at least 1.5 mm of lining above the rivet heads. Check for loose rivets, distortion, cracks, broken springs and other obvious damage **(see illustration)**. As mentioned above, ordinarily the clutch friction disc is routinely renewed, so if in doubt about the condition, renew it.

10 The release bearing should also be renewed along with the clutch friction disc (see Section 7). This is also a good time to check the condition of the pilot bearing (see Section 6).

11 Check the machined surfaces and the diaphragm spring fingers of the pressure plate **(see illustrations)**. If the surface is grooved or otherwise damaged, renew the pressure plate. Also check for obvious damage, distortion, cracking, etc. Light glazing can be

removed with emery cloth or sandpaper. If a new pressure plate is required, new and factory-rebuilt units are available.

Refitting

12 Before refitting, clean the flywheel and pressure plate machined surfaces with brake cleaner or degreaser. It's important that no oil or grease is on these surfaces or the lining of the clutch friction disc. Handle the parts only with clean hands.

13 Position the clutch friction disc and pressure plate against the flywheel with the disc held in place with an alignment tool **(see illustration)**. Make sure the disc is installed properly (most renewal clutch discs will be marked 'flywheel side' or something similar – if not marked, fit the clutch friction disc with the damper springs toward the transmission).

14 Tighten the pressure plate-to-flywheel bolts only finger tight, working around the pressure plate.

15 Centre the clutch disc by ensuring the alignment tool extends through the splined hub

and into the pocket in the crankshaft. Wiggle the tool up, down or side-to-side as needed to centre the disc. Tighten the pressure plate-to-flywheel bolts a little at a time, working in a criss-cross pattern to prevent distorting the cover. After all of the bolts are snug, tighten them to the torque listed in this Chapter's Specifications. Remove the alignment tool.

16 Using clutch assembly grease, lubricate the inner groove of the release bearing (see Section 7). Also place grease on the release lever contact areas and the transmission input shaft bearing retainer.

17 Fit the clutch release bearing (see Section 7).

18 Fit the transmission and all components removed previously.

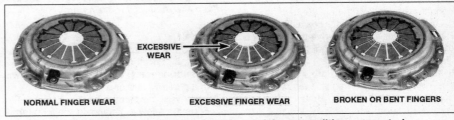

5.11a Renew the pressure plate if any of these conditions are noted

NORMAL FINGER WEAR   EXCESSIVE WEAR   EXCESSIVE FINGER WEAR   BROKEN OR BENT FINGERS

5.11b Inspect the pressure plate friction surface for score marks, cracks and signs of overheating

5.13 Centre the clutch disc in the pressure plate with a clutch alignment tool

6.4 Use a small slide-hammer puller to remove the pilot bearing

6.5 Tap the bearing into place with a bearing driver or a socket that is slightly smaller than the outside diameter of the bearing

6 Pilot bearing - inspection and renewal

1 The clutch pilot bearing is a ball-bearing which is pressed into the rear of the flywheel. It's greased at the factory and doesn't require additional lubrication. Its primary purpose is to support the front of the transmission input shaft. The pilot bearing should be inspected whenever the clutch components are removed from the engine. Because of its inaccessibility, renew it if you have any doubt about its condition.

2 Remove the clutch components (see Section 5).

3 Using a torch, inspect the bearing for excessive wear, scoring, dryness, roughness and any other obvious damage. If any of these conditions are noted, renew the bearing.

4 Remove the flywheel (see Chapter 2A). Using hammer and drift, drive the bearing out of the flywheel, from the front to the rear **(see illustration)**.

5 To fit a new bearing, lightly lubricate the outside surface with grease, then drive it into the recess with a bearing driver or a socket **(see illustration)**.

6 Fit the flywheel, if removed (see Chapter 2A). Fit the clutch components, transmission and other components removed previously. Tighten all fasteners to the recommended torque values where given.

7 Release bearing and fork – removal, inspection and refitting

⚠️ **Warning: Dust produced by clutch wear and deposited on clutch components is hazardous to your health. DO NOT blow it out with compressed air and DO NOT inhale it. DO NOT use petrol or petroleum-based solvents to remove the dust. Brake system cleaner or degreaser should be used to flush the dust into a drain pan.**

Removal

1 Unbolt the clutch release cylinder (see Section 3), but don't disconnect the fluid line. Suspend the release cylinder out of the way with a piece of wire or string.

2 Remove the transmission (see Chapter 7A).

3 Slide the release bearing off the input shaft,

disengage the clutch release fork retention spring from the ball-stud and remove the fork **(see illustration)**.

Inspection

4 Hold the bearing by the outer race and rotate the inner race while applying pressure. If the bearing doesn't turn smoothly or if it's noisy, renew the bearing/hub assembly **(see illustration)**.

5 Wipe the bearing with a clean rag and inspect it for damage, wear and cracks. It's common practice to renew the bearing with a new one whenever a clutch overhaul is performed, to decrease the possibility of a bearing failure in the future. Don't immerse the bearing in solvent – it's sealed for life and to do so would ruin it. Also check the release lever for cracks and bends.

Refitting

6 Fill the inner groove of the release bearing with clutch assembly grease. Also apply a light coat of the same grease to the transmission input shaft splines and the input shaft bearing retainer **(see illustration)**.

7 Lubricate the release fork ball socket, fork ends and release cylinder pushrod socket

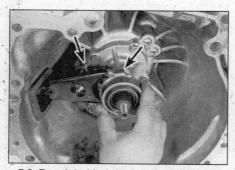

7.3 Reach behind the release lever and disengage the retention spring (left arrow), then remove the lever and slide the bearing tangs (right arrow) off the lever

7.4 To check the bearing, hold it by the outer race and rotate the inner race while applying pressure; if the bearing doesn't turn smoothly or if it's noisy, renew it

7.6 Apply clutch assembly grease to the bearing surface of the retainer

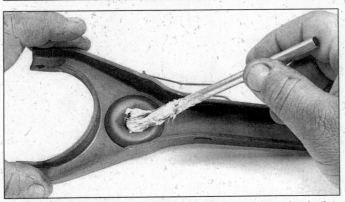

7.7a Apply clutch assembly grease to the ball-stud socket in the rear of the release lever . . .

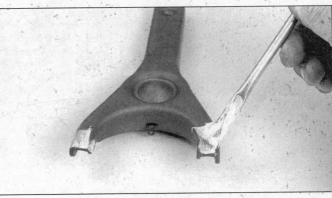

7.7b . . . the lever ends, the depression for the release cylinder pushrod . . .

with clutch assembly grease **(see illustrations)**.

8 Attach the release bearing to the release fork.

9 Slide the release bearing onto the transmission input shaft front bearing retainer while passing the end of the release fork through the opening in the clutch housing. Push the clutch release fork onto the ball-stud until it's firmly seated.

10 Apply a light coat of clutch assembly grease to the face of the release bearing where it contacts the pressure plate diaphragm fingers.

11 The remainder of refitting is the reverse of the removal procedure.

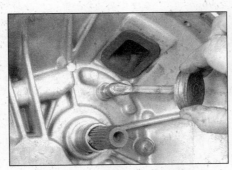

7.7c . . . and the ball-stud

8.1 Pedal height is the distance between the pedal pad and the floor

| 8 | Clutch pedal adjustment | |

Pedal height

1 The height of the clutch pedal is the distance the pedal sits off the floor **(see**

illustration). If the pedal height is not as specified, it must be adjusted.

2 To adjust the clutch pedal, loosen the locknut on the clutch switch or adjusting bolt and back the switch out until it no longer touches the pedal, then loosen the locknut on the clutch pushrod **(see illustration)**. Turn the pushrod to adjust the pedal height, then tighten the locknut.

3 Turn the switch or bolt clockwise until it just contacts the pedal arm, then turn it in an additional 3/4 to 1 turn. Tighten the locknut.

4 Adjust the starter/clutch interlock switch as described in Section 9.

Pedal freeplay

5 The freeplay is the pedal slack, or the distance the pedal can be depressed before it begins to have any effect on the clutch system **(see illustration)**. If the pedal freeplay is not within the specified range, it must be adjusted.

6 To adjust the pedal freeplay, loosen the locknut on the clutch pushrod. Then back off

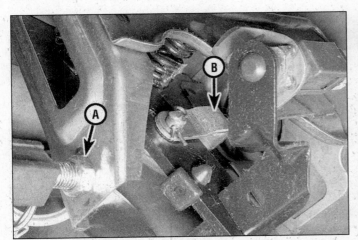

8.2 Undo the stopper bolt or switch (A) for clearance, then slacken the locknut just behind the clevis pin (B). Turn the pushrod to adjust the pedal height

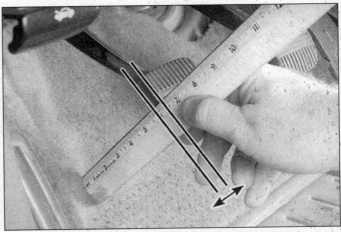

8.5 Pedal freeplay is the distance the pedal travels before resistance is felt

the pushrod to adjust the pedal freeplay to the specified range and retighten the locknut.

7 Check and, if necessary, adjust the starter/interlock switch (see Section 9).

9 Starter/clutch interlock switch – testing, renewal and adjustment

Testing

1 The starter/clutch interlock switch is located near the upper end of the clutch pedal **(see illustration)**. It has two wires – one coming from the starter relay and one going to earth. When the ignition switch key is turned to the Start position and the clutch pedal is depressed, the starter relay's path to earth is closed by the starter/clutch interlock switch and the starter motor is activated.

2 If the engine won't crank when the clutch pedal is depressed, adjust the switch (see Paragraph 6) and try again. If it still won't turn over, check the switch (see Paragraph 3) and, if necessary, renew it (see Paragraph 5). If the engine rotates when the clutch pedal isn't depressed, adjust the switch and try again.

3 If the engine won't start when the clutch pedal is depressed, either there's no voltage from the starter relay to the switch, or there's no continuity between the two terminals on the switch.

4 Check the voltage to the switch with a voltmeter or test light. When you turn the ignition key to the Start position and depress the clutch pedal, there should be voltage in the wire from the starter relay. If there isn't, look for an open- or short-circuit condition somewhere between the starter relay and the switch. If there is voltage in this wire, check the other side of the switch for voltage (with the pedal depressed). If there's voltage on both sides of the switch, the switch should be operating correctly. Try adjusting it (see Paragraph 6). If voltage isn't present on both sides, the switch may be defective.

Renewal

5 Unplug the electrical connector, loosen the adjustment nut and unscrew the switch from its mounting bracket. Refitting is the reverse of removal.

9.1 The interlock switch (arrowed) is located on a bracket near the top of the clutch pedal; it's secured to the bracket by a pair of nuts, one above the bracket, one below, which are also used to adjust the position of the switch plunger in relation to the stopper on the pedal

Adjustment

6 Loosen the locknut and turn the switch in or out, as necessary, to provide continuity through the switch when the clutch pedal is depressed.

Chapter 7 Part A:
Manual transmission

Contents

Degrees of difficulty

Easy, suitable for novice with little experience		**Fairly easy,** suitable for beginner with some experience		**Fairly difficult,** suitable for competent DIY mechanic
	Difficult, suitable for experienced DIY mechanic		**Very difficult,** suitable for expert DIY or professional	

Specifications

General
Type . . . . Manual, five forward speeds and reverse. Synchromesh on all forward speeds

Lubrication
Oil type . . . . See *Lubricants and fluids*
Oil capacity . . . . See Chapter 1

Torque wrench settings	Nm	lbf ft
Engine-to-transmission support bracket:		
8 mm	24	18
10 mm	44	32
12 mm	57	42
Flywheel lower cover nuts	12	9
Lower rear engine-to-transmission bolts:		
14 x 1.5 mm bolts*	84	62
12 x 1.25 mm bolts	64	47
Right-hand front transmission mounting:		
Mounting to transmission	64	47
Mounting bracket to body	44	32
Starter bolts	44	32
Upper transmission-to-engine bolts:		
12 mm	64	47
10 mm	40	30
Mounting bolt and nuts	64	47
Engine bracket-to-mounting through-bolt	74	55

*Do not re-use

1.1 Underside view of the manual transmission and its related components

1 Transmission   2 Gearchange rod   3 Extension rod   4 Driveshaft

1 General information

1 The transmission is contained in a cast-aluminium alloy casing bolted to the engine's right-hand end, and consists of the gearbox and final drive differential – often called a transmission **(see illustration)**.

2 Drive is transmitted from the crankshaft via the clutch to the input shaft, which has a splined extension to accept the clutch friction disc, and rotates in tapered roller bearings. From the input shaft, drive is transmitted to the output shaft, which also rotates in tapered roller bearings. From the output shaft, the drive is transmitted to the differential crownwheel, which rotates with the differential case and planetary gears, thus driving the sun gears and driveshafts. The rotation of the planetary gears on their shaft allows the inner roadwheel to rotate at a slower speed than the outer roadwheel when the car is cornering.

3 The input and output shafts are arranged side-by-side, parallel to the crankshaft and driveshafts, so that their gear pinion teeth are in constant mesh. In the neutral position, the output shaft gear pinions rotate freely, so that drive cannot be transmitted to the crownwheel.

4 Gear selection is via a floor-mounted lever and linkage. The selector linkage causes the appropriate selector fork to move its respective synchro-sleeve along the shaft, to lock the gear pinion to the synchro-hub. Since the synchro-hubs are splined to the output shaft, this locks the pinion to the shaft, so that drive can be transmitted. To ensure that gearchanging can be made quickly and quietly, a synchromesh system is fitted to all gears, consisting of baulk rings and spring-loaded fingers, as well as the gear pinions and synchro-hubs. The synchromesh cones are formed on the mating faces of the baulk rings and gear pinions.

Caution: If the radio in your vehicle is equipped with an anti-theft system, make sure you have the correct activation code before disconnecting the battery.

2 Driveshaft oil seals – renewal

1 Oil leaks frequently occur due to wear of the driveshaft oil seals. Renewal of these seals is relatively easy, since the repair can usually be performed without removing the transmission from the vehicle.

2 Driveshaft oil seals are located at the sides of the transmission, where the driveshafts are attached. If leakage at the seal is suspected, raise the vehicle and support it securely on axle stands (see *Jacking and vehicle support*). If the seal is leaking, lubricant will be found on the sides of the transmission, below the seals.

3 Refer to Chapter 8 and remove the driveshaft(s).

4 Use a screwdriver or lever bar to carefully prise the oil seal out of the transmission casing **(see illustration)**.

5 Using a large section of pipe or a large deep socket (slightly smaller than the outside diameter of the seal) as a drift, fit the new oil seal **(see illustration)**. Ensure that the spring side of the seal faces into the transmission casing. Drive it into the bore squarely and

2.4 Insert the tip of a large screwdriver behind the oil seal and carefully lever it out

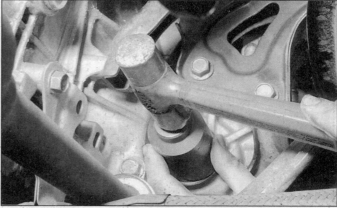

2.5 Using a large socket or a section of pipe, drive the new seal squarely into the bore

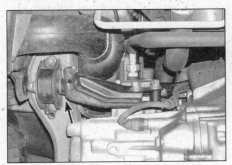

3.2 Insert a large screwdriver (arrowed) and try to move the transmission; if it moves appreciably, renew the mounting

4.1 Remove this gearchange lever boot and the dust seal underneath

4.3 Undo the bolt (arrowed) and disconnect the extension rod

make sure it's completely seated. Coat the seal lip with transmission lubricant.

6 Refit the driveshaft(s). Be careful not to damage the lip of the new seal.

3 Transmission mountings – inspection and renewal

1 Raise the front of the vehicle and place it securely on axle stands (see *Jacking and vehicle support*).

2 Insert a large screwdriver or lever bar between the mounting support arm and the frame and try to lever the support arm **(see illustration)**.

3 The transmission support arm should not move up more than about 12 to 18 mm within the mounting. If it does, renew the mounting.

4 To renew the mounting, support the transmission with a trolley jack, remove the nuts and bolts and remove the mounting.

⚠️ *Warning: Do not place any part of your body under the transmission when it's supported only by a jack.*

5 Refitting is the reverse of removal.

4 Gearchange mechanism – removal and refitting

Removal

1 Unscrew the gear lever knob. Remove the centre console (see Chapter 11). Remove the rubber gearchange lever boot and the dust seal underneath **(see illustration)**.

2 Raise the vehicle and place it securely on axle stands (see *Jacking and vehicle support*).

3 To disconnect the extension rod from the transmission, simply remove the bolt that attaches it to the extension bracket **(see illustration)**.

4 To disconnect the gearchange rod from the transmission, push the dust boot forward **(see illustration)**, remove the clip and drive out the roll-pin with a pin punch. Discard the spring pin – do not re-use it.

5 To disconnect the rear end of the

4.4 Push the dust boot forward, remove the clip and drive out the roll-pin (arrowed)

gearchange rod from the gear lever, remove the nuts and bolts **(see illustration)**.

6 Remove the two nuts and washers that retain the change ball holder to the underside of the extension rod **(see illustration 4.5)** and remove the change ball holder, lower gear lever dust seal, gear lever ball seat, gear lever and extension rod.

7 Inspect the bushing at the front end of the extension rod and renew it if it's cracked, torn or worn.

8 Renew the O-rings in the base of the gear lever.

Refitting

9 Refitting is the reverse of removal. Lubricate the new O-rings and the bushings with silicone grease. Use a new roll-pin to attach the gearchange rod to the transmission. Tighten all fasteners securely.

10 Check the operation of the gear lever.

5 Reversing light switch – testing and renewal

Testing

1 Before testing the reversing light switch, check the fuse in the passenger compartment fuse/relay box.

2 Put the gear lever in Reverse and turn the ignition switch to the ON position. The reversing lights should go on. Turn off the ignition switch.

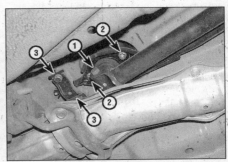

4.5 Remove the nut and bolt (1) and disconnect the gearchange rod from the gear lever; to disconnect the extension rod, remove the nuts (2) and the two bolts (3)

3 If the reversing lights don't go on, check the light bulbs in the tail light assembly (see Chapter 12).

4 If the fuse and bulbs are both okay, locate the reversing light switch on top (SOHC engines) or end (DOHC engines) of the transmission **(see illustration)**, trace the leads back to the electrical connector, unplug the connector and connect up an ohmmeter or continuity tester across the two terminals.

5 With the gear lever in Reverse, there should be continuity; with the lever in any other gear, there should be no continuity.

6 If the switch fails this test, renew it (see below).

7 If the switch is OK, but the reversing lights aren't coming on, check for power to the

5.4 The reversing light switch (arrowed) is located on the side of the transmission housing

6.4 Unplug the electrical connector (arrowed) from the Vehicle Speed Sensor

6.10 Remove the clutch hydraulic pipe bracket bolts (arrowed)

6.12 Remove the engine support bracket bolts (arrowed)

switch. If voltage is not available, trace the circuit between the switch and the fuse block. If power is present, trace the circuit between the switch and the reversing lights for an open-circuit condition.

Renewal

8 Unplug the reversing light switch electrical connector.
9 Unscrew the reversing light switch.
10 Discard the old washer.
11 Using a new washer, fit the new switch.
12 Plug in the connector.

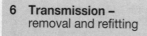

6 Transmission – removal and refitting

Removal

1 Remove the battery as described in Chapter 5A.
2 Remove the intake air duct and air cleaner housing (see Chapter 4A).
3 Disconnect the starter motor cables and remove the upper starter motor mounting bolt (see Chapter 5A).
4 Disconnect the transmission earth cable, unplug the reversing light switch connector (see Section 5) and detach the wiring harness clamp from the transmission. Unplug the Vehicle Speed Sensor electrical connector **(see illustration)**.
5 Slacken the driveshaft nut (see Chapter 8). Loosen the front roadwheel nuts, raise the vehicle and support it securely on axle stands

(see *Jacking and vehicle support*). Remove the front wheels.
6 Remove the engine splash shield, if fitted.
7 Remove the front section of the exhaust pipe (see Chapter 4A).
8 Drain the transmission oil (see Chapter 1).
9 Disconnect the gearchange and extension rods from the transmission (see Section 4).
10 Undo the bolts securing the clutch hydraulic pipe brackets to the transmission casing **(see illustration)**, undo the retaining bolts and move the release cylinder and pipe to one side, without disconnecting the pipe (see Chapter 6).
Caution: Be careful not to bend or kink the clutch hydraulic pipe, and don't depress the clutch pedal while the release cylinder is removed.
11 Remove the driveshafts (see Chapter 8).
12 Remove the engine-to-transmission support bracket (where fitted) **(see illustration)**.
13 Undo the retaining bolts, and remove the lower flywheel cover.
14 Remove the distributor top mounting bolt and attach an engine hoist to the cylinder head to support the engine, then lift the engine slightly to take the load off the engine and transmission mountings.
15 Support the transmission with a trolley jack. Raise the transmission just enough to take the weight off the mountings.
16 Remove the right-hand side transmission mounting bracket bolts and nuts **(see illustration)**.
17 Remove the four upper transmission-to-engine mounting bolts **(see illustration)**.

18 Remove the rear lower transmission-to-engine bolt immediately above the right driveshaft.
19 Remove the lower transmission-to-engine bolt and transmission mounting bracket bolts **(see illustration)**.
20 Make a final check that all wires and hoses have been disconnected from the transmission, then carefully pull the transmission and jack away from the engine.
21 Once the input shaft is clear, lower the transmission and remove it from under the vehicle.
22 With the transmission removed, the clutch components are now accessible and can be inspected. In most cases, new clutch components should be routinely installed when the transmission is removed (see Chapter 6).

Refitting

23 If removed, fit the clutch components (see Chapter 6).
24 Make sure the two locating dowels are installed in the transmission mating face. With the transmission on a trolley jack, raise it into position behind the engine, then carefully slide it forward, engaging the two locating dowels on the transmission with the corresponding holes in the block, and the input shaft with the clutch disc hub splines. Do not use excessive force to refit the transmission – if the input shaft does not slide into place, readjust the angle of the transmission so it is level and/or turn the input shaft so the splines engage properly with the clutch friction disc hub.

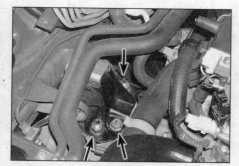

6.16 Remove the transmission mounting retaining bolts and nuts (arrowed)

6.17 Remove the upper transmission-to-engine bolts (arrowed)

6.19 Remove the lower transmission bolt and mounting bracket bolts (arrowed)

25 Refit the transmission housing-to-engine bolts and the transmission rear mounting bracket bolts and tighten them to the torque listed in this Chapter's Specifications.

26 Refit the three upper transmission-to-engine bolts and the lower starter motor mounting bolt, then tighten them to the torque listed in this Chapter's Specifications.

27 Raise the transmission slightly, then refit the right-hand transmission mounting bracket and the bracket bolt and nuts. Tighten the bolts and nuts to the torque listed in this Chapter's Specifications.

28 Refit the front mounting bracket and tighten the bolts to the torque listed in this Chapter's Specifications.

29 Remove the chain hoist and refit the distributor mounting bolt.

30 Refit the lower flywheel cover and, on models so equipped, refit the engine-to-transmission support brackets. Tighten the cover and bracket bolts to the torque listed in this Chapter's Specifications.

31 The remainder of refitting is the reverse of removal.

32 Refill the transmission with the specified amount of lubricant (see Chapter 1).

33 Check the operation of the clutch, and if necessary, bleed the clutch hydraulic system (see Chapter 6).

34 Road test the vehicle for proper operation and check for leaks.

7 Transmission overhaul – general information

1 Overhauling a manual transmission unit is a difficult and involved job for the DIY home mechanic. In addition to dismantling and reassembling many small parts, clearances must be precisely measured and, if necessary, changed by selecting shims and spacers. Internal transmission components are also often difficult to obtain, and in many instances, extremely expensive. Because of this, if the transmission develops a fault or becomes noisy, the best course of action is to have the unit overhauled by a specialist repairer, or to obtain an exchange reconditioned unit.

2 Nevertheless, it is not impossible for the more experienced mechanic to overhaul the transmission, provided the special tools are available, and the job is done in a deliberate step-by-step manner, so that nothing is overlooked.

3 The tools necessary for an overhaul include internal and external circlip pliers, bearing pullers, a slide hammer, a set of pin punches, a dial test indicator, and possibly a hydraulic press. In addition, a large, sturdy workbench and a vice will be required.

4 During dismantling of the transmission, make careful notes of how each component is fitted, to make reassembly easier and more accurate.

5 Before dismantling the transmission, it will help if you have some idea what area is malfunctioning. Certain problems can be closely related to specific areas in the transmission, which can make component examination and renewal easier. Refer to the *Fault finding* Section of this manual for more information.

Chapter 7 Part B: Automatic and Constantly Variable Transmissions

Contents

Degrees of difficulty

Easy, suitable for novice with little experience	Fairly easy, suitable for beginner with some experience	Fairly difficult, suitable for competent DIY mechanic	Difficult, suitable for experienced DIY mechanic	Very difficult, suitable for expert DIY or professional

Specifications

General

Transmission type:

S1LA	4-speed automatic with lock-up clutch
S4PA, S4MA	4-speed automatic with electronic control
S4XA	4-speed automatic with Transmission Control Module
AR4A	4-speed automatic controlled by Powertrain Control Module (PCM)
M4VA	Constantly Variable Transmission (CVT)
Selector lock solenoid clearance	2.4 ± 0.4 mm
Lock-up control solenoid resistance	12 to 25 ohms
Selector control solenoid resistance	12 to 25 ohms

Torque wrench settings

	Nm	lbf ft
Driveplate/torque converter cover	12	9
Driveplate-to-torque converter bolts	12	9
Engine to transmission support bracket:		
Bolts to transmission	57	42
Bolt to engine	24	18
Flywheel-to-driveplate bolts (Constantly Variable Transmission)	12	9
Lock-up control solenoid bolts	12	9
Rear engine/transmission mounting bolts	74	55
Right-hand side front mounting bracket:		
Long Bolts*	64	47
Short bolts	44	32
Selector control solenoid bolts	12	9
Selector lock solenoid self-locking nuts	10	7
Transmission mounting nuts	64	47
Transmission mounting through-bolt	74	55
Transmission-to-engine bolts	64	47

*Do not re-use

1 General information

The automatic transmissions **(see illustration)** fitted to the Civic have four forward speeds (and one reverse). The automatic gearchanges are either controlled hydraulically or electronically depending on the transmission type – see Specifications at the start of this Chapter. A kickdown facility is also provided, to enable a faster acceleration response when required. On S4XA and AR4A transmissions, the ECM employs 'Fuzzy logic' to determine the gear up-shift and down-shift points. Instead of having predetermined points for up-shift and down-shift, the ECM takes into account several influencing factors before deciding to shift up or down. These factors include engine speed, driving 'resistance' (engine load), brake pedal position, throttle position, and the rate at which the throttle pedal position is changed. This results in an almost infinite number of shift points, which the ECM can tailor to match the driving style, be that sporty or economic.

The automatic transmission consists of three main assemblies, these being the torque converter, which is directly coupled to the engine; the final drive unit, which incorporates the differential unit; and the planetary gearbox, with its multi-disc clutches and brake bands. The transmission is lubricated with automatic transmission fluid (ATF), which should be changed at regular intervals as described in Chapter 1.

The torque converter incorporates a lock-up feature, which eliminates any possibility of converter slip in all four forward gears; this aids performance and economy.

Civic models equipped with the 1.6 litre SOHC engine may be fitted with a Constantly Variable Transmission (CVT). This is a combination of drive and driven pulleys, a steel belt, and a three speed automatic transmission. By varying the effect diameter of the driven and drive pulleys, the transmission provides seamless overall ratio variation, with three diving modes.

Because of the need for special test equipment, the complexity of some of the parts, and the need for scrupulous cleanliness when servicing these transmissions, the amount which the owner can do is limited. Repairs to the final drive differential are also not recommended. Most major repairs and overhaul operations should be left to a Honda dealer or specialist, who will be equipped with the necessary equipment for fault diagnosis and repair. The information in this Chapter is therefore limited to a description of the removal and refitting of the transmissions as a complete unit, the transmission range sensor, and interlock system. The removal, refitting and adjustment of the kickdown cable is also described.

In the event of a transmission problem occurring, consult a Honda dealer or transmission specialist before removing the transmission from the vehicle, since the majority of fault diagnosis is carried out with the transmission *in situ*.

Caution: If the radio in your vehicle is equipped with an anti-theft system, make sure you have the correct activation code before disconnecting the battery.

2 Fault finding – general

Note: *Automatic transmission or Constantly Variable Transmission malfunctions may be caused by five general conditions: poor engine performance, improper adjustments, hydraulic malfunctions, mechanical malfunctions or malfunctions in the computer or its signal network. Diagnosis of these problems should always begin with a check of the easily repaired items: fluid level and condition (see Chapter 1), selector control cable adjustment and throttle control cable adjustment. Next, perform a road test to determine if the problem has been corrected or if more diagnosis is necessary. If the problem persists after the preliminary tests and corrections are completed, additional diagnosis should be done by a dealer service department or transmission specialist.*

Preliminary checks

1 Drive the vehicle to warm the transmission to normal operating temperature.

2 Check the fluid level as described in Chapter 1:

a) *If the fluid level is unusually low, add enough fluid to bring the level within the designated area of the dipstick, then check for external leaks (see below).*

b) *If the fluid level is abnormally high, drain off the excess, then check the drained fluid for contamination by coolant. The presence of engine coolant in the automatic transmission fluid indicates that a failure has occurred in the internal radiator walls that separate the coolant from the transmission fluid.*

c) *If the fluid is foaming, drain it and refill the transmission, then check for coolant in the fluid, or a high fluid level.*

3 Check the engine idle speed. **Note:** *If the engine is malfunctioning, do not proceed with the preliminary checks until it has been repaired and runs normally.*

4 Check the throttle control cable for freedom of movement. Adjust it if necessary (see Section 3). **Note:** *The cable may function properly when the engine is turned off and cold, but it may malfunction once the engine*

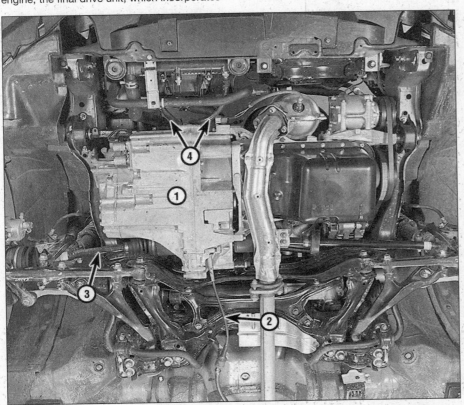

1.1 Underside view of the automatic transmission and its related components

| 1 Transmission | 2 Selector cable | 3 Driveshaft | 4 Cooler pipes |

is hot. Check it cold and at normal engine operating temperature.

5 Inspect the selector cable linkage (see Section 4). Make sure that it's properly adjusted and that the linkage operates smoothly.

Fluid leak diagnosis

6 Most fluid leaks are easy to locate visually. Repair usually consists of renewing a seal or gasket. If a leak is difficult to find, the following procedure may help.

7 Identify the fluid. Make sure it's transmission fluid and not engine oil or brake fluid (automatic transmission fluid is a deep red colour).

8 Try to pinpoint the source of the leak. Drive the vehicle several miles, then park it over a large sheet of cardboard. After a minute or two, you should be able to locate the leak by determining the source of the fluid dripping onto the cardboard.

9 Make a careful visual inspection of the suspected component and the area immediately around it. Pay particular attention to gasket mating surfaces. A mirror is often helpful for finding leaks in areas that are hard to see.

10 If the leak still cannot be found, clean the suspected area thoroughly with a degreaser, then dry it.

11 Drive the vehicle for several miles at normal operating temperature and varying speeds. After driving the vehicle, visually inspect the suspected component again.

12 Once the leak has been located, the cause must be determined before it can be properly repaired. If a gasket is renewed but the sealing flange is bent, the new gasket will not stop the leak. The bent flange must be straightened.

13 Before attempting to repair a leak, check

to make sure that the following conditions are corrected or they may cause another leak. **Note:** Some of the following conditions cannot be fixed without highly specialised tools and expertise. Such problems must be referred to a transmission specialist or a dealer service department.

Gasket leaks

14 Check the right-hand side cover periodically. Make sure the bolts are tight, no bolts are missing, the gasket is in good condition and the cover is not damaged.

15 If the leak is from the right-hand side cover area, the bolts may be too tight, the sealing surface of the transmission housing may be damaged, the gasket may be damaged or the transmission casting may be cracked or porous. If sealant instead of gasket material has been used to form a seal between the cover and the transmission housing, it may be the wrong sealant.

Seal leaks

16 If a transmission seal is leaking, the fluid level or pressure may be too high, the vent may be blocked, the seal bore may be damaged, the seal itself may be damaged or improperly installed, the surface of the shaft protruding through the seal may be damaged or a loose bearing may be causing excessive shaft movement.

17 Make sure the dipstick tube seal is in good condition and the tube is properly seated. Periodically check the area around the vehicle speed sensor for leakage. If transmission fluid is evident, check the O-ring for damage.

Housing leaks

18 If the housing itself appears to be leaking, the casting is porous and will have to be repaired or renewed.

19 Make sure the oil cooler hose fittings are tight and in good condition.

Fluid comes out vent pipe or filler tube

20 If this condition occurs, the transmission is overfilled, there is coolant in the fluid, the housing is porous, the dipstick is incorrect, the vent is blocked or the drain-back holes are blocked.

Fault diagnosis

21 On models equipped with the S1LA, S4PA or S4MA transmissions, fault diagnosis is limited to road testing, carrying out the component checks listed in this Chapter, or consulting an automatic transmission specialist. However, the electronic modules which control the S4XA, AR4A, and M4VA transmissions are equipped with a self diagnosis system.

22 Should a fault be recognised by the module, a Diagnostic Trouble Code (DTC) will be generated and stored in the Transmission Control Module (TCM) or Powertrain Control Module (PCM), and the position D4 light of the Selector indicator display on the instrument panel will flash.

23 To retrieve the DTC, locate the 2-pin Service Check Connector behind the passenger side kick panel/under the facia, and bridge the two connectors using a length of wire, turn the ignition key to position II, and observe the D4 indicator light on the instrument panel.

24 The light will blink a longer blink to represent the first digit of a two digit number and then will blink short for the second digit (for example, 1 long blink then 6 short blinks for the code 16). **Note:** If the system has more than one problem, the codes will be displayed in sequence, then a there will be pause, then the codes will repeat.

Diagnostic Trouble Codes (DTCs)

Trouble code	Component or system	Corrective action
Code 1	Lock-up clutch faulty	Check lock-up control solenoid (A)
Code 2	Lock-up clutch does not engage	Check lock-up control solenoid (B)
Code 3	Lock-up clutch does not engage	Check Throttle Position Sensor
Code 4	Lock-up clutch does not engage	Check the Vehicle Speed Sensor
Code 5	Shift failure (except 2nd to 4th)	Check gear position switch
Code 6	Shift failure (except 2nd to 4th)	Check gear position switch
Code 7	Shift failure (1st to 4th, 2nd to 4th or 2nd to 3rd only)	Check selector control solenoid (A)
Code 8	Stuck in 1st or 4th gear	Check selector control solenoid (B)
Code 9	Lock-up clutch does not engage	Check the countershaft speed sensor
Code 10	Lock-up clutch does not engage	Check engine coolant temperature sensor
Code 11	Lock-up clutch does not engage	Check ignition coil
Code 14	Rough gearchanges	Check TCM/PCM and wiring
Code 15	Rough gearchanges	Check mainshaft speed sensor
Code 16	Rough gearchanges	Check the linear solenoid

Clearing codes

25 When the TCM/PCM sets DTC, the indicator light will come on and a trouble code will be stored in the memory. The trouble code will stay in the TCM/PCM memory until the voltage to the TCM/PCM is interrupted. To clear the memory, remove the BACK-UP fuse from the fuse/relay box located in the engine compartment for at least ten seconds (see Chapter 12 for fusebox location). **Note:** *Unplugging the BACK-UP fuse also cancels the radio preset stations and the clock setting. Be sure to make a note of the various radio stations that are programmed into the memory before removing the fuse.*

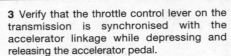

3 Throttle control cable – inspection and adjustment

Note: *The throttle control cable regulates the gearchange points of the S1LA, S4PA and S4XA automatic transmissions. Don't confuse it with the accelerator cable, which actuates the air intake throttle body for the fuel injection system.*

Inspection

1 Before you check the throttle control cable, make sure the accelerator cable freeplay (see Chapter 4A) and the idle speed (see Chapter 1) are correct.
2 Warm-up the engine to normal operating temperature.

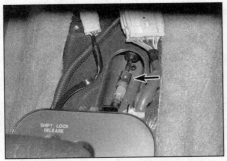

4.2 Detach the selector cable retaining clip (arrowed)

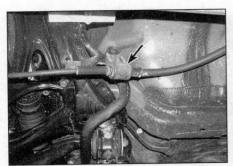

4.4 Detach the selector cable from the brace (arrowed)

3 Verify that the throttle control lever on the transmission is synchronised with the accelerator linkage while depressing and releasing the accelerator pedal.
4 If the throttle control lever isn't synchronised with the accelerator linkage, adjust the throttle control cable (see below).
5 Have an assistant depress the accelerator pedal to the full-throttle position, then verify that there's a little freeplay in the throttle control lever (on the transmission).
6 Disconnect the end of the throttle control cable from the throttle control lever at the transmission.
7 Verify that the throttle control lever moves smoothly. If it doesn't, take the vehicle to an automatic transmission specialist.
8 Reconnect the throttle control cable to the throttle control lever.

Adjustment

9 Follow Paragraphs 1 and 2 above.
10 Verify that the accelerator lever is in the fully closed position.
11 Loosen the throttle control cable locknut at the upper end, near the throttle body.
12 While pushing the throttle control lever to the fully closed position, remove all freeplay from the throttle control cable by tightening the adjusting nut.
13 Tighten the locknut.
14 After the locknut is tightened, check the synchronisation and throttle control lever movement. Also, make sure there is a little freeplay in the throttle control lever at the

4.3 Remove the selector cable bracket bolts (arrowed)

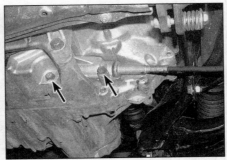

4.5 Remove the selector cable cover bolts (arrowed)

transmission when the accelerator pedal is fully depressed (if there isn't, the lever or the control mechanism in the transmission may become damaged).

4 Selector cable – renewal and adjustment

Renewal

1 Remove the centre console as described in Chapter 11.
2 Put the selector lever in the Neutral position, then remove the retaining clip from the cable adjuster **(see illustration)**.
3 Raise the front of the vehicle and support it securely on axle stands (see *Jacking and vehicle support*). Unbolt the selector cable bracket **(see illustration)**.
4 Detach the selector cable holder from the floor and detach the cable from the brace **(see illustration)**.
5 Remove the selector cable cover **(see illustration)**.
6 Remove the nut and detach the control lever from the control shaft, then remove the selector cable **(see illustration)**. Be careful not to bend the cable when removing or refitting it.
7 Refitting is the reverse of removal. Be sure to adjust the selector cable when you're through.

Adjustment

8 Remove the centre console, if not already done (see Chapter 11). Move the selector lever to the Neutral position, then remove the retaining clip from the cable adjuster **(see illustration 4.2)**.
9 There are two holes in the end of the selector cable. They're positioned 90° apart to allow cable adjustments in 1/4-turn increments. Verify that the hole in the adjuster is perfectly aligned with the hole in the selector cable **(see illustration)**.
10 If the two holes aren't perfectly aligned, loosen the locknut on the selector cable and adjust it as required, then retighten the locknut.

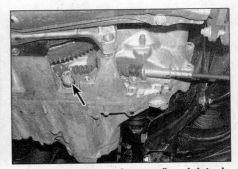

4.6 Remove the nut (arrowed) and detach the control lever from the control shaft

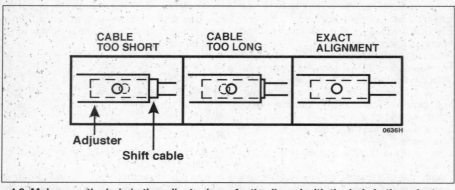

4.9 Make sure the hole in the adjuster is perfectly aligned with the hole in the selector cable

4.14 Make sure the white index mark (arrowed) at the base of the shift lever aligns with the corresponding neutral mark on the selector indicator panel

11 Fit the retaining clip on the adjuster. If the clip feels as if it's binding as you refit it, the cable is still out of adjustment and must be readjusted.

12 Remove the selector indicator panel mounting screws and align the marks by moving the panel.

13 Refit the panel screws and tighten them securely.

14 Verify that the selector lever is aligned with the Neutral mark on the selector indicator panel when the transmission is in Neutral **(see illustration)**. If they're not aligned, adjust the selector indicator panel.

15 Start the engine and check the selector lever in all gears. If any gear doesn't work properly, refer to Section 2.

5 Gear position switch – testing, adjustment and renewal

Testing

1 Remove the centre console (see Chapter 11).

2 Unplug the electrical connector from the gear position switch **(see illustrations)**.

3 Check for continuity between the indicated terminals (on the switch side of the harness) in each switch position in accordance with the accompanying tables **(see illustration)**. Move the selector lever back-and-forth at each switch position without touching the push-button and check for continuity within the range of selector lever freeplay (about 2.0 mm).

4 If there's no continuity within the range of selector lever freeplay at each selector lever position, adjust the position of the switch.

Adjustment

5 Move the selector lever to the Park position and loosen the switch mounting nuts **(see illustration 5.11)**.

6 Slide the switch toward the Drive positions until there's continuity between terminals 2 and 14 within the range of selector lever freeplay (about 2.0 mm).

5.2a Terminal guide for the gear position switch connector – 2, 3 and 4-door models

5.2b Terminal guide for the gear position switch connector – 5-door models

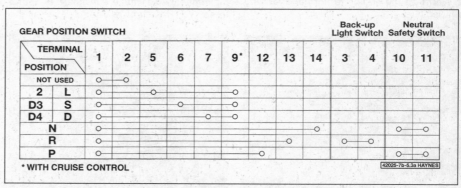

GEAR POSITION SWITCH

TERMINAL / POSITION	1	2	5	6	7	9*	12	13	14	Back-up Light Switch 3	Back-up Light Switch 4	Neutral Safety Switch 10	Neutral Safety Switch 11
NOT USED	o	o											
2 L	o		o			o							
D3 S	o			o		o							
D4 D	o				o	o							
N	o								o			o	o
R	o						o			o	o		
P	o							o		o		o	o

* WITH CRUISE CONTROL

5.3a Continuity table for the gear position switch – 2, 3 and 4-door models

GEAR POSITION SWITCH (Without cruise control)

TERMINAL ▶ / POSITION ▼	A	B	E	F	G	N	M	L	BACK-UP LIGHT SWITCH C	BACK-UP LIGHT SWITCH D	NEUTRAL SAFETY SWITCH J	NEUTRAL SAFETY SWITCH K
1	o	o										
2	o		o									
D3	o			o								
D4	o				o							
N	o					o					o	o
R	o						o		o	o		
P	o							o			o	o

5.3b Continuity table for the gear position switch – 5-door models without cruise control

GEAR POSITION SWITCH (With cruise control)										Back-up Light Switch		Neutral Safety Switch	
TERMINAL POSITION	I	A	B	E	F	G	N	M	L	C	D	J	K
1		○	○										
2	○	○		○									
D3	○	○			○								
D4	○	○				○							
N		○					○					○	○
R		○						○	○	○	○		
P		○							○			○	○

42025-7b-5.3c HAYNES

5.3c Continuity table for the gear position switch – 5-door models with cruise control

5.11 Remove the two nuts (arrowed) and detach the gear position switch (note the position in which the switch slider must be when refitting the switch)

7 Recheck continuity as described above in Paragraph 3. Make sure the engine starts when the selector lever is in the Neutral position.

8 If there's still no continuity at each selector lever position, inspect the selector lever detent and bracket for damage. If they're undamaged, the switch may be faulty.

Renewal

9 Remove the centre console (see Chapter 11).

10 Unplug the 14-pin connector **(see illustrations 5.2a and 5.2b)**.

11 Remove the two switch mounting nuts and washers **(see illustration)**.

12 Position the switch slider at the Neutral position.

13 Move the selector lever to the Neutral position, then fit the new switch.

14 Attach the new switch with the two nuts and washers.

15 Test the new switch as described above in Paragraph 3. Make sure the engine starts when the selector lever is in the Neutral position.

16 Reconnect the electrical connector. Clamp the harness.

17 Refit the centre console (see Chapter 11).

---

6 Interlock system – description, testing, and solenoid renewal and adjustment

Description

1 Vehicles equipped with an automatic transmission have an interlock system to prevent unintentional gear changing. The interlock system consists of two subsystems: a selector lock system and a key interlock system.

Key interlock system

2 The key interlock system prevents the ignition key from being removed from the ignition switch unless the selector lever is in the Park position. If you insert the key when the selector lever is in any position other than Park, a solenoid is activated, making it impossible for you to remove the key until the selector lever is moved to the Park position.

Selector lock system

3 The selector lock system prevents the selector lever from moving from the Park position unless the brake pedal is depressed. Nor can the selector lever be moved when the brake pedal and the accelerator pedal are depressed at the same time. In the event of a system malfunction, you can release the selector lever by inserting a key into the release slot near the selector lever.

Testing

Note: *Applies to S1LA, S4PA, S4MA transmissions only*

4 The following checks are simple tests of the key interlock solenoid and the selector lock solenoid you can do at home. Further testing of the interlock system should be left to a dealer service department or automatic transmission specialist.

Key interlock solenoid

5 Remove the lower instrument panel (see Chapter 11).

6 Unplug the 7-pin connector **(see illustration)** from the main wiring harness.

7 Check for continuity between the terminals in each switch position. With the key pushed in, there should be continuity between terminals 5, 6 and 7; with the key released, there should be continuity only between terminals 5 and 6.

8 Verify that the key can't be removed when battery voltage is connected to terminal 7 and terminal 5 is earthed.

Caution: Apply voltage only long enough to perform this check.

9 If the key can't be removed, the key interlock solenoid is okay; if the key can be removed, the steering lock assembly needs to be renewed (the key interlock solenoid isn't available separately).

Selector lock solenoid

10 Remove the centre console (see Chapter 11).

11 Unplug the two-pin connector from the selector lock solenoid **(see illustration)**.

12 Using a pair of bridging wires, momentarily touch a positive battery lead to the number 1 terminal of the two-pin connector and a negative lead to the number 2 terminal and note whether the solenoid clicks on or not.

Caution 1: Be very careful when applying battery voltage to an electrical component. Disconnect the component from the main wiring harness and apply voltage directly to the component. Do not apply voltage to the connector on the vehicle harness-side or damage to the Powertrain Control Module may result.

6.6 Terminal guide for the key interlock solenoid connector (as seen from the rear of the connector)

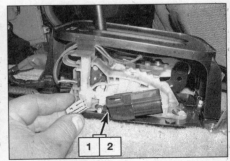

6.11 Terminal guide for the selector lock solenoid

6.18 Energise the solenoid, check the clearance between the selector lock lever and the lock pin groove (arrowed) and compare your measurement to the clearance listed in this Chapter's Specifications

Caution 2: Make sure you don't connect the battery voltage lead to the wrong connector terminal. Reversing the polarity can damage or destroy the diode inside the solenoid.

 a) *If the solenoid doesn't operate, renew it.*
 b) *If the solenoid does operate, but you have been having problems with the selector lock system, it may be necessary to adjust the solenoid at its OFF and ON positions (see below).*

13 While the solenoid is on, it's a good idea to check the clearance between the selector lock lever and the lock pin groove (see Paragraph 18).

14 With the solenoid turned off, note whether or not the lock pin is blocked by the selector lock lever. If it isn't, adjust the position of the selector lock solenoid until it is (see below).

Solenoid renewal

Note: *The following procedure pertains only to the selector lock solenoid. For information on how to renew the key interlock solenoid, refer to the 'Ignition switch and lock cylinder renewal' Section in Chapter 12. The key interlock solenoid isn't available separately.*

15 Remove the selector lock collar and the solenoid pin.

16 Remove the self-locking nuts and the selector lock solenoid. Discard the old nuts.

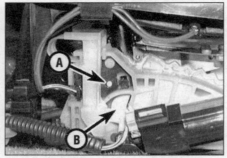

6.19 When the selector lock solenoid is OFF, ensure the lock pin (A) is blocked by the selector lock lever (B)

17 Refitting is the reverse of removal. Don't tighten the new nuts until you have adjusted the solenoid as follows.

Adjustment

18 To adjust the selector lock solenoid, energise the solenoid and check the clearance between the selector lock lever and the lock pin groove **(see illustration)** and compare your measurement to the clearance listed in this Chapter's Specifications. Position the solenoid so the clearance is correct, then tighten the new self-locking nuts to the torque listed in this Chapter's Specifications. **Note:** *Be sure to use new self-locking nuts.*

19 With the solenoid turned off, note whether or not the lock pin is blocked by the selector lock lever **(see illustration)**. If it isn't, readjust the position of the selector lock solenoid until it is.

---

7 Lock-up solenoid and selector control solenoid – testing and renewal

Testing

Note: *Applies to S1LA, S4PA, S4MA transmissions only*
Caution: Be very careful when applying battery voltage to an electrical component. Disconnect the component from the main

wiring harness and apply voltage directly to the component or to the harness connector leading to the component. Do not apply voltage to the connector on the vehicle harness-side or damage to the Powertrain Control/Transmission Control Module may result.

Lock-up control solenoid

1 Unplug the connector from the lock-up control solenoid valve assembly **(see illustration)**.

2 Measure the resistance between each of the connector terminals (solenoid side) and earth, and compare your measurements to the resistance listed in this Chapter's Specifications. If the resistance is out of specification for either terminal, it may be necessary to renew the entire solenoid assembly.

3 Connect each of the connector terminals (of the solenoid side of the connector) to the battery positive terminal with a bridging wire. You should hear a clicking sound as each solenoid valve is energised. If you don't, renew the solenoid assembly.

Selector control solenoid

4 Unplug the connector from the selector control solenoid valve assembly **(see illustration)**.

5 Measure the resistance between each of the connector terminals (solenoid side) and earth, and compare your measurements to the resistance listed in this Chapter's Specifications. If the resistance is out of specification for either terminal, it may be necessary to renew the entire solenoid assembly.

6 Connect each of the connector terminals to the battery positive terminal with a bridging cable. You should hear a clicking sound as each solenoid valve is energised. If you don't, renew the solenoid assembly.

Renewal

Note: *You cannot renew only one solenoid valve; both the lock-up and selector control solenoid valve assemblies must be renewed as a single unit.*

7 Remove the mounting bolts and remove the solenoid valve assembly **(see illustration)**

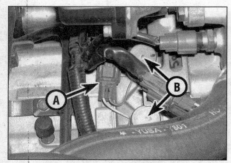

7.1 Unplug the connector (A) from the lock-up control solenoid valve assembly (B) located on top of the transmission

7.4 Unplug the electrical connector from the selector control solenoid assembly (A)

7.7 The lock-up and selector control solenoid valve assemblies are retained by three bolts (arrowed) – lock-up assembly shown

8.7 Remove the transmission-to-engine mounting bolts (arrowed)

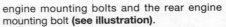

8.14 Remove the support bracket bolts (arrowed)

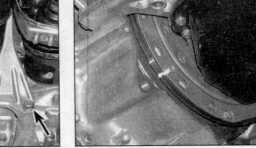

8.16 Prior to removing the driveplate-to-torque converter (or CVT driveplate and flywheel) bolts, mark the edge of the driveplate and torque converter or flywheel to ensure they're reattached in the same relationship when the transmission is refitted

8 Clean the mounting surface and oil passages; make sure all dirt and dust is removed.

9 Fit a new base gasket and fit the new solenoid valve assembly. Tighten the solenoid valve bolts to the torque listed in this Chapter's Specifications.

10 Check the electrical connector for dirt, corrosion and oil; clean it thoroughly if necessary. Reconnect it.

11 Check the solenoid valves as described above and make sure the new unit is functioning properly.

---

8 Automatic transmission or CVT – removal and refitting

Removal

1 Disconnect the negative cable from the battery (see Chapter 5A).

2 Remove the intake air duct and air cleaner housing (see Chapter 4A).

3 Remove the starter motor (see Chapter 5A).

4 Disconnect the earth cable from the transmission.

5 Unplug the electrical connector from the lock-up control solenoid (see Section 7).

6 Unplug the speed sensor electrical connector.

7 Remove the three upper transmission-to-

engine mounting bolts and the rear engine mounting bolt **(see illustration)**.

8 Remove the both front driveshafts as described in Chapter 8.

9 Remove the front exhaust pipe section from underneath the engine (see Chapter 4A).

10 Remove the selector cable cover, then detach the cable from the transmission (see Section 4).

11 Remove the right-hand front transmission mounting/bracket.

12 Disconnect the throttle control cable from the throttle control lever (where applicable; see Section 3).

13 Disconnect the transmission fluid cooler hoses from the cooler lines. Turn the hoses up to prevent fluid from flowing out, then plug the lines to prevent contamination.

14 Remove the engine-to-transmission support bracket(s) **(see illustration)**.

15 Remove the torque converter (conventional transmission) or flywheel (CVT) access plate. Unplug any electrical connectors still connected to the transmission.

16 Mark the relationship of the torque converter (conventional transmission) or flywheel (CVT) to the driveplate so that they can be refitted to their original positions **(see illustration)**.

17 Remove the torque converter- or flywheel-to-driveplate bolts one at a time by rotating the crankshaft pulley for access to each bolt.

18 Remove the distributor top mounting bolt,

then attach an engine hoist or support fixture to the engine.

19 Place a trolley jack under the transmission. Raise the transmission assembly just enough to take the load off the transmission mounting.

20 Remove the transmission side mounting **(see illustration)**.

21 Remove the lower transmission-to-engine bolt, the lower engine-to-transmission bolt and the rear engine mounting bolts **(see illustration)**.

22 Move the transmission back to disengage it from the engine block locating dowels and make sure the torque converter is detached from the driveplate. Secure the torque converter to the transmission so it will not fall out during removal. Lower the transmission from the vehicle. **Note:** *It may be necessary to slowly lower the engine while the jack supporting the transmission is being lowered. This will provide more clearance between the transmission and the body.*

Refitting

23 Honda recommends flushing the transmission cooler and the cooler hoses and pipes with degreaser whenever the transmission is removed from the vehicle. Flush the pipes and fluid cooler thoroughly and make sure no degreaser remains in the pipes or cooler after flushing. It's a good idea to repeat the flushing procedure with clean automatic transmission fluid to ensure that no degreaser remains in the pipes or cooler.

24 Refit the starter motor (see Chapter 5A).

25 Prior to refitting, make sure that the torque converter hub is securely engaged in the pump. Raise the transmission into position. Be sure to keep it level so the torque converter does not slide out.

26 Turn the torque converter to line it up with the driveplate. The marks you made on the torque converter and the driveplate must align.

8.20 Undo the transmission side mounting bolts and nuts (arrowed)

8.21 Remove the rear engine mounting bolts (arrowed)

27 Make sure the two locating dowels are still installed, then move the transmission forward carefully until the dowels and the torque converter are engaged.

28 Refit the lower transmission-to-engine bolt and the lower engine-to-transmission bolt. Tighten them to the torque listed in this Chapter's Specifications.

Caution: Don't use the bolts to force the transmission and engine together. If the transmission doesn't slide easily up against the engine, find out why before you tighten the bolts.

29 The remainder of refitting is the reverse of removal.

30 Refill the transmission with fluid to the specified level (see Chapter 1). Note that the transmission may require more fluid than in a normal fluid and filter change, since the torque converter may be empty (the converter is not drained during a fluid change).

31 Start the engine, set the handbrake and move the selector lever through all gears three times. Make sure the selector cable is working properly (see Section 4).

32 Check and, if necessary, adjust the ignition timing (see Chapter 5B).

33 Allow the engine to reach its proper operating temperature with the transmission in Park or Neutral, then turn it off and check the fluid level.

34 Road test the vehicle and check for fluid leaks.

9 Transmission Control Module (TCM) – removal and refitting

Removal

1 Disconnect the battery negative cable (see Chapter 5A).

2 Remove the driver's side footwell kick panel, below the facia, as described in Chapter 11, Section 31.

3 Disconnect the wiring plug, and remove the module.

Refitting

4 Refitting is a reversal of removal.

Chapter 8
Driveshafts

Contents

Degrees of difficulty

Easy, suitable for novice with little experience	**Fairly easy,** suitable for beginner with some experience	**Fairly difficult,** suitable for competent DIY mechanic	**Difficult,** suitable for experienced DIY mechanic	**Very difficult,** suitable for expert DIY or professional

Specifications

Lubrication

Type of grease .... CV joint grease
Quantity of grease per joint:
  Outer joint:
    SOHC models .... 100 to 118 g
    DOHC models .... 90 to 100 g
  Inner joint .... 120 to 130 g

Driveshafts

Driveshaft length:
  SOHC models:
    Left .... 774 to 779 mm
    Right .... 501 to 506 mm
  DOHC models .... 475 to 480 mm

Torque wrench settings

	Nm	lbf ft
Driveshaft-to-hub nut*	181	134
Intermediate shaft bearing support bolts	39	29

*Do not re-use

1 General information

Drive is transmitted from the differential to the front wheels by means of two steel driveshafts of either solid or hollow construction (depending on model). Both driveshafts are splined at their outer ends, to accept the wheel hubs, and are secured to the hub by a large nut. The inner end of each driveshaft is a push fit secured by a circlip. The left-hand driveshaft is splined to accept the end of the intermediate shaft. The intermediate shaft engages with the transmission differential, and is supported by a bearing and bracket bolted to the rear of the cylinder block.

Constant velocity (CV) joints are fitted to each end of the driveshafts, to ensure the smooth and efficient transmission of drive at all the angles possible as the roadwheels move up-and-down with the suspension, and as they turn from side-to-side under steering. On all models, the outer joint is of the ball-and-cage type, but the inner joint is of the tripod type.

Rubber or plastic gaiters are secured over both CV joints with steel clips. The gaiters contain the grease which lubricates the joints, and also protect the joints from the entry of dirt and debris.

2 Driveshafts – removal and refitting

Removal

1 Remove the wheel cover or hub cap. If the driveshaft/hub nut is staked, unstake it with a punch or chisel **(see illustration)**; if it's secured by locking tabs, bend the tabs out.

2 Slacken the hub nut with a socket and large breaker bar **(see illustration)**.

3 Loosen the roadwheel nuts, raise the

2.7b . . . if you're remove the left-hand driveshaft from a model equipped with an intermediate shaft, insert the screwdriver or lever bar between the intermediate shaft bearing and the driveshaft to pop it loose

vehicle and support it securely on axle stands (see *Jacking and vehicle support*). Remove the wheel. Drain the transmission lubricant (see Chapter 1).

4 Disconnect the damper fork from the shock absorber assembly and the lower control arm (see Chapter 10).

5 Using a balljoint splitter, separate the lower control arm from the hub (see Chapter 10). Now remove the driveshaft/hub nut.

6 Swing the hub assembly out (away from the vehicle) until the end of the driveshaft is free of the hub **(see illustration)**. **Note:** *If the driveshaft splines stick in the hub, tap on the end of the driveshaft with a plastic hammer.* Support the outer end of the driveshaft with a piece of wire to avoid unnecessary strain on the inner CV joint.

2.1 If the driveshaft nut is 'staked', use a centre punch to unstake it (wheel removed for clarity)

2.6 Swing the hub assembly out (away from the vehicle) and pull the driveshaft from the hub

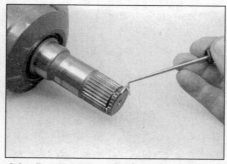

2.8a Pry the old circlip from the inner end of the driveshaft with a small screwdriver

7 Carefully lever the inner end of the driveshaft from the transmission – or, on models so equipped, the intermediate shaft – using a large screwdriver or lever bar positioned between the transmission or bearing support and the CV joint housing **(see illustrations)**. Support the CV joints and carefully remove the driveshaft from the vehicle. To prevent damage to the intermediate shaft seal or the differential seal, hold the inner CV joint horizontal until the driveshaft is clear of the intermediate shaft or transmission.

Refitting

8 Lever the old circlip from the inner end of the driveshaft and fit a new one **(see illustrations)**. Lubricate the differential or

2.2 Slacken the driveshaft nut with a long breaker bar

2.7a Use a large screwdriver or a lever bar to pop the end of the driveshaft from the transmission, or . . .

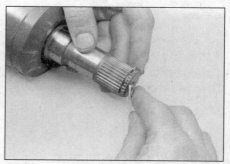

2.8b To install the new circlip, start one end in the groove and work the clip over the end of the shaft, and into the groove

3.5 Location of the intermediate shaft bearing support bolts (arrowed)

intermediate shaft seal with multi-purpose grease and raise the driveshaft into position while supporting the CV joints.

9 Insert the splined end of the inner CV joint into the differential side gear or the intermediate shaft and make sure the circlip locks in its groove.

10 Apply a light coat of multi-purpose grease to the outer CV joint splines, pull out on the strut/hub knuckle assembly and refit the driveshaft into the hub.

11 Insert the stud of the hub balljoint into the lower control arm and tighten the nut (see the torque specifications in Chapter 10). Be sure to use a new split pin. Refit the damper fork (see Chapter 10).

12 Fit a new driveshaft/hub nut (and, if applicable, a new locking tab washer). Tighten the hub nut securely, but don't try to tighten it to the actual torque specification until you've lowered the vehicle to the ground.

13 Grasp the inner CV joint housing (not the driveshaft) and pull out to make sure the driveshaft has seated securely in the transmission.

14 Refit the roadwheel and nuts, then lower the vehicle.

15 Tighten the roadwheel nuts to the torque listed in the Chapter 1 Specifications. Tighten the hub nut to the torque listed in this Chapter's Specifications. Using a hammer and punch, stake the nut to the groove in the driveshaft. If the hub nut uses a locking tab, be sure to bend the tabs up against the nut. Refit the wheel cover (if applicable).

16 Refill the transmission with the recommended type and amount of lubricant (see Chapter 1).

3 Intermediate shaft – removal and refitting

Removal

1 Loosen the left-hand side front road wheel lug, raise the front of the vehicle and support it securely on axle stands (see *Jacking and vehicle support*). Remove the wheel.

2 Drain the transmission lubricant (see Chapter 1).

3 Using a balljoint splitter, separate the left-hand lower control arm from the steering hub (see Chapter 10).

4 Carefully lever the inner CV joint housing from the intermediate shaft. Position the driveshaft out of the way and suspend it with a piece of wire. Do not allow it to hang unsupported, as the outer CV joint may be damaged.

5 Remove the three bearing support-to-engine block bolts **(see illustration)** and slide the intermediate shaft out of the transmission. Be careful not to damage the differential seal when pulling the shaft out.

6 Check the support bearing for smooth operation by turning the shaft while holding the bearing. If you feel any roughness, take the bearing support to a dealer service department or specialist to have a new bearing installed. To do the job at home, you'd need specialised tools.

Refitting

7 Lubricate the lips of the differential seal with multi-purpose grease. Carefully guide the intermediate shaft into the differential side gear then refit the mounting bolts through the bearing support. Tighten the bolts to the torque listed in this Chapter's Specifications.

8 Fit a new circlip on the inner CV joint **(see illustrations 2.8a and 2.8b)** and seat the driveshaft into the intermediate shaft splines.

9 Connect the lower control arm to the steering hub and tighten the balljoint stud nut to the torque listed in the Chapter 10 Specifications.

10 Refit the roadwheel and nuts, lower the vehicle and tighten the nuts to the torque listed in the Chapter 1 Specifications.

11 Refill the transmission with the proper type and amount of lubricant (see Chapter 1).

4 Driveshaft gaiters – renewal

Note: *Some automotive parts retailers carry 'split' type renewal gaiters, which can be installed without removing the driveshaft from the vehicle. This is a convenient alternative; however, the driveshaft should be removed and the CV joint dismantled and cleaned to ensure the joint is free from contaminants such as moisture and dirt which will accelerate CV joint wear.*

1 Remove the driveshaft from the vehicle (see Section 2).

2 Mount the driveshaft in a vice. The jaws of the vice should be lined with wood or rags to prevent damage to the driveshaft.

Inner CV joint and gaiter

Dismantling

3 If you have any doubts about the condition of the outer gaiter this would be a good time to renew it as well. Cut off both gaiter clamps and slide the gaiter towards the centre of the driveshaft **(see illustrations)**.

4 Scribe or paint alignment marks on the outer race and the tripod bearing assembly so they can be returned to their original position, then slide the outer race off the tripod bearing assembly.

5 Remove the circlip from the end of the driveshaft.

6 Secure the bearing rollers with tape, then remove the tripod bearing assembly from the driveshaft with a brass drift and a hammer **(see illustration)**. Remove the tape, but don't let the rollers fall off and get mixed up.

7 Remove the stop ring (if equipped), slide the old gaiter off the driveshaft and discard it.

Inspection

8 Clean the old grease from the outer race and the tripod bearing assembly. Carefully

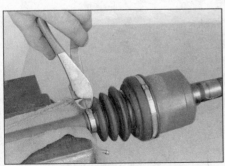

4.3a Cut off the gaiter clamps and discard them

4.3b Slide the gaiter towards the centre of the driveshaft

4.6 Secure the bearing rollers with tape and drive the tripod bearing assembly off the shaft, then remove the stop ring

4.10a Wrap the splined area of the driveshaft with tape to prevent damage to the gaiter when installing it

4.10b Install the stop ring on the driveshaft, ensuring it seats in its groove (not all driveshafts have stop rings)

4.12 Refit the tripod on the driveshaft, then install the circlip

dismantle each section of the tripod assembly, one at a time so as not to mix up the parts, and clean the needle bearings with degreaser.

9 Inspect the rollers, tripod, bearings and outer race for scoring, pitting or other signs of abnormal wear, which will warrant the renewal of the inner CV joint.

Reassembly

10 Wrap the splines of the driveshaft with tape to avoid damaging the new gaiter, then slide the gaiter onto the driveshaft **(see illustration)**. Remove the tape and slide the inner stop ring (if equipped) into place **(see illustration)**.

11 Slide the tripod assembly onto the driveshaft.

12 Fit the outer circlip **(see illustration)**.

13 Apply a coat of CV joint grease to the inner bearing surfaces to hold the needle bearings in place when reassembling the tripod assembly **(see illustration)**. Make sure each roller is refitted on the same post as before. **Note:** *If the rollers are equipped with a flat, rectangular shaped surface, make sure the flat sides are positioned closest to the driveshaft.*

14 Pack the outer race with half of the grease supplied with the new gaiter and place the remainder in the gaiter. Refit the outer race **(see illustration)**. Make sure the marks you made on the tripod assembly and the outer race are aligned.

15 Seat the gaiter in the grooves in the outer race and the driveshaft, then adjust the driveshaft to the proper length **(see illustration)**.

16 With the driveshaft set to the proper length, equalise the pressure in the gaiter by inserting a blunt screwdriver between the gaiter and the outer race **(see illustration)**.

4.13 Use plenty of CV joint grease to hold the needle bearings in place when you install the roller assemblies on the tripod, and ensure each roller is refitted in its original position

4.14 Pack the outer race with grease and slide it over the tripod assembly – ensure the match marks on the outer race and tripod line up

4.15 Adjust the driveshaft length to the dimension listed in this Chapter's Specifications before tightening the gaiter clamps

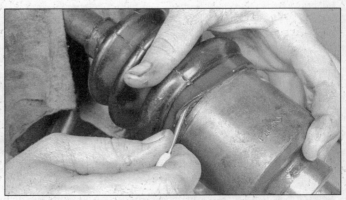

4.16 Equalise the pressure inside the gaiter by inserting a small, blunt screwdriver between the gaiter and the outer race

4.17a To install the fold-over type clamps, bend the tang down . . .

4.17b . . . and flatten the tabs to hold it in place

4.17c You may need a special tool to install 'band' type gaiter clamps: Install the band with its end pointing in the direction of driveshaft rotation and tighten it securely . . .

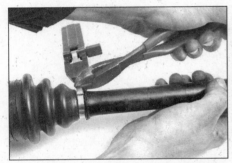

4.17d . . . bend back the end of the clamp, cut off the excess, then place a dimple in the centre of the folded-over portion with a hammer and a centre punch

4.17e If you're installing crimp-type gaiter clamps, use a pair of crimping pliers

4.23 Inspect the bearing surfaces for signs of wear

Don't damage the gaiter with the tool.

17 Fit and tighten the new gaiter clamps **(see illustrations)**.

18 Refit the driveshaft assembly (see Section 2).

Outer CV joint and gaiter

Dismantling

19 Following Paragraphs 3 to 7, remove the inner CV joint from the driveshaft and dismantle it.

20 If the driveshaft is equipped with a dynamic damper, scribe or paint a location mark on the driveshaft along the outer edge of the damper (the side facing the outer CV joint), cut the retaining clamp and slide the damper off. **Note:** *If you're planning to renew the driveshaft and outer CV joint assembly, measure the distance between the inner CV joint boot and the dynamic damper so the damper can be placed in the proper position on the new driveshaft.*

21 Cut the gaiter clamps from the outer CV joint. Slide the gaiter off the shaft. **Note:** *The outer CV joint can't be dismantled or removed from the shaft.*

Inspection

22 Thoroughly wash the inner and outer CV joints in degreaser and blow them dry with compressed air, if available. **Note:** *Because the outer joint can't be dismantled, it is difficult to wash away all the old grease and to rid the bearing of degreaser once it's clean. But it is imperative that the job be done thoroughly.*

 Warning: Wear eye protection when using compressed air.

23 Bend the outer CV joint housing at an angle to the driveshaft to expose the bearings, inner race and cage. Inspect the bearing surfaces for signs of wear **(see illustration)**. If the bearings are damaged or worn, renew the driveshaft.

Reassembly

24 Slide the new outer gaiter onto the driveshaft. It's a good idea to wrap tape around the splines of the shaft to prevent damage to the gaiter **(see illustration 4.10a)**. When the gaiter is in position, add the specified amount of grease (included in the gaiter renewal kit) to the outer joint and the gaiter (pack the joint with as much grease as it will hold and put the rest into the gaiter). Slide the gaiter on the rest of the way and fit the new clamps **(see illustrations 4.17a to 4.17e)**.

25 Slide the dynamic damper, if equipped, onto the shaft. Make sure its outer edge is aligned with the previously applied mark. **Note:** *If you're using a new driveshaft and outer CV joint assembly, refit the damper on the shaft to the distance from the inner CV joint gaiter measured in Paragraph 20. Fit a new retaining clamp.*

26 Clean and reassemble the inner CV joint by following Paragraphs 8 to 17, then refit the driveshaft as outlined in Section 2.

Notes

Chapter 9
Braking system

Contents

Degrees of difficulty

| **Easy,** suitable for novice with little experience | | **Fairly easy,** suitable for beginner with some experience | | **Fairly difficult,** suitable for competent DIY mechanic | | **Difficult,** suitable for experienced DIY mechanic | | **Very difficult,** suitable for expert DIY or professional | |

Specifications

General

Brake pedal:	
Freeplay	1 to 5 mm
Height (with floor mat removed):	
Manual transmission:	
3-door Hatchback, 2-door Coupe, 4-door Saloon	156.5 mm
5-door Estate, 5-door Hatchback	154.0 mm
Automatic transmission:	
3-door Hatchback, 2-door Coupe, 4-door Saloon	161.0 mm
5-door Estate, 5-door Hatchback	159.0 mm
Handbrake lever travel	6 to 9 clicks
Servo pushrod-to-master cylinder piston clearance (with a vacuum of 500 mmHg applied to servo)	0.04 mm
Servo input rod length (from servo mounting surface to centre of hole in clevis pin)	116 ± 0.5 mm
Wheel speed sensor air gap	0.4 to 1.0 mm

Disc brakes

Brake pad minimum thickness (excluding backing plate)	1.6 mm
Disc minimum thickness:	
Front:	
1.8 litre DOHC models	21.0 mm
All other models	19.0 mm
Rear	8.0 mm
Thickness variation (parallelism)	0.016 mm
Run-out limit	0.1 mm

Drum brakes

Brake lining minimum thickness (excluding backing plate)	2.0 mm

Torque wrench settings

	Nm	lbf ft
Brake hose-to-caliper banjo bolt (front or rear)	34	25
Front caliper bolts:		
1.8 litre DOHC models	49	36
Nissin caliper (casting stamped Nissin)	23	17
Akebono caliper (casting not stamped):		
14 in and 15 in wheels	32	24
13 in wheel:		
Upper bolt	34	25
Lower bolt	26	19
Front caliper mounting bracket bolts	108	80
Master cylinder mounting nuts	15	11
Rear caliper bolts	27	20
Rear caliper mounting bracket bolts:		
5-door Hatchback '97-on, 5-door Estate	55	41
All other models	38	28
Roadwheel bolts	108	80
Servo mounting nuts	12	9
Wheel cylinder nuts	9	7
Wheel sensor retaining bolt	10	7

1 General information

General

All vehicles covered by this manual are equipped with hydraulically-operated servo-assisted brake systems. All front brake systems are disc type **(see illustration)**. Some models use drum type brakes at the rear, others are equipped with rear disc brakes **(see illustration)**.

All brakes are self-adjusting. The front and rear disc brakes automatically compensate for pad wear, while the rear drum brakes incorporate an adjustment mechanism which is activated as the brakes are applied, either through the pedal or the handbrake lever.

The hydraulic system is a diagonally-split design, meaning there are separate circuits for the left front/right rear and the right front/left rear brakes. If one circuit fails, the other circuit will remain functional and a warning indicator will light up on the dashboard when a substantial amount of brake fluid is lost, showing that a failure has occurred.

Master cylinder

The master cylinder is bolted to the servo unit, which is mounted on the driver's side of the bulkhead. To locate the master cylinder, look for the large fluid reservoir on top. The fluid reservoir is a removable plastic cup, secured to the master cylinder by a clamp.

The master cylinder is designed for the 'split system' mentioned earlier and has separate piston assemblies for each circuit.

Proportioning valve

The proportioning valve assembly is located on the bulkhead. On vehicles equipped with the Anti-lock Brake System (ABS), it's an integral part of the modulator/solenoid unit, which is located on the right-hand side of the engine compartment.

The proportioning valve regulates the hydraulic pressure to the rear brakes during heavy braking to eliminate rear wheel lock-up. Under normal braking conditions, it allows full pressure to the rear brake system until a predetermined pedal pressure is reached. Above that point, the pressure to the rear brakes is limited.

The proportioning valve is not serviceable – if a problem develops with the valve, it must be renewed as an assembly.

Servo

The servo, which uses engine manifold vacuum and atmospheric pressure to provide assistance to the hydraulically-operated brakes, is mounted on the bulkhead in the engine compartment.

1.1a Typical front disc brake components

1 Brake hose   2 Caliper   3 Disc   4 Caliper bolt

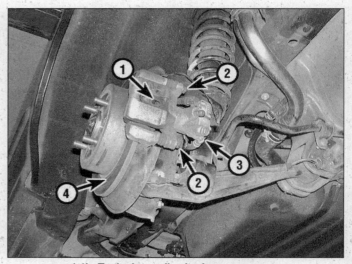

1.1b Typical rear disc brake components

1 Caliper   2 Caliper bolts   3 Hose   4 Disc

Handbrake

A handbrake lever inside the vehicle operates a single front cable attached to a pair of rear cables, each of which is connected to its respective rear brake. When the handbrake lever is pulled up on drum brake models, each rear cable pulls on a lever attached to the brake shoe assembly, causing the shoes to expand against the drum. When the lever is pulled on models with rear disc brakes, the rear cables pull on levers that are attached to screw-type actuators in the caliper housings, which apply force to the caliper pistons, clamping the brake pads against the brake disc.

Precautions

There are some general **Cautions** and **Warnings** involving the brake system on these vehicles:

a) *Use only brake fluid conforming to DOT 3 or DOT 4 specifications.*

b) *The brake pads and linings may contain asbestos fibres which are hazardous to your health if inhaled. Whenever you work on brake system components, clean all parts with brake system cleaner. Do not allow the fine dust to become airborne.*

c) *Safety should be paramount whenever any servicing of the brake components is performed. Do not use parts or fasteners which are not in perfect condition, and be sure that all clearances and torque specifications are adhered to. If you are at all unsure about a certain procedure, seek professional advice. Upon completion of any brake system work, test the brakes carefully in a controlled area before putting the vehicle into normal service.*

d) *If a problem is suspected in the brake system, don't drive the vehicle until it's fixed.*

Caution: If the radio in your vehicle is equipped with an anti-theft system, make sure you have the correct activation code before disconnecting the battery.

2 Anti-lock Brake System (ABS) – general information and trouble codes

General information

In a conventional braking system, if you press the brake pedal too hard, the wheels can 'lock up' (stop turning) and the vehicle can go into a skid. If the wheels lock up, you can lose control of the vehicle. The Anti-lock Brake System (ABS) prevents the wheels from locking up by modulating (pulsing on and off) the pressure of the brake fluid at each caliper.

The Anti-lock Brake System has two basic subsystems: One is an electrical system and the other is hydraulic. The electrical half has four wheel speed sensors, a computer and an electrical circuit connecting all the components. The hydraulic part of the system consists of a solenoid/modulator, the disc brake calipers and the hydraulic fluid lines between the solenoid/modulator and the calipers.

In principle, the system is simple: Each wheel has a wheel speed sensor monitoring a reluctor (pulser) ring (a ring with evenly-spaced raised ridges cast into its circumference). The wheel speed sensor 'counts' the ridges of the reluctor ring as they pass by, converts this information into an electrical output and transmits it back to the computer. The computer constantly 'samples' the voltage inputs from all four wheel speed sensors and compares them to each other. As long as the reluctor rings at all four wheels are rotating at the same speed, the Anti-lock Brake System is inactive. But when a wheel locks up, the voltage signal from that wheel speed sensor deviates from the signals coming from the other wheels. So the computer 'knows' the wheel is locking up. It sends an electrical signal to the solenoid/modulator assembly, which releases the brake fluid pressure to the brake caliper at that wheel. As soon as the wheel unlocks and resumes turning at the same rate of speed as the other wheels, its wheel sensor voltage output once again matches the output of the other wheels and the computer deactivates the signal to the solenoid/modulator.

In reality, the Anti-lock Brake System is far more complex than it sounds, so we don't recommend that you attempt to diagnose or service it. If the Anti-lock Brake System on your vehicle develops problems, take it to a dealer service department or specialist.

Obtaining ABS trouble codes

1 Normally, the ABS indicator light should come on when the engine is started, then go off after a couple of seconds. Under certain conditions, however, the indicator light may remain on. If this occurs, the ABS computer has stored a diagnostic trouble code (DTC) because it has detected a problem in the ABS system. You can have the ABS indicator display the diagnostic trouble code as follows:

2 Unplug the 2-pin service check connector or 5-pin data link connector from the connector cover located underneath the glovebox (see Chapter 4A, Section 19). On models using the 5-pin data link connector, a special ABS connector harness (available from Honda dealers) is required to plug into the connector to retrieve the DTCs.

5-door Hatchback models up to '96 model year – service check connector.

3-door Hatchback, 2-door Coupe, 4-door Saloon – service check connector.

5-door Hatchback '96 model year-on – data link connector.

5-door Estate – data link connector.

3 Bridge the two terminals of the service check connector with a bridging wire, or plug in the special ABS connector harness into the 5-pin data link connector (where applicable).

Service check connector

4 Turn the ignition switch to ON, but don't start the engine. Two seconds after you turn on the ignition, the ABS computer will begin displaying any stored diagnostic trouble code(s) by blinking the ABS indicator light on and off. The sequence begins with a two-second pause, followed by a series of blinks representing the main code, followed by a one-second pause, followed by another series of blinks representing the sub-code (if any), followed by a five-second pause, then the next main code/sub-code blinks, another five second pause, the next main code/sub-code combination, etc. The ABS computer can indicate up to three codes.

5 If you miscount, turn the ignition switch to OFF, then back to ON, to recycle the ABS computer. Record the number of main code and sub-code blinks and compare them to the accompanying lists. Most ABS repairs must be performed by a dealer service department or specialist.

Data link connector

6 Turn the ignition switch to ON, but don't start the engine. Two seconds after you turn on the ignition, the ABS computer will begin displaying any stored diagnostic trouble code(s) by blinking the ABS indicator light on and off. The sequence begins with a 3.6-second pause, followed by a series of blinks representing the code, followed by a 3.6 second pause, followed by another series of blinks representing the next code (if any), etc. The ABS light will blink a longer blink to represent the first digit of a two digit number, then blink short for the second digit (for example, one long blink, pause, followed by six short blinks indicates a Code 16).

7 Record the number of code blinks and refer to the following lists.

8 Not all codes apply to all models.

ABS Trouble Codes

All models except 5-door Hatchback up to '96

Code	Probable cause
11	Right front wheel sensor (open/short to body earth or short to power)
12	Right front wheel sensor (electrical noise or intermittent interruption)
13	Left front wheel sensor (open/short to body earth or short to power)
14	Left front wheel sensor (electrical noise or intermittent interruption)
15	Right rear wheel sensor (open/short to body earth or short to power)
16	Right rear wheel sensor (electrical noise or intermittent interruption)
17	Left rear wheel sensor (open/short to body earth or short to power)
18	Left rear wheel sensor (electrical noise or intermittent interruption)
21	Right front reluctor ring
22	Left front reluctor ring
23	Right rear reluctor ring
24	Left rear reluctor ring
31	Right front inlet solenoid
32	Right front outlet solenoid
33	Left front inlet solenoid

Code	Probable cause
34	Left front outlet solenoid
35	Right rear inlet solenoid
36	Right rear outlet solenoid
37	Left rear inlet solenoid
38	Left rear outlet solenoid
41	Right front wheel lock
42	Left front wheel lock
43	Right rear wheel lock
44	Left rear wheel lock
51	Motor lock
52	Motor remains OFF
53	Motor remains ON
54	Fail safe relay
61	Low ignition voltage
62	High ignition voltage
71	Different diameter tyre
81	Central Processing Unit and ROM/RAM diagnostics

5-door Hatchback up to '96

Code/Subcode	Probable cause
1 / 2	Pump motor
1 / 3	High pressure leakage
1 / 4	Pressure switch
1 / 8	High pressure system
2 / 1	Handbrake
3 / 1	Right front reluctor ring
3 / 2	Left front reluctor ring
3 / 4	Right rear reluctor ring
3 / 8	Left rear reluctor ring
4 / 1	Right front wheel speed sensor
4 / 2	Left front wheel speed sensor
4 / 4	Right rear wheel speed sensor
4 / 8	Left rear wheel speed sensor
5 / 4	Right rear wheel lock
5 / 8	Left rear wheel lock
6 / 1	Front fail-safe relay
6 / 4	Rear fail-safe relay
7 / 1	Right front solenoid
7 / 2	Left front solenoid
7 / 4	Rear solenoid
8 / 1	ABS function
8 / 2	CPU comparison (faulty ECM)
8 / 4	IC (Integrated circuit – faulty ECM)

Erasing diagnostic codes

9 Diagnostic codes must be cleared from the computer memory after the repairs have been performed.

5-door Hatchback (up to '96)

10 Clear the diagnostic codes by removing the bridging wire from the service check connector, then remove the 15 amp ABS B2 fuse (located in the engine compartment fusebox) for at least three seconds. Refit the fuse.

3-door Hatchback, Coupe and Saloon

11 With the bridging wire still installed and the ignition off, press on the brake pedal and then turn the ignition on. When the ABS indicator light goes out, release the brake pedal until the light comes on again and press on the brake pedal. Hold the pedal down until the indicator light goes out and release the pedal.

12 The indicator light should blink twice to indicate that the codes are erased. Turn off the ignition, remove the bridging wire.

5-door Hatchback (from '96) and Estate

13 On these models, erase the DTCs by turning the ignition switch ON and OFF 20 times or more.

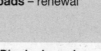

3 Disc brake pads – renewal

⚠ *Warning: Disc brake pads must be replaced on both front or rear wheels at the same time – never renew the pads on only one wheel. Also, the dust created by the brake system is harmful to your health. Never blow it out with compressed air and don't inhale any of it. Do not, under any circumstances, use petroleum-based solvents to clean brake parts. Use brake system cleaner only.*

1 Remove the cap from the brake fluid reservoir.

2 Loosen the roadwheel nuts, raise the front, or rear, of the vehicle and support it securely on axle stands (see *Jacking and vehicle support*).

3 Remove the front, or rear, wheels. Work on one brake assembly at a time, using the assembled brake for reference if necessary.

4 Inspect the brake disc carefully as outlined in Section 5. If machining is necessary, follow

3.6a Before removing anything, spray the assembly with brake system cleaner to remove the dust produced by brake pad wear – DO NOT blow the dust off with compressed air

3.6c Swing the caliper up . . .

3.5 Using a large G-clamp, push the piston back into the caliper – note that one end of the clamp is on the rear side of the caliper and the other end screw end) is pressing on the outer brake pad

the information in that Section to remove the disc, at which time the calipers and pads can be removed as well.

Front pads

5 Push the piston back into the bore to provide room for the new brake pads. A G-clamp can be used to accomplish this **(see illustration)**. As the piston is depressed to the bottom of the caliper bore, the fluid in the master cylinder will rise. Make sure it doesn't overflow. If necessary, syphon off some of the fluid.

6 Follow **the illustrations, beginning with 3.6a**, for the actual pad renewal procedure. Be sure to stay in order and read the caption under each illustration. Once you have installed the new pads, proceed to Paragraph 14.

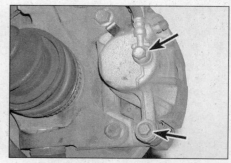

3.6b Remove the lower caliper bolt (lower arrow) (upper arrow points to the banjo fitting for the brake hose, which should not be disconnected unless you're removing the caliper from the vehicle)

3.6d . . . and support it in this position

3.6e Remove the outer brake pad and shim

3.6f Remove the inner brake pad (some models don't have a shim on the inner pad)

3.6g Remove and inspect the upper and lower brake pad retainer clips

3.6h The pad retainer clips should fit snugly into their respective grooves in the caliper mounting bracket; if they don't, renew them

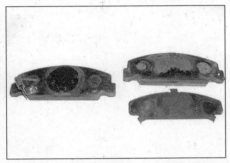

3.6i Inner pad (left) and outer pad and shim layout – some models have inner pad shims

3.6j Apply anti-squeal compound to the rear of the pads, then install the shim(s)

3.6k Install the new inner pad; ensure the 'ears' on the upper and lower ends of the pad are fully engaged with their respective grooves and the pad retainer clips

3.6l Install the new outer pad and shim (if the new pad has no shim, take the old shim off the old pad and install it on the new outer pad)

3.6m Before installing the caliper, remove the caliper bolt dust boots and inspect them for tears and cracks; if they're damaged, renew them

3.6n Clean off the caliper bolts, or sliding pins, and coat them with brake assembly grease

3.6o Swing the caliper down over the disc and new pads (if the caliper hits the inner pad, depress the piston further into the caliper bore with your G-clamp)

3.6p Refit the lower bolt and tighten it to the torque listed in this Chapter's Specifications

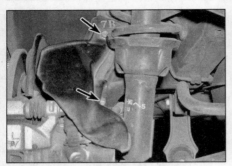

3.7a Remove the caliper shield bolts (arrowed) and the shield, then clean the brake as shown in illustration 3.6a

3.7b Remove the two caliper bolts (arrowed) . . .

3.7c . . . and lift the caliper from its mounting bracket; hang the caliper out of the way with a piece of wire (see illustration 3.6d)

3.7d Remove the outer pad and shim

3.7e Remove the inner pad and shim

3.7f Remove the brake pad retainers from the caliper mounting bracket

Rear pads

7 Follow **the illustrations, beginning with 3.7a,** for the pad renewal procedure. Be sure to stay in order and read the caption under each illustration. When you have completed the Steps described in the accompanying photos, proceed to Paragraph 8.

8 Apply a thin coat of disc brake anti-squeal compound, in accordance with the manufacturer's recommendations, on the backing plates of the new pads **(see illustration).**

9 Fit the shims onto their respective pads.

10 Refit the pad retainers in the caliper mounting bracket. Lubricate the retainers with a thin film of silicone grease.

11 Fit the new pads and shims to the caliper mounting bracket.

12 Retract the piston by engaging the tips of a pair of thin-nose pliers with two of the grooves in the face of the piston and turning it clockwise whilst pushing, until it bottoms in the bore **(see illustration).** Alternatively, use a piston retraction tool. Now, rotate the piston out until one of its grooves is aligned with the tab on the inner brake pad when you fit the caliper. You may have to adjust the piston position by turning it back-and-forth to fit the tab in the groove. If the piston dust boot becomes distorted when the piston is turned, turn the piston in the opposite direction to restore the shape of the boot, but make sure

the groove is aligned properly. Refit the caliper and tighten the retaining bolts to the specified torque.

13 Refit the caliper protector.

Front or rear pads

14 Refit the roadwheels and nuts, lower the vehicle and tighten the specified torque.

15 Apply and release the brake pedal and (if you renewed rear pads) the handbrake lever several times to bring the pads into contact with the brake discs.

16 Check the brake fluid level and add fluid, if necessary (see Chapter 1). Check the operation of the brakes before driving the vehicle in traffic.

3.8 Before fitting the brake pads, apply a coat of disc brake anti-squeal compound to the backing plates or the pads – follow the manufacturer's instructions on the label

3.12 To provide clearance for the new pads, push the piston into the bore whilst rotating it clockwise with a pair of thin-nose pliers

4 Disc brake caliper – removal and refitting

⚠ *Warning: Dust created by the brake system is harmful to your health. Never blow it out with compressed air and don't inhale any of it. Do not, under any circumstances, use petroleum-based solvents to clean brake parts. Use brake system cleaner only.*

Removal

1 Slacken – but don't remove – the nuts on the front, or rear wheels. Raise the front or rear of the vehicle and place it securely on

4.2 The handbrake cable is attached to the rear caliper by a clevis pin that is secured by a split pin

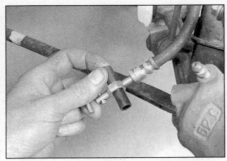

4.3 Using a short piece of rubber hose of the appropriate diameter, plug the brake pipe banjo fitting like this

axle stands (see *Jacking and vehicle support*). Remove the wheels.

2 If you're removing a rear caliper, remove the split pin from the clevis pin that connects the handbrake cable to the brake lever **(see illustration)**. Pull out the pin and detach the cable.

3 Use a clamp on the flexible rubber brake hose, then disconnect the brake pipe from the caliper **(see illustration 3.6b)** and plug it to keep contaminants out of the brake system, and to prevent losing any more brake fluid than is necessary **(see illustration)**.

4 Refer to Section 3 and remove the caliper (it's part of the brake pad renewal procedure).

Refitting

5 Refit the caliper by reversing the removal procedure. Remember to renew the sealing washer on either side of the brake pipe fitting (they should be included with the overhaul kit).

6 Bleed the brake system (see Section 10).

7 Refit the wheels, hand tighten the wheel nuts, remove the axle stands and lower the vehicle. Tighten the wheel to the specified torque.

---

5 Brake disc – inspection, removal and refitting

Inspection

1 Slacken the wheel nuts, raise the vehicle

and support it securely on axle stands (see *Jacking and vehicle support*). Remove the wheel and refit the nuts with 3 mm thick washers under them to hold the disc in place (if the two disc retaining screws are still in place, this will be unnecessary). If you're checking the rear disc, release the handbrake.

2 Remove the brake caliper (see Section 4). It's not necessary to disconnect the brake hose. After removing the caliper bolts, suspend the caliper out of the way with a piece of wire.

3 Visually inspect the disc surface for scoring or damage **(see illustration)**. Light scratches and shallow grooves are normal after use and

may not always be detrimental to brake operation, but deep scoring (over 0.3 mm) requires refinishing by an automotive engineering workshop or renewal. Be sure to check both sides of the disc.

4 If you've noted pulsation during braking, suspect disc run-out. To check disc run-out, place a dial indicator gauge (DTI) at a point about 12 mm from the outer edge of the disc **(see illustration)**. Set the DTI to zero and turn the disc. The DTI reading should not exceed the specified allowable run-out limit. If it does, have the disc refinished by an automotive engineering workshop or renew it. **Note:** *Consider having the discs resurfaced regardless of the DTI reading, as this will impart a smooth finish and ensure a perfectly flat surface, eliminating any brake pedal pulsation or other undesirable symptoms related to questionable discs. At the very least, if you elect not to have the discs resurfaced, remove the glazing from the surface with emery cloth or sandpaper using a swirling motion* **(see illustration)**.

5 It is absolutely critical that the disc not be machined to a thickness less than the minimum allowable thickness. The minimum wear (or discard) thickness is stamped on the disc **(see illustration)** and listed in the Specifications at the start of this Chapter. The disc thickness can be checked with a micrometer **(see illustration)**.

5.3 The brake pads on this vehicle were obviously neglected, as they wore down completely and cut deep grooves into the disc – wear this severe means the disc must be renewed

5.4a Make sure the disc retaining screws or wheel nuts are tight, then rotate the disc and check the run-out with a DTI gauge

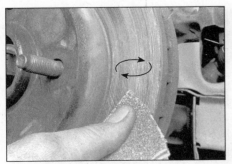

5.4b Using a swirling motion, remove the glaze from the disc with emery cloth or sandpaper

5.5a The minimum allowable thickness is stamped into the disc

5.5b A micrometer is used to measure disc thickness

5.6a Before removing the disc, remove the caliper mounting bracket bolts (arrowed), and the bracket

5.6b Remove the rear caliper bracket mounting bolts (arrowed)

5.7a If the disc retaining screws are stuck, use an impact driver to slacken them

Removal

6 Remove the two caliper mounting bracket-to-steering hub bolts **(see illustration)** or, on rear calipers, the bracket-to-trailing arm bolts **(see illustration)**, and remove the mounting bracket.

7 Remove the nuts which were installed to hold the disc in place, or the two disc retaining screws, if present **(see illustration)** and remove the disc from the hub. If the disc is stuck to the hub and won't come off, thread two bolts into the holes provided **(see illustration)** and tighten them. Alternate between the bolts, turning them a little at a time, until the disc is free **(see illustration)**.

Refitting

8 Place the disc in position over the threaded studs. Refit the disc retaining screws.
9 Refit the caliper mounting bracket, tightening the bolts to the torque listed in this Chapter's Specifications. Fit the brake pads and caliper over the disc. Tighten the caliper bolts to the specified torque.
10 Refit the wheel and nuts, then lower the vehicle to the earth. Tighten the nuts to the specified torque. Depress the brake pedal a few times to bring the brake pads into contact with the disc. Bleeding of the system will not be necessary unless the fluid hose was disconnected from the caliper. Check the operation of the brakes carefully before placing the vehicle into normal service.

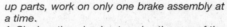

5.7b If the disc is stuck, thread two bolts into the disc and tighten them to force the disc off the hub

5.7c As you remove the disc, make sure you don't damage the threads on the studs for the wheel nuts

up parts, work on only one brake assembly at a time.
1 Slacken the wheel nuts, raise the rear of the vehicle and support it securely on axle stands (see *Jacking and vehicle support*). Block the front wheels to keep the vehicle from rolling. Remove the rear wheels. Release the handbrake.
2 Remove the brake drum. It should simply pull straight off the hub. If the drum won't come off, tap it carefully with a soft-faced mallet, or screw a couple of 8.0 mm bolts into the tapped holes **(see illustration)**. If it still won't budge, the shoes have probably carved wear grooves into the drum. To get the drum off, you'll have to retract the shoes. Remove the rubber plug in the backing plate. Use one screwdriver inserted through the hole in the

backing plate to hold the self-adjuster lever away from the adjuster bolt, then use another screwdriver to rotate the adjuster bolt until the drum can be removed.
3 Replacing the shoes is a lot easier if you remove the rear wheel bearing cap, spindle nut and washer, and slide off the hub unit (see Chapter 10). However, this is not absolutely necessary.
4 Follow **illustrations 6.4a through 6.4r** for the brake shoe renewal procedure. Be sure to stay in order and read the caption under each illustration. When you have finished refitting the new shoes, proceed to Paragraph 5.
5 Before refitting the drum it should be checked for cracks, score marks, deep scratches and hard spots, which will appear as small discoloured areas. If the hard spots

6 Drum brake shoes – renewal

Warning: Drum brake shoes must be renewed on both wheels at the same time – never renew the shoes on only one wheel. Also, the dust created by the brake system is harmful to your health. Never blow it out with compressed air and don't inhale any of it. Do not, under any circumstances, use petroleum-based solvents to clean brake parts. Use brake system cleaner only.
Note: *All four rear brake shoes must be renewed at the same time, but to avoid mixing*

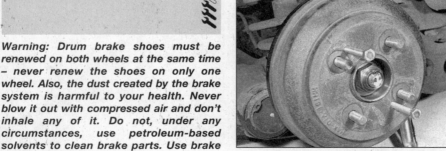

6.2 If the drum is hard to pull off, thread a pair of 8 mm bolts into the holes provided and press the drum off

6.4a Right-hand rear drum brake assembly

6.4b Before removing anything, clean the brake assembly with brake cleaner and allow it to dry

6.4c Push down on the retainer spring with a screwdriver, then turn the tension pin to align its blade with the slot in the retainer spring – the spring should pop off (repeat this on the other spring)

6.4d Pull the shoe assembly away from the backing plate (hub removed for clarity) . . .

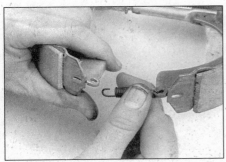

6.4e . . . and unhook the return spring

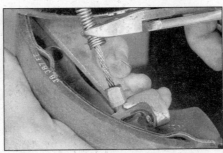

6.4f Pull back on the handbrake cable spring and squeeze the pliers just enough to grip the cable, holding the spring in the compressed position (be careful not to cut the cable); unhook the cable end from the handbrake lever

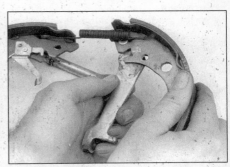

6.4g Swing the handbrake lever away from the trailing shoe, which will force the adjuster bolt clevis out of its groove in the shoe; the two shoes can now be separated

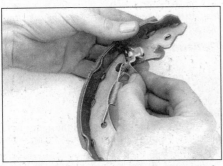

6.4h Remove the self-adjuster lever and spring from the leading shoe

6.4i Prise open the handbrake lever retaining clip and separate the lever from the shoe; be careful not to lose the wave washer that is under the clip

6.4j Put the new trailing shoe on the lever, place the wave washer over the pin, then install the retaining clip; crimp the ends of the clip together with a pair of thin-nose pliers

6.4k Clean the adjuster bolt and clevis, then lubricate the threads and ends with high-temperature grease

6.4l Connect the self-adjuster lever spring to the leading brake shoe, then insert the pin on the lever into its hole in the shoe

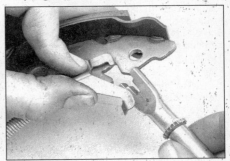

6.4m Insert the short clevis of the adjuster bolt into its slot in the leading shoe, making sure it catches the self-adjuster lever

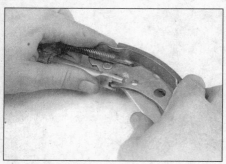

6.4n Connect the upper return spring between the two shoes, prise the lower ends of the shoes apart and insert the clevis at the other end of the adjuster bolt into the slot in the shoe; note the position of the stepped portion of the clevis opening

6.4o Lubricate the brake shoe contact areas on the backing plate with high-temperature grease

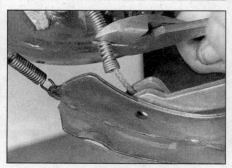

6.4p Compress the handbrake cable spring, hold it in position and connect the cable end to the handbrake lever

6.4q Place the brake shoe assembly against the backing plate, engaging the upper ends of the shoes in the slots in the wheel cylinder pistons. Connect the lower return spring between the shoes

6.4r With the brake shoes in position on the backing plate, pass the tension pins though the holes in the backing plate and brake shoes, then install the retainer springs (see illustration 6.4c) – make sure the handbrake cable spring and the lower return spring are seated behind the anchor plate

6.5 The maximum allowable diameter is cast into the drum (typical)

cannot be removed with sandpaper or emery cloth or if any of the other conditions listed above exist, the drum must be taken to an automotive engineering workshop to have it machined. **Note:** *Consider resurfacing the drums whenever a brake overhaul is done. Resurfacing will eliminate the possibility of out-of-round drums.* If the drums are worn so much that they can't be resurfaced without exceeding the maximum allowable diameter (stamped into the drum) **(see illustration)**, then new ones will be required. At the very least, if you elect not to have the drums resurfaced, remove the glazing from the surface with sandpaper or emery cloth using a swirling motion.

6 Refit the hub and bearing unit, the washer and a new spindle nut (if removed previously). Tighten the nut to the torque listed in the Chapter 10 Specifications.

7 When refitting the brake drum, adjust the brake shoes by turning the star wheel on the adjuster screw until the drum just slips over the shoes. When turning the drum, the shoes should not rub; if they do, remove the drum and back off the star wheel a little bit so they don't.

8 Refit the wheel, fit the nuts, then lower the vehicle. Tighten the wheel nuts to the specified torque.

9 Make a number of forward and reverse stops to adjust the brakes until satisfactory pedal action is obtained.

10 Check brake operation before driving the vehicle in traffic.

7 Wheel cylinder – removal and refitting

Removal

1 Raise the rear of the vehicle and support it securely on axle stands (see *Jacking and vehicle support*). Block the front wheels to keep the vehicle from rolling.

2 Remove the brake shoe assembly (see Section 6).

3 Remove all dirt and foreign material from around the wheel cylinder.

4 Clamp the flexible rubber hose, and unscrew the brake pipe fitting **(see illustration)**. Don't pull the brake pipe away from the wheel cylinder.

5 Remove the wheel cylinder mounting bolts.

6 Detach the wheel cylinder from the brake backing plate and place it on a clean workbench. Immediately plug the brake line to prevent fluid loss and contamination. **Note:** *If the*

brake shoe linings are contaminated with brake fluid, fit new brake shoes and clean the drums with brake system cleaner. If the wheel cylinders leak, they must be renewed – the manufacturer does not recommend rebuilding them.

Refitting

7 Apply RTV sealant to the mating surface of the wheel cylinder and the brake backing plate, place the cylinder in position and connect the brake pipe. Don't tighten the fitting completely yet.

8 Refit the mounting bolts, tightening them securely. Tighten the brake pipe fitting. Refit the brake shoe assembly.

9 Bleed the brakes (see Section 10).

10 Check brake operation before driving the vehicle in traffic.

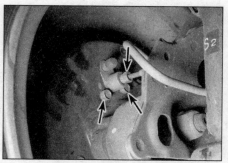

7.4 Unscrew the brake pipe fitting (upper arrow), then remove the two wheel cylinder retaining bolts (lower arrows)

8 Master cylinder – removal and refitting

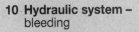

Removal

1 The master cylinder is located on the right-hand side of the engine compartment, mounted to the servo unit.

2 Remove as much fluid as you can from the reservoir with a syringe.

3 Place rags under the fluid fittings and prepare caps or plastic bags to cover the ends of the pipes once they are disconnected. *Caution: Brake fluid will damage paint. Cover all painted surfaces and be careful not to spill fluid during this procedure.*

4 Loosen the nuts at the ends of the brake pipes where they enter the master cylinder **(see illustration)**. To prevent rounding off the corners on these nuts, the use of a brake pipe nut spanner, which wraps around the nut, is preferred.

5 Pull the brake pipes slightly away from the master cylinder and plug the ends to prevent contamination.

6 Disconnect the electrical connector at the master cylinder, then remove the nuts attaching the master cylinder to the servo. Pull the master cylinder off the studs and out of the engine compartment. Again, be careful not to spill the fluid as this is done. **Note:** *If the master cylinder is defective, it must be renewed – the manufacturer does not recommend rebuilding it.*

Refitting

7 Fit the master cylinder over the studs on the servo and tighten the attaching nuts only finger tight at this time.

8 Thread the brake pipe fittings into the master cylinder. Since the master cylinder is still a bit loose, it can be moved slightly in order for the fittings to thread in easily. Do not strip the threads as the fittings are tightened.

9 Fully tighten the mounting nuts to the torque listed in this Chapter's Specifications, then the brake pipe fittings securely.

10 Fill the master cylinder reservoir with fluid, then bleed the master cylinder and the brake system as described in Section 10. Test the operation of the brake system carefully before placing the vehicle into normal service.

⚠ **Warning:** *Do not operate the vehicle if you are in doubt about the effectiveness of the brake system.*

9 Brake hoses and pipes – inspection and renewal

1 About every six months the flexible hoses which connect the steel brake pipes with the rear brakes and front calipers should be inspected for cracks, chafing of the outer cover, leaks, blisters, and other damage.

2 Check all brake pipes and fittings for rust, chafing or other damage. Renewal steel and flexible brake pipes are commonly available from dealer parts departments and automotive retailers.

3 When refitting the brake pipe, leave at least 18 mm clearance between the pipe and any moving or vibrating parts.

4 To disconnect a hose and pipe, use a brake pipe nut spanner **(see illustration)**. Then remove the clip and slide the hose out of the bracket **(see illustration)**.

5 When disconnecting two hoses, use normal spanners on the hose fittings. When connecting two hoses, make sure they are not twisted or strained.

6 Steel brake pipes are usually retained along their length with clips. Always remove these clips completely before removing a fixed brake pipe. Always refit these clips, or new ones if the old ones are damaged, when renewing a brake pipe, as they provide support and keep the pipes from vibrating, which can eventually break them.

7 When refitting a steel pipe, make sure it's securely supported in the brackets and has plenty of clearance between moving or hot components.

8 After refitting, check the fluid level in the master cylinder and add fluid as necessary. Bleed the brake system as described in Section 10 and test the brakes carefully before driving the vehicle in traffic.

10 Hydraulic system – bleeding

⚠ **Warning:** *Hydraulic fluid is poisonous; wash off immediately and thoroughly in the case of skin contact, and seek immediate medical advice if any fluid is swallowed or gets into the eyes. Certain types of hydraulic fluid are inflammable, and may ignite when allowed into contact with hot components; when servicing any hydraulic system, it is safest to assume that the fluid is inflammable, and to take precautions against the risk of fire as though it is petrol that is being handled. Hydraulic fluid is also an effective paint stripper, and will attack plastics; if any is spilt, it should be washed off immediately, using copious quantities of fresh water. Finally, it is hygroscopic (it absorbs moisture from the air) – old fluid may be contaminated and unfit for further use. When topping-up or renewing the fluid, always use the recommended type, and ensure that it comes from a freshly-opened sealed container.*

General

1 Bleeding the hydraulic system is necessary to remove any air that manages to find its way into the system when it's been opened during removal and refitting of a hose, pipe, caliper, wheel cylinder or master cylinder. It will probably be necessary to bleed the system at all four brakes if air has entered the system due to low fluid level, or if the brake pipe have been disconnected at the master cylinder.

2 If a brake pipe was disconnected only at a wheel, then only that caliper or wheel cylinder need be bled. If a brake pipe is disconnected at a fitting located between the master cylinder and any of the brakes, that part of the system served by the disconnected pipe must be bled.

3 Remove any residual vacuum from the servo unit by applying the brake several times with the engine off. Remove the master cylinder reservoir cover and fill the reservoir

8.4 Use a brake pipe spanner to unscrew the pipe fittings (1), then unplug the electrical connector for the brake fluid warning switch, then remove the two nuts (2)

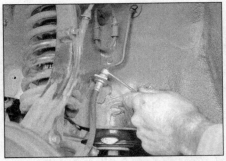

9.4a Use a brake pipe spanner to slacken the brake pipe-to-hose fitting . . .

9.4b . . . then remove the clip and slide the hose out of the bracket

with brake fluid. Refit the cover. **Note:** *Check the fluid level often during the bleeding operation and add fluid as necessary to prevent the fluid level from falling low enough to allow air bubbles into the master cylinder.*

4 Have an assistant on hand, as well as a supply of new brake fluid, a clear container partially-filled with clean brake fluid, a length of plastic, rubber or vinyl tubing to fit over the bleed screw and a spanner to open and close the bleed screw.

Models with ABS

5 If you're working on a vehicle equipped with an Anti-lock Brake System (ABS) and have removed and installed (or renewed) the master cylinder, or if the fluid level in the master cylinder became too low and allowed air into the system, begin the procedure by bleeding the pipes at the master cylinder. Have an assistant slowly depress the brake pedal and hold it there, then loosen the brake pipe fittings (one at a time) at the master cylinder, allowing fluid and air to escape. Repeat this procedure until the fluid coming out is free of air, then proceed to the next step.

5-door Hatchback models up to '96

6 On these models, bleed the hydraulic modulator. Attach a snug-fitting bleed hose to the bleeder valve on the hydraulic modulator unit. Start the engine to build-up pressure in the modulator, then slowly open the bleeder valve 1/8 to 1/4 turn to allow fluid and air to escape; do this in small increments, repeating the procedure until the fluid coming out of the modulator is free of air. Turn off the engine and proceed to bleed the remainder of the system. **Note:** *If the ABS light on the instrument panel comes on, repeat this step.*

⚠️ **Warning: The fluid in the modulator is under high pressure. Don't open the bleeder valve rapidly or more than 1/4 of a turn, or the brake fluid may squirt out with great force.**

All models

Note: *The brakes can also be bled using one-man kits, as described in Chapter 6 for bleeding the clutch.*

7 Beginning with the first wheel in the bleeding sequence, loosen the bleed screw slightly, then tighten it to a point where it is snug but can still be loosened quickly and easily. The bleeding sequence is as follows:

Estate models – Left front, right front, right rear, left rear.
All other models – Right rear, left front, left rear, right front.

8 Place one end of the tubing over the bleed screw and submerge the other end in brake fluid in the container **(see illustration).**

9 Have the assistant slowly depress the brake pedal and hold the pedal firmly depressed.

10 While the pedal is held depressed, open the bleed screw just enough to allow a flow of fluid to leave the screw. Watch for air bubbles to exit the submerged end of the tube. When the fluid flow slows after a couple of seconds, close the screw and have your assistant release the pedal.

11 Repeat Paragraphs 9 and 10 until no more air is seen leaving the tube, then tighten the bleed screw and proceed to bleed the rest of the brakes, following the sequence shown in Paragraph 7. Be sure to check the fluid in the master cylinder reservoir frequently.

12 Never use old brake fluid. It contains moisture which can boil during (or after) heavy braking, rendering the brakes inoperative.

13 Refill the master cylinder with fluid at the end of the operation.

14 Check the operation of the brakes. The pedal should feel solid when depressed, with no sponginess. If necessary, repeat the entire process.

---

11 Servo – testing, removal and refitting 🔧

Testing

1 Depress the brake pedal several times with the engine off and make sure there is no change in the pedal reserve distance.

2 Depress the pedal and start the engine. If the pedal goes down slightly, operation is normal.

3 Start the engine and turn it off after one or two minutes. Depress the brake pedal several times slowly. If the pedal goes down farther the first time but gradually rises after the second or third depression, the servo is airtight, operation is normal.

4 Depress the brake pedal while the engine is running, then stop the engine with the pedal depressed. If there is no change in the pedal reserve travel after holding the pedal for 30 seconds, the servo is airtight, operation is normal.

Removal

5 Servo units should not be dismantled. They require special tools not normally found in most repair workshops. They are fairly complex and because of their critical relationship to brake performance it is best to renew a defective servo unit or fit a rebuilt one.

6 To remove the servo, first remove the brake master cylinder as described in Section 8.

7 Disconnect the hose leading from the engine to the servo. Be careful not to damage the hose when removing it from the servo fitting.

8 Locate the pushrod clevis pin connecting the servo to the brake pedal. This is accessible from under the facia panel in front of the driver's seat.

9 Remove the split pin with pliers and pull out the clevis pin.

10 Remove the four nuts **(see illustration)** holding the brake servo to the bulkhead. You may need a torch to see them, because they're up under the facia area.

11 Slide the servo straight out from the bulkhead until the studs clear the holes and pull the servo, brackets and gaskets from the engine compartment area.

Refitting

12 If a new servo is being installed, measure the length of the input rod, from the booster

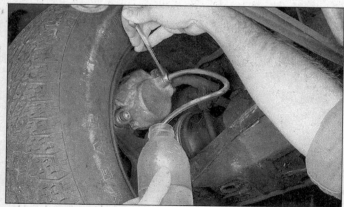

10.8 When bleeding the brakes, a hose is connected to the bleed screw at the caliper or wheel cylinder and then submerged in brake fluid – air will be seen as bubbles in the tube and container

11.10 To remove the brake servo, remove the split pin and clevis pin that connect the pushrod to the brake pedal, then remove the four mounting nuts (arrowed)

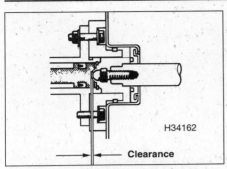

11.14a The servo pushrod-to-master cylinder clearance must be as specified – if there is interference between the two, the brakes may drag; if there is too much clearance there will be excessive pedal travel

mounting surface to the hole in the clevis; it should be as listed in this Chapter's Specifications. If it isn't, loosen the locknut and turn the clevis one way or the other until the length is correct.

13 Refitting procedures are basically the reverse of those for removal. Tighten the servo mounting nuts to the torque listed in this Chapter's Specifications. Also, be sure to use a new split pin on the clevis pin.

14 If a new servo unit is being installed, also check the pushrod clearance **(see illustration)** as follows:

a) *Using a hand-held vacuum pump, apply a vacuum of 500 mmHg to the servo. Measure the distance that the pushrod protrudes from the master cylinder mounting surface on the front of the servo, including the gasket (if used). Write down this measurement **(see illustration)**. This is dimension A.*

b) *Measure the distance from the mounting flange to the end of the master cylinder **(see illustration)**. Write down this measurement. This is dimension B.*

c) *Measure the distance from the end of the master cylinder to the bottom of the pocket in the piston **(see illustration)**. Write down this measurement. This is dimension C.*

d) *Subtract measurement B from*

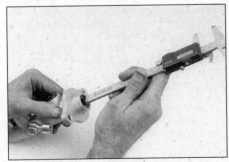

11.14d Measure the distance from the piston pocket to the end of the master cylinder

11.14b Measure the distance that the pushrod protrudes from the servo at the master cylinder mounting surface (including the gasket, if fitted)

measurement C, then subtract measurement A from the difference between B and C. This the pushrod clearance.

e) *Compare your calculated pushrod clearance to the pushrod clearance listed in this Chapter's Specifications. If necessary, adjust the pushrod length to achieve the correct clearance (see the next Paragraph).*

15 If the clearance is more or less than specified, loosen the star locknut and turn the adjuster on the servo pushrod until the clearance is within the specified limit **(see illustration)**. After adjustment, tighten the locknut. Recheck the clearance. Repeat this step as often as necessary until the clearance is correct.

16 After the final refitting of the master cylinder and brake hoses and pipes, bleed the brakes as described in Section 10.

12 Handbrake – adjustment

1 Remove the centre console as described in Chapter 11.

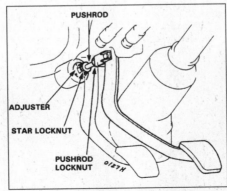

11.15 To adjust the length of the servo pushrod, slacken the star locknut and turn the adjuster in or out, as necessary, to achieve the desired setting

11.14c Measure the distance from the mounting flange to the end of the master cylinder

2 Block the front wheels, raise the rear of the vehicle and support it securely on axle stands (see *Jacking and vehicle support*). Apply the handbrake lever until you hear one click.

3 Turn the adjusting nut on the equaliser **(see illustration)** clockwise while rotating the rear wheels. Stop turning the nut when the brakes just start to drag on the rear wheels.

4 Release the handbrake lever and check to see that the brakes don't drag when the rear wheels are turned. The handbrake should be fully applied after the lever has been pulled up and 6 to 10 clicks have been heard.

5 Lower the vehicle and refit the console (see Chapter 11).

13 Handbrake cable(s) – renewal

1 Block the front wheels and loosen the rear roadwheel nuts. Raise the rear of the vehicle and support it securely on axle stands (see *Jacking and vehicle support*).

2 On vehicles with rear drum brakes, remove the brake drum(s) (see Section 6).

3 Following the procedure in the previous Section, slacken the cable adjusting nut. Remove the cable clamps from the cable

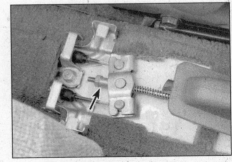

12.3 The handbrake adjusting nut (arrowed) is on the equaliser assembly

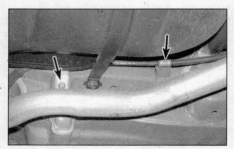

13.3 Slacken the bolts and detach the handbrake cable from the clips (arrowed)

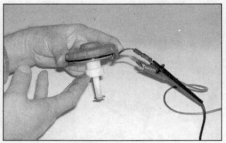

15.3a Raise the float and make sure there is no continuity

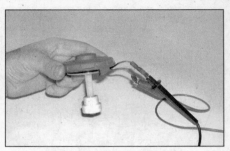

15.3b Make sure there is continuity with the float lowered

outer **(see illustration)**. Unhook the cable from the equaliser.

4 On models with rear drum brakes, remove the brake shoes (see Section 6) and disconnect the cable end from the lever on the trailing brake shoe **(see illustration 6.4f)**. Depress the tangs on the cable retainer and pass the cable through the backing plate. You can do this by passing an offset 12 mm spanner over the end of the cable and onto the retainer. This compresses all the tangs simultaneously.

5 On models with rear disc brakes, remove the clip and clevis to disconnect the cable end from the actuator lever on the caliper **(see illustration 4.2)**, then remove the spring clip to free the cable outer from the support bracket.

6 Unbolt the outer cable clamps from the underbody, noting how the cable is routed, then remove the cable from the vehicle. It may be necessary to remove the exhaust pipe heat shield bolts at the rear to allow cable removal.

7 If both cables are to be removed, repeat the above steps to remove the remaining cable.

8 Refitting is the reverse of the removal procedure. After the cable(s) are refitted, be sure to adjust them according to the procedure described in Section 12.

14 Brake light switch – testing, renewal and adjustment

Testing

1 To check the brake light switch, push on the brake pedal and verify that the brake lights come on.

2 If they don't, check the brake light fuse (see Chapter 12 or check your owner's handbook for fuse locations). Also check the brake light bulbs in both tail light assemblies (don't forget to check the high-mounted brake light).

3 If the fuse and the bulbs are okay, locate the brake light switch at the top of the brake pedal.

4 Unplug the switch wiring plug.

5 Check for continuity across the switch terminals. When the brake pedal is depressed, there should be continuity; when it's released, there should be no continuity. If the switch doesn't operate as described, renew it.

Renewal

6 Disconnect the electrical connector from the switch, if you haven't already done so.

7 Remove the locknut on the pedal side of the switch and unscrew the switch from the bracket.

8 Refitting of the brake light switch is the reverse of the removal procedure.

Adjustment

9 Loosen the brake light switch locknut and unscrew the brake light switch until there's clearance between the switch plunger and the brake pedal.

10 Loosen the pushrod locknut and screw the pushrod in or out with pliers until the pedal height from the floor is correct (as listed in this Chapter's Specifications).

11 Tighten the locknut securely.

12 Screw in the brake light switch until the plunger is fully depressed (threaded end touching the pad on the pedal arm), then unscrew the switch 1/2-turn and tighten the locknut securely.

13 Depress the pedal with your hand and measure the pedal freeplay. It should be within the dimensions listed in this Chapter's Specifications. Make sure the brake lights operate when the pedal is depressed and go off when the pedal is released.

15 Brake fluid level switch – testing and renewal

1 Unplug the switch wiring plug and remove the brake fluid reservoir cap and switch assembly.

2 Make sure the fluid level float moves up and down easily, if it doesn't, renew the assembly.

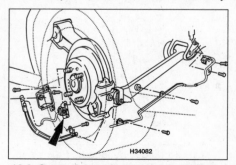

16.3 On models with rear disc brakes, the wheel speed sensor (arrowed) is fitted beneath a shield retained by two bolts

3 Connect the leads of an ohmmeter to the electrical connectors of the fluid level switch. Raise and lower the float and check for continuity. When the float is raised, there should be no continuity; when it's lowered, there should be continuity **(see illustrations)**. If the float assembly doesn't operate as described, renew it.

16 Wheel speed sensors – removal and refitting

Removal

1 Apply the handbrake, then jack up the front or rear of the vehicle as applicable, and support securely on axle stands (see *Jacking and vehicle support*). To improve access, remove the roadwheel.

2 Trace the wiring back from the sensor, releasing it from all the relevant clips and ties whilst noting its correct routing, and disconnect the wiring connector.

3 Slacken and remove the retaining bolt(s), then carefully pull the sensor out from the hub carrier/drum assembly and remove it from the vehicle. On models with rear disc brakes, the sensor is fitted beneath a shield retained by two bolts **(see illustration)**.

Refitting

4 Ensure that the mating faces of the sensor and hub carrier are clean and dry then lubricate the wheel sensor surfaces with a small quantity of copper-based grease.

5 Insert the wheel speed sensor and tighten the retaining bolt(s) to the specified torque.

6 Ensure the sensor is securely retained then work along the sensor wiring, making sure it is correctly routed, securing it in position with all the relevant clips, ties and screws. Reconnect the wiring connector.

7 In order for the sensor to function correctly, the air gap between the sensor tip and the reluctor (pulser) wheel teeth must be 0.4 to 1.0 mm. Measure the gap with feeler gauges. if the gap is incorrect, check for incorrect seating of the sensor, damage to the reluctor wheel/teeth, and distorted wheel hub/brake drum.

8 Refit the wheel (where removed) then lower the vehicle and (where necessary) tighten the wheel bolts to the specified torque.

Chapter 10
Suspension and steering

Contents

Degrees of difficulty

Easy, suitable for novice with little experience	**Fairly easy,** suitable for beginner with some experience	**Fairly difficult,** suitable for competent DIY mechanic	**Difficult,** suitable for experienced DIY mechanic	**Very difficult,** suitable for expert DIY or professional

Specifications

Front suspension
Type . . . . Independent with upper and lower control arms, shock absorber/coil spring, and an anti-roll bar

Rear suspension
Type . . . . Trailing arm with upper and lower control arms, coil spring/shock absorber units, and one some models, an anti-roll bar

Steering
Type . . . . Rack-and-pinion, hydraulically power-assisted on some models

Front wheel alignment and steering angles
Camber angle:
  5-door models:
    1.6i SR VTEC . . . . 0° 00' ± 1°
    All other 5-door models . . . . –0° 07' ± 1°
  2, 3 or 4-door models . . . . 0° 00' ± 1°
Castor angle:
  2, 3 and 4-door models . . . . 1° 40' ± 1°
  5-door models . . . . 1° 10' ± 1 °
Front wheel alignment – total toe-in:
  2, 3 and 4-door models . . . . 1.0 ± 3.0 mm
  5-door models . . . . 0.0 ± 2.0 mm

Rear wheel alignment
Camber angle:
  2, 3 and 4-door models . . . . –1° 00' ± 1°
  5-door models . . . . –0° 50' ± 0° 45'
Rear wheel alignment – total toe-in . . . . 2.3 ± 2.0 mm

Roadwheels

Type .... Pressed-steel or aluminium alloy

Tyres

Pressures .... See the label on the door aperture

Torque wrench settings

	Nm	lbf ft
Front suspension		
Anti-roll bar:		
Link nuts (upper and lower):		
Rubber bushing type*	22	16
Balljoint type	29	21
Bush clamp bolts	22	16
Damper fork:		
Pinch-bolt	43	32
Fork-to-lower arm through-bolt nut*	64	47
Lower control arm:		
Front pivot bolt		
5-door Hatchback and Estate	64	47
All others	103	76
Rear pivot stud nut*	83	61
Bush housing/clamp bolts	89	66
Shock absorber:		
Shock absorber-to-body mounting nuts:		
5-door Hatchback and Estate	38	28
All others	49	36
Shock absorber damper rod upper nut*	29	21
Steering hub carrier (lower) balljoint nut	49 to 59	36 to 44
Upper control arm:		
Balljoint nut	39 to 47	29 to 35
Pivot bolts (3-door Hatchback, 2-door Coupe, 4-door Saloon)	54	40
Control arm-to-shock tower nuts (5-door Hatchback and Estate)* ..	64	47
Rear suspension		
Anti-roll bar:		
Upper link nuts	29	21
Lower link nuts	39	29
Upper link bolt	14	10
Lower link bolt	45	33
Bush clamp bolts	22	16
Compensator arm bolts:		
5-door Hatchback and Estate models	45	33
All others	64	47
Hub-to-spindle nut*	181	134
Lower arm bolts:		
5-door Hatchback and Estate models	47	35
All others	54	40
Shock absorber:		
Damper rod nut*	29	21
Shock-to-lower arm bolt:		
5-door Hatchback and Estate models	47	35
All others	54	40
Shock upper mounting nuts:		
5-door Hatchback and Estate models	38	28
All others	49	36
Trailing arm bush bracket-to-body bolts:		
5-door Hatchback and Estate models	78	58
All others	64	47
Upper arm:		
Bush bracket-to-body bolts:		
5-door Hatchback and Estate models	30	22
All others	39	29
Upper arm-to-trailing arm bolt:		
5-door Hatchback and Estate models	45	33
All others	54	40

Torque wrench settings (continued)

	Nm	lbf ft
Steering system		
Airbag module Torx bolts*	10	7
Anti-roll bar clamp bolts	22	16
Chassis stiffener bracket/brace	38	28
Intermediate shaft pinch-bolt:		
5-door Hatchback and Estate models	28	21
All others	22	16
Steering gear mounting bolts:		
5-door Hatchback and Estate models:		
Right-hand side	58	43
Left-hand side	39	29
All others:		
Right-hand side	43	32
Left-hand side	39	29
Steering wheel bolt	39	29
Steering wheel nut*	49	36
Track rod end-to-hub carrier nut	39 to 47	29 to 35

*Do not re-use

1 General information

The front suspension (see illustration) is a fully independent design with upper and lower control arms, shock absorber/coil spring assemblies and an anti-roll bar.

The rear suspension uses trailing arms, upper and lower control arms, 'compensator' arms, an anti-roll bar (on some models), and shock absorber/coil spring units (see illustration overleaf).

All models use rack-and-pinion steering. Some models are power-assisted. The power steering system employs an engine-driven pump connected by hoses to the steering gear.

Frequently, when working on the suspension or steering system components, you may come across fasteners which seem impossible to loosen. These fasteners on the underside of the vehicle are continually subjected to water, road grime, mud, etc, and can become rusted or 'seized,' making them extremely difficult to remove. In order to unscrew these stubborn fasteners without damaging them (or other components), be

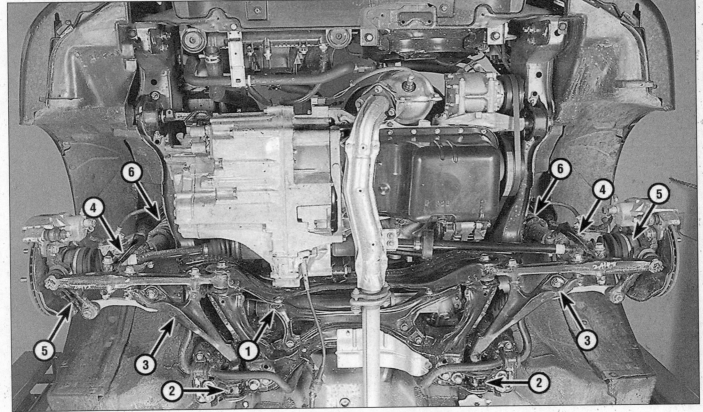

1.1 Front suspension and steering components

1 Steering rack	3 Lower control arm	5 Steering hub carrier
2 Lower control arm bush clamp	4 Damper fork	6 Shock absorber/coil spring assembly

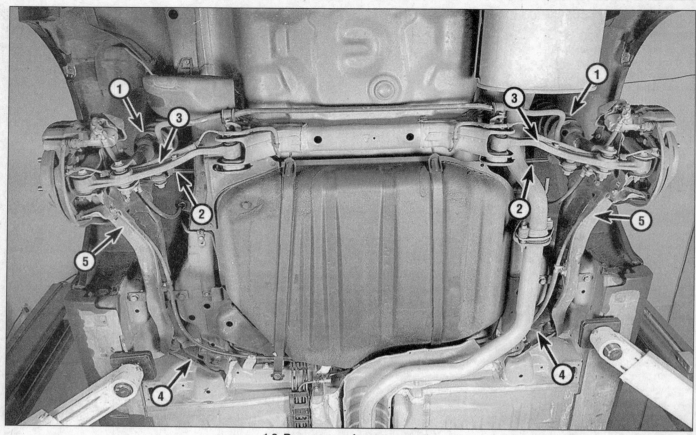

1.2 Rear suspension components

1 Shock absorber/coil spring assembly   2 Upper arm   3 Lower arm   4 Compensator arm   5 Trailing arm

sure to use lots of penetrating oil and allow it to soak in for a while. Using a wire brush to clean exposed threads will also ease removal of the nut or bolt and prevent damage to the threads. Sometimes a sharp blow with a hammer and punch is effective in breaking the bond between a nut and bolt threads, but care must be taken to prevent the punch from slipping off the fastener and ruining the threads. Heating the stuck fastener and surrounding area sometimes helps too, but isn't recommended because of the obvious dangers associated with fire. Long breaker bars and extension pipes will increase leverage, but never use an extension pipe on a ratchet – the ratcheting mechanism could be damaged. Sometimes, turning the nut or bolt in the tightening (clockwise) direction first will help to break it loose. Fasteners that require drastic measures to loosen should always be renewed.

Caution: Since most of the procedures that are dealt with in this chapter involve jacking up the vehicle and working underneath it, a good pair of axle stands will be needed. A trolley jack is the preferred type of jack to lift the vehicle, and it can also be used to support certain components during various operations.

⚠️ *Warning: Never, under any circumstances, rely on a jack to support the vehicle while working on it. Whenever any of the suspension or steering fasteners are loosened or removed they must be inspected and, if necessary, renewed with ones of the same part number or of original equipment quality and design. Torque specifications must be followed for proper reassembly and component retention. Never attempt to heat or straighten any suspension or steering component. Instead, renew any bent or damaged part.*

Caution: If the stereo in your vehicle is equipped with an anti-theft system, make sure you have the correct activation code before disconnecting the battery.

 2 Front shock absorber/coil spring assembly – removal and refitting

Removal

1 Loosen the roadwheel nuts, raise the vehicle and support it securely on axle stands (see *Jacking and vehicle support*). Remove the wheel.

2 Unbolt the brake hose from the shock absorber assembly.

3 Disconnect the anti-roll bar from the lower control arm (see Section 4).

4 Place a trolley jack under the lower control arm to support it when the shock absorber assembly is removed. Remove the shock absorber fork pinch-bolt **(see illustration)**.

5 Remove the shock absorber fork-to-lower control arm bolt and remove the fork (see

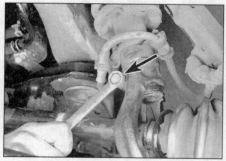

2.4 Remove the damper fork pinch-bolt (arrowed)

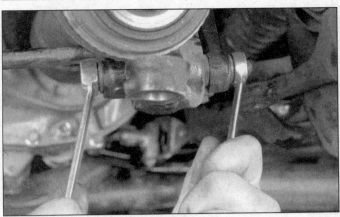

2.5a Remove the through-bolt that connects the damper fork to the lower control arm

2.5b Detach the damper fork from the shock absorber

illustrations). It may be necessary to tap the fork from the shock absorber.

6 Support the shock absorber and coil spring assembly and remove the two upper mounting nuts **(see illustration)**. Remove the unit from the wheelarch.

Refitting

7 Guide the shock absorber assembly up into the wheelarch and insert the upper mounting studs through the holes in the body. Once the studs protrude from the holes, refit the nuts so the assembly won't fall back through, but don't tighten the nuts completely yet. The shock absorber is heavy and awkward, so get an assistant to help you, if possible.

8 Insert the lower end of the shock absorber into the shock absorber fork. Make sure the aligning tab on the back of the shock body enters the slot in the shock absorber fork.

9 Connect the shock absorber fork to the lower control arm. Raise the lower control arm with the trolley jack to simulate normal ride height, then tighten the self-locking nut to the torque listed in this Chapter's Specifications. Now tighten the shock absorber fork pinch-

bolt to the torque listed in this Chapter's Specifications.

10 Connect the anti-roll bar to the control arm (see Section 4). Attach the brake hose to its bracket and tighten the bolt securely.

11 Refit the wheel and nuts, lower the vehicle and tighten the nuts to the torque listed in the Chapter 1 Specifications.

12 Tighten the upper mounting nuts to the torque listed in this Chapter's Specifications.

3 Shock absorber or coil spring – renewal

1 Remove the shock absorber/coil spring assembly (see Section 2 or 10).

2 Check the shock absorber for leaking fluid, dents, cracks or other obvious damage. Check the coil spring for chips or cracks which could cause premature failure and inspect the spring seats for hardness or general deterioration. The shock absorber assemblies, complete with the coil springs, are available on an exchange basis which eliminates much time and work. So, before

dismantling your shock to renew individual components, check on the availability of parts and the price of a complete rebuilt unit.

⚠ *Warning: Dismantling a shock absorber/coil spring assembly is potentially dangerous and utmost attention must be directed to the job, or serious injury may result. Use only a high-quality spring compressor and carefully follow the manufacturer's instructions furnished with the tool. After removing the coil spring from the shock absorber, set it aside in a safe, isolated area.*

3 Mount the shock absorber assembly in a vice. Line the vice jaws with wood or rags to prevent damage to the unit and don't tighten the vice excessively.

4 Mark the relationship of the damper mounting base to the spring (or if the spring is being renewed, put the mark on the damper unit). This will ensure correct positioning of the mounting base when the unit is reassembled.

5 Following the tool manufacturer's instructions, fit the spring compressor on the spring and compress it sufficiently to relieve all pressure from the damper mounting base **(see illustration)**.

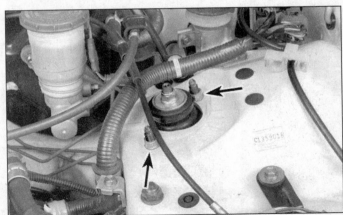

2.6 Remove the nuts (arrowed) from the shock absorber mounting studs – don't remove the larger nut in the centre

3.5 Fit the spring compressor according to the tool manufacturer's instructions and compress the spring until all pressure is relieved from the mounting base

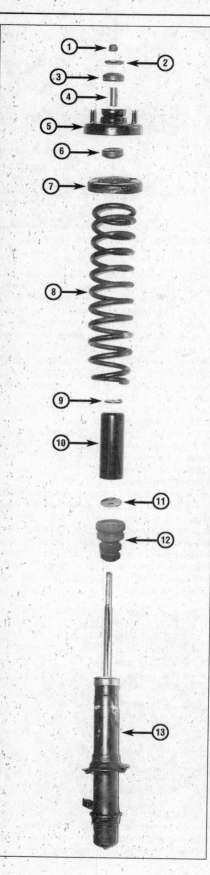

3.6 Typical shock absorber/coil spring assembly

1 Self-locking nut
2 Damper mounting washer
3 Damper mounting rubber
4 Damper mounting collar
5 Damper mounting base
6 Damper mounting rubber
7 Spring mounting rubber
8 Spring
9 Dust cover plate
10 Dust cover
11 Bump stop plate
12 Bump stop
13 Damper unit

6 Unscrew the self-locking nut while holding the damper shaft with an Allen key to prevent it from turning. Remove the parts from the upper part of the shock and lay them out in the exact order in which they're removed **(see illustration)**.

7 Carefully lift the compressed spring from the assembly and set it in a safe place.

8 Slide the rest of the parts off the damper shaft and lay them out in the exact order in which they're removed.

9 Refit the bump stop, bump stop plate (if equipped), dust cover and dust cover plate onto the new damper unit. Extend the damper shaft as far as it will go and slide the components down to the damper body.

10 Carefully place the coil spring onto the shock absorber body, with the end of the spring resting in the lowest part of the seat.

11 Refit the spring mounting rubber, lower mounting rubber, damper mounting collar, damper mounting base, seal, upper mounting rubber, damper mounting washer and a new self-locking nut. Before tightening the nut, align the previously applied marks on the mounting base and the spring (or damper body).

12 Tighten the self-locking nut to the torque listed in this Chapter's Specifications, again using the Allen key to prevent the shaft from turning. Remove the spring compressor.

13 Refit the shock absorber/coil spring assembly (see Section 2 or 10).

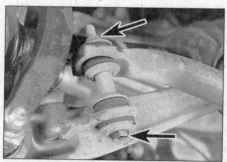

4.2a Some models use rubber bush type links; remove the nut and bolt (arrowed) and remove the anti-roll bar link assembly

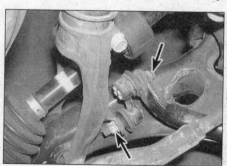

4.2b Other models use ball-stud type links (arrowed)

4 Front anti-roll bar and bushes – removal and refitting

Removal

1 Apply the handbrake. Loosen the front wheel nuts, raise the front of the vehicle and support it securely on axle stands (see *Jacking and vehicle support*). Remove the wheels.

2 Detach the anti-roll bar links from the bar **(see illustrations)**. Note the order in which the spacers, washers and bushes are arranged on the link bolt.

3 Remove the bolts which attach the anti-roll bar brackets to the underside of the vehicle **(see illustration)**.

4 Remove the bar from under the vehicle.

5 Pull the brackets off the anti-roll bar and inspect the bushes for cracks, hardness and other signs of deterioration. If the bushes are damaged, renew them.

Refitting

6 Refitting is the reverse of removal.

5 Upper control arm (front) – removal and refitting

Removal

1 Loosen the front wheel nuts, raise the vehicle, place it securely on axle stands (see

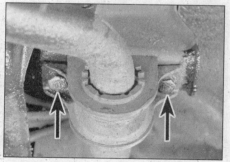

4.3 Remove the bolts (arrowed) attaching the anti-roll bar bracket to the chassis

5.2 Slacken – but don't remove – the upper balljoint nut (arrowed)

5.3 Using a balljoint splitter, separate the upper control arm balljoint stud from the hub carrier

5.4a Remove the front pivot bolt (arrowed) . . .

Jacking and vehicle support) and remove the wheel. Support the lower control arm with a trolley jack. If you're working on an 5-door Hatchback or Estate model, remove the shock absorber assembly (see Section 2).

2 Remove the split pin and loosen, but do not remove, the castellated nut **(see illustration)** from the upper balljoint stud. The nut will prevent the upper control arm and the steering hub carrier from separating violently in the next step.

3 Separate the upper control arm from the steering hub carrier with a balljoint splitter **(see illustration)**. Remove the castellated nut. Don't let the top of the steering hub carrier fall outwards. If necessary, secure it to the shock absorber (if still fitted) with a piece of wire.

4 If you're working on a 3-door Hatchback, 2-door Coupe or 4-door Saloon, remove the upper control arm pivot bolts from inside the engine compartment **(see illustrations)**, then remove the upper control arm.

5 If you're working on an 5-door Hatchback or Estate model, remove the upper control arm-to-shock absorber tower nuts **(see illustration)**.

Refitting

6 Refitting is the reverse of removal. Be sure to tighten all of the fasteners to the torque values listed in this Chapter's Specifications.

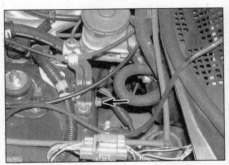

5.4b . . . and the rear pivot bolt (arrowed)

Note: *If you're working on a 3-door Hatchback, 2-door Coupe or 4-door Saloon, raise the front suspension with a trolley jack to simulate normal ride height before tightening the control arm pivot bolts.*

---

6 Lower control arm (front) – removal and refitting

Removal

1 Loosen the front wheel nuts, raise the vehicle, place it securely on axle stands (see

5.5 Remove the two upper control arm mounting bolts (arrowed)

Jacking and vehicle support) and remove the wheel.

2 Detach the anti-roll bar link from the lower control arm (see Section 4).

3 Detach the damper fork from the control arm (see Section 2).

4 Remove the split pin from the castellated nut on the lower balljoint stud. Loosen the nut, but don't remove it yet. Using a balljoint splitter, separate the lower control arm from the balljoint in the steering hub carrier **(see illustration)**. Remove the nut.

5 Remove the pivot bolt from the inner end of the lower control arm **(see illustration)**.

6 Remove the nut from the rear pivot stud

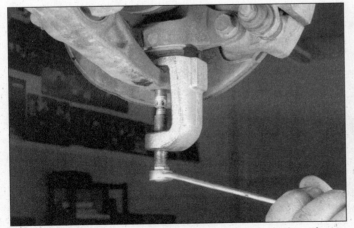

6.4 Separate the lower control arm from the hub carrier using a balljoint splitter

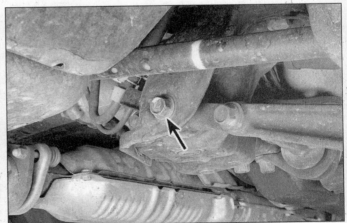

6.5 Remove the pivot bolt (arrowed) from the inner end of the lower control arm

6.6 To detach the lower control arm's pivot stud from its bush, remove the large nut (arrowed); it's not necessary to remove the three bush clamp bolts (arrowed) unless you need to renew the bush itself

7.1 Slacken the driveshaft/hub nut with a socket and breaker bar

8.3 Drive the hub from the hub carrier

(see illustration), pull the stud out of the bush housing/clamp and remove the arm noting which way the washers face. **Note:** *It's not necessary to remove the three bush housing/clamp retaining bolts unless the bushing is to be renewed.*

Refitting

7 Refitting is the reverse of removal. Raise the lower control arm with a trolley jack to simulate normal ride height before tightening the front pivot bolt or the rear pivot stud nut. Tighten the castellated nut to the lower torque specification, then tighten it only far enough to align the slot with the split pin hole. Do not align the nut by slackening it.

7 Steering hub carrier assembly – removal and refitting

Removal

1 Remove the wheel trim, if equipped. Loosen the driveshaft/hub nut **(see illustration)**. Loosen the wheel nuts, raise the front of the vehicle and support it securely on axle stands (see *Jacking and vehicle support*). Remove the wheel and the driveshaft/hub nut.
2 Unbolt the brake hose bracket from the steering hub carrier. Unbolt the brake caliper,

hang it out of the way with a piece of wire, remove the caliper mounting bracket and remove the brake disc (see Chapter 9).
3 Disconnect the steering track rod end from the steering hub carrier (see Section 15).
4 Separate the lower control arm from the balljoint in the bottom of the steering hub carrier (see Section 6).
5 Separate the upper end of the hub carrier from the upper control arm balljoint (see Section 5).
6 Carefully pull the hub carrier assembly off the driveshaft. Tap the end of the driveshaft with a soft-faced hammer to free the driveshaft from the hub. Support the driveshaft with a piece of wire to prevent damage to the inner CV joint.

Refitting

7 Apply a light coat of grease to the driveshaft splines. Insert the driveshaft through the splined bore of the hub while guiding the hub carrier assembly into position.
8 Connect the upper end of the hub carrier to the upper control arm balljoint (see Section 5). Tighten the balljoint stud nut to the torque listed in this Chapter's Specifications.
9 Connect the balljoint on the bottom of the hub carrier to the lower control arm (see Section 6).
10 Refit the brake disc, caliper mount and caliper (see Chapter 9). Attach the brake hose bracket.
11 Refit the driveshaft/hub nut and tighten it securely.
12 Refit the wheel and nuts, lower the vehicle

and tighten the nuts to the torque listed in the Chapter 1 Specifications.
13 Tighten the driveshaft/hub nut to the torque specified in Chapter 8.

8 Front hub and bearing assembly – removal and refitting

Removal

1 Remove the steering hub carrier from the vehicle as described in Section 7.
2 Remove the brake disc as described in Chapter 9.
3 Mount the hub carrier securely in a vice, and using a suitable drift (such as a large socket) drive out the hub flange from the inboard side **(see illustration)**.
4 Prise out the sealing ring from the inboard side of the hub carrier **(see illustration)**.
5 Mount the drive flange in a vice, then with careful use of a chisel, progressively tap off the bearing race **(see illustration)**. If a bearing puller is available, this is preferable, to avoid risking any damage to the drive flange surfaces.
6 Remove the bearing retaining circlip from the outboard side of the hub **(see illustration)**.
7 Undo the three retaining screws and remove the brake disc splash shield.
8 Mount the hub carrier in a vice, and drive out the bearing from the inboard side, using a suitable drift.

8.4 Prise out the sealing ring

8.5 Use a chisel to remove the bearing inner race

8.6 Remove the circlip

8.10 Drive the new bearing into the hub carrier

8.11 Refit the disc shield

8.12 Ensure that the hub is pressed squarely into the new bearing

Refitting

9 Clean up the hub and drive flange, removing all old grease, and any metal debris from removing the old bearing.

10 Support the inboard side of the hub below the bearing location, and progressively press in the new bearing using a suitable socket or tube which bears only on the bearing outer race. Make sure that the bearing is kept square in the hub until it is fully seated (**see illustration**).

11 Secure the bearing using a new circlip (usually supplied with the new bearing), then refit the brake disc shield and secure with the screws (**see illustration**).

12 Again supporting the inboard side of the hub below the bearing location, align the drive flange squarely into the hub, and tap/press it fully into position (**see illustration**).

13 Fit the new sealing ring to the inboard side of the hub carrier.

14 Refitting the hub is a reversal of removal, noting the following points:

a) *Tighten all fasteners to the specified torque.*

b) *Use a new hub-to-driveshaft nut. Tighten the nut when the weight of the vehicle is on its wheels again.*

c) *Refit the hub carrier as described in Section 7.*

d) *Refit the brake disc and as described in Chapter 9.*

9 Balljoints – renewal

1 The front suspension uses two balljoints. The upper balljoint, located in the upper control arm, can't be removed. If it's worn or damaged, renew the upper control arm (see Section 5).

2 The lower balljoint, located in the steering carrier, can be removed, but special tools are needed. If it's worn or damaged, remove the carrier (see Section 7) and take it to a Honda dealer or automotive engineering workshop to have it renewed.

10 Rear shock absorber/coil spring assembly – removal and refitting

Removal

1 Loosen the rear wheel nuts, raise the vehicle, place it securely on axle stands (see *Jacking and vehicle support*) and remove the rear wheels. Support the trailing arm with a trolley jack.

2 On some models a cover is fitted in the luggage compartment side panel. Remove the panel to gain access to the upper shock absorber mounting (**see illustration**). On other models, remove the luggage compartment side panel as described in Chapter 11, Section 31.

3 Remove the shock absorber upper mounting nuts (**see illustration**).

4 Remove the shock absorber lower mounting bolt (**see illustration**).

5 Lower the jack and the lower arm and remove the shock absorber/coil spring assembly.

6 To inspect or renew the shock absorber or coil spring, see Section 3.

Refitting

7 Refitting is the reverse of removal. Be sure to tighten all fasteners to the torque values listed in this Chapter's Specifications. **Note:** *Before tightening the shock absorber lower mounting bolt, raise the rear of the trailing arm with the trolley jack to simulate normal ride height.*

11 Rear anti-roll bar – removal and refitting

Removal

1 Loosen the rear wheel nuts, raise the vehicle, place it securely on axle stands and

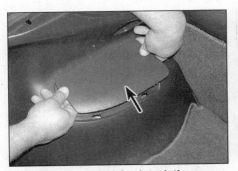

10.2 On some models, detach the cover (arrowed) for access to the upper shock absorber mounting nuts

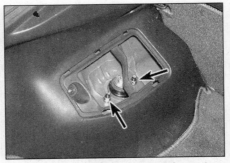

10.3 Remove the upper mounting nuts (arrowed) – don't remove the large centre nut

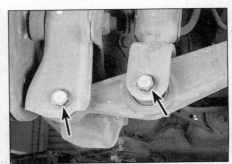

10.4 Remove the mounting bolt (right arrow) that attaches the lower end of the shock absorber to the lower arm; to disconnect the lower arm from the trailing arm, remove the left bolt (left arrow)

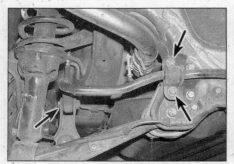

11.2 Remove the anti-roll bar-to-link bolts and the clamp bolts (arrowed)

12.3 Using a hammer and chisel, remove the dust cover

12.4a Unstake the hub nut

12.4b The hub assembly should come off easily, but if it's stuck, pull it from the hub carrier with a slide hammer

12.5 Stake the hub nut back into place

remove the rear wheels (see *Jacking and vehicle support*).
2 Remove the anti-roll bar-to-link bolts/nuts and the anti-roll bar-to-body clamp bolts and remove the bar **(see illustration)**.
3 Pull the brackets off the anti-roll bar and inspect the bushes for cracks, hardness and other signs of deterioration. If the bushes are damaged, renew them.

Refitting

4 Refitting is the reverse of removal.

12 Rear hub and bearing assembly – removal and refitting

Removal

Note: *The rear hub and bearing are combined into a single assembly. The bearing is sealed for life and requires no lubrication or attention. If the bearing is worn or damaged, renew the entire hub and bearing assembly.*
1 Loosen the rear wheel nuts, raise the vehicle, place it securely on axle stands and remove the rear wheel (see *Jacking and vehicle support*).
2 Remove the brake drum or caliper and disc (see Chapter 9).
3 Remove the dust cover **(see illustration)**.
4 Unstake the hub retaining nut **(see illustration)**, unscrew the nut, then remove the thrustwasher and the hub assembly **(see illustration)**.

Refitting

5 Fit the new hub assembly and thrustwasher, tighten the new nut to the torque listed in this Chapter's Specifications, then stake its edge into the groove in the spindle **(see illustration)**.
6 Refit the dust cover by tapping lightly around the edge until it is seated.
7 The remainder of refitting is the reverse of removal.

13 Suspension arms (rear) – removal and refitting

1 Loosen the rear wheel nuts, raise the vehicle, place it securely on axle stands and remove the wheel (see *Jacking and vehicle support*).

Upper arm

2 Remove the upper arm-to-trailing arm bolt and nut **(see illustration)**.
3 Remove the mounting bolts from the upper arm inner bush and remove the upper arm.
4 Inspect the bushes for cracking or deterioration. If it's worn, have it pressed out,

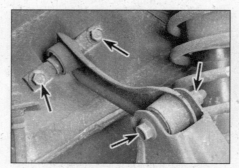

13.2 to remove the upper arm, remove the bolt and nut (right arrow) that attach it to the trailing arm, then remove the two bolts (left arrows) that attach the inner end to the body

and a new one installed, by a Honda dealer or automotive engineering workshop.
5 Refitting is the reverse of removal. Be sure to tighten all fasteners to the torque listed in this Chapter's Specifications. **Note:** *Before tightening the upper arm-to-trailing arm bolt, raise the rear of the trailing arm with a trolley jack to simulate normal ride height.*

Lower arm

6 Remove the lower arm-to-trailing arm bolt and the shock absorber-to-lower arm bolt (see Section 10).
7 Remove the inner pivot bolt and nut from the lower arm **(see illustration)**, then remove the lower arm.
8 Inspect the lower arm bushes for cracks and deterioration. If any of them are worn,

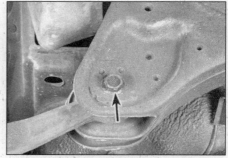

13.7 To disconnect the inner end of the lower arm from the chassis, remove the pivot bolt (arrowed)

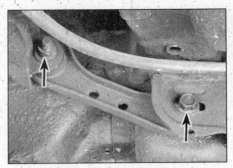

13.10 To remove the compensator arm, remove the bolt that attaches the arm to the body (right arrow), then remove the bolt that attaches the compensator arm to the trailing arm (left arrow)

13.18a Remove the left bush shaft bolt (arrowed) . . .

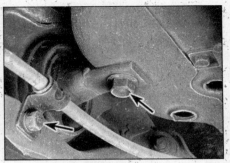

13.18b . . . and the right bolt (arrowed); detach the handbrake cable bracket by removing the bolt (arrowed)

have them pressed out, and new ones installed, by a Honda dealer or an automotive engineering workshop.

9 Refitting is the reverse of removal. Be sure to tighten all fasteners to the torque listed in this Chapter's Specifications. **Note:** *Before tightening the lower arm-to-trailing arm, lower arm inner pivot bolt and shock absorber-to-lower arm bolt, raise the rear of the trailing arm with a trolley jack to simulate normal ride height.*

Compensator arm

10 Remove the compensator arm-to-trailing arm bolt **(see illustration)**.
11 Remove the compensator arm-to-body nut and bolt and remove the compensator arm.

12 Inspect the compensator arm bushes for wear and deterioration. If either of them need to be renewed, have them pressed out, and new ones installed, by a Honda dealer or an automotive engineering workshop.
13 Refitting is the reverse of removal. **Note:** *Before tightening the compensator arm-to-body bolt or compensator arm-to-trailing arm bolt, raise the rear of the trailing arm with a trolley jack to simulate normal ride height.*

Trailing arm

14 Disconnect the brake hose from the wheel cylinder or rear caliper and plug the hose to prevent leakage or contamination. Remove the brake drum and brake shoes, or the rear caliper and disc. Disconnect the handbrake cable (see Chapter 9).

15 Remove the rear hub and bearing assembly (see Section 12).
16 Remove the brake backing plate.
17 Detach the upper, lower and compensator arms from the trailing arm.
18 Disconnect the handbrake cable bracket from the trailing arm, then remove the bolts from the trailing arm bush shaft **(see illustrations)** and remove the trailing arm.
19 Inspect the trailing arm bush for cracks and deterioration. If it needs to be renewed, have it pressed out, and a new one installed, by a Honda dealer or an automotive engineering workshop.
20 Refitting is the reverse of removal, noting the following points:
a) *Before tightening the fasteners to the torque values listed in this Chapter's Specifications, raise the rear of the trailing arm with a trolley jack to simulate normal ride height.*
b) *Bleed the brake hydraulic system (see Chapter 9).*

14.2a Remove the access plate from the underside of the steering wheel – on some models its secured by a screw

14.2b Unplug the yellow connector for the airbag module (arrowed)

14 Steering wheel –
 removal and refitting

Warning: Models covered by this manual are equipped with a Supplemental Restraint System (SRS), more commonly known as an airbag(s). Always disable the airbag system before working in the vicinity of the airbag unit(s), steering column or instrument panel to avoid the possibility of accidental deployment of the airbag, which could cause personal injury (see Chapter 12).

Removal

1 Disconnect the cable from the negative battery terminal, then disconnect the positive battery cable and wait at least three minutes before proceeding (see Chapter 5A).
2 Rotate the wheel 180° so the access plate is facing up. Remove the access plate and unplug the connector for the airbag module **(see illustrations)**. On 1995 5-door Hatchback models, remove the shorting connector from the access plate and plug it

14.2c On 1995 model year 5-door Hatchbacks, the shorting connector is stored on the inside of the access plate . . .

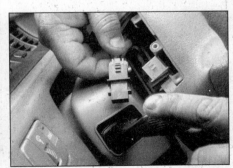

14.2d . . . plug the connector into the airbag module connector

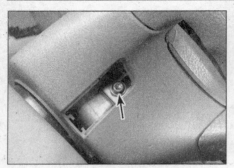

14.3a Remove the left Torx screw (arrowed) that attaches the airbag module to the steering wheel . . .

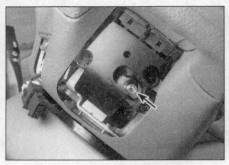

14.3b . . . then remove the right Torx screw (arrowed)

14.4 Remove the airbag module

into the airbag module connector **(see illustrations)**. **Note:** *On all other models the airbag automatically is shorted when the connector is unplugged.*

3 Turn the steering wheel back so it is centred again and the front wheels are straight, then pry off the small panel on each side of the steering wheel. Remove both Torx screws from the side of the steering wheel facing toward the dash **(see illustrations)**. These screws retain the airbag module.

4 Pull off the module **(see illustration)** and carefully set the module in a safe location with the trim side facing up.

> ⚠️ *Warning: When carrying the airbag module, make sure the trim side is facing away from you. When you set it down, place it in an isolated area with the trim side facing up. Also, don't set any objects on top of the airbag module.*

5 Unplug the electrical connectors for the horn and, if equipped, the cruise control system.

6 Remove the steering wheel retaining nut or bolt. Paint or scribe a mark indicating the relationship of the steering wheel hub to the steering column shaft **(see illustration)**.

7 Remove the wheel by pulling it straight off the shaft, using a side-to-side rocking motion. Don't attempt to remove the wheel by

hammering on the steering column shaft or steering wheel.

> ⚠️ *Warning: While the steering wheel is removed, DO NOT turn the steering column shaft. If you do so, the airbag cable reel could be damaged.*

Refitting

8 Make sure that the wheels are pointed straight-ahead.

9 Make absolutely sure that the cable reel is centred with the arrow on the cable reel pointing up **(see illustration)**. This shouldn't be a problem as long as you have not turned the steering column shaft while the wheel was removed. If for some reason the shaft was turned, centre the cable reel as follows:

a) *Rotate the cable reel clockwise until it stops.*

b) *Rotate the cable reel anti-clockwise about two turns until the yellow gear tooth lines up with the mark on the cover (some models) and the arrow on the cable reel points straight up.*

10 Be sure to align the index mark on the steering wheel hub with the mark on the column shaft when you slip the wheel onto the shaft. Also, make sure the pins on the cable reel engage the corresponding holes in the

steering wheel, and the projections on the direction indicator cancelling cam line up with the slots on the steering wheel hub. Fit the new mounting nut or bolt and tighten it to the torque listed in this Chapter's Specifications.

11 Plug in the horn connector and, if equipped, the cruise control connector.

12 Reattach the airbag module with NEW Torx bolts and tighten the bolts to the torque listed in this Chapter's Specifications. Refit the Torx bolt access panels.

13 If you're working on a 1995 5-door Hatchback model, unplug the shorting connector from the airbag connector.

14 Plug the airbag and cable reel connector halves together.

15 Secure the shorting connector (if equipped) to the access plate and refit the access plate.

---

15 Track rod ends – removal and refitting

Removal

1 Slacken the wheel nuts. Raise the front of the vehicle, support it securely on axle stands and remove the wheel (see *Jacking and vehicle support*).

14.6 After removing the steering wheel nut or bolt, mark the relationship of the wheel to the column shaft

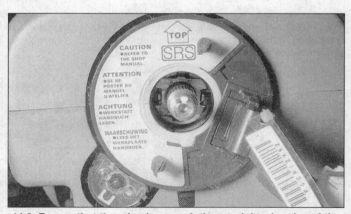

14.9 Ensure that the wheels are pointing straight-ahead, and the TOP mark points straight up on the cable reel for the airbag system; note that on some models the yellow gear tooth at 7 o'clock is aligned with the mark on the cover

15.2a Counterhold the track rod end with a second spanner

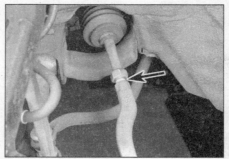

15.2b Make an alignment mark on the exposed threads, along the edge of the track rod end, so the new track rod end will be fitted in the exact same position

15.4 Use a balljoint splitter to separate the track rod end from the hub carrier arm

2 Hold the track rod end with a open-ended spanner and loosen the locknut enough to mark the position of the track rod end in relation to the threads **(see illustrations)**.
3 Remove the split pin and loosen the nut on the track rod end balljoint. Don't completely remove the nut.
4 Separate the track rod from the hub carrier arm with a balljoint splitter **(see illustration)**. Remove the nut and detach the track rod.
5 Unscrew the track rod end from the track rod.

Refitting

6 Thread the track rod end on to the marked position and insert the track rod balljoint stud into the hub carrier arm. Don't tighten the lock nut yet.
7 Refit the nut on the stud and tighten it to the torque listed in this Chapter's Specifications. Fit a new split pin. **Note:** If necessary, turn the nut a little more to align a slot in the nut with the hole in the stud. Don't loosen the nut to allow split pin insertion.
8 Tighten the lock nut securely.
9 Refit the wheel and nuts. Lower the vehicle and tighten the nuts to the torque listed in the Chapter 1 Specifications.
10 Have the wheel alignment checked by a dealer service department or specialist.

16 Steering rack gaiters – renewal

1 Remove the track rod end and locknut (see Section 15).
2 Remove the steering rack gaiter clamps and slide off the gaiter **(see illustration)**.
3 Before refitting the new gaiter, wrap the threads and serrations on the end of the track rod with a layer of tape so the small end of the new gaiter isn't damaged.
4 Slide the new gaiter into position on the steering rack until it seats in the groove in the steering rod and fit new clamps.
5 Remove the tape and refit the track rod end (see Section 15).
6 Refit the wheel and nuts. Lower the vehicle and tighten the nuts to the torque listed in the Chapter 1 Specifications.

17 Steering rack – removal and refitting

Removal

1 Park the vehicle with the front wheels pointing straight-ahead. Working under the dash, remove the steering column universal joint cover **(see illustration)**. Lock the steering wheel by removing the ignition key or loop the seat belt through the steering wheel to prevent the steering wheel from rotating.
Caution: Failure to do this could result in damage to the airbag system cable reel.
2 Mark the relationship of the intermediate shaft universal joint to the steering gear input shaft **(see illustration)**. Remove the upper and lower pinch-bolts from the intermediate shaft and slide the intermediate shaft up and off the steering gear input shaft.
3 Apply the handbrake. Loosen the front wheel nuts, raise the front of the vehicle and

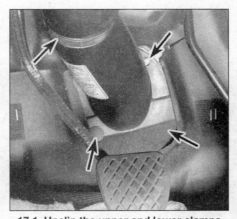

17.1 Unclip the upper and lower clamps (upper left arrow points to lower clamp; upper clamp not visible in this photo), remove the single plastic retaining clip (lower left arrow) and slide off the cover; when refitting, make sure the two holes (right arrows) in the flange at the lower end of the shield engage with the locating pins in the bulkhead

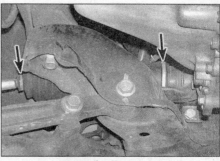

16.2 Cut the steering rack gaiter clamps (arrowed)

support it securely on axle stands (see *Jacking and vehicle support*). Remove the wheels.
4 Detach the gearchange and extension rods (manual transmission) or selector cable (automatic transmission) from the transmission (see Chapter 7A or 7B).
5 Remove the catalytic converter (see Chapter 4A).
6 Remove the track rod ends (see Section 15). Extend the steering rack all the way to the right-hand side.
7 On models with power steering, place a drain pan under the steering gear. Disconnect the power steering fluid pipes **(see**

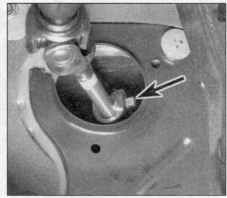

17.2 Mark the relationship of the intermediate shaft to the steering rack input pinion and remove the pinch-bolts (arrow indicates lower bolt)

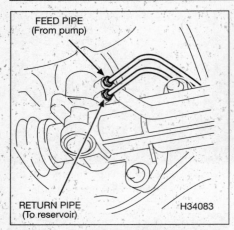

17.7 Disconnect the power steering fluid pipes

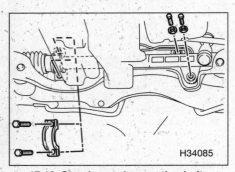

17.10 Steering rack mounting bolts (arrowed)

illustration) and cap them to prevent contamination and excessive loss of fluid.

8 On 3-door Hatchback, 2-door Coupe and 4-door Saloon models, remove the chassis stiffener bracket **(see illustration)**.

9 On 5-door Hatchback and Estate models, undo the bolts and remove the rear chassis brace, and detach the power steering return pipe bracket **(see illustration)**. Remove the

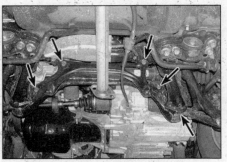

17.8 Remove the bolts (arrowed) and detach the chassis bracket

clamp bolts and lower the front anti-roll bar. There is no need to disconnect the anti-roll bar from the links at each end.

10 On all models, check that any power steering pipes are free from their retaining clips, then support the steering rack and remove the mounting bolts **(see illustration)**. Move the steering rack as far as possible to the right-hand side, then rotate the steering rack so that the pinion shaft is facing forward. Lower the left-hand end of the steering rack past the chassis and guide it out toward the left-hand side of the vehicle.

Refitting

11 Refitting is the reverse of removal, noting the following points:

a) *After mounting the steering rack, centre the rack within the housing.*

b) *When connecting the intermediate shaft to the steering gear pinion shaft, be sure to align the previously applied alignment marks.*

c) *Tighten all steering fasteners to the torque values listed in this Chapter's Specifications.*

d) *Fill the power steering pump reservoir with the recommended fluid (see 'Weekly checks'). Bleed the steering system (see Section 19).*

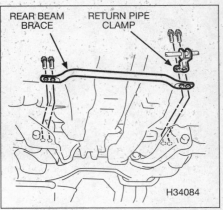

17.9 Remove the rear chassis brace and return pipe bracket

18 Power steering pump – removal and refitting

Removal

1 Disconnect the fluid hoses at the pump **(see illustrations)**. Note the difference between the pressure and the return hoses; the return hose is held to the pump with a spring type clamp, and the pressure pipe has two bolts holding it to the pump body. Cap or plug both hoses to prevent leakage or contamination. Fit a new O-ring on the end of the pressure pipe.

2 Remove the pump adjusting bolt.

3 Remove the pump mounting bolt(s) and remove the pump from the engine. Do not turn the steering wheel with the pump removed.

Refitting

4 Refitting is the reverse of removal. Be sure to adjust the drivebelt tension (see Chapter 1) and bleed the power steering system (see Section 19).

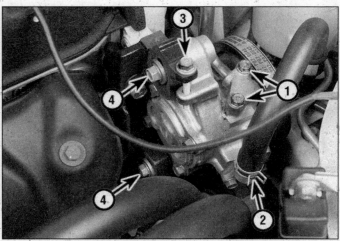

18.1a To remove the power steering pump on early models, disconnect the pressure pipe bolts (1) and the return pipe clamp (2), then remove the adjuster bolt (3) and the mounting bolts (4)

18.1b On later models, disconnect the pressure pipe bolts (1) and the return pipe clamp (2), then remove the adjuster bolt (3) and the mounting bolt (4)

19 Power steering system – bleeding

1 Following any operation in which the power steering fluid lines have been disconnected, the power steering system must be bled to remove all air and obtain proper steering performance.

2 With the front wheels in the straight-ahead position, check the power steering fluid level (see Chapter 1). If it's low, add fluid until it reaches the lower mark on the reservoir.

3 Start the engine and allow it to run at fast idle. Recheck the fluid level and add more if necessary to reach the Cold mark on the dipstick.

4 Bleed the system by turning the wheels from side-to-side, without hitting the stops. This will work the air out of the system. Keep the reservoir full of fluid as this is done.

5 When the air is worked out of the system, return the wheels to the straight-ahead position and leave the vehicle running for several more minutes before turning it off.

6 Road test the vehicle to be sure the steering system is functioning normally and noise free.

7 Recheck the fluid level (see *Weekly checks*).

20 Wheels and tyres – general information

All vehicles covered by this manual are equipped with steel belted radial tyres **(see illustration)**. Use of other size or type of tyres may affect the ride and handling of the vehicle. Don't mix different types of tyres, such as radials, cross ply and/or bias belted

on the same vehicle as handling may be seriously affected. It's recommended that tyres be renewed in pairs on the same axle, but if only one tyre is being renewed, be sure it's the same size, structure and tread design as the other.

Because tyre pressure has a substantial effect on handling and wear, the pressure on all tyres should be checked regularly or before any extended trips (see *Weekly checks*).

Wheels must be renewed if they are bent, dented, leak air, have elongated bolt holes, are heavily rusted, out of vertical symmetry or if the nuts won't stay tight. Wheel repairs that use welding or peening are not recommended.

Tyre and wheel balance is important to the overall handling, braking and performance of the vehicle. Unbalanced wheels can adversely affect handling and ride characteristics as well as tyre life. Whenever a tyre is fitted on a wheel, the tyre and wheel should be balanced by a specialist with the proper equipment.

21 Wheel alignment – general information

Wheel alignment refers to the adjustments made to the wheels so they are in proper angular relationship to the suspension and the earth. Wheels that are out of proper alignment not only affect steering control, but also increase tyre wear. Toe-in can be adjusted on the front and rear wheels. The front and rear camber and caster angles should be checked to determine if any of the suspension components are worn out or bent **(see illustration)**.

Getting the proper wheel alignment is a very exacting process, one in which

complicated and expensive machines are necessary to perform the job properly. Because of this, you should have a technician with the proper equipment perform these tasks. We will, however, use this space to give you a basic idea of what is involved with wheel alignment so you can better understand the process and deal intelligently with the workshop that does the work.

Toe-in is the turning in of the wheels. The purpose of a toe specification is to ensure parallel rolling of the wheels. In a vehicle with zero toe-in, the distance between the front edges of the wheels will be the same as the distance between the rear edges of the wheels. The actual amount of toe-in is normally only a fraction of an inch. At the front end, toe-in is controlled by the track rod end position on the track rod. At the rear it is adjusted by moving the compensator arm within its bracket on the body. Incorrect toe-in will cause the tyres to wear improperly by making them scrub against the road surface.

Camber is the tilting of the wheels from the vertical when viewed from the front or rear of the vehicle. When the wheels tilt out at the top, the camber is said to be positive (+). When the wheels tilt in at the top the camber is negative (–). The amount of tilt is measured in degrees from the vertical and this measurement is called the camber angle. This angle affects the amount of tyre tread which contacts the road and compensates for changes in the suspension geometry when the vehicle is cornering or travelling over an undulating surface. Camber isn't adjustable on these vehicles.

Caster is the tilting of the top of the steering axis from the vertical. A tilt toward the rear is positive caster and a tilt toward the front is negative caster. Caster isn't adjustable on these vehicles.

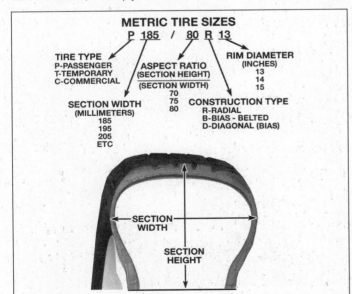

20.1 Tyre size code

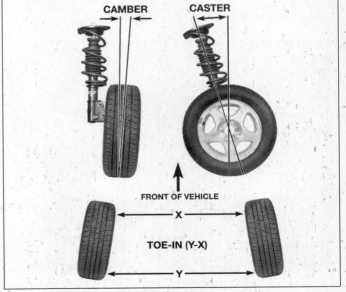

21.1 Wheel alignment details

Chapter 11
Bodywork and fittings

Contents

Degrees of difficulty

Easy, suitable for novice with little experience	**Fairly easy,** suitable for beginner with some experience	**Fairly difficult,** suitable for competent DIY mechanic	**Difficult,** suitable for experienced DIY mechanic	**Very difficult,** suitable for expert DIY or professional

Specifications

Torque wrench settings

	Nm	lbf ft
Seat belt buckle bolts	32	24
Seat belt reel bolt	32	24
Seat belt pretensioner	32	24

1 General information

These models feature a 'unibody' layout, using a floorpan with front and rear frame side rails which support the body components, front and rear suspension systems and other mechanical components.

Certain components are particularly vulnerable to accident damage and can be unbolted and repaired or replaced. Among these parts are the body mouldings, bumpers, front wings, the bonnet and boot lid (or tailgate) and all glass.

Only general body maintenance practices and body panel repair procedures within the scope of the home mechanic are included in this Chapter.

Caution: If the radio in your vehicle is equipped with an anti-theft system, make sure you have the correct activation code before disconnecting the battery.

2 Maintenance – bodywork and underframe

The general condition of a vehicle's bodywork is the one thing that significantly affects its value. Maintenance is easy, but needs to be regular. Neglect, particularly after minor damage, can lead quickly to further deterioration and costly repair bills. It is important also to keep watch on those parts of the vehicle not immediately visible, for instance the underside, inside all the wheelarches, and the lower part of the engine compartment.

The basic maintenance routine for the bodywork is washing – preferably with a lot of water, from a hose. This will remove all the loose solids which may have stuck to the vehicle. It is important to flush these off in such a way as to prevent grit from scratching the finish. The wheelarches and underframe need washing in the same way, to remove any accumulated mud, which will retain moisture and tend to encourage rust. Paradoxically enough, the best time to clean the underframe and wheelarches is in wet weather, when the mud is thoroughly wet and soft. In very wet weather, the underframe is usually cleaned of large accumulations automatically, and this is a good time for inspection.

Periodically, except on vehicles with a wax-based underbody protective coating, it is a good idea to have the whole of the underframe of the vehicle steam-cleaned, engine compartment included, so that a thorough inspection can be carried out to see what minor repairs and renovations are necessary. Steam-cleaning is available at many garages, and is necessary for the removal of the accumulation of oily grime, which sometimes is allowed to become thick in certain areas. If steam-cleaning facilities are not available, there are some excellent grease solvents available which can be brush-applied; the dirt can then be simply hosed off. Note that these methods should not be used on vehicles with wax-based underbody protective coating, or the coating will be removed. Such vehicles should be inspected annually, preferably just prior to Winter, when the underbody should be washed down, and any damage to the wax coating repaired. Ideally, a completely fresh coat should be applied. It would also be worth considering the use of such wax-based protection for injection into door panels, sills, box sections, etc, as an additional safeguard against rust damage, where such protection is not provided by the vehicle manufacturer.

After washing paintwork, wipe off with a chamois leather to give an unspotted clear finish. A coat of clear protective wax polish will give added protection against chemical pollutants in the air. If the paintwork sheen has dulled or oxidised, use a cleaner/polisher combination to restore the brilliance of the shine. This requires a little effort, but such dulling is usually caused because regular washing has been neglected. Care needs to be taken with metallic paintwork, as special non-abrasive cleaner/polisher is required to avoid damage to the finish. Always check that the door and ventilator opening drain holes and pipes are completely clear, so that water can be drained out. Windscreens and windows can be kept clear of the smeary film which often appears, by the use of proprietary glass cleaner. Never use any form of wax or other body polish on glass.

3 Maintenance – upholstery and carpets

Mats and carpets should be brushed or vacuum-cleaned regularly, to keep them free of grit. If they are badly stained, remove them from the vehicle for scrubbing or sponging, and make quite sure they are dry before refitting. Seats and interior trim panels can be kept clean by wiping with a damp cloth. If they do become stained (which can be more apparent on light-coloured upholstery), use a little liquid detergent and a soft nail brush to scour the grime out of the grain of the material. Do not forget to keep the headlining clean in the same way as the upholstery.

When using liquid cleaners inside the vehicle, do not over-wet the surfaces being cleaned. Excessive damp could get into the seams and padded interior, causing stains, offensive odours or even rot.

> **HAYNES HINT** *If the inside of the vehicle gets wet accidentally, it is worthwhile taking some trouble to dry it out properly, particularly where carpets are involved. Do not leave oil or electric heaters inside the vehicle for this purpose.*

4 Minor body damage – repair

Repair of minor scratches in the vehicle's bodywork

If the scratch is very superficial, and does not penetrate to the metal of the bodywork, repair is very simple. Lightly rub the area of the scratch with a paintwork renovator, or a very fine cutting paste, to remove loose paint from the scratch and to clear the surrounding bodywork of wax polish. Rinse the area with clean water.

In the case of metallic paint, the most commonly-found 'scratches' are not in the paint, but in the lacquer top coat, and appear white. If care is taken , these can sometimes be rendered less obvious by very careful use of paintwork renovator (which would otherwise not be used on metallic paintwork); otherwise, repair of these scratches can be achieved by applying lacquer with a fine brush.

Apply touch-up paint to the scratch using a thin paintbrush; continue to apply thin layers of paint until the surface of the paint in the scratch is level with the surrounding paintwork. Allow the new paint at least two weeks to harden, then blend it into the surrounding paintwork by rubbing the paintwork in the scratch area with a paintwork renovator or a very fine cutting paste. Finally, apply wax polish.

Where the scratch has penetrated right through to the metal of the bodywork, causing the metal to rust, a different repair technique is required. Remove any loose rust from the bottom of the scratch with a penknife, then apply rust-inhibiting paint, to prevent the formation of rust in the future. Using a rubber or nylon applicator fill the scratch with bodystopper paste. If required, this paste can be mixed with cellulose thinners, to provide a very thin paste which is ideal for filling narrow scratches. Before the stopper-paste in the scratch hardens, wrap a piece of smooth cotton rag around the top of a finger. Dip the finger in cellulose thinners, and then quickly sweep it across the surface of the stopper-paste in the scratch; this will ensure that the surface of the stopper-paste is slightly

hollowed. The scratch can now be painted over as described earlier in this Section.

Repair of dents in bodywork

When deep denting of the vehicle's bodywork has taken place, the first task is to pull the dent out, until the affected bodywork almost attains its original shape. There is little point in trying to restore the original shape completely, as the metal in the damaged area will have stretched on impact, and cannot be reshaped fully to its original contour. It is better to bring the level of the dent up to a point which is about 3 mm below the level of the surrounding bodywork. In cases where the dent is very shallow anyway, it is not worth trying to pull it out at all. If the underside of the dent is accessible, it can be hammered out gently from behind, using a mallet with a wooden or plastic head. Whilst doing this, hold a suitable block of wood firmly against the outside of the panel to absorb the impact from the hammer blows and thus prevent a large area of the bodywork from being 'belled-out'.

Should the dent be in a section of the bodywork which has a double skin or some other factor making it inaccessible from behind, a different technique is called for. Drill several small holes through the metal inside the area – particularly in the deeper section. Then screw long self-tapping screws into the holes just sufficiently for them to gain a good purchase in the metal. Now the dent can be pulled out by pulling on the protruding heads of the screws with a pair of pliers.

The next stage of the repair is the removal of the paint from the damaged area, and from an inch or so of the surrounding 'sound' bodywork. This is accomplished most easily by using a wire brush or abrasive pad on a power drill, although it can be done just as effectively by hand using sheets of abrasive paper. To complete the preparation for filling, score the surface of the bare metal with a screwdriver or the tang of a file, or alternatively, drill small holes in the affected area. This will provide a really good 'key' for the filler paste.

To complete the repair, see the Section on filling and re-spraying.

Repair of rust holes or gashes in bodywork

Remove all paint from the affected area, and from an inch or so of the surrounding 'sound' bodywork, using an abrasive pad or a wire brush on a power drill. If these are not available, a few sheets of abrasive paper will do the job just as effectively. With the paint removed, you will be able to gauge the severity of the corrosion, and therefore decide whether to renew the whole panel (if this is possible) or to repair the affected area. New body panels are not as expensive as most people think, and it is often quicker and more satisfactory to fit a new panel than to attempt to repair large areas of corrosion.

Remove all fittings from the affected area, except those which will act as a guide to the original shape of the damaged bodywork. Then, using tin snips or a hacksaw blade, remove all loose metal and any other metal badly affected by corrosion. Hammer the edges of the hole inwards in order to create a slight depression for the filler paste.

Wire-brush the affected area to remove the powdery rust from the surface of the remaining metal. Paint the affected area with rust-inhibiting paint; if the back of the rusted area is accessible treat this also.

Before filling can take place, it will be necessary to block the hole in some way. This can be achieved by the use of aluminium or plastic mesh, or aluminium tape.

Aluminium or plastic mesh or glass fibre matting is probably the best material to use for a large hole. Cut a piece to the approximate size and shape of the hole to be filled, then position it in the hole so that its edges are below the level of the surrounding bodywork. It can be retained in position by several blobs of filler paste around its periphery.

Aluminium tape should be used for small or very narrow holes. Pull a piece off the roll and trim it to the approximate size and shape required, then pull off the backing paper (if used) and stick the tape over the hole; it can be overlapped if the thickness of one piece is insufficient. Burnish down the edges of the tape with the handle of a screwdriver or similar, to ensure that the tape is securely attached to the metal underneath.

Before using this Section, see the Sections on dent, deep scratch, rust holes and gash repairs.

Many types of bodyfiller are available, but generally speaking those proprietary kits which contain a tin of filler paste and a tube of resin hardener are best for this type of repair; some can be used directly from the tube. A wide, flexible plastic or nylon applicator will be found invaluable for imparting a smooth and well contoured finish to the surface of the filler.

Mix up a little filler on a clean piece of card or board – measure the hardener carefully (follow the maker's instructions on the pack) otherwise the filler will set too rapidly or too slowly. Using the applicator, apply the filler paste to the prepared area; draw the applicator across the surface of the filler to achieve the correct contour and to level the filler surface. As soon as a contour that approximates to the correct one is achieved, stop working the paste – if you carry on too long the paste will become sticky and begin to 'pick up' on the applicator. Continue to add thin layers of filler paste at twenty-minute intervals until the level of the filler is just proud of the surrounding bodywork.

Once the filler has hardened, excess can be removed using a metal plane or file. From then on, progressively finer grades of abrasive paper should be used, starting with a 40-grade production paper and finishing with 400-grade wet-and-dry paper. Always wrap the abrasive paper around a flat rubber, cork, or wooden block – otherwise the surface of the filler will not be completely flat. During the smoothing of the filler surface the wet-and-dry paper should be periodically rinsed in water. This will ensure that a very smooth finish is imparted to the filler at the final stage.

At this stage the 'dent' should be surrounded by a ring of bare metal, which in turn should be encircled by the finely 'feathered' edge of the good paintwork. Rinse the repair area with clean water, until all of the dust produced by the rubbing-down operation has gone.

Spray the whole repair area with a light coat of primer – this will show up any imperfections in the surface of the filler. Repair these imperfections with fresh filler paste or bodystopper, and once more smooth the surface with abrasive paper. If bodystopper is used, it can be mixed with cellulose thinners to form a really thin paste which is ideal for filling small holes. Repeat this spray and repair procedure until you are satisfied that the surface of the filler, and the feathered edge of the paintwork are perfect. Clean the repair area with clean water and allow to dry fully.

The repair area is now ready for final spraying. Paint spraying must be carried out in a warm, dry, windless and dust free atmosphere. This condition can be created artificially if you have access to a large indoor working area, but if you are forced to work in the open, you will have to pick your day very carefully. If you are working indoors, dousing the floor in the work area with water will help to settle the dust which would otherwise be in the atmosphere. If the repair area is confined to one body panel, mask off the surrounding panels; this will help to minimise the effects of a slight mis-match in paint colours. Bodywork fittings (e.g. chrome strips, door handles etc) will also need to be masked off. Use genuine masking tape and several thicknesses of newspaper for the masking operations.

Before commencing to spray, agitate the aerosol can thoroughly, then spray a test area (an old tin, or similar) until the technique is mastered. Cover the repair area with a thick coat of primer; the thickness should be built up using several thin layers of paint rather than one thick one. Using 400 grade wet-and-dry paper, rub down the surface of the primer until it is really smooth. While doing this, the work area should be thoroughly doused with water, and the wet-and-dry paper periodically rinsed in water. Allow to dry before spraying on more paint.

Spray on the top coat, again building up the thickness by using several thin layers of paint. Start spraying in the centre of the repair area and then, with a single side-to-side motion, work outwards until the whole repair area and about 50 mm of the surrounding original paintwork is covered. Remove all masking material 10 to 15 minutes after spraying on the final coat of paint.

Allow the new paint at least two weeks to harden, then, using a paintwork renovator or a very fine cutting paste, blend the edges of the paint into the existing paintwork. Finally, apply wax polish.

Plastic components

With the use of more and more plastic body components by the vehicle manufacturers (e.g. bumpers, spoilers, and in some cases major body panels), rectification of more serious damage to such items has become a matter of either entrusting repair work to a specialist in this field, or renewing complete components. Repair of such damage by the DIY owner is not really feasible owing to the cost of the equipment and materials required for effecting such repairs. The basic technique involves making a groove along the line of the crack in the plastic using a rotary burr in a power drill. The damaged part is then welded back together by using a hot-air gun to heat up and fuse a plastic filler rod into the groove. Any excess plastic is then removed and the area rubbed down to a smooth finish. It is important that a filler rod of the correct plastic is used, as body components can be made of a variety of different types (e.g. polycarbonate, ABS, polypropylene).

Damage of a less serious nature (abrasions, minor cracks etc) can be repaired by the DIY owner using a two-part epoxy filler repair material. Once mixed in equal proportions, this is used in similar fashion to the bodywork filler used on metal panels. The filler is usually cured in twenty to thirty minutes, ready for sanding and painting.

If the owner is renewing a complete component himself, or if he has repaired it with epoxy filler, he will be left with the problem of finding a suitable paint for finishing which is compatible with the type of plastic used. At one time the use of a universal paint was not possible owing to the complex range of plastics encountered in body component applications. Standard paints, generally speaking, will not bond to plastic or rubber satisfactorily. However, it is now possible to obtain a plastic body parts finishing kit which consists of a pre-primer treatment, a primer and coloured top coat. Full instructions are normally supplied with a kit, but basically the method of use is to first apply the pre-primer to the component concerned and allow it to dry for up to 30 minutes. Then the primer is applied and left to dry for about an hour before finally applying the special coloured top coat. The result is a correctly-coloured component where the paint will flex with the plastic or rubber, a property that standard paint does not normally possess.

5 Major body damage – repair

Where serious damage has occurred, or large areas need renewal due to neglect, it means that complete new panels will need welding in, and this is best left to professionals. If the damage is due to impact, it will also be necessary to check completely the alignment of the bodyshell, and this can

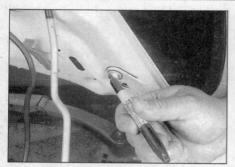

8.2 Scribe or draw alignment marks around the bonnet hinge bolt heads

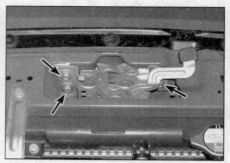

8.10 Scribe a line around the bonnet latch so you can judge the movement, then slacken the bolts (arrowed) and adjust the latch position

8.11 Turn each edge cushion to adjust the vertical height of the bonnet's leading edge

only be carried out accurately by a Honda dealer using special jigs. If the body is left misaligned, it is primarily dangerous, as the car will not handle properly. Secondly, uneven stresses will be imposed on the steering, suspension and possibly transmission, causing abnormal wear, or complete failure, particularly to such items as the tyres.

6 Hinges and locks – maintenance

The hinges and latch assemblies on the doors, bonnet and boot (or tailgate) should be given a few drops of light oil or lock lubricant at regular intervals (see Chapter 1). The door latch strikers should also be lubricated with a thin coat of grease to reduce wear and ensure free movement. Lubricate the door and boot (or tailgate) locks with spray-on graphite lubricant.

7 Windscreen and fixed glass – renewal

Renewal of the windscreen and fixed glass requires the use of special fast-setting adhesive materials and some specialised tools and techniques. These operations should be left to a windscreen renewal specialist.

8 Bonnet – removal, refitting and adjustment

Note: *The bonnet is heavy and somewhat awkward to remove and fit – at least two people should perform this procedure.*

Removal

1 Use blankets or pads to cover the wings and scuttle areas. This will protect the body and paint as the bonnet is lifted off.
2 Scribe or draw alignment marks around the

bolt heads to ensure proper alignment during refitting **(see illustration)**.
3 Disconnect any cables or wiring harnesses, which will interfere with removal.
4 Have an assistant support the weight of the bonnet. Remove the hinge-to-bonnet bolts and any shims, if already installed. If there are any shims, make sure you keep the shims for each side with their respective bolts. Don't mix them up.
5 Lift off the bonnet.

Refitting

6 Refitting is the reverse of removal. If you fit the bonnet so that the hinges fit within the alignment marks you made before loosening the bolts and if you fit the shims, if any, in the same number and location they were in prior to removal, then the bonnet should still be aligned. Of course, if you're fitting a new bonnet, or forgot to mark the hinge positions, or mixed up the shims, etc, then you'll need to readjust the bonnet position.

Adjustment

7 You can adjust the bonnet fore-and-aft and right-and-left by means of the elongated holes in the hinges.
8 Scribe a line around the entire hinge plate so you can judge the amount of movement.
9 Loosen the bolts and move the bonnet into correct alignment. Move it only a little at a time. Tighten the hinge bolts or nuts and carefully lower the bonnet to check the alignment.

9.2 Detach the cable and unhook the end from the catch

10 If necessary after fitting, the entire bonnet latch assembly can be adjusted up-and-down as well as from side-to-side on the upper radiator support so the bonnet closes securely and is flush with the wings **(see illustration)**. To do this, scribe a line around the bonnet latch mounting bolts to provide a reference point. Then loosen the bolts and reposition the latch assembly as necessary. Following adjustment, retighten the mounting bolts.
11 Adjust the vertical height of the leading edge of the bonnet by screwing the edge cushions in or out so that the bonnet, when closed, is flush with the wings **(see illustration)**. Finally, adjust the rear edge of the bonnet until it's flush with the wings by using shims (available at a Honda dealer parts department) between the bonnet and the hinge plates.
12 The bonnet latch assembly, as well as the hinges, should be periodically lubricated with white lithium-base grease to prevent sticking and wear.

9 Bonnet release catch and cable – removal and refitting

Catch

1 Remove the radiator grille opening cover (if equipped), then scribe a line around the catch to aid alignment when refitting, detach the catch retaining bolts from the radiator support **(see illustration 8.10)** and remove the catch.
2 Disconnect the bonnet release cable by disengaging the cable from the catch assembly **(see illustration)**.
3 Refitting is reverse of the removal. **Note:** *Adjust the catch so the bonnet engages securely when closed and the bonnet bumpers are slightly compressed.*

Cable

4 Disconnect the bonnet release cable from the catch assembly **(see illustration 9.2)**.
5 Working in the passenger's compartment, remove the driver's side kick panel from the

9.5 Remove the release lever bolts (arrowed) and detach the cable

10.2a Bumper cover lower retaining bolts

10.2b Some models have screws securing the lower corners of the bumper cover

footwell. Then remove the two release lever mounting bolts and detach the bonnet release lever **(see illustration)**. Detach the cable from the lever.

6 Attach a piece of stiff wire to the release lever end of the cable, then detach all the cable retaining clips.

7 Push the grommet through the bulkhead and pull the cable into the engine compartment. Ensure that the new cable has a grommet attached, then remove the old cable from the wire and renew it with the new cable.

8 Pull the wire back through the bulkhead.

9 Refitting is the reverse of the removal. **Note:** *Push on the grommet to seat it in the bulkhead completely.*

10 Bumper covers and bumper – removal and refitting

Front

1 Apply the handbrake, raise the vehicle and support it securely on axle stands (see *Jacking and vehicle support*).

2 Working under the vehicle, detach the bolts or screws securing the lower edges of the bumper cover **(see illustrations)**.

3 Working in the front wheelarch, detach the plastic retaining screws securing the bumper

cover to inner wheelarch splash shields **(see illustration)**.

4 Remove the screws (or the plastic retaining rivets on some models) securing the upper portion of the bumper cover **(see illustrations)** and pull the bumper cover assembly out and away from the vehicle. **Note:** *To remove plastic retaining rivets, pull the centre portion out, then pry the entire rivet out.*

5 Disconnect any electrical connections which would interfere with removal. If necessary, remove the bumper beam gussets from each side of the bumper, then remove the four bolts and detach the bumper from the vehicle.

6 Refitting is the reverse of removal.

Rear

7 Apply the handbrake, raise the vehicle and support it securely on axle stands (see *Jacking and vehicle support*).

8 Working under the vehicle, detach the plastic clips and screws securing the lower edge of the bumper cover **(see illustration)**.

9 Remove the screws securing the bumper cover in the rear wheelarches **(see illustration)**.

10 Open the boot or tailgate and remove the screws and clips securing the upper edge of

10.3 The ends of the bumper cover are retained by screws (arrowed)

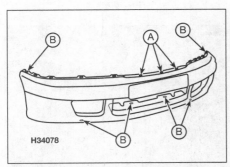

10.4b Bumper cover fasteners (later 5-door Hatchback and Estates)
A Plastic clips   B Screws

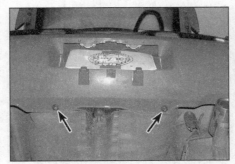

10.8 Remove the plastic clips (arrowed) and screws from the lower half of the rear bumper cover

10.9 The forward ends for the bumper cover are retained by bolts (arrowed) in the wheelarch

10.4a Bumper cover retaining screws (except later 5-door Hatchback and Estates)

the bumper cover **(see illustration)**. Pull the bumper cover assembly out and away from the vehicle. **Note:** *Estate model rear bumper covers are also retained by two bolts at the top of the cover, either side of the tailgate aperture **(see illustration)**.*

11 To remove the bumper beam, drill out the rivets securing the foam isolator (if necessary), then remove the bumper retaining bolts and pull the bumper assembly out and away from the vehicle.

12 Refitting is the reverse of removal.

11 Tailgate catch, lock cylinder and support struts – removal and refitting

1 Open the tailgate.

Catch

3-door Hatchback

2 Remove the trim cover and catch mounting screws **(see illustrations)**.
3 Disconnect the actuating rod, detach any electrical connectors, then remove the catch from the tailgate.
4 Refitting is the reverse of removal.

Estate and 5-door Hatchback

5 Carefully pull the upper trim and side trims from each side of the tailgate **(see illustration)**.
6 Undo the single screw from the lower edge of the tailgate and remove the handle recess from the trim **(see illustration)**.

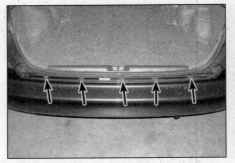

10.10a Remove the screws or clips along the upper edge of the rear bumper cover (arrowed)

7 Release the various retaining clips and remove the tailgate trim panel. Some clips simply pull to release them, whilst those along the lower edge of the panel are released by pulling out/unscrewing the centre portion, then prising out the entire clip.
8 Remove the three retaining bolts/screws, disconnect the actuating rod, unplug any electrical connectors, and remove the catch from the tailgate.
9 Refitting is the reverse of removal.

Lock cylinder

3-door Hatchback

10 Remove the tailgate trim cover.
11 Remove the bolt securing the lock cylinder **(see illustration)**.
12 Detach the actuating rod, rotate the lock cylinder and pull it out to remove it.

10.10b On Estate models, the bumper cover is also retained by one bolt (arrowed) either side of the tailgate aperture

13 Refitting is the reverse of removal.

Estate and 5-door Hatchback

14 Remove the tailgate upper, side trims and trim panel as described in Paragraphs 5 to 7 of this Section.
15 Detach the actuating rod and any electrical connections from the lock cylinder.
16 Undo the single retaining bolt, and manoeuvre the cylinder from the tailgate.
17 Refitting is the reverse of removal.

Support struts

18 Open the tailgate and support it securely.

3-door Hatchback

19 Using an open-end spanner, remove the balljoint nut securing the upper end of the strut **(see illustration)**.

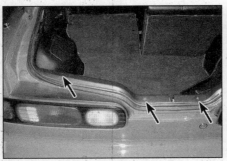

11.2a Remove the plastic rivets (arrowed) and detach the trim panel . . .

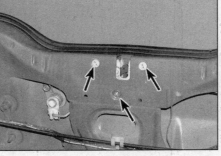

11.2b . . . then remove the catch screws (arrowed)

11.5 Pull the side trims from each side of the tailgate

11.6 Undo the screw and remove the handle recess

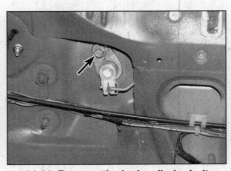

11.11 Remove the lock cylinder bolt (arrowed)

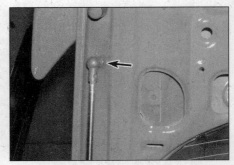

11.19 Undo the balljoint nut (arrowed)

11.20 Detach the lower strut cover and remove the retaining clip

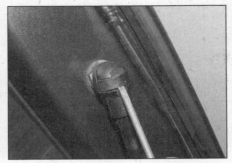

11.22 Prise out the strut retaining clips

12.2 Remove the upper trim moulding

20 Detach the trim cover and pry the retaining clip off the locating pin at the lower end. Pull the lower end of the strut off the locating pin and remove it from the vehicle (**see illustration**). Note: *Some models have retaining bolts securing the upper and lower ends of the strut to the tailgate. On these models, simply remove the bolts to detach the strut from the vehicle.*
21 Refitting is the reverse of removal.

Estate and 5-door Hatchback

22 Prise out the retaining clips, and detach the strut from the mounting stud (**see illustration**).
23 Refitting is the reverse of removal.

12 Tailgate – removal, refitting and adjustment

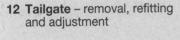

Note: *The tailgate is heavy and somewhat awkward to hold – at least two people should perform this procedure.*

Removal and refitting

1 Open the tailgate and support it securely.

3-door Hatchback

2 Remove the upper trim moulding from the tailgate opening (**see illustration**) and disconnect all wiring harness connectors leading to the tailgate.

Estate and 5-door Hatchback

3 Remove the tailgate upper trim, side trims and trim panel as described in Section 11.
4 Disconnect the wiring harness from the various electrical components, labelling each connector to aid refitting. Note its routing, then release the harness from any retaining clips.
5 Prise out the grommet at the top of the tailgate, and pull the harness out of the hole, and out of the tailgate.

All models

6 While an assistant supports the tailgate, detach both ends of the support struts as described in the previous Section.
7 Detach the hinge-to-tailgate nuts (**see illustration**) and remove the tailgate from the vehicle.
8 Refitting is the reverse of removal.

Adjustment

9 Adjustments are made by loosening the hinge-to-tailgate bolts and moving the tailgate. Proper alignment is achieved when the edges of the tailgate are parallel with the rear quarter panels and the roof panel.
10 Adjust the latch striker assembly as necessary to provide positive engagement with the latch mechanism (**see illustration**).

11 Finally, adjust the height of the tailgate in relation to the body by screwing the rubber bumpers in-or-out (**see illustration**).

13 Boot lid catch, lock cylinder and support struts – removal and refitting

Boot lid catch

1 Open the boot and scribe a line around the boot lid catch assembly for a reference point to aid the refitting procedure.
2 Remove the bolt and nut retaining the boot lid catch (**see illustration**).

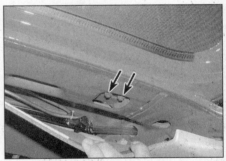

12.7 Remove the tailgate retaining nuts (arrowed)

12.10 To adjust the tailgate striker, slacken the screws (arrowed) and move the striker as necessary

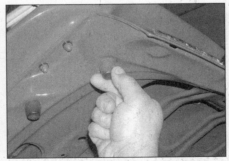

12.11 Rotate the rubber bumpers to make the final adjustments to the tailgate

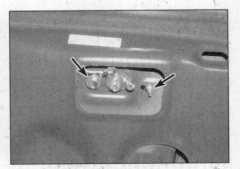

13.2 Boot lid catch retaining screw and bolt (arrowed)

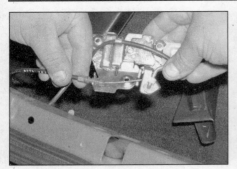

13.3 Detach the cable and unhook the end from the catch

14.3 Make alignment marks (arrowed) around the hinge

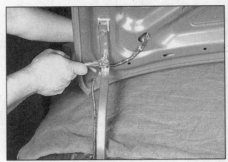

14.4 Remove the four boot lid retaining bolts

3 Remove the catch and disconnect the cable, lock cylinder rod and electrical connections **(see illustration)**.
4 Refitting is the reverse of removal.

Boot lock cylinder

5 Open the boot. Look upward through the boot lid access hole and detach the rod from the lock cylinder.
6 Remove the bolt and turn the cylinder clockwise to align the tab on the lock cylinder with the slot in the body, then remove it from the boot lid.
7 Refitting is the reverse of removal.

Boot lid support struts

8 Open the boot and support it securely.
9 Remove the two bolts and detach the upper end of the support strut.
10 Use a small screwdriver to detach the cover and remove the retaining bolt at the lower end, then remove the strut.
11 Refitting is the reverse of removal.

14 Boot lid – removal, refitting and adjustment

Note: *The boot lid is heavy and somewhat awkward to remove and fit – at least two people should perform this procedure.*

15.1 Remove the screws (arrowed) and detach the release assembly

Removal and refitting

1 Open the boot lid and cover the edges of the boot compartment with pads or cloths to protect the painted surfaces when the lid is removed.
2 Disconnect any cables or wire harness connectors attached to the boot lid that would interfere with removal.
3 Make alignment marks around the hinge **(see illustration)**.
4 While an assistant supports the boot lid, remove the lid-to-hinge bolts on both sides and lift it off **(see illustration)**.
5 Refitting is the reverse of removal. **Note:** *When refitting the boot lid, align the lid-to-hinge bolts with the marks made during removal.*

Adjustment

6 Fore-and-aft and side-to-side adjustment of the boot lid is accomplished by moving the lid in relation to the hinge after loosening the bolts or nuts.
7 Scribe a line around the hinge plate as described earlier in this Section so you can determine the amount of movement.
8 Loosen the bolts or nuts and move the boot lid into correct alignment. Move it only a little at a time. Tighten the hinge bolts or nuts and carefully lower the boot lid to check the alignment.
9 If necessary after refitting, the entire boot lid striker assembly can be adjusted up and down as well as from side-to-side on the boot

15.4 Working in the luggage compartment/boot, rotate the fuel filler flap release cable 90° so that the tabs line up with the slots in the body, then withdraw it

lid so the lid closes securely and is flush with the rear quarter panels. To do this, scribe a line around the boot lid striker assembly to provide a reference point. Then loosen the bolts and reposition the striker as necessary. Following adjustment, retighten the mounting bolts.
10 The boot lid catch assembly, as well as the hinges, should be periodically lubricated with white lithium-base grease to prevent sticking and wear.
11 Finally, adjust the height of the boot lid in relation to the body by screwing the rubber bumpers in-or-out.

15 Boot lid/tailgate and fuel filler flap release cables – removal and refitting

Release lever

1 Working in the driver's side, remove the screw and detach the trim panel for access the release cable and lever retaining bolts. Then remove the lever retaining bolts **(see illustration)**. Detach the cable(s) from the release assembly.
2 Refitting is the reverse of removal.

Cables

3 Working in the boot or luggage compartment, remove plastic clips securing the driver's side and rear luggage compartment/boot trim panels to allow access to the fuel door assembly.
4 Twist the cable 90° to align the tabs on the striker assembly with the slots in the body and withdraw it into the rear compartment **(see illustration)**. Detach the boot/tailgate release cable from the boot lid/tailgate catch.
5 Remove the right-hand front and rear door (where applicable) sill plate, B-pillar lower trim, the rear seat and the left rear quarter panel trim. Pull the carpet back and detach all the cable retaining clips.
6 Working in the boot/luggage compartment, pull the cable assembly towards the rear of the vehicle.
7 Refitting is the reverse of removal.

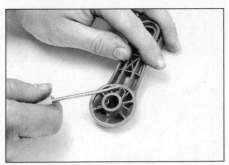

16.1 Remove the window winder handle by pulling this clip off with a wire hook (handle removed for clarity)

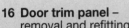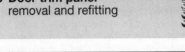

16 Door trim panel –
removal and refitting

HAYNES HiNT *It is a good idea to obtain a few trim panel retaining clips before starting, as they are often broken in the course of removal, or will be found to have broken during previous removal attempts.*

1 On manual window models, remove the window handle **(see illustration)**.
2 Remove the inner door handle retaining screw, Pull the handle outward and disconnect the handle actuating rods and the door lock switch electrical connector **(see illustration 18.11b)**. Remove the handle from the door

Saloon

3 Prise away the front door speaker cover (where applicable), undo the speaker retaining screws and disconnect the wiring plug as the speaker is withdrawn.
4 Release the retaining tab at the front edge of the door inner grip handle outer cover, and pull the outer half of the grip away **(see illustration)**.
5 Undo the screw at the rear of the grip and at the front **(see illustrations)**.

Coupe and 3-door Hatchback

6 Undo the retaining screw in the base of the armrest pocket.

16.4 Release the retaining tab and pull the outer half of the door grip handle away

7 Prise off the speaker cover (where fitted), and remove the three speaker retaining screws.

Estate and 5-door Hatchback

8 Undo the two screws securing the inner pull handle, and the screw adjacent to the top door hinge **(see illustrations)**.

All models

9 Carefully release the door trim retaining clips with a trim pad remover or a putty knife between the trim panel and the door. Work slowly and carefully around the outer edge of the trim panel until it's free **(see illustration)**.
10 After all of the clips are disengaged, pull the trim panel up, unplug any wire harness connectors and remove the panel.
11 For access to the door inner panel, carefully pry out the retainers and detach the plastic shield/water deflector.
12 Prior to refitting the door trim panel, be sure to refit any clips in the panel which may have come out when you removed the panel.
13 Plug in the wire harness connectors for the door locking switch and the electric window switch, if equipped, and place the panel in position in the door. Press the door panel into place until the clips are seated. The remainder of refitting is the reverse of removal.

16.5a Undo the screw at the rear of the grip handle . . .

17 Door – removal, refitting and adjustment

Note: *The door is heavy and somewhat awkward to remove and fit – at least two people should perform this procedure.*

Removal and refitting

1 Lower the window completely in the door, then disconnect the negative cable from the battery (see Chapter 5A).
2 Open the door all the way and support it on jacks or blocks covered with rags to prevent damaging the paint.
3 Remove the door trim panel and water deflector as described in Section 16.
4 Disconnect all electrical connections, earth wires and harness retaining clips from the

16.5b . . . and at the front

16.8b . . . and the screw adjacent to the door hinge (5-door models)

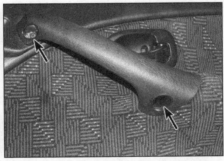

16.8a Undo the two screws (arrowed) securing the inner pull handle . . .

16.9 Carefully prise the clips free so the door trim panel can be removed

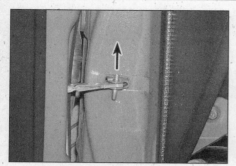

17.6 On some models it will be necessary to use a small hammer to tap out the retaining pin (tap it upwards only) – on other models it will be necessary to remove the door strut retaining bolt

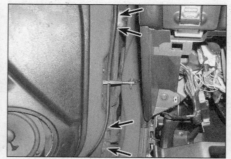

17.8 Remove the door hinge bolts (arrowed)

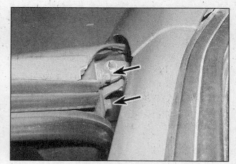

17.11 Slacken the hinge-to-body bolts (arrowed) to adjust the doors

door. **Note:** *It is a good idea to label all connections to aid the reassembly process.*

5 From the door side, detach the rubber conduit between the body and the door. Then pull the wiring harness through conduit hole and remove from the door.

6 Remove the door stop strut **(see illustration)**.

7 Mark around the door hinges with a pen or a scribe to facilitate realignment during reassembly.

8 With an assistant holding the door, remove the hinge-to-door bolts **(see illustration)** and lift the door off.

9 Refitting is the reverse of removal.

Adjustment

10 Having proper door-to-body alignment is a critical part of a well-functioning door assembly. First check the door hinge pins for excessive play. Fully open the door and lift up on the door without lifting the body. If a door has 2 mm or more excessive play, the hinges should be renewed.

11 Door-to-body alignment adjustments are made by loosening the hinge-to-body bolts **(see illustration)** or hinge-to-door bolts and moving the door. Proper body alignment is achieved when the top of the doors are parallel with the roof section, the front door is flush with the wing, the rear door is flush with

the rear quarter panel and the bottom of the doors are aligned with the lower sill panel. If these goals can't be reached by adjusting the hinge-to-body or hinge-to-door bolts, body alignment shims may have to be purchased and inserted behind the hinges to achieve correct alignment.

12 To adjust the door closed position, scribe a line or mark around the striker plate to provide a reference point, then check that the door catch is contacting the centre of the catch striker. If not adjust the up-and-down position first.

13 Finally adjust the catch striker sideways position, so that the door panel is flush with the B-pillar or rear quarter panel and provides positive engagement with the catch mechanism **(see illustration)**.

18 Door catch, lock cylinder and handles – removal and refitting

Door catch

1 Raise the window then remove the door trim panel and water deflector panel as described in Section 16.

2 Remove the bolt securing the base of the rear window guide channel to the door **(see illustration 19.4)**.

3 Disconnect the inner handle operating rod

from the catch, then remove the outside handle as described in this Section.

4 Remove the screws securing the catch to the door **(see illustration)**. Label and disconnect the electrical connector and harness clips (where applicable) from the catch. Remove the catch assembly from the door.

5 Refitting is the reverse of removal.

Outside handle and door lock cylinder

6 To remove the outside handle and lock cylinder assembly, raise the window and remove the door trim panel and water deflector as described in Section 16.

7 Remove the outside handle retaining bolts **(see illustration)**.

8 Pull the handle assembly from the door, then disengage the plastic clips that secure the outside handle-to-catch rod and the outside door lock-to-catch rod **(see illustration 18.7)**.

9 Remove the handle and lock cylinder assembly from the vehicle. To remove the lock cylinder, slide out the retaining clip and lift the cylinder from the outer handle.

10 Refitting is the reverse of removal.

Inside handle

11 Remove the door handle retaining screw, pull the handle outward and disconnect the handle actuating rods and the door lock

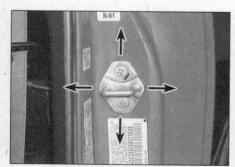

17.13 Adjust the door lock striker by slackening the mounting screws and gently tapping the striker in the desired direction (arrowed)

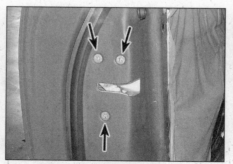

18.4 Remove the catch screws (arrowed) from the end of the door and pull the catch assembly through the access hole

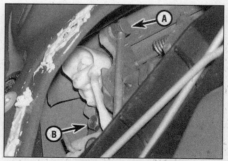

18.7 Detach the actuating rod (A) and outside handle fasteners (B)

18.11a Undo the door handle retaining screw . . .

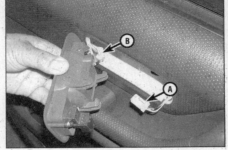

18.11b . . . and pull the handle outward to access the door lock switch electrical connector (A) and the door handle actuating rods (B)

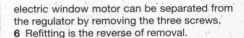

19.4 Remove the rear guide channel bolts and screws (arrowed)

switch electrical connector **(see illustrations)**. Remove the handle from the door.

12 Refitting is the reverse of removal.

19 Door window glass – removal and refitting

Drop glass

1 Remove the door trim panel and the plastic water deflector (see Section 16).

2 On models with manual windows, refit the window winder handle. On models with electric windows, temporarily reconnect the window switch. Lower the window glass all the way down into the door.

3 Carefully prise out the weatherstrip out of the door window opening.

4 Remove the nut(s)/bolt(s) and detach the rear guide channel from the door **(see illustration)**.

5 Raise the window just enough to access the window retaining bolts through the hole in the door frame **(see illustration)**.

6 On 5-door Estate rear door windows, undo the screw, release the retaining clip, and remove the lock rod protector from the door frame.

7 Place a rag over the glass to help prevent scratching the glass and remove the two glass mounting bolts.

8 Remove the glass by pulling it up and out.
9 Refitting is the reverse of removal.

Quarterlight glass

10 Remove the window drop glass as described previously.

11 Carefully pull the quarterlight glass and rubber surround from the door frame.

12 Separate the glass from the rubber surround.

13 Refitting is the reverse of removal.

20 Door window glass regulator – removal and refitting

1 Remove the door trim panel and the plastic water deflector (see Section 16).

2 Remove the window glass assembly (see Section 19).

3 On electric windows, disconnect the electrical connector from the window regulator motor.

4 On electric windows, remove the equaliser arm bracket and the regulator mounting bolts **(see illustrations)**. On manually operated windows remove the regulator mounting bolts, then slide the regulator assembly out of the lower channel guide.

5 Pull the equaliser arm and regulator assemblies through the service hole in the door frame to remove it. If necessary the

electric window motor can be separated from the regulator by removing the three screws.

6 Refitting is the reverse of removal.

21 Rear view mirrors – removal and refitting

Exterior mirrors

1 Remove the door trim panel and the plastic water deflector (see Section 16).

2 Prise off the mirror trim cover **(see illustration)**. On non-electric mirrors, prise out the cap, undo the control knob retaining

19.5 Raise the window to access the glass retaining bolts (arrowed) through the holes in the door frame

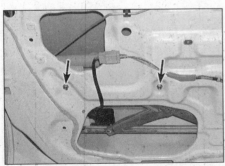

20.4a Detach the window equaliser arm bracket retaining bolts (arrowed) . . .

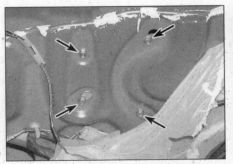

20.4b . . . then remove the window regulator bolts (arrowed) (electric window model)

21.2 Use a small screwdriver to prise off the mirror cover

21.4 Remove the three fasteners (arrowed) and detach the mirror

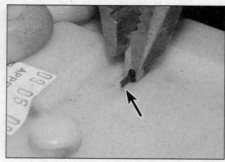

21.7 Remove the retaining pin (arrowed) and pull the glass from the actuator

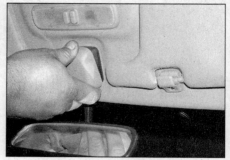

21.8 Remove the mirror cover

21.9 Undo the three screws (arrowed) and detach the mirror

22.1 Prise up the cover and remove the two screws (arrowed)

22 Centre console – removal and refitting

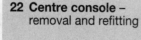

screw, pull the knob from the control arm and remove the trim cover.

3 Disconnect the electrical connector from the mirror (if equipped).

4 Remove the three mirror retaining fasteners and detach the mirror from the vehicle (see illustration).

5 Refitting is the reverse of removal.

Glass renewal

6 Examine the underside of the mirror housing. If there is an access hole, insert a cross-head screwdriver and slacken the mirror actuator retaining screw sufficiently to allow the mirror to be removed. Where no access hole is provided, the mirror is clipped to the actuator. Press in the inboard edge of the mirror glass, and using a flat-bladed screwdriver from the outside edge, carefully prise the mirror glass from the actuator. Note that on vehicles

equipped with heated mirrors, the mirror glass is not available separately from the actuator.

7 With powered windows, remove the retaining pin and pull the glass from the actuator (see illustration).

Interior mirror

Coupe, Saloon and 3-door Hatchback

8 Using a flat-bladed screwdriver, carefully prise off the mirror mounting cover (see illustration). Where fitted, disconnect the remote central locking receiver connector.

9 Remove the screws and lower the mirror (see illustration).

Estate and 5-door Hatchback

10 Slide the mirror mounting bracket up from the windscreen plate, and remove it.

All models

11 Refitting is the reverse of removal.

Rear console

1 On 5-door models, prise up the cover and remove the two rear console screws (see illustration).

2 On 2, 3 and 4-door models, undo the screws at either side of the front of the console.

3 Remove the screws along both sides of console (see illustrations).

4 Pull up on the handbrake handle. Remove the rear half of the console by lifting it up and toward the rear. Disconnect any electrical connectors as the console is withdrawn.

Front console

2, 3 and 4-door models

5 Remove the gear lever knob (see Chapter 7A).

6 Remove the console retaining screws (see illustrations).

7 Remove the front console screws and lift the console up and over the gear/selector lever (see illustration). Disconnect any electrical connections and remove the console from the vehicle.

5-door models

8 Remove the rear console as described previously.

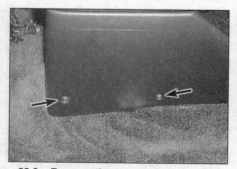

22.3a Remove the screws (arrowed) on each side of the rear console

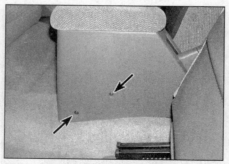

22.3b On some models, it's easier to move the front seat forward for access to the rear console screws (arrowed)

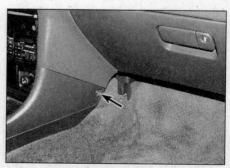

22.6a Remove the screws along the sides (arrowed) . . .

22.6b . . . and (if equipped) along the front of the front edge of the console (arrowed)

22.7 Lift up the rear of the console, then pull it out

22.12 Undo the centre console upper screws (arrowed)

9 Carefully prise the switches from the centre console, and remove the audio unit (see Chapter 12).

10 On manual transmission models, unscrew the gear knob from the lever.

11 On models with automatic transmission, carefully working from the front edge, prise out the trim panel surrounding the selector lever.

12 On all models, the console is secured by two screws at the top (by the switch apertures), one in the centre of the audio unit aperture, and one screw each side approximately halfway up the console **(see illustration)**. Lift the console over the gear change/selector lever. Disconnect any electrical connectors as the console is withdrawn.

All models

13 Refitting is the reverse of removal.

23 Facia trim panels – removal and refitting

Instrument cluster surround

1 Tilt the steering wheel down to the lowest position.

2 Where fitted prise out the switches in the surround and disconnect the wiring plugs **(see illustration)**.

3 Remove the cross-head screws **(see illustration)**, then grasp the surround securely and pull back to detach the clips from the facia. On 5-door models, there are two more retaining screws at the base of the surround **(see illustration)**.

4 Unplug any electrical connectors that interfere with removal.

5 Refitting is the reverse of removal.

Facia lower trim panel

6 On 5-door models, open the driver's storage compartment lid in the panel, and lift it from the hinges.

7 Remove the screws securing the lower part of the facia trim panel **(see illustrations)**.

8 On 2, 3 and 4-door models, lift the lower edge of the panel upward and detach the clips or fasteners on the upper edge.

9 On 5-door models, lift the panel upwards and remove it.

10 Unplug any electrical connectors, then lower the trim panel from the instrument panel.

11 Refitting is the reverse of removal.

Glovebox

12 To remove the glovebox, simply remove the screws from the hinge **(see illustration)**. Open the glovebox door, squeeze the plastic sides in and lower the glovebox from the instrument panel. **Note:** *On some models it*

23.2 Prise out the switches (where fitted) and disconnect the wiring plugs

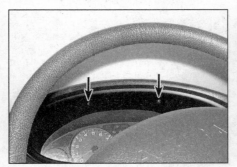

23.3a Remove the cluster surround retaining screws (arrowed)

23.3b On 5-door models, two more screws retain the base of the surround (arrowed)

23.7a Lower facia trim panel screws (arrowed) – 2, 3 and 4-door models (LHD)

23.7b Lower facia trim panel screws (arrowed) – 5-door models

23.12 Glovebox hinge retaining screws (arrowed)

will be necessary to unsnap the door stops from the glovebox.
13 Refitting is the reverse of the removal.

Centre lower cover

2, 3 and 4-door models

14 Remove the facia lower panel trim and glovebox as described previously in this Section.
15 Open the ashtray and remove the screws in the roof of the ashtray aperture.
16 There are four more screws securing the cover to the facia above. Remove the screws and bolt and detach the cover from the facia **(see illustration)**.
17 Refitting is the reverse of the removal.

Front ashtray assembly

5-door models

18 Remove the front console as described in Section 22.
19 Undo the five screws and pull the ashtray out from the facia, disconnecting any electrical connectors as the assembly is withdrawn **(see illustration)**.
20 Refitting is the reverse of removal.

---

24 Steering column shrouds –
removal and refitting

Removal

1 Remove the facia lower trim panel (see Section 23).

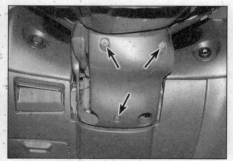

24.3 Remove the steering column shroud screws (arrowed)

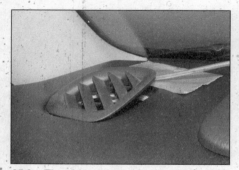

25.9a The side and centre air vents should be prised out front edge first . . .

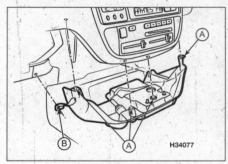

23.16 Centre lower cover

A Screws   *B Bolt*

2 On tilt steering columns, move the column to the lowest position.
3 Remove the retaining screws, then separate the halves and remove the covers **(see illustration)**.

Refitting

4 Refitting is the reverse of the removal procedure.

---

25 Facia –
removal and refitting

Removal

1 Disconnect the cable from the negative terminal of the battery (see Chapter 5A).
2 Remove the steering wheel (see Chapter 10).

25.8 Steering column retaining nuts (arrowed)

25.9b . . . and the driver and passenger vents, lower edge first

---

23.19 Undo the five screws (arrowed) and remove the ashtray assembly

3 Remove the front and rear centre consoles (see Section 22).
4 Remove the instrument cluster surround (see Section 23).
5 Remove the instrument cluster (see Chapter 12).
6 Remove all of the dashboard trim panels described in Section 23.
7 Detach the nuts and bolts securing the fusebox and the bonnet release handle (see Chapter 12 and Section 9).
8 Remove the nuts and lower the steering column **(see illustration)**.
9 Carefully prise out the air vents from the facia. The side demisters and centre air vent should be prised out at the front edge first **(see illustration)**. Note that when refitting the centre vent, align the vent position arm with the heater link arm. The drivers and passengers vents are prised from place along with their surround trims. Prise them out at the lower edge first **(see illustration)**.
10 Prise/unscrew up the front door sill trims, then prise out the driver's and passenger side lower kick panels.
11 On 2, 3 and 4-door models, working at the driver's end of the facia, prise up the centre pin of the retaining clip, then carefully lever off the facia end cover.
12 On 5-door models, prise open the access panels at each end of the facia to reveal the securing screws **(see illustration)**.
13 Remove the screws from each end of the facia **(see illustration)**.
14 Disconnect the yellow connector for the passenger side airbag (where fitted), then remove the three (2, 3 and 4-door models) or

25.12 Prise open the access panels to expose the screws – 5-door models

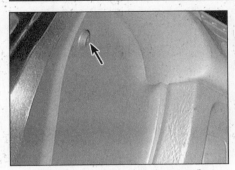

25.13 Remove the screw (arrowed) at each end of the facia

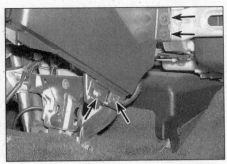

25.16 Remove the screws (arrowed) along the lower edge of the facia

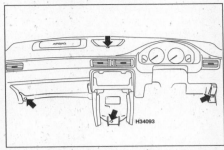

25.18 The facia is secured by two screws in the centre and two more at the lower outer edges (arrowed)

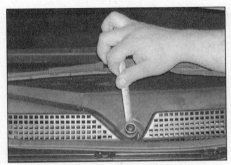

26.1 Remove the nuts and detach the wiper arms

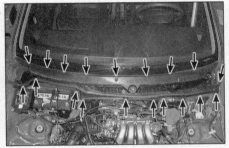

26.2 Remove the plastic rivets (upper arrows) and the clips (lower arrows), then detach the cover

two (5-door models) nuts to separate the airbag from its mounting (see Chapter 12).
15 Remove the audio unit (see Chapter 12) and the heater control assembly (see Chapter 3).

2, 3 and 4-door models
16 Remove the screws securing the lower centre part of the facia **(see illustration)**.
17 Remove the bolts retaining the upper front edge of facia to the bulkhead

5-door models
18 The facia is secured by two screws in the centre (one upper screw in the centre air vent aperture, and one lower), and one screw each side at the lower part of the facia **(see illustration)**.

All models
19 Pull facia towards the rear of the vehicle and detach any electrical connectors

interfering with removal.
20 Lift the facia over the steering column and remove it from the vehicle.

Refitting
21 Refitting is the reverse of removal.

26 Scuttle cover – removal and refitting

Removal
1 Mark the positions of the windscreen wiper arms on the windscreen with pieces of tape. Remove the wiper arm retaining nuts and remove the wiper arms **(see illustration)**.
2 Pull out the centres of the plastic rivets securing the rear of the scuttle cover, then prise the rivets out **(see illustration)**.
3 Carefully remove the clips securing the

bonnet seal **(see illustration 26.2)** and remove the scuttle cover from the vehicle. Prise directly underneath the clips, being careful not to tear the bonnet seal.

Refitting
4 Refitting is the reverse of removal. Be sure to align the wiper arms with the tape marks on the windscreen.

27 Seats – removal and refitting

Front seat
1 Position the seat all the way forward, then all the way to the rear to access the seat retaining bolts **(see illustrations)**.
2 Detach any bolt trim covers and remove the retaining bolts.
3 Tilt the seat upward to access the underneath, then disconnect any electrical connectors and lift the seat from the vehicle.
4 Refitting is the reverse of removal.

Rear seat
5 On 2, 3 and 4-door models, remove the seat cushion bolts and remove the cushion **(see illustration)**. Fold the seats forward, and undo the bolts securing the pivot brackets to the back of the seats. Lift the seats from the vehicle.
6 On 5-door models, undo the cushion retaining bolts at the front hinges **(see**

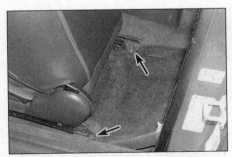

27.1a Move the front seat all the way forward to access the rear retaining bolts (arrowed) . . .

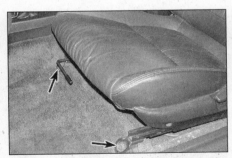

27.1b . . . the move the seat all the way to the rear to access the front retaining bolts (arrowed)

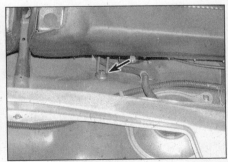

27.5 Remove the rear seat cushion retaining bolts (arrowed)

illustration). On Hatchback models it may be necessary to prise up hinge covers. Fold the seat back forward, prise up the hinge covers, and undo the mounting bolts (see illustration).
7 Refitting is the reverse of removal.

28 Radiator grille – removal and refitting

2, 3 and 4-door models

1 Remove the front bumper as described in Section 10.
2 Undo the screws, release the retaining clips and separate the grille from the bumper.

5-door Hatchback

Up to '97

3 Remove the front bumper as described in Section 10.
4 Undo the screws, release the retaining clips and separate the grille from the bumper.

From '97

5 Open the bonnet, and undo the six nuts, and two clips securing the grille to the bonnet. To release the clips, prise out the centre pin, then prise the entire clip out.

All models

6 Refitting is the reverse of removal.

29 Sunroof – general information

1 Removal and refitting, and adjustments to the roof panel, are best entrusted to a Honda garage, as specialised tools are required, and the complete headlining must be removed.
2 The sunroof panel motor can be removed and refitted as described in Chapter 12. If the motor malfunctions when the roof panel is in the open position, it can be wound shut manually. To do this, use a screwdriver or coin to unscrew the round plug in the centre of the headlining. Obtain the cranking tool from the vehicle's toolkit (see illustrations). Insert the cranking tool into the hole and into

27.6a Undo the cushion retaining bolts at the front hinges . . .

the socket. The tool can then be turned to close the sunroof as required.
3 If the sunroof water drain hoses become blocked, they may be cleared by probing them with a length of suitable cable (an old speedometer drive cable is ideal). Insert the cleaning tool into the top of the hoses, accessible when the sunroof is fully open. The front drain tubes terminates just in front of the A-pillars, behind the wheelarch liners. The rear drain tubes terminate behind the rear wheelarch liners, ahead the bumper.

30 Seat belts – general information

1 Periodically check the belts for fraying or other damage. If evident, renew the belt.
2 If the belts become dirty, wipe them with a damp cloth, using a little liquid detergent only.
3 Check the tightness of the anchor bolts, and if they are ever disconnected, make quite sure that the original sequence of fitting of washers, bushes, and anchor plate is retained.
4 Access to the front belt height adjuster and inertia reel units can be made by removing the trim from the B-pillar on the side concerned (see Section 31).
5 The rear seat belt anchorages/inertia reel units can be checked by removing the C-pillar trims, and the luggage compartment side trims (see Section 31).
6 The torque wrench settings for the seat belt anchor bolts and other attachments are given in the Specifications at the start of this

27.6b . . . then fold the seat forward, prise up the hinge covers and undo the bolts

Chapter. Not that the upper seat belt anchorage bolt threads should by coated with thread locking compound prior to refitting.
7 Never modify the seat belts, or alter the attachments to the body, in any way.
8 Note that the front seat belt anchorages incorporate pyrotechnic pretensioners. If a pretensioner must be removed, the B-pillar trim and door sill scuff plate should be removed, and the tensioner and inertia reel removed at the same time. The tensioner is retained by one bolt (see illustration). Take great care not to knock the tensioner against anything. Due to the risk of injury, we recommend removal and renewal of the pretensioners should be entrusted to a Honda dealer or specialist.

31 Interior trim panels – removal and refitting

General

1 The interior trim panels are secured using either screws or various types of trim fasteners, usually studs or clips.
2 Check that there are no other panels overlapping the one to be removed; usually there is a sequence to be followed that will become obvious on close inspection.
3 Remove all obvious fasteners, such as screws. If the panel will not come free, it is held by hidden clips or fasteners. These are usually situated around the edge of the panel, and can be prised up to release them. Note, however, that they can

29.2a Unscrew the centre plug from the headlining . . .

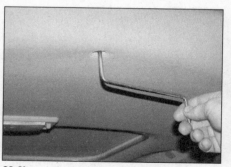

29.2b . . . then insert the cranked tool from the toolkit

30.4 The seat belt pretensioner is retained by one bolt (arrowed)

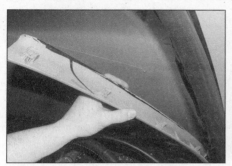

31.6 Carefully prise the A-pillar trim away

31.7 The B-pillar trim is secured by push-on clips

31.13 Undo the rear side upper trim retaining screws (arrowed) – Estate models

break quite easily, so renewals should be available. The best way of releasing such clips in the absence of the correct type of tool, is to use a large flat-bladed screwdriver. Note in many cases that an adjacent sealing strip (such as the rubber door seal) must be prised back to release a panel.

4 When removing a panel, **never** use excessive force, or the panel may be damaged. Always check carefully that all fasteners have been removed or released before attempting to withdraw a panel.

5 Refitting is the reverse of the removal procedure; secure the fasteners by pressing them firmly into place, and ensure that all disturbed components are correctly secured, to prevent rattles.

A-pillar trim panel

6 Peel off the rubber door seal adjoining the trim panel, then carefully prise the panel away from the A-pillar. The panel is held by push-on clips **(see illustration)**.

B-pillar trim panels

Lower panel

7 Peel off the rubber door seals adjoining the trim panel, carefully prise up/unscrew the front and rear door sill trims, and gently prise the panel from its location **(see illustration)**.

Upper panel

8 Remove the lower panel as described in Paragraph 7.

9 Prise off the plastic cover, and undo the seat belt upper anchorage bolt, then prise the trim panel from its location. The panel is secured by push-on clips.

Rear side window surround panel

2 and 3-door models

10 Remove the rear side trim panel as described in this Section.

11 Undo the front and rear (where applicable) upper seat belt anchorage bolts.

12 The panel is secured by several different types of clip. On some, prise up the centre pin, then lever the entire clip out. Carefully pull the panel from its location.

Estate

13 Undo the two screws securing the rear side upper trim from the luggage compartment, and pull the trim from its retaining clips **(see illustration)**.

14 Peel the rubber door seals from the rear door and tailgate apertures, adjacent to the window surround panel.

15 Undo the two screws and remove the lower trim panel adjacent to the rear seat **(see illustrations)**.

16 The window surround panel is secured by push-on clips. Carefully pull the panel from its location.

C-pillar trim panel

17 Peel away the rubber door and tailgate (where applicable) seals from the rear door aperture adjacent to the panel.

18 The panel is secured by push-on clips. Carefully pull the panel from its location. On 5-door models, undo the rear lower seat belt anchorage bolt, and thread the seat belt back through the panel.

19 Prise out the seat belt access panel from the panel – this is clipped in very tightly.

20 The trim panel is held by a total of four push-on clips down the middle of the panel. Carefully prise the panel away from the body **(see illustration)**. To remove the panel completely, the rear seat belt lower mounting will have to be removed.

Rear side trim panel

21 Remove the rear seat as described in Section 27.

2-door models

22 Remove the rear parcel shelf as described in this Section.

23 Unscrew the rear seat pivots brackets from the rear side trim panel.

24 The rear side trim panel is secured by a combination of self-tapping screws, and push-on clips. Undo the screws and carefully prise the panel from its location.

3-door models

25 Carefully pull the rear side shelf panel from its location.

26 Peel away the rubber door seal from the rear door and tailgate aperture adjacent to the side trim panel.

27 The rear trim panel beneath the tailgate aperture must be removed. The panel is secured by push-on clips, and prise-out clips, where the centre pin must be levered out, followed by the entire clip.

28 Unscrew the rear seat pivot bracket.

29 The rear side panel trim is secured by a combination of self-tapping screws and push-on clips. Undo the screws and carefully pull the panel from its location.

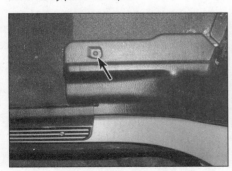

31.15a Undo the lower trim panel screw (arrowed) . . .

31.15b . . . and upper trim panel screw (arrowed) – Estate models

31.20 Carefully prise the C-pillar trim away

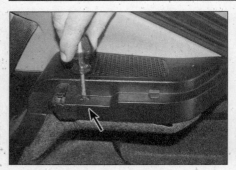

31.30 Undo the single screw (arrowed) and carefully pull the rear side shelf panel away – 5-door Hatchback models

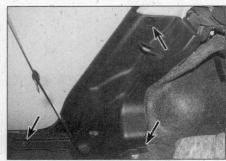

31.35 Undo the rear seat side trim panel screws and clips (arrowed)

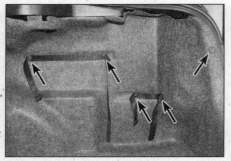

31.36a The rear side panel trim is secured by screws and clips (arrowed)

31.36b With prise-out clips, lever up the centre pin, flowed by the entire clip

Luggage area side trim panel

5-door Hatchback

30 Undo the single screw and carefully pull the rear side shelf panel from its location (see illustration).

31 Peel away the rubber door seal from the tailgate aperture adjacent to the side trim panel.

32 The rear trim panel beneath the tailgate aperture must be removed. The panel is secured prise-out clips, where the centre pin must be levered out, followed by the entire clip.

33 Remove the rear seat back as described in Section 27.

34 Remove the rear door sill trim. The trim is secured by push-on clips or screws.

35 Undo the screws and pull the rear seat

side trim panel from its location (see illustration).

36 The rear side panel trim is secured by a combination of self-tapping screws, push-on clips and prise-out clips, where the centre pin must be levered out, followed by the entire clip. Undo the screws, remove the prise-out clips and carefully pull the panel from its location (see illustrations).

Estate

37 Undo the two screws and remove the rear side upper trim panel, under the rear side window.

38 Remove the luggage compartment floor lid, and rear side storage space lid (where fitted).

39 Undo the single screw and pull the rear trim panel from its location at the rear of the luggage compartment.

40 Undo the screw and remove the 'tie-down' hook from the side panel.

41 The side panel trim is secured by push-on clips. Carefully pull the panel from its location.

Headlining

42 The rigid headlining is clipped to the roof, and can only be withdrawn once all fittings such as the grab handles, sunvisors, interior light, and related trim panels have been removed, and the door, tailgate and sunroof aperture sealing strips have been prised clear.

43 As with carpet removal, taking out the headlining is not especially difficult, just time-consuming.

Grab handles

44 Slide off the plastic covers either end of the handles, and undo the retaining screws (see illustration).

45 Refitting is a reversal of removal.

Rear parcel shelf

46 Remove the rear seat back as described in Section 27.

47 Parcel shelf is secured by seven push-on clips. Carefully pull the shelf from its location, and disconnect the high-level brake light connector as the shelf is withdrawn.

Footwell kick panels

48 Prise up/unscrew the front door sill trims, then prise out the driver's and passenger side lower kick panels (see illustration)

32 Sunvisors – removal and refitting

1 Release the relevant sunvisor from the its retaining clip, undo the two screws, and remove the sunvisor (see illustration). Disconnect the wiring plug as the visor is removed.

2 If necessary, undo and remove the screw securing the sunvisor retaining clip to the roof.

3 Refitting is a reversal of removal.

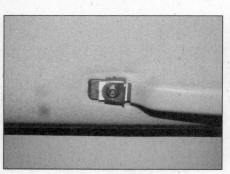

31.44 Undo the grab handle screws

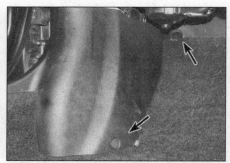

31.48 Remove the clips (arrowed) and carefully prise off the footwell kick panel

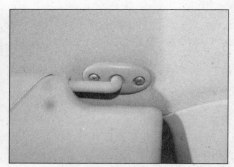

32.1 Undo the sunvisor screws

Chapter 12
Body electrical system

Contents

Degrees of difficulty

Easy, suitable for novice with little experience	Fairly easy, suitable for beginner with some experience	Fairly difficult, suitable for competent DIY mechanic	Difficult, suitable for experienced DIY mechanic	Very difficult, suitable for expert DIY or professional

Specifications

System type	12 volt, negative earth

Bulbs	Power rating (watts)
Brake and tail lights	21/5 (bayonet)
Foglight:	
Front	55 (H3 type)
Rear	21 (bayonet)
Glovebox light	3 (festoon)
Headlights (halogen)	60/55 (H4 type)
High-mounted brake light	5 (capless) or LED
Indicators	21 (bayonet)
Instrument cluster	3.4, 1.4 or 0.9 (capless)
Interior lights	5 (festoon)
Interior mirror light	3 (festoon)
Luggage compartment	5 (festoon)
Number plate light	5 (capless)
Reversing light	21 (bayonet)
Sidelights	5 (capless)
Side repeaters	5 (capless)

Torque wrench setting	Nm	lbf ft
Passenger side airbag	10	7

1 General information and precautions

⚠️ **Warning: Before carrying out any work on the electrical system, read through the precautions given in 'Safety first!' at the beginning of this manual, and in Chapter 5A.**

1 The electrical system is of 12 volt negative earth type. Power for the lights and all electrical accessories is supplied by a lead-acid type battery which is charged by the alternator.

2 This Chapter covers repair and service procedures for the various electrical components not associated with the engine. Information on the battery, alternator and starter motor can be found in Chapter 5A.

3 It should be noted that prior to working on any component in the electrical system, the battery negative terminal should first be disconnected to prevent the possibility of electrical short-circuits and/or fires (see Chapter 5A).

Caution: If the vehicle has a security-coded radio, check that you have a copy of the code number before disconnecting the battery. Refer to your Honda dealer if in doubt.

2 Electrical fault finding – general information

Note: Refer to the precautions given in 'Safety first!' and in Chapter 5 before starting work. The following tests relate to testing of the main electrical circuits, and should not be used to test delicate electronic circuits (such as anti-lock braking systems), particularly where an electronic control unit is used.

General

1 Typically, electrical circuit consists of an electrical component, any switches, relays, motors, fuses, fusible links or circuit breakers related to that component, and the wiring and connectors which link the component to both the battery and the chassis. To help to pinpoint a problem in an electrical circuit, wiring diagrams are included at the end of this Chapter.

2 Have a good look at the appropriate wiring diagram, before attempting to diagnose an electrical fault, to obtain a complete understanding of the components included in the particular circuit concerned. The possible sources of a fault can be narrowed down by noting if other components related to the circuit are operating properly. If several components or circuits fail at one time, the problem is likely to be related to a shared fuse or earth connection.

3 An electrical problem will usually stem from simple cause, such as loose or corroded connections, a faulty earth connection, a blown fuse, a melted fusible link, or a faulty relay (refer to Section 4 for details of testing relays). Visually inspect the condition of all fuses, wires and connections in a problem circuit before testing the components. Use the wiring diagrams to determine which terminal connections will need to be checked in order to pinpoint the trouble spot.

4 The basic tools required for electrical fault finding include a circuit tester or voltmeter (a 12 volt bulb with a set of test leads can also be used for certain tests); a self-powered test light (sometimes known as a continuity tester); an ohmmeter (to measure resistance); a battery and set of test leads; and a jumper wire, preferably with a circuit breaker or fuse incorporated, which can be used to bypass suspect wires or electrical components. Before attempting to locate a problem with test instruments, use the wiring diagram to determine where to make the connections.

5 Sometimes, an intermittent wiring fault (usually caused to a poor or dirty connection, or damaged wiring insulation) can be pinpointed by performing a wiggle test on the wiring. This involves wiggling the wiring by hand to see if the fault occurs as the wiring is moved. It should be possible to narrow down the source of the fault to a particular section of wiring. This method of testing can be used in conjunction with any of the tests described in the following sub-Sections.

6 Apart from problems due to poor connections, two basic types of fault can occur in an electrical circuit: open-circuit, or short-circuit.

7 Largely, open-circuit faults are caused by a break somewhere in the circuit, which prevents current from flowing. An open-circuit fault will prevent a component from working, but will not cause the relevant circuit fuse to blow.

8 Low resistance or short-circuit faults are caused by a 'short'; a failure point which allows the current flowing in the circuit to 'escape' along an alternative route, somewhere in the circuit. This typically occurs when a positive supply wire touches either an earth wire, or an earthed component such as the bodyshell. Such faults are normally caused by a breakdown in wiring insulation, A short-circuit fault will normally cause the relevant circuit fuse to blow.

9 Fuses are designed to protect a circuit from being overloaded. A blown fuse indicates that there may be problem in that particular circuit and it is important to identify and rectify the problem before renewing the fuse. Always renew a blown fuse with one of the correct current rating; fitting a fuse of a different rating may cause an overloaded circuit to overheat and even catch fire.

Finding an open-circuit

10 One of the most straightforward ways of finding an open circuit fault is by using a circuit test meter or voltmeter. Connect one lead of the meter to either the negative battery terminal or a known good earth. Connect the other lead to a connector in the circuit being tested, preferably nearest to the battery or fuse. Switch on the circuit, bearing in mind that some circuits are live only when the ignition switch is moved to a particular position. If voltage is present (indicated either by the tester bulb lighting or a voltmeter reading, as applicable), this means that the section of the circuit between the relevant connector and the battery is problem-free. Continue to check the remainder of the circuit in the same fashion. When a point is reached at which no voltage is present, the problem must lie between that point and the previous test point with voltage. Most problems can be traced to a broken, corroded or loose connection.

Finding a short-circuit

11 Loading the circuit during testing will produce false results and may damage your test equipment, so all electrical loads must be disconnected from the circuit before it can be checked for short circuits. Loads are the components which draw current from a circuit, such as bulbs, motors, heating elements, etc.

12 Keep both the ignition and the circuit under test switched off, then remove the relevant fuse from the circuit, and connect a circuit test meter or voltmeter to the fuse connections.

13 Switch on the circuit, bearing in mind that some circuits are live only when the ignition switch is moved to a particular position. If voltage is present (indicated either by the tester bulb lighting or a voltmeter reading, as applicable), this means that there is a short-circuit. If no voltage is present, but the fuse still blows with the load(s) connected, this indicates an internal fault in the load(s).

Finding an earth fault

14 The battery negative terminal is connected to 'earth' – the metal of the engine/transmission and the car body – and most systems are wired so that they only receive a positive feed, the current returning through the metal of the car body. This means that the component mounting and the body form part of that circuit. Loose or corroded mountings can therefore cause a range of electrical faults, ranging from total failure of a circuit, to a puzzling partial fault. In particular, lights may shine dimly (especially when another circuit sharing the same earth point is in operation), motors (eg, wiper motors or the radiator cooling fan motor) may run slowly, and the operation of one circuit may have an apparently unrelated effect on another. Note that on many vehicles, earth straps are used between certain components, such as the engine/transmission and the body, usually where there is no metal-to-metal contact between components due to flexible rubber mountings, etc.

3.1a Passenger compartment fuse block

3.1b Engine compartment fuse block

15 To check whether a component is properly earthed, disconnect the battery and connect one lead of an ohmmeter to a known good earth point. Connect the other lead to the wire or earth connection being tested. The resistance reading should be zero; if not, check the connection as follows.

16 If an earth connection is thought to be faulty, dismantle the connection and clean back to bare metal both the bodyshell and the wire terminal or the component earth connection mating surface. Be careful to remove all traces of dirt and corrosion, then use a knife to trim away any paint, so that a clean metal-to-metal joint is made. On reassembly, tighten the joint fasteners securely; if a wire terminal is being refitted, use serrated washers between the terminal and the bodyshell to ensure a clean and secure connection. When the connection is remade, prevent the onset of corrosion in the future by applying a coat of petroleum jelly or silicone-based grease or by spraying on (at regular intervals) a proprietary ignition sealer or a water dispersant lubricant.

3 Fuses – general information

1 The electrical circuits of the vehicle are protected by a combination of fuses and circuit breakers. The two fuse blocks (three fuse blocks on models equipped with ABS) are located under the driver's side of the facia (behind the storage box) and on the left-hand side of the engine compartment **(see illustrations)**.

2 Each of the fuses is designed to protect a specific circuit (or circuits), and the various circuits are identified on the fuse panel itself.

3 Miniaturised fuses are employed in the fuse blocks. These compact fuses, with blade terminal design, are removed using the tool provided in the fusebox. If an electrical component fails, always check the fuse first. To check the fuses, turn the ignition key to the

3.1c ABS fusebox

ON position and, using a test light, probe each exposed terminal of each fuse. If the test light glows on both terminals of a fuse, the fuse is good. If power is available on one side of the fuse but not the other, the fuse is blown. When removed, a blown fuse is easily identified through the clear plastic body **(see illustration)**. Visually inspect the element for evidence of damage.

4 Be sure to renew blown fuses with the correct type. Fuses of different ratings are physically interchangeable, but only fuses of the proper rating should be used. Replacing a fuse with one of a higher or lower value than specified is not recommended. Each electrical circuit needs a specific amount of protection. The amperage value of each fuse is moulded into the fuse body.

5 If the new fuse immediately fails, don't renew it again until the cause of the problem is isolated and corrected. In most cases, the cause will be a short circuit in the wiring caused by a broken or deteriorated wire.

6 All models are equipped with main fusible links which protect all the circuits coming from the battery. If these circuits are overloaded, the fusible links blow, preventing damage to the main wiring harness. The fusible links consist of a metal strip which will be visibly melted when overloaded. Always disconnect the battery before renewing a main fuse (available from your dealer). The fusible links are located in the engine

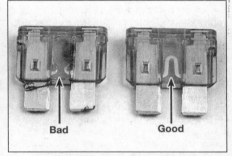

3.3 The fuses can be visually inspected to see if they are blown

compartment fuse block. To remove the fusible link, unscrew the fixing screws. Make sure you fit a unit that's equivalent to the old fuse. In other words, if the old fusible link is an 80A unit, renew it with an 80A fuse.

4 Relays – general information

General information

1 Several electrical accessories in the vehicle, such as the fuel injection system, horns, starter, and cooling fans use relays to transmit the electrical power to the component. Relays use a low-current circuit (the control circuit) to open and close a high-current circuit (the power circuit). If the relay is defective, that component will not operate properly. The various relays are mounted in engine compartment fusebox **(see illustration 3.1b)** and several locations throughout the vehicle. If a faulty relay is suspected, it can be removed and tested using the procedure below. Defective relays must be renewed as a unit.

Testing

2 It's best to refer to the wiring diagram for the circuit to determine the proper connections for the relay you're testing. However, if you're not able to determine the

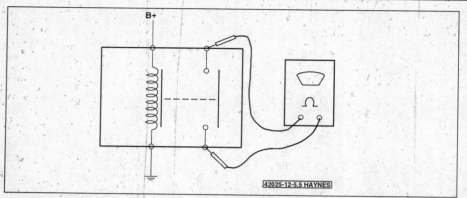

4.5 To test a typical four terminal normally open relay, connect an ohmmeter to the two terminals of the power circuit – the meter will indicate no continuity until battery power and earth are connected to the two terminals of the control circuit, then the relay will click and continuity will be indicated

correct connections from the wiring diagrams, you may be able to determine the test connections from the information that follows.

3 On most relays, two of the terminals are the relay's control circuit (they connect to the relay coil which, when energised, closes the large contacts to complete the circuit). The other terminals are the power circuit (they are connected together within the relay when the control-circuit coil is energised).

4 Most relays are marked as an aid to help you determine which terminals are the control circuit and which are the power circuit.

5 Connect an ohmmeter to the two terminals of the power circuit. Connect a fused bridging wire between one of the two control circuit terminals and the positive battery terminal. Connect another bridging wire between the other control circuit terminal and earth. When the connections are made, the relay should click and continuity will be indicated on the meter (see illustration). On some relays, polarity may be critical, so, if the relay doesn't click, try swapping the bridging wires on the control circuit terminals.

6 If the relay fails the above test, renew it.

5 Indicator flasher/hazard relay – testing and renewal

1 The hazard/indicator relay is located in the interior fusebox under the right-hand side of the facia (see illustration).

2 If the relay is functioning properly, you can hear an audible clicking sound when it's operating. If the indicators fail on one side or the other and the relay doesn't make its characteristic clicking sound, look for a faulty indicator bulb.

3 If both indicators fail to flash, the problem may be due to a blown fuse (in the engine compartment fusebox), a faulty relay, a broken switch or a loose or open connection. If a quick check of the fusebox indicates that the direction indicator fuse has blown, check the wiring for a short circuit before refitting a new fuse.

4 To renew the flasher, simply pull it out of the fusebox.

5 Make sure that the new unit is identical to the original. Compare the old one to the new one before refitting it.

6 Refitting is the reverse of removal.

6 Steering column switches – testing and renewal

⚠ Warning: The models covered by this manual are equipped with a Supplemental Restraint system (SRS), more commonly known as airbags. Always disable the airbag system before working in the vicinity of the impact sensors, steering column or instrument panel to avoid the possibility of accidental deployment of the airbag, which could cause personal injury (see Section 23). Do not use electrical test equipment on any of the airbag system wiring or tamper with them in any way.

Light & wiper/washer switch
Testing

1 The exterior lighting and wiper switches are located on the steering column. The combination light switch incorporates the direction indicator, headlight, dip switch and sidelight switches into one switch on the left side of the column. The windscreen wiper/washer functions are incorporated into another switch on the right side of the column.

2 Remove the switch(es) (see Paragraph 4).

3 Using an ohmmeter or self-powered test light and the accompanying diagrams, check for continuity between the indicated switch terminals with the switch in each of the indicated positions (see illustrations). If the continuity isn't as specified, renew the switch.

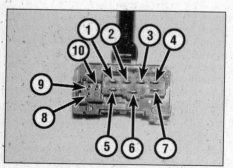

5.1 The hazard/turn signal flasher relay (arrowed) is located on the interior fusebox

6.3a Combination light switch terminal identification

Swich Position	Continuity Between
Parking Lights	1 and 2
Headlights (dipped beam)	1 and 2, 4 and 6, 3
Headlights (main beam)	1 and 2, 5 and 6, 4, 5
Headlight Flash	5 and 6
Right Direction Indicator	8 and 10
Left Direction Indicator	8 and 9

H34079

6.3b Combination light switch continuity table

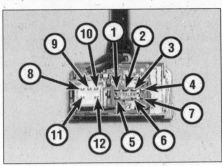

6.3c Windscreen and rear window wiper/washer switch terminal identification

SWITCH POSITION	CONTINUITY BETWEEN
Off	1 and 6
intermittent	1 and 6 ; 3 and 4
Low	1 and 5
High	2 and 5
Wash	4 and 7
Mist	2 and 5
WINDSHIELD WIPER/WASHER SWITCH	

SWITCH POSITION	CONTINUITY BETWEEN
Off	8 and 9
On	8 and 10
Wash	11 and 12
REAR WINDOW WIPER/WASHER SWITCH	

42025-12-7.3D HAYNES

6.3d Wiper/washer switch continuity table

Renewal

4 Remove the steering column shrouds (see Chapter 11). Use a small screwdriver to carefully detach the electrical connectors from the switch. Remove the two retaining screws and detach the switch from the steering column **(see illustrations)**.
5 Refitting is the reverse of removal.

Cruise control switch

Testing

6 Remove the switch from the steering wheel (see below).
7 Using an ohmmeter or self-powered test light check for continuity between the indicated terminals on the switch in each of the indicated positions **(see illustration)**. If the continuity isn't as specified, renew the switch.

Renewal

8 Disconnect the negative battery cable (see Chapter 5A), then the positive battery cable and wait at least three minutes before proceeding any further (see **Warning** above).
9 Remove the cover over the cruise control switch.
10 Detach the switch retaining screws **(see illustration)**. Then disconnect the electrical connections and remove the switch from the steering wheel.
11 Refitting is the reverse of removal.

6.4a Remove the two retaining screws (arrowed) (steering wheel removed for clarity only, position the spokes vertically to access the screws) . . .

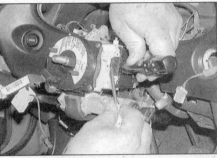

6.4b . . . and carefully prise the switch out of the steering column bracket

Always disable the airbag system before working in the vicinity of the impact sensors, steering column or instrument panel to avoid the possibility of accidental deployment of the airbag, which could cause personal injury (see Section 23). Do not use electrical test equipment on any of the airbag system wiring or tamper with them in any way.

Ignition switch

1 Disconnect the negative battery cable (see

7 Ignition switch and lock cylinder – testing and renewal

⚠️ *Warning: The models covered by this manual are equipped with a Supplemental Restraint system (SRS), more commonly known as airbags.*

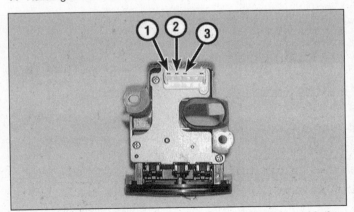

6.7 Cruise control Set/Resume switch terminal guide – with the switch in the Set position there should be continuity between terminals 1 and 3; with the switch in the Resume position there should be continuity between terminals 1 and 2

6.10 Undo the two mounting screws (arrowed) and remove the switch

Swich Position	Continuity Between
Accesory 2, 3 and 4 door models 5 door models	3 and 8 3 and 11
On 2, 3 and 4 door models 5 door models	3, 8, 10 and 12 3, 8, 9 and 11
Start 2, 3 and 4 door models 5 door models	1, 3 and 12 1, 3 and 8

H34080

8	9
10	11	12

5 Pin Connector

1	2	3
4	5	6	7

7 Pin Connector

7.4 Ignition switch terminal guide and continuity table

7.7 Remove the two ignition switch screws (arrowed) and remove the switch

7.14 Remove the two shear-bolts (arrowed) to remove the steering lock and key lock cylinder

Chapter 5A), then the positive battery cable (see **Warning** above).
2 Remove the lower facia trim panel and the steering column shrouds (see Chapter 11).

3 Follow the wire harness for the ignition switch down the steering column and disconnect the connectors from the fusebox and wiring harness.

4 Check the ignition switch for continuity between the indicated connector terminals with the ignition switch in each position (**see illustration**).
5 If the continuity is not as specified, renew the switch.
6 Insert the key and turn it to the Lock position.
7 Remove the two retaining screws and detach the switch (**see illustration**).
8 Refitting is the reverse of removal.

Steering column lock

9 Check the lock cylinder in each position to make sure it isn't worn or loose and that the key position corresponds to the markings on the housing. If the lock cylinder is faulty, the entire steering column lock assembly will have to be renewed.
10 Disconnect the negative battery cable (see Chapter 5A), then the positive battery cable (see **Warning** above).
11 Remove the steering column shrouds and facia lower trim panel (see Chapter 11).
12 Remove the ignition switch (see above).
13 Remove the retaining nuts and lower the steering column.
14 The lock assembly is clamped to the steering column by two shear-bolts (**see illustration**). Use a centre punch to make a dimple in the head of each bolt, then drill the head off the bolt with a 5 mm bit. Separate the clamp and remove the assembly from the steering column.
15 Place the new lock assembly in position without the key inserted and tighten the bolts until they are snug.
16 Insert the key and check the lock cylinder for proper operation.
17 Tighten the bolts until their heads break off.
18 Raise the steering column into position and fit the nuts/bolts. Tighten the steering column-to-instrument panel flange nuts to 13 Nm. Tighten the retaining collar clamp bolts to 22 Nm.
19 Fit the ignition switch, facia trim panel and steering column shrouds.
20 Connect the positive battery cable, followed by the negative cable.

8 Facia-mounted switches – testing and renewal

Cruise control on/off switch
Testing

1 To check the switch it must first be removed (see Paragraph 3).
2 Using an ohmmeter or self-powered test lamp and the accompanying diagram, check for continuity between each of the indicated switch terminals with the switch in each of the indicated positions (**see illustration**). If the continuity isn't as specified, renew the switch.

Swich Position	Continuity Between
Accesory 2, 3 and 4 door models 5 door models	3 and 8 3 and 11
On 2, 3 and 4 door models 5 door models	3, 8, 10 and 12 3, 8, 9 and 11
Start 2, 3 and 4 door models 5 door models	1, 3 and 12 1, 3 and 8

H34081

8	9
10	11	12

5 Pin Connector

1	2	3
4	5	6	7

7 Pin Connector

8.2 Cruise control on/off switch terminal guide and continuity table

8.3 Carefully prise the cruise control switch from the facia (LHD)

Renewal

3 To remove the switch, carefully prise it out of the dash and disconnect its electrical connector **(see illustration)**.
4 Refitting is the reverse of removal.

Heated rear window switch

Testing

5 Remove the switch from the facia (see Paragraph 8).
6 On 2, 3, and 4-door models, the timer circuitry is contained within the switch, so the switch can not be checked using conventional methods. If the heater rear window does not operate, turn the ignition ON but don't start the engine. Place the positive probe of a voltmeter at terminal number 1 and the negative probe at terminal number 4 on the wiring harness connector **(see illustration)**. Battery voltage should be indicated. If there's

no voltage, check the wiring harness and fuse. If there's battery voltage, connect a jumper wire between terminal numbers 1 and 4. If the heated rear window now works, renew the switch. If the heated rear window still doesn't work, check the heated rear window relay (see Section 4) and related circuit.
7 If you're working on a 5-door model, use an ohmmeter or self-powered test lamp and the accompanying diagram to check for continuity between the indicated switch terminals with the switch in the indicated positions **(see illustration)**. If the continuity isn't as specified, renew the switch.

Renewal

8 Carefully prise the switch out of the instrument panel and disconnect the electrical connector **(see illustration)**.
9 Refitting is the reverse of removal.

Instrument panel dimmer

Testing

10 Remove the switch from the facia (see Paragraph 16).
11 The control circuitry is contained within the switch, so the switch cannot be checked using conventional methods. The following check tests each individual circuit. If there is a

problem with the system and the circuits are good, the switch is assumed defective. Inspect the switch terminals, if they're corroded or bent, repair them if possible or renew the switch.
12 Working on the wiring harness connector, connect an ohmmeter between terminal number 2 and a good chassis earth **(see illustration)**. There should be continuity. If not, check the circuit for an open or bad connection.
13 With the headlight switch ON, connect a voltmeter between terminal number 1 and earth. There should be battery voltage. If not, check the circuit back to the under-facia fusebox and combination switch.
14 With the headlight switch ON, connect a bridging wire between terminal number 3 and a good chassis earth. The instrument panel lights should come on at full brightness.
15 If the wiring test results were correct and the switch doesn't work properly, renew the switch.

Renewal

16 To remove the switch, carefully prise it out of the facia and disconnect the electrical connector **(see illustration)**.
17 Refitting is the reverse of removal.

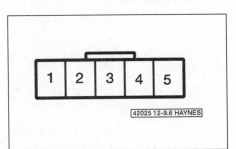

8.6 Heated rear window switch wiring harness connector terminal identification

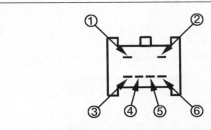

SWITCH POSITION	CONTINUITY BETWEEN
On	4 and 6
Off (bulb check)	1 and 3; 2 and 5

8.7 Heated rear window switch terminal identification and continuity table – 5-door models

8.8 Carefully prise the heated rear window switch out from the facia with a small screwdriver

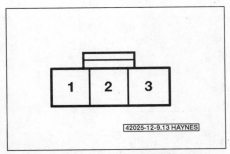

8.12 Instrument cluster panel lights dimmer switch wiring harness identification – looking from the rear of the connector

8.16 Carefully prise the instrument cluster light dimmer switch from the facia with a small screwdriver

9.3a Remove the instrument cluster screws (arrowed) – 2, 3 and 4-door models

9.3b Instrument cluster retaining screws (arrowed) – 5-door models

9.3c Pull the cluster from the facia, turn it over and unplug the electrical connectors from the rear

9 Instrument cluster – removal and refitting

Removal

1 Disconnect the negative battery cable, then the positive cable and wait three minutes before proceeding further (see Chapter 5A).
2 Tilt the steering wheel to its lowest position and remove the instrument cluster surround (see Chapter 11, Section 23).
3 Remove the cluster mounting screws, carefully pull it straight out of the instrument panel and disconnect the electrical connectors (see illustrations).

Refitting

4 Refitting is the reverse of removal.

10 Radio/cassette player and speakers – removal and refitting

Radio/cassette player

2, 3 and 4-door models

1 Remove the facia centre lower cover (see Chapter 11, Section 23).
2 Reach under the radio/cassette player and remove the two retaining screws (see illustration). Pull out the radio and unplug the electrical connector and aerial lead.
3 Refitting is the reverse of removal.

5-door models

4 The radio/cassette player is fitted with special mounting clips, requiring the use of special removal tools, which should be supplied with the vehicle, or may be obtained from an in-car entertainment specialist.
5 Insert the removal rods in the holes provided on the upper and lower edges of the radio/cassette player unit.
6 Slide the removal tools fully into the slots until they locate (see illustration).
7 Withdraw the radio/cassette player from the mounting case, then disconnect the loudspeaker, supply and aerial plugs. Note that some radio units also have a fuse fitted on the rear face.
8 Refitting is a reversal of removal, but push the radio fully into its case until the spring clips are engaged.

Speakers

Front main speakers

9 On 2, 3 and 4-door models, remove the speaker trim cover. Remove the speaker mounting screws, pull out the speaker and unplug the electrical connector (see illustration).
10 On 5-door models, remove the door inner trim panel as described in Chapter 11. Remove the speaker mounting screws, pull out the speaker and unplug the electrical connector.
11 On all models, refitting is the reverse of removal.

Front tweeters

12 Remove the door trim panel (see Chapter 11).

10.2 Reach under the audio unit and remove the retaining screws (arrowed)

10.6 Slide the removal tools into the audio unit

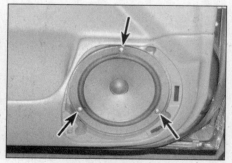

10.9 Remove the screws (arrowed), pull the speaker out and unplug it

11.3 Remove the aerial retaining screws

11.6 Tape the wing to protect it and remove the aerial nut with circlip pliers

11.7 With the ignition key and the radio in the ON position, guide the aerial mast out of the motor assembly

13 Disconnect the tweeter electrical connector.
14 Remove the side mirror trim.
15 Remove the tweeter mounting screws and take it out.
16 Refitting is the reverse of removal.

Rear speakers

17 If you're working on a 2, 3, or 4-door model, remove the rear side trim (Hatchback) or rear shelf (Coupe/Saloon).
18 If you're working on an 5-door Estate, remove the speaker trim cover.
19 If you're working on an 5-door Hatchback, undo the single screw and remove the rear side shelf, then lift off the speaker cover.
20 Remove the speaker mounting screws and lift the speaker out.
21 Refitting is the reverse of removal.

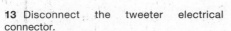

11 Aerial – removal and refitting

2, 3, and 4-door models

Manual aerial

1 Remove the radio/cassette player as described in the previous Section.
2 Connect a piece of string or wire to the aerial lead at the radio end.
3 Remove the mounting screws and pull the aerial out of the body pillar **(see illustration)**.
4 Fasten the wire or string to the lead of the new aerial. Lower the aerial into place while

11.8 Insert the new aerial so that the aerial cable teeth face the rear of the vehicle

pulling the new lead into the pillar with the wire or string.
5 Disconnect the string or wire and connect the aerial lead to the radio. Refit the aerial mounting screws and tighten them securely.

Power aerial mast

6 Tape the wing to protect it from scratches. Remove the nut and spacer **(see illustration)**.
7 Have an assistant switch the radio ON to extend the aerial. Guide the mast as it extends, then remove it from the vehicle **(see illustration)**.
8 Fit the aerial with teeth facing the rear of the vehicle and engage the aerial teeth with the drive cable. Switch the radio ON and let the aerial motor pull the mast into the wing **(see illustration)**.
9 Refit the spacer and aerial nut. **Note:** *If the spacer has a flat seal, it goes inside the collar, below the spacer. If the spacer has an O-ring, it goes on top of the spacer.*

Power aerial motor

10 Remove the luggage compartment side trim panel from the vehicle interior (see Chapter 11, Section 31).
11 Remove the aerial nut and washer **(see illustration 11.6)**. Remove the aerial motor mounting nut **(see illustration)**. Disconnect the electrical connector and aerial lead and withdraw the assembly.
12 Refitting is the reverse of removal.

5-door models

13 Carefully prise off the interior light lens,

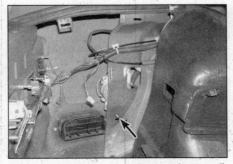

11.11 Remove the mounting nut (arrowed) to detach the aerial motor

and undo the two screws securing the light to the roof. Disconnect the wiring plugs as the light is withdrawn.
14 Prise off the plastic cap, then undo the nut securing the aerial lead.
15 Undo the three nuts and remove the aerial assembly from the roof.
16 Refitting is the reverse of removal.

12 Headlight bulb – renewal

⚠ *Warning: Halogen gas-filled bulbs are under pressure and may shatter if the surface is scratched or the bulb is dropped. Wear eye protection and handle the bulbs carefully, grasping only the base whenever possible. Do not touch the surface of the bulb with your fingers because the oil from your skin could cause it to overheat and fail prematurely. If you do touch the bulb surface, clean it with methylated spirit.*

1 Open the bonnet. **Note:** *On 5-door models, to access the right-hand side headlight bulb, remove the air intake pipe by pulling it straight up. On 2, 3 and 4-door models, to access the left-hand side headlight bulb, remove the power steering reservoir by pulling it up from its mounting bracket.*
2 Reach behind the headlight assembly, unplug the electrical connector, then remove the rubber boot **(see illustration)**.
3 Release the bulbholder retaining clip, then

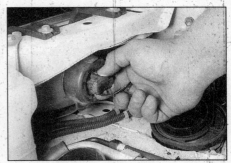

12.2 Unplug the electrical connector and remove the rubber boot

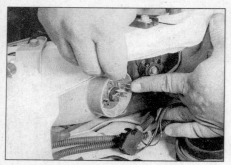

12.3a Release the retaining clip . . .

12.3b . . . then pull the bulb straight out of the housing

13.2a Vertical headlight adjuster (2, 3 and 4-door models) . . .

pull out the bulb/holder assembly **(see illustrations)**.

4 Refitting is the reverse of removal (see **Warning** above).

13 Headlight beam adjustment – general information

1 Accurate adjustment of the headlight beam is only possible using optical beam setting equipment, and this work should therefore be carried out by a Honda dealer or suitably-equipped workshop.

2 For reference, the headlights can be adjusted using the adjuster screws, accessible via the top of each light unit on 5-door models, or from the rear of the headlight on 2, 3, and 4-door models **(see illustrations)**.

3 Some models are equipped with an electrically-operated headlight beam adjustment system which is controlled through the switch in the facia. On these models, ensure that the switch is set to the basic 0 position before adjusting the headlight aim.

14 Headlights – removal and refitting

Removal

1 Unplug the electrical connectors, and remove the halogen bulbs (see Section 12).

2 Remove the front bumper cover (see Chapter 11).

3 Remove the headlight housing mounting bolts/nuts and remove the housing **(see illustrations)**.

Refitting

4 Refitting is the reverse of removal. After you're done, adjust the headlights (see Section 13).

15 Bulb renewal

Front direction indicator

1 If you're renewing the left-hand side bulb, start the engine, turn the wheels all the way to the right and stop the engine. If you're renewing the right-hand side bulb, start the

13.2b . . . and horizontal adjuster

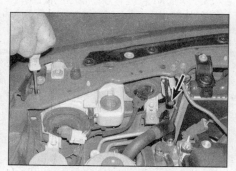

13.2c 5-door models headlight adjusters (arrowed)

14.3a On 2, 3 and 4-door models, remove the bolt at the bottom centre (arrowed) . . .

14.3b . . . at the outside . . .

14.3c . . . and at the top (arrowed)

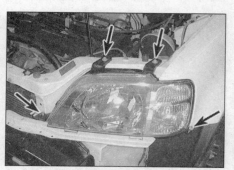

14.3d On 5-door models, remove the headlight retaining bolts (arrowed)

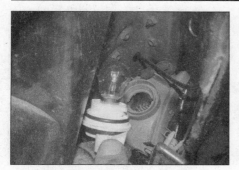

15.2 Pull back the wheelarch liner to expose the front indicator bulbholder

15.5 Disconnect the sidelight bulb connector (arrowed)

15.13 Tail light retaining screws (arrowed)

engine, turn the wheels all the way to the left and stop the engine.

2 Prise off the clips, remove the screws and remove the front section of the inner wheelarch liner **(see illustration)**.

3 Rotate the bulbholder 1/4-turn anti-clockwise and remove it from the housing. Push in on the bulb and turn it anti-clockwise, then pull it out of the bulbholder. Refitting is the reverse of removal.

Sidelight

4 Open the bonnet. **Note:** *On 5-door models, to access the right-hand side bulb, remove the air intake pipe by pulling it straight up. On 2, 3 and 4-door models, to access the left-hand side bulb, remove the power steering reservoir by pulling it up from its mounting bracket.*

5 Reach behind the headlight assembly, and pull the connector from the sidelight bulb **(see illustration)**.

6 Rotate the bulbholder 1/4 turn anti-clockwise and pull it from the headlight shell. The bulb is 'capless' and pulls straight out of the bulbholder.

7 Refitting is the reverse of removal.

Tail/brake/reversing/foglight

4-door Saloon models

8 On these models the rear lights are fitted into the rear wing and the boot lid. For the rear wing lights see Paragraph 17 to 20.

9 To renew the bulb(s) fitted into the boot lid light assembly, open the boot and undo the

single screw securing the cover to the light assembly.

10 Rotate the relevant bulbholder anti-clockwise and pull it from the light.

11 Push in the bulb and turn it anti-clockwise, then pull it from the bulbholder.

12 Refitting is the reverse of removal.

Estate models

13 Open the tailgate, and undo the two screws securing the tail light assembly **(see illustration)**. Manoeuvre the tail light from the quarter panel.

14 Rotate the bulbholder 1/4 turn anti-clockwise, and pull it from the tail light assembly.

15 Push in on the bulb and turn it anti-clockwise, then pull it from the bulbholder.

16 Refitting is the reverse of removal.

All other models

17 Open the boot or rear hatch and remove the access cover.

18 Turn the bulbholder 1/8-turn anti-clockwise and pull it out of the housing **(see illustrations)**.

19 Push in on the bulb and turn it anti-clockwise, then pull it out of the bulbholder.

20 Refitting is the reverse of removal.

High-mounted brake light

2 and 3-door models

21 Remove the two screws and pull the assembly from the rear hatch. Twist the bulbholder anti-clockwise, remove it from the housing and pull out the capless bulb.

22 Refitting is the reverse of removal.

4-door Saloon models

23 Remove the parcel shelf as described in Chapter 11, Section 31.

24 Undo the two screws and remove the light assembly from the parcel shelf.

25 Twist the bulbholder anti-clockwise, remove it from the light unit and pull out the capless bulb.

26 Refitting is the reverse of removal.

5-door models

27 On these models, the high-level brake light is of the LED type. If defective the complete unit must be renewed.

Instrument panel lights

28 To gain access to the instrument panel lights, the instrument cluster will have to be removed first (see Section 9).

29 Rotate the bulbholder anti-clockwise and remove it from the instrument cluster **(see illustration)**.

30 Pull the bulb straight out of the holder.

31 Refitting is the reverse of removal.

Number plate lights

5-door Hatchback models

32 Undo the two screws and remove the lens.

33 The bulb is 'capless' and pulls straight out of the bulbholder.

34 Refitting is the reverse of removal.

All other models

35 Remove the two screws and pull out the lens.

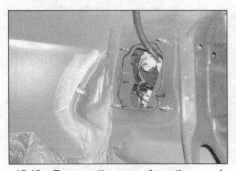

15.18a Remove the cover from the panel to access the bulbs

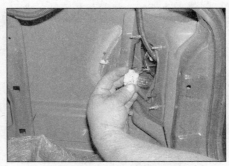

15.18b Rotate the bulbholder anti-clockwise, pull it out and remove the bulb

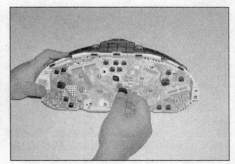

15.29 Depress the bulbholder and turn it anti-clockwise to remove it

15.36 Remove the number plate light and turn the bulbholder anti-clockwise to remove it

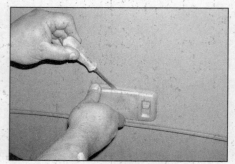

15.39 Carefully prise the interior light lens out to access the bulb

15.42 Push the side repeater light forward, and lever out the rear edge

36 Rotate the bulbholder 1/8-turn anti-clockwise and detach it from the lens housing **(see illustration)**.
37 Pull the bulb straight out of the holder.
38 Refitting is the reverse of removal.

Interior/luggage area lights

39 Carefully prise the lens off for access to the bulb **(see illustration)**.
40 Remove the bulb from the terminals. It may be necessary to prise the bulb out – if this is the case, lever only on the ends of the bulb (otherwise the glass may shatter).
41 Refitting is the reverse of removal.

Side repeater light

42 Gently push the rear edge of the repeater

lens to the front of the vehicle, compressing the retaining clip, and lever the rear edge of the lens from the wing **(see illustration)**.
43 Rotate the bulbholder anti-clockwise and remove it from the lens. The bulb is 'capless' and pull straight out of the bulbholder.
44 Push the new bulb into the holder, and refit the bulbholder into the lens. Check the light for correct operation.
45 Insert the front edge of the lens into the vehicle wing, and push the rear edge in until it clicks into place.

Front foglight

46 Some models are fitted with foglights in the front bumper cover. To renew the bulb on 5-door Hatchback models up to '97 model year, undo the two retaining screws and remove the trim around the light unit. On other models, the trim simply prises out.
47 Undo the three mounting screws and remove the light unit from the bumper. Disconnect the wiring plug.
48 Undo the three screws and remove the cover from the rear of the light unit.
49 Release the retaining clip, and remove the halogen bulb from the light.
50 Refitting is the reverse of removal, noting that the cut-outs in the bulb flange must align with the corresponding lugs in the light fitting.

16 Wiper motor(s) – removal and refitting

Front

1 Remove the windscreen wiper arm **(see illustration)**.
2 Remove the scuttle cover (see Chapter 11).
3 Disconnect the electrical connector from the wiper motor.
4 Undo the four bolts and remove the wiper linkage complete with motor **(see illustration)**.
5 Remove the wiper motor retaining bolts **(see illustration)**.
6 Remove the wiper motor from the wiper linkage assembly.
7 Refitting is the reverse of removal.

Rear

8 Pull the rear wiper arm cover back to access the wiper arm retaining nut. Detach the nut and pull the wiper arm straight off the shaft to remove it **(see illustration)**.
9 Open the rear hatch/tailgate and remove the trim panel (see Section 11 of Chapter 11).
10 Disconnect the electrical connector from the wiper motor.
11 Remove the wiper motor mounting

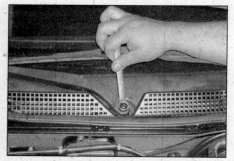

16.1 To remove a wiper arm, remove the nut and pull the arm from the shaft

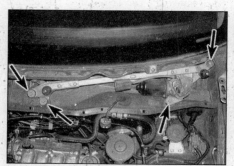

16.4 Remove the wiper-to-body mounting bolts (arrowed) and remove the complete assembly from the vehicle (LHD; RHD is symmetrical)

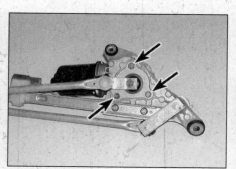

16.5 Remove the motor mounting bolts (arrowed), and remove the motor from the linkage assembly

16.8 Flip up the cover, and remove the wiper arm nut

16.11a Rear wiper motor retaining bolts (arrowed) – Hatchback models

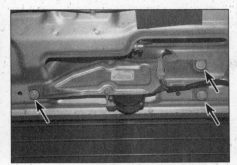

16.11b Rear wiper motor retaining bolts (arrowed) – Estate models

17.2 Horn mounting bolt (arrowed)

bracket bolts and remove the motor **(see illustrations)**.

12 Refitting is the reverse of removal.

17 Horn – removal and refitting

1 Remove the front bumper cover as described in Chapter 11. On post '97 model year vehicles, there is no need to remove the bumper, simply reach through the front grille aperture.

2 Disconnect the electrical connectors and remove the bracket bolt **(see illustration)**.

3 Refitting is the reverse of removal.

18 Cruise control system – description and testing

1 The cruise control system maintains vehicle speed with a servo located in the engine compartment on the driver's side inner wing. An electronic control module controls the operation of the servo. The system consists of the servo, control module (in the passenger compartment fusebox), brake switch, control switches, speed sensor and related circuits

(see illustrations). The servo is connected to the accelerator pedal by a cable. 5-door models use an electronic servo, while 2, 3 and 4-door models use a vacuum-operated servo. Some features of the system require special testers and diagnostic procedures which are beyond the scope of this manual. Listed below are some general procedures that may be used to locate common problems.

2 Locate and check the cruise control system fuses in both the interior fusebox and the underbonnet fusebox (see Section 3). Check the cruise control ON/OFF switch and Set/Resume switch (see Section 6).

3 The brake pedal switch (or stop-lamp switch) deactivates the cruise control system. Have an assistant press the brake pedal while you check the stop-lamp operation.

4 If the brake lights do not operate properly, correct the problem and retest the cruise control.

5 Check the control cable between the cruise control servo and the accelerator pedal and renew as necessary.

6 The cruise control system uses a speed sensing device. The speed sensor is located in the transmission.

7 Test drive the vehicle to determine if the cruise control is now working. If it isn't, take it to a dealer service department or an automotive electrical specialist for further diagnosis.

19 Electric window system – description and testing

Description

1 The electric window system operates electric motors, mounted in the doors, which lower and raise the windows. The system consists of the control switches, the motors, regulators, glass mechanisms and associated wiring.

2 The electric windows can be lowered and raised from the master control switch by the driver or by remote switches located at the individual windows. Each window has a separate motor which is reversible. The position of the control switch determines the polarity and therefore the direction of operation.

3 The circuit is protected by a fuse. Each motor is also equipped with an internal circuit breaker, which prevents one stuck window from disabling the whole system.

4 The electric window system will only operate when the ignition switch is ON. In addition, many models have a window lockout switch at the master control switch which, when activated, disables the switches at the

18.1a On 5-door models, the electronic cruise control servo is located in the left-hand front corner of the engine compartment . . .

18.1b . . . other models use a vacuum-operated cruise control servo

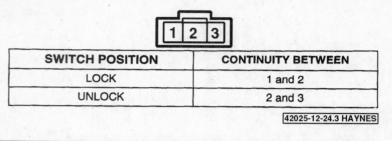

SWITCH POSITION	CONTINUITY BETWEEN
LOCK	1 and 2
UNLOCK	2 and 3

42025-12-24.3 HAYNES

20.3 Central locking switch terminal guide and continuity table

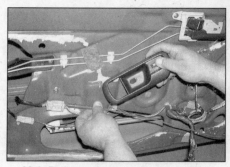

20.6 Remove the door trim panel and check for power to the door lock solenoid while the switch is depressed

rear windows and, sometimes, the switch at the passenger's window also. Always check these items before diagnosing a window problem.

5 These procedures are general in nature, so if you can't find the problem using them, take the vehicle to a dealer service department or automotive electrical specialist.

Testing

6 If the electric windows won't operate, always check the fuse first.

7 If only the rear windows are inoperative, or if the windows only operate from the master control switch, check the rear window lockout switch for continuity in the unlocked position. Renew it if it doesn't have continuity.

8 Check the wiring between the switches and fuse panel for continuity. Repair the wiring, if necessary.

9 If only one window is inoperative from the master control switch, try the other control switch at the window. **Note:** *This doesn't apply to the driver's door window.*

10 If the same window works from one switch, but not the other, check the switch for continuity.

11 If the switch tests OK, check for a short or open in the circuit between the affected switch and the window motor.

12 If one window is inoperative from both switches, remove the trim panel from the affected door and check for voltage at the switch and at the motor while the switch is operated. If a defective switch is suspected, remove the switch and check it for continuity.

13 If voltage is reaching the motor, disconnect the glass from the regulator (see Chapter 11). Move the window up-and-down by hand while checking for binding and damage. Also check for binding and damage to the regulator. If the regulator is not damaged and the window moves up-and-down smoothly, renew the motor. If there's binding or damage, lubricate, repair or renew parts, as necessary. **Note:** *The window motor is an integral part of the window regulator assembly. See Chapter 11 for the removal procedures.*

14 If voltage isn't reaching the motor, check the wiring in the circuit for continuity between the switches and motors. You'll need to consult the wiring diagram for the vehicle. If the circuit is equipped with a relay, check that the relay is earthed properly and receiving voltage.

15 Test the windows after you are done to confirm proper repairs.

20 Central door locking system – description and testing

Description

The central door locking system operates the door lock actuators mounted in each door. The system consists of the switches, actuators, a control unit and associated wiring. Diagnosis can usually be limited to simple checks of the wiring connections and actuators for minor faults which can be easily repaired. Since this system uses an electronic control unit, in-depth diagnosis should be left to a dealership service department or automotive electrical specialist. The door lock control unit is located behind the facia, to the left of the fusebox.

Central door locking systems are operated by bi-directional solenoids located in the doors. The lock switches have two operating positions: Lock and Unlock. When activated, the switch sends a earth signal to the door lock control unit to lock or unlock the doors. Depending on which way the switch is activated, the control unit reverses polarity to the solenoids, allowing the two sides of the circuit to be used alternately as the feed (positive) and earth side.

Some vehicles may have an anti-theft systems incorporated into the door locks. If you are unable to locate the trouble using the following general Steps, consult your a dealer service department or automotive electrical specialist.

Testing

1 Always check the fuse(s) first.

2 Operate the door lock switches in both directions (Lock and Unlock) with the engine off. Listen for the click of the solenoids operating.

3 Test the switches for continuity **(see illustration)**. Renew the switch if there's not continuity in both switch positions.

4 Check the wiring between the switches, control unit and solenoids for continuity. Repair the wiring if there's no continuity.

5 Check for a bad earth connections at the switches or the control unit.

6 If all but one lock solenoids operate, remove the trim panel from the affected door (see Chapter 11) and check for voltage at the solenoid while the lock switch is operated. One of the wires should have voltage in the Lock position; the other should have voltage in the Unlock position **(see illustration)**.

7 If the inoperative solenoid is receiving voltage, renew the solenoid.

8 If the inoperative solenoid isn't receiving voltage, check for an open or short-circuit in the wire between the lock solenoid and the control unit. **Note:** *It's common for wires to break in the portion of the harness between the body and door (opening and closing the door fatigues and eventually breaks the wires).*

21 Electric rear view mirrors – description and testing

1 Electric rear view mirrors use two motors to move the glass; one for up-and-down adjustments and one for left-to-right adjustments.

2 The control switch has a selector portion which sends voltage to the left or right side mirror. With the ignition ON, engine OFF, roll down the windows and operate the mirror control switch through all functions (left-right and up-down) for both the left and right side mirrors.

3 Listen carefully for the sound of the electric motors running in the mirrors.

4 If the motors can be heard but the mirror glass doesn't move, there's probably a problem with the drive mechanism inside the mirror.

5 If the mirrors don't operate and no sound comes from the mirrors, check the fuse (see Section 3).

6 If the fuse is OK, remove the mirror control switch from its mounting without disconnecting the wires attached to it. Turn the ignition ON and check for voltage at the

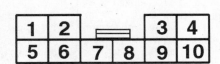

SWITCH POSITION	CONTINUITY BETWEEN
Left	
UP	2 and 5; 3 and 4
DOWN	2 and 3; 4 and 5
LEFT	2 and 3; 4 and 6
RIGHT	2 and 6; 3 and 4
Right	
UP	2 and 9; 3 and 4
DOWN	2 and 3; 4 and 9
LEFT	2 and 3; 4 and 8
RIGHT	2 and 8; 3 and 4

42025-12-25.7A HAYNES

21.7a Electric mirror switch terminal guide and continuity table – 2, 3 and 4-door models

A - - - - - - - - - - - - -▶ J

SWITCH POSITION	CONTINUITY BETWEEN
Left	
UP	J, D and G; I and E
DOWN	I, D and G; J and E
LEFT	I, E and G; J and D
RIGHT	J, E and G; I and D
Right	
UP	J, C and F; I and E
DOWN	I, C and F; J and E
LEFT	I, E and F; J and C
RIGHT	J, E and F; I and C

42025-12-25.7B HAYNES

21.7b Electric mirror switch terminal guide and continuity table – 5-door models

switch. There should be voltage at one terminal. If there's no voltage at the switch, check for an open or short-circuit in the wiring between the fuse panel and the switch.

7 If there's voltage at the switch, disconnect it. Check the switch for continuity in all its operating positions **(see illustrations)**. If the switch does not have continuity, renew it.

8 Reconnect the switch. Locate the wire going from the switch to earth. Leaving the switch connected, connect a bridging wire between this wire and earth. If the mirror works normally with this wire in place, repair the faulty earth connection.

9 If the mirror still doesn't work, remove the cover and check the wires at the mirror for voltage with a test light. Check with ignition ON and the mirror selector switch on the appropriate side. Operate the mirror switch in all its positions. There should be voltage at one of the switch-to-mirror wires in each switch position (except the neutral position).

10 If there's not voltage in each switch position, check the wiring between the mirror and control switch for open and short-circuits.

11 If there's voltage, remove the mirror and test it off the vehicle with bridging wires. Renew the mirror if it fails this test (see Chapter 11).

22 Sunroof motor – removal and refitting

Closing sunroof manually

1 If the motor malfunctions when the roof panel is in the open position, it can be wound shut manually. To do this, undo the circular plug in the centre of the headlining. Insert the cranking tool (from the vehicle tool kit) into the hole at the end of the motor shaft. The tool can then be turned to close the sunroof as required – see Chapter 11, Section 29.

Motor

Removal

2 Ensure that the sunroof is fully closed – refer to paragraph 1 if the motor has failed. Disconnect the battery negative lead (refer to Chapter 5A).

3 Remove the complete headlining as described in Chapter 11, Section 31.

4 Disconnect the motor wiring plug.

5 Undo the mounting screws/nuts and remove the motor. **Note:** On 2, 3 and 4-door models the motor is secured by two bolts as well as three nuts. On other models, the motor is secured by three bolts.

Refitting

6 Refit in the reverse order of removal, noting the following points:

a) *As with removal, it is important that the roof panel be in the closed position to ensure correct engagement. If the motor was activated whilst it was removed, or if a new motor is being fitted, it must be set for correct engagement before fitting. To do this, connect up the switch wiring to it and turn the switch to the closed position. This will activate the motor so that it is set at the closed position, ready for fitting.*

b) *Check for satisfactory operation of the sunroof on completion.*

23 Airbag system – general information and precautions

⚠ *Warning: Before carrying out any operations on the airbag system, disconnect the battery negative terminal (see Chapter 5A), and wait at least 3 minutes before starting any operation. Ensure that the battery negative lead cannot accidentally be reconnected. Before working on the airbag(s) or seat belt pretensioners, ensure you are electrostatically discharged, by touching a suitable metal part, eg, a metal bench, or mains water pipe.*

• *Do not use a 'code saver' device when working on the supplementary restraint system. When operations are complete, make sure no one is inside the vehicle when the battery is reconnected.*

• *Note that the airbag(s) must not be subjected to temperatures in excess of 90°C (194°F). When the airbag is removed, ensure that it is stored the correct way up to prevent possible inflation.*

• *Do not allow any solvents or cleaning agents to contact the airbag assemblies. They must be cleaned using only a damp cloth.*

• *The airbags and control unit are both sensitive to impact. If either is dropped or damaged they should be renewed.*

• *Disconnect the airbag control unit wiring plug prior to using arc-welding equipment on the vehicle.*

23.8 To disable the driver's airbag, remove the access panel on the steering wheel and disconnect the 2-pin airbag connector – if equipped with a red shorting connector (arrowed), install the shorting connector in the airbag connector

1 All models are equipped with a Supplemental Restraint System (SRS), more commonly known as an airbag. Some models have two airbags, one for the driver and one for the front seat passenger. The SRS system is designed to protect the driver (and passenger) from serious injury in the event of a head-on or frontal collision.

2 The SRS system consists of an SRS unit – which contains an impact sensor, safing sensor, self-diagnosis circuit and a back-up power circuit – located under the dash, right in front of the floor console, an airbag assembly in the centre of the steering wheel and a second airbag assembly for the front seat passenger, located in the top of the facia right above the glovebox. Some models are equipped with front seat belt pretensioner units which are similar in operation to an airbag. During an impact that would trigger the airbag system, the airbag control unit also activates the seatbelt pretensioners. When activated, the tensioners instantly take up the slack in the seat belts, preparing the driver and front seat passenger for impact.

Operation

3 For the airbag(s) to deploy, the impact and safing sensors must be activated. When this condition occurs, the circuit to the airbag inflator is closed and the airbag inflates. If the battery is destroyed by the impact, or is too low to power the inflator, a back-up power unit inside the SRS unit provides power.

Self-diagnosis system

4 A self-diagnosis circuit in the SRS unit displays a light when the ignition switch is turned to the ON position. If the system is operating normally, the light should go out after about six seconds. If the light doesn't come on, or doesn't go out after six seconds, or if it comes on while you're driving the vehicle, there's a malfunction in the SRS system. Have it inspected and repaired as soon as possible. Do not attempt to diagnose or service the SRS system yourself. Even a small mistake could cause the SRS system to malfunction when you need it.

Servicing components near the SRS system

5 There are times when you need to remove the steering wheel, radio or service other components on or near the dashboard or front seats. At these times, you'll be working around components and wire harnesses for the SRS system. Do not disconnect any of the SRS system electrical connectors unless absolutely necessary. And do not use electrical test equipment on SRS wires or components. **ALWAYS DISABLE THE SRS SYSTEM BEFORE WORKING NEAR THE SRS SYSTEM COMPONENTS OR RELATED WIRING.**

Disabling the SRS system

6 Disconnect the battery negative cable (see Chapter 5A), then disconnect the positive cable and wait three minutes.

7 Carefully disconnect the airbag system connectors as described in the following steps.

Driver's airbag

8 Remove the access panel on the steering wheel below the airbag (see illustration).

9 Disconnect the driver's airbag module two-pin connector.

10 On 1995 5-door models, remove the red shorting connector from the holder and insert it into the airbag side of the connector. 1996 and later models are automatically shorted when disconnected.

Passenger's airbag

11 Remove the glovebox (see Chapter 11, Section 23).

12 Disconnect the passenger's airbag module two-pin connector (see illustration). On 1995 5-door models remove the red shorting connector from the holder and insert it into the airbag side of the connector. 1996 and later models are automatically shorted when disconnected.

Front seat belt pretensioners

13 Remove the centre B-pillar lower trim panel (see Chapter 11, Section 31).

14 Disconnect the seat belt pretensioner two-pin connector (see illustration).

Enabling the SRS system

15 After you've disabled the SRS system and performed the necessary service, reconnect the two-pin airbag module and seat belt pretensioner connectors. Refit the cover to the underside of the steering wheel, refit the glovebox and refit the centre pillar lower trim panels as required.

16 Make sure the ignition switch is in the OFF position.

17 Attach the positive battery cable first, then the negative battery cable (see Chapter 5A).

Airbag removal and refitting

⚠ *Warning: Always use extra caution when handling an airbag module. When carrying an airbag module, keep the trim side facing away from your body. Store the airbag module in a safe location with the trim side facing up, never place the airbag module on the floor or a bench with the trim side down.*

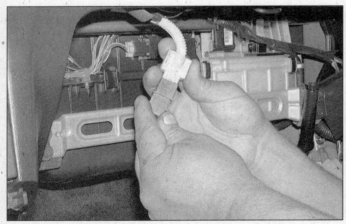

23.12 When disabling the passenger's airbag, unplug the 2-pin connector from the SRS main harness

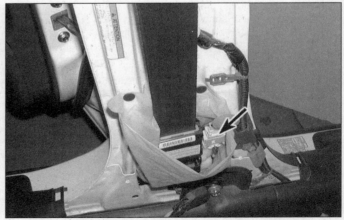

23.14 Disconnect the tensioner 2-pin plug (arrowed)

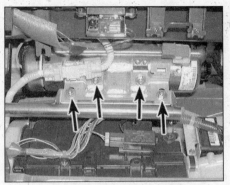

23.20 Typical passenger's side airbag mounting screws (arrowed)

18 Disable the SRS system (see above).
19 To remove the driver's side airbag, refer to *Steering wheel – removal and refitting* in Chapter 10.
20 To remove the passenger's side airbag, remove the passenger side glovebox, remove the mounting nuts and carefully remove the airbag module from the facia **(see illustration)**.
21 Refitting is the reverse of removal. Enable the SRS system as described above.

24 Anti-theft alarm system – general information

An engine immobiliser is fitted as standard, and a volumetric sensing perimeter alarm is available as an option.

Should the system(s) become faulty, the vehicle should be taken to a Honda dealer for examination. They will have access to a special diagnostic tester which will quickly trace any fault present in the system.

25 Clock – removal and refitting

Removal

2, 3 and 4-door models

1 Remove the heater control panel as described in Chapter 3.
2 Disconnect the wiring plug from the rear of the clock.
3 Undo the two screws and remove the clock from the control panel.

5-door models

4 Remove the front centre console as described in Chapter 11.
5 Disconnect the wiring plug from the rear of the clock.
6 Undo the two screws and remove the clock from the console.

Refitting

7 Refitting is a reversal of removal.

26 Wiring diagrams – general information

Since it isn't possible to include all wiring diagrams for every year and model covered by this manual, the following diagrams are those that are typical and most commonly needed.

Prior to troubleshooting any circuits, check the fuses to make sure they're in good condition. Make sure the battery is properly charged and check the cable connections.

When checking a circuit, make sure that all connectors are clean, with no broken or loose terminals. When unplugging a connector, do not pull on the wires. Pull only on the connector housing.

HONDA CIVIC 1995 to 2001 wiring diagrams
3 door, 4 door and coupé models

Diagram 1

Key to symbols

Bulb	
Switch	
Multiple contact switch (ganged)	
Fuse/fusible link and current rating	F5 30A
Resistor	
Variable resistor	
Connecting wires	
Plug and socket contact	
Item no.	2
Pump/motor	M
Earth point and location	E12
Gauge/meter	
Diode	
Wire splice or soldered joint	
Solenoid actuator	
Light emitting diode (LED)	
Wire colour and wire size (brown with black tracer, 4mm²)	Br/Sw 4
Screened cable	

Dashed outline denotes part of a
larger item, containing in this case
an electronic or solid state device.
2 - unspecified connector
pin 2.
182 1 - Connector C182, pin 1.

Earth points

E1	Battery earth	E7	LH engine bulkhead
E2	RH wing	E8	LH wing
E3	Behind dashboard	E9	Behind dashboard LH centre
E4	Rear boot bulkhead	E10	RH front engine compartment
E5	Behind dashboard RH centre	E11	Engine rear
E6	Drivers footwell	E12	Drivers door sill

Key to circuits

Diagram 1	Information for wiring diagrams
Diagram 2	Front and rear wash/wipe, airbag, clock, electric windows and cigarette lighter
Diagram 3	Central locking, sunroof and ABS
Diagram 4	Interior lights, headlights, sidelights, licence plate light and tail lights, brake light, control illumination and horn
Diagram 5	Headlight leveling, direction indicator lights, integrated control unit power hazard warning, reverse lights, foglights and heated rear window
Diagram 6	Radio, electric windows and heater blower
Diagram 7	Air conditioning, engine cooling fan, charging system, Cruise control, starting and ignition system
Diagram 8	Instrument module

Fuse tables

Engine fuse box

Fuses	Rating	Circuit protected
F41	80A	Power distribution
F42	40A	Ignition switch
F43	7.5A	Interior light, data link connector
F44	15A	Fuel injection relay
F45	-	Not used
F46	40A	Electric windows
F47	7.5A	Radio, automatic transmission, clock, engine control module
F48	30A	Passenger fuse box, headlights
F49	-	Not used
F50	30A	Heated rear window
F51	20A	Central locking, sunroof
F52	15A	Horn, ABS
F53	10A	Direction indicators
F54	40A	Passenger fuse box
F55	40A	Blower motor
F56	20A	Air conditioning
F57	20A	Radiator fan motor

ABS fuse box

Fuses	Rating	Circuit protected
F61	40A	ABS pump
F62	7.5A	ABS control module
F63	20A	ABS control module

Passenger fuse box

Fuses	Rating	Circuit protected
F1	-	Not used
F2	-	Not used
F3	10A	Rear window wiper, washer
F4	10A	RH high beam
F5	10A	LH high beam
F6	-	Not used
F7	20A	Electric windows
F8	20A	Electric windows
F9	15A	Ignition coil
F10	20A	Electric windows
F11	20A	Electric windows
F12	7.5A	Direction indicators
F13	15A	Engine control module, airbag
F14	7.5A	Cruise control, central locking
F15	7.5A	Charging and starting
F16	7.5A	ABS, heated rear window
F17	-	Not used
F18	-	Not used
F19	7.5A	Reversing light, interlock unit
F20	7.5A	Rear fog lights
F21	10A	RH low beam
F22	10A	LH low beam
F23	10A	Airbag
F24	7.5A	Sunroof, headlight adjuster, electric windows
F25	-	Not used
F26	20A	Windscreen wash/wipe, integrated control unit
F27	10A	Cigarette lighter
F29	7.5A	Integrated control unit
F30	7.5A	Instrument lights, light dimmer
F31	-	Not used
F32	7.5A	Parking lights, tail lights, number plate lights
F33	7.5A	Light switch

MTS
H32644

Wire colours

Br	Brown	LGn	Light green
Bl	Blue	Gr	Gray
LBl	Light blue	Or	Orange
Ro	Red	Pk	Pink
Ge	Yellow	Pu	Purple
Gn	Green	Sw	Black
		Ws	White

MTS
H32645

Key to items

1 Battery
2 Engine fuse box
3 Passenger fuse box
4 Ignition switch
5 Intergrated control unit
6 Data link connector
7 Cigarette lighter
8 Washer pump
9 Windscreen wiper
10 Wiper switch
11 Rear wiper controller
12 Rear washer pump
13 Rear wiper switch
14 Rear wiper motor
15 Clock
16 Drivers door switch
17 Drivers airbag
18 Passengers airbag
19 Memory erase connector
20 Service check connector
21 Airbag sensor module
22 Clock spring
23 Power mirror switch
24 Retractable mirror unit
25 LH power mirror
26 RH power mirror

Diagram 2

Wash/wipe

Cigarette lighter

Clock

Airbags

Power mirrors

See diagram 8 Instrument module

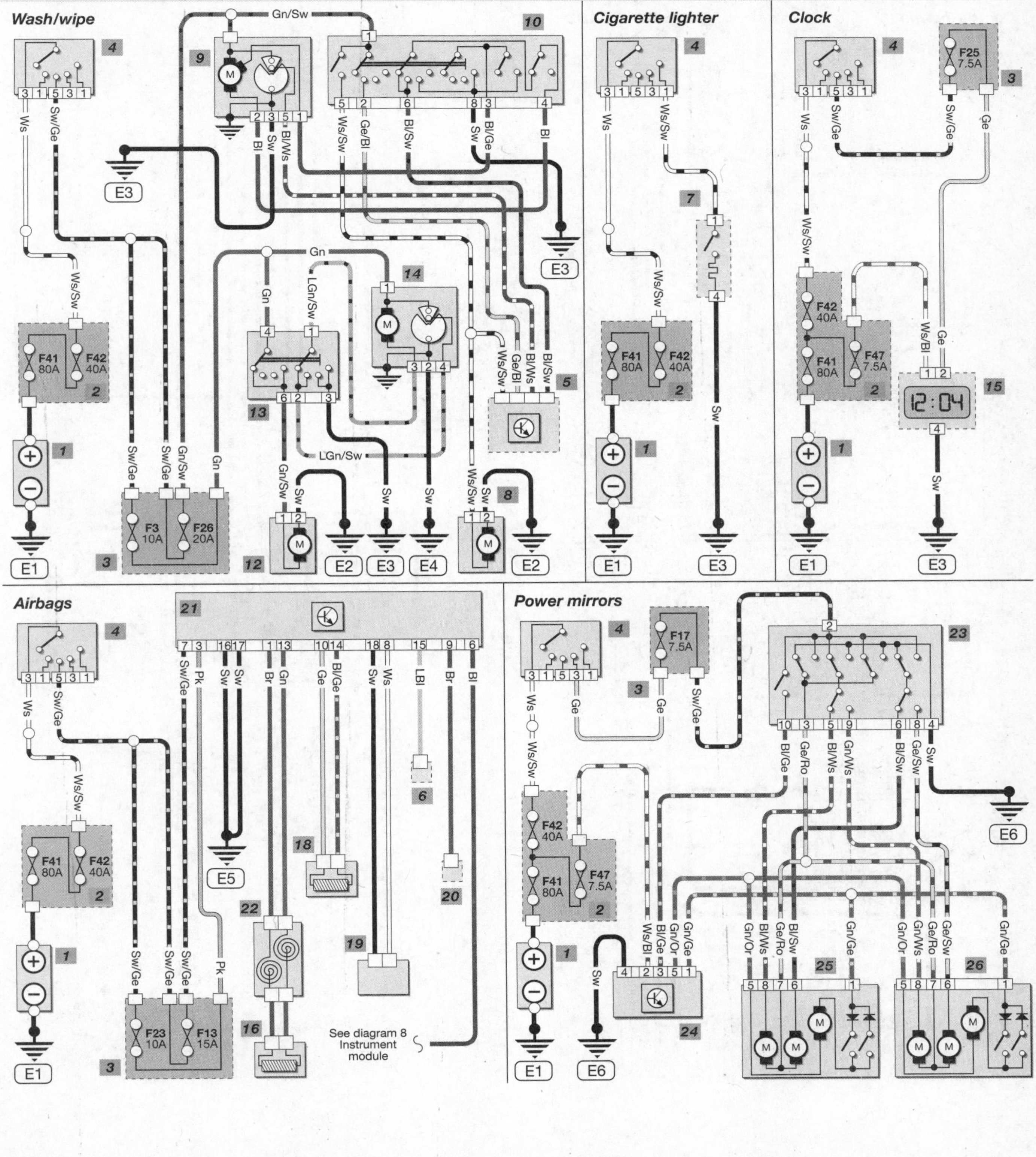

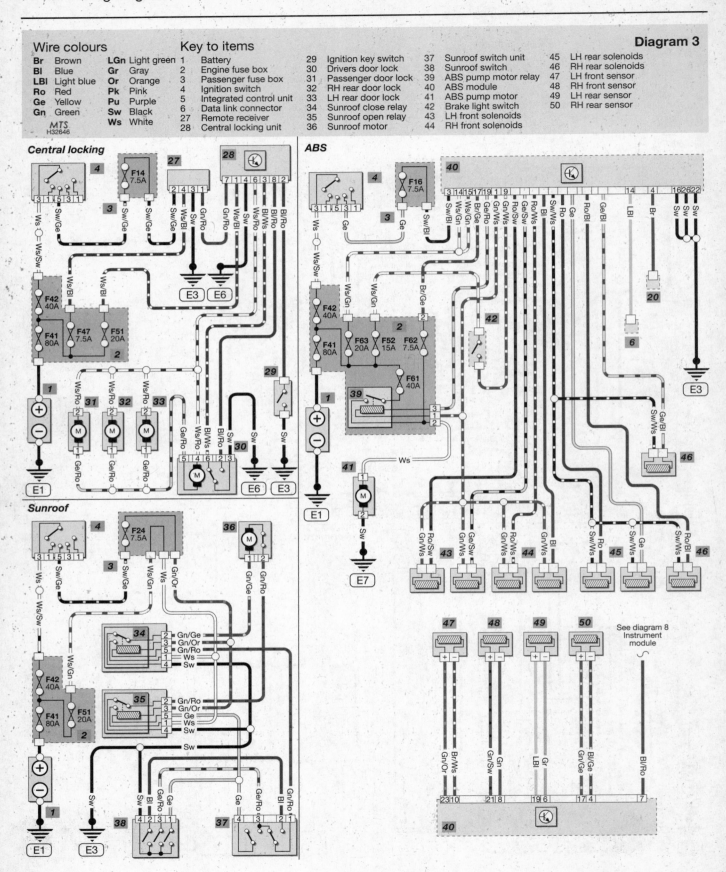

Wire colours

Br Brown
Bl Blue
LBl Light blue
Ro Red
Ge Yellow
Gn Green

LGn Light green
Gr Gray
Or Orange
Pk Pink
Pu Purple
Sw Black
Ws White

MTS
H32646

Key to items

1 Battery
2 Engine fuse box
3 Passenger fuse box
4 Ignition switch
5 Integrated control unit
6 Data link connector
27 Remote receiver
28 Central locking unit

29 Ignition key switch
30 Drivers door lock
31 Passenger door lock
32 RH rear door lock
33 LH rear door lock
34 Sunroof close relay
35 Sunroof open relay
36 Sunroof motor

37 Sunroof switch unit
38 Sunroof switch
39 ABS pump motor relay
40 ABS module
41 ABS pump motor
42 Brake light switch
43 LH front solenoids
44 RH front solenoids

45 LH rear solenoids
46 RH rear solenoids
47 LH front sensor
48 RH front sensor
49 LH rear sensor
50 RH rear sensor

Diagram 3

Central locking

ABS

Sunroof

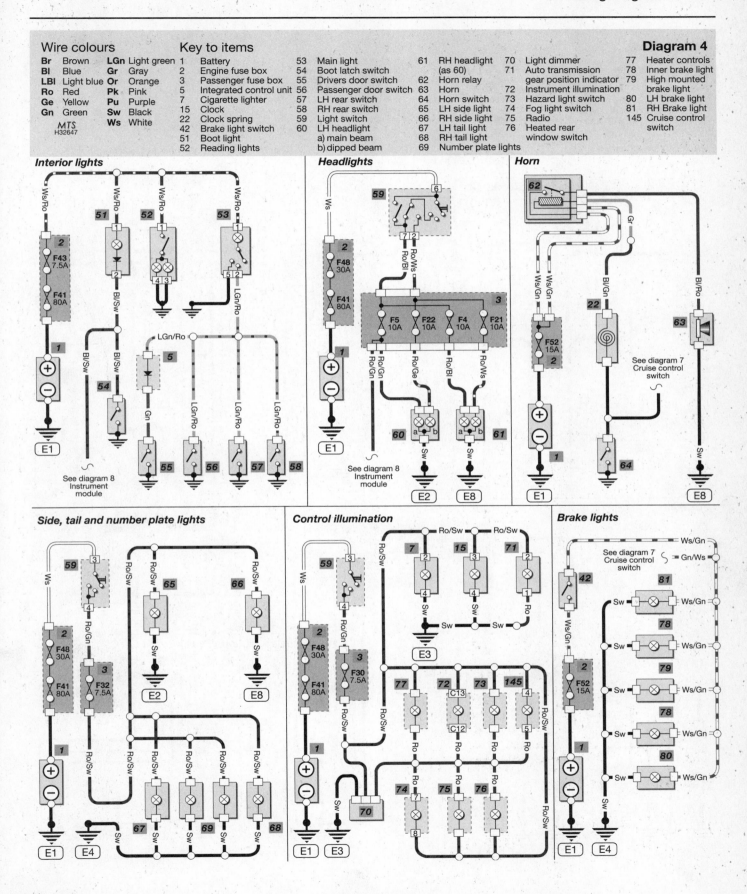

Diagram 4

Wire colours

Br	Brown	**LGn**	Light green
Bl	Blue	**Gr**	Gray
LBl	Light blue	**Or**	Orange
Ro	Red	**Pk**	Pink
Ge	Yellow	**Pu**	Purple
Gn	Green	**Sw**	Black
		Ws	White

MTS
H32647

Key to items

1 Battery
2 Engine fuse box
3 Passenger fuse box
5 Integrated control unit
7 Cigarette lighter
15 Clock
22 Clock spring
42 Brake light switch
51 Boot light
52 Reading lights

53 Main light
54 Boot latch switch
55 Drivers door switch
56 Passenger door switch
57 LH rear switch
58 RH rear switch
59 Light switch
60 LH headlight
   a) main beam
   b) dipped beam

61 RH headlight
   (as 60)
62 Horn relay
63 Horn
64 Horn switch
65 LH side light
66 RH side light
67 LH tail light
68 RH tail light
69 Number plate lights

70 Light dimmer
71 Auto transmission
   gear position indicator
72 Instrument illumination
73 Hazard light switch
74 Fog light switch
75 Radio
76 Heated rear
   window switch

77 Heater controls
78 Inner brake light
79 High mounted
   brake light
80 LH brake light
81 RH Brake light
145 Cruise control
    switch

Interior lights

Headlights

Horn

See diagram 8
Instrument
module

See diagram 8
Instrument
module

See diagram 7
Cruise control
switch

Side, tail and number plate lights

Control illumination

Brake lights

See diagram 7
Cruise control
switch

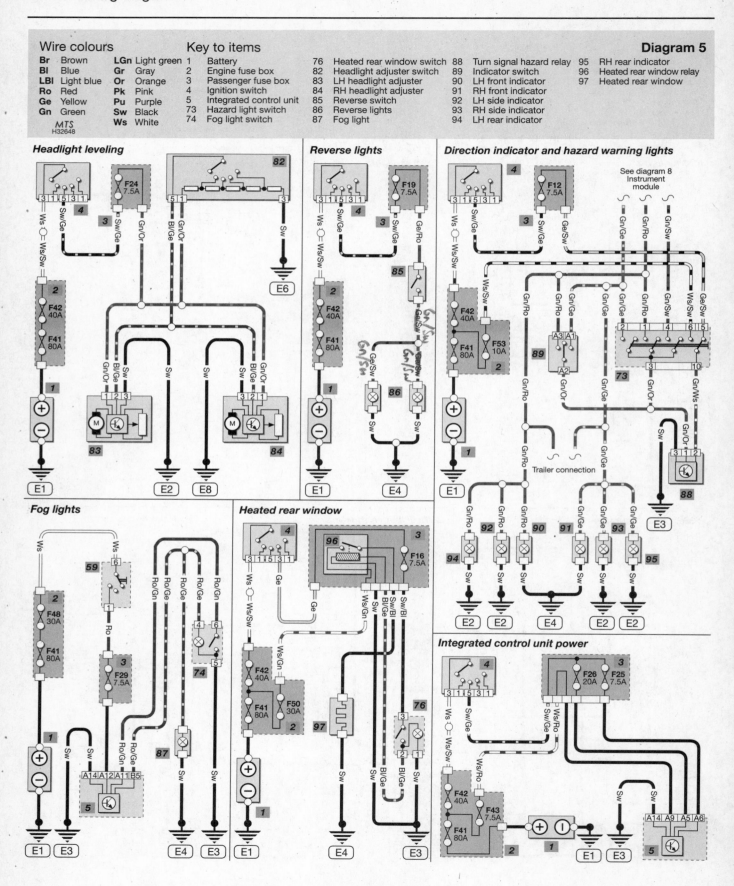

Wire colours

Br	Brown	**LGn**	Light green
Bl	Blue	**Gr**	Gray
LBl	Light blue	**Or**	Orange
Ro	Red	**Pk**	Pink
Ge	Yellow	**Pu**	Purple
Gn	Green	**Sw**	Black
		Ws	White

MTS
H32648

Key to items

1	Battery
2	Engine fuse box
3	Passenger fuse box
4	Ignition switch
5	Integrated control unit
73	Hazard light switch
74	Fog light switch
76	Heated rear window switch
82	Headlight adjuster switch
83	LH headlight adjuster
84	RH headlight adjuster
85	Reverse switch
86	Reverse lights
87	Fog light
88	Turn signal hazard relay
89	Indicator switch
90	LH front indicator
91	RH front indicator
92	LH side indicator
93	RH side indicator
94	LH rear indicator
95	RH rear indicator
96	Heated rear window relay
97	Heated rear window

Diagram 5

Headlight leveling

Reverse lights

Direction indicator and hazard warning lights

Fog lights

Heated rear window

Integrated control unit power

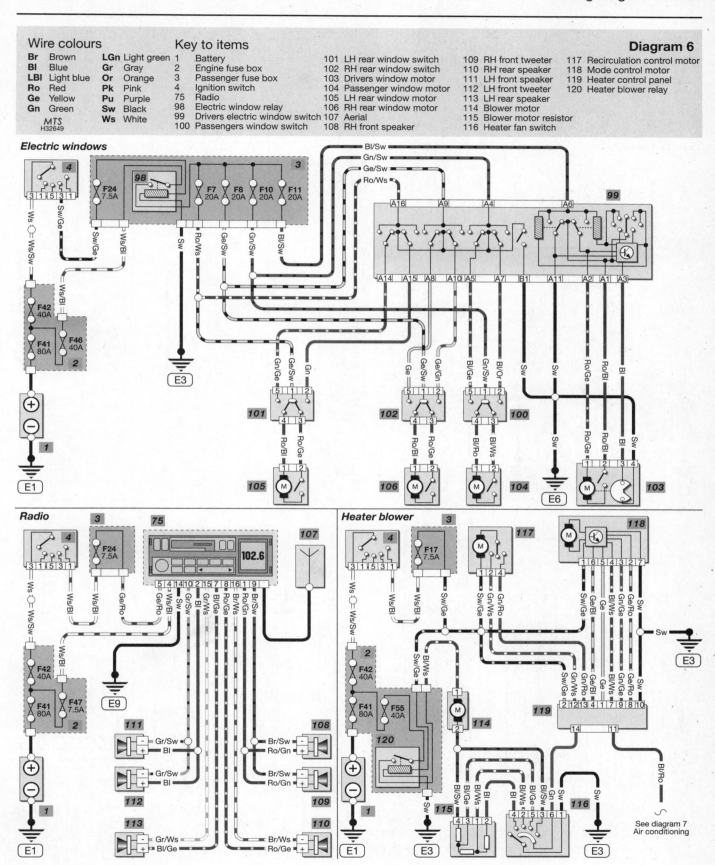

Diagram 6

Wire colours

Br Brown
Bl Blue
LBl Light blue
Ro Red
Ge Yellow
Gn Green

LGn Light green
Gr Gray
Or Orange
Pk Pink
Pu Purple
Sw Black
Ws White

MTS
H32649

Key to items

1 Battery
2 Engine fuse box
3 Passenger fuse box
4 Ignition switch
75 Radio
98 Electric window relay
99 Drivers electric window switch
100 Passengers window switch

101 LH rear window switch
102 RH rear window switch
103 Drivers window motor
104 Passenger window motor
105 LH rear window motor
106 RH rear window motor
107 Aerial
108 RH front speaker

109 RH front tweeter
110 RH rear speaker
111 LH front speaker
112 LH front tweeter
113 LH rear speaker
114 Blower motor
115 Blower motor resistor
116 Heater fan switch

117 Recirculation control motor
118 Mode control motor
119 Heater control panel
120 Heater blower relay

Electric windows

Radio

Heater blower

See diagram 7
Air conditioning

Wire colours

Br	Brown	LGn	Light green
Bl	Blue	Gr	Gray
LBl	Light blue	Or	Orange
Ro	Red	Pk	Pink
Ge	Yellow	Pu	Purple
Gn	Green	Sw	Black
		Ws	White

MTS
H32650

Key to items

1 Battery
2 Engine fuse box
3 Passenger fuse box
4 Ignition switch
22 Clock spring
42 Brake switch
121 Compressor clutch relay
122 Condenser fan relay
123 Condenser fan
124 Compressor clutch
125 A/C thermostat
126 A/C pressure switch
127 Radiator fan relay
128 Radiator fan motor
129 Engine coolant
    temperature switch
130 Starter motor
131 Auto gear position switch
132 Distributor
133 Cruise control module
134 Set/resume switch
135 Cruise control switch
136 Cruise control actuator
137 Gear position switch*
137 Clutch switch**
138 Electrical load detector
139 Alternator

★   Automatic only
★★ Manual only

Diagram 7

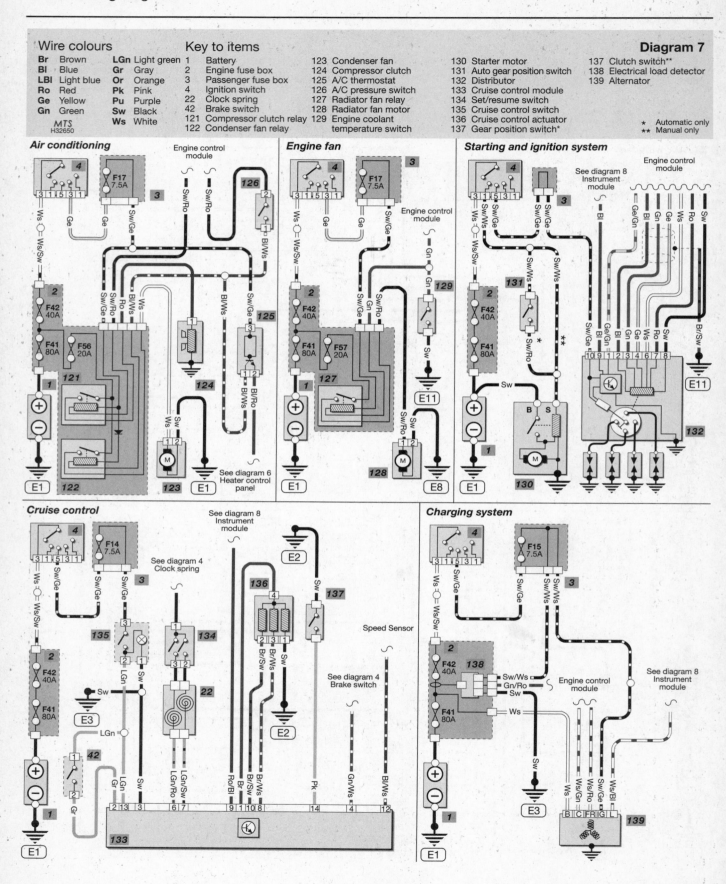

Air conditioning

Engine fan

Starting and ignition system

Cruise control

Charging system

Wire colours

Br	Brown	**LGn**	Light green
Bl	Blue	**Gr**	Gray
LBl	Light blue	**Or**	Orange
Ro	Red	**Pk**	Pink
Ge	Yellow	**Pu**	Purple
Gn	Green	**Sw**	Black
		Ws	White

MTS
H32651

Key to items

1 Battery
2 Engine fuse box
3 Passenger fuse box
4 Ignition switch
5 Integrated control unit
140 Instrument module
  a) charge indicator
  b) speedometer
  c) tachometer
  d) engine coolant
    temperature gauge

140 Instrument module cont.
  e) fuel gauge
  f) low fuel indicator
  g) high beam indicator
  h) LH turn indicator
  i) RH turn indicator
  j) brake fault indicator
  k) boot open indicator
  l) oil pressure indicator
  m) malfunction indicator
  n) seat belt indicator

140 Instrument module cont.
  o) airbag fault indicator
  p) ABS indicator
  q) cruise control light or
    economy indicator
  s) hazard warning light
  r) immobiliser indicator
141 Vehicle speed sensor
142 Engine coolant
    temperature sensor
143 Fuel unit

144 Brake fluid level switch
145 Hand brake switch
146 Oil pressure switch
147 Drivers seat belt switch

Diagram 8

Instrument module

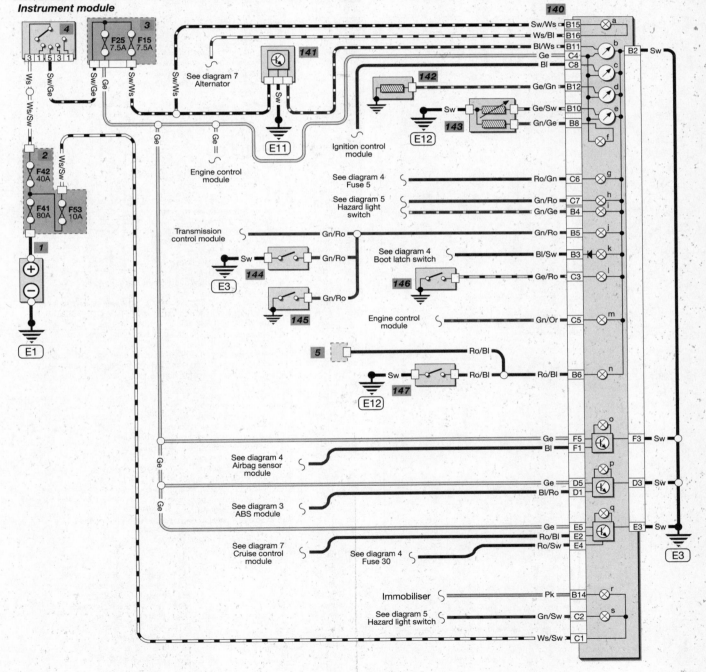

Civic 5 door and Aerodeck wiring diagrams

Diagram 1

Key to symbols

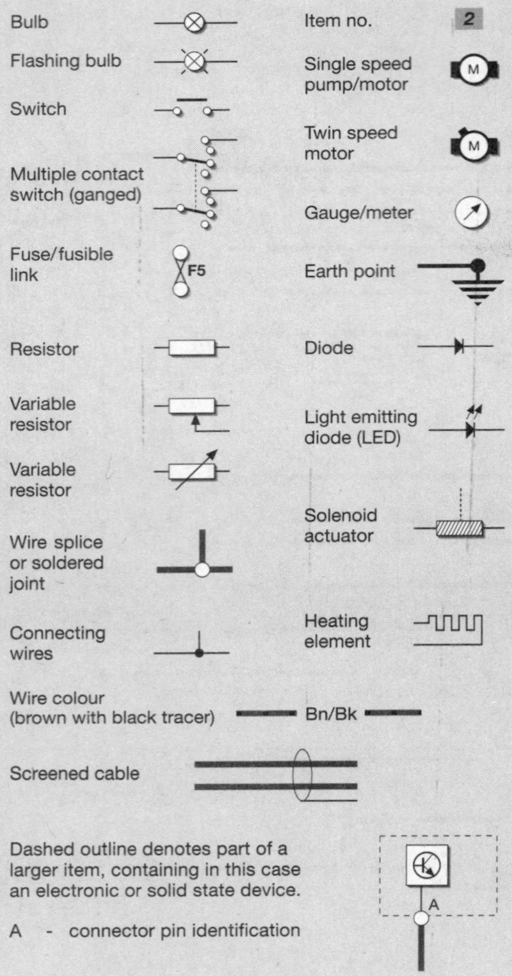

Bulb	⊗	Item no.	2
Flashing bulb	⊗	Single speed pump/motor	Ⓜ
Switch		Twin speed motor	Ⓜ
Multiple contact switch (ganged)		Gauge/meter	⊘
Fuse/fusible link	F5	Earth point	
Resistor		Diode	
Variable resistor		Light emitting diode (LED)	
Variable resistor		Solenoid actuator	
Wire splice or soldered joint		Heating element	
Connecting wires			
Wire colour (brown with black tracer)	Bn/Bk		
Screened cable			

Dashed outline denotes part of a larger item, containing in this case an electronic or solid state device.

A - connector pin identification

Key to circuits

Diagram 1 Information for wiring diagrams.
Diagram 2 Starting, charging, horn, auto.trans. shift lever position indicator, cigar lighter & clock.
Diagram 3 Instrument cluster.
Diagram 4 Side, tail, stop, reversing & headlights, front & rear foglights (1995 model).
Diagram 5 Front & rear foglights (Aerodeck & models from 1996), headlight levelling, direction indicators & hazard warning lights.
Diagram 6 Interior lighting, glove box light, interior light dimmer & integrated control unit (1995 model).
Diagram 7 Integrated control unit (Aerodeck & models from 1996), heated rear window, engine cooling fan & radio/cassette.
Diagram 8 Heater blower/air conditioning, sunroof & headlight levelling.
Diagram 9 Front & rear wash/wipe & safety restraint system.
Diagram 10 Electric mirrors, electric windows & central locking.

Engine fusebox

Fuse	Rating	Circuit protected
F31	15A	Fuel injection main relay, immobiliser
F32	7.5A	Engine management control unit, clock, radio/cassette memory
F33	30A	Heated rear window
F34	30A	Engine cooling fan
F35	20A	A/C condenser fan & compressor
F36	50A	Passenger fusebox
F37	30A	Heater blower motor
F38	-	Not used
F39	50A	Ignition switch
F40	40A	Integrated control unit, rear fog light, light switch
F41	100/80A	Battery power distribution
F42	20A	Horn relay, alarm, horn, stop lights
F43	10A	Hazard warning lights, direction indicators, alarm, immobiliser warning light
F44	-	Not used
F45	-	Not used
F46	-	Not used

Passenger fusebox

Fuse	Rating	Circuit protected
F1	30A	Sunroof
F2	20A	Headlight washer
F3	7.5A	Interior lighting, data link connector, ignition lock illumination, central locking remote receiver
F4	20A	RH rear electric window
F5	20A	Driver's electric window, electric window control unit
F6	20A	Central locking control unit, alarm
F7	20A	LH rear electric window
F8	20A	Passenger's electric window
F9	10A	RH headlight high beam
F10	10A	LH headlight high beam, high beam warning light
F11	15A	Front foglights
F12	15A	Inertia switch, vehicle speed sensor, alternator & instruments
F13	7.5A	Electric mirrors, heated rear window warning light, A/C switch indicator light, A/C recirculation motor, A/C thermostat, A/C compressor clutch relay, A/C condenser fan relay, engine cooling fan relay, heater blower relay
F14	20A	Sunroof relays, front & rear wash/wipe, electric window relay
F15	10A	Clock, direction indicators/hazard warning lights, instruments, A/T gear position indicator, headlight levelling, reversing lights
F16	10A	ABS
F17	10A	Integrated control unit
F18	7.5A	Engine management
F19	10A	Instrument illumination, glove box light, interior lighting dimmer, switch illumination, cigar lighter, side & tail lights, number plate lights, integrated control unit
F20	7.5A	Rear foglight, headlight washer control unit
F21	10A	RH headlight dip beam
F22	10A	LH headlight dip beam
F23	15A	Radio/cassette, cigar lighter
F24	15A	Safety restraint system, inertia switch, vehicle speed sensor, alternator & instrument cluster
F25	10A	Safety restraint system
F26	15A	Alternator, vehicle speed sensor, instrument cluster
F27	10A	ABS

Earth locations

E1	Near battery	E11	Behind instrument cluster
E2	Behind LH headlight	E12	Under centre console
E3	RH inner wing	E13	Near LH wheel arch
E4	Behind front bumber LHS	E14	Top of RHS kick panel
E5	Engine bulkhead near steering rack	E15	Under driver's seat
E6	LH front inner wing	E16	Near RH rear wheel arch
E7	RH front inner wing	E17	LHS tailgate
E8	RH front inner wing	E18	LH rear of roof
E9	'A' pillar RHS	E19	RHS lower tailgate
E10	'A' pillar RHS		

H32662

Wire colours

Bk	Black	Rd	Red
Wh	White	Pk	Pink
Bu	Blue	Gr	Grey
Gn	Green	Bn	Brown
Ye	Yellow	Lt.Gn	Light green
Or	Orange	Lt.Bu	Light blue

* 1995 model only
** Aerodeck only

Key to items

1 Battery
2 Ignition switch
3 Engine fusebox
4 Passenger fusebox
5 Starter motor
6 Alternator
7 Starter relay
8 Horn
9 Horn relay
10 Steering wheel slip ring
11 Steering wheel clock spring
12 Horn switch
13 Auto.trans. shift lever position indicator (in instrument cluster)
14 Auto.trans. shift lever position switch
15 Auto.trans. switch stage illumination
16 Cigar lighter
17 Clock
18 Neutral position switch

Diagram 2

H32663

Starting & charging

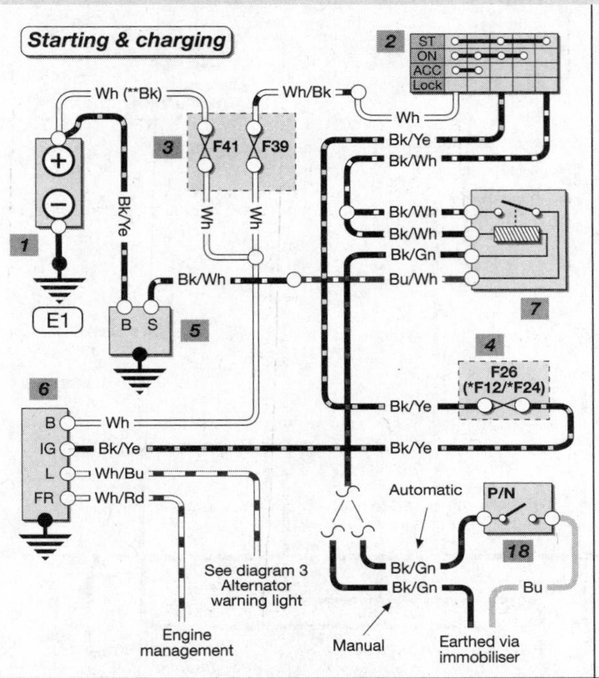

Auto. trans. shift lever position indicator

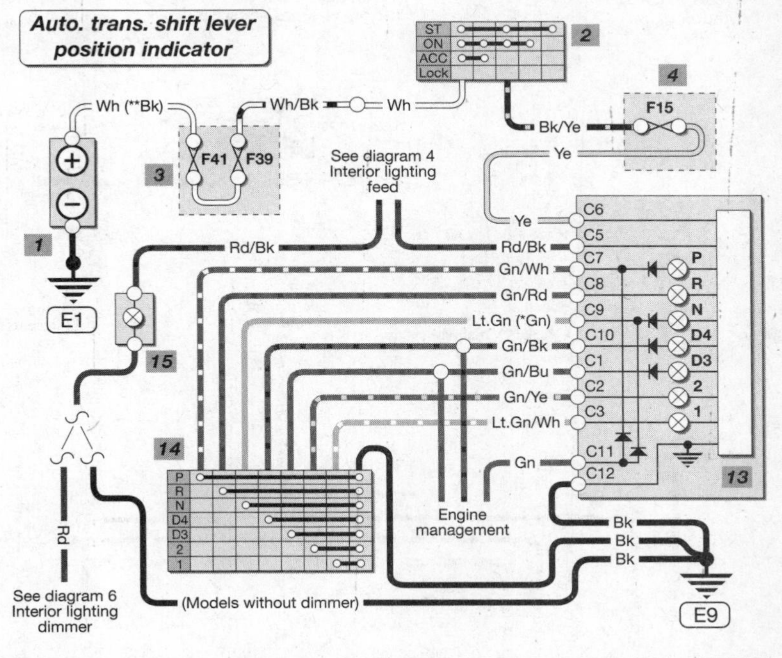

Horn - without airbag

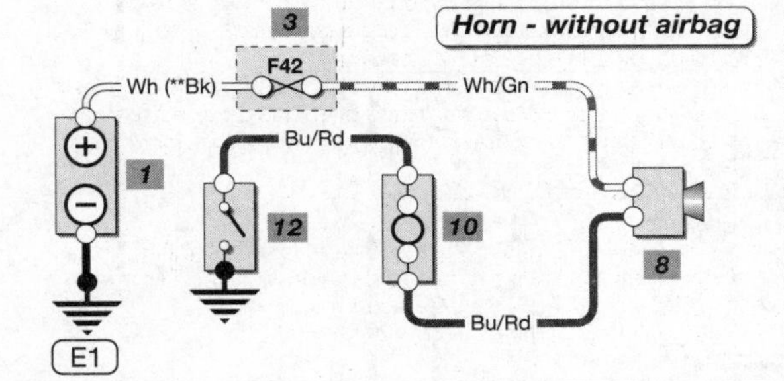

Horn - with airbag

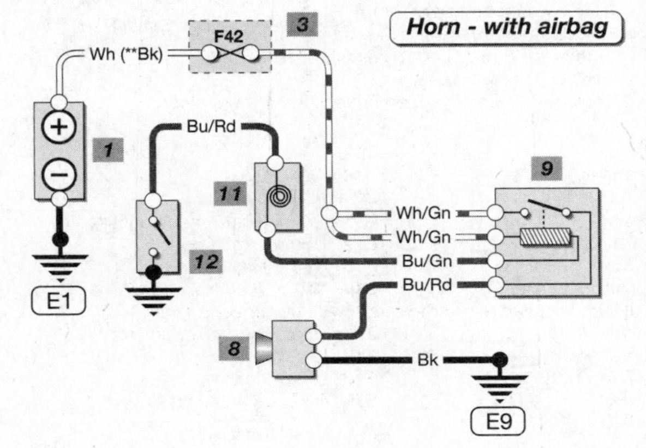

Cigar lighter

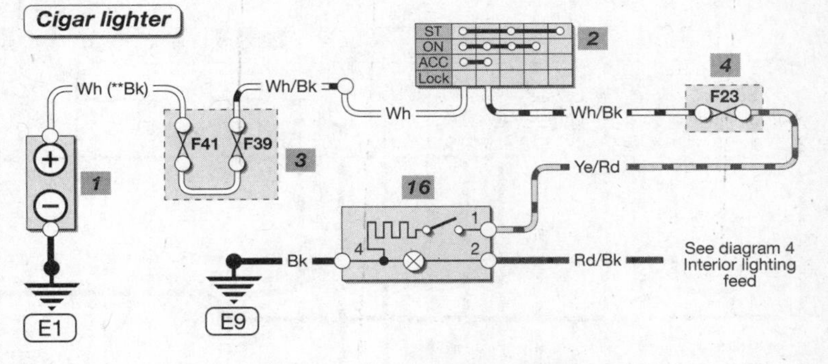

Clock

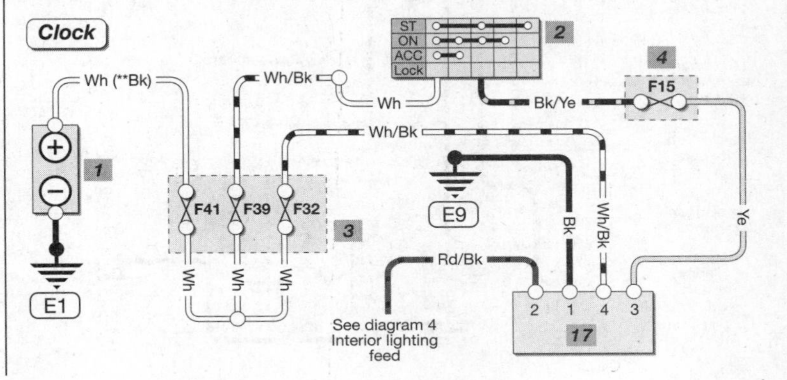

Wire colours

Bk	Black	**Rd**	Red
Wh	White	**Pk**	Pink
Bu	Blue	**Gr**	Grey
Gn	Green	**Bn**	Brown
Ye	Yellow	**Lt.Gn**	Light green
Or	Orange	**Lt.Bu**	Light blue

* 1995 model only
** Aerodeck only

Key to items

1 = Battery
2 = Ignition switch
3 = Engine fusebox
4 = Passenger fusebox
20 = Instrument cluster
  a = instrument illumination
  b = immobiliser warning light
  c = hazard warning light
  d = alternator warning light
  e = door ajar warning light
  f = tailgate open warning light
  g = brake system warning light

h = low oil pressure warning light
i = engine management warning light
j = ABS warning light
k = SRS warning light control unit
l = SRS warning light
m = economy light control unit
n = economy light
o = LH indicator warning light
p = RH indicator warning light
q = high beam warning light
r = tachometer
s = fuel gauge

t = low fuel warning light
u = speedometer
v = coolant temperature gauge
21 = Handbrake switch
22 = Brake fluid level switch
23 = Oil pressure switch
24 = Fuel gauge sender unit
25 = Low fuel level sensor
26 = Engine coolant temp. sensor
27 = Vehicle speed sensor

Diagram 3

H32664

Instrument cluster

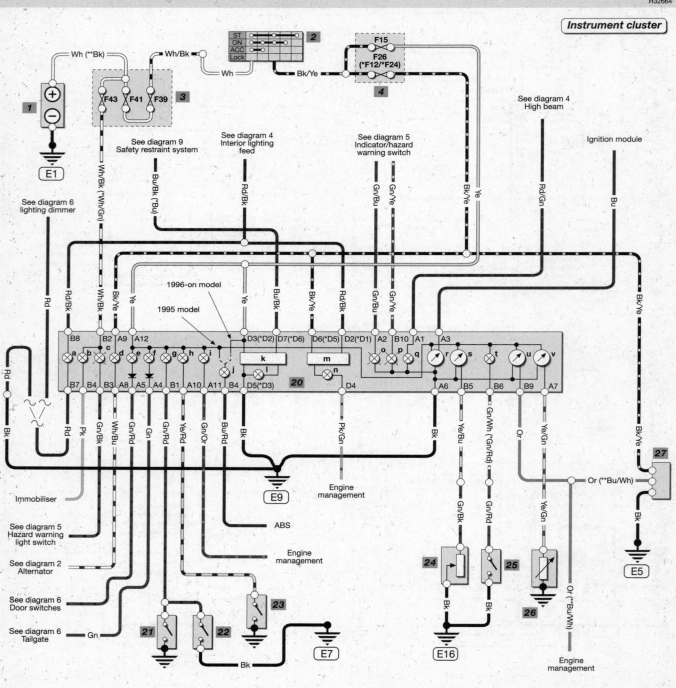

Wire colours

Bk	Black	**Rd**	Red
Wh	White	**Pk**	Pink
Bu	Blue	**Gr**	Grey
Gn	Green	**Bn**	Brown
Ye	Yellow	**Lt.Gn**	Light green
Or	Orange	**Lt.Bu**	Light blue

* 1995 model only
** Aerodeck only

Key to items

1 Battery
2 Ignition switch
3 Engine fusebox
4 Passenger fusebox
30 Light switch
 a = side/headlight
 b = headlight flasher
 c = high/low beam
31 LH front sidelight
32 RH front sidelight
33 LH tail light

34 RH tail light
35 Number plate light
36 LH headlight
37 RH headlight
38 LH stop light
39 RH stop light
40 LH reversing light
41 RH reversing light
42 High level stop light
43 Stop light switch
44 Reversing light switch

45 Auto.trans. gear position switch
46 Front foglight relay
47 Rear foglight relay
48 Front/rear foglight switch
 a = rear foglight switch
 b = switch illumination
 c = front foglight switch
49 LH front foglight
50 RH front foglight
51 Rear foglight

Diagram 4

H32665

Side & tail lights

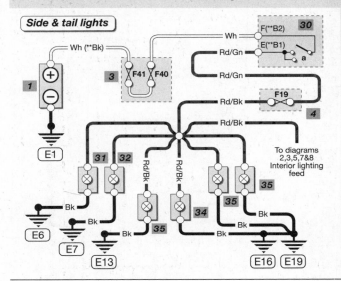

Headlights

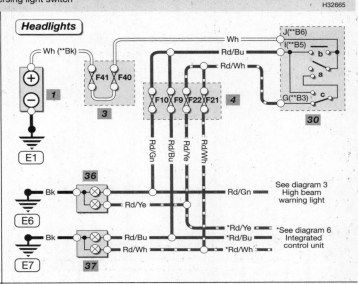

Stop & reversing lights

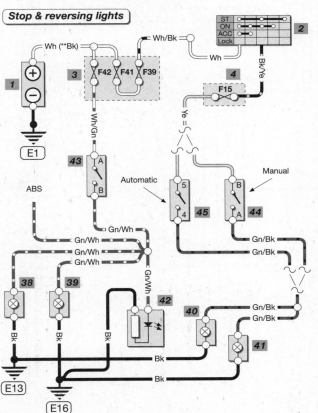

Front & rear foglights - 1995 model

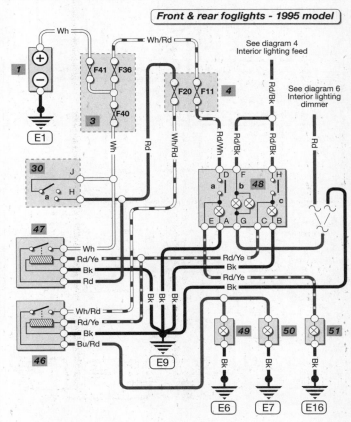

Wire colours

Bk	Black	Rd	Red
Wh	White	Pk	Pink
Bu	Blue	Gr	Grey
Gn	Green	Bn	Brown
Ye	Yellow	Lt.Gn	Light green
Or	Orange	Lt.Bu	Light blue

* 1995 model only
** Aerodeck only

Key to items

1	Battery
2	Ignition switch
3	Engine fusebox
4	Passenger fusebox
30	Light switch
	a = side/headlight
46	Front foglight relay
47	Rear foglight relay
48	Front/rear foglight switch
	a = rear foglight switch
	b = switch illumination
	c = front foglight switch

49	LH front foglight
50	RH front foglight
51	Rear foglight
52	Rear foglight control unit
55	LH headlight levelling motor
56	RH headlight levelling motor
57	Headlight levelling switch
58	Hazard warning switch
59	Direction indicator switch
60	Direction indicator flasher relay
61	LH front direction indicator
62	LH indicator side repeater

63	LH rear direction indicator
64	RH front direction indicator
65	RH indicator side repeater
66	RH rear direction indicator

Diagram 5

H32666

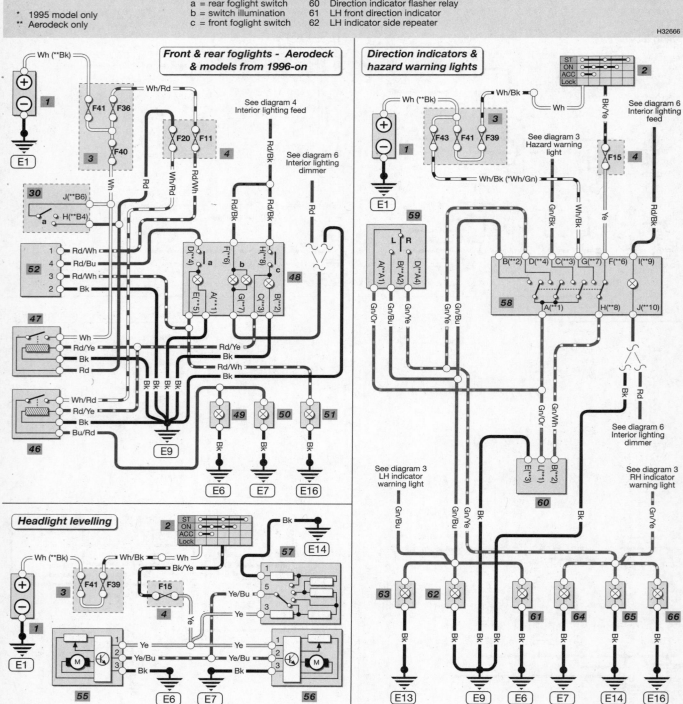

Front & rear foglights - Aerodeck & models from 1996-on

Direction indicators & hazard warning lights

Headlight levelling

Wire colours

Bk	Black	**Rd**	Red
Wh	White	**Pk**	Pink
Bu	Blue	**Gr**	Grey
Gn	Green	**Bn**	Brown
Ye	Yellow	**Lt.Gn**	Light green
Or	Orange	**Lt.Bu**	Light blue

Key to items

1 Battery
2 Ignition switch
3 Engine fusebox
4 Passenger fusebox
30 Light switch
   a = side/headlight
70 Interior light timer unit
71 Ignition lock illumination

72 Interior light
73 Rear interior light (Aerodeck)
74 Luggage compartment light
75 LH front door switch
76 LH rear door switch
77 RH rear door switch
78 Tailgate switch
79 Interior lighting dimmer unit

80 Glove box light
81 Integrated control unit
   a = wiper relay circuit
   b = lights on buzzer
   c = lights on buzzer circuit
   d = dim-dip relay circuit
82 Driver's door switch
83 Dim-dip resistor

Diagram 6

* 1995 model only
** Aerodeck only

H32667

Interior lighting

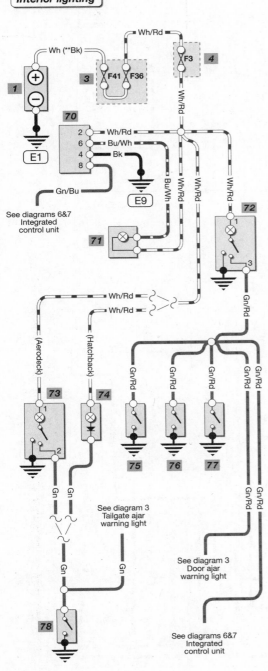

Glovebox light & interior light dimmer

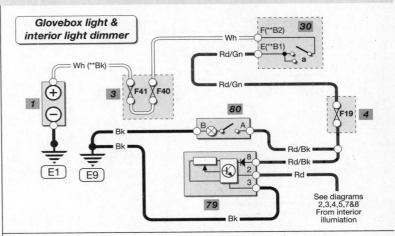

Integrated control unit - 1995 model

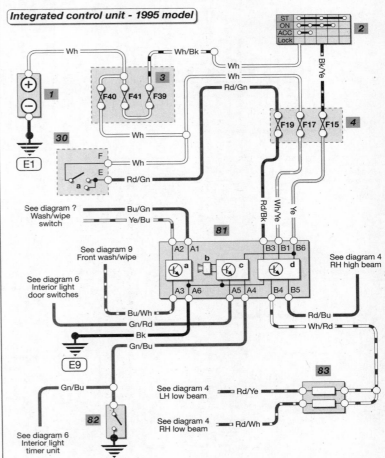

Wire colours

Bk	Black	**Rd**	Red
Wh	White	**Pk**	Pink
Bu	Blue	**Gr**	Grey
Gn	Green	**Bn**	Brown
Ye	Yellow	**Lt.Gn**	Light green
Or	Orange	**Lt.Bu**	Light blue

* 1995 model only
** Aerodeck only

Key to items

1	Battery	82	Driver's door switch
2	Ignition switch	85	Engine cooling fan
3	Engine fusebox	86	Engine cooling fan switch
4	Passenger fusebox	87	Engine cooling fan relay
30	Light switch	88	Heated rear window relay
	a = side/headlight	89	Heated rear window
81	Integrated control unit	90	Heated rear window switch
	a = wiper relay circuit	91	Radio/cassette unit
	b = lights on buzzer	92	LH front tweeter
	c = lights on buzzer circuit	93	LH front speaker

94	LH rear speaker
95	RH front tweeter
96	RH front speaker
97	RH rear speaker

Diagram 7

H32668

Integrated control unit - Aerodeck & models from 1996-on

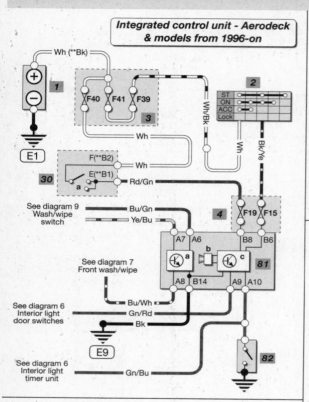

Heated rear window

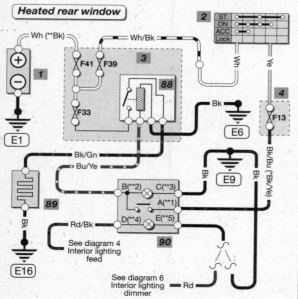

Engine cooling fan

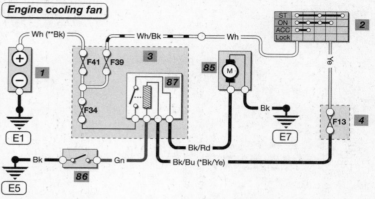

Radio/cassette

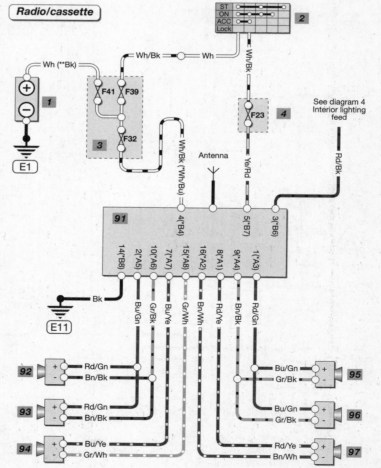

Wire colours

Bk	Black	Rd	Red
Wh	White	Pk	Pink
Bu	Blue	Gr	Grey
Gn	Green	Bn	Brown
Ye	Yellow	Lt.Gn	Light green
Or	Orange	Lt.Bu	Light blue

* 1995 model only
** Aerodeck only

Key to items

1	Battery	104	Compressor clutch thermal protection
2	Ignition switch	105	Compressor clutch
3	Engine fusebox	106	Air conditioning thermostat
4	Passenger fusebox	107	Heater blower motor
30	Light switch	108	Heater blower resistors
a = side/headlight		109	Recirculation motor
99	Heater blower relay	110	Heater blower switch
100	Condenser fan relay	111	Air conditioning switch
101	Condenser fan	112	Heater panel illumination
102	Diode	113	Recirculation switch
103	Compressor clutch relay	114	Air conditioning pressure switch

115	Sunroof close relay
116	Sunroof switch
117	Sunroof open relay
118	Sunroof assembly
	a = sunroof motor
	b = close limit switch 1
	c = close limit switch 2
119	Headlight washer control unit
120	Headlight washer switch
121	Headlight washer pump

Diagram 8

H32669

Heater blower/air conditioning

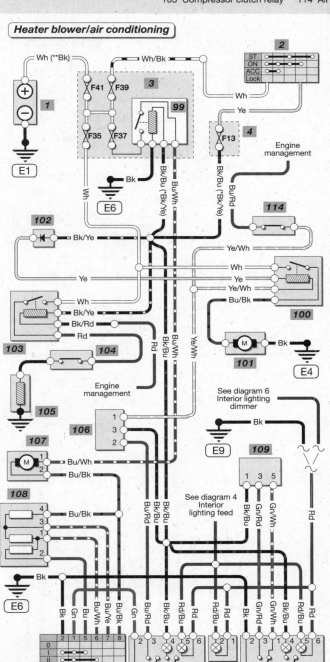

Sunroof

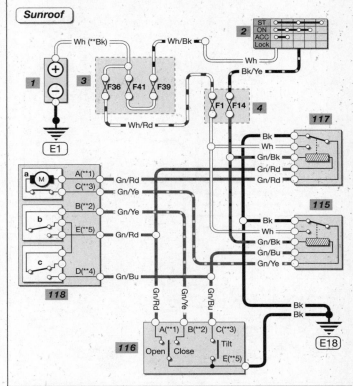

Headlight levelling

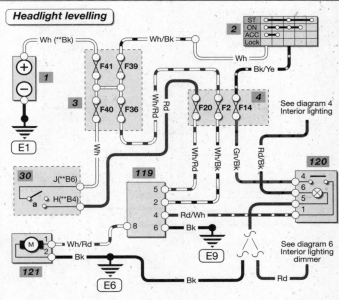

Wire colours

Bk	Black	**Rd**	Red
Wh	White	**Pk**	Pink
Bu	Blue	**Gr**	Grey
Gn	Green	**Bn**	Brown
Ye	Yellow	**Lt.Gn**	Light green
Or	Orange	**Lt.Bu**	Light blue

* 1995 model only
** Aerodeck only

Key to items

1 Battery
2 Ignition switch
3 Engine fusebox
4 Passenger fusebox
11 Steering wheel clock spring
125 Windscreen wash/wipe switch
   a = washer
   b = wiper
   c = flick wipe
126 Intermittent wiper control unit
   (if fitted)

127 Front wiper motor
128 Washer pump
129 Rear wash/wipe switch
130 Rear wiper motor
131 Rear washer pump
132 Airbag control unit
133 Driver's airbag
134 Passenger's airbag
135 Memory erase connector

Diagram 9

H32670

Front wash/wipe

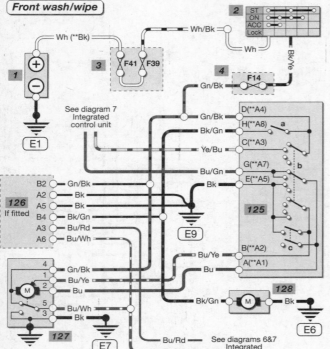

Rear wash/wipe – without intermittent wiper control unit

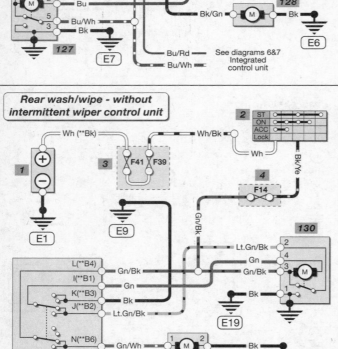

Rear wash/wipe – with intermittent wiper control unit

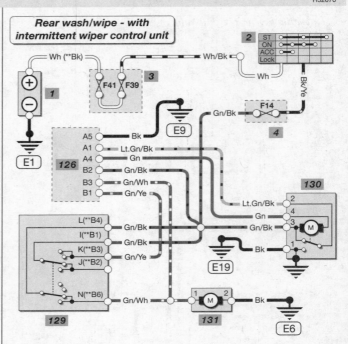

Safety restraint system

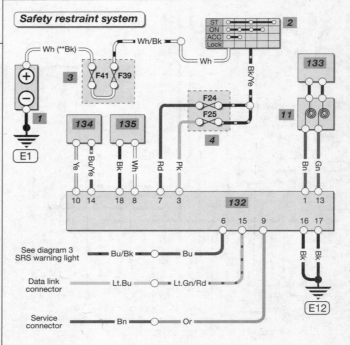

Wire colours

Bk	Black	**Rd**	Red
Wh	White	**Pk**	Pink
Bu	Blue	**Gr**	Grey
Gn	Green	**Bn**	Brown
Ye	Yellow	**Lt.Gn**	Light green
Or	Orange	**Lt.Bu**	Light blue

* 1995 model only
** Aerodeck only

Key to items

1 Battery
2 Ignition switch
3 Engine fusebox
4 Passenger fusebox
137 Mirror control switch
138 Heated mirror switch (not Aerodeck)
139 LH mirror assembly
140 RH mirror assembly
141 Central locking control unit
142 Remote receiver
143 Driver's door lock assembly
144 Passenger's door lock motor
145 LH rear door lock motor
146 RH rear door lock motor
147 Tailgate lock motor
148 Electric window relay
149 Driver's window control switch
150 Driver's window control unit
151 Driver's electric window
152 LH rear door switch
153 RH rear door switch
154 Electric window master switch
   a = LH rear window
   b = RH rear window
   c = front passenger's window
   d = main switch
155 LH rear window motor
156 RH rear window motor
157 Passenger's window motor

Diagram 10

H32671

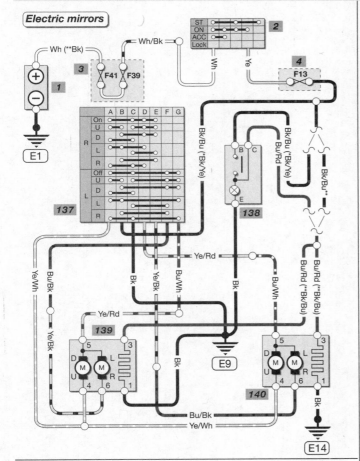

Electric mirrors

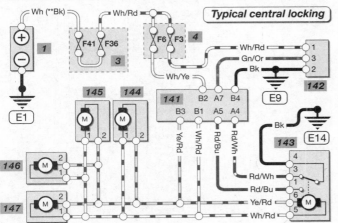

Typical central locking

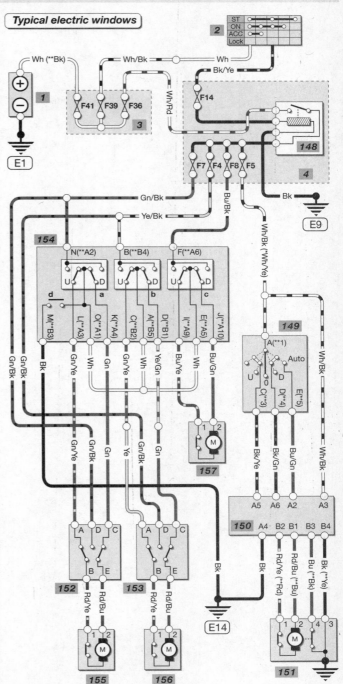

Typical electric windows

Dimensions and weights

Note: *All figures are approximate, and may vary according to model. Refer to manufacturer's data for exact figures.*

Dimensions

Length:
  3-door Hatchback . . . . .4190 mm
  4-door Saloon . . . . .4460 mm
  2-door Coupe . . . . .4460 mm
  5-door Hatchback . . . . .4325 mm
  5-door Estate . . . . .4425 mm
Width:
  All models . . . . .1695 mm
Height:
  3-door Hatchback . . . . .1375 mm
  4-door Saloon . . . . .1390 mm
  2-door Coupe . . . . .1375 mm
  5-door Hatchback . . . . .1390 mm
  5-door Estate . . . . .1440 mm

Weights

Kerb weight:
  3-door Hatchback . . . . .970 to 1180 kg
  4-door Saloon . . . . .995 to 1195 kg
  2-door Coupe . . . . .1034 to 1095 kg
  5-door Hatchback . . . . .1090 to 1155 kg
  5-door Estate . . . . .1143 to 1281 kg
Permissible gross weight:
  3-door Hatchback . . . . .1500 kg
  4-door Saloon . . . . .1575 kg
  2-door Coupe . . . . .1550 kg
  5-door Hatchback . . . . .1600 kg
  5-door Estate . . . . .1600 kg

Conversion factors

Length (distance)

Inches (in)	x 25.4	= Millimetres (mm)	x 0.0394	= Inches (in)
Feet (ft)	x 0.305	= Metres (m)	x 3.281	= Feet (ft)
Miles	x 1.609	= Kilometres (km)	x 0.621	= Miles

Volume (capacity)

Cubic inches (cu in; in³)	x 16.387	= Cubic centimetres (cc; cm³)	x 0.061	= Cubic inches (cu in; in³)
Imperial pints (Imp pt)	x 0.568	= Litres (l)	x 1.76	= Imperial pints (Imp pt)
Imperial quarts (Imp qt)	x 1.137	= Litres (l)	x 0.88	= Imperial quarts (Imp qt)
Imperial quarts (Imp qt)	x 1.201	= US quarts (US qt)	x 0.833	= Imperial quarts (Imp qt)
US quarts (US qt)	x 0.946	= Litres (l)	x 1.057	= US quarts (US qt)
Imperial gallons (Imp gal)	x 4.546	= Litres (l)	x 0.22	= Imperial gallons (Imp gal)
Imperial gallons (Imp gal)	x 1.201	= US gallons (US gal)	x 0.833	= Imperial gallons (Imp gal)
US gallons (US gal)	x 3.785	= Litres (l)	x 0.264	= US gallons (US gal)

Mass (weight)

Ounces (oz)	x 28.35	= Grams (g)	x 0.035	= Ounces (oz)
Pounds (lb)	x 0.454	= Kilograms (kg)	x 2.205	= Pounds (lb)

Force

Ounces-force (ozf; oz)	x 0.278	= Newtons (N)	x 3.6	= Ounces-force (ozf; oz)
Pounds-force (lbf; lb)	x 4.448	= Newtons (N)	x 0.225	= Pounds-force (lbf; lb)
Newtons (N)	x 0.1	= Kilograms-force (kgf; kg)	x 9.81	= Newtons (N)

Pressure

Pounds-force per square inch (psi; lbf/in²; lb/in²)	x 0.070	= Kilograms-force per square centimetre (kgf/cm²; kg/cm²)	x 14.223	= Pounds-force per square inch (psi; lbf/in²; lb/in²)
Pounds-force per square inch (psi; lbf/in²; lb/in²)	x 0.068	= Atmospheres (atm)	x 14.696	= Pounds-force per square inch (psi; lbf/in²; lb/in²)
Pounds-force per square inch (psi; lbf/in²; lb/in²)	x 0.069	= Bars	x 14.5	= Pounds-force per square inch (psi; lbf/in²; lb/in²)
Pounds-force per square inch (psi; lbf/in²; lb/in²)	x 6.895	= Kilopascals (kPa)	x 0.145	= Pounds-force per square inch (psi; lbf/in²; lb/in²)
Kilopascals (kPa)	x 0.01	= Kilograms-force per square centimetre (kgf/cm²; kg/cm²)	x 98.1	= Kilopascals (kPa)
Millibar (mbar)	x 100	= Pascals (Pa)	x 0.01	= Millibar (mbar)
Millibar (mbar)	x 0.0145	= Pounds-force per square inch (psi; lbf/in²; lb/in²)	x 68.947	= Millibar (mbar)
Millibar (mbar)	x 0.75	= Millimetres of mercury (mmHg)	x 1.333	= Millibar (mbar)
Millibar (mbar)	x 0.401	= Inches of water (inH₂O)	x 2.491	= Millibar (mbar)
Millimetres of mercury (mmHg)	x 0.535	= Inches of water (inH₂O)	x 1.868	= Millimetres of mercury (mmHg)
Inches of water (inH₂O)	x 0.036	= Pounds-force per square inch (psi; lbf/in²; lb/in²)	x 27.68	= Inches of water (inH₂O)

Torque (moment of force)

Pounds-force inches (lbf in; lb in)	x 1.152	= Kilograms-force centimetre (kgf cm; kg cm)	x 0.868	= Pounds-force inches (lbf in; lb in)
Pounds-force inches (lbf in; lb in)	x 0.113	= Newton metres (Nm)	x 8.85	= Pounds-force inches (lbf in; lb in)
Pounds-force inches (lbf in; lb in)	x 0.083	= Pounds-force feet (lbf ft; lb ft)	x 12	= Pounds-force inches (lbf in; lb in)
Pounds-force feet (lbf ft; lb ft)	x 0.138	= Kilograms-force metres (kgf m; kg m)	x 7.233	= Pounds-force feet (lbf ft; lb ft)
Pounds-force feet (lbf ft; lb ft)	x 1.356	= Newton metres (Nm)	x 0.738	= Pounds-force feet (lbf ft; lb ft)
Newton metres (Nm)	x 0.102	= Kilograms-force metres (kgf m; kg m)	x 9.804	= Newton metres (Nm)

Power

Horsepower (hp)	x 745.7	= Watts (W)	x 0.0013	= Horsepower (hp)

Velocity (speed)

Miles per hour (miles/hr; mph)	x 1.609	= Kilometres per hour (km/hr; kph)	x 0.621	= Miles per hour (miles/hr; mph)

Fuel consumption*

Miles per gallon, Imperial (mpg)	x 0.354	= Kilometres per litre (km/l)	x 2.825	= Miles per gallon, Imperial (mpg)
Miles per gallon, US (mpg)	x 0.425	= Kilometres per litre (km/l)	x 2.352	= Miles per gallon, US (mpg)

Temperature

Degrees Fahrenheit = (°C x 1.8) + 32   Degrees Celsius (Degrees Centigrade; °C) = (°F - 32) x 0.56

It is common practice to convert from miles per gallon (mpg) to litres/100 kilometres (l/100km), where mpg x l/100 km = 282

Spare parts are available from many sources, including maker's appointed garages, accessory shops, and motor factors. To be sure of obtaining the correct parts, it will sometimes be necessary to quote the vehicle identification number. If possible, it can also be useful to take the old parts along for positive identification. Items such as starter motors and alternators may be available under a service exchange scheme – any parts returned should be clean.

Our advice regarding spare parts is as follows.

Officially appointed garages

This is the best source of parts which are peculiar to your car, and which are not otherwise generally available (eg, badges, interior trim, certain body panels, etc). It is also the only place at which you should buy parts if the vehicle is still under warranty.

Accessory shops

These are very good places to buy materials and components needed for the maintenance of your car (oil, air and fuel filters, light bulbs, drivebelts, greases, brake pads, touch-up paint, etc). Components of this nature sold by a reputable shop are of the same standard as those used by the car manufacturer.

Besides components, these shops also sell tools and general accessories, usually have convenient opening hours, charge lower prices, and can often be found close to home. Some accessory shops have parts counters where components needed for almost any repair job can be purchased or ordered.

Motor factors

Good factors will stock all the more important components which wear out comparatively quickly, and can sometimes supply individual components needed for the overhaul of a larger assembly (eg, brake seals and hydraulic parts, bearing shells, pistons, valves). They may also handle work such as cylinder block reboring, crankshaft regrinding, etc.

Tyre and exhaust specialists

These outlets may be independent, or members of a local or national chain. They frequently offer competitive prices when compared with a main dealer or local garage, but it will pay to obtain several quotes before making a decision. When researching prices, also ask what extras may be added – for instance fitting a new valve and balancing the wheel are both commonly charged on top of the price of a new tyre.

Other sources

Beware of parts or materials obtained from market stalls, car boot sales or similar outlets. Such items are not invariably sub-standard, but there is little chance of compensation if they do prove unsatisfactory. In the case of safety-critical components such as brake pads, there is the risk not only of financial loss, but also of an accident causing injury or death.

Second-hand components or assemblies obtained from a car breaker can be a good buy in some circumstances, but this sort of purchase is best made by the experienced DIY mechanic.

Vehicle identification

The vehicle identification plate is located on the left-hand side of the engine compartment bulkhead . . .

Modifications are a continuing and unpublicised process in vehicle manufacture, quite apart from major model changes. Spare parts manuals and lists are compiled upon a numerical basis, the individual vehicle identification numbers being essential to correct identification of the component concerned.

When ordering spare parts, always give as much information as possible. Quote the car model, year of manufacture, body and engine numbers as appropriate.

The *vehicle identification plate* is situated on the left-hand side of the engine compartment bulkhead **(see illustration)**. The *vehicle identification number* is also repeated in the form of plate visible through the windscreen on the passenger's side **(see illustration)**, and stamped into the vehicle body in the centre of the bulkhead **(see illustration)**.

The *engine number* is stamped on the front side of the cylinder block, adjacent to the transmission joint **(see illustration)**. *Other identification numbers* or codes are stamped on major items such as the gearbox, etc. These numbers are unlikely to be needed by the home mechanic.

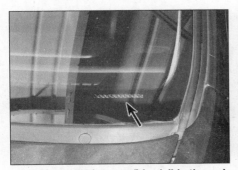

. . . and the VIN (arrowed) is visible through the windscreen . . .

. . . and stamped into the centre of the bulkhead

Engine number

Whenever servicing, repair or overhaul work is carried out on the car or its components, observe the following procedures and instructions. This will assist in carrying out the operation efficiently and to a professional standard of workmanship.

Joint mating faces and gaskets

When separating components at their mating faces, never insert screwdrivers or similar implements into the joint between the faces in order to prise them apart. This can cause severe damage which results in oil leaks, coolant leaks, etc upon reassembly. Separation is usually achieved by tapping along the joint with a soft-faced hammer in order to break the seal. However, note that this method may not be suitable where dowels are used for component location.

Where a gasket is used between the mating faces of two components, a new one must be fitted on reassembly; fit it dry unless otherwise stated in the repair procedure. Make sure that the mating faces are clean and dry, with all traces of old gasket removed. When cleaning a joint face, use a tool which is unlikely to score or damage the face, and remove any burrs or nicks with an oilstone or fine file.

Make sure that tapped holes are cleaned with a pipe cleaner, and keep them free of jointing compound, if this is being used, unless specifically instructed otherwise.

Ensure that all orifices, channels or pipes are clear, and blow through them, preferably using compressed air.

Oil seals

Oil seals can be removed by levering them out with a wide flat-bladed screwdriver or similar implement. Alternatively, a number of self-tapping screws may be screwed into the seal, and these used as a purchase for pliers or some similar device in order to pull the seal free.

Whenever an oil seal is removed from its working location, either individually or as part of an assembly, it should be renewed.

The very fine sealing lip of the seal is easily damaged, and will not seal if the surface it contacts is not completely clean and free from scratches, nicks or grooves. If the original sealing surface of the component cannot be restored, and the manufacturer has not made provision for slight relocation of the seal relative to the sealing surface, the component should be renewed.

Protect the lips of the seal from any surface which may damage them in the course of fitting. Use tape or a conical sleeve where possible. Lubricate the seal lips with oil before fitting and, on dual-lipped seals, fill the space between the lips with grease.

Unless otherwise stated, oil seals must be fitted with their sealing lips toward the lubricant to be sealed.

Use a tubular drift or block of wood of the appropriate size to install the seal and, if the seal housing is shouldered, drive the seal down to the shoulder. If the seal housing is unshouldered, the seal should be fitted with its face flush with the housing top face (unless otherwise instructed).

Screw threads and fastenings

Seized nuts, bolts and screws are quite a common occurrence where corrosion has set in, and the use of penetrating oil or releasing fluid will often overcome this problem if the offending item is soaked for a while before attempting to release it. The use of an impact driver may also provide a means of releasing such stubborn fastening devices, when used in conjunction with the appropriate screwdriver bit or socket. If none of these methods works, it may be necessary to resort to the careful application of heat, or the use of a hacksaw or nut splitter device.

Studs are usually removed by locking two nuts together on the threaded part, and then using a spanner on the lower nut to unscrew the stud. Studs or bolts which have broken off below the surface of the component in which they are mounted can sometimes be removed using a stud extractor. Always ensure that a blind tapped hole is completely free from oil, grease, water or other fluid before installing the bolt or stud. Failure to do this could cause the housing to crack due to the hydraulic action of the bolt or stud as it is screwed in.

When tightening a castellated nut to accept a split pin, tighten the nut to the specified torque, where applicable, and then tighten further to the next split pin hole. Never slacken the nut to align the split pin hole, unless stated in the repair procedure.

When checking or retightening a nut or bolt to a specified torque setting, slacken the nut or bolt by a quarter of a turn, and then retighten to the specified setting. However, this should not be attempted where angular tightening has been used.

For some screw fastenings, notably cylinder head bolts or nuts, torque wrench settings are no longer specified for the latter stages of tightening, "angle-tightening" being called up instead. Typically, a fairly low torque wrench setting will be applied to the bolts/nuts in the correct sequence, followed by one or more stages of tightening through specified angles.

Locknuts, locktabs and washers

Any fastening which will rotate against a component or housing during tightening should always have a washer between it and the relevant component or housing.

Spring or split washers should always be renewed when they are used to lock a critical component such as a big-end bearing retaining bolt or nut. Locktabs which are folded over to retain a nut or bolt should always be renewed.

Self-locking nuts can be re-used in non-critical areas, providing resistance can be felt when the locking portion passes over the bolt or stud thread. However, it should be noted that self-locking stiffnuts tend to lose their effectiveness after long periods of use, and should then be renewed as a matter of course.

Split pins must always be replaced with new ones of the correct size for the hole.

When thread-locking compound is found on the threads of a fastener which is to be re-used, it should be cleaned off with a wire brush and solvent, and fresh compound applied on reassembly.

Special tools

Some repair procedures in this manual entail the use of special tools such as a press, two or three-legged pullers, spring compressors, etc. Wherever possible, suitable readily-available alternatives to the manufacturer's special tools are described, and are shown in use. In some instances, where no alternative is possible, it has been necessary to resort to the use of a manufacturer's tool, and this has been done for reasons of safety as well as the efficient completion of the repair operation. Unless you are highly-skilled and have a thorough understanding of the procedures described, never attempt to bypass the use of any special tool when the procedure described specifies its use. Not only is there a very great risk of personal injury, but expensive damage could be caused to the components involved.

Environmental considerations

When disposing of used engine oil, brake fluid, antifreeze, etc, give due consideration to any detrimental environmental effects. Do not, for instance, pour any of the above liquids down drains into the general sewage system, or onto the ground to soak away. Many local council refuse tips provide a facility for waste oil disposal, as do some garages. If none of these facilities are available, consult your local Environmental Health Department, or the National Rivers Authority, for further advice.

With the universal tightening-up of legislation regarding the emission of environmentally-harmful substances from motor vehicles, most vehicles have tamperproof devices fitted to the main adjustment points of the fuel system. These devices are primarily designed to prevent unqualified persons from adjusting the fuel/air mixture, with the chance of a consequent increase in toxic emissions. If such devices are found during servicing or overhaul, they should, wherever possible, be renewed or refitted in accordance with the manufacturer's requirements or current legislation.

OIL CARE
FOLLOW THE CODE
OIL BANK LINE
0800 66 33 66
www.oilbankline.org.uk

Note: It is antisocial and illegal to dump oil down the drain. To find the location of your local oil recycling bank, call this number free.

The jack supplied with the vehicle tool kit should only be used for changing the roadwheels – see *Wheel changing* at the front of this manual. When carrying out any other kind of work, raise the vehicle using a hydraulic trolley jack, and always supplement the jack with axle stands positioned under the vehicle jacking points.

When using a trolley jack or axle stands, always position the jack head or axle stand head under, or adjacent to one of the relevant wheel changing jacking points under the sills or under the front or rear central jacking points **(see illustrations)**. Use a block of wood between the jack or axle stand and the sill.

Do not attempt to jack the vehicle under the sump, or any of the suspension components.

The jack supplied with the vehicle locates in the jacking points on the underside of the sills – see *Wheel changing* at the front of this manual. Ensure that the jack head is correctly engaged before attempting to raise the vehicle.

Never work under, around, or near a raised vehicle, unless it is adequately supported in at least two places.

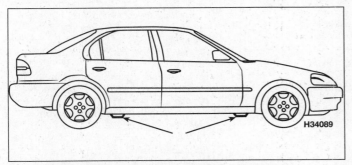

Vehicle jacking points under the sills (vehicle jack) . . .

. . . and at the front and rear (trolley jack)

Radio/cassette unit anti-theft system - precaution

The radio/cassette unit fitted as standard equipment by Honda is equipped with a built-in security code to deter thieves. If the power source to the unit is cut, the anti-theft system will activate. Even if the power source is immediately reconnected, the radio/cassette unit will not function until the correct security code has been entered. Therefore, if you do not know the correct security code for the unit, do not disconnect the battery negative lead, or remove the radio/cassette unit from the vehicle.

Introduction

A selection of good tools is a fundamental requirement for anyone contemplating the maintenance and repair of a motor vehicle. For the owner who does not possess any, their purchase will prove a considerable expense, offsetting some of the savings made by doing-it-yourself. However, provided that the tools purchased meet the relevant national safety standards and are of good quality, they will last for many years and prove an extremely worthwhile investment.

To help the average owner to decide which tools are needed to carry out the various tasks detailed in this manual, we have compiled three lists of tools under the following headings: *Maintenance and minor repair, Repair and overhaul,* and *Special.* Newcomers to practical mechanics should start off with the *Maintenance and minor repair* tool kit, and confine themselves to the simpler jobs around the vehicle. Then, as confidence and experience grow, more difficult tasks can be undertaken, with extra tools being purchased as, and when, they are needed. In this way, a *Maintenance and minor repair* tool kit can be built up into a *Repair and overhaul* tool kit over a considerable period of time, without any major cash outlays. The experienced do-it-yourselfer will have a tool kit good enough for most repair and overhaul procedures, and will add tools from the *Special* category when it is felt that the expense is justified by the amount of use to which these tools will be put.

Maintenance and minor repair tool kit

The tools given in this list should be considered as a minimum requirement if routine maintenance, servicing and minor repair operations are to be undertaken. We recommend the purchase of combination spanners (ring one end, open-ended the other); although more expensive than open-ended ones, they do give the advantages of both types of spanner.

☐ *Combination spanners:*
  Metric - 8 to 19 mm inclusive
☐ *Adjustable spanner - 35 mm jaw (approx.)*
☐ *Spark plug spanner (with rubber insert) - petrol models*
☐ *Spark plug gap adjustment tool - petrol models*
☐ *Set of feeler gauges*
☐ *Brake bleed nipple spanner*
☐ *Screwdrivers:*
  Flat blade - 100 mm long x 6 mm dia
  Cross blade - 100 mm long x 6 mm dia
  Torx - various sizes (not all vehicles)
☐ *Combination pliers*
☐ *Hacksaw (junior)*
☐ *Tyre pump*
☐ *Tyre pressure gauge*
☐ *Oil can*
☐ *Oil filter removal tool*
☐ *Fine emery cloth*
☐ *Wire brush (small)*
☐ *Funnel (medium size)*
☐ *Sump drain plug key (not all vehicles)*

Repair and overhaul tool kit

These tools are virtually essential for anyone undertaking any major repairs to a motor vehicle, and are additional to those given in the *Maintenance and minor repair* list. Included in this list is a comprehensive set of sockets. Although these are expensive, they will be found invaluable as they are so versatile - particularly if various drives are included in the set. We recommend the half-inch square-drive type, as this can be used with most proprietary torque wrenches.

The tools in this list will sometimes need to be supplemented by tools from the *Special* list:

☐ *Sockets (or box spanners) to cover range in previous list (including Torx sockets)*
☐ *Reversible ratchet drive (for use with sockets)*
☐ *Extension piece, 250 mm (for use with sockets)*
☐ *Universal joint (for use with sockets)*
☐ *Flexible handle or sliding T "breaker bar" (for use with sockets)*
☐ *Torque wrench (for use with sockets)*
☐ *Self-locking grips*
☐ *Ball pein hammer*
☐ *Soft-faced mallet (plastic or rubber)*
☐ *Screwdrivers:*
  Flat blade - long & sturdy, short (chubby), and narrow (electrician's) types
  Cross blade – long & sturdy, and short (chubby) types
☐ *Pliers:*
  Long-nosed
  Side cutters (electrician's)
  Circlip (internal and external)
☐ *Cold chisel - 25 mm*
☐ *Scriber*
☐ *Scraper*
☐ *Centre-punch*
☐ *Pin punch*
☐ *Hacksaw*
☐ *Brake hose clamp*
☐ *Brake/clutch bleeding kit*
☐ *Selection of twist drills*
☐ *Steel rule/straight-edge*
☐ *Allen keys (inc. splined/Torx type)*
☐ *Selection of files*
☐ *Wire brush*
☐ *Axle stands*
☐ *Jack (strong trolley or hydraulic type)*
☐ *Light with extension lead*
☐ *Universal electrical multi-meter*

Sockets and reversible ratchet drive

Brake bleeding kit

Torx key, socket and bit

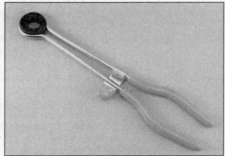

Hose clamp

Angular-tightening gauge

Special tools

The tools in this list are those which are not used regularly, are expensive to buy, or which need to be used in accordance with their manufacturers' instructions. Unless relatively difficult mechanical jobs are undertaken frequently, it will not be economic to buy many of these tools. Where this is the case, you could consider clubbing together with friends (or joining a motorists' club) to make a joint purchase, or borrowing the tools against a deposit from a local garage or tool hire specialist. It is worth noting that many of the larger DIY superstores now carry a large range of special tools for hire at modest rates.

The following list contains only those tools and instruments freely available to the public, and not those special tools produced by the vehicle manufacturer specifically for its dealer network. You will find occasional references to these manufacturers' special tools in the text of this manual. Generally, an alternative method of doing the job without the vehicle manufacturers' special tool is given. However, sometimes there is no alternative to using them. Where this is the case and the relevant tool cannot be bought or borrowed, you will have to entrust the work to a dealer.

- [ ] Angular-tightening gauge
- [ ] Valve spring compressor
- [ ] Valve grinding tool
- [ ] Piston ring compressor
- [ ] Piston ring removal/installation tool
- [ ] Cylinder bore hone
- [ ] Balljoint separator
- [ ] Coil spring compressors (where applicable)
- [ ] Two/three-legged hub and bearing puller
- [ ] Impact screwdriver
- [ ] Micrometer and/or vernier calipers
- [ ] Dial gauge
- [ ] Stroboscopic timing light
- [ ] Dwell angle meter/tachometer
- [ ] Fault code reader
- [ ] Cylinder compression gauge
- [ ] Hand-operated vacuum pump and gauge
- [ ] Clutch plate alignment set
- [ ] Brake shoe steady spring cup removal tool
- [ ] Bush and bearing removal/installation set
- [ ] Stud extractors
- [ ] Tap and die set
- [ ] Lifting tackle
- [ ] Trolley jack

Buying tools

Reputable motor accessory shops and superstores often offer excellent quality tools at discount prices, so it pays to shop around.

Remember, you don't have to buy the most expensive items on the shelf, but it is always advisable to steer clear of the very cheap tools. Beware of 'bargains' offered on market stalls or at car boot sales. There are plenty of good tools around at reasonable prices, but always aim to purchase items which meet the relevant national safety standards. If in doubt, ask the proprietor or manager of the shop for advice before making a purchase.

Care and maintenance of tools

Having purchased a reasonable tool kit, it is necessary to keep the tools in a clean and serviceable condition. After use, always wipe off any dirt, grease and metal particles using a clean, dry cloth, before putting the tools away. Never leave them lying around after they have been used. A simple tool rack on the garage or workshop wall for items such as screwdrivers and pliers is a good idea. Store all normal spanners and sockets in a metal box. Any measuring instruments, gauges, meters, etc, must be carefully stored where they cannot be damaged or become rusty.

Take a little care when tools are used. Hammer heads inevitably become marked, and screwdrivers lose the keen edge on their blades from time to time. A little timely attention with emery cloth or a file will soon restore items like this to a good finish.

Working facilities

Not to be forgotten when discussing tools is the workshop itself. If anything more than routine maintenance is to be carried out, a suitable working area becomes essential.

It is appreciated that many an owner-mechanic is forced by circumstances to remove an engine or similar item without the benefit of a garage or workshop. Having done this, any repairs should always be done under the cover of a roof.

Wherever possible, any dismantling should be done on a clean, flat workbench or table at a suitable working height.

Any workbench needs a vice; one with a jaw opening of 100 mm is suitable for most jobs. As mentioned previously, some clean dry storage space is also required for tools, as well as for any lubricants, cleaning fluids, touch-up paints etc, which become necessary.

Another item which may be required, and which has a much more general usage, is an electric drill with a chuck capacity of at least 8 mm. This, together with a good range of twist drills, is virtually essential for fitting accessories.

Last, but not least, always keep a supply of old newspapers and clean, lint-free rags available, and try to keep any working area as clean as possible.

Micrometers

Dial test indicator ("dial gauge")

Strap wrench

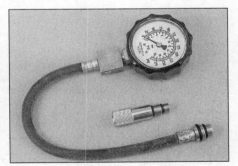

Compression tester

Fault code reader

This is a guide to getting your vehicle through the MOT test. Obviously it will not be possible to examine the vehicle to the same standard as the professional MOT tester. However, working through the following checks will enable you to identify any problem areas before submitting the vehicle for the test.

Where a testable component is in borderline condition, the tester has discretion in deciding whether to pass or fail it. The basis of such discretion is whether the tester would be happy for a close relative or friend to use the vehicle with the component in that condition. If the vehicle presented is clean and evidently well cared for, the tester may be more inclined to pass a borderline component than if the vehicle is scruffy and apparently neglected.

It has only been possible to summarise the test requirements here, based on the regulations in force at the time of printing. Test standards are becoming increasingly stringent, although there are some exemptions for older vehicles.

An assistant will be needed to help carry out some of these checks.

The checks have been sub-divided into four categories, as follows:

1 Checks carried out **FROM THE DRIVER'S SEAT**

2 Checks carried out **WITH THE VEHICLE ON THE GROUND**

3 Checks carried out **WITH THE VEHICLE RAISED AND THE WHEELS FREE TO TURN**

4 Checks carried out on **YOUR VEHICLE'S EXHAUST EMISSION SYSTEM**

---

1 Checks carried out **FROM THE DRIVER'S SEAT**

Handbrake

☐ Test the operation of the handbrake. Excessive travel (too many clicks) indicates incorrect brake or cable adjustment.

☐ Check that the handbrake cannot be released by tapping the lever sideways. Check the security of the lever mountings.

Footbrake

☐ Depress the brake pedal and check that it does not creep down to the floor, indicating a master cylinder fault. Release the pedal, wait a few seconds, then depress it again. If the pedal travels nearly to the floor before firm resistance is felt, brake adjustment or repair is necessary. If the pedal feels spongy, there is air in the hydraulic system which must be removed by bleeding.

☐ Check that the brake pedal is secure and in good condition. Check also for signs of fluid leaks on the pedal, floor or carpets, which would indicate failed seals in the brake master cylinder.

☐ Check the servo unit (when applicable) by operating the brake pedal several times, then keeping the pedal depressed and starting the engine. As the engine starts, the pedal will move down slightly. If not, the vacuum hose or the servo itself may be faulty.

Steering wheel and column

☐ Examine the steering wheel for fractures or looseness of the hub, spokes or rim.

☐ Move the steering wheel from side to side and then up and down. Check that the steering wheel is not loose on the column, indicating wear or a loose retaining nut. Continue moving the steering wheel as before, but also turn it slightly from left to right.

☐ Check that the steering wheel is not loose on the column, and that there is no abnormal

movement of the steering wheel, indicating wear in the column support bearings or couplings.

Windscreen, mirrors and sunvisor

☐ The windscreen must be free of cracks or other significant damage within the driver's field of view. (Small stone chips are acceptable.) Rear view mirrors must be secure, intact, and capable of being adjusted.

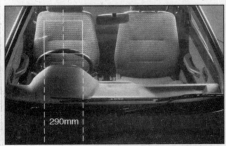

☐ The driver's sunvisor must be capable of being stored in the "up" position.

Seat belts and seats

Note: *The following checks are applicable to all seat belts, front and rear.*

☐ Examine the webbing of all the belts (including rear belts if fitted) for cuts, serious fraying or deterioration. Fasten and unfasten each belt to check the buckles. If applicable, check the retracting mechanism. Check the security of all seat belt mountings accessible from inside the vehicle.

☐ Seat belts with pre-tensioners, once activated, have a "flag" or similar showing on the seat belt stalk. This, in itself, is not a reason for test failure.

☐ The front seats themselves must be securely attached and the backrests must lock in the upright position.

Doors

☐ Both front doors must be able to be opened and closed from outside and inside, and must latch securely when closed.

2 Checks carried out WITH THE VEHICLE ON THE GROUND

Vehicle identification

☐ Number plates must be in good condition, secure and legible, with letters and numbers correctly spaced – spacing at (A) should be at least twice that at (B).

☐ The VIN plate and/or homologation plate must be legible.

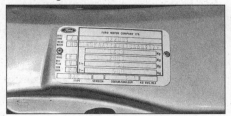

Electrical equipment

☐ Switch on the ignition and check the operation of the horn.

☐ Check the windscreen washers and wipers, examining the wiper blades; renew damaged or perished blades. Also check the operation of the stop-lights.

☐ Check the operation of the sidelights and number plate lights. The lenses and reflectors must be secure, clean and undamaged.

☐ Check the operation and alignment of the headlights. The headlight reflectors must not be tarnished and the lenses must be undamaged.

☐ Switch on the ignition and check the operation of the direction indicators (including the instrument panel tell-tale) and the hazard warning lights. Operation of the sidelights and stop-lights must not affect the indicators - if it does, the cause is usually a bad earth at the rear light cluster.

☐ Check the operation of the rear foglight(s), including the warning light on the instrument panel or in the switch.

☐ The ABS warning light must illuminate in accordance with the manufacturers' design. For most vehicles, the ABS warning light should illuminate when the ignition is switched on, and (if the system is operating properly) extinguish after a few seconds. Refer to the owner's handbook.

Footbrake

☐ Examine the master cylinder, brake pipes and servo unit for leaks, loose mountings, corrosion or other damage.

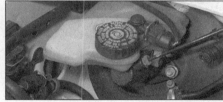

☐ The fluid reservoir must be secure and the fluid level must be between the upper (**A**) and lower (**B**) markings.

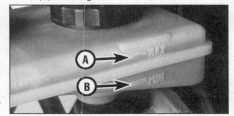

☐ Inspect both front brake flexible hoses for cracks or deterioration of the rubber. Turn the steering from lock to lock, and ensure that the hoses do not contact the wheel, tyre, or any part of the steering or suspension mechanism. With the brake pedal firmly depressed, check the hoses for bulges or leaks under pressure.

Steering and suspension

☐ Have your assistant turn the steering wheel from side to side slightly, up to the point where the steering gear just begins to transmit this movement to the roadwheels. Check for excessive free play between the steering wheel and the steering gear, indicating wear or insecurity of the steering column joints, the column-to-steering gear coupling, or the steering gear itself.

☐ Have your assistant turn the steering wheel more vigorously in each direction, so that the roadwheels just begin to turn. As this is done, examine all the steering joints, linkages, fittings and attachments. Renew any component that shows signs of wear or damage. On vehicles with power steering, check the security and condition of the steering pump, drivebelt and hoses.

☐ Check that the vehicle is standing level, and at approximately the correct ride height.

Shock absorbers

☐ Depress each corner of the vehicle in turn, then release it. The vehicle should rise and then settle in its normal position. If the vehicle continues to rise and fall, the shock absorber is defective. A shock absorber which has seized will also cause the vehicle to fail.

Exhaust system

☐ Start the engine. With your assistant holding a rag over the tailpipe, check the entire system for leaks. Repair or renew leaking sections.

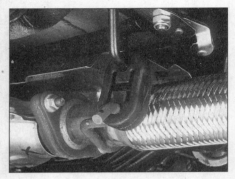

3 Checks carried out **WITH THE VEHICLE RAISED AND THE WHEELS FREE TO TURN**

Jack up the front and rear of the vehicle, and securely support it on axle stands. Position the stands clear of the suspension assemblies. Ensure that the wheels are clear of the ground and that the steering can be turned from lock to lock.

Steering mechanism

☐ Have your assistant turn the steering from lock to lock. Check that the steering turns smoothly, and that no part of the steering mechanism, including a wheel or tyre, fouls any brake hose or pipe or any part of the body structure.

☐ Examine the steering rack rubber gaiters for damage or insecurity of the retaining clips. If power steering is fitted, check for signs of damage or leakage of the fluid hoses, pipes or connections. Also check for excessive stiffness or binding of the steering, a missing split pin or locking device, or severe corrosion of the body structure within 30 cm of any steering component attachment point.

Front and rear suspension and wheel bearings

☐ Starting at the front right-hand side, grasp the roadwheel at the 3 o'clock and 9 o'clock positions and rock gently but firmly. Check for free play or insecurity at the wheel bearings, suspension balljoints, or suspension mountings, pivots and attachments.

☐ Now grasp the wheel at the 12 o'clock and 6 o'clock positions and repeat the previous inspection. Spin the wheel, and check for roughness or tightness of the front wheel bearing.

☐ If excess free play is suspected at a component pivot point, this can be confirmed by using a large screwdriver or similar tool and levering between the mounting and the component attachment. This will confirm whether the wear is in the pivot bush, its retaining bolt, or in the mounting itself (the bolt holes can often become elongated).

☐ Carry out all the above checks at the other front wheel, and then at both rear wheels.

Springs and shock absorbers

☐ Examine the suspension struts (when applicable) for serious fluid leakage, corrosion, or damage to the casing. Also check the security of the mounting points.

☐ If coil springs are fitted, check that the spring ends locate in their seats, and that the spring is not corroded, cracked or broken.

☐ If leaf springs are fitted, check that all leaves are intact, that the axle is securely attached to each spring, and that there is no deterioration of the spring eye mountings, bushes, and shackles.

☐ The same general checks apply to vehicles fitted with other suspension types, such as torsion bars, hydraulic displacer units, etc. Ensure that all mountings and attachments are secure, that there are no signs of excessive wear, corrosion or damage, and (on hydraulic types) that there are no fluid leaks or damaged pipes.

☐ Inspect the shock absorbers for signs of serious fluid leakage. Check for wear of the mounting bushes or attachments, or damage to the body of the unit.

Driveshafts (fwd vehicles only)

☐ Rotate each front wheel in turn and inspect the constant velocity joint gaiters for splits or damage. Also check that each driveshaft is straight and undamaged.

Braking system

☐ If possible without dismantling, check brake pad wear and disc condition. Ensure that the friction lining material has not worn excessively, (A) and that the discs are not fractured, pitted, scored or badly worn (B).

☐ Examine all the rigid brake pipes underneath the vehicle, and the flexible hose(s) at the rear. Look for corrosion, chafing or insecurity of the pipes, and for signs of bulging under pressure, chafing, splits or deterioration of the flexible hoses.

☐ Look for signs of fluid leaks at the brake calipers or on the brake backplates. Repair or renew leaking components.

☐ Slowly spin each wheel, while your assistant depresses and releases the footbrake. Ensure that each brake is operating and does not bind when the pedal is released.

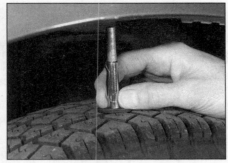

☐ Examine the handbrake mechanism, checking for frayed or broken cables, excessive corrosion, or wear or insecurity of the linkage. Check that the mechanism works on each relevant wheel, and releases fully, without binding.

☐ It is not possible to test brake efficiency without special equipment, but a road test can be carried out later to check that the vehicle pulls up in a straight line.

Fuel and exhaust systems

☐ Inspect the fuel tank (including the filler cap), fuel pipes, hoses and unions. All components must be secure and free from leaks.

☐ Examine the exhaust system over its entire length, checking for any damaged, broken or missing mountings, security of the retaining clamps and rust or corrosion.

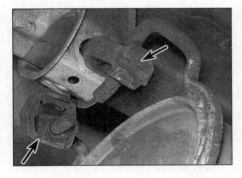

Wheels and tyres

☐ Examine the sidewalls and tread area of each tyre in turn. Check for cuts, tears, lumps, bulges, separation of the tread, and exposure of the ply or cord due to wear or damage. Check that the tyre bead is correctly seated on the wheel rim, that the valve is sound and properly seated, and that the wheel is not distorted or damaged.

☐ Check that the tyres are of the correct size for the vehicle, that they are of the same size and type on each axle, and that the pressures are correct.

☐ Check the tyre tread depth. The legal minimum at the time of writing is 1.6 mm over at least three-quarters of the tread width. Abnormal tread wear may indicate incorrect front wheel alignment.

Body corrosion

☐ Check the condition of the entire vehicle structure for signs of corrosion in load-bearing areas. (These include chassis box sections, side sills, cross-members, pillars, and all suspension, steering, braking system and seat belt mountings and anchorages.) Any corrosion which has seriously reduced the thickness of a load-bearing area is likely to cause the vehicle to fail. In this case professional repairs are likely to be needed.

☐ Damage or corrosion which causes sharp or otherwise dangerous edges to be exposed will also cause the vehicle to fail.

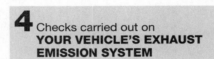

4 Checks carried out on **YOUR VEHICLE'S EXHAUST EMISSION SYSTEM**

Petrol models

☐ Have the engine at normal operating temperature, and make sure that it is in good tune (ignition system in good order, air filter element clean, etc).

☐ Before any measurements are carried out, raise the engine speed to around 2500 rpm, and hold it at this speed for 20 seconds. Allow the engine speed to return to idle, and watch for smoke emissions from the exhaust tailpipe. If the idle speed is obviously much too high, or if dense blue or clearly-visible black smoke comes from the tailpipe for more than 5 seconds, the vehicle will fail. As a rule of thumb, blue smoke signifies oil being burnt (engine wear) while black smoke signifies unburnt fuel (dirty air cleaner element, or other carburettor or fuel system fault).

☐ An exhaust gas analyser capable of measuring carbon monoxide (CO) and hydrocarbons (HC) is now needed. If such an instrument cannot be hired or borrowed, a local garage may agree to perform the check for a small fee.

CO emissions (mixture)

☐ At the time of writing, for vehicles first used between 1st August 1975 and 31st July 1986 (P to C registration), the CO level must not exceed 4.5% by volume. For vehicles first used between 1st August 1986 and 31st July 1992 (D to J registration), the CO level must not exceed 3.5% by volume. Vehicles first

used after 1st August 1992 (K registration) must conform to the manufacturer's specification. The MOT tester has access to a DOT database or emissions handbook, which lists the CO and HC limits for each make and model of vehicle. The CO level is measured with the engine at idle speed, and at "fast idle". The following limits are given as a general guide:

At idle speed -
CO level no more than 0.5%
At "fast idle" (2500 to 3000 rpm) -
CO level no more than 0.3%
(Minimum oil temperature 60ºC)

☐ If the CO level cannot be reduced far enough to pass the test (and the fuel and ignition systems are otherwise in good condition) then the carburettor is badly worn, or there is some problem in the fuel injection system or catalytic converter (as applicable).

HC emissions

☐ With the CO within limits, HC emissions for vehicles first used between 1st August 1975 and 31st July 1992 (P to J registration) must not exceed 1200 ppm. Vehicles first used after 1st August 1992 (K registration) must conform to the manufacturer's specification. The MOT tester has access to a DOT database or emissions handbook, which lists the CO and HC limits for each make and model of vehicle. The HC level is measured with the engine at "fast idle". The following is given as a general guide:

At "fast idle" (2500 to 3000 rpm) -
HC level no more than 200 ppm
(Minimum oil temperature 60ºC)

☐ Excessive HC emissions are caused by incomplete combustion, the causes of which can include oil being burnt, mechanical wear and ignition/fuel system malfunction.

Diesel models

☐ The only emission test applicable to Diesel engines is the measuring of exhaust smoke density. The test involves accelerating the engine several times to its maximum unloaded speed.

Note: It is of the utmost importance that the engine timing belt is in good condition before the test is carried out.

☐ The limits for Diesel engine exhaust smoke, introduced in September 1995 are:
Vehicles first used before 1st August 1979:
Exempt from metered smoke testing, but must not emit "dense blue or clearly visible black smoke for a period of more than 5 seconds at idle" or "dense blue or clearly visible black smoke during acceleration which would obscure the view of other road users".
Non-turbocharged vehicles first used after 1st August 1979: $2.5m^{-1}$
Turbocharged vehicles first used after 1st August 1979: $3.0m^{-1}$

☐ Excessive smoke can be caused by a dirty air cleaner element. Otherwise, professional advice may be needed to find the cause.

Engine

- ☐ Engine fails to rotate when attempting to start
- ☐ Engine rotates, but will not start
- ☐ Engine difficult to start when cold
- ☐ Engine difficult to start when hot
- ☐ Starter motor noisy or excessively-rough in engagement
- ☐ Engine starts, but stops immediately
- ☐ Engine idles erratically
- ☐ Engine misfires at idle speed
- ☐ Engine misfires throughout the driving speed range
- ☐ Engine hesitates on acceleration
- ☐ Engine stalls
- ☐ Engine lacks power
- ☐ Engine backfires
- ☐ Oil pressure warning light illuminated with engine running
- ☐ Engine runs-on after switching off
- ☐ Engine noises

Cooling system

- ☐ Overheating
- ☐ Overcooling
- ☐ External coolant leakage
- ☐ Internal coolant leakage
- ☐ Corrosion

Fuel and exhaust systems

- ☐ Excessive fuel consumption
- ☐ Fuel leakage and/or fuel odour
- ☐ Excessive noise or fumes from exhaust system

Clutch

- ☐ Pedal travels to floor – no pressure or very little resistance
- ☐ Clutch fails to disengage (unable to select gears)
- ☐ Clutch slips (engine speed increases, with no increase in vehicle speed)
- ☐ Judder as clutch is engaged
- ☐ Noise when depressing or releasing clutch pedal

Manual transmission

- ☐ Noisy in neutral with engine running
- ☐ Noisy in one particular gear
- ☐ Difficulty engaging gears
- ☐ Jumps out of gear
- ☐ Vibration
- ☐ Lubricant leaks

Automatic transmission

- ☐ Fluid leakage
- ☐ General gear selection problems
- ☐ Transmission will not downshift (kickdown) with accelerator pedal fully depressed
- ☐ Engine will not start in any gear, or starts in gears other than Park or Neutral
- ☐ Transmission slips, shifts roughly, is noisy, or has no drive in forward or reverse gears

Driveshafts

- ☐ Vibration when accelerating or decelerating
- ☐ Clicking or knocking noise on turns (at slow speed on full-lock)

Braking system

- ☐ Vehicle pulls to one side under braking
- ☐ Noise (grinding or high-pitched squeal) when brakes applied
- ☐ Excessive brake pedal travel
- ☐ Brake pedal feels spongy when depressed
- ☐ Excessive brake pedal effort required to stop vehicle
- ☐ Judder felt through brake pedal or steering wheel when braking
- ☐ Pedal pulsates when braking hard
- ☐ Brakes binding

Steering and suspension

- ☐ Vehicle pulls to one side
- ☐ Wheel wobble and vibration
- ☐ Excessive pitching and/or rolling around corners, or during braking
- ☐ Wandering or general instability
- ☐ Excessively-stiff steering
- ☐ Excessive play in steering
- ☐ Lack of power assistance
- ☐ Tyre wear excessive

Electrical system

- ☐ Battery will not hold a charge for more than a few days
- ☐ Ignition/no-charge warning light remains illuminated with engine running
- ☐ Ignition/no-charge warning light fails to come on
- ☐ Lights inoperative
- ☐ Instrument readings inaccurate or erratic
- ☐ Horn inoperative, or unsatisfactory in operation
- ☐ Windscreen/tailgate wipers inoperative, or unsatisfactory in operation
- ☐ Windscreen washers inoperative, or unsatisfactory in operation
- ☐ Electric windows inoperative, or unsatisfactory in operation

Introduction

The vehicle owner who does his or her own maintenance according to the recommended service schedules should not have to use this section of the manual very often. Modern component reliability is such that, provided those items subject to wear or deterioration are inspected or renewed at the specified intervals, sudden failure is comparatively rare. Faults do not usually just happen as a result of sudden failure, but develop over a period of time. Major mechanical failures in particular are usually preceded by characteristic symptoms over hundreds or even thousands of miles. Those components which do

occasionally fail without warning are often small and easily carried in the vehicle.

With any fault-finding, the first step is to decide where to begin investigations. Sometimes this is obvious, but on other occasions, a little detective work will be necessary. The owner who makes half a dozen haphazard adjustments or replacements may be successful in curing a fault (or its symptoms), but will be none the wiser if the fault recurs, and ultimately may have spent more time and money than was necessary. A calm and logical approach will be found to be more satisfactory in the long

run. Always take into account any warning signs or abnormalities that may have been noticed in the period preceding the fault – power loss, high or low gauge readings, unusual smells, etc – and remember that failure of components such as fuses or spark plugs may only be pointers to some underlying fault.

The pages which follow provide an easy-reference guide to the more common problems which may occur during the operation of the vehicle. These problems and their possible causes are grouped under headings denoting various components or systems, such as Engine, Cooling system, etc. The general Chapter which deals with the problem is also shown in brackets; refer to the relevant part of that Chapter for system-specific information. Whatever the fault, certain basic principles apply. These are as follows:

☐ *Verify the fault*. This is simply a matter of being sure that you know what the symptoms are before starting work. This is particularly important if you are investigating a fault for someone else, who may not have described it very accurately.

☐ *Don't overlook the obvious*. For example, if the vehicle won't start, is there fuel in the tank? (Don't take anyone else's word on this particular point, and don't trust the fuel gauge either!) If an electrical fault is indicated, look for loose or broken wires before digging out the test gear.

☐ *Cure the disease, not the symptom*. Substituting a flat battery with a fully-charged one will get you off the hard shoulder, but if the underlying cause is not attended to, the new battery will go the same way. Similarly, changing oil-fouled spark plugs for a new set

will get you moving again, but remember that the reason for the fouling (if it wasn't simply an incorrect grade of plug) will have to be established and corrected.

☐ *Don't take anything for granted*. Particularly, don't forget that a new component may itself be defective (especially if its been rattling around in the boot for months), and don't leave components out of a fault diagnosis sequence just because they are new or recently-fitted. When you do finally diagnose a difficult fault, you'll probably realise that all the evidence was there from the start.

Engine

Engine fails to rotate when attempting to start

☐ Battery terminal connections loose or corroded (see *Weekly checks*).
☐ Battery discharged or faulty (Chapter 5A).
☐ Broken, loose or disconnected wiring in the starting circuit (Chapter 5A).
☐ Defective starter solenoid or switch (Chapter 5A).
☐ Defective starter motor (Chapter 5A).
☐ Starter pinion or flywheel/driveplate ring gear teeth loose or broken (Chapter 2 and 5A).
☐ Engine earth strap broken or disconnected (Chapter 5A).

Engine rotates, but will not start

☐ Fuel tank empty.
☐ Battery discharged (engine rotates slowly) (Chapter 5A).
☐ Battery terminal connections loose or corroded (see *Weekly checks*).
☐ Ignition components damp or damaged (Chapters 1 and 5B).
☐ Broken, loose or disconnected wiring in the ignition circuit (Chapters 1 and 5B).
☐ Worn, faulty or incorrectly-gapped spark plugs (Chapter 1).
☐ Fuel injection system fault (Chapter 4A).
☐ Major mechanical failure (e.g. timing chain/belt) (Chapter 2).

Engine difficult to start when cold

☐ Battery discharged (Chapter 5A).
☐ Battery terminal connections loose or corroded (see *Weekly checks*).
☐ Worn, faulty or incorrectly-gapped spark plugs (Chapter 1).
☐ Fuel injection system fault (Chapter 4A).
☐ Other ignition system fault (Chapters 1 and 5B).
☐ Low cylinder compressions (Chapter 2).

Engine difficult to start when hot

☐ Air filter element dirty or clogged (Chapter 1).
☐ Fuel injection system fault (Chapter 4A).
☐ Low cylinder compressions (Chapter 2).

Starter motor noisy or excessively-rough in engagement

☐ Starter pinion or flywheel ring gear teeth loose or broken (Chapter 2 and 5A).
☐ Starter motor mounting bolts loose or missing (Chapter 5A).
☐ Starter motor internal components worn or damaged (Chapter 5A).

Engine starts, but stops immediately

☐ Loose or faulty electrical connections in the ignition circuit (Chapters 1 and 5B).
☐ Vacuum leak at the throttle body or inlet manifold (Chapter 4A).
☐ Blocked injector/fuel injection system fault (Chapter 4A).

Engine idles erratically

☐ Air filter element clogged (Chapter 1).
☐ Vacuum leak at the throttle body, inlet manifold or associated hoses (Chapter 4A).
☐ Worn, faulty or incorrectly-gapped spark plugs (Chapter 1).
☐ Uneven or low cylinder compressions (Chapter 2).
☐ Camshaft lobes worn (Chapter 2).
☐ Timing chain/belt incorrectly fitted (Chapter 2).
☐ Blocked injector/fuel injection system fault (Chapter 4A).

Engine misfires at idle speed

☐ Worn, faulty or incorrectly-gapped spark plugs (Chapter 1).
☐ Faulty spark plug HT leads (Chapter 1).
☐ Vacuum leak at the throttle body, inlet manifold or associated hoses (Chapter 4A).
☐ Blocked injector/fuel injection system fault (Chapter 4A).
☐ Uneven or low cylinder compressions (Chapter 2).
☐ Disconnected, leaking, or perished crankcase ventilation hoses (Chapter 4B).

Engine misfires throughout the driving speed range

☐ Fuel filter choked (Chapter 1).
☐ Fuel pump faulty, or delivery pressure low (Chapter 4A).
☐ Fuel tank vent blocked, or fuel pipes restricted (Chapter 4).
☐ Vacuum leak at the throttle body, inlet manifold or associated hoses (Chapter 4A).
☐ Worn, faulty or incorrectly-gapped spark plugs (Chapter 1).
☐ Faulty spark plug HT leads (Chapter 1).
☐ Faulty ignition coil(s) – petrol models (Chapter 5B).
☐ Uneven or low cylinder compressions (Chapter 2).
☐ Blocked injector/fuel injection system fault (Chapter 4A).

Engine hesitates on acceleration

☐ Worn, faulty or incorrectly-gapped spark plugs (Chapter 1).
☐ Vacuum leak at the throttle body, inlet manifold or associated hoses (Chapter 4A).
☐ Blocked injector/fuel injection system fault (Chapter 4A).

Engine stalls

☐ Vacuum leak at the throttle body, inlet manifold or associated hoses (Chapter 4A).
☐ Fuel filter choked (Chapter 1 and 4).
☐ Fuel pump faulty, or delivery pressure low (Chapter 4A).
☐ Fuel tank vent blocked, or fuel pipes restricted (Chapter 4).
☐ Blocked injector/fuel injection system fault Chapter 4A).

Engine (continued)

Engine lacks power

- [ ] Timing chain/belt incorrectly fitted or tensioned (Chapter 2).
- [ ] Fuel filter choked (Chapter 1 and 4).
- [ ] Fuel pump faulty, or delivery pressure low (Chapter 4A).
- [ ] Uneven or low cylinder compressions (Chapter 2).
- [ ] Worn, faulty or incorrectly-gapped spark plugs (Chapter 1).
- [ ] Vacuum leak at the throttle body, inlet manifold or associated hoses (Chapter 4A).
- [ ] Blocked injector/fuel injection system fault (Chapter 4A).
- [ ] Brakes binding (Chapters 1 and 9).
- [ ] Clutch slipping (Chapter 6).
- [ ] Air filter element clogged (Chapter 1).

Engine backfires

- [ ] Timing chain/belt incorrectly fitted or tensioned (Chapter 2).
- [ ] Vacuum leak at the throttle body, inlet manifold or associated hoses (Chapter 4A).
- [ ] Incorrect HT firing sequence (Chapter 5B)
- [ ] Blocked injector/fuel injection system fault (Chapter 4A).

Oil pressure warning light illuminated with engine running

- [ ] Low oil level, or incorrect oil grade (*Weekly checks*).
- [ ] Faulty oil pressure switch (Chapter 2).
- [ ] Worn engine bearings and/or oil pump (Chapter 2).
- [ ] High engine operating temperature (Chapter 3).
- [ ] Oil pressure relief valve defective (Chapter 2).
- [ ] Oil pick-up strainer clogged (Chapter 2).

Engine runs-on after switching off

- [ ] Excessive carbon build-up in engine (Chapter 2).
- [ ] High engine operating temperature (Chapter 3).
- [ ] Fuel injection system fault (Chapter 4A).

Engine noises

Pre-ignition (pinking) or knocking during acceleration or under load

- [ ] Ignition system fault (Chapters 1 and 5B).
- [ ] Incorrect grade of spark plug (Chapter 1).
- [ ] Vacuum leak at the throttle body, inlet manifold or associated hoses (Chapter 4A).
- [ ] Excessive carbon build-up in engine (Chapter 2).
- [ ] Blocked injector/fuel injection system fault (Chapter 4A).

Whistling or wheezing noises

- [ ] Leaking inlet manifold or throttle body gasket (Chapter 4A).
- [ ] Leaking exhaust manifold gasket or pipe-to-manifold joint (Chapter 4).
- [ ] Leaking vacuum hose (Chapters 4 and 9).
- [ ] Blowing cylinder head gasket (Chapter 2).

Tapping or rattling noises

- [ ] Worn or defective lost motion adjusters (Chapter 2).
- [ ] Worn valve gear or camshaft (Chapter 2).
- [ ] Ancillary component fault (coolant pump, alternator, etc) (Chapters 3, 5, etc).

Knocking or thumping noises

- [ ] Worn big-end bearings (regular heavy knocking, perhaps less under load) (Chapter 2).
- [ ] Worn main bearings (rumbling and knocking, perhaps worsening under load) (Chapter 2).
- [ ] Piston slap (most noticeable when cold) (Chapter 2).
- [ ] Ancillary component fault (coolant pump, alternator, etc) (Chapters 3, 5, etc).

Cooling system

Overheating

- [ ] Insufficient coolant in system (*Weekly checks*).
- [ ] Thermostat faulty (Chapter 3).
- [ ] Radiator core blocked, or grille restricted (Chapter 3).
- [ ] Electric cooling fan or thermostatic switch faulty (Chapter 3).
- [ ] Inaccurate temperature gauge sender unit (Chapter 3).
- [ ] Airlock in cooling system.
- [ ] Expansion tank pressure cap faulty (Chapter 3).

Overcooling

- [ ] Thermostat faulty (Chapter 3).
- [ ] Inaccurate temperature gauge sender unit (Chapter 3).

External coolant leakage

- [ ] Deteriorated or damaged hoses or hose clips (Chapter 1).

- [ ] Radiator core or heater matrix leaking (Chapter 3).
- [ ] Pressure cap faulty (Chapter 3).
- [ ] Coolant pump internal seal leaking (Chapter 3).
- [ ] Coolant pump-to-housing seal leaking (Chapter 3).
- [ ] Boiling due to overheating (Chapter 3).
- [ ] Core plug leaking (Chapter 2).

Internal coolant leakage

- [ ] Leaking cylinder head gasket (Chapter 2).
- [ ] Cracked cylinder head or cylinder block (Chapter 2).

Corrosion

- [ ] Infrequent draining and flushing (Chapter 1).
- [ ] Incorrect coolant mixture or inappropriate coolant type (see *Weekly checks*).

Fuel and exhaust systems

Excessive fuel consumption

- [ ] Air filter element dirty or clogged (Chapter 1).
- [ ] Fuel injection system fault (Chapter 4A).
- [ ] Ignition system fault (Chapters 1 and 5B).
- [ ] Brakes binding (Chapter 9).
- [ ] Tyres under-inflated (see *Weekly checks*).

Fuel leakage and/or fuel odour

- [ ] Damaged fuel tank, pipes or connections (Chapter 4).

Excessive noise or fumes from exhaust system

- [ ] Leaking exhaust system or manifold joints (Chapters 1 and 4).
- [ ] Leaking, corroded or damaged silencers or pipe (Chapters 1 and 4).
- [ ] Broken mountings causing body or suspension contact (Chapter 1).

Clutch

Pedal travels to floor – no pressure or very little resistance

☐ Faulty master or slave cylinder (Chapter 6).
☐ Faulty hydraulic release system (Chapter 6).
☐ Broken clutch release bearing or arm (Chapter 6).
☐ Broken diaphragm spring in clutch pressure plate (Chapter 6).

Clutch fails to disengage (unable to select gears)

☐ Faulty master or slave cylinder (Chapter 6).
☐ Faulty hydraulic release system (Chapter 6).
☐ Clutch disc sticking on gearbox input shaft splines (Chapter 6).
☐ Clutch disc sticking to flywheel or pressure plate (Chapter 6).
☐ Faulty pressure plate assembly (Chapter 6).

Clutch slips (engine speed increases, with no increase in vehicle speed)

☐ Faulty hydraulic release system (Chapter 6).

☐ Clutch disc linings excessively worn (Chapter 6).
☐ Clutch disc linings contaminated with oil or grease (Chapter 6).
☐ Faulty pressure plate or weak diaphragm spring (Chapter 6).

Judder as clutch is engaged

☐ Clutch disc linings contaminated with oil or grease (Chapter 6).
☐ Clutch disc linings excessively worn (Chapter 6).
☐ Faulty or distorted pressure plate or diaphragm spring (Chapter 6).
☐ Worn or loose engine or gearbox mountings (Chapter 2).
☐ Clutch disc hub or gearbox input shaft splines worn (Chapter 6).

Noise when depressing or releasing clutch pedal

☐ Worn clutch release bearing (Chapter 6).
☐ Worn or dry clutch pedal pivot (Chapter 6).
☐ Faulty pressure plate assembly (Chapter 6).
☐ Pressure plate diaphragm spring broken (Chapter 6).
☐ Broken clutch friction plate cushioning springs (Chapter 6).

Manual transmission

Noisy in neutral with engine running

☐ Input shaft bearings worn (noise apparent with clutch pedal released, but not when depressed) (Chapter 7A).*
☐ Clutch release bearing worn (noise apparent with clutch pedal depressed, possibly less when released) (Chapter 6).

Noisy in one particular gear

☐ Worn, damaged or chipped gear teeth (Chapter 7A).*

Difficulty engaging gears

☐ Clutch fault (Chapter 6).
☐ Worn or damaged gear linkage (Chapter 7A).
☐ Worn synchroniser units (Chapter 7A).*

Jumps out of gear

☐ Worn or damaged gear linkage (Chapter 7A).

☐ Worn synchroniser units (Chapter 7A).*
☐ Worn selector forks (Chapter 7A).*

Vibration

☐ Lack of oil (Chapter 1).
☐ Worn bearings (Chapter 7A).*

Lubricant leaks

☐ Leaking oil seal (Chapter 7A).
☐ Leaking housing joint (Chapter 7A).*
☐ Leaking input shaft oil seal (Chapter 7A).

*Although the corrective action necessary to remedy the symptoms described is beyond the scope of the home mechanic, the above information should be helpful in isolating the cause of the condition, so that the owner can communicate clearly with a professional mechanic.

Automatic transmission/Constantly variable transmission

Note: *Due to the complexity of the automatic transmission/constantly variable transmission, it is difficult for the home mechanic to properly diagnose and service this unit. For problems other than the following, the vehicle should be taken to a dealer service department or automatic transmission specialist. Do not be too hasty in removing the transmission if a fault is suspected, as most of the testing is carried out with the unit still fitted.*

Fluid leakage

☐ Automatic transmission fluid is usually dark in colour. Fluid leaks should not be confused with engine oil, which can easily be blown onto the transmission by airflow.
☐ To determine the source of a leak, first remove all built-up dirt and grime from the transmission housing and surrounding areas using a degreasing agent, or by steam-cleaning. Drive the vehicle at low speed, so airflow will not blow the leak far from its source. Raise and support the vehicle, and determine where the leak is coming from.

General gear selection problems

☐ Chapter 7B deals with checking and adjusting the selector mechanism on automatic transmissions. The following are common problems which may be caused by a poorly-adjusted mechanism:
a) *Engine starting in gears other than Park or Neutral.*
b) *Indicator panel indicating a gear other than the one actually being used.*

c) *Vehicle moves when in Park or Neutral.*
d) *Poor gear shift quality or erratic gear changes.*
☐ Refer to Chapter 7B for the selector mechanism adjustment procedure.

Transmission will not downshift (kickdown) with accelerator pedal fully depressed

☐ Low transmission fluid level (Chapter 1).
☐ Incorrect selector mechanism adjustment (Chapter 7B).

Engine will not start in any gear, or starts in gears other than Park or Neutral

☐ Incorrect selector mechanism adjustment (Chapter 7B).

Transmission slips, shifts roughly, is noisy, or has no drive in forward or reverse gears

☐ There are many probable causes for the above problems, but unless there is a very obvious reason (such as a loose or corroded wiring plug connection on or near the transmission), the car should be taken to a franchise dealer or automatic transmission specialist for the fault to be diagnosed. The transmission control unit incorporates a self-diagnosis facility, and any fault codes can quickly be read and interpreted by a dealer or specialist with the proper diagnostic equipment.

Driveshafts

Vibration when accelerating or decelerating

- [ ] Worn inner constant velocity joint (Chapter 8).
- [ ] Bent or distorted driveshaft (Chapter 8).

Clicking or knocking noise on turns (at slow speed on full-lock)

- [ ] Worn outer constant velocity joint (Chapter 8).
- [ ] Lack of constant velocity joint lubricant, possibly due to damaged gaiter (Chapter 8).

Braking system

Note: *Before assuming that a brake problem exists, make sure that the tyres are in good condition and correctly inflated, that the front wheel alignment is correct, and that the vehicle is not loaded with weight in an unequal manner. Apart from checking the condition of all pipe and hose connections, any faults occurring on the anti-lock braking system should be referred to a Honda dealer or specialist for diagnosis.*

Vehicle pulls to one side under braking

- [ ] Worn, defective, damaged or contaminated front or rear brake pads/shoes on one side (Chapters 1 and 9).
- [ ] Seized or partially-seized front or rear brake caliper/wheel cylinder (Chapter 9).
- [ ] A mixture of brake pad/shoe lining materials fitted between sides (Chapter 9).
- [ ] Leaking wheel cylinder (Chapter 9).
- [ ] Brake caliper mounting bolts loose (Chapter 9).
- [ ] Worn or damaged steering or suspension components (Chapters 1 and 10).

Noise (grinding or high-pitched squeal) when brakes applied

- [ ] Brake pad/shoe friction lining material worn down to metal backing (Chapters 1 and 9).
- [ ] Excessive corrosion of brake disc/drum – may be apparent after the vehicle has been standing for some time (Chapters 1 and 9).
- [ ] Foreign object (stone chipping, etc) trapped between brake disc and shield (Chapters 1 and 9).

Excessive brake pedal travel

- [ ] Faulty master cylinder (Chapter 9).
- [ ] Air in hydraulic system (Chapter 9).
- [ ] Faulty vacuum servo unit (Chapter 9).

Brake pedal feels spongy when depressed

- [ ] Air in hydraulic system (Chapter 9).

- [ ] Deteriorated flexible rubber brake hoses (Chapters 1 and 9).
- [ ] Master cylinder mountings loose (Chapter 9).
- [ ] Faulty master cylinder (Chapter 9).

Excessive brake pedal effort required to stop vehicle

- [ ] Faulty vacuum servo unit (Chapter 9).
- [ ] Disconnected, damaged or insecure brake servo vacuum hose (Chapters 1 and 9).
- [ ] Primary or secondary hydraulic circuit failure (Chapter 9).
- [ ] Seized brake caliper/wheel cylinder (Chapter 9).
- [ ] Brake pads/shoes incorrectly fitted (Chapter 9).
- [ ] Incorrect grade of brake pads/shoes fitted (Chapter 9).
- [ ] Brake pads/shoes contaminated (Chapter 9).

Judder felt through brake pedal or steering wheel when braking

- [ ] Excessive run-out or distortion of brake disc(s)/drum(s) (Chapter 9).
- [ ] Brake pad/shoe linings worn (Chapters 1 and 9).
- [ ] Brake caliper mounting bolts loose (Chapter 9).
- [ ] Wear in suspension or steering components or mountings (Chapters 1 and 10).

Pedal pulsates when braking hard

- [ ] Normal feature of ABS – no fault

Brakes binding

- [ ] Seized brake caliper piston(s)/ wheel cylinder (Chapter 9).
- [ ] Incorrectly-adjusted handbrake mechanism (Chapter 9).
- [ ] Faulty master cylinder (Chapter 9).

Rear wheels locking under normal braking

- [ ] Rear brake pad/shoe linings contaminated (Chapters 1 and 9).
- [ ] Rear brake discs/shoes warped (Chapters 1 and 9).

Steering and suspension

Note: *Before diagnosing suspension or steering faults, be sure that the trouble is not due to incorrect tyre pressures, mixtures of tyre types, or binding brakes.*

Vehicle pulls to one side

- [ ] Defective tyre (see *Weekly checks*).
- [ ] Excessive wear in suspension or steering components (Chapters 1 and 10).
- [ ] Incorrect front wheel alignment (Chapter 10).
- [ ] Accident damage to steering or suspension components (Chapters 1 and 10).

Wheel wobble and vibration

- [ ] Front roadwheels out of balance (vibration felt mainly through the steering wheel) (Chapter 10).
- [ ] Rear roadwheels out of balance (vibration felt throughout the vehicle) (Chapter 10).
- [ ] Roadwheels damaged or distorted (Chapter 10).
- [ ] Faulty or damaged tyre (*Weekly checks*).
- [ ] Worn steering or suspension joints, bushes or components (Chapters 1 and 10).
- [ ] Wheel bolts loose (Chapter 1 and 10).

Excessive pitching and/or rolling around corners, or during braking

- [ ] Defective shock absorbers (Chapters 1 and 10).
- [ ] Broken or weak coil spring and/or suspension component (Chapters 1 and 10).
- [ ] Worn or damaged anti-roll bar or mountings (Chapter 10).

Wandering or general instability

- [ ] Incorrect front wheel alignment (Chapter 10).
- [ ] Worn steering or suspension joints, bushes or components (Chapters 1 and 10).
- [ ] Roadwheels out of balance (Chapter 10).
- [ ] Faulty or damaged tyre (*Weekly checks*).
- [ ] Wheel bolts loose (Chapter 10).
- [ ] Defective shock absorbers (Chapters 1 and 10).

Excessively-stiff steering

- [ ] Seized track rod end balljoint or suspension balljoint (Chapters 1 and 10).

- [ ] Broken or incorrectly adjusted auxiliary drivebelt (Chapter 1).
- [ ] Incorrect front wheel alignment (Chapter 10).
- [ ] Steering gear damaged (Chapter 10).

Excessive play in steering

- [ ] Worn steering column universal joint(s) (Chapter 10).
- [ ] Worn steering track rod end balljoints (Chapters 1 and 10).
- [ ] Worn steering gear (Chapter 10).
- [ ] Worn steering or suspension joints, bushes or components (Chapters 1 and 10).

Lack of power assistance

- [ ] Broken or incorrectly-adjusted auxiliary drivebelt (Chapter 1).
- [ ] Incorrect power steering fluid level (*Weekly checks*).
- [ ] Restriction in power steering fluid hoses (Chapter 10).
- [ ] Faulty power steering pump (Chapter 10).
- [ ] Faulty steering gear (Chapter 10).

Tyre wear excessive

Tyres worn on inside or outside edges

- [ ] Incorrect camber or castor angles (Chapter 10).
- [ ] Worn steering or suspension joints, bushes or components (Chapters 1 and 10).
- [ ] Excessively-hard cornering.
- [ ] Accident damage.

Tyre treads exhibit feathered edges

- [ ] Incorrect toe setting (Chapter 10).

Tyres worn in centre of tread

- [ ] Tyres over-inflated (*Weekly checks*).

Tyres worn on inside and outside edges

- [ ] Tyres under-inflated (*Weekly checks*).
- [ ] Worn shock absorbers (Chapter 10).

Tyres worn unevenly

- [ ] Tyres/wheels out of balance (*Weekly checks*).
- [ ] Excessive wheel or tyre run-out (Chapter 10).
- [ ] Worn shock absorbers (Chapters 1 and 10).
- [ ] Faulty tyre (*Weekly checks*).

Electrical system

Note: *For problems associated with the starting system, refer to the faults listed under Engine earlier in this Section.*

Battery will not hold a charge for more than a few days

- [ ] Battery defective internally (Chapter 5A).
- [ ] Battery electrolyte level low – where applicable (*Weekly checks*).
- [ ] Battery terminal connections loose or corroded (*Weekly checks*).
- [ ] Auxiliary drivebelt worn – or incorrectly adjusted, where applicable (Chapter 1).
- [ ] Alternator not charging at correct output (Chapter 5A).
- [ ] Alternator or voltage regulator faulty (Chapter 5A).
- [ ] Short-circuit causing continual battery drain (Chapters 5 and 12).

Ignition/no-charge warning light remains illuminated with engine running

- [ ] Auxiliary drivebelt broken, worn, or incorrectly adjusted (Chapter 1).
- [ ] Internal fault in alternator or voltage regulator (Chapter 5A).
- [ ] Broken, disconnected, or loose wiring in charging circuit (Chapter 5A).

Ignition/no-charge warning light fails to come on

- [ ] Broken, disconnected, or loose wiring in warning light circuit (Chapter 12).
- [ ] Alternator faulty (Chapter 5A).

Lights inoperative

- [ ] Bulb blown (Chapter 12).
- [ ] Corrosion of bulb or bulbholder contacts (Chapter 12).
- [ ] Blown fuse (Chapter 12).
- [ ] Faulty relay (Chapter 12).
- [ ] Broken, loose, or disconnected wiring (Chapter 12).
- [ ] Faulty switch (Chapter 12).

Instrument readings inaccurate or erratic

Fuel or temperature gauges give no reading

- [ ] Faulty gauge sender unit (Chapters 3 and 4).
- [ ] Wiring open-circuit (Chapter 12).
- [ ] Faulty gauge (Chapter 12).

Fuel or temperature gauges give continuous maximum reading

- [ ] Faulty gauge sender unit (Chapters 3 and 4).
- [ ] Wiring short-circuit (Chapter 12).
- [ ] Faulty gauge (Chapter 12).

Horn inoperative, or unsatisfactory in operation

Horn operates all the time

- [ ] Horn contacts permanently bridged or horn buttons stuck down (Chapter 12).

Horn fails to operate

- [ ] Blown fuse (Chapter 12).
- [ ] Cable or cable connections loose, broken or disconnected (Chapter 12).
- [ ] Faulty horn (Chapter 12).

Horn emits intermittent or unsatisfactory sound

- [ ] Cable connections loose (Chapter 12).
- [ ] Horn mountings loose (Chapter 12).
- [ ] Faulty horn (Chapter 12).

Windscreen/tailgate wipers inoperative, or unsatisfactory in operation

Wipers fail to operate, or operate very slowly

- [ ] Wiper blades stuck to screen, or linkage seized or binding (*Weekly checks* and Chapter 12).

- [ ] Blown fuse (Chapter 12).
- [ ] Cable or cable connections loose, broken or disconnected (Chapter 12).
- [ ] Faulty relay (Chapter 12).
- [ ] Faulty wiper motor (Chapter 12).

Wiper blades sweep over too large or too small an area of the glass

- [ ] Wiper arms incorrectly positioned on spindles (Chapter 12).
- [ ] Excessive wear of wiper linkage (Chapter 12).
- [ ] Wiper motor or linkage mountings loose or insecure (Chapter 12).

Wiper blades fail to clean the glass effectively

- [ ] Wiper blade rubbers worn or perished (*Weekly checks*).
- [ ] Wiper arm tension springs broken, or arm pivots seized (Chapter 12).
- [ ] Insufficient windscreen washer additive to adequately remove road film (*Weekly checks*).

Windscreen washers inoperative, or unsatisfactory in operation

One or more washer jets inoperative

- [ ] Blocked washer jet (Chapter 12).
- [ ] Disconnected, kinked or restricted fluid hose (Chapter 12).
- [ ] Insufficient fluid in washer reservoir (*Weekly checks*).

Washer pump fails to operate

- [ ] Broken or disconnected wiring or connections (Chapter 12).
- [ ] Blown fuse (Chapter 12).
- [ ] Faulty washer switch (Chapter 12).
- [ ] Faulty washer pump (Chapter 12).

Electric windows inoperative, or unsatisfactory in operation

Window glass will only move in one direction

- [ ] Faulty switch (Chapter 12).

Window glass slow to move

- [ ] Regulator seized or damaged, or in need of lubrication (Chapter 11).
- [ ] Door internal components or trim fouling regulator (Chapter 11).
- [ ] Faulty motor (Chapter 11).

Window glass fails to move

- [ ] Blown fuse (Chapter 12).
- [ ] Faulty relay (Chapter 12).
- [ ] Broken or disconnected wiring or connections (Chapter 12).
- [ ] Faulty motor (Chapter 12).

Central locking system inoperative, or unsatisfactory in operation

Complete system failure

- [ ] Blown fuse (Chapter 12).
- [ ] Faulty relay (Chapter 12).
- [ ] Broken or disconnected wiring or connections (Chapter 12).

Latch locks but will not unlock, or unlocks but will not lock

- [ ] Faulty switch (Chapter 12).
- [ ] Broken or disconnected latch operating rods or levers (Chapter 11).
- [ ] Faulty relay (Chapter 12).

One lock fails to operate

- [ ] Broken or disconnected wiring or connections (Chapter 12).
- [ ] Faulty motor (Chapter 11).
- [ ] Broken, binding or disconnected lock operating rods or levers (Chapter 11).
- [ ] Fault in door lock (Chapter 11).

A

ABS (Anti-lock brake system) A system, usually electronically controlled, that senses incipient wheel lockup during braking and relieves hydraulic pressure at wheels that are about to skid.

Air bag An inflatable bag hidden in the steering wheel (driver's side) or the dash or glovebox (passenger side). In a head-on collision, the bags inflate, preventing the driver and front passenger from being thrown forward into the steering wheel or windscreen.

Air cleaner A metal or plastic housing, containing a filter element, which removes dust and dirt from the air being drawn into the engine.

Air filter element The actual filter in an air cleaner system, usually manufactured from pleated paper and requiring renewal at regular intervals.

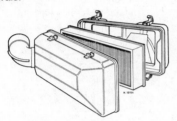

Air filter

Allen key A hexagonal wrench which fits into a recessed hexagonal hole.

Alligator clip A long-nosed spring-loaded metal clip with meshing teeth. Used to make temporary electrical connections.

Alternator A component in the electrical system which converts mechanical energy from a drivebelt into electrical energy to charge the battery and to operate the starting system, ignition system and electrical accessories.

Alternator (exploded view)

Ampere (amp) A unit of measurement for the flow of electric current. One amp is the amount of current produced by one volt acting through a resistance of one ohm.

Anaerobic sealer A substance used to prevent bolts and screws from loosening. Anaerobic means that it does not require oxygen for activation. The Loctite brand is widely used.

Antifreeze A substance (usually ethylene glycol) mixed with water, and added to a vehicle's cooling system, to prevent freezing of the coolant in winter. Antifreeze also contains chemicals to inhibit corrosion and the formation of rust and other deposits that would tend to clog the radiator and coolant passages and reduce cooling efficiency.

Anti-seize compound A coating that reduces the risk of seizing on fasteners that are subjected to high temperatures, such as exhaust manifold bolts and nuts.

Anti-seize compound

Asbestos A natural fibrous mineral with great heat resistance, commonly used in the composition of brake friction materials. Asbestos is a health hazard and the dust created by brake systems should never be inhaled or ingested.

Axle A shaft on which a wheel revolves, or which revolves with a wheel. Also, a solid beam that connects the two wheels at one end of the vehicle. An axle which also transmits power to the wheels is known as a live axle.

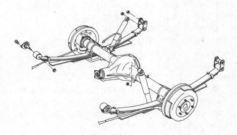

Axle assembly

Axleshaft A single rotating shaft, on either side of the differential, which delivers power from the final drive assembly to the drive wheels. Also called a driveshaft or a halfshaft.

B

Ball bearing An anti-friction bearing consisting of a hardened inner and outer race with hardened steel balls between two races.

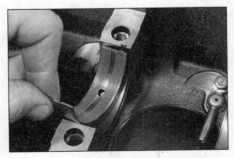

Bearing

Bearing The curved surface on a shaft or in a bore, or the part assembled into either, that permits relative motion between them with minimum wear and friction.

Big-end bearing The bearing in the end of the connecting rod that's attached to the crankshaft.

Bleed nipple A valve on a brake wheel cylinder, caliper or other hydraulic component that is opened to purge the hydraulic system of air. Also called a bleed screw.

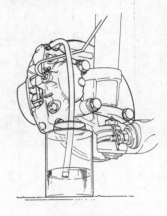

Brake bleeding

Brake bleeding Procedure for removing air from lines of a hydraulic brake system.

Brake disc The component of a disc brake that rotates with the wheels.

Brake drum The component of a drum brake that rotates with the wheels.

Brake linings The friction material which contacts the brake disc or drum to retard the vehicle's speed. The linings are bonded or riveted to the brake pads or shoes.

Brake pads The replaceable friction pads that pinch the brake disc when the brakes are applied. Brake pads consist of a friction material bonded or riveted to a rigid backing plate.

Brake shoe The crescent-shaped carrier to which the brake linings are mounted and which forces the lining against the rotating drum during braking.

Braking systems For more information on braking systems, consult the *Haynes Automotive Brake Manual*.

Breaker bar A long socket wrench handle providing greater leverage.

Bulkhead The insulated partition between the engine and the passenger compartment.

C

Caliper The non-rotating part of a disc-brake assembly that straddles the disc and carries the brake pads. The caliper also contains the hydraulic components that cause the pads to pinch the disc when the brakes are applied. A caliper is also a measuring tool that can be set to measure inside or outside dimensions of an object.

Camshaft A rotating shaft on which a series of cam lobes operate the valve mechanisms. The camshaft may be driven by gears, by sprockets and chain or by sprockets and a belt.

Canister A container in an evaporative emission control system; contains activated charcoal granules to trap vapours from the fuel system.

Canister

Carburettor A device which mixes fuel with air in the proper proportions to provide a desired power output from a spark ignition internal combustion engine.

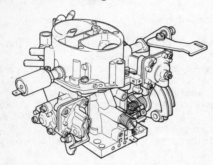

Carburettor

Castellated Resembling the parapets along the top of a castle wall. For example, a castellated balljoint stud nut.

Castellated nut

Castor In wheel alignment, the backward or forward tilt of the steering axis. Castor is positive when the steering axis is inclined rearward at the top.

Catalytic converter A silencer-like device in the exhaust system which converts certain pollutants in the exhaust gases into less harmful substances.

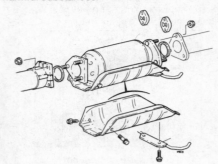

Catalytic converter

Circlip A ring-shaped clip used to prevent endwise movement of cylindrical parts and shafts. An internal circlip is installed in a groove in a housing; an external circlip fits into a groove on the outside of a cylindrical piece such as a shaft.

Clearance The amount of space between two parts. For example, between a piston and a cylinder, between a bearing and a journal, etc.

Coil spring A spiral of elastic steel found in various sizes throughout a vehicle, for example as a springing medium in the suspension and in the valve train.

Compression Reduction in volume, and increase in pressure and temperature, of a gas, caused by squeezing it into a smaller space.

Compression ratio The relationship between cylinder volume when the piston is at top dead centre and cylinder volume when the piston is at bottom dead centre.

Constant velocity (CV) joint A type of universal joint that cancels out vibrations caused by driving power being transmitted through an angle.

Core plug A disc or cup-shaped metal device inserted in a hole in a casting through which core was removed when the casting was formed. Also known as a freeze plug or expansion plug.

Crankcase The lower part of the engine block in which the crankshaft rotates.

Crankshaft The main rotating member, or shaft, running the length of the crankcase, with offset "throws" to which the connecting rods are attached.

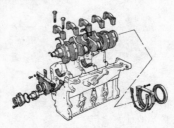

Crankshaft assembly

Crocodile clip See Alligator clip

D

Diagnostic code Code numbers obtained by accessing the diagnostic mode of an engine management computer. This code can be used to determine the area in the system where a malfunction may be located.

Disc brake A brake design incorporating a rotating disc onto which brake pads are squeezed. The resulting friction converts the energy of a moving vehicle into heat.

Double-overhead cam (DOHC) An engine that uses two overhead camshafts, usually one for the intake valves and one for the exhaust valves.

Drivebelt(s) The belt(s) used to drive accessories such as the alternator, water pump, power steering pump, air conditioning compressor, etc. off the crankshaft pulley.

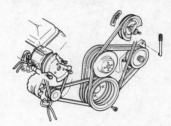

Accessory drivebelts

Driveshaft Any shaft used to transmit motion. Commonly used when referring to the axleshafts on a front wheel drive vehicle.

Driveshaft

Drum brake A type of brake using a drum-shaped metal cylinder attached to the inner surface of the wheel. When the brake pedal is pressed, curved brake shoes with friction linings press against the inside of the drum to slow or stop the vehicle.

Drum brake assembly

E

EGR valve A valve used to introduce exhaust gases into the intake air stream.

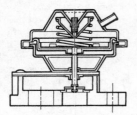

EGR valve

Electronic control unit (ECU) A computer which controls (for instance) ignition and fuel injection systems, or an anti-lock braking system. For more information refer to the *Haynes Automotive Electrical and Electronic Systems Manual.*

Electronic Fuel Injection (EFI) A computer controlled fuel system that distributes fuel through an injector located in each intake port of the engine.

Emergency brake A braking system, independent of the main hydraulic system, that can be used to slow or stop the vehicle if the primary brakes fail, or to hold the vehicle stationary even though the brake pedal isn't depressed. It usually consists of a hand lever that actuates either front or rear brakes mechanically through a series of cables and linkages. Also known as a handbrake or parking brake.

Endfloat The amount of lengthwise movement between two parts. As applied to a crankshaft, the distance that the crankshaft can move forward and back in the cylinder block.

Engine management system (EMS) A computer controlled system which manages the fuel injection and the ignition systems in an integrated fashion.

Exhaust manifold A part with several passages through which exhaust gases leave the engine combustion chambers and enter the exhaust pipe.

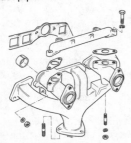

Exhaust manifold

F

Fan clutch A viscous (fluid) drive coupling device which permits variable engine fan speeds in relation to engine speeds.

Feeler blade A thin strip or blade of hardened steel, ground to an exact thickness, used to check or measure clearances between parts.

Feeler blade

Firing order The order in which the engine cylinders fire, or deliver their power strokes, beginning with the number one cylinder.

Flywheel A heavy spinning wheel in which energy is absorbed and stored by means of momentum. On cars, the flywheel is attached to the crankshaft to smooth out firing impulses.

Free play The amount of travel before any action takes place. The "looseness" in a linkage, or an assembly of parts, between the initial application of force and actual movement. For example, the distance the brake pedal moves before the pistons in the master cylinder are actuated.

Fuse An electrical device which protects a circuit against accidental overload. The typical fuse contains a soft piece of metal which is calibrated to melt at a predetermined current flow (expressed as amps) and break the circuit.

Fusible link A circuit protection device consisting of a conductor surrounded by heat-resistant insulation. The conductor is smaller than the wire it protects, so it acts as the weakest link in the circuit. Unlike a blown fuse, a failed fusible link must frequently be cut from the wire for replacement.

G

Gap The distance the spark must travel in jumping from the centre electrode to the side

Adjusting spark plug gap

electrode in a spark plug. Also refers to the spacing between the points in a contact breaker assembly in a conventional points-type ignition, or to the distance between the reluctor or rotor and the pickup coil in an electronic ignition.

Gasket Any thin, soft material - usually cork, cardboard, asbestos or soft metal - installed between two metal surfaces to ensure a good seal. For instance, the cylinder head gasket seals the joint between the block and the cylinder head.

Gasket

Gauge An instrument panel display used to monitor engine conditions. A gauge with a movable pointer on a dial or a fixed scale is an analogue gauge. A gauge with a numerical readout is called a digital gauge.

H

Halfshaft A rotating shaft that transmits power from the final drive unit to a drive wheel, usually when referring to a live rear axle.

Harmonic balancer A device designed to reduce torsion or twisting vibration in the crankshaft. May be incorporated in the crankshaft pulley. Also known as a vibration damper.

Hone An abrasive tool for correcting small irregularities or differences in diameter in an engine cylinder, brake cylinder, etc.

Hydraulic tappet A tappet that utilises hydraulic pressure from the engine's lubrication system to maintain zero clearance (constant contact with both camshaft and valve stem). Automatically adjusts to variation in valve stem length. Hydraulic tappets also reduce valve noise.

I

Ignition timing The moment at which the spark plug fires, usually expressed in the number of crankshaft degrees before the piston reaches the top of its stroke.

Inlet manifold A tube or housing with passages through which flows the air-fuel mixture (carburettor vehicles and vehicles with throttle body injection) or air only (port fuel-injected vehicles) to the port openings in the cylinder head.

J

Jump start Starting the engine of a vehicle with a discharged or weak battery by attaching jump leads from the weak battery to a charged or helper battery.

L

Load Sensing Proportioning Valve (LSPV) A brake hydraulic system control valve that works like a proportioning valve, but also takes into consideration the amount of weight carried by the rear axle.

Locknut A nut used to lock an adjustment nut, or other threaded component, in place. For example, a locknut is employed to keep the adjusting nut on the rocker arm in position.

Lockwasher A form of washer designed to prevent an attaching nut from working loose.

M

MacPherson strut A type of front suspension system devised by Earle MacPherson at Ford of England. In its original form, a simple lateral link with the anti-roll bar creates the lower control arm. A long strut - an integral coil spring and shock absorber - is mounted between the body and the steering knuckle. Many modern so-called MacPherson strut systems use a conventional lower A-arm and don't rely on the anti-roll bar for location.

Multimeter An electrical test instrument with the capability to measure voltage, current and resistance.

N

NOx Oxides of Nitrogen. A common toxic pollutant emitted by petrol and diesel engines at higher temperatures.

O

Ohm The unit of electrical resistance. One volt applied to a resistance of one ohm will produce a current of one amp.

Ohmmeter An instrument for measuring electrical resistance.

O-ring A type of sealing ring made of a special rubber-like material; in use, the O-ring is compressed into a groove to provide the sealing action.

O-ring

Overhead cam (ohc) engine An engine with the camshaft(s) located on top of the cylinder head(s).

Overhead valve (ohv) engine An engine with the valves located in the cylinder head, but with the camshaft located in the engine block.

Oxygen sensor A device installed in the engine exhaust manifold, which senses the oxygen content in the exhaust and converts this information into an electric current. Also called a Lambda sensor.

P

Phillips screw A type of screw head having a cross instead of a slot for a corresponding type of screwdriver.

Plastigage A thin strip of plastic thread, available in different sizes, used for measuring clearances. For example, a strip of Plastigage is laid across a bearing journal. The parts are assembled and dismantled; the width of the crushed strip indicates the clearance between journal and bearing.

Plastigage

Propeller shaft The long hollow tube with universal joints at both ends that carries power from the transmission to the differential on front-engined rear wheel drive vehicles.

Proportioning valve A hydraulic control valve which limits the amount of pressure to the rear brakes during panic stops to prevent wheel lock-up.

R

Rack-and-pinion steering A steering system with a pinion gear on the end of the steering shaft that mates with a rack (think of a geared wheel opened up and laid flat). When the steering wheel is turned, the pinion turns, moving the rack to the left or right. This movement is transmitted through the track rods to the steering arms at the wheels.

Radiator A liquid-to-air heat transfer device designed to reduce the temperature of the coolant in an internal combustion engine cooling system.

Refrigerant Any substance used as a heat transfer agent in an air-conditioning system. R-12 has been the principle refrigerant for many years; recently, however, manufacturers have begun using R-134a, a non-CFC substance that is considered less harmful to the ozone in the upper atmosphere.

Rocker arm A lever arm that rocks on a shaft or pivots on a stud. In an overhead valve engine, the rocker arm converts the upward movement of the pushrod into a downward movement to open a valve.

Rotor In a distributor, the rotating device inside the cap that connects the centre electrode and the outer terminals as it turns, distributing the high voltage from the coil secondary winding to the proper spark plug. Also, that part of an alternator which rotates inside the stator. Also, the rotating assembly of a turbocharger, including the compressor wheel, shaft and turbine wheel.

Runout The amount of wobble (in-and-out movement) of a gear or wheel as it's rotated. The amount a shaft rotates "out-of-true." The out-of-round condition of a rotating part.

S

Sealant A liquid or paste used to prevent leakage at a joint. Sometimes used in conjunction with a gasket.

Sealed beam lamp An older headlight design which integrates the reflector, lens and filaments into a hermetically-sealed one-piece unit. When a filament burns out or the lens cracks, the entire unit is simply replaced.

Serpentine drivebelt A single, long, wide accessory drivebelt that's used on some newer vehicles to drive all the accessories, instead of a series of smaller, shorter belts. Serpentine drivebelts are usually tensioned by an automatic tensioner.

Serpentine drivebelt

Shim Thin spacer, commonly used to adjust the clearance or relative positions between two parts. For example, shims inserted into or under bucket tappets control valve clearances. Clearance is adjusted by changing the thickness of the shim.

Slide hammer A special puller that screws into or hooks onto a component such as a shaft or bearing; a heavy sliding handle on the shaft bottoms against the end of the shaft to knock the component free.

Sprocket A tooth or projection on the periphery of a wheel, shaped to engage with a chain or drivebelt. Commonly used to refer to the sprocket wheel itself.

Starter inhibitor switch On vehicles with an automatic transmission, a switch that prevents starting if the vehicle is not in Neutral or Park.

Strut See MacPherson strut.

T

Tappet A cylindrical component which transmits motion from the cam to the valve stem, either directly or via a pushrod and rocker arm. Also called a cam follower.

Thermostat A heat-controlled valve that regulates the flow of coolant between the cylinder block and the radiator, so maintaining optimum engine operating temperature. A thermostat is also used in some air cleaners in which the temperature is regulated.

Thrust bearing The bearing in the clutch assembly that is moved in to the release levers by clutch pedal action to disengage the clutch. Also referred to as a release bearing.

Timing belt A toothed belt which drives the camshaft. Serious engine damage may result if it breaks in service.

Timing chain A chain which drives the camshaft.

Toe-in The amount the front wheels are closer together at the front than at the rear. On rear wheel drive vehicles, a slight amount of toe-in is usually specified to keep the front wheels running parallel on the road by offsetting other forces that tend to spread the wheels apart.

Toe-out The amount the front wheels are closer together at the rear than at the front. On front wheel drive vehicles, a slight amount of toe-out is usually specified.

Tools For full information on choosing and using tools, refer to the *Haynes Automotive Tools Manual.*

Tracer A stripe of a second colour applied to a wire insulator to distinguish that wire from another one with the same colour insulator.

Tune-up A process of accurate and careful adjustments and parts replacement to obtain the best possible engine performance.

Turbocharger A centrifugal device, driven by exhaust gases, that pressurises the intake air. Normally used to increase the power output from a given engine displacement, but can also be used primarily to reduce exhaust emissions (as on VW's "Umwelt" Diesel engine).

U

Universal joint or U-joint A double-pivoted connection for transmitting power from a driving to a driven shaft through an angle. A U-joint consists of two Y-shaped yokes and a cross-shaped member called the spider.

V

Valve A device through which the flow of liquid, gas, vacuum, or loose material in bulk may be started, stopped, or regulated by a movable part that opens, shuts, or partially obstructs one or more ports or passageways. A valve is also the movable part of such a device.

Valve clearance The clearance between the valve tip (the end of the valve stem) and the rocker arm or tappet. The valve clearance is measured when the valve is closed.

Vernier caliper A precision measuring instrument that measures inside and outside dimensions. Not quite as accurate as a micrometer, but more convenient.

Viscosity The thickness of a liquid or its resistance to flow.

Volt A unit for expressing electrical "pressure" in a circuit. One volt that will produce a current of one ampere through a resistance of one ohm.

W

Welding Various processes used to join metal items by heating the areas to be joined to a molten state and fusing them together. For more information refer to the *Haynes Automotive Welding Manual.*

Wiring diagram A drawing portraying the components and wires in a vehicle's electrical system, using standardised symbols. For more information refer to the *Haynes Automotive Electrical and Electronic Systems Manual.*

Haynes Manuals – The Complete UK Car List

Title	Book No.
ALFA ROMEO Alfasud/Sprint (74 - 88) up to F *	0292
Alfa Romeo Alfetta (73 - 87) up to E *	0531
AUDI 80, 90 & Coupe Petrol (79 - Nov 88) up to F	0605
Audi 80, 90 & Coupe Petrol (Oct 86 - 90) D to H	1491
Audi 100 & 200 Petrol (Oct 82 - 90) up to H	0907
Audi 100 & A6 Petrol & Diesel (May 91 - May 97) H to P	3504
Audi A3 Petrol & Diesel (96 - May 03) P to 03	4253
Audi A4 Petrol & Diesel (95 - 00) M to X	3575
Audi A4 Petrol & Diesel (01 - 04) X to 54	4609
AUSTIN A35 & A40 (56 - 67) up to F *	0118
Austin/MG/Rover Maestro 1.3 & 1.6 Petrol (83 - 95) up to M	0922
Austin/MG Metro (80 - May 90) up to G	0718
Austin/Rover Montego 1.3 & 1.6 Petrol (84 - 94) A to L	1066
Austin/MG/Rover Montego 2.0 Petrol (84 - 95) A to M	1067
Mini (59 - 69) up to H *	0527
Mini (69 - 01) up to X	0646
Austin/Rover 2.0 litre Diesel Engine (86 - 93) C to L	1857
Austin Healey 100/6 & 3000 (56 - 68) up to G *	0049
BEDFORD CF Petrol (69 - 87) up to E	0163
Bedford/Vauxhall Rascal & Suzuki Supercarry (86 - Oct 94) C to M	3015
BMW 316, 320 & 320i (4-cyl) (75 - Feb 83) up to Y *	0276
BMW 320, 320i, 323i & 325i (6-cyl) (Oct 77 - Sept 87) up to E	0815
BMW 3- & 5-Series Petrol (81 - 91) up to J	1948
BMW 3-Series Petrol (Apr 91 - 99) H to V	3210
BMW 3-Series Petrol (Sept 98 - 03) S to 53	4067
BMW 520i & 525e (Oct 81 - June 88) up to E	1560
BMW 525, 528 & 528i (73 - Sept 81) up to X *	0632
BMW 5-Series 6-cyl Petrol (April 96 - Aug 03) N to 03	4151
BMW 1500, 1502, 1600, 1602, 2000 & 2002 (59 - 77) up to S *	0240
CHRYSLER PT Cruiser Petrol (00 - 03) W to 53	4058
CITROËN 2CV, Ami & Dyane (67 - 90) up to H	0196
Citroën AX Petrol & Diesel (87 - 97) D to P	3014
Citroën Berlingo & Peugeot Partner Petrol & Diesel (96 - 05) P to 55	4281
Citroën BX Petrol (83 - 94) A to L	0908
Citroën C15 Van Petrol & Diesel (89 - Oct 98) F to S	3509
Citroën C3 Petrol & Diesel (02 - 05) 51 to 05	4197
Citroën CX Petrol (75 - 88) up to F	0528
Citroën Saxo Petrol & Diesel (96 - 04) N to 54	3506
Citroën Visa Petrol (79 - 88) up to F	0620
Citroën Xantia Petrol & Diesel (93 - 01) K to Y	3082
Citroën XM Petrol & Diesel (89 - 00) G to X	3451
Citroën Xsara Petrol & Diesel (97 - Sept 00) R to W	3751
Citroën Xsara Picasso Petrol & Diesel (00 - 02) W to 52	3944
Citroën ZX Diesel (91 - 98) J to S	1922
Citroën ZX Petrol (91 - 98) H to S	1881
Citroën 1.7 & 1.9 litre Diesel Engine (84 - 96) A to N	1379
FIAT 126 (73 - 87) up to E *	0305
Fiat 500 (57 - 73) up to M *	0090
Fiat Bravo & Brava Petrol (95 - 00) N to W	3572
Fiat Cinquecento (93 - 98) K to R	3501
Fiat Panda (81 - 95) up to M	0793
Fiat Punto Petrol & Diesel (94 - Oct 99) L to V	3251
Fiat Punto Petrol (Oct 99 - July 03) V to 03	4066
Fiat Regata Petrol (84 - 88) A to F	1167
Fiat Tipo Petrol (88 - 91) E to J	1625
Fiat Uno Petrol (83 - 95) up to M	0923
Fiat X1/9 (74 - 89) up to G *	0273
FORD Anglia (59 - 68) up to G *	0001
Ford Capri II (& III) 1.6 & 2.0 (74 - 87) up to E *	0283
Ford Capri II (& III) 2.8 & 3.0 V6 (74 - 87) up to E	1309

Title	Book No.
Ford Cortina Mk I & Corsair 1500 ('62 - '66) up to D*	0214
Ford Cortina Mk III 1300 & 1600 (70 - 76) up to P *	0070
Ford Escort Mk I 1100 & 1300 (68 - 74) up to N *	0171
Ford Escort Mk I Mexico, RS 1600 & RS 2000 (70 - 74) up to N *	0139
Ford Escort Mk II Mexico, RS 1800 & RS 2000 (75 - 80) up to W *	0735
Ford Escort (75 - Aug 80) up to V *	0280
Ford Escort Petrol (Sept 80 - Sept 90) up to H	0686
Ford Escort & Orion Petrol (Sept 90 - 00) H to X	1737
Ford Escort & Orion Diesel (Sept 90 - 00) H to X	4081
Ford Fiesta (76 - Aug 83) up to Y	0334
Ford Fiesta Petrol (Aug 83 - Feb 89) A to F	1030
Ford Fiesta Petrol (Feb 89 - Oct 95) F to N	1595
Ford Fiesta Petrol & Diesel (Oct 95 - Mar 02) N to 02	3397
Ford Fiesta Petrol & Diesel (Apr 02 - 05) 02 to 54	4170
Ford Focus Petrol & Diesel (98 - 01) S to Y	3759
Ford Focus Petrol & Diesel (Oct 01 - 05) 51 to 05	4167
Ford Galaxy Petrol & Diesel (95 - Aug 00) M to W	3984
Ford Granada Petrol (Sept 77 - Feb 85) up to B *	0481
Ford Granada & Scorpio Petrol (Mar 85 - 94) B to M	1245
Ford Ka (96 - 02) P to 52	3570
Ford Mondeo Petrol (93 - Sept 00) K to X	1923
Ford Mondeo Petrol & Diesel (Oct 00 - Jul 03) X to 03	3990
Ford Mondeo Petrol & Diesel (July 03 - 07) 03 to 56	4619
Ford Mondeo Diesel (93 - 96) L to N	3465
Ford Orion Petrol (83 - Sept 90) up to H	1009
Ford Sierra 4-cyl Petrol (82 - 93) up to K	0903
Ford Sierra V6 Petrol (82 - 91) up to J	0904
Ford Transit Petrol (Mk 2) (78 - Jan 86) up to C	0719
Ford Transit Petrol (Mk 3) (Feb 86 - 89) C to G	1468
Ford Transit Diesel (Feb 86 - 99) C to T	3019
Ford 1.6 & 1.8 litre Diesel Engine (84 - 96) A to N	1172
Ford 2.1, 2.3 & 2.5 litre Diesel Engine (77 - 90) up to H	1606
FREIGHT ROVER Sherpa Petrol (74 - 87) up to E	0463
HILLMAN Avenger (70 - 82) up to Y	0037
Hillman Imp (63 - 76) up to R *	0022
HONDA Civic (Feb 84 - Oct 87) A to E	1226
Honda Civic (Nov 91 - 96) J to N	3199
Honda Civic Petrol (Mar 95 - 00) M to X	4050
Honda Civic Petrol & Diesel (01 - 05) X to 55	4611
Honda Jazz (01 - Feb 08) 51 - 57	4735
HYUNDAI Pony (85 - 94) C to M	3398
JAGUAR E Type (61 - 72) up to L *	0140
Jaguar MkI & II, 240 & 340 (55 - 69) up to H *	0098
Jaguar XJ6, XJ & Sovereign; Daimler Sovereign (68 - Oct 86) up to D	0242
Jaguar XJ6 & Sovereign (Oct 86 - Sept 94) D to M	3261
Jaguar XJ12, XJS & Sovereign; Daimler Double Six (72 - 88) up to F	0478
JEEP Cherokee Petrol (93 - 96) K to N	1943
LADA 1200, 1300, 1500 & 1600 (74 - 91) up to J	0413
Lada Samara (87 - 91) D to J	1610
LAND ROVER 90, 110 & Defender Diesel (83 - 07) up to 56	3017
Land Rover Discovery Petrol & Diesel (89 - 98) G to S	3016
Land Rover Discovery Diesel (Nov 98 - Jul 04) S to 04	4606
Land Rover Freelander Petrol & Diesel (97 - Sept 03) R to 53	3929
Land Rover Freelander Petrol & Diesel (Oct 03 - Oct 06) 53 to 56	4623
Land Rover Series IIA & III Diesel (58 - 85) up to C	0529
Land Rover Series II, IIA & III 4-cyl Petrol (58 - 85) up to C	0314

Title	Book No.
MAZDA 323 (Mar 81 - Oct 89) up to G	1608
Mazda 323 (Oct 89 - 98) G to R	3455
Mazda 626 (May 83 - Sept 87) up to E	0929
Mazda B1600, B1800 & B2000 Pick-up Petrol (72 - 88) up to F	0267
Mazda RX-7 (79 - 85) up to C *	0460
MERCEDES-BENZ 190, 190E & 190D Petrol & Diesel (83 - 93) A to L	3450
Mercedes-Benz 200D, 240D, 240TD, 300D & 300TD 123 Series Diesel (Oct 76 - 85)	1114
Mercedes-Benz 250 & 280 (68 - 72) up to L *	0346
Mercedes-Benz 250 & 280 123 Series Petrol (Oct 76 - 84) up to B *	0677
Mercedes-Benz 124 Series Petrol & Diesel (85 - Aug 93) C to K	3253
Mercedes-Benz C-Class Petrol & Diesel (93 - Aug 00) L to W	3511
MGA (55 - 62) *	0475
MGB (62 - 80) up to W	0111
MG Midget & Austin-Healey Sprite (58 - 80) up to W *	0265
MINI Petrol (July 01 - 05) Y to 05	4273
MITSUBISHI Shogun & L200 Pick-Ups Petrol (83 - 94) up to M	1944
MORRIS Ital 1.3 (80 - 84) up to B	0705
Morris Minor 1000 (56 - 71) up to K	0024
NISSAN Almera Petrol (95 - Feb 00) N to V	4053
Nissan Almera & Tino Petrol (Feb 00 - 07) V to 56	4612
Nissan Bluebird (May 84 - Mar 86) A to C	1223
Nissan Bluebird Petrol (Mar 86 - 90) C to H	1473
Nissan Cherry (Sept 82 - 86) up to D	1031
Nissan Micra (83 - Jan 93) up to K	0931
Nissan Micra (93 - 02) K to 52	3254
Nissan Primera Petrol (90 - Aug 99) H to T	1851
Nissan Stanza (82 - 86) up to D	0824
Nissan Sunny Petrol (May 82 - Oct 86) up to D	0895
Nissan Sunny Petrol (Oct 86 - Mar 91) D to H	1378
Nissan Sunny Petrol (Apr 91 - 95) H to N	3219
OPEL Ascona & Manta (B Series) (Sept 75 - 88) up to F *	0316
Opel Ascona Petrol (81 - 88)	3215
Opel Astra Petrol (Oct 91 - Feb 98)	3156
Opel Corsa Petrol (83 - Mar 93)	3160
Opel Corsa Petrol (Mar 93 - 97)	3159
Opel Kadett Petrol (Nov 79 - Oct 84) up to B	0634
Opel Kadett Petrol (Oct 84 - Oct 91)	3196
Opel Omega & Senator Petrol (Nov 86 - 94)	3157
Opel Rekord Petrol (Feb 78 - Oct 86) up to D	0543
Opel Vectra Petrol (Oct 88 - Oct 95)	3158
PEUGEOT 106 Petrol & Diesel (91 - 04) J to 53	1882
Peugeot 205 Petrol (83 - 97) A to P	0932
Peugeot 206 Petrol & Diesel (98 - 01) S to X	3757
Peugeot 206 Petrol & Diesel (02 - 06) 51 to 06	4613
Peugeot 306 Petrol & Diesel (93 - 02) K to 02	3073
Peugeot 307 Petrol & Diesel (01 - 04) Y to 54	4147
Peugeot 309 Petrol (86 - 93) C to K	1266
Peugeot 405 Petrol (88 - 97) E to P	1559
Peugeot 405 Diesel (88 - 97) E to P	3198
Peugeot 406 Petrol & Diesel (96 - Mar 99) N to T	3394
Peugeot 406 Petrol & Diesel (Mar 99 - 02) T to 52	3982
Peugeot 505 Petrol (79 - 89) up to G	0762
Peugeot 1.7/1.8 & 1.9 litre Diesel Engine (82 - 96) up to N	0950
Peugeot 2.0, 2.1, 2.3 & 2.5 litre Diesel Engines (74 - 90) up to H	1607
PORSCHE 911 (65 - 85) up to C	0264

* Classic reprint

Title	Book No.
Porsche 924 & 924 Turbo (76 - 85) up to C	0397
PROTON (89 - 97) F to P	3255
RANGE ROVER V8 Petrol (70 - Oct 92) up to K	0606
RELIANT Robin & Kitten (73 - 83) up to A *	0436
RENAULT 4 (61 - 86) up to D *	0072
Renault 5 Petrol (Feb 85 - 96) B to N	1219
Renault 9 & 11 Petrol (82 - 89) up to F	0822
Renault 18 Petrol (79 - 86) up to D	0598
Renault 19 Petrol (89 - 96) F to N	1646
Renault 19 Diesel (89 - 96) F to N	1946
Renault 21 Petrol (86 - 94) C to M	1397
Renault 25 Petrol & Diesel (84 - 92) B to K	1228
Renault Clio Petrol (91 - May 98) H to R	1853
Renault Clio Diesel (91 - June 96) H to N	3031
Renault Clio Petrol & Diesel (May 98 - May 01) R to Y	3906
Renault Clio Petrol & Diesel (June '01 - '05) Y to 55	4168
Renault Espace Petrol & Diesel (85 - 96) C to N	3197
Renault Laguna Petrol & Diesel (94 - 00) L to W	3252
Renault Laguna Petrol & Diesel (Feb 01 - Feb 05) X to 54	4283
Renault Mégane & Scénic Petrol & Diesel (96 - 99) N to T	3395
Renault Mégane & Scénic Petrol & Diesel (Apr 99 - 02) T to 52	3916
Renault Megane Petrol & Diesel (Oct 02 - 05) 52 to 55	4284
Renault Scenic Petrol & Diesel (Sept 03 - 06) 53 to 06	4297
ROVER 213 & 216 (84 - 89) A to G	1116
Rover 214 & 414 Petrol (89 - 96) G to N	1689
Rover 216 & 416 Petrol (89 - 96) G to N	1830
Rover 211, 214, 216, 218 & 220 Petrol & Diesel (Dec 95 - 99) N to V	3399
Rover 25 & MG ZR Petrol & Diesel (Oct 99 - 04) V to 54	4145
Rover 414, 416 & 420 Petrol & Diesel (May 95 - 98) M to R	3453
Rover 45 / MG ZS Petrol & Diesel (99 - 05) V to 55	4384
Rover 618, 620 & 623 Petrol (93 - 97) K to P	3257
Rover 75 / MG ZT Petrol & Diesel (99 - 06) S to 06	4292
Rover 820, 825 & 827 Petrol (86 - 95) D to N	1380
Rover 3500 (76 - 87) up to E *	0365
Rover Metro, 111 & 114 Petrol (May 90 - 98) G to S	1711
SAAB 95 & 96 (66 - 76) up to R *	0198
Saab 90, 99 & 900 (79 - Oct 93) up to L	0765
Saab 900 (Oct 93 - 98) L to R	3512
Saab 9000 (4-cyl) (85 - 98) C to S	1686
Saab 9-3 Petrol & Diesel (98 - Aug 02) R to 02	4614
Saab 9-5 4-cyl Petrol (97 - 04) R to 54	4156
SEAT Ibiza & Cordoba Petrol & Diesel (Oct 93 - Oct 99) L to V	3571
Seat Ibiza & Malaga Petrol (85 - 92) B to K	1609
SKODA Estelle (77 - 89) up to G	0604
Skoda Fabia Petrol & Diesel (00 - 06) W to 06	4376
Skoda Favorit (89 - 96) F to N	1801
Skoda Felicia Petrol & Diesel (95 - 01) M to X	3505
Skoda Octavia Petrol & Diesel (98 - Apr 04) R to 04	4285
SUBARU 1600 & 1800 (Nov 79 - 90) up to H *	0995
SUNBEAM Alpine, Rapier & H120 (67 - 74) up to N *	0051
SUZUKI SJ Series, Samurai & Vitara (4-cyl) Petrol (82 - 97) up to P	1942
Suzuki Supercarry & Bedford/Vauxhall Rascal (86 - Oct 94) C to M	3015
TALBOT Alpine, Solara, Minx & Rapier (75 - 86) up to D	0337

Title	Book No.
Talbot Horizon Petrol (78 - 86) up to D	0473
Talbot Samba (82 - 86) up to D	0823
TOYOTA Avensis Petrol (98 - Jan 03) R to 52	4264
Toyota Carina E Petrol (May 92 - 97) J to P	3256
Toyota Corolla (80 - 85) up to C	0683
Toyota Corolla (Sept 83 - Sept 87) A to E	1024
Toyota Corolla (Sept 87 - Aug 92) E to K	1683
Toyota Corolla Petrol (Aug 92 - 97) K to P	3259
Toyota Corolla Petrol (July 97 - Feb 02) P to 51	4286
Toyota Hi-Ace & Hi-Lux Petrol (69 - Oct 83) up to A	0304
Toyota Yaris Petrol (99 - 05) T to 05	4265
TRIUMPH GT6 & Vitesse (62 - 74) up to N *	0112
Triumph Herald (59 - 71) up to K *	0010
Triumph Spitfire (62 - 81) up to X	0113
Triumph Stag (70 - 78) up to T *	0441
Triumph TR2, TR3, TR3A, TR4 & TR4A (52 - 67) up to F *	0028
Triumph TR5 & 6 (67 - 75) up to P *	0031
Triumph TR7 (75 - 82) up to Y *	0322
VAUXHALL Astra Petrol (80 - Oct 84) up to B	0635
Vauxhall Astra & Belmont Petrol (Oct 84 - Oct 91) B to J	1136
Vauxhall Astra Petrol (Oct 91 - Feb 98) J to R	1832
Vauxhall/Opel Astra & Zafira Petrol (Feb 98 - Apr 04) R to 04	3758
Vauxhall/Opel Astra & Zafira Diesel (Feb 98 - Apr 04) R to 04	3797
Vauxhall/Opel Astra Petrol (04 - 07) 04 - 07	4732
Vauxhall/Opel Astra Diesel (04 - 07) 04 - 07	4733
Vauxhall/Opel Calibra (90 - 98) G to S	3502
Vauxhall Carlton Petrol (Oct 78 - Oct 86) up to D	0480
Vauxhall Carlton & Senator Petrol (Nov 86 - 94) D to L	1469
Vauxhall Cavalier Petrol (81 - Oct 88) up to F	0812
Vauxhall Cavalier Petrol (Oct 88 - 95) F to N	1570
Vauxhall Chevette (75 - 84) up to B	0285
Vauxhall/Opel Corsa Diesel (Mar 93 - Oct 00) K to X	4087
Vauxhall Corsa Petrol (Mar 93 - 97) K to R	1985
Vauxhall/Opel Corsa Petrol (Apr 97 - Oct 00) P to X	3921
Vauxhall/Opel Corsa Petrol & Diesel (Oct 00 - Sept 03) X to 53	4079
Vauxhall/Opel Corsa Petrol & Diesel (Oct 03 - Aug 06) 53 to 06	4617
Vauxhall/Opel Frontera Petrol & Diesel (91 - Sept 98) J to S	3454
Vauxhall Nova Petrol (83 - 93) up to K	0909
Vauxhall/Opel Omega Petrol (94 - 99) L to T	3510
Vauxhall/Opel Vectra Petrol & Diesel (95 - Feb 99) N to S	3396
Vauxhall/Opel Vectra Petrol & Diesel (Mar 99 - May 02) T to 02	3930
Vauxhall/Opel Vectra Petrol & Diesel (June 02 - Sept 05) 02 to 55	4618
Vauxhall/Opel 1.5, 1.6 & 1.7 litre Diesel Engine (82 - 96) up to N	1222
VW 411 & 412 (68 - 75) up to P *	0091
VW Beetle 1200 (54 - 77) up to S	0036
VW Beetle 1300 & 1500 (65 - 75) up to P	0039
VW 1302 & 1302S (70 - 72) up to L *	0110
VW Beetle 1303, 1303S & GT (72 - 75) up to P	0159
VW Beetle Petrol & Diesel (Apr 99 - 01) T to 51	3798
VW Golf & Jetta Mk 1 Petrol 1.1 & 1.3 (74 - 84) up to A	0716
VW Golf, Jetta & Scirocco Mk 1 Petrol 1.5, 1.6 & 1.8 (74 - 84) up to A	0726

Title	Book No.
VW Golf & Jetta Mk 1 Diesel (78 - 84) up to A	0451
VW Golf & Jetta Mk 2 Petrol (Mar 84 - Feb 92) A to J	1081
VW Golf & Vento Petrol & Diesel (Feb 92 - Mar 98) J to R	3097
VW Golf & Bora Petrol & Diesel (April 98 - 00) R to X	3727
VW Golf & Bora 4-cyl Petrol & Diesel (01 - 03) X to 53	4169
VW Golf & Jetta Petrol & Diesel (04 - 07) 53 to 07	4610
VW LT Petrol Vans & Light Trucks (76 - 87) up to E	0637
VW Passat & Santana Petrol (Sept 81 - May 88) up to E	0814
VW Passat 4-cyl Petrol & Diesel (May 88 - 96) E to P	3498
VW Passat 4-cyl Petrol & Diesel (Dec 96 - Nov 00) P to X	3917
VW Passat Petrol & Diesel (Dec 00 - May 05) X to 05	4279
VW Polo & Derby (76 - Jan 82) up to X	0335
VW Polo (82 - Oct 90) up to H	0813
VW Polo Petrol (Nov 90 - Aug 94) H to L	3245
VW Polo Hatchback Petrol & Diesel (94 - 99) M to S	3500
VW Polo Hatchback Petrol (00 - Jan 02) V to 51	4150
VW Polo Petrol & Diesel (02 - May 05) 51 to 05	4608
VW Scirocco (82 - 90) up to H *	1224
VW Transporter 1600 (68 - 79) up to V	0082
VW Transporter 1700, 1800 & 2000 (72 - 79) up to V *	0226
VW Transporter (air-cooled) Petrol (79 - 82) up to Y *	0638
VW Transporter (water-cooled) Petrol (82 - 90) up to H	3452
VW Type 3 (63 - 73) up to M *	0084
VOLVO 120 & 130 Series (& P1800) (61 - 73) up to M *	0203
Volvo 142, 144 & 145 (66 - 74) up to N *	0129
Volvo 240 Series Petrol (74 - 93) up to K	0270
Volvo 262, 264 & 260/265 (75 - 85) up to C *	0400
Volvo 340, 343, 345 & 360 (76 - 91) up to J	0715
Volvo 440, 460 & 480 Petrol (87 - 97) D to P	1691
Volvo 740 & 760 Petrol (82 - 91) up to J	1258
Volvo 850 Petrol (92 - 96) J to P	3260
Volvo 940 petrol (90 - 98) H to R	3249
Volvo S40 & V40 Petrol (96 - Mar 04) N to 04	3569
Volvo S40 & V50 Petrol & Diesel (Mar 04 - Jun 07) 04 to 07	4731
Volvo S70, V70 & C70 Petrol (96 - 99) P to V	3573
Volvo V70 / S80 Petrol & Diesel (98 - 05) S to 55	4263

AUTOMOTIVE TECHBOOKS

Title	Book No.
Automotive Electrical and Electronic Systems Manual	3049
Automotive Gearbox Overhaul Manual	3473
Automotive Service Summaries Manual	3475
Automotive Timing Belts Manual – Austin/Rover	3549
Automotive Timing Belts Manual – Ford	3474
Automotive Timing Belts Manual – Peugeot/Citroën	3568
Automotive Timing Belts Manual – Vauxhall/Opel	3577

DIY MANUAL SERIES

Title	Book No.
The Haynes Air Conditioning Manual	4192
The Haynes Car Electrical Systems Manual	4251
The Haynes Manual on Bodywork	4198
The Haynes Manual on Brakes	4178
The Haynes Manual on Carburettors	4177
The Haynes Manual on Diesel Engines	4174
The Haynes Manual on Engine Management	4199
The Haynes Manual on Fault Codes	4175
The Haynes Manual on Practical Electrical Systems	4267
The Haynes Manual on Small Engines	4250
The Haynes Manual on Welding	4176

* Classic reprint

CL23.12/07

Preserving Our Motoring Heritage

< The Model J Duesenberg Derham Tourster. Only eight of these magnificent cars were ever built – this is the only example to be found outside the United States of America

Almost every car you've ever loved, loathed or desired is gathered under one roof at the Haynes Motor Museum. Over 300 immaculately presented cars and motorbikes represent every aspect of our motoring heritage, from elegant reminders of bygone days, such as the superb Model J Duesenberg to curiosities like the bug-eyed BMW Isetta. There are also many old friends and flames. Perhaps you remember the 1959 Ford Popular that you did your courting in? The magnificent 'Red Collection' is a spectacle of classic sports cars including AC, Alfa Romeo, Austin Healey, Ferrari, Lamborghini, Maserati, MG, Riley, Porsche and Triumph.

A Perfect Day Out

Each and every vehicle at the Haynes Motor Museum has played its part in the history and culture of Motoring. Today, they make a wonderful spectacle and a great day out for all the family. Bring the kids, bring Mum and Dad, but above all bring your camera to capture those golden memories for ever. You will also find an impressive array of motoring memorabilia, a comfortable 70 seat video cinema and one of the most extensive transport book shops in Britain. The Pit Stop Cafe serves everything from a cup of tea to wholesome, home-made meals or, if you prefer, you can enjoy the large picnic area nestled in the beautiful rural surroundings of Somerset.

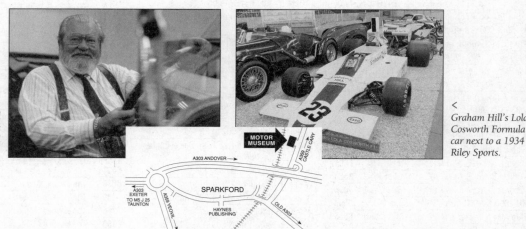

John Haynes O.B.E., Founder and Chairman of the museum at the wheel of a Haynes Light 12. >

< Graham Hill's Lola Cosworth Formula 1 car next to a 1934 Riley Sports.

The Museum is situated on the A359 Yeovil to Frome road at Sparkford, just off the A303 in Somerset. It is about 40 miles south of Bristol, and 25 minutes drive from the M5 intersection at Taunton.
Open 9.30am - 5.30pm (10.00am - 4.00pm Winter) 7 days a week, *except Christmas Day, Boxing Day and New Years Day*
Special rates available for schools, coach parties and outings Charitable Trust No. 292048